EYEWITNESS TO AMERICA

EYEWITNESS TO AMERICA

*500 Years
of America
in the Words
of Those
Who Saw It
Happen*

EDITED BY

DAVID COLBERT

Pantheon Books   New York

Compilation copyright: © 1997 by David Colbert

All rights reserved under International and Pan-American Copyright Conventions. Published in the United States by Pantheon Books, a division of Random House, Inc., New York, and simultaneously in Canada by Random House of Canada Limited, Toronto.

Permissions Acknowledgments begin on page 567.

Library of Congress Cataloging-in-Publication Data

Eyewitness to America : 500 years of America in the words of those who saw it happen / edited by David Colbert.

        p.   cm.
  Includes bibliographical references and index.
  ISBN 0-679-44224-3
   1. United States—History—Sources.   I. Colbert, David.
E173.E9   1997
973—dc20   96-24150
                                     CIP

Random House Web Address: http://www.randomhouse.com/

Book design by M. Kristen Bearse

Printed in the United States of America
First Edition
9 8 7 6 5 4 3 2 1

For my parents

CONTENTS

ACKNOWLEDGMENTS

I AM GRATEFUL to talented friends who researched essential contributions to this book: Rachel Lehmann-Haupt, Jay Leibold, Desa Philadelphia, and Damian Sharp. Thanks also to Jay for his expert comments on the manuscript.

Thanks to Marty Asher and Laurie Brown, who made a home for the idea at Pantheon, and to their colleagues who made the idea into a book: Marge Anderson, Kristen Bearse, Marian Brown, Fearn Cutler, Joy Dallanegra-Sanger, Dan Frank, Janice Goldklang, Kathy Grasso, Evelyn Grossberg, Lisa Healy of S.W. Cohen & Associates, Altie Karper, Edward Kastenmeier, Anne McCormick, Claudine O'Hearn, and Suzanne Williams.

Thank you to my agent, Joy Harris, and to her staff. Thanks also to copyeditor Chuck Antony, to illustrators Peter Guarnaccia and Mirko Ilic, to Randall Park for his hard work on the permissions and to Wayne Furman and the New York Public Library for granting use of the Wertheim Study.

Family and many friends dug up facts, corrected errors, helped make selections, and offered advice and comfort—some of them daily. They made this book possible. Thank you to: Véronique Bardach, Ursula Bollini, Stanley H. Brown, Ani Chamichian, Christine Dowson, Lisa Feuer, Amy Hertz, Daniel Huang, Henry Huang, Shannon Kaye, Lyuba Konopasek, Matthew Kronby, Miles Kronby, Marc de La Bruyère, Garrett Loubé, Theresa Menders, Anne Millman, Neil Millman, Bonnie Nadell, Cliff Palefsky, Peter Pfau, Carolyn Pittis, Tim Porter, Katie Rabin, Bob Rochelle, Marcia Rodgers, Leslie Rossman, Zina Scarpulla, Stacy Schiff, Karen Scofield, Ben Shykind, Kim Starr, Lena Tabori, Frank Takao, Wanda Takao, my sisters, Jan and Melanie Colbert, and my parents, Stanley and Nancy.

And I must give special thanks to my thoughtful, thorough editor, Alan D. Williams. Receiving his guidance was the most rewarding experience of compiling this book.

INTRODUCTION

THE RUSSIANS HAVE A PROVERB: *He lies like an eyewitness.* Few eyewitnesses see it all, fewer still understand all the implications. And their reports are always personal.

Yet what they see is essential. History begins with people caught in the moment-by-moment rush of events. The correspondent on the scene shares the jolt of joy or horror in watching the world change in an instant. Personal bias becomes part of the story, and often makes the account more vivid. In this book, for example, Howard Smith's view of the Stonewall gay rights riot is hardly compassionate, but it accurately reflects the attitudes of 1969. And Langston Hughes's account of a visit to the Scottsboro Boys' prison in Alabama is wholly subjective—*"For a moment the fear came: even for me, a Sunday morning visitor, the doors might never open again."* That is the point of reading Langston Hughes.

Newspaper reporters like to say they write "the first draft of history." Every fact may not be in the story. Every consequence may not have been questioned. Yet the eyewitness's story evokes unforgettable urgency and energy, and a sense of truth.

Just over a hundred years ago only one Ivy League university had a full-time American history professor. Now the question is, *Which* American history? Revisionist? Marxist? History of peoples of color? The unfashionable history of now-pilloried "dead white males"? For this book, the answer is all of the above. There are more than a few old white men here; and there are also some women like Susan B. Anthony, who gave those men hell. The Vietnam War comes under fire; but the eyewitness is Admiral James Stockdale, a self-described war hawk who says we were right to fight there. Ernie Pyle's elegy to Captain Henry Waskow is sentimental, patriotic, and a beautiful piece of writing; yet the accounts of Japanese American concentration camps and the McCarthy hearings, both of which occurred in the name of the same patriotism, are accurately presented here as indecent acts. Dr. Martin Luther King, Jr.'s, "I Have a Dream" speech is here, adored by a white reporter and deplored by Malcolm X. Native Americans kill and are killed. So it goes.

A simple, essential observation by historian Daniel Boorstin has shaped this book's structure: "The historian's neat categories parse experience in ways never found among living people." In this volume, events are ordered chronologically, without chapters and sections to segregate them. The story of America unfolds as it happened, with events and issues competing for attention just as they did when people were living them. Some of the fun is in the surprise of what will come next, and the odd coincidence of people and events.

The starting point is Columbus, rather than the great origin myths of the Native Americans, who were here long before him, and the sagas of the Norsemen, whose voyages preceded his by half a millennium. The origin myths and sagas are fascinating and valuable to read, but they aren't accounts from eyewitnesses. The immediacy of experiencing an event is at the heart of this volume.

Confirming stonecut words on the National Archives building, Washington, D.C.— WHAT IS PAST IS PROLOGUE—patterns emerge.

—The pursuit of gold and other forms of the quick buck is the American Holy Grail. Columbus came looking for gold, the California Forty-niners opened the west in hopes of finding it, and the Almighty dollar drives Wall Street today.

—Americans seem to believe society can be negotiated into perfection, and try to get the deal on paper. The night before disembarking from the *Mayflower,* the Pilgrims negotiated and signed the Mayflower Compact, following a pattern that had already been started by Virginia's first representative assembly in 1619, and which would continue through the Constitutional Convention to the many Constitutional amendments.

—Slavery and ethnic politics have been national preoccupations since before the colonies broke from Britain. The antislavery clause struck from the Declaration of Independence foreshadows the slavery debates at the Constitutional Convention, the various "compro-

mises," the Civil War, the Scottsboro Boys, and the civil rights movements and race riots of the present day.

—*Americans get angry and then move west.* Or, as Davey Crockett said about his critics after his unsuccessful term in Congress, "They can go to hell. I'm going to Texas." (Unfortunately, he went to the Alamo.) The west means freedom, from the first arrivals, who wanted freedom from Europe; to Roger Williams, who stormed from the civilization of Massachusetts to the wilderness of Rhode Island; to the Kentucky and Ohio settlers, the Oregon Trail pioneers, the Mormons, and on to present-day California, where people go to reinvent themselves.

—*At times, the whole country seems to chant a single mantra: faster faster faster.* The locomotive, the telegraph, the Pony Express, the computer were all born of the ongoing national need for speed.

Five hundred years of history leave a big stack of paper. What to keep? What to toss? Boorstin once complained, "A democratic society like ours, a community of voluntary mobile communities, leaves a random record of its past." He was writing about the loss of diaries, letters, and similar artifacts from the age of print. The electronic age offers a different sort of random record, one that is random not because anything is lost, but because everything is included. Computers promise to create a democracy of information, as if all information were created equal. Anyone with a thought or picture (even an artificially concocted photo) will be able to make it appear as relevant as any other thought or picture, publishing it instantly all over the world.

Everyone would select differently from this great mass of themes and material. An editor is as subjective as a source. Sometimes a single account had to suffice for a topic that offered several possibilities. Several "essential" events are gone altogether. (Otherwise the 1960s might have read like a long string of assassinations: Medgar Evers, JFK, Malcolm X, Dr. King, RFK.) Yet there has to be room for the amusing side of American life. Three hundred years ago New Yorkers frightened visitors with their pushiness. (1679—*"We heard a minister preach . . . but he was so rough that even the roughest and most godless of our sailors were astonished."*) More than two hundred years ago John Adams complained about long-winded congressmen. (1774—*"In Congress, nibbling and quibbling as usual . . . these great wits, these subtle critics, these refined geniuses, these learned lawyers, these*

wise statesmen are so fond of showing their parts and powers, as to make their con-
sultations very tedious.") More than a hundred years ago Japan's first trade
negotiators confounded Commodore Matthew Perry's gunboat delegation. (1858—"*If this friendly letter of the President to the Emperor is not*
received and duly replied to, he will consider his country insulted.")

Some of the writers are famous, often with distinctive styles. Others
are anonymous. Some of the events are familiar and some are arcane. Yet
every piece, regardless of the source, regardless of the familiarity of the
event, delivers on the implicit contract between writer and reader, taking
you to a different time and place, turning you into the eyewitness.

EYEWITNESS TO AMERICA

"The Admiral saw a light ..."

THE OLD WORLD DISCOVERS THE NEW WORLD

October 10–12, 1492
San Salvador, Bahamas

BARTOLOMÉ DE LAS CASAS

*C*olumbus sailed due east from the Canary Islands in hopes of reaching Japan. He wanted to find a direct ocean route to the palaces of gold Marco Polo had described hundreds of years earlier.

The shape of the Earth was not an issue. Educated geographers already agreed the planet was round, not flat. But contemporary estimates set the distance to Japan at about 7,500 miles, too great for ships of the day. Nonetheless, Columbus arrogantly made his own calculations, which showed he would reach Japan in about 2,500 miles—just where he sighted the New World. (The reward for first sighting of land, mentioned in this account, was kept by Columbus himself.) Columbus did not reach the mainland of North America. Although the exact location of the landing is a matter of controversy, it was probably the Bahamian island now known as San Salvador.

No copies of Columbus's diary still exist, but we do have the history written by Las Casas, who had a copy and paraphrased it.

Las Casas was associated with Columbus most of his life. As an eight-year-old he watched Columbus's triumphant return to Seville on Palm Sunday 1493, when Columbus marched through the streets with his crew and native captives. Las Casas's father and three uncles were part of Columbus's second voyage, and when Las Casas came of age, he went to Hispaniola to manage his family's property there. Eventually he became an advocate for freedom for the native slaves.

He refers to Columbus as "the Admiral."

OCTOBER 10

The Admiral sailed west-southwest, at the rate of ten miles an hour and occasionally twelve, and at other times seven, running between day and night fifty-nine leagues; he told the men only forty-four. Here the crew could stand it no longer, they complained of the long voyage, but the

Admiral encouraged them as best he could, giving them hopes of the profits that they might have. And he added that it was useless to murmur because he had come in search of the Indies, and was going to continue until he found them with God's help.

OCTOBER II

He sailed to the west-southwest, had a high sea, higher than before. They saw sandpipers and floating by the vessel a green rush. The men of the *Pinta* saw a reed and a stick, and got a small stick apparently cut or marked with an iron instrument, and a piece of cane, and some other grass which grows on the land, and a small board. Those of the caravel *Niña* also saw other indications of land and a little stick loaded with dog roses. In view of such signs they breathed more freely and grew cheerful.

The land was first seen by a sailor called Rodrigo de Triana. But the Admiral, at ten o'clock at night, standing on the castle of the poop, saw a light, though it was so indistinct that he did not dare to affirm that it was land. He called Pero Gutierrez, a King's butler, and told him there seemed to be a light. It was like a small wax candle that was being hoisted and raised, which would seem to few to be an indication of land. The Admiral however was quite convinced of the proximity of land. In consequence of that when they said the Salve which they used to say and sing it in their way, all the sailors and all being present, the Admiral requested and admonished them to keep a sharp lookout at the castle of the bow, and to look well for land, and said that he would give to him who first saw land a silk doublet, besides the other rewards that the King and Queen had promised.

Two hours after midnight the land appeared, about two leagues off. They lowered all the sails, leaving only a storm square sail, which is the mainsail without bonnets, and lay to until Friday when they reached a small island of the Lucayos, called Guanahani by the natives. They soon saw people naked, and the Admiral went on shore in the armed boat, also Martin Alonso Pinzon and Vincente Anes, his brother, who was commander of the *Niña*. The Admiral took the Royal standard and the captains with two banners of the Green Cross, which the Admiral carried on all the ships as a distinguishing flag having an F and a Y [for Ferdinand and Ysabella]: each letter surmounted by its crown, one at one arm of the cross, and the other at the other arm.

As soon as they had landed they saw trees of a brilliant green abundance of water and fruits of various kinds. The Admiral called the two captains and the rest who had come on shore, and Rodrigo Descovedo, the Notary of all the fleet, and Rodrigo Sanchez de Segovia, and he called them as witnesses to certify that he in the presence of them all, was taking, as he in fact took possession of said island for the King and Queen his masters, making the declarations that were required. Soon after a large crowd of natives congregated there.

"They received everything and gave whatever they had . . ."

COLUMBUS MEETS THE NATIVE AMERICANS

October 12, 1492
San Salvador, Bahamas

CHRISTOPHER COLUMBUS

*T*he natives Columbus met were Taino, Arawaks who began to migrate from South America about 2,500 years ago. They were living in Puerto Rico, Jamaica, Cuba, and the Bahamas at the time Columbus arrived. They were among the estimated several million people then living in North, Central, and South America and the West Indies.

This section of the Las Casas history quotes directly from Columbus's diary.

In order to win the friendship and affection of that people, and because I was convinced that their conversion to our Holy Faith would be better promoted through love than through force; I presented some of them with red caps and some strings of glass beads which they placed around their necks, and with other trifles of insignificant worth that delighted them and by which we have got a wonderful hold on their affections. They afterwards came to the boats of the vessels swimming, bringing us parrots, cotton thread in balls, and spears, and many other things, which they bartered for others we gave them, as glass beads and little bells. Finally they received everything and gave whatever they had with good will. But I thought them to be a very poor people. . . .

I saw some with scars on their bodies, and to my signs asking them what these meant, they answered in the same manner, that people from neighboring islands wanted to capture them, and they had defended themselves; and I did believe, and do believe, that they came from the mainland to take them prisoners.

They must be good servants and very intelligent, because I see that they repeat very quickly what I told them, and it is my conviction that they would easily become Christians, for they seem not to have any sect.

If it please our Lord, I will take six of them from here to your Highnesses on my departure, that they may learn to speak. The people are totally unacquainted with arms, as your Highnesses will see by observing the seven which I have caused to be taken in. With fifty men all can be kept in subjection, and made to do whatever you desire.

"A most horrible and pitiful case ..."

EPIDEMIC AT STADACONA, AND A CURE

February 1536

JACQUES CARTIER

Cartier was the first European to navigate the St. Lawrence River. Eventually the foothold he established led to outposts that rivaled the British and Spanish settlements in North America.

This epidemic occurred on the second of his three voyages. The illness seems to have been scurvy, which had afflicted sea travelers for centuries, leaving historians puzzled at Cartier's failure to recognize it.

Although Cartier noted the name of the tree that provided the cure, and returned to France with a sample for the royal garden at Fontainebleau, he did not describe it in his account. This proved fatal for many of the men on Samuel de Champlain's expedition about eighty years later, who knew of Cartier's experience but could not identify the tree. It was the eastern white cedar, which has leaves that brew a tea rich in vitamin C.

The account refers to Cartier in the third person because it was edited by one of his sailors before being translated by Richard Hakluyt, Oxford University's first professor of modern geography, whose anthologies of voyagers' logs, first published in the 1580s, greatly influenced exploration and settlement of the New World.

Stadacona is now Quebec City.

In the month of December we understood that the pestilence was come among the people of Stadacona, in such sort that before we knew it, according to their confession, there were dead above 50; whereupon we charged them neither to come near our fort, nor about our ships, or us. And albeit we had driven them from us, the said unknown sickness began to spread itself amongst us after the strangest sort that ever was either heard of or seen, insomuch as some did lose all their strength and could not stand on their feet; then did their legs swell, their sinews shrink as black as any coal. Others also had all their skins spotted with spots of blood of a purple colour; then did it ascend up to their ankles, knees, thighs, shoulders, arms, and neck; their mouth became stinking, their gums so rotten that all the flesh did fall off, even to the roots of the teeth, which did also almost all fall out.

With such infection did this sickness spread itself in our three ships that about the middle of February, of 110 persons that we were, there were not ten whole, so that one could not help the other—a most horrible and pitiful case.

Philip Rougemont, born in Amboise, died, being twenty-two years old; and, because the sickness was to us unknown, our Captain caused him to be ripped to see if by any means possible we might know what it was, and so seek means to save and preserve the rest of the company; he was found to have his heart white but rotten and more than a quart of red water about it; his liver was indifferent fair, but his lungs black and mortified; his blood was altogether shrunk about the heart so that, when he was opened, great quantity of rotten blood issued out from about his heart; his spleen toward the back was somewhat deteriorated, rough as if it had been rubbed against a stone. Moreover, because one of his thighs was very black without, it was opened, but within it was whole and sound; that done as well as we could, he was buried.

In such sort did the sickness continue and increase that there were not above three sound men in the ships, and none was able to go under hatches to draw drink for himself nor for his fellows. Sometimes we were constrained to bury some of the dead under the snow because we were not able to dig any graves for them, the ground was so hard frozen and we so weak.

Besides this, we did greatly fear that the people of the country would perceive our weakness and misery, which to hide, our captain would make all his men make a great noise with knocking sticks, stones, hammers, and other things together.

Our captain, considering our estate (and how that sickness was increased and hot amongst us), one day went forth of the fort and, walking upon the ice, he saw a troupe of those countrymen coming from Stadacona, among which was Domagaia, who, not passing ten or 12 days afore, had been very sick with that disease and had his knees swollen as big as a child of two years old, all his sinews shrunk together, his teeth spoiled, his gums rotten and stinking. Our captain, seeing him whole and sound, was thereat marvellous glad, hoping to understand and know of him how he had healed himself, to the end he might ease and help his men. So soon as they were come near him, he asked Domagaia how he had done to heal himself; he answered that he had taken the juice and sap of the leaves of a certain tree and therewith had healed himself, for it is a singular remedy against that disease. Then our captain asked of him if any were to be had thereabout, desiring him to show him for to heal a servant of his who, whilst he was in Canada with Donnacona, was stricken with that disease. That he did because he would not show the number of his sick men. Domagaia straight sent two women to fetch some of it, which brought ten or 12 branches of it and therewithal showed the way how to use it, and that is thus: to take the bark and leaves of the said tree and boil them together, then to drink of the said decoction every other day and to put the dregs of it upon his legs that is sick; moreover, they told us that the virtue of that tree was to heal any other disease. The tree is in their language called *ameda* or *hanneda;* this is thought to be the sassafras tree.

Our captain presently caused some of that drink to be made for his men to drink of it, but there was none durst taste for it except one or two who ventured the drinking of it only to taste and prove it. The others, seeing that, did the like and presently recovered their health and were delivered of that sickness and what other disease soever, in such sort that there were some had been diseased and troubled with the French pox [syphilis] four or five years and with this drink were clean healed.

After this medicine was found and proved to be true, there was such strife about it who should be first to take it that they were ready to kill one another, so that a tree as big as any oak in France was spoiled and lopped bare and occupied all in five or six days; and it wrought so well that if all the physicians of Montpellier and Louvain had been there with all the drugs of Alexandria, they would not have done so much in one year as that tree did in six days; for it did so prevail that as many as used of it by the grace of God recovered their health.

"When the general disembarked, he was quite surprised ..."

THE FOUNDING OF ST. AUGUSTINE

August 25—September 8, 1565

FRANCISCO LÓPEZ DE MENDOZA GRAJALES

*A*round 1539, the Spanish made two forays northward from their established *settlements in Mexico and the West Indies. Francisco Váquez Coronado led a group of conquistadors north from Mexico into what is now the southwestern United States, to look for the rumored Cities of Gold. And Hernando de Soto, Spanish governor of Cuba, landed six hundred soldiers near Tampa Bay to conquer Florida, which to the Spanish at the time meant all of the eastern continent. De Soto's expedition headed north, crossed the Mississippi River near Memphis, reached into Arkansas, and may have come close to present-day Oklahoma.*

When French explorers established Fort Caroline near present-day Jacksonville, Florida, in 1563, the Spanish considered it an encroachment on their claims. Spanish forces based in Havana set out to engage the French, played cat and mouse with the superior French fleet, and then were forced by a storm to seek shelter on the Florida coast. They built a fort to protect themselves until help could arrive. That fort became St. Augustine, the oldest surviving European city in America. The rival French fort disappeared after the Spanish slaughtered all the inhabitants.

Grajales was chaplain of the fleet led by Captain General Pedro Menéndez de Avilés.

On Monday, August 27, while we were near the entrance to the Bahama Channel, God showed to us a miracle from heaven. About nine o'clock in the evening a comet appeared, which showed itself directly above us, a little eastward, giving so much light that it might have been taken for the sun. It went towards the west,—that is, towards Florida,—and its brightness lasted long enough to repeat two Credos. According to the sailors, this was a good omen.

Wednesday morning, September 5, at sunrise, so great a storm arose that we feared we should be shipwrecked. The same evening, about sunset, we perceived a sail afar off, which we supposed was one of our galleys, and which was a great subject of rejoicing; but, as the ship approached, we discovered it was the French flagship *Trinity* we had fired at the night before. At first we thought she was going to attack us; but she did not dare to do it, and anchored between us and the shore, about a league from us. That night the pilots of our other ships came on board, to consult with the Admiral. The next morning, being fully persuaded that the storm had made a wreck of our galley, or that, at least, she had been driven a hundred leagues out to sea, we decided that so soon as daylight came we would weigh anchor and withdraw to a river which was below the French colony, and there disembark, and construct a fort, which we would defend until assistance came to us.

Our fort is at a distance of about fifteen leagues from that of the enemy. The energy and talents of these two brave captains, joined to the efforts of their brave soldiers, who had no tools with which to work the earth, accomplished the construction of this fortress of defence; and, when the general disembarked, he was quite surprised with what had been done.

"A monument of our being there . . ."

SIR FRANCIS DRAKE CLAIMS A KINGDOM

June 17, 1579
Northern California Coast

FRANCIS FLETCHER

*D*rake was the first Englishman to round Cape Horn and sail up the Pacific coasts of South and North America. He may have reached as far north as the state of Washington. Having failed to find a Northwest Passage to Asia, he turned back, and on that leg of the trip made this landing. The actual site is unclear, but claims have been made for several points near San Francisco.

The plate of brass described in this account was "discovered" near San Quentin in 1936 and put on display at the Bancroft Library in Berkeley, California. Tests show it is probably a fake.

Fletcher was chaplain on the ship.

This country our general named Albion, and that for two causes; the one in respect of the white banks and cliffs, which lie toward the sea; the other, that it might have some affinity, even in name also, with our own country, which was sometime so called.

Before we went from there, our general caused to be set up, a monument of our being there; as also of her majesties, and successors right and title to that kingdom, namely, a plate of brass, fast nailed to a great and firm post; whereon is engraven her graces name, and the day and year of our arrival there, and of the free giving up, of the province and kingdom, both by the king and people, into her majesties hands; together with her highness' picture, and arms in a piece of sixpence current English money, showing itself by a hole made of purpose through the plate: underneath was likewise engraven the name of our general &c.

The Spaniards never had any dealing, or so much as set a foot in this country; the utmost of their discoveries, reaching only to many degrees Southward of this place.

The Plate of Brass:

BEE IT KNOWNE VNTO ALL MEN BY THESE PRESENTS

IVNE 17 1579

BY THE GRACE OF GOD AND IN THE NAME OF HERR

MAIESTY QVEEN ELIZABETH OF ENGLAND AND HERR

SVCCESSORS FOREVER I TAKE POSSESSION OF THIS

KINGDOME WHOSE KING AND PEOPLE FREELY RESIGNE

THEIR RIGHT AND TITLE IN THE WHOLE LAND VNTO HERR

MAIESTIES KEEPEING NOW NAMED BY ME AN TO BEE

KNOWNE VNTO ALL MEN AS NOVA ALBION

FRANCIS DRAKE

"In the midst of some delicate garden ..."

VIRGINIA

July 2–4, 1584

CAPTAIN ARTHUR BARLOWE

*T*he English arrived late. Almost 100 years after Columbus's voyage, well after the Spanish had established colonies in North and South America and the West Indies, Sir Walter Raleigh sent the expedition that gave this report of Virginia, Raleigh's all-encompassing name for whatever land England could claim in North America. Raleigh had inherited the royal charter to "remote and heathen barbarous *lands" after the death of his half brother, Sir Humphrey Gilbert, who had drowned on an earlier expedition. Notably, that original charter decreed that settlers "would enjoy all the privileges of free denizens and persons native of England."*

The area described in this account is now the coast of North Carolina.

The second of July, we found shallow water, where we smelled so sweet and so strong a smell, as if we had been in the midst of some delicate garden abounding with all kind of odoriferous flowers, by which we were assured, that the land could not be far distant: and keeping good watch, and bearing but slack sail, the fourth of the same month we arrived upon the coast, which we supposed to be a continent and firm land, and we sailed along the same a hundred and twenty English miles before we could find any entrance, or river issuing into the sea. The first that appeared unto us, we entered, though not without some difficulty, and cast anchor about three harquebuz-shot within the haven's mouth, on the left hand of the same: and after thanks given to God for our safe arrival there, we manned our boats, and went to view the land next adjoining, and to take possession of the same, in the right of the Queen's most excellent Majesty, as rightful Queen.

This land, which lay stretching it self to the west, we found to be but an island of twenty miles long, and not above six miles broad. Under the bank or hill whereon we stood, we beheld the valleys replenished with goodly cedar trees, and having discharged our harquebuz-shot, such a flock of cranes (the most part white) arose under us, with such a cry redoubled by many echoes, as if an army of men had shouted all together.

The next day there came unto us many boats, and in one of them the King's brother, accompanied with forty or fifty men, very handsome and goodly people, and in their behavior as mannerly and civil as any in Europe. His name was Granganimeo, and the king is called Wingina, the country Wingandacoa, and now by her Majesty Virginia. . . .

A day or two after this, we fell to trading with them, exchanging some things that we had, for chamois and deer skins. When we showed him all our packet of merchandise, of all things that he saw, a bright tin dish most pleased him, which he presently took up and clapped it before his breast, and after made a hole in the brim and hung it about his neck, making signs that it would defend him against his enemies' arrows, for those people maintain a deadly and terrible war with the people and King adjoining. We exchanged our tin dish for twenty skins worth twenty crowns, or twenty nobles, and a copper kettle for fifty skins worth fifty crowns.

The King's brother had great liking of our armor, a sword, and many other things which we had, and offered to lay a great box of pearls in exchange for them, but we refused it for this time, because we would not make them know, that we esteemed thereof, until we had understood in what places of the country the pearl grew, which now your Worship does very well understand.

We brought home also two of the Savages being lusty men, whose names were Wanchese and Manteo.

"We could perceive no sign of them . . ."

THE LOST COLONY

1590
Roanoke, Virginia

JOHN WHITE

T *he successful voyage of Barlowe and Amadas in 1584 led Raleigh to venture another expedition in 1587, this time to colonize Virginia with about one hundred settlers.*

The colonists, led by Governor John White, soon ran into difficulty. They could barely feed themselves and had lost skirmishes with the Indians.

White returned to England with plans to raise support for the colony. Although he had left behind his wife and children, he did not return for three years, perhaps prevented by Britain's battles with the Spanish Armada. When he did return, he found nothing. The colonists had vanished.

Many years later the mystery of the Lost Colony was at least partially solved. Apparently some of the colonists had gone to live among the Croatoan natives, now the Lumbee.

AUGUST 15, 1590

Towards evening we came to an anchor at Hatorask. We saw a great smoke rise in the isle Roanoke near the place where I left our colony in the year 1587, which smoke put us in good hope that some of the colony were there expecting my return out of England.

AUGUST 17

Our boats and all things fitted again, we put off from Hatorask, being the number of 19 persons in both boats; but before we could get to the place where our planters were left, it was so exceeding dark that we overshot the place a quarter of a mile. There we espied toward the north end of the island the light of a great fire through the woods, to which we presently rode. When we came right over against it, we let fall our grapnel near the shore and sounded with a trumpet a call, and afterwards many familiar English tunes of songs, and called to them friendly. But we had no answer. We therefore landed at daybreak, and coming to the fire, we found the grass and sundry rotten trees burned about the place.

From hence we went through the woods, and from there we returned by the waterside, round about the north point of the island, until we came to the place where I left our colony in the year 1587.

In all this way we saw in the sand the print of the savages' feet of two or three sorts trodden the night, and as we entered up the sandy bank, upon a tree, in the very brow thereof, were curiously carved these fair Roman letters CRO; which letters presently we knew to signify the place where I should find the planters seated, according to a secret token agreed upon between them and me at my last departure from them, which was that they should not fail to write or carve on the trees or posts of the doors the name of the place where they should be seated; for at my coming away they were prepared to remove from Roanoke 50 miles in the main.

Therefore at my departure from them in 1587 I willed them that if they should happen to be distressed in any of those places, that then they should carve over the letters or name a cross; but we found no such sign of distress. And having well considered of this, we passed towards the place where they were left in sundry houses, but we found the houses taken down, and the place very strongly enclosed with a high palisade of great trees, with curtains and flankers, very fort-like, and one of the chief trees or posts at the right side of the entrance had the bark taken off, and five foot from the ground in fair capital letters was graven CROATOAN without any cross or sign of distress; this done, we entered into the palisade, where we found many bars of iron, two pigs of lead, four iron fowlers, iron sacker-shot (for large cannon) and such like heavy things, thrown here and there, almost overgrown with grass and weeds.

From there we went along by the waterside, towards the point of the creek to see if we could find any of their boats or pinnace, but we could perceive no sign of them, nor any of the last falcons and small ordnance which were left with them at my departure from them.

At our return from the creek, some of our sailors meeting us, told us that they had found where divers chests had been hidden, and long since digged up again and broken up, and much of the goods in them spoiled and scattered about, but nothing left of such things as the savages knew any use of, undefaced.

Presently Captain Cook and I went to the place, which was in the end of an old trench made two years past by Captain Amadas, where we found five chests that had been carefully hidden of the planters, and of the same chests three were my own, and about this place many of my things spoiled and broken, and my books torn from the covers, the frames of some of my pictures and maps rotten and spoiled with rain, and my armor almost eaten through with rust.

This could be no other but the deed of the savages our enemies.

"Their orders for government were put in a box, not to be opened."

THE FOUNDING OF JAMESTOWN

May 13, 1607
Virginia Colony

JOHN SMITH

*A*fter defeating the Spanish Armada, Britain turned again to America. In this renewed effort, Captain Christopher Newport set out from England with 103 men and boys. But the Jamestown venture encountered difficulties just as earlier expeditions had. More than half the colonists died in the first year.

John Smith, who has become the best-known leader of the Jamestown colony, was already a seasoned explorer by the time he sailed for America. He had traveled through Europe while still a teenager, had fought as a mercenary in Transylvania, been captured by the Turks and made a slave, had escaped and traveled into Russia, and finally had returned to England shortly before the London Company launched the Jamestown effort. Although he viewed world events with great self-interest his accounts of the major events are considered reasonably accurate. And to some extent, survival of the colony depended on Smith's political sense, because he was able to forge an alliance with Chief Powhatan when Newport went back to England for supplies.

Smith wrote this account in the third person. Remnants of the fort he describes were unearthed in 1996.

Captain Bartholomew Gosnoll, one of the first movers of this plantation, having many years solicited many of his friends, but found small assistants; at last prevailed with some gentlemen, as Captain John Smith, Master Edward-Maria Wingfield, Master Robert Hunt, and many others, who depended a year upon his projects, but nothing could be effected, till by their great charge and industries it came to be apprehended by certain of the nobility, gentry, and merchants, so that his Majesty by his letters patents, gave commission for establishing councils, to direct here; and to govern, and to execute there. To effect this, was spent another year, and by that, three ships were provided, one of 100 tons, another of 40, and a pinnace of 20. The transportation of the company was committed to Captain Christopher Newport, a mariner well practiced for the western parts of America. But their orders for government were put in a box, not to be opened, nor the governors known until they arrived in Virginia.

The first land they made they called Cape Henry; where thirty of them recreating themselves on shore, were assaulted by five savages, who hurt two of the English very dangerously.

That night was the box opened, and the orders read, in which Bartholomew Gosnoll, John Smith, Edward Wingfield, Christopher Newport, John Ratliffe, John Martin, and George Kendall, were named to be the Council, and to choose a President amongst them for a year, who with the Council should govern. Matters of moment were to be examined by a jury, but determined by the major part of the Council, in which the President had two voices.

Until the 13 of May they sought a place to plant in; then the Council was sworn, Master Wingfield was chosen President, and an oration made, why Captain Smith was not admitted of the Council as the rest.

Now fell every man to work, the Council contrive the Fort, the rest cut down trees to make place to pitch their tents; some provide clapboard to relade the ships. some make gardens, some nets, etc. The savages often visited us kindly. The Presidents overweening jealousy would admit no exercise at arms, or fortification but the boughs of trees cast together in the form of a half moon by the extraordinary pains and diligence of Captain Kendall.

Newport, Smith, and twenty others, were sent to discover the head of the river: by divers small habitations they passed, in six days they arrived at a town called Powhatan, consisting of some twelve houses, pleasantly seated on a hill; before it three fertile isles, about it many of their cornfields, the place is very pleasant, and strong by nature, of this place the Prince is called Powhatan, and his people Powhatans. To this place the river is navigable: but higher within a mile, by reason of the rocks and Isles, there is not passage for a small boat, this they call The Falls. The people in all parts kindly entreated them, till being returned within twenty miles of James town, they gave just cause of jealousy: but had God not blessed the discoverers otherwise than those at the Fort, there had then been an end of that plantation; for at the Fort, where they arrived the next day, they found 17 men hurt, and a boy slain by the savages, and had it not chanced a cross barre shot from the Ships struck down a bough from a tree amongst them, that caused them to retire, our men would have all been slain since they were all at work and their arms were stored away.

Hereupon the President was contented the Fort should be palisaded, the ordnance mounted, his men armed and exercised: for many were the assaults, and ambushes of the savages, and our men by their disorderly straggling were often hurt, when the savages by the nimbleness of their heels well escaped.

"Pocahontas got his head in her arms . . ."

POCAHONTAS SAVES JOHN SMITH

January 1608
Jamestown, Virginia, and Environs

JOHN SMITH

Some historians believe Pocahontas, daughter of Chief Powhatan, did not save John Smith—that Smith instead misinterpreted or misrepresented an initiation ceremony.

By all accounts Pocahontas was extraordinary. Yet Smith abandoned her, leaving for England and allowing her to think that he was dead. She went on to marry John Rolfe, who had become successful as the first European tobacco farmer.

Pocahontas was shocked and hurt to see Smith alive when she traveled with Rolfe to London in 1615. Smith later admitted he deserved her angry tirade. The realization that she had been duped may have contributed to her deep unhappiness in London. She soon fell ill and died there.

Six or seven weeks those barbarians kept [Smith] prisoner, many strange triumphs and conjurations they made of him, yet he so demeaned himself amongst them, as he not only diverted them from surprising the fort but procured his own liberty, and got himself and his company such estimation amongst them that those savages admired him more than their own Quiyouckosucks.

The manner how they used and delivered him is as follows. . . .

He demanding for their captain, they showed him Opechankanough, king of Pamaunkee, to whom he gave a round ivory double compass dial. Much they marveled at the playing of the fly and needle, which they could see so plainly and yet not touch it because of the glass that covered them. But when he demonstrated by that globe-like jewel the roundness of the earth and skies, the sphere of the sun, moon, and stars, and how the sun did chase the night round about the world continually; the greatness of the land and sea, the diversity of nations, variety of complexions, and how we were to them antipodes, and many other such like matters, they all stood as amazed with admiration. Notwithstanding, within an hour after they tied him to a tree, and as many as could stand about him prepared to shoot him: but the king holding up the compass in his hand, they all laid down their bows and arrows, and in a triumphant manner led him to Orapaks, where he was after their manner kindly feasted, and well used.

At last they brought him to Werowocomoco, where was Powhatan, their emperor. Here more than two hundred of those grim courtiers stood wondering at him, as he had been a monster; till Powhatan and his train had put themselves in their greatest braveries. Before a fire upon a seat like a bedstead, he sat covered with a great robe, made of raccoon skins, and all the tails hanging by. On either hand did sit a young wench of sixteen or eighteen years, and along on each side the house, two rows of men and behind them as many women, with all their heads and shoulders painted red, many of their heads bedecked with the white down of birds, but every one with something, and a great chain of white beads about their necks. At his entrance before the king, all the people gave a great shout. The queen of Appamatuck was appointed to bring him water to wash his hands, and another brought him a bunch of feathers, instead of a towel to dry them. Having feasted him after their best barbarous manner they could, a long consultation was held, but the conclusion was, two great stones were brought before Powhatan: then as many as could laid hands on him, dragged him to them, and thereon laid his head, and being ready with their clubs to beat out his brains, Pocahontas, the king's dearest daughter, when no entreaty could prevail, got his head in her arms, and laid her own upon his to save him from death: whereat the emperor was contented he should live to make him hatchets, and her bells, beads, and copper; for they thought him as well of all occupations as themselves. For the king himself will make his own robes, shoes, bows, arrows, pots; plant, hunt, or do anything so well as the rest.

Two days after, Powhatan having disguised himself in the most fearfulest manner he could, caused Captain Smith to be brought forth to a great house in the woods, and there upon a mat by the fire to be left alone. Not long after, from behind a mat that divided the house was made the most dolefulest noise he ever heard; then Powhatan, more like a devil than a man, with some two hundred more as black as himself, came unto him and told him now they were friends, and presently he should go to Jamestown, to send him two great guns, and a grindstone, for which he would give him the county of Capahowosick, and for ever esteem him as his son Wantaquoud.

"This great Charter is to bind us and our heirs for ever . . ."

THE FIRST REPRESENTATIVE ASSEMBLY IN AMERICA

July 30, 1619
Jamestown, Virginia

JOHN TWINE

When first organized, the Virginia Colony was merely a company town. The colonists held no property of their own. They were practically employees of the Virginia Company's stockholders in England. "Twice a day," wrote historian Samuel Eliot Morison, "the men were marched to the fields or woods by the beat of a drum, twice marched back and into church."

These military methods failed. In about a decade the Virginia Company realized profits would come only after the pioneers had a stake in their own fate. Soon after, the colonists asked for a voice in government.

This first representative assembly in the United States was composed of two members—called burgesses—from each of the eleven settlements in Virginia, along with Governor George Yeardley and his council. At the time it was established, the European population of the colony was just under one thousand persons.

The most convenient place we could find to sit in was the choir of the church, where Sir George Yeardley, the governor, being set down in his accustomed place, those of the Council of Estate sat next him on both hands. Forasmuch as men's affairs do little prosper where God's service is neglected, all the burgesses took their places in the choir, till a prayer was said by Mr. Bucke, the minister, that it would please God to guide and sanctify all our proceedings to His own glory, and the good of this plantation.

Which done, [the Speaker] read unto [the Assembly] the commission for establishing the Counsel of Estate and the general Assembly, wherein their duties were described to the life.

Having thus prepared them, he read over unto them the great Charter, or commission of privileges, orders and laws, sent by Sir George Yeardly out of England . . . and so they were referred to the perusal of two committees . . . and accordingly brought in their opinions.

But some men may here object: To what end we should presume to refer that to the examination of the committees what the Counsel and Company in England had already resolved to be perfect, and did expect nothing but our assent thereunto? To this we answer that we did it not to the end to correct or control anything therein contained, but only in case we should find ought not perfectly squaring with the state of this Colony or any law which did press or bind too hard, that we might by way of humble petition, seek to have it redressed, especially because this great Charter is to bind us and our heirs for ever.

"In these hard and difficult beginnings . . ."

THE PILGRIMS' LANDING AND FIRST WINTER

November 21, 1620–March 20, 1621
Plymouth, Massachusetts

WILLIAM BRADFORD

*T*he first European colony in New England was not supposed to be in New England at all.

The Mayflower *left Plymouth, England, on September 1620 with 102 passengers who had received a grant to settle in Virginia. Most, but not all, were members of the Separatists, a dissident Protestant sect that had been persecuted in England and had settled briefly in Holland.*

Poor navigation, or perhaps a desire to avoid the rule of the British authorities that controlled the Virginia Colony, brought them to the coast of Massachusetts. They dropped anchor near what is now Provincetown on November 21, then explored Cape Cod before formally landing and founding Plymouth Colony on December 21.

Because the Mayflower *passengers were outside the jurisdiction of the London Company, they decided to establish their own government. The men on the ship drafted the Mayflower Compact—an early American Constitution—to create a "civil body politic" binding the settlers together and to the rule of law.*

The arrival of an English-speaking Native American to save the settlement would seem a far-fetched plot twist in a novel. How did it happen? Though some of the early details are sketchy, Squanto, also known as Tisquantum, may have been taken to England by a British sea captain as early as 1605, and returned to North America a few years later by Captain John Smith. Around 1615 he was captured along with a few dozen other natives by slavers associated with Smith, and taken to Spain to be sold. He escaped and made his way to England, then returned to North America in 1619 as a pilot for an English ship. Because plague—perhaps smallpox—had killed the members of his Pawtuxet tribe, he went to live with the Wampanoags of Cape Cod. With no family ties to the "Wampanoags, Squanto devoted much of his time to aiding the European settlers.

Bradford became governor of the colony in the spring of 1621 and was reelected to that post thirty times in the following thirty-five years. This account comes from his History of Plymouth Plantation.

The Plymouth Colony became part of the Massachusetts Bay Colony in 1691.

Being thus arrived at Cap-Cod, and necessity calling them to look out a place for habitation, (as well as the masters and mariners importunity), they having brought a large ship with them out of England, stowed in quarters in the ship, they now got her out, and set their carpenters to work to trim her up, but being much bruised and shattered in the ship with foul weather, they saw she would be long in mending. Whereupon a few of them tendered themselves, to go by land and discover those nearest places, while the ship was in mending. . . . It was conceived there might be some danger in the attempt, yet seeing them resolute they were permitted to go, being 16 of them well armed under the conduct of Captain Standish. . . . After some hours sailing, it began to snow and rain, and about the middle of the afternoon, the wind increased, and the sea became very rough; and they broke their rudder, and it was as much as two men could do to steer her with a couple of oars. But their pilot bade them be of good cheer for he saw the harbor, but the storm increasing, and night drawing on, they bore what sail they could to get in, while they could see; but herewith they broke their mast in three pieces and their sail fell overboard, in a very high sea. . . .

But a lusty seaman which steered, bade those which rowed if they were men, about with her, or else they were all cast away; which they did with speed, so he bid them be of good cheer, and row justly for there was a fair sound before them, and he doubted not, but they should find one place or other, where they might ride in safety. And though it was very dark, and rained sore; yet in the end they got under the lee of a small island and remained there all that night in safety. . . .

But though this had been a day and night of much trouble, and danger unto them; yet God gave them a morning of comfort and refreshing (as usually he does to his children) for the next day was a fair sunshining day, and they found themselves to be on an island secure from the Indians; where they might dry their stuff, fix their pieces, and rest themselves, and gave God thanks for his mercies, in their manifold deliverances. And this being the last day of the week, they prepared there to keep the Sabbath; on Monday they sounded the harbor, and found it fit for shipping; and marched into the land, and found many cornfields, and little running brooks, a place (as they supposed) fit for situation, at least it was the best they could find, and the season, and their present necessity made them glad to accept of it. So they returned to their ship again with this news to the rest of their people, which did much comfort their hearts. . . .

Afterwards [they] took better view of the place, and resolved where to pitch their dwelling; and the 25th day began to erect the first house, for common use to receive them, and their goods. . . .

In these hard and difficult beginnings they found some discontents and murmurings arise amongst some, and mutinous speeches and carriages in other; but they were soon quelled, and overcome, by the wisdom, patience, and just and equal carriage of things, by the Governor and the better part which clave faithfully together in the main. But that which was most sad, and lamentable, was, that in two or three months the half of their company died, especially in January and February, being the depth of winter, and wanting houses and other comforts; being infected with the scurvy and other diseases, which this long voyage and their inaccommodate condition had brought upon them; so as there died some times two or three of a day, in the foresaid time; that of one hundred and odd persons scarce fifty remained: and of these in the time of most distress there was but six or seven sound persons; who to their great commendations, be it spoken, spared no pains, night nor day, but with abundance of toil and hazard of their own health, fetched them wood, made them fires, dressed their meat, made their beads, washed their loathsome clothes, clothed and unclothed them. In a word did all the homely, and necessary offices for them, which dainty and queasy stomachs cannot endure to hear named and all this willingly and cheerfully, without any grudging in the least, showing herein their true love unto their friends and brethren. A rare example and worthy to be remembered, two of these seven were Mr. William Brewster, their Reverend Elder, and Miles Standish, their Captain and military commander, (unto whom myself, and many others were much beholden in our low, and sick condition). . . . And what I have said of these, I may say of many others who died in this general visitation and others yet living; that while they had health . . . or any strength continuing they were not wanting to any that had need of them; And I [doubt] not but their recompense is with the Lord. . . .

All this while the Indians came skulking about them, and would sometimes show themselves aloof, but when any approached near them, they would run away; and once they stole away their tools when they had been at work and were gone to diner. But about the 16th of March a certain Indian came boldly amongst them, and spoke to them in broken English which they could well understand, but marveled at it; at length they understood by discourse with him, that he was not of these parts, but belonged to the eastern parts where some English ships came to fish, with whom he was acquainted, and could name sundry of them by their names, amongst whom he had got his language. He became profitable to them in acquainting them with many things concerning the state of the country in the east parts where he lived . . . of the people here, of their names, number and strength, of their situation and distance from this place, and who was chief amongst them. His name was Samasett; he told them also of another Indian whose name was Squanto, a native of this place, who had been in England and could speak better English then himself. Being after some time of entertainment, and gifts dismissed, a while after he came again, and five more with him, and they brought again all the tools that were stolen away before, and made way for the coming of their great Sachem, called Massasoyt. Who about four or five days after came with the chief of his friends, and other attendance with the aforesaid Squanto. With whom after friendly entertainment, and some gifts given him, they made a peace with him (which has now continued this 24 years) in these terms:

1. That neither he nor any of his, should injure or do hurt, to any of their people.

2. That if any of his, did any hurt to any of theirs; he should send the offender, that they might punish him.

3. That if any thing were taken away from any of theirs, he should cause it to be restored; and they should do the like to his.

4. If any did unjustly war against him, they would aide him; if any did war against them, he should aide them.

5. He should send to his neighbors confederates to certify them of this [treaty], that they might not wrong them [the Pilgrims], but might be likewise comprised in the conditions of peace.

6. That when [Massasoyt's] men came to [the Pilgrims,] they should leave their bows and arrows behind them. . . .

They [the Pilgrims] began now to gather in the small harvest they had; and to fit up their houses and dwellings, against winter, being all well recovered in health and strength; and had all things in good plenty, for as some were thus employed in affairs abroad; others were exercised in fishing, about cod, and bass, other fish of which they took good store, of which every family had their portion; all the summer there was no want; and now began to come in store of fowl, as winter approached, of which this place did abound when they came first, (but afterward decreased by degrees), and besides water fowl, there was great store of wild turkeys, of which they took many, besides venison etc. Besides they had about a peck a meal a week to a person, or now since harvest, Indian corn to that proportion, which made many afterwards write so largely of their plenty here to their friends in England, which were not fained, but true reports.

"Drink and be merry, merry, merry boys . . ."

THE MAYPOLE OF MERRY-MOUNT

May 1, 1628
Merry-Mount, Massachusetts Colony

THOMAS MORTON

*M*orton, who had been an attorney in London, was a great annoyance to the Massachusetts authorities because he ridiculed their religious beliefs and sold rifles to the natives. He was forcibly returned to England and imprisoned, but eventually returned to the colony. His exploits are the subject of a story by Nathaniel Hawthorne, two novels, and a 1934 opera by Howard Hanson.
  Merry-Mount is now Quincy.

The Inhabitants of Pasonagessit (having translated the name of their habitation from that ancient savage name to Merry-Mount) did devise amongst themselves to have it performed in a solemn manner with revels and merriment after the old English custom. They prepared to set up a Maypole upon the festival day of Philip and Jacob; and brewed a barrel of excellent beer, and provided a case of bottles to be spent, with other good cheer, for all comers of that day. And because they would have it in a complete form, they had prepared a song fitting to the time and present occasion. And upon Mayday they brought the Maypole to the place appointed, with drums, guns, pistols, and other fitting instruments, for that purpose; and there erected it with the help of Savages, that came there to see the manner of our revels. A goodly pine tree, eighty feet long, was reared up, with a pair of buck's horns nailed on, somewhat near unto the top of it: where it stood as a fair sea mark for directions; how to find out the way to my host of Merry-Mount.

And because it should more fully appear to what end it was placed there, they had a poem in readiness made, which was fixed to the Maypole, to show the new name confirmed upon that plantation. . . .

The setting up of this Maypole was a lamentable spectacle to the precise separatists that lived at new Plymouth. They termed it an Idol; yea they called it the Calf of Horeb, and stood at defiance with the place, naming it Mount Dagon; threatening to make it a woeful mount and not a merry mount. . . .

There was likewise a merry song made, which (to make their revels more fashionable) was sung with a chorus, every man bearing his part; which they performed in a dance, hand in hand about the Maypole while one of the Company sung, and filled out the good liquor like Gamedes and Jupiter:

> Drink and be merry, merry, merry boys,
> Let all your delight be in Hymen's joys,
> Joy to Hymen now the day is come,
> About the merry Maypole take a room.
>
> Make greene garlands, bring bottles out;
> And fill sweet Nectar, freely about,
> Uncover thy head, and fear no harm,
> For here's good liquor to keep it warm. . . .

This harmless mirth made by young men (that lived in hope to have wives brought over to them . . .) was much distasted by the precise Separatists . . . troubling their brains more than reason would require about things that are indifferent, and from that time sought occasion against my honest host of Merry-Mount to overthrow his undertakings, and to destroy his plantation quite and clean.

"Many dangerous opinions ..."

ROGER WILLIAMS DEMANDS FREEDOM OF RELIGION

1634–1636
Massachusetts and Rhode Island

NATHANIEL MORTON

*W*illiams, like two other famous dissenters, Anne Hutchinson and John Wheel-wright, challenged the rule of the church in Massachusetts. After being banished from Plymouth Colony and the Massachusetts Bay Colony, Williams founded Rhode Island, establishing a government that guaranteed religious freedom. Wheelwright, banished from Massachusetts a short time later, founded a settlement in

New Hampshire. Hutchinson was the last of the three to be expelled. She settled in southern Rhode Island and then on Long Island.

Eyewitness Nathaniel Morton was raised by the Bradford family and later served as secretary of the Massachusetts Bay Colony.

In the year 1634, Mr. Roger Williams removed from Plymouth to Salem. He had lived about three years at Plymouth, where he was well accepted as an assistant in the Ministry to Mr. Ralph Smith, then Pastor of the Church there, but by expressing many of his own singular opinions, and seeking to impose them upon others, he not finding such a concurrence as he expected, he desired his dismission to the Church of Salem. Fearing that his continuance amongst them might cause divisions, the Church of Plymouth consented to his dismission, and such as did adhere to him were also dismissed, and removed with him, or not long after him to Salem.

But he having in one years time, filled that place with principles of rigid separation, and tending to Anabaptistry, the prudent Magistrates of the Massachusetts Jurisdiction, sent to the Church of Salem, desiring them to forbear calling him to office, which they not hearkening to, was a cause of much disturbance; for Mr. Williams had begun, and then being in office, he proceeded more vigorously to vent many dangerous opinions, as amongst many others these were some . . . that there should be a general and unlimited toleration of all religions, and for any man to be punished for any matters of his conscience, was persecution.

He not only persisted, but grew more violent in his way, insomuch as he staying at home in his own house, sent a letter, which was delivered and read in the public Church assembly, the scope of which was to give them notice, that if the Church of Salem would not separate not only from the Churches of Old-England, but the Churches of New-England too, he would separate from them. The more prudent and sober part of the Church being amazed at his way, could not yield unto him. Whereupon he never came to the Church Assembly more, professing separation from them as Antichristian, and not only so, but he withdrew all private religious Communion from any that would hold Communion with the Church there, insomuch as he would not pray nor give thanks at meals with his own wife nor any of his family, because they went to the Church Assemblies.

The prudent Magistrates understanding, and seeing things grow more and more towards a general division and disturbance, after all other means used in vain, they passed a sentence of Banishment against him out of the Massachusetts Colony, as against a disturber of the peace, both of the Church and Commonwealth.

After which Mr. Williams sat down in a place called Providence, out of the Massachusetts Jurisdiction, and was followed by many of the members of the Church of Salem, who did zealously adhere to him, and who cried out of the Persecution that was against him, keeping that one principle, that every one should have the liberty to worship God according to the light of their own consciences.

"Stuyvesant's first arrival ... was like a peacock ..."

STUYVESANT'S BAD GOVERNMENT

1647
New Amsterdam

JUNKER VAN DER DONCK AND OTHERS

Between the English colonies of New England and Virginia were colonies of New Sweden and the New Netherlands. Van der Donck, who had been a lawyer in the Netherlands, was a member of a committee that reported on conditions in the colony. He predicted that mismanagement would lead to the fall of the New Netherlands Colony. He was right. In 1664, Governor Peter Stuyvesant, facing four ships of British sailors, surrendered its capital, New Amsterdam, without a fight. The city was quickly renamed New York.

Stuyvesant's first arrival—for what passed on the voyage is not for us to speak of—was like a peacock, with great state and pomp. The appellation of *Lord General,* and similar titles, were never before known here. Almost every day he caused proclamations of various import to be published, which were for the most part never observed, and have long since been a dead letter, except the Fine excise, as that yielded a profit. . . . At one time, after leaving the house of the minister, where the consistory had been sitting and had risen, it happened that Arnoldus Van Herdenbergh related the proceedings relative to the estate of Zeger Teunisz, and how he himself, as curator, had appealed from the sentence; whereupon the Director, who had been sitting there with them as an elder, interrupted him and replied, "It may during my administration be contemplated to appeal, but if any one should do it, I will *make him a foot shorter,* and send the pieces to Holland, and let him appeal in that way."

In our opinion this country will never flourish under the government of the Honorable Company, but will pass away and come to an end of itself, unless the Honorable Company be reformed.

"She had been a queen in her own country . . ."

AN ANGRY SLAVE

October 2, 1663
Massachusetts

JOHN JOSSELYN

*T*he first African slaves were brought to the shores of America in 1619, when a group of twenty were put to work at the Jamestown settlement. (That same year the white citizens of Jamestown demanded and received representation in Virginia's government. See page 19.)

Josselyn was an Englishman, possibly a physician, who wrote two notable books about his visits to the colonies.

The second of October, about nine of the clock in the morning, Mr. Maverick's Negro woman came to my chamber window, and in her own country language and tune sang very loud and shrill. Going out to her, she used a great deal of respect towards me, and willingly would have expressed her grief in English. But I apprehended it by her countenance and deportment, whereupon I repaired to my host, to learn of him the cause, and resolved to entreat him in her behalf, for that I understood before that she had been a queen in her own country, and observed a very humble and dutiful garb used towards her by another Negro who was her maid. Mr. Maverick was desirous to have a breed of Negroes, and therefore seeing she would not yield by persuasions to company with a young Negro man he had in his house, he commanded him, willed she nilled she, to go to bed to her, which was no sooner done but she kicked him out again. This she took in high disdain beyond her slavery, and this was the cause of her grief.

"We saw also a hideous monster . . ."

JOLLIET AND MARQUETTE
TRAVEL THE MISSISSIPPI

June 10–17, 1673

FATHER JACQUES MARQUETTE

*T*he Jesuit Jacques Marquette founded missions at Sault Ste. Marie and St. Ignace in
present-day Michigan before joining the voyage of Louis Jolliet, a Jesuit-educated
explorer, down the Mississippi. They started from the Bay of Puan, now Green Bay.

   The explorations of Jolliet, Marquette, and others such as Robert Cavelier and
Sieur de La Salle helped the French establish outposts in the Great Lakes and Mississippi regions. (In 1682 La Salle claimed the river and all of its tributaries for
France. He named the region Louisiana, after King Louis XIV. He also tried to
honor Jean-Baptiste Colbert, the king's legendary minister of finance, by renaming
the river "Le Colbert.")

   The French outposts hindered the westward movement of the British colonists,
leading to the French and Indian War in the 1750s (see page 45).

This bay is about thirty leagues long, and eight broad in its greatest
breadth, for it grows narrower and forms a cone at the extremity. It has
tides that ebb as regular as the sea. We left this bay to go to a river [the
Fox River] that discharges itself therein. . . . It flows very gently. . . . We
next came to a village of the Maskoutens, or nation of fire. . . .

   The next day, being the 10th of June, the two guides [from the Miami
tribe] embarked with us in sight of all the village, who were astonished at
our attempting so dangerous an expedition. We were informed that at
three leagues from the Maskoutens, we should find a river which runs
into the Mississippi, and that we were to go to the west-south-west to find
it, but there were so many marshes and lakes, that if it had not been for
our guides we could not have found it.

   The river upon which we rowed and had to carry our canoes from
one to the other, looked more like a corn-field than a river, insomuch that
we could hardly find its channel. As our guides had been frequently at this
portage, they knew the way, and helped us to carry our canoes overland
into the other river, distant about two miles and a half; from whence they
returned home, leaving us in an unknown country, having nothing to rely

upon but Divine Providence. We now left the waters which extend to Quebec, about five or six hundred leagues, to take those which would lead us hereafter into strange lands.

Before embarking we all offered up prayers to the Holy Virgin, which we continued to do every morning, placing ourselves and the events of the journey under her protection, and after having encouraged each other, we got into our canoes. The river upon which we embarked is called Mesconsin [Wisconsin]; the river is very wide, but the sand bars make it very difficult to navigate, which is increased by numerous islands covered with grape vines.

The country through which it flows is beautiful; the groves are so dispersed in the prairies that it makes a noble prospect; and the fruit of the trees shows a fertile soil. These groves are full of walnut, oak, and other trees unknown to us in Europe. We saw neither game nor fish, but roebuck and buffaloes in great numbers. After having navigated thirty leagues we discovered some iron mines, and one of our company who had seen such mines before, said these were very rich in ore. They are covered with about three feet of soil, and situate near a chain of rocks, whose base is covered with fine timber. After having rowed ten leagues further, making forty leagues from the place where we had embarked, we came into the Mississippi on the 17th of June.

Behold us, then, upon this celebrated river, whose singularities I have attentively studied. The Mississippi takes its rise in several lakes in the North. Its channel is very narrow at the mouth of the Mesconsin, and runs south until it is affected by very high hills. Its current is slow, because of its depth. In sounding we found nineteen fathoms of water. A little further on it widens nearly three-quarters of a league, and the width continues to be more equal. We slowly followed its course to the south and south-east to the 42° N. lat. Here we perceived the country change its appearance. There were scarcely any more woods or mountains. The islands are covered with fine trees, but we could not see any more roebucks, buffaloes, bustards, and swans.

We met from time to time monstrous fish, which struck so violently against our canoes, that at first we took them to be large trees, which threatened to upset us. We saw also a hideous monster; his head was like that of a tiger, his nose was sharp, and somewhat resembled a wildcat; his beard was long; his ears stood upright; the color of his head was gray; and his neck black. He looked upon us for some time, but as we came near him our oars frightened him away.

When we threw our nets into the water we caught an abundance of sturgeons, and another kind of fish like our trout, except that the eyes and nose are much smaller, and they have near the nose a bone like a woman's busk, three inches broad and a foot and a half long, the end of which is flat and broad, and when it leaps out of the water the weight of it throws it on its back.

Having descended the river as far as $41°28'$ we found that turkeys took the place of game, and the Pisikious that of other animals. We called the Pisikious wild buffaloes, because they very much resemble our domestic oxen; they are not so long, but twice as large. We shot one of them, and it was as much as thirteen men could do to drag him from the place where he fell.

About the end of June, we embarked in presence of all the village, who admired our birch canoes, as they had never before seen anything like them. We descended the river, looking for another called Pekitanoni [the Missouri] which runs from the north-west into the Mississippi, of which I will speak more hereafter.

As we were descending the river we saw high rocks with hideous monsters painted on them, and upon which the bravest Indians dare not look. They are as large as a calf, with head and horns like a goat; their eyes red; beard like a tiger's; and a face like a man's. Their tails are so long that they pass over their heads and between their fore legs, under their belly, and ending like a fish's tail. They are painted red, green, and black. They are so well drawn that I cannot believe they were drawn by the Indians. And for what purpose they were made seems to me a great mystery.

As we fell down the river, and while we were discoursing upon these monsters, we heard a great rushing and bubbling of waters, and small islands of floating trees coming from the mouth of the Pekitanoni [Missouri], with such rapidity that we could not trust ourselves to go near it. The water of this river is so muddy that we could not drink it. It so discolors the Mississippi as to make the navigation of it dangerous. This river comes from the north-west, and empties into the Mississippi, and on its banks are situated a number of Indian villages. We judged by the compass, that the Mississippi discharged itself into the Gulf of Mexico.

Having satisfied ourselves, we resolved to return home. We considered that the advantage of our travels would be altogether lost to our nation if we fell into the hands of the Spaniards, from whom we could expect no other treatment than death or slavery.

"Now is the dreadful hour come ..."

KING PHILIP'S WAR: MARY ROWLANDSON IS CAPTURED

February 10, 1675
Lancaster, Massachusetts

MARY ROWLANDSON

*T*he many book-length accounts of kidnapping and captivity such as Rowland-son's thrilled readers in Britain and became a staple of early American litera-ture. As historian John Demos remarked in The Unredeemed Captive, "at some deeper (mostly unacknowledged) level" Europeans were fascinated with the possibil-ity that "instead of their civilizing the wilderness (and its savage inhabitants), the wilderness might change, might uncivilize them. . . . that some captives will come to prefer Indian ways."

Rowlandson was taken captive during King Philip's War (1675–1676), one of the most devastating conflicts between the European settlers and the Native Ameri-cans. The war was named for Metacom, chief of the Wampanoags, who was called Philip by the Europeans. Although Metacom's father, Massasoit, had been a friend of the Puritans, Metacom was tired of accommodating the expansionist settlers. He forged an alliance with tribes such as the Naragansett, and together they com-pletely destroyed a dozen New England cities and killed hundreds of settlers. Half the towns in New England suffered some damage. One of every sixteen European men of military age was killed. The Native Americans suffered as badly or worse during the war and ultimately lost the struggle to limit the inland drive of the set-tlers. The war officially ended when Metacom was killed in August 1676, but back-and-forth raids continued.

Rowlandson, wife of Lancaster's minister, was ransomed after eleven weeks of being marched around New England.

On the 10th of February, 1675, came the Indians with great numbers upon Lancaster. Their first coming was about sunrising.

Hearing the noise of some guns, we looked out; several houses were burning, and the smoke ascending to heaven. There were five persons taken in one house; the father and the mother and a suckling child they knocked on the head; the other two they took and carried away alive. There were two others, who, being out of their garrison upon some occasion, were set upon; one was knocked on the head, the other escaped. Another there was who, running along, was shot and wounded, and fell down; he begged of them his life, promising them money (as they told me), but they would not hearken to him, but knocked him in the head, and stripped him naked, and split open his bowels. Another seeing many of the Indians about his barn ventured and went out, but was quickly shot down. There were three others belonging to the same garrison who were killed; the Indians, getting up upon the roof of the barn, had advantage to shoot down upon them over their fortification. Thus these murderous wretches went on burning and destroying before them.

At length they came and beset our own house, and quickly it was the dolefulest day that ever mine eyes saw. The house stood upon the edge of a hill; some of the Indians got behind the hill, others into the barn, and others behind anything that could shelter them; from all which places they shot against the house, so that the bullets seemed to fly like hail, and quickly they wounded one man among us, then another, and then a third. About two hours (according to my observation in that amazing time) they had been about the house before they prevailed to fire it; they fired it once, and one ventured out and quenched it, but they quickly fired it again, and that took. Now is the dreadful hour come that I have often heard of, but now mine eyes see it. Some in our house were fighting for their lives, others wallowing in their blood, the house on fire over our heads, and the bloody heathen ready to knock us on the head if we stirred out. Now might we hear mothers and children crying out for themselves and one another, "Lord, what shall we do?" Then I took my children (and one of my sisters hers) to go forth and leave the house, but, as soon as we came to the door and appeared, the Indians shot so thick that the bullets rattled against the house as if one had taken a handful of stones and threw them, so that we were forced to give back. We had six stout dogs belonging to our garrison, but none of them would stir, though another time if any Indian had come to the door, they were ready to fly upon him and tear him down. The Lord hereby would make us the more to acknowledge His hand, and to see that our help is always in Him. But out we must go, the fire increasing, and coming along behind us roaring, and the Indians gaping before us with their guns, spears, and hatchets to devour us.

No sooner were we out of the house but my brother-in-law (being before wounded in defending the house, in or near the throat) fell down dead, whereat the Indians scornfully shouted and hallooed, and were presently upon him, stripping off his clothes. The bullets flying thick, one went through my side, and the same (as would seem) through the bowels and hand of my dear child in my arms. One of my elder sister's children (named William) had then his leg broke, which the Indians perceiving they knocked him on the head. Thus were we butchered by those merciless heathen, standing amazed, with the blood running down to our heels. My eldest sister being yet in the house, and seeing those woeful sights, the infidels hauling mothers one way and children another, and some wallowing in their blood; and her elder son telling her that her son William was dead, and myself was wounded, she said, "And, Lord, let me die with them"; which was no sooner said, but she was struck with a bullet, and fell down dead over the threshold. I hope she is reaping the fruit of her good labors, being faithful to the service of God in her place.

I had often before this said, that if the Indians should come, I should choose rather to be killed by them than taken alive, but when it came to the trial, my mind changed; their glittering weapons so daunted my spirit, that I chose rather to go along with those (as I may say) ravenous bears, than that moment to end my days.

"A wild worldly world . . ."

NEW YORK AND ENVIRONS

September 24–October 11, 1679

JASPAR DANCKAERTS AND PETER SLUYTER

*D*anckaerts and Sluyter had come to America from the Netherlands to find a site for a colony for their small Protestant sect. (The sect eventually settled in Maryland but did not last long.)
Many of the place names and characteristics they describe survive to this day.

As it was Sunday, in order to avoid scandal and for other reasons, we did not wish to absent ourselves from church. We therefore went, and found there truly a wild worldly world. I say wild, not only because the people are wild, as they call it in Europe, but because most all the people who go there to live, or who are born there, partake somewhat of the nature of the country, that is, peculiar to the land where they live. We heard a minister preach, who had come from the up-river country, from

Fort Orange, where his residence is, an old man, named Domine Schaats, of Amsterdam. As it is not strange in these countries to have men as ministers who drink, we could imagine nothing else than that he had been drinking a little this morning. His text was, Come unto me all ye, etc., but he was so rough that even the roughest and most godless of our sailors were astonished.

The church being in the fort, we had an opportunity to look through the latter, as we had come too early for preaching. It is not large; it has four points or batteries; it has no moat outside, but is enclosed with a double row of palisades. It is built from the foundation with quarry stone. The parapet is of earth. It is well provided with cannon, for the most part of iron, though there were some small brass pieces, all bearing the mark or arms of the Netherlanders. The garrison is small. There is a well of fine water dug in the fort by the English, contrary to the opinion of the Dutch, who supposed the fort was built upon rock, and had therefore never attempted any such thing. . . . It has only one gate, and that is on the land side, opening upon a broad plain or street, called the Broadway or Beaverway.

27th. Wednesday. We started at two o'clock for Long Island. We went on, up the hill, along open roads and a little woods, through the first village, called Breukelen, which has a small and ugly little church standing in the middle of the road. Having passed through here, we struck off to the right, in order to go to Gouanes. We went upon several plantations where Gerrit was acquainted with most all of the people, who made us very welcome, sharing with us bountifully whatever they had.

On [our] return home, we went from the city, following the Broadway. Upon both sides of this way were many habitations of negroes, mulattoes and whites. These negroes were formerly the proper slaves of the (West India) company, but, in consequence of the frequent changes and conquests of the country, they have obtained their freedom and settled themselves down where they have thought proper, and thus on this road, where they have ground enough to live on with their families. We left the village, called the Bouwerij, lying on the right hand, and went through the woods to New Harlem, a tolerably large village situated on the south side of the island [now reckoned as the east side], directly opposite the place where the northeast creek and the East river come together, situated about three hours journey from New Amsterdam.

11th [October], Wednesday. We embarked early this morning in his boat and rowed over to Staten Island, where we arrived about eight o'clock. . . . There are now about a hundred families on the island, of which the English constitute the least portion, and the Dutch and French divide between them about equally the greater portion. They have neither church nor minister, and live rather far from each other, and inconveniently to meet together. The English are less disposed to religion and inquire little after it, but in case there were a minister, would contribute to his support. The French and Dutch are very desirous and eager for one, for they spoke of it wherever we went.

When we arrived at Gouanes, we heard a great noise, shouting and singing in the huts of the Indians, who as we mentioned before, were living there. They were all lustily drunk, raving, striking, shouting, jumping, fighting each other, and foaming at the mouth like raging wild beasts. Some who did not participate with them, had fled with their wives and children to Simon's house, where the drunken brutes followed, bawling in the house and before the door, which we finally closed. And this was caused by Christians [selling liquor]. Simon and his wife also do their best in the same way, although we spoke to them severely on the subject. They brought forward this excuse, that if they did not do it, others would, and then they would have the trouble and others the profit; but if they must have the trouble, they ought to have the profit, and so they all said, and for the most part falsely, for they all solicit the Indians as much as they can, and after begging their money from them, compel them to leave their blankets, leggings, and coverings of their bodies in pawn, yes, their guns and hatchets, the very instruments by which they obtain their subsistence. This subject is so painful and so abominable, that I will forbear saying anything more for the present.

". . . I said, this is certainly a tavern."

HARVARD STUDENTS

July 9, 1680
Cambridge, Massachusetts

JASPAR DANCKAERTS AND PETER SLUYTER

To be fair, it should be noted that Harvard was in a slump when Danckaerts and Sluyter visited—not long after King Philip's War had disrupted most aspects of New England life. The college had been without a president for a few years, and only four or five students were enrolled in each class. The student body soon became larger and more energetic. In 1723, Judge Samuel Sewall, head of a committee looking into student life, was able to report, "There has been a practice of general immoralities, particularly stealing, lying, swearing, idleness, picking of locks, and too frequent use of strong drink."

We started out to go to Cambridge, lying to the northeast of Boston, in order to see their college, and printing office. We reached Cambridge, about eight o'clock. It is not a large village, and the houses stand very much apart. The college building is the most conspicuous among them. We went to it, expecting to see something curious, as it is the only college, or would-be academy of the Protestants in all America, but we found ourselves mistaken. In approaching the house, we neither heard nor saw anything mentionable; but, going to the other side of the building, we heard noise enough in an upper room, to lead my comrade to suppose they were engaged in disputation.

We entered, and went up stairs, when a person met us, and requested us to walk in, which we did. We found there, eight or ten young fellows, sitting around, smoking tobacco, with the smoke of which the rooms was so full, that you could hardly see; and the whole house smelled so strong of it, that when I was going up stairs, I said, this is certainly a tavern. We excused ourselves, that we could speak English only a little, but understood Dutch or French, which they did not. However, we spoke as well as we could. We inquired how many professors there were, and they replied not one, that there was no money to support one. We asked how many students there were. They said at first, thirty, and then came down to twenty; I afterwards understood there are probably not ten. They could hardly speak a word of Latin, so that my comrade could not converse with them. They took us to the library where there was nothing particular. We looked over it a little. They presented us with a glass of wine. This is all we ascertained there. The minister of the place goes there morning and evening to make prayer, and has charge over them. The students have tutors or masters.

Our visit was soon over, and we left them to go and look at the land about there. We found the place beautifully situated on a large plain, more than eight miles square, with a fine stream in the middle of it, capable of bearing heavily laden vessels. As regards the fertility of the soil, we consider the poorest in New York, superior to the best here. As we were tired, we took a mouthful to eat, and left. We passed by the printing office, but there was nobody in it; the paper sash however being broken, we looked in; and saw two presses with six or eight cases of type. There is not much work done there. Our printing office is well worth two of it, and even more.

"Did you at any time ride upon a stick or pole?"

TRIAL OF "WITCHES" SUSANNAH MARTIN AND MARY LACEY

1692
Salem Village, Massachusetts

EZEKIEL CHEEVER AND COTTON MATHER

*T*he witch mania in Salem Village (now Danvers) did not differ much from the bloodier witch hunts in Europe, but it occurred at the time that the Europeans were becoming enlightened. Twenty "witches" were executed before the trials were halted by Governor William Phips. More than a hundred were in jail waiting their turn at the bar and likely death.

A few years after the trials, some of the judges repudiated the prosecutions and a public fast was called in penance. In 1711, descendants of those who had been executed were awarded compensation.

Mather, supposedly the most learned colonist—he wrote hundreds of books—followed his usual course of combining superstition with passionate intensity. More than merely chronicling the madness, he helped foster it. Cheever was a clerk of the court.

Susannah Martin, a sixty-seven-year old widow who "spoke her mind freely, and with strength of expression," was hanged. Mary Lacey confessed and was spared.

Susannah Martin pleaded Not Guilty to the indictment of witchcraft brought in against her.

The evidence of many persons very sensibly and grievously bewitched was produced. They all complained of the prisoner as the person whom they believed at the cause of their miseries. And now, as well as in the other trials, there was an extraordinary endeavor by witchcraft, with cruel and frequent fits, to hinder the poor sufferers from giving their complaints. The cast of Martin's eye struck people to the ground, whether they saw that cast or not.

These were among the passages between the Magistrates and the Accused:

MAGISTRATE: "Pray, what ails these people?"
MARTIN: "I don't know."

MAGISTRATE: "But what do you think ails them?"

MARTIN: "I don't desire to spend my judgment upon it."

MAGISTRATE: "Don't you think they are bewitched?"

MARTIN: "No, I do not think they are."

MAGISTRATE: "Tell us your thoughts about them then."

MARTIN: "No, my thoughts are my own, when they are in; but when they are out they are another's. Their Master—"

MAGISTRATE: "Their Master? Who do you think is their Master?"

MARTIN: "If they be dealing in the Black Art, then you may know as well as I."

MAGISTRATE: "Well, what have you done towards this?"

MARTIN: "Nothing at all."

MAGISTRATE: "Why, 'tis you or your Appearance."

MARTIN: "I cannot help it."

MAGISTRATE: "Is it not your Master? How comes your Appearance to hurt these?"

MARTIN: "How do I know? He that appeared in the shape of Samuel, a glorified Saint, may appear in anyone's shape."

It was noted that in her, as in others like her, that if the afflicted went to approach her, they were flung down to the ground. And, when she was asked the reason of it, she said, "I cannot tell. It may be the Devil bears me more malice than another."

. . . Mary Lacey was brought in, and Mary Warren in a violent fit.

MAGISTRATE: "You are here accused for practising witchcraft upon Goo Ballard; which way do you do it?"

LACEY: "I cannot tell. Where is my mother that made me a witch, and I knew it not?"

MAGISTRATE: "Can you look upon that maid, Mary Warren, and not hurt her? Look upon her in a friendly way."

She trying so to do, struck her down with her eyes.

MAGISTRATE: "Do you acknowledge now you are a witch?"

LACEY: "Yes."

MAGISTRATE: "How long have you been a witch?"

LACEY: "Not above a week."

MAGISTRATE: "Did the Devil appear to you?"

LACEY: "Yes."

MAGISTRATE: "In what shape?"

LACEY: "In the shape of a horse."

MAGISTRATE: "What did he say to you?"

LACEY: "He bid me not to be afraid of any thing, and he would bring me out; but he has proved a liar from the beginning."

MAGISTRATE: "Did he bid you worship him?"

LACEY: "Yes; he bid me also to afflict persons."

MAGISTRATE: "Who did the Devil bid you afflict?"

LACEY: "Timothy Swan. Richard Carrier comes often a-nights and has me to afflict persons."

MAGISTRATE: "Did you at any time ride upon a stick or pole?"

LACEY: "Yes."

MAGISTRATE: "How high?"

LACEY: "Sometimes above the trees."

"... A sword in the hands of a wicked kind."

FREEDOM OF THE PRESS

August 4, 1735
New York City

JOHN PETER ZENGER

*Z*enger *was the editor and printer of the* New-York Weekly Journal, *founded in opposition to Governor William Cosby. He was arrested for printing statements critical of Cosby, among them "We see men's deeds destroyed, judges arbitrarily displaced, new courts erected, without consent of the legislature, by which it seems to me, trials by jury are taken away when a governor pleases. . . ."*

He was in prison for ten months before his case went to trial. During that time he continued to publish the Journal *by giving instructions to his wife and servants through a hole in the prison door.*

When his first lawyers were disbarred for daring to defend him, Andrew Hamilton, the most prominent lawyer in America (and no relation to Alexander), was secretly secured to make the arguments. His appearance in court surprised the justices, and his arguments won the case. Benjamin Franklin called Hamilton "the day-star of the Revolution."

Hamilton offered the jurors the extraordinary and successful argument to ignore the law and instead consider the truthfulness of the statements Zenger printed. *While freedom of the press was not entirely secured by the Zenger decision, the case laid the foundation.*

The chief justice was Cosby appointee James De Lancey. "Mr. Attorney" was Richard Bradley, attorney-general of New York.

ATTORNEY GENERAL BRADLEY: . . . The case before the Court is, whether Mr. Zenger is guilty of libelling his Excellency the Governor of New-York, and indeed the whole Administration of the Government. Mr. Hamilton has confessed the printing and publishing, and I think nothing is plainer, than that the words in the information are scandalous, and tend to sedition, and to disquiet the minds of the people of this province. And if such papers are not libels, I think it may be said, there can be no such thing as a libel.

MR. HAMILTON: May it please your Honour; I cannot agree with Mr. Attorney. For tho' I freely acknowledge, that there are such things as libels, yet I must insist at the same time, that what my client is charged with, is not a libel; and I observed just now, that Mr. Attorney in defining a libel, made use of the words *scandalous, seditious,* and *tend to disquiet the people;* but (whether with design or not I will not say) he omitted the word "false." . . .

MR. CHIEF JUSTICE: You cannot be admitted, Mr. Hamilton, to give the truth of a libel in evidence. A libel is not to be justified; for it is nevertheless a libel that it is true.

MR. HAMILTON: I am sorry the Court has so soon resolved upon that piece of law; I expected first to have been heard to that point. I have not in all my reading met with an authority that says, we cannot be admitted to give the truth in evidence, upon an information for a libel.

MR. CHIEF JUSTICE: The law is clear, That you cannot justify a libel. . . .

MR. HAMILTON: I thank your Honour. Then, gentlemen of the jury, it is to you we must now appeal, for witnesses, to the truth of the facts we have offered, and are denied the liberty to prove; and let it not seem strange, that I apply my self to you in this manner, I am warranted so to do both by law and reason. The last supposes you to be summoned, out of the neighbourhood where the fact is alleged to be committed; and the reason of your being taken out of the neighbourhood is, because you are supposed to have the best knowledge of the fact that is to be tried. And were you to find a verdict against my client, you must take upon you to say, the papers referred to in the information, and which we acknowledge we printed and published, are false, scandalous and seditious; but of this I can have no apprehension. You are citizens of New-York; you are really what the law supposes you to be, honest and lawful men; and, according to my brief, the facts which we offer to prove were not committed in a corner; they are notoriously known to be true; and therefore in your justice lies our safety. And as we are denied the liberty of giving evidence, to prove the truth of what we have published, I will beg leave to lay it down as a standing rule in such cases, that the suppressing of evidence ought always to be taken for the strongest evidence; and I hope it will have that weight with you. . . .

It is true in times past it was a crime to speak truth, and in that terrible Court of Star-Chamber, many worthy and brave men suffered for so doing; and yet even in that court, and in those bad times, a great and good man dared to say, what I hope will not be taken amiss of me to say in this place, to wit, the practice of informations for libels is a sword in the hands of a wicked King, and an arrant coward to cut down and destroy the innocent; the one cannot, because of his high station, and the other dares not, because of his want of courage, revenge himself in another manner.

ATTORNEY GENERAL BRADLEY: Pray Mr. Hamilton, have a care what you say, don't go too far neither, I don't like those liberties.

MR. HAMILTON: I hope to be pardon'd, Sir, for my zeal upon this occasion: It is an old and wise caution, that when our neighbour's house is on fire, we ought to take care of our own. For tho', blessed be God, I live in a government where liberty is well understood, and freely enjoy'd; yet experience has shown us all (I'm sure it has to me) that a bad precedent in one government, is soon set up for an authority in another; and therefore I cannot but think it mine, and every honest man's duty, that (while we pay all due obedience to men in authority) we ought at the same time to be upon our guard against power, wherever we apprehend that it may affect ourselves or our fellow-subjects. . . .

I should think it my duty, if required, to go to the utmost part of the land, where my service could be of any use in assisting to quench the flame of prosecutions upon informations, set on foot by the government, to deprive a people of the right of remonstrating (and complaining too) of the arbitrary attempts of men in power. Men who injure and oppress the people under their administration provoke them to cry out and complain; and then make that very complaint the foundation for new oppressions and prosecutions. I wish I could say there were no instances of this kind. But to conclude; the question before the court and you, gentlemen of the jury, is not of small nor private concern, it is not the cause of a poor printer, nor of New-York alone, which you are now trying; No! It may in its consequence, affect every freeman that lives under a British government on the main of America. It is the best cause. It is the cause of liberty; and I make no doubt but your upright conduct, this day, will not only entitle you to the love and esteem of your fellow-citizens; but every man, who prefers freedom to a life of slavery, will bless and honour you, as men who have baffled the attempt of tyranny; and by an impartial and uncorrupt verdict, have laid a noble foundation for securing to ourselves, our posterity, and our neighbours, that to which nature and the laws of our country have given us a right—the liberty—both of exposing and opposing arbitrary power (in these parts of the world, at least) by speaking and writing truth. . . .

MR. CHIEF JUSTICE: Gentlemen of the jury. The great pains Mr. Hamilton has taken, to show how little regard juries are to pay to the opinion of the judges; and his insisting so much upon the conduct of some judges in trials of this kind; is done, no doubt, with a design that you should take but very little notice of what I may say upon this occasion. I shall therefore only observe to you that, as the facts or words in the information are confessed: the only thing that can come in question before you is, whether the words, as set forth in the information, make a libel. And that is a matter of law, no doubt, and which you may leave to the court. . . .

The Jury withdrew, and in a small time returned, and being asked by the clerk, whether they were agreed of their verdict, and whether John Peter Zenger was guilty of printing and publishing the libels in the information mentioned? They answered by Thomas Bunt, their Foreman, Not Guilty. Upon which there were three Huzzas in the hall which was crowded with people, and the next day I was discharged from my imprisonment.

"A day of great fatigue and trouble."

THE MARCH OF THE ACADIANS DURING THE FRENCH AND INDIAN WAR

August 30–September 5, 1755
Grand Pré, Nova Scotia

COLONEL JOHN WINSLOW

*A*t the time of the French and Indian War (1756–1763), America was at a crossroads. The British colonists wanted to expand westward, but the French dominated the west by virtue of three key advantages: outposts in the territory; dominance of strategic rivers, secured by ports at New Orleans and Quebec City; and good relations with the Native Americans, who became their allies in the war.

By the time the war was over—after involving much of Europe, where it was known as the Seven Years' War—the future course of America was influenced in ways big and small. The most obvious result of the war was that British colonists were free to move west. Moreover, the cost of the war to the British treasury led Parliament to levy on America the "intolerable" taxes that sparked the Revolution. And the conflict gave a young soldier named George Washington several opportunities to distinguish himself, creating a reputation that led directly to his selection as commander in chief of the revolutionary army.

Another lasting effect of the French and Indian War is Louisiana's Cajun culture. Cajuns are descendants of the Acadians, French settlers in Nova Scotia who remained after the British took control of the region in 1710. During the war, the British government, fearful of resistance from the Acadians, sent them on a forced march to scatter them throughout the colonies. About six thousand were exiled. The march was later memorialized by Henry Wadsworth Longfellow in "Evangeline."

Colonel Winslow was an officer from Massachusetts.

AUGUST 30TH

Last evening Captain Murray arrived and brought with him the instructions and letters. I consulted [with him on] methods for removing the whole inhabitants of the villages of Grand Pre, Mines, Rivers Cannard, Habbertong and Gaspereau, and agreed that it would be most convenient to cite all the male inhabitants of said villages to assemble at the

Church in this place on the 5th of September next to hear the King's orders, and that at the same time Captain Murray to collect the inhabitants of Piziquid, and villages adjacent to Fort Edward for the same purpose.

SEPTEMBER 4TH

A fine day and the inhabitants very busy about their harvest, etcetera.

SEPTEMBER 5TH

This morning received the powder horns of several companies and divvied out gunpowder at half a pound and twelve balls [of shot] to each half pound of powder. Ordered the whole camp to lie upon their arms this day.

At 3:00 in the afternoon the French inhabitants appeared, agreeable to their citation, at the Church in Grand Pre, amounting to 418 of their best men, upon which I ordered a table to be set in the center of the Church and attended with those of my officers who were off guard. I delivered to them through interpreters the King's orders in the following words:

"*Gentlemen*—

"I have received from his Excellency Governor Lawrence the King's commission which I have in my hand and by whose orders you are convened together to manifest to you his Majesty's final resolution to the French inhabitants of this his Province of Nova Scotia, who for almost half a century have had more indulgence granted them than any of his subjects in any part of his Dominion. . . .

"The part of duty I am now upon is, though necessary, very disagreeable to my nature and temper as I know it must be grievous to you who are of the same kind. But it is not my business to criticize, but rather to obey such orders as I receive. . . .

"Your land and tenements, cattle of all kinds and livestock of all sorts are forfeited to the Crown with all other effects saving your money and household goods and you are to be removed from this province. . . .

"I shall do everything in my power that all money and household goods be secured to you and that you are not molested in carrying them and also that all families shall go in the same vessel, and to make this removal, which I know must give you a great deal of trouble, as easy as his Majesty's service will admit. I hope that in whatever part of the world you may fall you may be faithful subjects, and peaceful and happy people.

"I must also inform you that it is his Majesty's pleasure that you remain in security under the inspection and direction of the troops that I have the honor to command."

I then declared them the King's prisoners. . . .

I returned to my quarters and the French inhabitants soon moved by their elders that it was a great grief to them that they had incurred his Majesty's displeasure, and that they were fearful the surprise of their detention here would quite overcome their families, whom they had no means to apprise of these melancholy circumstances. They asked that some of them might be returned as hostages, and the rest and bigger number admitted to go home to their families. I informed them I would consider their motion. . . .

SEPTEMBER 5TH [EVENING]

The French people not having any provisions with them and pleading hunger begged for bread which I gave them.

Thus ended the memorable fifth of September, a day of great fatigue and trouble.

"American independence was then and there born."

JAMES OTIS STARTS A FIRE

February 24, 1761
Boston

JOHN ADAMS

*A*n early graduate of Harvard, Otis became well known as a lawyer and was advocate general of the vice-admiralty court. When the British Parliament decided in 1761 to improve its tax collection efforts by giving customs officers wide enforcement powers, Otis resigned his post to argue the legal case against these powers, called the Writs of Assistance.

Although Otis lost the case, his speech became famous: "A man's house is his castle; and while he is quiet, he is as well guarded as a prince in his castle. This writ, if it should be declared legal, would totally annihilate this privilege. Custom-house officers may enter our houses when they please; we are commanded to permit their entry. Their menial servants may enter—may break locks, bars, everything in their way; and whether they break through malice or revenge, no man, no court can inquire. . . . I am determined to sacrifice estate, ease, health, applause and even life, in opposition. . . ." (Otis was artfully embellishing the famous phrase of the English jurist Sir Edward Coke from more than a hundred years earlier: "The house of everyone is to him as his castle and fortress.")

Otis quickly became the leading political figure in Massachusetts. But even more suddenly, his career had a tragic end. In 1769, after he had published an article that criticized the customs officers, one of the officers assaulted him with a cane, striking Otis's head so hard that he was deranged for most of the rest of his life.

Parliament . . . sent orders and instructions to the collector of the customs in Boston, Mr. Charles Paxton, to apply to the civil authority for writs of assistance, to enable the custom-house officers, tidewaiters, land-waiters, and all, to command all sheriffs and constables, etc., to attend and aid them in breaking open houses, stores, shops, cellars, ships, bales, trunks, chests, casks, packages of all sorts, to search for goods, wares, and merchandises which had been imported against the prohibitions or without paying the taxes imposed by certain acts of Parliament, called "The Acts of Trade." . . .

An alarm was spread far and wide. Merchants of Salem and Boston applied [for legal assistance] to Mr. Pratt, who refused, and to Mr. Otis and Mr. Thacher, who accepted, to defend them against this terrible menacing Monster, the writ of assistance. Great fees were offered, but Otis, and I believe Thacher, would accept of none. "In such a cause," said Otis, "I despise all fees."

Mr. Gridley argued [for the British government] with his characteristic learning, ingenuity, and dignity, and said everything that could be said in favor of [deputy collector at Salem] Cockle's petition, all depending, however, on the question "If the Parliament of Great Britain is the sovereign legislature of all the British empire."

Mr. Thacher followed him on the other side, and argued with the softness of manners, the ingenuity, and the cool reasoning which were remarkable in his amiable character.

But Otis was a flame of fire! With a promptitude of classical allusions, a depth of research, a rapid summary of historical events and dates, a profusion of legal authorities, a prophetic glance of his eye into futurity, and a torrent of impetuous eloquence he hurried away everything before him. American independence was then and there born; the seeds of patriots and heroes were then and there sown. . . .

Every man of a crowded audience appeared to me to go away, as I did, ready to take arms against writs of assistance. Then and there was the first scene of the first act of opposition to the arbitrary claims of Great Britain. Then and there the child Independence was born. In fifteen years, namely in 1776, he grew up to manhood and declared himself free.

Mr. Otis' popularity was without bounds. In May, 1761, he was elected into the House of Representatives by an almost unanimous vote. On the week of his election, I happened to be at Worcester attending a Court of Common Pleas, of which Brigadier Ruggles was Chief Justice, when the news arrived from Boston of Mr. Otis' election.

Justice Ruggles, at dinner at Colonel Chandler's on that day, said, "Out of this election will arise a d——d faction, which will shake this province to its foundation."

"A cry was heard—'Let us rush in.' "

A MOB CONFRONTS A STAMP DISTRIBUTOR

October 30, 1765
Williamsburg, Virginia

FRANCIS FAUQUIER

"*T*he French and Indian War," *wrote historian Carl Van Doren,* "which made the British government think of the colonies as important enough to be taxed, *had made the Americans think of themselves as important enough to say how they should be taxed."*

The Stamp Act was a tax requiring that fifty-five items, including all business papers, publications, and even cards and dice, display a stamp bought from the government. A stamp for dice cost just ten shillings; for a college diploma, two pounds; and for a grant from the governor, six pounds.

The stamp distributor who was met by the mob in this account, Colonel Hugh Mercer, became a true patriot. He helped organize the Virginia militia, fought heroically at the Battle of Trenton in 1776, and lost his life a few days later in the Battle of Princeton.

Eyewitness Lieutenant-Governor Francis Fauquier was acting governor of Virginia for several years. He dissolved the colony's legislature for passing a resolution by Patrick Henry against the Stamp Act. Angry leaders from several colonies then organized the Stamp Act Congress. That illegal assembly adopted the Declaration of Rights and Grievances, which proclaimed that the colonists could not be taxed without being represented in Parliament.

My Lords—

The present unhappy state of this Colony, will, to my great concern, oblige me to trouble Your Lordships with a long and very disagreeable letter. We were for some time in almost daily expectations of the arrival of Colonel Mercer with the Stamps for the use of this Colony, and rumours were industriously thrown out that at the time of the General Court parties would come down from most parts of the country to seize on and destroy all Stamped Papers.

Very unluckily, Colonel Mercer arrived at the time this town was the fullest of Strangers. On Wednesday the 30th October he came up to town. I then thought proper to go to the Coffee house, that I might be an eye witness of what did really pass, and not receive it by relation from others. The mercantile people were all assembled as usual. The first word I heard was "One and all"; upon which, as at a word agreed on before between themselves, they all quitted the place to find Colonel Mercer at his Father's lodgings where it was known he was. This concourse of people I should call a mob, did I not know that it was chiefly if not altogether composed of gentlemen of property in the Colony, some of them at the head of their respective Counties, and the merchants of the country, whether English, Scotch or Virginian; for few absented themselves. They met Colonel Mercer on the way, just at the Capitol: there they stopped and demanded of him an answer whether he would resign or act in this office as Distributor of the Stamps. He said it was an affair of great moment to him; he must consult his friends; and promised to give them an answer at 10 o'clock on Friday morning at that place.

This did not satisfy them; and they followed him to the Coffee house, in the porch of which I had seated myself with many of the Council and the Speaker, who had posted himself between the crowd and myself. We all received him with the greatest marks of welcome; with which, if one may be allowed to judge by their countenances, they were not well pleased, tho' they remained quiet and were silent. Now and then a voice was heard from the crowd that Friday was too late; the Act would take place, they would have an answer tomorrow. Several messages were brought to Mr. Mercer by the leading men of the crowd, to whom he constantly answered he had already given an answer and he would have no other extorted from him. After some little time a cry was heard, "let us rush in." Upon this we that were at the top of the [steps], knowing the advantage our situation gave us to repel those who should attempt to mount them, advanced to the edge of the Steps, of which number I was one. I immediately heard a cry, "See the Governor, take care of him." Those who before were pushing up the steps, immediately fell back, and left a small space between me and them. If your Lordships will not accuse me of vanity I would say that I believe this to be partly owing to the respect they bore to my character and partly to the love they bore to my person.

After much entreaty of some of his friends, Mr. Mercer was, against his own inclination, prevailed upon to promise them an answer at the Capitol the next evening at five. The crowd did not yet disperse; it was growing dark, and I did not think it safe to have to leave Mr. Mercer behind me, so I again advanced to the edge of the steps and said aloud I believed no man there would do me any hurt, and turned to Mr. Mercer and told him if he would walk with me through the people I believed I could conduct him safe to my house; and we accordingly walked side by side through the thickest of the people, who did not molest us, tho' there was some little murmurs. By me thus taking him under my protection, I believe I saved him from being insulted at least. When we got home we had much discourse on the subject. . . . He left me that night in a state of uncertainty what part he should act.

Accordingly Mr. Mercer appeared at the Capitol at 5, as he had promised. The number of people assembled there was much increased, by messengers having been sent into the neighborhood for that purpose. Colonel Mercer then read to them the answer [he resigned] which is printed in the Supplement of the Gazette, of which I enclose your Lordships a copy, to which I beg leave to refer.

If I accepted the resignation, I must appoint another, and I was well convinced I could not find one to accept of it, in those circumstances, which would render the office cheap. Besides if I left Mr. Mercer in possession of the place he would be always ready to distribute the Stamped papers, whenever peoples eyes should be opened and they should come to their senses, so as to receive them.

I will do my duty to His Majesty and save the stamps from being destroyed, to the best of my power, tho' I can by no means answer for the success of my endeavours. . . .

"They will never submit to it."

FRANKLIN ARGUES AGAINST THE STAMP ACT IN THE BRITISH PARLIAMENT

February 13, 1766
London, England

UNOFFICIAL TRANSCRIPT

During the Stamp Act crisis, Benjamin Franklin was in London to represent Pennsylvania on other matters. Historian Carl Van Doren remarked, "Trying to draw two parts of the Empire together, he found himself suspected by each of being a partisan of the other." Franklin hurt his own cause by making some rare political missteps. When his first attempt to persuade the British to repeal the Stamp Act taxes was unsuccessful, he bought stamps for his own printing company and nominated a friend to become a stamp distributor.

Franklin's political enemies spread rumors that he was the architect of the Stamp Act, and mobs in Philadelphia flirted with the thought of burning down his new house. His wife sent their daughter to New Jersey, then fortified herself in an upstairs room with guns and ammunition.

His testimony before Parliament—answering 174 questions over the course of four hours—marked a moment of both political crisis for the country and personal crisis for himself. Because he and the colonies had some allies in Parliament, parts of the interrogation were as carefully scripted as many of today's congressional hearings. But he could not plan for all of the questions by his antagonists. (James Hewitt, for instance, who started the questioning, was an ally. He was the son of a cloth manufacturer whose goods were among those boycotted by the colonists in response to the Act. But British prime minister George Grenville was skeptical of the colonists.)

Franklin's performance was outstanding. When an unofficial transcript of his testimony was published, his reputation at home was more than restored. Pennsylvania extended his commission as agent to England. Massachusetts, New Jersey, and Georgia appointed him to the same role. He became essentially an ambassador for all the colonies.

The Stamp Act was repealed.

Q. What is your Name, and Place of abode?
A. Franklin, of Philadelphia.

Q. Do the Americans pay any considerable taxes among themselves?

A. Certainly many, and very heavy taxes.

Q. What are the present taxes in Pennsylvania, laid by the laws of the Colony?

A. There are taxes on all estates real and personal, a poll-tax, a tax on all offices, professions, trades and businesses, according to their profits; an excise upon all wine, rum and other spirits; and a duty of ten pounds per head on all negroes imported, with some other duties. . . .

Q. Are not the Colonies, from their circumstances, very able to pay the stamp-duty?

A. In my opinion, there is not gold and silver enough in the Colonies to pay the stamp duty for one year.

Q. Don't you know that the money arising from the stamps was all to be laid out in America?

A. I know it is appropriated by the act to the American service; but it will be spent in the conquered Colonies, where the soldiers are, not in the Colonies that pay it.

Q. Is there not a balance of trade due from the Colonies where the troops are posted, that will bring back the money to the old Colonies?

A. I think not. I believe very little would come back. I know of no trade likely to bring it back. I think it would come from the Colonies where it was spent directly to England; for I have always observed, that in every Colony the more plenty the means of remittance to England the more goods are sent for, and the more trade with England carried on. . . .

Q. How many white men do you suppose there are in North America?

A. About 300,000 from sixteen to sixty years of age.

Q. What may be the amount of one year's imports into Pennsylvania from Britain?

A. I have been informed that our merchants compute the imports from Britain to be above 500,000 pounds.

Q. What may be the amount of the produce of your province exported to Britain?

A. It must be small, as we produce little that is wanted in Britain. I suppose it cannot exceed 40,000 pounds.

Q. How then do you pay the balance?

A. The balance is paid by our produce carried to the West-Indies, and sold in our own islands, or to the French, Spaniards, Danes and Dutch; by the same carried to other colonies in North-America, as to New-England, Nova-Scotia, Newfoundland, Carolina and Georgia. . . .

Q. Have you heard of any difficulties lately laid on the Spanish trade?

A. Yes, I have heard that it has been greatly obstructed by some new regulations, and by the English men of war and cutters stationed all along the coast of America.

Q. Do you think it right America should be protected by this country, and pay no part of the expense?

A. That is not the case. The colonies raised, clothed and paid, during the last war, near 25,000 men, and spent many millions.

Q. Were you not reimbursed by Parliament?

A. We were reimbursed what, in your opinion, we had advanced beyond our proportion, or beyond what might be reasonably expected from us; and it was a very small part of what we spent. Pennsylvania, in particular, disbursed about 500,000 pounds, and the reimbursements, in the whole, did not exceed 60,000 pounds. . . .

Q. Do not you think the people of America would submit to pay the stamp duty, if it was moderated?

A. No, never, unless compelled by force of arms. . . .

Q. What was the temper of America towards Great Britain before the year 1763?

A. The best in the world. They submitted willingly to the government of the Crown, and paid, in all their courts, obedience to acts of Parliament. Numerous as the people are in the several old provinces, they cost you nothing in forts, citadels, garrisons or armies, to keep them in subjection. They were governed by this country at the expense only of a little pen, ink and paper. They were led by a thread. They had not only a respect, but an affection, for Great Britain, for its laws, its customs and manners, and even a fondness for its fashions, that greatly increased the commerce. Natives of Britain were always treated with particular regard; to be an Old Englandman, was, of itself, a character of some respect, and gave a kind of rank among us.

Q. And what is their temper now?

A. Oh, very much altered.

Q. Did you ever hear the authority of Parliament to make laws for America questioned till lately?

A. The authority of Parliament was allowed to be valid in all laws, except such as should lay internal taxes. It was never disputed in laying duties to regulate commerce. . . .

Q. In what light did the people of America use to consider the Parliament of Great Britain?

A. They considered the Parliament as the great bulwark & security of their liberties and privileges, and always spoke of it with the utmost respect and veneration: arbitrary ministers, they thought, might possibly, at times, attempt to oppress them, but they relied on it, that the Parliament, on application, would always give redress. They remembered, with gratitude, a strong instance of this, when a bill was brought into Parliament, with a clause to make royal instructions laws in the colonies, which the House of Commons would not pass, and it was thrown out.

Q. And have they not still the same respect for Parliament?

A. No; it is greatly lessened.

Q. To what cause is that owing?

A. To a concurrence of causes; the restraints lately laid on their trade, by which the bringing of foreign gold and silver into the colonies was prevented; the prohibition of making paper money among themselves; and then demanding a new and heavy tax by stamps; taking away at the same time, trials by juries, and refusing to receive & hear their humble petitions.

Q. Don't you think they would submit to the stamp-act, if it was modified, the obnoxious parts taken out, and the duties reduced to some particulars, of small moment?

A. No; they will never submit to it. . . .

Q. Was it an opinion in America before 1763, that the Parliament had no right to lay taxes and duties there?

A. I never heard any objection to the right of laying duties to regulate commerce; but a right to lay internal taxes was never supposed to be in Parliament, as we are not represented there. . . .

Q. If the stamp-act should be repealed, would it induce the assemblies of America to acknowledge the rights of Parliament to tax them, and would they erase their resolutions?

A. No, never.

Q. Is there no means of obliging them to erase those resolutions?

A. None that I know of; they will never do it unless compelled by force of arms.

Q. Is there no power on earth that can force them to erase them?

A. No power, how great soever, can force men to change their opinions.

*"This unhappy affair began
by boys and young fellows throwing snow balls ..."*

THE BOSTON MASSACRE

March 5, 1770

JOHN TUDOR

Patriot John Adams acted as defense attorney for the British soldiers who fired on the Americans. In a remarkable turnabout that dismayed many colonists, he won their acquittal.

Tudor was a Boston merchant.

On Monday evening the 5th current, a few minutes after 9 o'clock a most horrid murder was committed in King Street before the Customhouse door by eight or nine soldiers, under the command of Captain Thomas Preston, drawn from the main guard on the south side of the Townhouse.

This unhappy affair began by some boys & young fellows throwing snow balls at the sentry placed at the Customhouse door, upon which eight or nine soldiers came to his assistance. Soon after a number of people collected, when the Captain commanded the soldiers to fire, which they did and three men were killed on the spot and several mortally wounded, one of which died next morning. The Captain soon drew off his soldiers up to the main guard, or the consequences might have been terrible, for on the guns firing the people were alarmed and set the bells a-ringing as if for fire, which drew multitudes to the place of action. Lieutenant Governor Hutchinson, who was Commander in Chief, was sent for and came to the Council Chamber, where some of the magistrates attended. The Governor desired the multitude about 10 o'clock to separate and go home peaceably and [said] he would do all in his power that justice should be done etc. The 29th Regiment were then under arms on the south side of the Townhouse. But the people insisted that the soldiers should be ordered to their barracks first before they would separate, which being done the people separated about 1 o'clock. Captain Preston was taken up by a warrant given to the High Sheriff by Justice Dana and Tudor and came under examination about 2 o'clock and we sent him to jail soon after 3 o'clock, having evidence sufficient to commit him, on his ordering the soldiers to fire. So about 4 o'clock the town became quiet. The next forenoon the eight soldiers that fired on the inhabitants was also sent to jail.

Tuesday A.M. The inhabitants met at Faneuil Hall and after some pertinent speeches, chose a committee of fifteen gentlemen to wait on the Lieutenant Governor in council to request the immediate removal of the troops. The message was in these words: That it is the unanimous opinion of this meeting, that the inhabitants and soldiery can no longer live together in safety; that nothing can rationally be expected to restore the peace of the town and prevent blood and carnage, but the removal of the troops; and that we most fervently pray his honor that his power and influence may be exerted for their instant removal.

His honor's reply was: Gentlemen I am extremely sorry for the unhappy difference and especially of the last evening and signifying that it was not in his power to remove the troops etc., etc.

The above reply was not satisfactory to the inhabitants, as but one regiment should be removed to the castle barracks. In the afternoon the town adjourned to Dr. Sewall's Meetinghouse, for Faneuil Hall was not large enough to hold the people, there being at least 3,000, some supposed near 4,000, when they chose a committee to wait on the Lieutenant Governor to let him and the council know that nothing less will satisfy the people, than a total and immediate removal of the troops out of the town.

His Honor laid before the Council the vote of the town. The Council thereon expressed themselves to be unanimously of opinion that it was absolutely necessary for his Majesty's service, the good order of the town etc., that the troops should be immediately removed out of the town.

His honor communicated this advice of the council to Colonel Dalrymple and desired he would order the troops down to Castle William. After the Colonel had seen the vote of the Council he gave his word and honor to the town's committee that both the regiments should be removed without delay. The committee returned to the town meeting and Mr. Hancock, chairman of the committee read their report as above, which was received with a shout and clap of hands, which made the Meetinghouse ring. So the meeting was dissolved and a great number of gentlemen appeared to watch the center of the town and the prison, which continued for eleven nights and all was quiet again, as the soldiers were all moved off to the castle.

(Thursday) Agreeable to a general request of the inhabitants, were followed to the grave (for they were all buried in one) in succession the four bodies of Messrs. Samuel Gray, Samuel Maverick, James Caldwell and Crispus Attucks, the unhappy victims who fell in the bloody massacre. On this sorrowful occasion most of the shops and stores in town were shut, all the bells were ordered to toll a solemn peal in Boston, Charleston, Cambridge and Roxbury. The several hearses forming a junction in King Street, the theater of that inhuman tragedy, proceeded from there through the main streets lengthened by an immense concourse of people, so numerous as to be obliged to follow in ranks of four and six abreast and brought up by a long train of carriages. The sorrow visible in the countenances, together with the peculiar solemnity, surpass description. It was supposed that the spectators and those that followed the corps amounted to 15,000, some supposed 20,000.

"Every chest from the three vessels was knocked to pieces."

THE BOSTON TEA PARTY

December 16, 1773

JOHN ANDREWS

*I*n response to protests, the British Parliament repealed most of the import taxes imposed on the colonies. But it left the tax on imported tea to prove its authority. The colonists were not amused. When three British ships arrived in Boston in November 1773, with 342 chests of tea, the Bostonians refused to let the tea be unloaded. Governor Thomas Hutchinson demanded the duty be paid anyway and made the ships sit in the harbor. So Samuel Adams and friends, disguised as Indians, threw a party.

Andrews, a selectman of Boston, wrote this account to a relative.

November 29th. Hall and Bruce arrived Saturday evening with each a hundred and odd chests of the detested Tea. What will be done with it, can't say: but I tremble for the consequences should the consignees still persist in their obstinacy and not consent to reship it. They have softened down so far as to offer it to the care of Council or the town, till such times as they hear from their friends in England, but am persuaded, from the present dispositions of the people, that no other alternative will do, than to have it immediately sent back to London again. . . . the bells are ringing for a general muster, and a third vessel is now arrived in Nan-tasket road. Handbills are stuck up, calling upon Friends! Citizens! and Countrymen!

December 1st. Having just returned from Fire Club, and am now, in company with the two Miss Masons and Mr. Williams of your place, at Sam. Eliot's, who has been dining with him at Col. Hancock's, and acquaints me that Mr. Palfrey sets off express for New York and Philadel-phia at five o'clock tomorrow morning, to communicate the transactions of this town respecting the tea. I acquainted you that Bruce and Hall had arrived, which was a mistake, as only Hall has arrived; which has caused the most spirited and firm conduct to be observed that ever was known: the regularity and particulars of which proceedings Mr. Palfrey will be able to tell you. The consignees have all taken their residence at the Cas-tle, as they still persist in their refusal to take the tea back. It's not only the town, but the country are unanimous against the landing it, and at the Monday and Tuesday Meetings, they attended to the number of some hundreds from all the neighboring towns within a dozen miles. 'T'would puzzle any person to purchase a pair of pistols in town, as they are all bought up, with a full determination to repel force by force.

December 18th. However precarious our situation may be, yet such is the present calm composure of the people that a stranger would hardly think that ten thousand pounds sterling of the East India Company's tea was destroyed the night, or rather evening before last, yet it's a serious truth; and if yours, together with the other Southern provinces, should rest satisfied with their quota being stored, poor Boston will feel the whole weight of ministerial vengeance. However, it's the opinion of most people that we stand an equal chance now, whether troops are sent in conse-quence of it or not; whereas, had it been stored, we should inevitably have had 'em, to enforce the sale of it.

The affair was transacted with the greatest regularity and despatch. Mr. Rotch finding he exposed himself not only to the loss of his ship but for the value of the tea in case he sent her back with it, without a clearance from the custom house, as the Admiral kept a ship in readiness to make a seizure of it whenever it should sail under these circumstances; therefore declined complying with his former promises, and absolutely declared his vessel should not carry it, without a proper clearance could be procured or he to be indemnified for the value of her.

When a general muster was assembled, from this and all the neighbor-ing towns, to the number of five or six thousand, at 10 o'clock Thursday morning in the Old South Meeting house, where they passed a unanimous vote that the Sea should go out of the harbor that afternoon, and sent a committee with Mr. Rotch to the Custom house to demand a clearance, which the collector told 'em was not in his power to give, without the duties being first paid. They then sent Mr. Rotch to Milton, to ask a pass from the Governor, who sent for answer, that "consistent with the rules of government and his duty to the King he could not grant one without they produced a previous clearance from the office." By the time he returned with this message the candles were light in [the] house, and upon reading it, such prodigious shouts were made, that induced me, while drinking tea at home, to go out and know the cause of it. The house was so crowded I could get no farther than the porch, when I found the moderator was just declaring the meeting to be dissolved, which caused another general shout, outdoors and in, and three cheers. What with that, and the consequent noise of breaking up the meeting, you'd thought that the inhabitants of the infernal regions had broke loose.

They mustered, I'm told, upon Fort Hill, to the number of about two hundred, and proceeded, two by two, to Griffin's wharf, where Hall, Bruce, and Coffin lay, each with 114 chests of the ill-fated article on board; the two former with only that article, but the latter, arrived at the wharf only the day before, was freighted with a large quantity of other goods, which they took the greatest care not to injure in the least, and before nine o'clock in the evening, every chest from on board the three vessels was knocked to pieces and flung over the sides. They say the actors were Indians from Narragansett. Whether they were or not, to a transient observer they appeared as such, being clothed in Blankets with the heads muffled, and copper colored countenances, being each armed with a hatchet or ax, and pair pistols, nor was their dialect different from what I conceive these geniuses to speak, as their jargon was unintelligible to all but themselves. Not the least insult was offered to any person, save one Captain Conner, a letter of horses in this place, not many years since removed from dear Ireland, who had ripped up the lining of his coat and waistcoat under the arms, and watching his opportunity had nearly filled 'em with tea, but being detected, was handled pretty roughly. They not only stripped him of his clothes, but gave him a coat of mud, with a severe bruising into the bargain; and nothing but their utter aversion to make any disturbance prevented his being tarred and feathered.

Should not have troubled you with this, by this Post, hadn't I thought you would be glad of a more particular account of so important a transaction, than you could have obtained by common report; and if it affords my brother but a temporary amusement, I shall be more than repaid for the trouble of writing it.

"In Congress, nibbling and quibbling as usual."

THE FIRST CONTINENTAL CONGRESS

September–October 1774
Philadelphia

JOHN ADAMS

*F*ollowing the Boston Tea Party, Britain passed five laws that came to be called the Intolerable Acts. Among these were the Boston Port Act, which closed the city to shipping, and a law allowing British troops to be billeted in American homes.

The other colonies quickly came to the aid of Massachusetts with food and other provisions. They also began to organize resistance. In the Virginia legislature, the occupation of Boston was decreed a "hostile invasion."

In illegal elections the British authorities could not prevent, fifty-five members were selected from the individual colonies to meet in Philadelphia as a Continental Congress. From the start, the difficulty of establishing a federal system was apparent. Yet as resistance turned to revolution, this congress and the one that followed in 1775 became the American government.

John Adams, later president, was a delegate to the first congress.

[September] 5. Monday. At ten the delegates all met at the City Tavern, and walked to the Carpenters' Hall, where they took a view of the room, and of the chamber where is an excellent library; there is also a long entry where gentlemen may walk, and a convenient chamber opposite to the library. The general cry was, that this was a good room, and the question was put, whether we were satisfied with this room? and it passed in the affirmative. A very few were for the negative, and they were chiefly from Pennsylvania and New York. Then Mr. Lynch arose, and said there was a gentleman present who had presided with great dignity over a very respectable society, greatly to the advantage of America, and he therefore proposed that the Honorable Peyton Randolph, Esquire, one of the delegates from Virginia, and the late Speaker of their House of Burgesses, should be appointed Chairman, and he doubted not it would be unanimous.

The question was put, and he was unanimously chosen.

Mr. Randolph then took the chair, and the commissions of the delegates were all produced and read.

Then Mr. Lynch proposed that Mr. Charles Thomson, a gentleman of family, fortune, and character in this city, should be appointed Secretary, which was accordingly done without opposition, though Mr. Duane and Mr. Jay discovered at first an inclination to seek further.

Mr. Duane then moved that a committee should be appointed to prepare regulations for this Congress. Several gentlemen objected.

I then arose and asked leave of the President to request of the gentleman from New York an explanation, and that he would point out some particular regulations which he had in his mind. He mentioned particularly the method of voting, whether it should be by Colonies, or by the poll, or by interests.

Mr. Henry then arose, and said this was the first General Congress which had ever happened; that no former Congress could be a precedent; that we should have occasion for more general congresses, and therefore that a precedent ought to be established now; that it would be great injustice if a little Colony should have the same weight in the councils of America as a great one, and therefore he was for a committee.

Major Sullivan observed that a little Colony had its all at stake as well as a great one. . . .

Mr. Henry: "Government is dissolved. Fleets and armies and the present state of things show that government is dissolved. Where are your landmarks, your boundaries of Colonies? We are in a state of nature, sir. I did propose that a scale should be laid down; that part of North America which was once Massachusetts Bay, and that part which was once Virginia, ought to be considered as having a weight. Will not people complain? Ten thousand Virginians have not outweighed one thousand others.

"I will submit, however; I am determined to submit, if I am over-ruled.

"A worthy gentleman near me [Henry was referring to Adams himself] seemed to admit the necessity of obtaining a more adequate representation.

"I hope future ages will quote our proceedings with applause. It is one of the great duties of the democratical part of the constitution to keep itself pure. It is known in my Province that some other Colonies are not so numerous or rich as they are. I am forgoing all the satisfaction in my power.

"The distinctions between Virginians, Pennsylvanians, New Yorkers, and New Englanders, are no more. I am not a Virginian, but an American.

"Slaves are to be thrown out of the question, and if the freemen can be represented according to their numbers, I am satisfied."

Mr. Lynch: "I differ in one point from the gentleman from Virginia, that is, in thinking that numbers only ought to determine the weight of Colonies. I think that property ought to be considered, and that it ought to be a compound of numbers and property that should determine the weight of the Colonies. I think it cannot be now settled."

Mr. Rutledge: "We have no legal authority; and obedience to our determinations will only follow the reasonableness, the apparent utility and necessity of the measures we adopt. We have no coercive or legislative authority. Our constituents are bound only in honor to observe our determinations."

Governor Ward: "There are a great number of counties, in Virginia, very unequal in point of wealth and numbers, yet each has a right to send two members."

Mr. Lee: "But one reason, which prevails with me, and that is, that we are not at this time provided with proper materials. [I] am afraid we are not."

Mr. Gadsen: "I can't see any way of voting, but by Colonies."

Colonel Bland: "I agree with the gentleman [Adams] who spoke near me, that we are not at present provided with materials to ascertain the importance of each Colony. The question is, whether the rights and liberties of America shall be contended for, or given up to arbitrary powers."

Mr. Pendelton: "If the committee should find themselves unable to ascertain the weight of the Colonies, by their numbers and property, they will report this, and this will lay the foundation for the Congress to take some other steps to procure evidence of numbers and property at some future time."

Mr. Henry: "I agree that authentic accounts cannot be had, if by authenticity is meant attestations of officers of the Crown.

"I go upon the supposition that government is at an end. All distinctions are thrown down. All America is thrown into one mass."

Mr. Jay: "Could I suppose that we came to frame an American constitution, instead of endeavoring to correct the faults in an old one—I can't yet think that all government is at an end. The measure of arbitrary power is not full, and I think it must run over, before we undertake to frame a new constitution.

"To the virtue, spirit, and abilities of Virginia, we owe much. I should always, therefore, from inclination as well as justice, be for giving Virginia its full weight.

"I am not clear that we ought not to be bound by a majority, though ever so small, but I only mentioned it as a matter of danger, worthy of consideration. . . ."

10. Saturday. Mr. Reed . . . says we never were guilty of a more mas-

terly stroke of policy, than in moving that Mr. Duche might read prayers; it has had a very good effect, etc. He says the sentiments of people here are growing more and more favorable every day.

1 1. Sunday. There is such a quick and constant succession of new scenes, characters, persons, and events, turning up before me, that I can't keep any regular account. . . .

1 7. Saturday. This was one of the happiest days of my life. In Congress we had generous, noble sentiments, and manly eloquence. This day convinced me that America will support Massachusetts or perish with her. . . .

[October] 1 o. Monday. The deliberations of the Congress are spun out to an immeasurable length. There is so much wit, sense, learning, acuteness, subtlety, eloquence, etc. among fifty gentlemen, each of whom has been habituated to lead and guide in his own province, that an immensity of time is spent unnecessarily.

2 o. Thursday. Dined with the whole Congress, at the City Tavern, at the invitation of the House of Representatives of the Province of Pennsylvania. The whole House dined with us, making near one hundred guests in the whole; a most elegant entertainment. A sentiment was given: "May the sword of the parent never be stained with the blood of her children." . . .

2 4. Monday. In Congress, nibbling and quibbling as usual. There is no greater mortification than to sit with half a dozen wits, deliberating upon a petition, address, or memorial. These great wits, these subtle critics, these refined geniuses, these learned lawyers, these wise statesmen, are so fond of showing their parts and powers, as to make their consultations very tedious. . . .

2 8. Friday. Took our departure, in a very great rain, from the happy, the peaceful, the elegant, the hospitable, and polite city of Philadelphia. It is not very likely that I shall ever see this part of the world again, but I shall ever retain a most grateful, pleasing sense of the many civilities I have received in it, and shall think myself happy to have an opportunity of returning them.

"Give me liberty or give me death!"

PATRICK HENRY'S SPEECH

March 23, 1775
Richmond, Virginia

EDMUND RANDOLPH

*I*n the the spring of 1775, most members of the Virginia legislature were antici-
pating the upcoming meeting of the Second Continental Congress, scheduled for
May 10 in Philadelphia. But some could not wait for action. Patrick Henry made
his famous speech in response to a proposed resolution:"That this colony be immedi-
ately put into a state of defense, and that . . . a committee to prepare a plan for
embodying, arming, and disciplining such a number of men as may be sufficient for
that purpose." Less than a month later, the battles at Lexington and Concord proved
him right.

It was a proud [day] to a Virginian feeling and acting with his country.
The multitude, many of whom had traveled to the convention from a distance, could not suppress their emotion.

Henry was his pure self. Those who had toiled in the artifices of
scholastic rhetoric were involuntarily driven into an inquiry within themselves whether rules and forms and niceties of elocution would not have
choked his native fire. It blazed so as to warm the coldest heart. . . . It
was Patrick Henry, born in obscurity, poor, and without the advantages of
literature, rousing the genius of his country, and binding a band of patriots
together to hurl defiance at the tyranny of so formidable a nation as Great
Britain. . . . When he sat down, his sounds vibrated so loudly, if not in the
ears at least in the memory of his audience, that no other member, not
even his friend [Lee] who was to second him, was yet adventurous enough
to interfere with that voice which had so recently subdued and captivated.
After a few minutes, Richard Henry Lee fanned and refreshed with a gale
of pleasure; but the vessel of the revolution was still under the impulse of
the tempest which Henry had created. Artificial oratory fell in copious
streams from the mouth of Lee, and rules of persuasion accomplished
everything which rules could effect. If elegance had been personified, Lee
would have been chosen. But Henry had trampled upon rules and yet tri-
umphed, at this time perhaps beyond his own expectation. Jefferson was

not silent. He argued closely, profoundly and warmly on the same side. The post in this revolutionary debate belonging to him was that at which the theories of republicanism were deposited. Washington was prominent, though silent. His looks bespoke a mind absorbed in meditation on his country's fate; but a positive concert between him and Henry could not more effectually have exhibited him to view, than when Henry with indignation ridiculed the idea of peace "when there was no peace," and enlarged on the duty of preparing for war. . . .

"Mr. President," Henry began, "it is natural for man to indulge in the illusions of hope. We are apt to shut our eyes against a painful truth, and listen to the song of that siren till she transforms us into beasts. Is this the part of wise men, engaged in a great and arduous struggle for liberty? Are we disposed to be of the number of those who, having eyes, see not, and having ears, hear not, the things which so nearly concern their temporal salvation? For my part, whatever anguish of spirit it may cost, I am willing to know the whole truth; to know the worst, and to provide for it.

"I have but one lamp by which my feet are guided, and that is the lamp of experience. I know of no way of judging of the future but by the past. And, judging by the past, I wish to know what there has been in the conduct of the British ministry for the last ten years to justify those hopes with which the gentlemen have been pleased to solace themselves and the House? Is it that insidious smile with which our petition has been lately received? Trust it not, sir; it will prove a snare to your feet. Suffer not yourselves to be betrayed with a kiss. Ask yourselves how this gracious reception of our petition comports with those warlike preparations which cover our waters and darken our land. Are fleets and armies necessary to a work of love and reconciliation? Have we shown ourselves so unwilling to be reconciled that force must be called in to win back our love? Let us not deceive ourselves, sir. These are the implements of war and subjugation, the last arguments to which kings resort.

"I ask the gentlemen, sir, what means this martial array, if its purpose be not to force us to submission? Can the gentlemen assign any other possible motive for it? Has Great Britain any enemy in this Quarter of the world, to call for all this accumulation of navies and armies? No, sir, she has none. They are meant for us; they can be meant for no other. They are sent over to bind and rivet upon us those chains which the British ministry have been so long forging. And what have we to oppose to them? Shall we try argument? Sir, we have been trying that for the last ten years. Have we anything new to offer upon the subject? Nothing. We have held the subject up in every light of which it is capable; but it has been all in vain.

"Shall we resort to entreaty and humble supplication? What terms shall we find which have not been already exhausted? Let us not, I beseech you, sir, deceive ourselves longer. Sir, we have done everything that could be done, to avert the storm which is now coming on. We have petitioned, we have remonstrated, we have supplicated; we have prostrated ourselves before the throne, and have implored its interposition to arrest the tyrannical hands of the ministry and Parliament. Our petitions have been slighted; our remonstrances have produced additional violence and insult; our supplications have been disregarded; and we have been spurned, with contempt, from the foot of the throne. . . . There is no longer any room for hope.

"If we wish to be free; if we mean to preserve inviolate those inestimable privileges for which we have been so long contending; if we mean not basely to abandon the noble struggle in which we have been so long engaged, and which we have pledged ourselves never to abandon until the glorious object of our contest shall be obtained—we must fight! I repeat it, sir, we must fight! An appeal to arms, and to the God of hosts, is all that is left us.

"They tell us, sir, that we are weak—unable to cope with so formidable an adversary. But when shall we be stronger? Will it be the next week or the next year? Will it be when we are totally disarmed, and when a British guard shall be stationed in every house? Shall we gather strength by irresolution and inaction? Shall we acquire the means of effectual resistance by lying supinely on our backs, and hugging the delusive phantom of hope, until our enemies shall have bound us hand and foot? Sir, we are not weak, if we make a proper use of those means which the God of nature hath placed in our power. Three millions of people, armed in the holy cause of Liberty, and in such a country as that which we possess, are invincible by any force which our enemy can send against us.

"Besides, sir, we shall not fight our battles alone. There is a just God, who presides over the destinies of nations, and who will raise up friends to fight our battles for us. The battle, sir, is not to the strong alone; it is to the vigilant, the active, the brave. Besides, sir, we have no election. If we were base enough to desire it, it is now too late to retire from the contest. There is no retreat but in submission and slavery! Our chains are forged. Their clanking may be heard on the plains of Boston! The war is inevitable—and let it come! I repeat it, sir, let it come!

"It is vain, sir, to extenuate the matter. The gentlemen may cry, Peace, peace! but there is no peace. The war has actually begun! The next gale that sweeps from the north will bring to our ears the clash of resounding arms! Our brethren are already in the field! Why stand we here idle?

What is it that the gentlemen wish? What would they have? Is life so dear or peace so sweet as to be purchased at the price of chains and slavery? Forbid it, Almighty God. I know not what course others may take, but as for me, give me liberty or give me death!"

**"If I did not give him true answers,
he would blow my brains out."**

LANTERNS IN THE NORTH CHURCH STEEPLE

April 18, 1775
Massachusetts

PAUL REVERE

*R*evere, *who had been active in the Sons of Liberty and had taken part in the Boston Tea Party before carrying news of the event to New York City, was an express rider for the Boston Committee of Public Safety at the time of the battles of Lexington and Concord. Although he and his compatriot William Dawes never reached Concord, Dr. Samuel Prescott, whose aid they enlisted after a chance meeting on the way, reached the town with the news that the British were coming.*

Revere was also an accomplished artisan. He is primarily remembered as a silversmith, but he also designed and engraved the official seal of the colonies and their first paper money.

He wrote this account in a 1798 letter to Dr. Jeremy Belknap, one of America's first historians.

In the fall of 1774 and winter of 1775, I was one of upwards of thirty, chiefly mechanics, who formed ourselves into a committee for the purpose of watching the movements of the British soldiers, and gaining every intelligence of the movements of the Tories. We held our meetings at the Green Dragon tavern. We were so careful that our meetings should be kept secret that every time we met, every person swore upon the Bible that they would not discover any of our transactions but to Messrs. Hancock, Adams, Doctors Warren, Church and one or two more.

In the winter, towards the spring, we frequently took turns, two and two, to watch the soldiers by patrolling the streets all night. The Saturday night preceding the 18th of April, about 12 o'clock at night, the boats belonging to the transports were all launched and carried under the sterns of the men-of-war. (They had been previously hauled up and repaired.) We likewise found that the grenadiers and light infantry were all taken off duty.

From these movements we expected something serious was to be transacted. On Tuesday evening, the 18th, it was observed that a number of soldiers were marching towards the bottom of the Common. About 10 o'clock, Dr. Warren sent in great haste for me and begged that I would immediately set off for Lexington, where Messrs. Hancock and Adams were, and acquaint them of the movement, and that it was thought they were the objects.

When I got to Dr. Warren's house, I found he had sent an express by land to Lexington—a Mr. William Dawes. The Sunday before, by desire of Dr. Warren, I had been to Lexington, to Messrs. Hancock and Adams, who were at the Rev. Mr. [Jonas] Clark's. I returned at night through Charlestown; there I agreed with a Colonel Conant and some other gentlemen that if the British went out by water, we would show two lanterns in the North Church steeple; and if by land, one, as a signal; for we were apprehensive it would be difficult to cross the Charles River or get over Boston Neck. I left Dr. Warren, called upon a friend and desired him to make the signals.

I then went home, took my boots and surtout, went to the north part of the town, where I had kept a boat; two friends rowed me across Charles River, a little to the eastward where the Somerset man-of-war lay. It was then young flood, the ship was winding, and the moon was rising. They landed me on the Charlestown side. When I got into town, I met Colonel Conant and several others; they said they had seen our signals. I told them what was acting, and went to get me a horse; I got a horse of Deacon Larkin. While the horse was preparing, Richard Devens, Esq., who was one of the Committee of Safety, came to me and told me that he came down the road from Lexington after sundown that evening; that he met ten British officers, all well mounted, and armed, going up the road.

I set off upon a very good horse; it was then about eleven o'clock and very pleasant. After I had passed Charlestown Neck, I saw two men on horseback under a tree. When I got near them, I discovered they were British officers. One tried to get ahead of me, and the other to take me. I turned my horse very quick and galloped towards Charlestown Neck, and then pushed for the Medford Road. The one who chased me, endeavoring to cut me off, got into a clay pond near where Mr. Russell's Tavern is now built. I got clear of him, and went through Medford, over the bridge and up to Menotomy. In Medford, I awaked the captain of the minute men; and after that, I alarmed almost every house, till I got to Lexington. I found Messrs. Hancock and Adams at the Rev. Mr. Clark's; I told them my errand and enquired for Mr. Dawes; they said he had not been there; I related the story of the two officers, and supposed that he must have been stopped, as he ought to have been there before me.

After I had been there about half an hour, Mr. Dawes came; we refreshed ourselves, and set off for Concord. We were overtaken by a young Dr. Prescott, whom we found to be a high Son of Liberty. I told them of the ten officers that Mr. Devens met, and that it was probable we might be stopped before we got to Concord; for I supposed that after night they divided themselves, and that two of them had fixed themselves in such passages as were most likely to stop any intelligence going to Concord. I likewise mentioned that we had better alarm all the inhabitants till we got to Concord. The young doctor much approved of it and said he would stop with either of us, for the people between that and Concord knew him and would give the more credit to what we said.

We had got nearly half way. Mr. Dawes and the doctor stopped to alarm the people of a house. I was about one hundred rods ahead when I saw two men in nearly the same situation as those officers were near Charlestown. I called for the doctor and Mr. Dawes to come up. In an instant I was surrounded by four. They had placed themselves in a straight road that inclined each way; they had taken down a pair of bars on the north side of the road, and two of them were under a tree in the pasture. The doctor being foremost, he came up and we tried to get past them; but they being armed with pistols and swords, they forced us into the pasture. The doctor jumped his horse over a low stone wall and got to Concord.

I observed a wood at a small distance and made for that. When I got there, out started six officers on horseback and ordered me to dismount. One of them, who appeared to have the command, examined me, where I came from and what my name was. I told him. He asked me if I was an express. I answered in the affirmative. He demanded what time I left Boston. I told him, and added that their troops had catched aground in passing the river, and that there would be five hundred Americans there in a short time, for I had alarmed the country all the way up. He immediately rode towards those who stopped us, when all five of them came down upon a full gallop. One of them, whom I afterwards found to be a Major Mitchel, of the 5th Regiment, clapped his pistol to my head, called me by name and told me he was going to ask me some questions, and if I did not give him true answers, he would blow my brains out. He then asked me similar questions to those above. He then ordered me to mount my horse, after searching me for arms. He then ordered them to advance and to lead me in front. When we got to the road, they turned down towards Lexington. When we had got about one mile, the major rode up to the officer that was leading me, and told him to give me to the sergeant. As soon as he took me, the major ordered him, if I attempted to run, or anybody insulted them, to blow my brains out.

We rode till we got near Lexington meeting-house, when the militia fired a volley of guns, which appeared to alarm them very much. The major inquired of me how far it was to Cambridge, and if there were any other road.

After some consultation, the major rode up to the sergeant and asked if his horse was tired. He answered him he was—he was a sergeant of grenadiers and had a small horse. "Then," said he, "take that man's horse." I dismounted, and the sergeant mounted my horse, when they all rode towards Lexington meeting-house.

I went across the burying-ground and some pastures and came to the Rev. Mr. Clark's house, where I found Messrs. Hancock and Adams. I told them of my treatment, and they concluded to go from that house towards Woburn. I went with them and a Mr. Lowell, who was a clerk to Mr. Hancock.

When we got to the house where they intended to stop, Mr. Lowell and myself returned to Mr. Clark's, to find what was going on. When we got there, an elderly man came in; he said he had just come from the tavern, that a man had come from Boston who said there were no British troops coming. Mr. Lowell and myself went towards the tavern, when we met a man on a full gallop, who told us the troops were coming up the rocks. We afterwards met another, who said they were close by. Mr. Lowell asked me to go to the tavern with him, to get a trunk of papers belonging to Mr. Hancock. We went up chamber, and while we were getting the trunk, we saw the British very near, upon a full march. We hurried towards Mr. Clark's house. In our way we passed through the militia. There were about fifty. When we had got about one hundred yards from the meeting-house, the British troops appeared on both sides of the meeting-house. In their front was an officer on horseback. They made a short halt; when I saw, and heard, a gun fired, which appeared to be a pistol. Then I could distinguish two guns, and then a continual roar of musketry; when we made off with the trunk.

"Alarm guns were fired,
and the drums beat to arms."

STANDOFF AT LEXINGTON

April 19, 1775

JONAS CLARK

*T*he British troops experienced a brief but unforgettable interruption in their
march to Concord. Joseph Warren, one of the key figures in this account and
other events leading to the Revolutionary War, was killed less than two months later
at the Battle of Bunker Hill.

Eyewitness Jonas Clark was pastor of the church in Lexington.

Between the hours of twelve and one, on the morning of the nineteenth of April, we received intelligence, by express, from the Honorable
Joseph Warren, Esq., at Boston, "that a large body of the king's troops
(supposed to be a brigade of about twelve or fifteen hundred) were
embarked in boats from Boston, and gone over to land on Lechmere's
Point (so called) in Cambridge; and that it was shrewdly suspected that
they were ordered to seize and destroy the stores belonging to the colony,
then deposited at Concord."

Upon this intelligence, as also upon information of the conduct of the
officers as above-mentioned, the militia of this town were alarmed and
ordered to meet on the usual place of parade.

Accordingly, about half an hour after four o'clock, alarm guns were
fired, and the drums beat to arms, and the militia were collecting together.
Some, to the number of about 50 or 60, or possibly more, were on the
parade, others were coming towards it. In the mean time, the troops having thus stolen a march upon us and, to prevent any intelligence of their
approach, having seized and held prisoners several persons whom they met
unarmed upon the road, seemed to come determined for murder and
bloodshed—and that whether provoked to it or not! When within about
half a quarter of a mile of the meeting-house, they halted, and the command was given to prime and load; which being done, they marched on till
they came up to the east end of said meeting-house, in sight of our militia
(collecting as aforesaid) who were about 12 or 13 rods distant.

Immediately upon their appearing so suddenly, Capt. Parker, who commanded the militia company, ordered the men to disperse and take care of themselves, and not to fire. Upon this, our men dispersed—but many of them not so speedily as they might have done, not having the most distant idea of such brutal barbarity and more than savage cruelty from the troops of a British king, as they immediately experienced! For, no sooner did they come in sight of our company, but one of them, supposed to be an officer of rank, was heard to say to the troops, "Damn them! We will have them!" Upon which the troops shouted aloud, huzza'd, and rushed furiously towards our men.

About the same time, three officers (supposed to be Col. Smith, Major Pitcairn and another officer) advanced on horse back to the front of the body, and coming within 5 or 6 rods of the militia, one of them cried out, "Ye villains, ye Rebels, disperse! Damn you, disperse!"—or words to this effect. One of them (whether the same or not is not easily determined) said, "Lay down your arms! Damn you, why don't you lay down your arms?" The second of these officers about this time, fired a pistol towards the militia as they were dispersing. The foremost, who was within a few yards of our men, brandishing his sword and then pointing towards them, with a loud voice said to the troops, "Fire! By God, fire"—which was instantly followed by a discharge of arms from the said troops, succeeded by a very heavy and close fire upon our party, dispersing, so long as any of them were within reach. Eight were left dead upon the ground! Ten were wounded. The rest of the company, through divine goodness, were (to a miracle) preserved unhurt in this murderous action!

"The firing then soon became general ..."

THE SHOT HEARD 'ROUND THE WORLD

April 20, 1775
Concord, Massachusetts

WILLIAM EMERSON

*F*rom Lexington, the British pressed on to Concord, where the famous shot was *fired. The sound really did travel. War began in Virginia and North Carolina; in Britain the event was taken very seriously; the French learned all the details from the newspapers and quickly recognized how it would affect their rivalry with* *the British for North America. Even in Venice a newspaper described* "la grande scaramucia"—*the great skirmish*—"a Concordia."

William Emerson was the grandfather of Ralph Waldo Emerson, who related his own version of the event in his famous poem "Concord Bridge."

1775, 19 April. This morning, between 1 and 2 o'clock, we were alarmed by the ringing of the bell, and upon examination found that the troops, to the number of 800, had stole their march from Boston, in boats and barges, from the bottom of the Common over to a point in Cambridge, near to Inman's farm, and were at Lexington Meeting-house, half an hour before sunrise, where they had fired upon a body of our men, and (as we afterward heard) had killed several.

This intelligence was brought us at first by Dr. Samuel Prescott, who narrowly escaped the guard that were sent before on horses, purposely to prevent all posts and messengers from giving us timely information. He, by the help of a very fleet horse, crossing several walls and fences, arrived at Concord at the time above mentioned; when several posts were immediately despatched, that returning confirmed the account of the regulars' arrival at Lexington, and that they were on their way to Concord.

Upon this, a number of our minute men belonging to this town, and Acton and Lyncoln, with several others that were in readiness, marched out to meet them, while the alarm company were preparing to receive them in the town. Capt. Minot, who commanded them, thought it proper to take possession of the hill above the meeting-house, as the most advantageous situation. No sooner had our men gained it than we were met by the companies that were sent out to meet the troops, who informed us that they were just upon us, and that we must retreat, as their number was more than treble ours.

We then retreated from the hill near the Liberty Pole and took a new post back of the town upon an eminence, where we formed into two battalions and waited the arrival of the enemy. Scarcely had we formed before we saw the British troops at the distance of a quarter of a mile, glittering in arms, advancing towards us with the greatest celerity. Some were for making a stand, notwithstanding the superiority of their number; but others more prudent thought best to retreat till our strength should be equal to the enemy's by recruits from neighboring towns that were continually coming to our assistance.

Accordingly we retreated over the bridge, when the troops came into the town, set fire to several carriages for the artillery, destroyed 60 barrels flour, rifled several houses, took possession of the town-house, destroyed 500 lbs. of balls, set a guard of 100 men at the North Bridge, and sent up a party to the house of Col. Barrett, where they were in expectation of finding a quantity of warlike stores. But these were happily secured just before their arrival, by transportation into the woods and other by-places.

In the meantime, the guard set by the enemy to secure the pass at the North Bridge were alarmed by the approach of our people, who had retreated, as mentioned before, and were now advancing with special orders not to fire upon the troops unless fired upon. These orders were so punctually observed that we received the fire of the enemy in three several and separate discharges of their pieces before it was returned by our commanding officer; the firing then soon became general for several minutes, in which skirmish two were killed on each side, and several of the enemy wounded.

It may here be observed, by the way, that we were the more cautious to prevent beginning a rupture with the King's troops, as we were then uncertain what had happened at Lexington, and knew that they had begun the quarrel there by first firing upon our people and killing eight men upon the spot.

The three companies of troops soon quitted their post at the bridge and retreated in the greatest disorder and confusion to the main body, who were soon upon the march to meet them. For half an hour, the enemy, by their marches and countermarches, discovered great fickleness and inconstancy of mind, sometimes advancing, sometimes returning to their former posts; till at length they quitted the town and retreated by the way they came. In the meantime, a party of our men (150) took the back way through the Great Fields into the east quarter and had placed themselves to advantage, lying in ambush behind walls, fences and buildings, ready to fire upon the enemy on their retreat.

"Mortification and resentment were expressed ..."

WASHINGTON IS CHOSEN FOR COMMAND

June 15, 1775
Philadelphia

JOHN ADAMS

John Hancock and Samuel Adams were not merely being presumptuous when they hesitated to support Washington. At that time their roles in the rebellion were more evident. They had even been singled out by British General Thomas Gage, who, just three days earlier, had specifically excluded Hancock and Adams from the pardon he offered all the other rebels.

The New England army investing Boston, the New England legislatures, congresses and conventions, and the whole body of the people were left without munitions of war, without arms, clothing, pay, or even countenance and encouragement. Every post brought me letters from my friends, urging in pathetic terms the impossibility of keeping their men together without the assistance of Congress.

I was urging all these things, but we were embarrassed with more than one difficulty, not only with the party in favor of the petition to the King and the party who were jealous of independence, but a third party, which was a Southern party, against a Northern, and a jealousy against a New England army under the command of a New England general.

Whether this jealousy was sincere, or whether it was mere pride and a haughty ambition of furnishing a Southern general to command the Northern army, the intention was very visible to me that Colonel Washington was their object, and so many of our staunchest men were in the plan that we could carry nothing without conceding to it.

Another embarrassment, which was never publicly known, and which was carefully concealed by those who knew it, the Massachusetts and other New England delegates were divided. Mr. Hancock and Mr. Cushing hung back; Mr. Paine did not come forward, and even Mr. Samuel Adams was irresolute.

Mr. Hancock himself had an ambition to be appointed commander-in-chief. Whether he thought an election a compliment due to him and intended to have the honor of declining it, or whether he would have accepted it, I know not. To the compliment he had some pretensions, for, at that time, his exertions, sacrifices, and general merits in the cause of his country had been incomparably greater than those of Colonel Washington.

But the delicacy of his health, and his entire want of experience in actual service, though an excellent militia officer, were decisive objections to him in my mind.

In canvassing this subject, out of doors, I found too that even among the delegates of Virginia there were difficulties. The apostolical reasonings among themselves, which should be greatest, were not less energetic among the saints of the ancient dominion than they were among us of New England.

In several conversations, I found more than one very cool about the appointment of Washington, and particularly Mr. Pendleton was very clear and full against it. Full of anxieties concerning these confusions, and apprehending daily that we should hear very distressing news from Boston, I walked with Mr. Samuel Adams in the Statehouse yard, for a little exercise and fresh air, before the hour of Congress, and there represented to him the various dangers that surrounded us.

He agreed to them all, but said, "What shall we do?" I answered him, that he knew I had taken great pains to get our colleagues to agree upon some plan, that we might be unanimous; but he knew that they would pledge themselves to nothing; but I was determined to take a step which should compel them and all the other members of Congress to declare themselves for or against something.

"I am determined this morning to make a direct motion that Congress should adopt the army before Boston and appoint Colonel Washington commander of it."

Mr. Adams seemed to think very seriously of it but said nothing.

Accordingly, when Congress had assembled, I rose in my place, and in as short a speech as the subject would admit, represented the state of the Colonies, the uncertainty in the minds of the people, their great expectation and anxiety, the distresses of the army, the danger of its dissolution, the difficulty of collecting another, and the probability that the British army would take advantage of our delays, march out of Boston, and spread desolation as far as they could go.

I concluded with a motion, in form, that Congress would adopt the army at Cambridge, and appoint a general; that though this was not the proper time to nominate a general, yet, as I had reason to believe, this was a point of the greatest difficulty, I had no hesitation to declare that I had but one gentleman in my mind for that important command, and that was a gentleman from Virginia who was among us and very well known to all of us, a gentleman whose skill and experience as an officer, whose independent fortune, great talents, and excellent universal character, would command the approbation of all Americans, and unite the cordial exertions of all the Colonies better than any other person in the Union.

Mr. Washington, who happened to sit near the door, as soon as he heard me allude to him, from his usual modesty, darted into the library room. Mr. Hancock—who was our President, which gave me an opportunity to observe his countenance while I was speaking on the state of the Colonies, the army at Cambridge, and the enemy—heard me with visible pleasure; but when I came to describe Washington for the commander, I never remarked a more sudden and striking change of countenance. Mortification and resentment were expressed as forcibly as his face could exhibit them.

Mr. Samuel Adams seconded the motion, and that did not soften the President's physiognomy at all. The subject came under debate, and several gentlemen declared themselves against the appointment of Mr. Washington, not on account of any personal objection against him, but because the army were all from New England, had a general of their own, appeared to be satisfied with him, and had proved themselves able to imprison the British army in Boston, which was all they expected or desired at that time.

Mr. Pendleton, of Virginia, Mr. Sherman, of Connecticut, were very explicit in declaring their opinion; Mr. Cushing and several others more faintly expressed their opposition and their fears of discontents in the army and in New England. Mr. Paine expressed a great opinion of General Ward and a strong friendship for him, having been his classmate at college, or at least his contemporary; but gave no opinion upon the question.

The subject was postponed to a future date. In the meantime, pains were taken out of doors to obtain a unanimity, and the voices were generally so clearly in favor of Washington, that the dissentient members were persuaded to withdraw their opposition, and Mr. Washington was nominated, I believe, by Mr. Thomas Johnson, of Maryland, unanimously elected, and the army adopted.

"What can be your reasons?"

JEFFERSON IS SELECTED TO WRITE THE DECLARATION OF INDEPENDENCE

June 1776
Philadelphia

JOHN ADAMS

*W*hen Washington's troops succeeded in driving the British army out of Boston *by March 1776, many colonists believed a compromise with Britain should be negotiated. But the Continental Congress continued to move toward independence. A committee was assembled to draft a declaration: John Adams of Massachusetts, Ben Franklin of Pennsylvania, Robert Livingstone of New York, Roger Sherman of Connecticut, and Thomas Jefferson of Virginia.*

Adams's note about "the Frankfort advice" refers to a meeting in 1774 between the Massachusetts representatives at the Continental Congress and some members of the Philadelphia branch of the Sons of Liberty, a political group.

You inquire why so young a man as Mr. Jefferson was placed at the head of the Committee for preparing a Declaration of Independence? I answer; It was the Frankfort advice, to place Virginia at the head of every thing. Mr. Richard Henry Lee might be gone to Virginia, to his sick family, for aught I know, but that was not the reason of Mr. Jefferson's appointment. There were three committees appointed at the same time. One for the Declaration of Independence, another for preparing articles of Confederation, and another for preparing a treaty to be proposed to France. Mr. Lee was chosen for the Committee of Confederation, and it was not thought convenient that the same person should be upon both. Mr. Jefferson came into Congress, in June, 1775, and brought with him a reputation for literature, science, and a happy talent of composition. Writings of his were handed about, remarkable for the peculiar felicity of expression. Though a silent member in Congress, he was so prompt, frank, explicit, and decisive upon committees and in conversation, not even Samuel Adams was more so, that he soon seized upon my heart; and upon this occasion I gave him my vote, and did all in my power to procure the votes of others. I think he had one more vote than any other, and that placed him at the head of the committee. I had the next highest number, and that placed me the second. The committee met, discussed the subject, and then appointed Mr. Jefferson and me to make the draught, I suppose because we were the two first on the list.

The sub-committee met. Jefferson proposed to me to make the draught. I said, "I will not."

"You should do it," he said.

"Oh! no."

"Why will you not? You ought to do it."

"I will not."

"Why?"

"Reasons enough," I said.

"What can be your reasons?"

"Reason first—You are a Virginian, and a Virginian ought to appear at the head of this business. Reason second—I am obnoxious, suspected, and unpopular. You are very much otherwise. Reason third—You can write ten times better than I can."

"Well," said Jefferson, "if you are decided, I will do as well as I can."

"Very well. When you have drawn it up, we will have a meeting."

A meeting we accordingly had, and looked the paper over. I was delighted with its high tone and the flights of oratory with which it abounded, especially that concerning negro slavery, which, though I knew his Southern brethren would never suffer to pass in Congress, I certainly never would oppose. There were other expressions which I would not have inserted, if I had drawn it up, particularly that which called the King tyrant. I thought this too personal; for I never believed George to be a tyrant in disposition and in nature; I always believed him to be deceived by his courtiers on both sides of the Atlantic, and in his official capacity only, cruel. I thought the expression too passionate, and too much like scolding, for so grave and solemn a document; but as Franklin and Sherman were to inspect it afterwards, I thought it would not become me to strike it out. I consented to report it, and do not now remember that I made or suggested a single alteration.

We reported it to the committee of five. It was read, and I do not remember that Franklin or Sherman criticized any thing. We were all in haste. Congress was impatient, and the instrument was reported, as I believe, in Jefferson's handwriting, as he first drew it. Congress cut off about a quarter of it, as I expected they would; but they obliterated some of the best of it, and left all that was exceptionable, if any thing in it was. I have long wondered that the original draught has not been published. I suppose the reason is, the vehement philippic against negro slavery.

. . . There is not an idea in it but what had been hackneyed in Congress for two years before. The substance of it is contained in the declaration of rights and the violation of those rights, in the Journals of Congress, in 1774. Indeed, the essence of it is contained in a pamphlet, voted and printed by the town of Boston, before the first Congress met, composed by James Otis, as I suppose, in one of his lucid intervals, and pruned and polished by Samuel Adams.

"I have made it a rule ..."

YOUNG JEFFERSON GETS SOME ADVICE FROM BEN FRANKLIN

July 1776
Philadelphia

THOMAS JEFFERSON

When the Declaration of Independence was under the consideration of Congress, there were two or three unlucky expressions in it which gave offense to some members. The words "Scotch and other foreign auxiliaries" excited the ire of a gentleman or two of that country. Severe strictures on the conduct of the British king, in negativing [vetoing] our repeated repeals of the law which permitted the importation of slaves, were disapproved by some Southern gentlemen, whose reflections were not yet matured to the full abhorrence of that traffic. Altho' the offensive expressions were immediately yielded, these gentlemen continued their depredations on other parts of the instrument. I was sitting by Dr. Franklin, who perceived that I was not insensible to these mutilations. "I have made it a rule," said he, "whenever in my power, to avoid becoming the draughtsman of papers to be reviewed by a public body. I took my lesson from an incident which I will relate to you. When I was a journeyman printer, one of my companions, an apprentice Hatter, having served out his time, was about to open shop for himself. His first concern was to have a handsome signboard, with a proper inscription. He composed it in these words 'John Thompson, Hatter, makes and sells hats for ready money,' with a figure of a hat subjoined. But he thought he would submit it to his friends for their amendments. The first he showed it to thought the word 'Hatter,' tautologous, because followed by the words 'makes hats' which show he was a Hatter. It was struck out. The next observed that the word 'makes' might as well be omitted, because his customers would not care who made the hats. If good and to their mind, they would buy, by whomsoever made. He struck it out. A third said he thought the words 'for ready money' were useless as it was not the custom of the place to sell on credit. Every one who purchased expected to pay. They were parted with, and the inscription now stood 'John Thomson sells hats.' 'Sells hats' says his next friend? Why nobody will expect you to give them away. What then is the use of that word? it was stricken out, and 'hats' followed it, as there was one painted on the board. So his inscription was reduced ultimately to 'John Thomson' with the figure of a hat."

"The clause . . . reprobating enslaving . . . was struck out."

THE DECLARATION'S MISSING CLAUSE

July 1776
Philadelphia

THOMAS JEFFERSON

*O*n the subject of slavery, Jefferson's words and actions were contradictory, and over the course of his life his thoughts on the issue wavered. Although he owned slaves, he wrote a strongly worded attack on slavery for the Declaration of Independence.

Historian Samuel Eliot Morison noted, "Of all the ironies in American history, the career and influence of Thomas Jefferson are the greatest. . . . His Southern supporters accepted Jefferson's principles with the reservation that they applied only to white men . . . but the Northerners whom Jefferson converted to his views took him seriously and literally. . . . When the issue really became acute in 1860–61, the society which Jefferson loved, and which still worshipped his name . . . was overthrown by the society which had taken those principles to heart."

The clause . . . reprobating enslaving the inhabitants of Africa was struck out in complaisance to South Carolina and Georgia, who had never attempted to restrain the importation of slaves, and who on the contrary still wished to continue it. Our Northern brethren also I believe felt a little tender under those censures; for tho' their people have very few slaves themselves yet they had been pretty considerable carriers of them to others.

Text of the clause—

He [King George] has waged cruel war against human nature itself, violating its most sacred rights of life and liberty in the persons of a distant people who never offended him, captivating and carrying them into slavery in another hemisphere, or to incur miserable death in their transportation there. This piratical warfare, the opprobrium of Infidel powers, is the warfare of the Christian King of Great Britain. Determined to keep open a market where men should be bought and sold, he has prostituted his [veto] for suppressing every legislative attempt to prohibit or to restrain this execrable commerce. And that this assemblage of horrors might want no fact of distinguished [caprice], he is now exciting those very people to rise in arms among us, and to purchase that liberty of which he has deprived them, by murdering the people on whom he has also obtruded them, thus paying off former crimes committed against the liberties of one people, with crimes which he urges them to commit against the lives of another.

**"The pensive and awful silence
which pervaded the house ..."**

SIGNING THE DECLARATION

August 2, 1776
Philadelphia

DR. BENJAMIN RUSH

*O*n *July 2, 1776, the Continental Congress adopted the resolution that "these United Colonies are, and, of right, ought to be Free and Independent States . . . absolved of all allegiance to the British Crown." Two days later, the final version of the Declaration was adopted. The Declaration was first read publicly in Philadelphia on July 8. Washington's troops in New York heard it the next day.*
Yet only two men signed it on July 4: John Hancock, president of the Congress,

and Charles Thomson, the secretary. Most of the fifty-six signers added their names on August 2. The identities of the signers were kept secret for several months to prevent revenge by the British or by Loyalists. Even that precaution did not keep all the signers safe from being singled out for vengeance. Several families were chased from farms and homes that were then destroyed. Some of the signers, and even their wives, were imprisoned. John Martin of Pennsylvania died following a breakdown caused by the strain of being shunned by friends. The wife of Francis Lewis died in prison.

Dr. Benjamin Rush, one of the signers, was an early social reformer. He opposed slavery and capital punishment and supported making education and health care widely available. (His reputation as a doctor suffers from his eagerness to bleed his patients.) This account comes from a letter Rush wrote to fellow signer John Adams. The Colonel Harrison he mentions was Benjamin Harrison, father of President William Henry Harrison and great-grandfather of President Benjamin Harrison.

Dear Old Friend—

The 4th of July has been celebrated in Philadelphia in the manner I expected. The military men, and particularly one of them, ran away with all the glory of the day. Scarcely a word was said of the solitude and labors and fears and sorrows and sleepless nights of the men who projected, proposed, defended, and subscribed the Declaration of Independence. Do you recollect your memorable speech upon the day on which the vote was taken? Do you recollect the pensive and awful silence which pervaded the house when we were called up, one after another, to the table of the President of Congress to subscribe what was believed by many at that time to be our own death warrants? The silence and the gloom of the morning were interrupted, I well recollect, only for a moment by Colonel Harrison of Virginia, who said to Mr. [Elbridge] Gerry at the table: "I shall have a great advantage over you, Mr. Gerry, when we are all hung for what we are now doing. From the size and weight of my body I shall die in a few minutes, but from the lightness of your body you will dance in the air an hour or two before you are dead." This speech procured a transient smile, but it was soon succeeded by the solemnity with which the whole business was conducted. . . .

Let us, my dear friend, console ourselves for the unsuccessful efforts of our lives to serve our fellow creatures by recollecting that we have aimed well.

"The object was to amuse themselves at our expense ..."

RECRUITING TROUBLE

1776
Frankfort, Pennsylvania

CAPTAIN ALEXANDER GRAYDON

" *A good part of the American people supported the war for independence as the only alternative to submission,"* wrote historian Samuel Eliot Morison, *"but by no standard, of that time or ours, was their support adequate. After Congress had declared independence, most of Washington's army expected to be discharged."* They were disappointed. Instead, recruiters such as this eyewitness secured more troops.

The object now was to raise my company, and as the streets of the city had been pretty well swept by the preceding and contemporary levies, it was necessary to have recourse to the country. My recruiting party was therefore sent out in various directions; and each of my officers as well as myself, exerted himself in the business. Among the many unpleasant peculiarities of the American service, it was not the least that the drudgery, which in old military establishments belongs to sergeants and corporals, here devolved on the commissioned officers; and that the whole business of recruiting, drilling, etc. required their unremitted personal attention. This was more emphatically the case in recruiting; since the common opinion was, that the men and the officers were never to be separated, and hence, to see the persons who were to command them, and above all, the captain, was deemed of vast importance by those inclining to enlist. For this reason I found it necessary, in common with my brother officers, to put my feelings most cruelly to the rack; and in an excursion I once made to Frankfort, they were tried to the utmost.

A number of fellows at the tavern, at which my party rendezvoused, indicated a desire to enlist, but although they drank freely of our liquor, they still held off. I soon perceived that the object was to amuse themselves at our expense, and that if there might be one or two among them really disposed to engage, the others would prevent them. One fellow in particular, who had made the greatest show of taking the bounty, presuming on the weakness of our party, consisting only of a drummer, corporal, my second lieutenant and myself, began to grow insolent, and manifested an intention to begin a quarrel, in the issue of which, he no doubt calculated on giving us a drubbing. The disgrace of such a circumstance, presented itself to my mind in colors the most dismal, and I resolved, that if a scuffle should be unavoidable, it should, at least, be as serious as the hangers which my lieutenant and myself carried by our sides, could make it. Our endeavor, however, was to guard against a contest; but the moderation we testified, was attributed to fear.

At length the arrogance of the principal ruffian rose to such a height, that he squared himself for battle and advanced towards me in an attitude of defiance. I put him by, with an admonition to be quiet, though with a secret determination, that, if he repeated the insult, to begin the war, whatever might be the consequence. The occasion was soon presented; when taking excellent aim, I struck him with the utmost force between the eyes and sent him staggering to the other end of the room. Then instantly drawing our hangers, and receiving the manful co-operation of the corporal and drummer, we were fortunate enough to put a stop to any further hostilities. It was some time before the fellow I had struck, recovered from the blow, but when he did, he was quite an altered man. He was as submissive as could be wished, begging my pardon for what he had done, and although he would not enlist, he hired himself to me for a few weeks as a fifer, in which capacity he had acted in the militia; and during the time he was in this employ, he bore about the effects of his insolence, in a pair of black eyes.

This incident would be little worthy of relating, did it not serve in some degree to correct the error of those who seem to conceive the year 1776 to have been a season of almost universal patriotic enthusiasm. It was far from prevalent in my opinion, among the lower ranks of the people, at least in Pennsylvania. At all times, indeed, licentious, levelling principles are much to the general taste, and were of course popular with us; but the true merits of the contest, were little understood or regarded. The opposition to the claims of Britain originated with the better sort: it was truly aristocratic in its commencement; and as the oppression to be apprehended, had not been felt, no grounds existed for general enthusiasm. The cause of liberty it is true, was fashionable, and there were great preparations to fight for it; but a zeal proportioned to the magnitude of the question was only to be looked for in the minds of those sagacious politicians, who inferred effects from causes, and who, as Mr. Burke expresses it, "snuffed the approach of tyranny in every tainted breeze."

"Dec. 25. Christmas—we are still in tents."

WINTER AT VALLEY FORGE

December 12, 1777–January 8, 1778
Pennsylvania

DR. ALBIGENCE WALDO

*T*he early battles of the War did not go well for the patriots. An eyewitness to
Washington's retreat from New York City in September 1776 said "the General
*was so exasperated that he struck several officers in their flight, three times dashed
his hat on the ground, and at last exclaimed "Good God, have I got such troops as
those! . . . It was with difficulty his friends could get him to quit the field, so great
were his emotions."A few months later Thomas Paine published the dramatic opening line of the first pamphlet of* The American Crisis:*"These are the times that
try men's souls."*

*Shortly afterward, American morale was bolstered by victories in the Battle of
Trenton and the Battle of Princeton. But by September 1777, the Continental Congress had been forced to flee Philadelphia. Washington decided his army was not yet
capable of defeating the British, so he encamped with twelve thousand tattered
troops at Valley Forge. A harsh winter and a lack of supplies led to starvation and
disease. This was the Revolution's lowest point. Yet Valley Forge was also where the
troops were trained and drilled into fighting trim. By June 1778 they were ready
for an advance on the British.*

Dr. Waldo was a surgeon from Connecticut.

Dec. 12th.—A bridge of wagons made across the Schuylkill last night
consisting of 36 wagons, with a bridge of rails between each. Some skir-
mishing over the river. Militia and draggoons brought into camp several
prisoners. Sun set.——We are order'd to march over the river—it snows—
I'm sick—eat nothing—no whiskey—no baggage—Lord—Lord—Lord.
The army were 'till sun rise crossing the river—some at the wagon
bridge, & some at the raft bridge below. Cold & uncomfortable.

Dec. 13th.——The army march'd three miles from the west side the
river and encamp'd near a place call'd the Gulph and not an improper
name neither—for this gulph seems well adapted by its situation to keep
us from the pleasure & enjoyments of this world, or being conversant
with any body in it—it is an excellent place to raise the ideas of a philoso-

pher beyond the glutted thoughts and reflexions of an epicurian. His reflexions will be as different from the common reflexions of mankind as if he were unconnected with the world, and only conversant with material beings. It cannot be that our superiors are about to hold consultation with spirits infinitely beneath their order—by bringing us into these utmost regions of the terraqueous sphere. No—it is, upon consideration, for many good purposes since we are to winter here—there is plenty of wood & water; there are but few families for the soldiery to steal from— tho, far be it from a soldier to steal; there are warm sides of hills to erect huts on; they will be heavenly minded like Jonah when in the belly of a great fish; they will not become home sick as is sometimes the case when men live in the open world—since the reflections which must naturally arise from their present habitation, will lead them to the more noble thoughts of employing their leisure hours in filling their knapsacks with such materials as may be necessary on the journey to another home.

Dec. 14th.—Prisoners & deserters are continually coming in. The army who have been surprisingly healthy hitherto—now begin to grow sickly from the continued fatigues they have suffered this campaign. Yet they still show spirit of alacrity & contentment not to be expected from so young troops. I am sick—discontented—and out of humour. Poor food—hard lodging—cold weather—fatigue—nasty cloaths—nasty cookery—vomit half my time—smoak'd out of my senses—the devil's in't—I can't endure it—why are we sent here to starve and freeze—what sweet felicities have I left at home;—a charming wife—pretty children— good beds—good food—good cookery—all agreeable—all harmonious. Here, all confusion—smoke cold—hunger & filthyness—a pox on my bad luck. Here comes a bowl of beef soup—full of burnt leaves and dirt, sickish enough to make a Hector spue,—away with it boys—I'll live like the chameleon upon air.

Dec. 18th.—Universal thanksgiving—a roasted pig at night. God be thanked for my health which I have pretty well recovered. How much better should I feel, were I assured my family were in health—but the same good being who graciously preserves me—is able to preserve them—& bring me to the ardently wish'd for enjoyment of them again.

Dec. 25th, Christmas.—We are still in tents—when we ought to be in huts—the poor sick, suffer much in tents this cold weather—but we now treat them differently from what they used to be at home, under the inspection of old women & Doct. Bolus Linctus. [A bolus was a large pill; a linctus was similar to a lozenge.] We give them mutton & grogg—and a capital medicine once in a while—to start the disease from its foundation

at once. We avoid—piddling pills, powders, bolus's linctus's—cordials—
and all such insignificant matters whose powers are only render'd important by causing the patient to vomit up his money instead of his disease.
But very few of the sick men die.

Dec. 26th.—The enemy have been some days the west Schuylkill
from opposite the city to derby—there intentions not yet known. The
city is at present pretty clear of them—why don't his Excellency rush in
& retake the city, in which he will doubtless find much plunder?—
Because he knows better than to leave his post and be catch'd like a . . .
fool cooped up in the city. He has always acted wisely hitherto—his conduct when closely scrutinised is uncensurable. Were his inferior generals
as skillfull as himself—we should have the grandest choir of officers ever
God made. . . .

Dec. 28th.—Yesterday upwards of fifty officers in Gen. Greene's
division resigned their commissions—six or seven of our regiment are
doing the like today. All this is occasion'd by officers families being so
much neglected at home on account of provisions.

The present circumstances of the soldier is better by far than the officer—for the family of the soldier is provided for at the public expence if
the articles they want are above the common price—but the officer's family, are obliged not only to beg in the most humble manner for the necessaries of life—but also to pay for them afterwards at the most exhorbitant
rates—and even in this manner, many of them who depend entirely on
their money, cannot procure half the material comforts that are wanted in
a family—this produces continual letters of complaint from home.

Dec. 31st.—Adjutant Selden learn'd me how to darn stockings—to
make them look like knit work—first work the thread in a parallel manner, then catch these over & over as above.

1778. January 1st.—New year. I am alive. I am well.

Huts go on briskly, and our camp begins to appear like a spacious city.

Bought an embroidered jacket.

How much we affect to appear of consequence by a superfluous
dress,—and yet custom—(that law which none may fight against) has
rendered this absolutely necessary & commendable. An officer frequently
fails of being duly noticed, merely from the want of a genteel dress.

Sunday, Jan. 4th.—Properly accouter'd I went to work at masonry—
none of my mess were to dictate me—and before night (being found with
mortar & stone) I almost compleated a genteel chimney to my magnificent hut—however, as we had short allowance of food & no grogg—my
back ached before night.

I was call'd to relieve a soldier tho't to be dying—he expir'd before I reach'd the hutt. He was an Indian—an excellent soldier—and an obedient good natur'd fellow. . . .

8th.—Unexpectedly got a furlow. Set out for home.

"I saw all the amazed inhabitants . . ."

YANKEES INVADE GREAT BRITAIN

April 22–23, 1778
Whitehaven, England

CAPTAIN JOHN PAUL JONES

*O*ne *of the oddities of the Revolutionary War was this intrepid raid on the northwest coast of England. Along with a less successful raid later that day— Jones was hoping to kidnap his former neighbor Lord Selkirk—it was the only combat on the British mainland during the war.*

Jones, born John Paul in Scotland in 1747, came to America in 1773 with a shady past. He had already been cleared of the murder of one seaman under his command when he killed another sailor, who was part of a mutiny. He fled to America to avoid another trial, and added "Jones" to his name.

The 22d introduced fair weather, though the three kingdoms [of Great Britain] were, as far as the eye could reach covered with snow. I now resolved once more to attempt Whitehaven; but the wind became very light, so that the ship would not in proper title approach so near as I intended. At midnight I left the ship with two boats and thirty-one volunteers; when we reached outer pier the day began to dawn; I would not, however, abandon my enterprise, but despatched one boat under the direction of Mr. Hill and Mr. Wallingford, with the necessary combustibles to set fire to the shipping on the north side of the harbor, while I went with the other party to attempt the south side. I was successful in scaling the walls and spiking up all the cannon in the first fort; finding the sentinels shut up in the guard house, they were secured without being hurt. Having fixed sentinels, I now took with me one man only (Mr. Green) and spiked up all the cannon in the southern forts distant from the Others a quarter of a mile.

On my returning from the business, I naturally expected to see the fire of the ships on the north side, as well as to find my own party with every thing in readiness to set fire to the shipping on the south; instead of this, I found the boat under the direction of Mr. Hill and Mr. Wallingford returned, and the party in some confusion, their light having burnt out at the instant when it became necessary.

By the strangest fatality my own party were in the same situation, the candles being all burnt out. The day too came on apace, yet I would by no means retract while any hopes of success remained. Having again placed sentinels, a light was obtained at a house disjoined from the town, and a fire was kindled in the steerage of a large ship, which was surrounded by at least one hundred and fifty others, chiefly from two to four hundred tons burden, and lying side by side, aground unsurrounded by the water. There were, beside from seventy to a hundred large ships on the north arm of the harbor, aground clear of the water, and divided from the rest only by a stone pier of a ship's height.

I should have kindled fires in other places if the time had permitted; as it did not, our care was to prevent the one kindled from being easily extinguished. After some search, a barrel of tar was found, and poured into the flames, which now ascended from all the hatchways. The inhabitants began to appear in thousands, and individuals ran hastily towards us. I stood between them and the ship on fire, with a pistol in my hand, and ordered them to retire, which they did with precipitation.

The flames had already caught in the rigging, and began to ascend the mainmast; the sun was a full hour's march above the horizon, and as sleep no longer ruled the world, it was time to retire. We re-embarked without opposition, having released a number of prisoners, as our boats could not carry them.

After all my people had embarked, I stood upon the pier for a considerable space, yet no person advanced; I saw all the eminences around the town covered with the amazed inhabitants.

Had it been possible to have landed a few hours sooner, my success would have been complete. Not a single ship, out of more than 200, could possibly have escaped, and all the world would not have been able to save the town.

"I have not yet begun to fight . . ."

JOHN PAUL JONES REFUSES TO SURRENDER

September 23, 1779
North Sea, near Flamborough Head

LIEUTENANT RICHARD DALE

*D*espite his daring raid at Whitehaven, politics prevented John Paul Jones from commanding a ship for more than a year. He finally received a weatherworn French merchant ship. He rebuilt it and named it Bonhomme Richard (Poor Richard) in honor of Ben Franklin, who had helped him receive the command.

The ship had a crew of 380 men from eleven different countries. Historian and U.S. Navy admiral Samuel Eliot Morison wrote, "This motley collection of professional sailors, beachcombers, and peasants" was forged by Jones into "as stout a force as ever served under the Stars and Stripes . . . [they] scared the daylights out of Edinburgh and Newcastle."

The famous battle began when Jones and his squadron spotted forty British merchant ships protected by the British navy ships Serapis and Countess of Scarborough. "For sheer grit," wrote historians Louis Snyder and Richard Morris, it was "unsurpassed in maritime history." Even Jones's victorious ship sank afterward—in part because the Alliance, an American ship, repeatedly fired upon it by mistake.

Jones ended his career as a captain for hire in the Russian navy, and was buried in an unmarked grave in Paris. In 1905, his remains were discovered and moved to the U.S. Naval Academy at Annapolis.

On the 23d of September, 1779, being below, I was roused by an unusual noise upon deck. This induced me to go upon deck, when I found the men were swaying up the royal yards, preparatory to making sail for a large fleet under our lee. I asked the coasting pilot what fleet it was. He answered:

"The Baltic fleet, under convoy of the *Serapis* of forty-four guns, and the *Countess of Scarborough* of twenty guns."

A general chase then commenced of the *Bonhomme Richard,* the *Vengeance,* the *Pallas,* and the *Alliance* [American ships in Jones's squadron].

At this time our fleet headed to the northward, with a light breeze, Flamborough Head being about two leagues distant. At 7 P.M. it was evident the Baltic fleet perceived we were in chase, from the signal of the

Serapis to the merchantmen to stand in shore. At the same time, the *Serapis* and *Countess of Scarborough* tacked ship, and stood off shore, with the intention of drawing off our attention from the convoy. When these ships had separated from the convoy about two miles, they again tacked and stood in shore after the merchantmen. At about eight, being within hail, the *Serapis* demanded,

"What ship is that?"

He was answered: "I can't hear what you say."

Immediately after the *Serapis* hailed again:

"What ship is that? Answer immediately, or I shall be under the necessity of firing into you."

At this moment I received orders from Commodore Jones to commence the action with a broadside, which indeed appeared to be simultaneous on board both ships. Our position being to windward of the *Serapis,* we passed ahead of her, and the *Serapis* coming up on our larboard quarter, the action commenced abreast of each other. The *Serapis* soon passed ahead of the *Bonhomme Richard,* and when he thought he had gained a distance sufficient to go down athwart the fore foot to rake us, found he had not enough distance . . . and the *Bonhomme Richard,* having headway, ran her bows into the stern of the *Serapis.* We had remained in this situation but a few minutes when we were again hailed by the Serapis:

"Has your ship struck?"

To which Captain Jones answered: *"I have not yet begun to fight."*

As we were unable to bring a single gun to bear upon the *Serapis,* our topsails were backed, while those of the *Serapis* being filled, the ships separated. The *Serapis* bore short round upon her heel, and her jib boom ran into the mizen rigging of the *Bonhomme Richard.* In this situation the ships were made fast together with a hawser, the bowsprit of the *Serapis* to the mizenmast of the *Bonhomme Richard,* and the action recommenced from the starboard sides of the two ships. . . . A novelty in naval combats was now presented to many witnesses, but to few admirers. . . .

From the commencement to the termination of the action, there was not a man on board the *Bonhomme Richard* ignorant of the superiority of the *Serapis,* both in weight of metal, and in the qualities of the crews. The crew of that ship was picked seamen, and the ship itself had been only a few months off the stocks; whereas the crew of the *Bonhomme Richard* consisted of part American, English, and French, and a part of Maltese, Portuguese, and Malays, these latter contributing, by their want of naval skill and knowledge of the English language, to depress rather than elevate the first hope of success in a combat under such circumstances. Neither the consideration of the relative force of the ships, the fact of the blowing up of the gundeck above them by the bursting of two of the eighteen pounders, nor the alarm that the ship was sinking, could depress the ardor or change the determination of the brave Captain Jones, his officers and men. Neither the repeated broadsides of the *Alliance,* given with a view of sinking or disabling the *Bonhomme Richard,* the frequent necessity of suspending the combat to extinguish the flames, which several times were within a few inches of the magazine, nor the liberation by the master-at-arms of nearly five hundred prisoners, could change or weaken the purpose of the American commander. At the moment of the liberation of the prisoners, one of them, a commander of a twenty-gun ship taken a few days before, passed through the ports on board the *Serapis,* and informed Captain Pearson that if he would hold out only a little while longer, the ship alongside would either strike or sink, and that all the prisoners had been released to save their lives. The combat was accordingly continued with renewed ardor by the *Serapis.*

The fire from the tops of the *Bonhomme Richard* was conducted with so much skill and effect as to destroy ultimately every man who appeared upon the quarter-deck of the *Serapis,* and induced her commander to order the survivors to go below. Nor even under shelter of the decks were they more secure. The powder-monkeys of the *Serapis,* finding no officer to receive the eighteen-pound cartridges brought from the magazines, threw them on the main deck, and went for more. These cartridges being scattered along the deck, and numbers of them broken, it so happened that some of the hand grenades thrown from the main-yard of the *Bonhomme Richard,* which was directly over the main hatch of the *Serapis,* fell upon this powder, and produced a most awful explosion. The effect was tremendous. More than twenty of the enemy were blown to pieces, and many stood with only the collars of their shirts upon their bodies. In less than an hour afterward the flag of England, which had been nailed to the mast of the *Serapis,* was struck by Captain Pearson's *own hands,* as none of his people would venture aloft on this duty; and this, too, when more than 1,500 persons were witnessing the conflict, and the humiliating termination of it, from Scarborough and Flamborough Head.

"I have the mortification to inform your Excellency . . ."

CORNWALLIS SURRENDERS

October 19, 1781
Yorktown, Virginia

LT. GENERAL CHARLES, MARQUIS CORNWALLIS

The appointment in 1780 of Nathanael Greene to lead the army in the south marked another turning point in the war. Greene quickly revitalized his troops. Although his force was already smaller than the British in the region, he divided it into two units, making the troops better able to live off the land and raid the British.

By the middle of 1781, the British, led in the south by Cornwallis, had been maneuvered into an encampment at Yorktown, Virginia. Washington gathered his army and navy there, along with the allied forces of France, to achieve the final victory. Cornwallis waited in vain for help from Sir Henry Clinton, Commander of the British forces in America, who was holding New York City. Clinton did not want to risk losing New York by sending troops to Virginia.

This letter to Clinton marked what was effectively the end of the war. Still, it took more than a year to negotiate and sign the actual peace treaty.

I have the mortification to inform your Excellency that I have been forced to give up the posts of York and Gloucester, and to surrender the troops under my command, by capitulation, on the 19th instant, as prisoners of war to the combined forces of America and France.

I never saw this post in a very favourable light, but when I found I was to be attacked in it in so unprepared a state, by so powerful an army and artillery, nothing but the hopes of relief would have induced me to attempt its defence, for I would either have endeavoured to escape to New York by rapid marches from the Gloucester side, immediately on the arrival of General Washington's troops at Williamsburg, or I would, notwithstanding the disparity of numbers, have attacked them in the open field, where it might have been just possible that fortune would have favoured the gallantry of the handful of troops under my command, but being assured by your Excellency's letters that every possible means would be tried by the navy and army to relieve us, I could not think myself at liberty to venture upon either of those desperate attempts;

therefore, after remaining for two days in a strong position in front of this place in hopes of being attacked, upon observing that the enemy were taking measures which could not fail of turning my left flank in a short time, and receiving on the second evening your letter of the 24th of September, informing me that the relief would sail about the 5th of October, I withdrew within the works on the night of the 29th of September, hoping by the labour and firmness of the soldiers to protract the defence until you could arrive.

On the night of the 6th of October they made their first parallel, extending from its right on the river, to a deep ravine on the left, nearly opposite to the centre of this place, and embracing our whole left at a distance of 600 yards. Having perfected this parallel, their batteries opened on the evening of the 9th against our left, and other batteries fired at the same time against a redoubt advanced over the creek upon our right. . . . On the evening of the 14th they assaulted. . . . Being perfectly sensible that our works could not stand many hours, we not only continued a constant fire with all our mortars and every gun that could be brought to bear upon it, but a little before daybreak on the morning of the 16th, I ordered a sortie of about 350 men, under the direction of Lieut.-Colonel Abercrombie, to attack two batteries which appeared to be in the greatest forwardness, and to spike the guns. A detachment succeeded in spiking 11 guns, and killing or wounding about 100 of the French troops, who had the guard of that part of the trenches, and with little loss on our side.

This action, though extremely honourable to the officers and soldiers who executed it, proved of little public advantage, for the cannon having been spiked in a hurry, were soon rendered fit for service again, and before dark the whole parallel and batteries appeared of the whole front attacked on which we could show a single gun, and our shells were nearly expended. I, therefore, had only to choose between preparing to surrender next day, or endeavouring to get off with the greatest part of the troops, and I determined to attempt the latter. . . . In this situation, with my little force divided, the enemy's batteries opened at daybreak.

Under all these circumstances, I thought it would have been wanton and inhuman to the last degree to sacrifice the lives of this small body of gallant soldiers, who had ever behaved with so much fidelity and courage, by exposing them to an assault which, from the numbers and precautions of the enemy, could not fail to succeed. I therefore proposed to capitulate; and I have the honour to enclose to your Excellency the copy of the correspondence between General Washington and me on that subject, and the terms of capitulation agreed upon. I sincerely lament that better could not be obtained, but I have neglected nothing in my power to alleviate the misfortune and distress of both officers and soldiers. The men are well clothed and provided with necessaries. The treatment, in general, that we have received from the enemy since our surrender has been perfectly good and proper, but the kindness and attention that has been shown to us by the French officers in particular—their delicate sensibility of our situation—their generous and pressing offer of money, both public and private, to any amount—has really gone beyond what I can possibly describe, and will, I hope, make an impression on the breast of every British officer, whenever the fortune of war should put any of them into our power.

"The hopes of all the Union center in this Convention."

THE EVE OF THE CONSTITUTIONAL CONVENTION

May 17–20, 1787
Philadelphia

GEORGE MASON

After the Revolutionary War, the colonies were first united under the "Articles of Confederation." The Articles, which made the Continental Congress a legal assembly, left the structure of the government heavily weighted toward the individual states, rather than creating a strong federal government.

By 1787, Congress had decided to call a special convention "for the sole and express purpose of revising the Articles of Confederation . . . to render the federal constitution adequate to the exigencies of government, and the preservation of the Union."

Along with more substantial matters, the convention debates ended a long-forgotten historical oddity: Technically the first "President of the United States" was not George Washington. Although the office of President as we know it was first established by the Constitution, and of course the first chief executive was George Washington, elected in 1789, eight years earlier Congress had voted Maryland's John Hanson "President of the United States in Congress Assembled." But the post was actually closer to speaker of the assembly than chief executive.

Eyewitness Mason, a delegate from Virginia, took an active role in the conven-

*tion debates. Ultimately he refused to sign the Constitution because he believed it
was too aristocratic. He wrote this account in a letter to his son, describing both the
issues of the day and the sense of apprehension felt by the delegates, who were
mindful of the failed Annapolis Convention of the previous year.*

Upon our arrival here on Thursday evening, seventeenth May, I found
only the States of Virginia and Pennsylvania fully represented; and there
are at this time only five—New York, the two Carolinas, and the two
before mentioned. All the States, Rhode Island excepted, have made their
appointments; but the members drop in slowly; some of the deputies
from the Eastern States are here, but none of them have yet a sufficient
representation, and it will probably be several days before the Convention
will be authorized to proceed to business. The expectations and hopes of
all the Union center in this Convention. God grant that we may be able to
concert effectual means of preserving our country from the evils which
threaten us.

The Virginia deputies (who are all here) meet and confer together
two or three hours every day, in order to form a proper correspondence
of sentiments; and for form's sake, to see what new deputies are arrived,
and to grow into some acquaintance with each other, we regularly meet
every day at three o'clock. These and some occasional conversations with
the deputies of different States, and with some of the general officers of
the late army, are the only opportunities I have hitherto had of forming
any opinion upon the great subject of our mission, and, consequently, a
very imperfect and indecisive one, Yet, upon the great principles of it, I
have reason to hope there will be greater unanimity and less opposition,
except from the little States, than was at first apprehended. The most
prevalent idea in the principal States seems to be a total alteration of the
present federal system, and substituting a great national council or parliament, consisting of two branches of the legislature, founded upon the
principles of equal proportionate representation, with full legislative
powers upon all the subjects of the Union; and an executive: and to make
the several State legislatures subordinate to the national, by giving the latter the power of a negative upon all such laws as they shall judge contrary
to the interest of the federal Union. It is easy to foresee that there will be
much difficulty in organizing a government upon this great scale, and at
the same time reserving to the State legislatures a sufficient portion of
power for promoting and securing the prosperity and happiness of their
respective citizens; yet with a proper degree of coolness, liberality and
candor (very rare commodities by the bye), I doubt not but it may be
effected. There are among a variety some very eccentric opinions upon

this great subject; and what is a very extraordinary phenomenon, we are likely to find the republicans, on this occasion, issue from the Southern and Middle States, and the anti-republican from the Eastern; however extraordinary this may at first seem, it may, I think be accounted for from a very common and natural impulse of the human mind. Men disappointed in expectations too hastily and sanguinely formed, tired and disgusted with the unexpected evils they have experienced, and anxious to remove them as far as possible, are very apt to run into the opposite extreme; and the people of the Eastern States, setting out with more republican principles, have consequently been more disappointed than we have been.

We found travelling very expensive—from eight to nine dollars per day. In this city the living is cheap. We are at the old Indian Queen in Fourth Street, where we are very well accommodated, have a good room to ourselves, and are charged only twenty-five Pennsylvania Currency per day, including our servants and horses, exclusive of club in liquors and extra charges; so that I hope I shall be able to defray my expenses with my public allowance, and more than that I do not wish.

"I meet with nobody but myself that is always in the right."

LAST-MINUTE DISSENTERS AT THE CONSTITUTIONAL CONVENTION

September 1 5–1 7, 1 7 8 7
Philadelphia

JAMES MADISON

To put the objections of dissenters in perspective: The Constitution prepared at the convention was certainly imperfect by modern standards. It failed to secure many crucial individual rights, later guaranteed in its first ten amendments, the Bill of Rights. It also failed to resolve the differences between the states that would lead to the Civil War.

But delegate Benjamin Franklin was a pragmatist. He knew a perfect document could not be created in the first attempt, given the many different views of the delegates. (His own suggestions for the government, such as a single federal legislature rather than both a House and Senate, had been ignored.) Just when the convention was on the verge of falling apart, the revered figure, almost eighty-two years old, rose from his seat to rally the delegates to a common cause, calling for them to ratify the Constitution despite their concerns and to move the country forward.

Franklin's speech was read by James Wilson, a younger Pennsylvania delegate considered an intellectual equal to Jefferson and Adams. Wilson played a key role in shaping the Constitution. He had worked to maintain a balance between federal power and states rights, and to ensure that the national government was elected directly by the people rather than by the state assemblies. He later became a justice of the Supreme Court.

SEPTEMBER 15

Mr. Gerry stated the objections which determined him to withhold his name from the Constitution: 1, the duration and reeligibility of the Senate; 2, the power of the House of Representatives to conceal their Journals; 3, the power of Congress over the places of election; 4, the unlimited power of Congress over their own compensation; 5, that Massachusetts has not a due share of representatives allotted to her; 6, that three-fifths of the blacks are to be represented, as if they were freemen; 7, that under the power over commerce, monopolies may be established; 8, the Vice-President being made head of the Senate. He could, however, he said, get over all these, if the rights of the citizens were not rendered insecure—first, by the general power of the legislature to make what laws they may please to call "necessary and proper;" secondly, to raise armies and money without limit; thirdly, to establish a tribunal without juries, which will be a Star Chamber as to civil cases. Under such a view of the Constitution, the best that could be done, he conceived, was to provide for a second General Convention. . . .

SEPTEMBER 17

The engrossed Constitution being read, Dr. Franklin rose with a speech in his hand, which he had reduced to writing for his own convenience, and which Mr. Wilson read in the words following:

"Mr. President: I confess that there are several parts of this Constitution which I do not at present approve, but I am not sure I shall never approve them. For, having lived long, I have experienced many instances of being obliged, by better information or fuller consideration, to change opinions, even on important subjects, which I once thought right, but found to be otherwise. It is therefore that, the older I grow, the more apt I am to doubt my own judgment, and to pay more respect to the judgment of others. Most men, indeed, as well as most sects in religion, think themselves in possession of all truth, and that wherever others differ from them, it is so far error. Steele, a Protestant, in a dedication, tells the Pope, that the only difference between our churches, in their opinions of the certainty of their doctrines, is, 'the Church of Rome is infallible, and the Church of England is never in the wrong.' But though many private persons think almost as highly of their own infallibility as of that of their sect, few express it so naturally as a certain French lady, who, in a dispute with her sister, said, 'I don't know how it happens, sister, but I meet with nobody but myself that is always in the right—*il n'y a que moi qui a toujours raison.*'

"In these sentiments, sir, I agree to this Constitution, with all its faults, if they are such; because I think a general government necessary for us, and there is no form of government, but what may be a blessing to the people if well administered; and believe further, that this is likely to be well administered for a course of years, and can only end in despotism, as other forms have done before it, when the people shall become so corrupted as to need despotic government, being incapable of any other. I doubt, too, whether any other Convention we can obtain may be able to make a better Constitution. For, when you assemble a number of men to have the advantage of their joint wisdom, you inevitably assemble with those men all their prejudices, their passions, their errors of opinion, their local interests, and their selfish views. From such an assembly can a perfect production be expected? It therefore astonishes me, sir, to find this system approaching so near to perfection as it does; and I think it will astonish our enemies, who are waiting with confidence to hear that our councils are confounded, like those of the builders of Babel; and that our states are on the point of separation, only to meet hereafter for the purpose of cutting one another's throats. Thus I consent, sir, to this Constitution, because I expect no better, and because I am not sure, that it is not the best. The opinions I have had of its errors I sacrifice to the public good. I have never whispered a syllable of them abroad. Within these walls they were born, and here they shall die. . . .

"On the whole, sir, I cannot help expressing a wish that every member of the Convention, who may still have objections to it, would with me, on this occasion, doubt a little of his own infallibility, and, to make manifest our unanimity, put his name to this instrument." He then moved that the Constitution be signed by the members, and offered the following as a convenient form, viz.:

"Done in Convention by the unanimous consent of the states present, the 17th of September, &c. In witness whereof, we have hereunto sub-scribed our names."

This ambiguous form had been drawn up by Mr. Gouverneur Morris, in order to gain the dissenting members, and put into the hands of Dr. Franklin, that it might have the better chance of success. . . .

Mr. Randolph then rose, and, with an allusion to the observations of Dr. Franklin, apologized for his refusing to sign the Constitution, notwithstanding the vast majority and venerable names that would give sanction to its wisdom and its worth. He said, however, that he did not mean by this refusal to decide that he should oppose the Constitution without doors. He meant only to keep himself free to be governed by his duty, as it should be prescribed by his future judgment. He refused to sign, because he thought the object of the Convention would be frustrated by the alternative which it presented to the people. Nine states will fail to ratify the plan, and confusion must ensue. . . .

Mr. Gouverneur Morris said, that he too had objections, but, consid-ering the present plan as the best that was to be attained, he should take it with all its faults. The majority had determined in its favor, and by that determination he should abide. The moment this plan goes forth, all other considerations will be laid aside, and the great question will be, shall there be a national government, or not? and this must take place, or a general anarchy will be the alternative. . . .

Mr. Williamson . . . did not think a better plan was to be expected, and had no scruples against putting his name to it.

Mr. Hamilton expressed his anxiety that every member should sign. A few characters of consequence, by opposing, or even refusing to sign the Constitution, might do infinite mischief, by kindling the latent sparks that lurk under an enthusiasm in favor of the Convention which may soon subside. No man's ideas were more remote from the plan than his own were known to be; but is it possible to deliberate between anarchy, and convulsion, on one side, and the chance of good to be expected from the plan, on the other?

Mr. Blount said, he . . . would, without committing himself, attest the fact that the plan was the unanimous act of the states in Convention.

Dr. Franklin . . . hoped that [Randolph] would yet lay aside his objections, and, by concurring with his brethren, prevent the great mis-chief which the refusal of his name might produce.

Mr. Randolph . . . repeated that, in refusing to sign the Constitution, he took a step which might be the most awful of his life; but it was dictated by his conscience, and it was not possible for him to hesitate, much less, to change. He repeated also his persuasion, that the holding out this plan, with a final alternative to the people of accepting or rejecting it in toto, would not really produce the anarchy and civil convulsions which were apprehended from the refusal of individuals to sign it.

Mr. Gerry described the painful feelings of his situation, and the embarrassments under which he rose to offer any further observations on the subject which had been finally decided. Whilst the plan was depending, he had treated it with all the freedom he thought it deserved. He now felt himself bound, as he was disposed, to treat it with the respect due to the act of the Convention. He hoped he should not violate that respect in declaring, on this occasion, his fears that a civil war may result from the present crisis of the United States. . . .

Gen. Pinckney [said] we are not likely to gain many converts by the ambiguity of the proposed form of signing. He thought it best to be candid, and let the form speak the substance. . . .

On the motion of Dr. Franklin:

New Hampshire, Massachusetts, Connecticut, New Jersey, Pennsylvania, Delaware, Maryland, Virginia, North Carolina, Georgia, aye, 10; South Carolina, divided. . . .

The members then proceeded to sign the Constitution, as finally amended.

The Constitution being signed by all the members, except Mr. Randolph, Mr. Mason, and Mr. Gerry, who declined giving it the sanction of their names, the Convention dissolved itself by an adjournment *sine die*.

Whilst the last members were signing, Dr. Franklin, looking towards the president's chair, at the back of which a rising sun happened to be painted, observed to a few members near him, that painters had found it difficult to distinguish, in their art, a rising from a setting sun. "I have," said he, "often and often, in the course of the session, and the vicissitudes of my hopes and fears as to its issue, looked at that behind the president, without being able to tell whether it was rising or setting; but now, at length, I have the happiness to know that it is a rising, and not a setting sun."

"He opened the cage and let the bird fly about the room."

JEFFERSON AT THE WHITE HOUSE

1801
Washington, D.C.

MARGARET BAYARD SMITH

*P*resident John F. Kennedy once quipped that the guests at a White House dinner were the greatest collection of talent ever assembled there, except when Thomas Jefferson dined alone. Yet Jefferson, "the most eloquent spokesman for the principles that underlie our whole political culture," according to historian Bernard Bailyn, almost did not become president.

The election of 1800 was not decided until two weeks before the scheduled inauguration. From early November 1800 until mid-February 1801, the Electoral College was deadlocked between Thomas Jefferson and Aaron Burr, both from the same party. The party leaders assumed Jefferson would be president and Burr vice president. But the election rules stated only that the man with the most votes would have the higher office. While Burr publicly supported Jefferson, he did not take himself out of the race.

The deadlock was sent to the House of Representatives to be broken. Burr hoped to win support from the rival Federalist party, because its leading light, Alexander Hamilton, was an old political enemy of Jefferson. But Hamilton liked Burr even less. On the thirty-sixth ballot, the House decided in favor of Jefferson. (The personal quarrel between Burr and Hamilton would be decided three years later in a fatal duel. See page 109.)

Margaret Bayard Smith, a prolific novelist and journalist, was from a prominent political family.

The apartment in which he took most interest was his cabinet; this he had arranged according to his own taste and convenience. It was a spacious room. In the center was a long table, with drawers on each side, in which were deposited not only articles appropriate to the place, but a set of carpenter's tools in one and small garden implements in another, from the use of which he derived much amusement. Around the walls were maps, globes, charts, books, etc. In the window recesses were stands for the flowers and plants which it was his delight to attend, and among his roses and geraniums was suspended the cage of his favorite mockingbird, which he cherished with peculiar fondness, not only for its melodious powers, but for its uncommon intelligence and affectionate disposition, of which qualities he gave surprising instances. It was the constant companion of his solitary and studious hours. Whenever he was alone, he opened the cage and let the bird fly about the room. After flitting for a while from one object to another, it would alight on his table and regale him with its sweetest notes, or perch on his shoulder and take its food from his lips. Often when he retired to his chamber it would hop up the stairs after him and while he took his siesta, would sit on his couch and pour forth its melodious strains. How he loved this bird! How he loved his flowers! He could not live without something to love, and in the absence of his darling grandchildren his bird and his flowers became objects of tender care. In a man of such dispositions, such tastes, who would recognize the rude, unpolished democrat which foreigners and political enemies described him to be? If his dress was plain, unstudied, and sometimes old-fashioned in its form, it was always of the finest materials; in his personal habits he was fastidiously neat; and if in his manners he was simple, affable, and unceremonious, it was not because he was ignorant of but because he despised the conventional and artificial usages of courts and fashionable life.

. . . The same fanciful disposition characterized all his architectural plans and domestic arrangements, and even in the President's House were introduced some of these favorite contrivances, many of them really useful and convenient. Among these, there was in his dining room an invention for introducing and removing the dinner without the opening and shutting of doors. A set of circular shelves were so contrived in the wall that on touching a spring they turned into the room loaded with the dishes placed on them by the servants without the wall, and by the same process the removed dishes were conveyed out of the room. When he had any persons dining with him with whom he wished to enjoy a free and unrestricted flow of conversation, the number of persons at table never exceeded four and by each individual was placed a dumb-waiter containing everything necessary for the progress of the dinner from beginning to end so as to make the attendance of servants entirely unnecessary, believing, as he did, that much of the domestic and even public discord was produced by the mutilated and misconstructed repetition of free conversation at dinner tables by these mute but not inattentive listeners.

"Bah! Who will buy it from him?"

THE BATHTUB DICTATOR SELLS LOUISIANA

1803

Paris, France

LUCIEN BONAPARTE

*I*n this account, Napoleon avoids explaining why the deal was so expedient: he was selling property that France did not own and could not defend.

In theory, Spain had ceded Louisiana to France. But France had not met its treaty obligations, and Spain was still governing the territory. If Napoleon didn't sell Louisiana quickly, Spain or England or America was very likely to ignore the dubious French claims altogether. So the deal was struck for 60 million francs (about $15 million), giving Napoleon ready cash for his war with Great Britain.

On the other side of the table, Jefferson was more nervous about buying than Napoleon was about selling. He anxiously philosophized about the federal government's right to purchase the 828,000 square miles of new territory on behalf of the states. The Constitution certainly didn't give him the right. Fortunately, Congress approved the deal. The purchase doubled the size of the country.

Lucien Bonaparte, eyewitness to and participant in this odd scene, was seven years younger than his brother Napoleon. When ambassador to Spain, he had negotiated the shaky transfer of Louisiana from Spain to France. Joseph Bonaparte, a year older than Napoleon, held several high positions during his career in the French government, including an unsuccessful reign as king of Spain.

"Here you are at last!" exclaimed my brother [Joseph], "I was afraid you were not coming. It is a fine time to go to the theater; I come to tell you a piece of news which will not make you feel like amusing yourself. No, you will not believe it, and yet it is true. I give you a thousand guesses; the general (we still called Napoleon in that way), the general wishes to alienate Louisiana."

"Bah! Who will buy it from him?"

"The Americans."

I was thunderstruck for a moment.

"The idea! If he could wish it, the Chambers would not consent to it."

"And therefore he expects to do without their consent. That is what he replied to me when I said to him, as you do now, that the Chambers would not consent to it. And, what is more, he added to me that this sale would furnish him the first funds for war."

. . . It had become late. The plan of going to the theater was up, and we separated not without having agreed that I first should go the next morning to pay a visit to the first Consul. . . .

I still believe firmly to-day that if the plan of the Consul had been submitted to the Chambers, it would have been rejected by a very large majority; for after all what worse thing could happen to us, in case of sacrifices necessary to obtain peace, if we were at war with the English, or with any other government, than to cede one of our finest colonies for eighteen millions?

The next morning I betook myself to the Tuileries where immediately I was shown up to my brother who had just got into his bath; I found him in excellent humor. He began by speaking to me of the first night [of the theater] at which he had been present, astonished and sorry that we had not gone to join him. . . .

It was almost time to leave the bath, and we had not discussed Louisiana. I was vexed at it, but the nearer the last moment of speaking of it approached, the more I put off doing so. The body-servant was already holding the sheet prepared to wrap his master in: I was about to leave the place, when Rustan scratched at the door like a cat. . . .

The person for whom Rustan had broken his nails at the door to the consular bath-room, was Joseph.

"Let him come in," said the first Consul, "I will stay in the water a quarter of an hour longer."

It is known that he liked very much to stay there a long time, when there was no pressing business. I had time to make a sign to the new-comer that I had not yet spoken of anything, and I saw that he was himself embarrassed as to when and how he was to broach the subject, if our brother did not give him some pretext for it.

His irresolution and my suppositions did not last long, for all at once the Consul said to Joseph:

"Well, brother, so you have not spoken to Lucien?"

"About what?" said Joseph.

"About our plan in regard to Louisiana, you know?"

"About yours, my dear brother, you mean? You cannot have forgotten that far from being mine . . ."

". . . Come, come, preacher. But I have no need of discussing that with you. You are so obstinate. With Lucien I speak more willingly of serious matters; for though he sometimes takes it into his head to oppose me, he knows how to give in to my opinion, Lucien does, when I see fit to try to make him change his."

Joseph was showing annoyance at our conversation, the tone of which was more friendly than anything else, when finally he said to the Consul, rather brusquely:

"Well, you still say nothing of your great plan?"

"Oh! yes," said the Consul, "Know merely, Lucien, that I have decided to sell Louisiana to the Americans."

I thought I ought to show very moderate astonishment at this piece of news supposed to be unknown to me. Knowing very well that an opportunity would be given me to show more, I mean at his intention to dispose of it by his own will, without speaking of it to the Chambers, I contented myself with saying: "Ah! ah!" in that tone of curiosity which shows the desire to know the rest of what has been begun rather than it signifies approbation or even the contrary.

This apparent indifference made the first Consul say: "Well, Joseph you see! Lucien does not make an outcry about that as you do. Yet he would almost have a right to do so, for his part; for after all Louisiana is his conquest."

"As for me, I assure you," replied Joseph, "that if Lucien says nothing, he thinks none the less."

"Truly? And why should he play the diplomat with me?"

Brought into prominence in a way that I did not expect, and as they say, at a standstill, I could not delay explaining myself, and, to tell the truth.

The discussion perhaps would have stopped there to our great regret and we were about to start for the door, to leave the Consul free to come out of his bath; he had already made a movement to do so—his body-servant was still holding his sheet spread out, ready to receive his master and to dry him by wrapping him in it—when this master, changing his mind all at once, said to us loud enough to make us turn round:

"And then, Gentlemen, think what you please about it, but give this affair up as lost both of you; you, Lucien, on account of the sale in itself, you, Joseph, because I shall get along without the consent of anyone whomsoever, do you understand?"

I admit that in the presence of the body-servant I felt hurt at this profession of faith on so delicate a subject, and that there escaped from me a smile of astonishment at least, which, I have reasons to believe, betrayed my thoughts and perhaps even more than my thought of the moment, and in spite of the absolute silence which I maintained, was perhaps the distant or preparatory cause of the tempest which was brewing, not in a tea-pot, according to the proverb, but rather in the bathtub of him who was beginning to make all the sovereigns of Europe quake.

"They measured the distance, ten full paces ..."

AARON BURR KILLS ALEXANDER HAMILTON

July 11, 1804
Weehawken Heights, New Jersey

NATHANIEL PENDLETON AND WILLIAM P. VAN NESS

Hamilton had thwarted Burr's intense ambitions twice—first in 1800, when Hamilton influenced the House of Representatives to choose Thomas Jefferson as president, and again in 1804, when Burr's run for governor of New York was hindered by statements Hamilton made about his character.

Burr then challenged Hamilton to the duel that ended Hamilton's life and Burr's career.

In this account prepared for the press, the seconds of the two men agreed in almost every respect. But they never agreed on whether Hamilton actually intended to fire at Burr, as Burr and his friends claimed, or deliberately fired to the side, as Hamilton's allies insisted.

Colonel Burr arrived first on the ground as had been previously agreed. When General Hamilton arrived the parties exchanged salutations and the Seconds proceeded to make their arrangements. They measured the distance, ten full paces, and cast lots for the choice of position as also to determine by whom the word should be given, both of which fell to the Second of General Hamilton. They then proceeded to load the pistols in each others presence, after which the parties took their stations. The Gentleman who was to give the word, then explained to the parties the rules which were to govern them in firing which were as follows:

The parties being placed at their stations—The Second who gives the word shall ask them whether they are ready—being answered in the affirmative, he shall say "present" after which the parties shall present & fire when they please. If one fires before, the opposite second shall say one, two, three, fire, and he shall fire or lose his fire.

And asked if they were prepared, being answered in the affirmative he gave the word present as had been agreed on, and both of the parties took aim and fired in succession. The intervening time is not expressed as the Seconds do not precisely agree on that point. The pistols were discharged within a few seconds of each other and the fire of Colonel Burr took effect; General Hamilton almost instantly fell, Colonel Burr then advanced toward General Hamilton with a manner and gesture that appeared to General Hamilton's friend to be expressive of regret, but without speaking turned about and withdrew—being urged from the field by his friend as has been subsequently stated, with a view to prevent his being recognised by the surgeon and bargemen who were then approaching. No farther communication took place between the principals and the barge that carried Colonel Burr immediately returned to [New York] City. We conceive it proper to add that the conduct of the parties in that interview was perfectly proper as suited the occasion.

"That ocean, the object of all our labors . . ."

LEWIS AND CLARK HEAD TO THE PACIFIC

August 12 and November 7, 1805

MERIWETHER LEWIS AND WILLIAM CLARK

*M*eriwether Lewis had been Thomas Jefferson's secretary. His friend William Clark was the younger brother of Revolutionary War hero George Rogers Clark. They had been instructed by President Jefferson himself to explore the vast Louisiana Territory. Their expedition set out from St. Louis, then a small village, in 1804. The twenty-nine men trekked 8,000 miles, across what would become ten states, reaching the Pacific coast in present-day Oregon.

Their experiences still excite the imagination: they met more than fifty Native American tribes, saw huge buffalo herds, canoed along the great rivers, and even discovered the bones of a large dinosaur. All but one of the party survived; and the one casualty died of a ruptured appendix. Crucial to their success was a Native American named Sacagawea and her Canadian husband, Toussaint Charbonneau. Sacagawea was a Shoshoni who had been kidnapped as a child by the Mandan natives of the upper Missouri River valley. Lewis and Clark met her and Charbon-neau when they wintered with the Mandans in 1804–1805.

Lewis and Clark were not quite at the Pacific coast when they saw the "ocean" in this account. They were at Gray's Bay, in the mouth of the Columbia River, which is so wide it seemed to be the ocean itself. The bay was named for Robert Gray, the first American to circumnavigate the globe, who discovered the Columbia in 1792, and named it after his ship.

This account comes from the edition of the journals compiled and edited by Nicholas Biddle, who, although not on the journey, "magnificently" produced a work "completely true to the original," in the assessment of Stephen Ambrose, author of the Lewis biography Undaunted Courage.

AUGUST 12

At the Continental Divide   This morning . . . Captain Lewis . . . wound along the foot of the mountains to the southwest, approaching obliquely the main stream he had left yesterday. The road was still plain, and as it led them directly on towards the mountain the stream gradually became smaller, till after going two miles it had so greatly diminished in width that one of the men in a fit of enthusiasm, with one foot on each side of the river, thanked God that he had lived to bestride the Missouri. As they went along their hopes of soon seeing the waters of the Columbia arose almost to painful anxiety, when after four miles from the last abrupt turn of the river, they reached a small gap formed by the high mountains which recede on each side, leaving room for the Indian road. . . . They had now reached the hidden sources of that river, which had never yet been seen by civilized man; and as they quenched their thirst at the chaste and icy fountain—as they sat down by the brink of that little rivulet, which yielded its distant and modest tribute to the parent ocean, they felt themselves rewarded for all their labours and all their difficulties. They left reluctantly this interest-ing spot, and pursuing the Indian road through the interval of the hills, arrived at the top of a ridge, from which they saw high mountains partially covered with snow still to the west of them. The ridge on which they stood formed the dividing line between the waters of the Atlantic and Pacific oceans. They followed a descent much steeper than that on the eastern side, and at the distance of three quarters of a mile reached a handsome bold creek of cold clear water running to the westward. They stopped to taste for the first time the waters of the Columbia; and after a few minutes followed the road across steep hills and low hollows, till they reached a spring on the side of a mountain.

NOVEMBER 7

Near the Pacific Ocean   The morning was rainy and the fog so thick that we could not see across the river. . . .

At a distance of twenty miles from our camp we halted at a village . . . behind two small marshy islands. . . . Opposite to these islands the hills on the left retire, and the river widens into a kind of bay crowded with low islands, subject to be overflowed occasionally by the tide. We had not gone far from this village when the fog cleared off, and we enjoyed the delightful prospect of the ocean; that ocean, the object of all our labours, the reward of all our anxieties. This cheering view exhilirated the spirits of all the party, who were still more delighted on hearing the distant roar of the breakers. We went on with great cheerfulness under the high mountainous country which continued along the right bank; the shore was however so bold and rocky, that we could not, until after going fourteen miles from the last village, find any spot fit for an encampment. At that distance, having made during the day thirty-four miles, we spread our mats on the ground, and passed the night in the rain.

"Some imagined it to be a sea monster . . ."

FIRST VOYAGE OF THE *CLERMONT*

August 7, 1807
Poughkeepsie, New York

H. FREELAND

*R*obert Fulton had already shown expertise as a gunsmith, a jeweler, and a *painter, and had built a working submarine—with torpedoes—before designing the* Clermont, *the first paddle wheel steamboat. Its first voyage was a round trip on the Hudson from New York City to Albany and back.*

This account was a recollection written when Freeland was an adult.

It was in the early autumn of the year 1807 that a knot of villagers was gathered on a high bluff just opposite Poughkeepsie, on the west bank of the Hudson, attracted by the appearance of a strange, dark looking craft, which was slowly making its way up the river. Some imagined it to be a sea monster, while others did not hesitate to express their belief that it was a sign of the approaching judgment. What seemed strange in the vessel was the substitution of lofty and straight black smoke-pipes rising from the deck, instead of the gracefully tapered masts that commonly stood on the vessels navigating the stream, and, in place of the spars and rigging, the curious play of the working-beam and pistons and the slow turning and splashing of the huge and naked paddle-wheels met the astonished gaze. The dense clouds of smoke, as they rose wave upon wave, added still more to the wonderment of the rustics.

This strange looking craft was the *Clermont* on her trial trip to Albany, and of the little knot of villagers mentioned above, the writer, then a boy in his eighth year, with his parents, formed a part; and I well remember the scene, one so well fitted to impress a lasting picture upon the mind of a child accustomed to watch the vessels that passed up and down the river.

The forms of four persons were distinctly visible on the deck as she passed the bluff,—one of whom, doubtless, was Robert Fulton, who had on board with him all the cherished hopes of years, the most precious cargo the wonderful boat could carry.

On her return trip the curiosity she excited was scarcely less intense. The whole country talked of nothing but the sea monster belching forth fire and smoke. The fishermen became terrified and rowed homewards, and they saw nothing but destruction devastating their fishing grounds, while the wreaths of black vapor and the rushing noise of the paddle-wheels, foaming with the stirred up waters, produced great excitement among the boatmen, until it was more intelligent than before; for the character of that curious boat, and the nature of the enterprise which she was pioneering, had been ascertained. From that time, Robert Fulton, Esq., became known and respected as the author and builder of the first steam packet from which we plainly see the rapid improvement in commerce and civilization. Who can doubt that Fulton's first packet boat has been the model steamer? Except in finer finish and greater size, there is no difference between it and the splendid steamships now crossing the Atlantic. Who can doubt that Fulton saw the meeting of all nations upon his boats, gathering together in unity and harmony, that the "freedom of the seas would be the happiness of the earth"? Who can doubt that Fulton saw the world circumnavigated by steam, and that his invention was carrying the messages of freedom to every land, that no man could tell all its benefits, or describe all its wonders? What a wonderful achievement! What a splendid triumph!

". . . One of those uncommon geniuses."

TECUMSEH

July–October 1811
Vincennes, Indiana Territory

WILLIAM HENRY HARRISON

S hawnee chief Tecumseh, among the most charismatic leaders in American his-
tory, built a confederation among several tribes to resist the westward movement
of white settlers. His great enemy was William Henry Harrison, governor of the
Indiana Territory, who had used various underhanded methods to secure land
treaties. Tecumseh first fought with legal arguments, declaring that the nomadic
tribes of the region could not cede lands that were not wholly theirs. When he was
ignored, he used force.

In 1811, during one of Tecumseh's trips away from the area to build support
for his confederation, his brother, known as the Prophet, capriciously attacked Har-
rison's forces to start the Battle of Tippecanoe. Harrison won the battle, breaking
the momentum of Tecumseh's movement. (The victory was so famous Harrison
became president in 1840 on a ticket with John Tyler, using the slogan "Tippecanoe
and Tyler too.")

Tecumseh died in the War of 1812, fighting alongside the British. The circum-
stances remain mysterious. As one early historian of the war wrote, "Here the heroic
Indian chieftain, the greatest of his race, doubtless fell. Yet no Indian that I have
met has admitted the fact; and no white man that I have seen has with certainty
known it."

Harrison recorded his observations after two meetings with Tecumseh at Vin-
cennes, capital of the Indiana Territory.

Tecumseh has taken for his model the celebrated Pontiac, and I am
persuaded he will bear a favorable comparison, in every respect, with that
far famed warrior. If it is his object to begin with the surprise of this
place, it is impossible that a more favorable situation could have been chosen, than the one he occupies: it is just so far off as to be removed from
immediate observation, and yet so near as to enable him to strike us,
when the water is high, in twenty-four hours, and even when it is low,
their light canoes will come fully as fast as the journey could be performed on horseback. The situation is in other respects admirable for the

purposes for which he has chosen it. It is nearly central with regard to the tribes which he wishes to unite. The water communication with Lake Erie, by means of the Wabash and Miami—with Lake Michigan and the Illinois, by the Tippecanoe, is a great convenience. It is immediately in the centre of the back line of that fine country which he wishes to prevent us from settling—and above all, he has immediately in his rear a country that has been but little explored, consisting principally of barren thickets, interspersed with swamps and lakes, into which our cavalry could not penetrate, and our infantry, only by slow, laborious efforts.

. . . The implicit obedience and respect which the followers of Tecumseh pay to him, is really astonishing, and more than any other circumstance bespeaks him one of those uncommon geniuses which spring up occasionally to produce revolutions, and overturn the established order of things. If it were not for the vicinity of the United States, he would, perhaps, be the founder of an empire that would rival in glory Mexico or Peru. No difficulties deter him. For four years he has been in constant motion. You see him to-day on the Wabash, and in a short time hear of him on the shores of lake Erie or Michigan, or on the banks of the Mississippi; and wherever he goes he makes an impression favorable to his purposes. He is now upon the last round to put a finishing stroke to his work. I hope, however, before his return that that part of the fabric which he considered complete, will be demolished and even its foundations rooted up. . . . The Prophet is impudent and audacious, but is deficient in judgment, talents and firmness.

"I insist on waiting . . ."

DOLLEY MADISON SAVES WASHINGTON'S PORTRAIT

August 23–24, 1814
Washington, D.C.

DOLLEY MADISON

*T*he War of 1812 followed from the harassment of American sailors by British
ships and the encouragement of Tecumseh by the British army.
The most dramatic event of the war was undoubtedly the British burning of

Washington, D.C., following a quick exit by the American politicians and generals. The citizens were not pleased with the lack of defense. In 1818, a traveler to Washington described graffiti on the Capitol building: "Some of the pencil drawings exhibit the military commander hanging upon a tree; others represent the President running off without his hat or wig; some, Admiral Cockburn robbing henroosts: to which are added such inscriptions as, 'The capital of the Union lost by cowardice,' 'Curse cowards,' 'A ———— sold the city for 5,000 dollars,' 'James Madison is a rascal, a coward, and a fool,' etcetera.")

But the military defeat also prompted the war's most romantic moment: First Lady Dolley Madison's rescue of a portrait of George Washington from the President's Residence.

Dear Sister—

My husband left me yesterday morning to join General Winder. He inquired anxiously whether I had courage or firmness to remain in the President's house until his return on the morrow, or succeeding day, and on my assurance that I had no fear but for him, and the success of our army, he left, beseeching me to take care of myself, and of the Cabinet papers, public and private. I have since received two despatches from him, written with a pencil. The last is alarming, because he desires I should be ready at a moment's warning to enter my carriage, and leave the city; that the enemy seemed stronger than had at first been reported, and it might happen that they would reach the city with the intention of destroying it. I am accordingly ready; I have pressed as many Cabinet papers into trunks as to fill one carriage; our private property must be sacrificed, as it is impossible to procure wagons for its transportation. I am determined not to go myself until I see Mr. Madison safe, so that he can accompany me, as I hear of much hostility towards him. Disaffection stalks around us. My friends and acquaintances are all gone, even Colonel C. with his hundred, who were stationed as a guard in this inclosure. French John (a faithful servant), with his usual activity and resolution, offers to spike the cannon at the gate, and lay a train of powder, which would blow up the British, should they enter the house. To the last proposition I positively object, without being able to make him understand why all advantages in war may not be taken.

Wednesday Morning, twelve o'clock.—Since sunrise I have been turning my spy-glass in every direction, and watching with unwearied anxiety, hoping to discover the approach of my dear husband and his friends; but, alas! I can descry only groups of military, wandering in all directions, as if there was a lack of arms, or of spirit to fight for their own fireside.

Three o'clock.—Will you believe it, my sister? we have had a battle, or skirmish, near Bladensburg, and here I am still, within sound of the cannon! Mr. Madison comes not. May God protect us! Two messengers, covered with dust, come to bid me fly; but here I mean to wait for him. . . . At this late hour a wagon has been procured, and I have had it filled with plate and the most valuable portable articles, belonging to the house. Whether it will reach its destination, the "Bank of Maryland," or fall into the hands of British soldiery, events must determine. Our kind friend, Mr. Carroll, has come to hasten my departure, and in a very bad humor with me, because I insist on waiting until the large picture of General Washington is secured, and it requires to be unscrewed from the wall. This process was found too tedious for these perilous moments; I have ordered the frame to be broken, and the canvas taken out. It is done! and the precious portrait placed in the hands of two gentlemen of New York, for safe keeping. And now, dear sister, I must leave this house, or the retreating army will make me a prisoner in it by filling up the road I am directed to take. When I shall again write to you, or where I shall be tomorrow, I cannot tell!

"A party of hungry soldiers . . ."

UNINVITED GUESTS FIND DINNER AT THE WHITE HOUSE

August 24, 1814

GEORGE ROBERT GLEIG

I f the British seem uncharacteristically rude in this account, one should remember that they considered the burning of the American capital to be merely a response to the earlier burning of York, Upper Canada's capital, by the American army.

Contrary to legend, the President's Residence was informally called the White House even before it was painted to cover damage from the fire. In 1901, President Theodore Roosevelt made the name official by engraving it on his stationery.

Eyewitness Gleig was an officer in the British army.

When the detachment sent out to destroy Mr. Madison's house entered his dining parlor, they found a dinner table spread and covers laid for forty guests. Several kinds of wine, in handsome cut-glass decanters, were cooling on the sideboard; plate holders stood by the fireplace, filled with dishes and plates; knives, forks, and spoons were arranged for immediate use; in short, everything was ready for the entertainment of a ceremonious party. Such were the arrangements in the dining room, whilst in the kitchen were others answerable to them in every respect. Spits, loaded with joints of various sorts, turned before the fire; pots, saucepans, and other culinary utensils stood upon the grate; and all the other requisites for an elegant and substantial repast were exactly in a state which indicated that they had been lately and precipitately abandoned.

You will readily imagine that these preparations were beheld by a party of hungry soldiers with no indifferent eye. An elegant dinner, even though considerably overdressed, was a luxury to which few of them, at least for some time back, had been accustomed, and which, after the dangers and fatigues of the day, appeared peculiarly inviting. They sat down to it, therefore, not indeed in the most orderly manner, but with countenances which would not have disgraced a party of aldermen at a civic feast, and, having satisfied their appetites with fewer complaints than would have probably escaped their rival gourmands and partaken pretty freely of the wines, they finished by setting fire to the house which had so liberally entertained them.

But, as I have just observed, this was a night of dismay to the inhabitants of Washington. They were taken completely by surprise; nor could the arrival of the flood be more unexpected to the natives of the antediluvian world than the arrival of the British army to them. The first impulse of course tempted them to fly, and the streets were in consequence crowded with soldiers and senators, men, women, and children, horses, carriages, and carts loaded with household furniture, all hastening towards a wooden bridge which crosses the Potomac. The confusion thus occasioned was terrible, and the crowd upon the bridge was such as to endanger its giving way. But Mr. Madison, having escaped among the first, was no sooner safe on the opposite bank of the river than he gave orders that the bridge should be broken down; which being obeyed, the rest were obliged to return and to trust to the clemency of the victors.

"The general manners and habits are very relaxed."

PUBLIC AMUSEMENTS IN NEW ORLEANS

1818

HENRY BRADSHAW FEARON

*F*earon, a British surgeon, had been hired by several English families to scout America for the best place to settle. He later published a book on his travels.

French language is still predominant in New Orleans. The population is said to be 30,000; two thirds of which do not speak English.

The general manners and habits are very relaxed. The first day of my residence here was Sunday, and I was not a little surprised to find in the United States the markets, shops, theatre, circus, and public ball-rooms open. Gambling houses throng the city: all coffee-houses, together with the exchange, are occupied from morning until night, by gamesters. It is said, that when the Kentuckians arrive at this place, they are in their glory, finding neither limit to, nor punishment of their excesses. The general style of living is luxurious. Houses are elegantly furnished. The ball-room, at Davis's hotel, I have never seen exceeded in splendour. Private dwellings partake of the same character, and the ladies dress with expensive elegance. The sources of public amusement are numerous and varied; among them I remark the following:

INTERESTING EXHIBITION

On Sunday the 9th inst. will be represented in the place where Fire-works are generally exhibited, near the Circus, an extraordinary fight of Furious Animals. The place where the animals will fight is a rotunda of 160 feet in circumference, with a railing 17 feet in height, and a circular gallery well conditioned and strong, inspected by the Mayor and surveyors by him appointed.

1st Fight—A strong Attakapas Bull, attacked and subdued by six of the strongest dogs of the country.

2d Fight—Six Bull-dogs against a Canadian Bear.

3d Fight—A beautiful Tiger against a black Bear.

4th Fight—Twelve dogs set against a strong and furious Opeloussas Bull.

If the Tiger is not vanquished in his fight with the Bear, he will be sent alone against the last Bull, and if the latter conquers all his enemies, several pieces of fire-works will be placed on his back, which will produce a very entertaining amusement.

In the Circus will be placed two Manakins, which, notwithstanding the efforts of the Bulls, to throw them down, will always rise again, whereby the animals will get furious.

The doors will be opened at three and the Exhibition begin at four o'clock precisely.

Admittance, one dollar for grown persons and 50 cents for children.

A military band will perform during the Exhibition.

If Mr. Renault is so happy as to amuse the spectators by that new spectacle, he will use every exertion to diversify and augment it, in order to prove to a generous public, whose patronage has been hitherto so kindly bestowed upon him how anxious he is to please them.

"*This Missouri question has betrayed the secret of their souls.*"

CALHOUN AND THE MISSOURI COMPROMISE

February 24, 1820
Washington, D.C.

JOHN QUINCY ADAMS

*M*issouri's impending admission to the Union as a slave state was about to upset the careful balance of power between free and slave states. To maintain the status quo, the Missouri Compromise created the free state of Maine out of northern Massachusetts and set a dividing line between north and south that would act as a line between free and slave states. Missouri would be the only slave state allowed north of the line.

The deal didn't solve any problems. It only delayed the Civil War. John Quincy Adams, James Monroe's secretary of state (later president), foresaw the eventual *results of the continual threats by the southern states to secede, as he makes clear in this sketch involving Secretary of War (later Vice President) John Calhoun.*

I had some conversation with Calhoun on the slave question pending in Congress. He said he did not think it would produce a dissolution of the Union, but, if it should, the South would be from necessity compelled to form an alliance, offensive and defensive, with Great Britain.

I said that would be returning to the colonial state.

He said, yes, pretty much, but it would be forced upon them. I asked him whether he thought, if by the effect of this alliance, offensive and defensive, the population of the North should be cut off from its natural outlet upon the ocean, it would fall back upon its rocks bound hand and foot, to starve, or whether it would not retain its powers of locomotion to move southward by land. Then, he said, they would find it necessary to make their communities all military. I pressed the conversation no further; but if the dissolution of the Union should result from the slave question, it is as obvious as anything that can be foreseen of futurity, that it must shortly afterwards be followed by the universal emancipation of the slaves. . . .

After this meeting, I walked home with Calhoun, who said that the principles which I had avowed were just and noble; but that in the Southern country, whenever they were mentioned, they were always understood as applying only to white men. Domestic labor was confined to the blacks, and such was the prejudice, that if he, who was the most popular man in his district, were to keep a white servant in his house, his character and reputation would be irretrievably ruined.

I said that this confounding of the ideas of servitude and labor was one of the bad effects of slavery; but he thought it attended with many excellent consequences. It did not apply to all kinds of labor—not, for example, to farming. He himself had often held the plough; so had his father. Manufacturing and mechanical labor was not degrading. It was only manual labor—the proper work of slaves. No white person could descend to that. And it was the best guarantee to equality among the whites. It produced an unvarying level among them. It not only did not excite, but did not even admit of inequalities, by which one white man could domineer over another.

I told Calhoun I could not see things in the same light. It is in truth, all perverted sentiment—mistaking labor for slavery, and dominion for freedom. The discussion of this Missouri question has betrayed the secret of their souls. In the abstract they admit that slavery is an evil, they disclaim all participation in the introduction of it, and cast it all upon the shoulder of our old Grandam Britain. But when probed to the quick upon it, they show at the bottom of their souls pride and vainglory in their condition of masterdom. They fancy themselves more generous and noble-hearted than the plain freemen who labor for subsistence. They look down upon the simplicity of a Yankee's manners, because he has no habits of overbearing like theirs and cannot treat negroes like dogs. . . . The impression produced upon any mind by the progress of this discussion is, that the bargain between freedom and slavery contained in the Constitution of the United States is morally and politically vicious, inconsistent with the principles upon which alone our Revolution can be justified; cruel and oppressive, by riveting the chains of slavery, by pledging the faith of freedom to maintain and perpetuate the tyranny of the master; and grossly unequal and impolitic, by admitting that slaves are at once enemies to be kept in subjection, property to be secured or restored to their owners, and persons not to be represented themselves, but for whom their masters are privileged with nearly a double share of representation. . . .

It would be no difficult matter to prove, by reviewing the history of the Union under this Constitution, that almost everything which has contributed to the honor and welfare of the nation has been accomplished in despite of them or forced upon them, and that everything unpropitious and dishonorable, including the blunders and follies of their adversaries, may be traced to them. I have favored this Missouri compromise, believing it to be all that could be effected under the present Constitution, and from extreme unwillingness to put the Union at hazard. But perhaps it would have been a wiser as well as a bolder course to have persisted in the restriction upon Missouri, till it should have terminated in a convention of the States to revise and amend the Constitution. This would have produced a new Union of thirteen or fourteen States unpolluted with slavery, with a great and glorious object to effect, namely, that of rallying to their standard the other States by the universal emancipation of their slaves. If the Union must be dissolved, slavery is precisely the question upon which it ought to break. For the present, however, this contest is laid asleep.

*"The head is shaped very much
like that of an elephant . . ."*

PEALE'S MUSEUM

1826
Philadelphia

ANNE ROYALL

C harles Willson Peale was a fascinating character. He was a famous portrait
painter, having produced works of Washington (including the first known portrait), Franklin, Jefferson, and most of the other leaders of the new country. He
organized the first American scientific expeditions, including one in 1801 that discovered the bones of a mastodon in upstate New York. He helped found the
Philadelphia Academy of Fine Arts. He wrote books. He was an accomplished natu-
ralist and taxidermist. He also invented innovative eyeglasses, false teeth, and, with
Thomas Jefferson, an early mimeograph machine.

    Anne Royall was just as interesting. She had entered William Royall's family as
a servant while still a child. He helped her get an education, eventually married
her, and left her most of his estate when he died. But other heirs fought a long legal
battle with her and forced her into poverty, so she became a journalist at the age of
fifty-five. By one description, "she became in time the conscience of Washington and
was a dangerous enemy of any corrupt politician, no matter how highly placed. She
was, in effect, the first of the great muckrakers, though she anticipated them by fifty
years."

It may readily be supposed, that the idea of seeing a place so celebrated as the museum of Philadelphia, inspired me with no common
curiosity.

    The museum is in Chestnut Street. I soon discovered it by a sign, and
after crossing a gallery, came to a stair-case, wide enough to admit a
wagon and team. I made but a few steps, before one of them springing
under my feet, rung a bell, to my great surprise, and upon gaining the
stairs, I was met by a man whose business it is to receive the money paid,
which is twenty-five cents. The first object of my inquiry was the mammoth skeleton, but I was greatly disappointed in its appearance. The
skeleton is indeed as large as is represented, but it had not that formidable, dread-inspiring aspect which my romantic turn led me to expect,

and with which I expected to be overwhelmed. I beheld it without surprise or emotion. It is standing upon its feet in a small room, which is lighted by a large window, enclosed with a rail as high as one's breast, and presenting its side foremost. I could not forbear smiling at a gentleman who, like myself, had formed extravagant notions of the mammoth. He stooped under the rail in order to examine it minutely, and scraping a part of the skeleton with his pen-knife, swore "it was nothing but wood," saying to his friend, that he was cheated out of his money; they both retired displeased. It has indeed the appearance of old smoky-looking hard white oak, and might impose upon wiser-looking people than Monsieur or myself. The whole has a very dark appearance, and in many parts it is quite black. In some instances the bone is as hard as iron, while other parts seem to be in a moldering condition. If anything, the head appears the most amazing; but I hasten to describe it. Height over the shoulders, 11 feet; length from the tusks to the end of the tails, following the curve of the backbone, 31 feet; width of the hips, 5 feet, 8 inches. The head is shaped very much like that of an elephant, wide at the top, and tapering off suddenly at the chin.

This skeleton was found by accident, in Ulster county on a farm. In 1801, Mr. C. W. Peale, of Philadelphia, purchased the right of digging for the skeleton, and after six weeks of intense labor, his efforts were crowned with success. He obtained the skeleton perfect, except [for two missing ribs].

Although I was not thrown into hysterics at the sight of the mammoth skeleton, I found enough of the marvelous in the museum to remunerate for the disappointment. Amongst these were the sea-lion, the skeleton of a horse, which, when living, measured twenty hands in height, with a human figure on its back, a sheep weighing 214 pounds, the devil-fish—in short, ten thousand things wonderful and pleasing. What Mr. Jefferson said of the natural bridge, might with as much propriety be said of Peale's museum, viz. that it was worth a trip across the Atlantic. Here are 1,100 birds of different kinds, 250 quadrupeds, 3,450 insects, fish, wax figures, and what was very pleasing to me, 200 portraits of our most distinguished men. The quadrupeds, birds and sea-animals, are stuffed. The hair, and even the gloss of the feathers, are perfect, and all standing upon their feet, in full size.

The most remarkable is the sea lion; what surprised me is the eye, which is of glass, very large, full, fierce, and as natural as though it were living; even the eye lash was entire. The animal in size is enormous, greater than the largest ox. Then there is the elephant seal, which is even larger! The devil fish is twelve feet in length, and fifteen round the body, weighing upwards of 2,000 pounds! There was a camel-leopard, of which I had often read; this has a very slender body. A great Missouri bear and the largest buffalo bull, an old buck elk, with his tremendous horns on his head. All those animals and many others, are standing on their feet, facing each other, and, as near as possible, presenting something like a furious combat of the most awful looking wild beasts, among which the tiger and the lion, which last with his dreadful jaws extended, seems to threaten the whole affair of them with instant destruction. I was gratified to find the hyena, such as it is described, with fury and vengeance its countenance; and under it a famished wolf standing over a lamb which he had just killed, and was in the act of tearing to pieces. This was the most natural representation of the whole; the bowels of the sheep looked as though they had that instant been torn out of the body, and the blood besmeared upon the wool seemed yet warm.

The museum was founded by Mr. Peale, in 1784; this indefatigable man has done more since that time, than one would suppose could be done by a whole nation—the collection is endless. Ores, fish, crocodiles, serpents, monsters, insects, shells, and coins of the whole known world are here exhibited daily. I had not the pleasure of seeing Mr. Peale, but was much gratified in the acquaintance of his son, and by seeing a full length portrait of the old gentleman, painted by himself—it stands in the museum. The young Mr. Peale is a small man, upon whom, however, nature and art have lavished their favors; I met with him in the museum, and received from him those marks of politeness and attention, which none but the learned and the refined know how to bestow; I was charmed by his conversation. After paying once, you have free liberty of the museum as often as you choose to call.

"An amazing clatter . . ."

LUNCH IN NEW YORK CITY

May 21, 1827

CAPTAIN BASIL HALL

*H*all, *a British seaman, wrote extensively about his visits to America.*

On the 21st of May, I accompanied two gentlemen, about three o'clock, to a curious place called the Plate House, in the very centre of the business part of the busy town of New York.

We entered a long, narrow, and rather dark room, or gallery, fitted up like a coffeehouse, with a row of boxes on each side made just large enough to hold four persons, and divided into that number by fixed arms limiting the seats. Along the passage, or avenue, between the rows of boxes, which was not above four feet wide, were stationed sundry little boys, and two waiters, with their jackets off—and good need too, as will be seen. At the time we entered, all the compartments were filled except one, of which we took possession. There was an amazing clatter of knives and forks; but not a word audible to us was spoken by any of the guests. The silence, however, on the part of the company, was amply made up for by the rapid vociferations of the attendants, especially of the boys, who were gliding up and down, and across the passage, inclining their heads for an instant, first to one box, then to another, and receiving the whispered wishes of the company, which they straightway bawled out in a loud voice, to give notice of what fare was wanted. It quite baffled my comprehension to imagine how the people at the upper end of the room, by whom a communication was kept up in some magical way with the kitchen, could contrive to distinguish between one order and the other. . . .

We had been told by old stagers of the excellence of the corned beef, and said to the boy we should all three take that dish. Off the gnome glanced from us like a shot, to attend to the beck of another set of guests, on the opposite side of the room; but, in flying across the passage, turned his face towards the upper end of the apartment and called out, "Three beef, 8!" the last word of his sentence referring to the number of our box. In a trice we saw the waiters gliding down the avenue to us, with three sets of little covered dishes, each containing a plate, on which lay a large, piping hot slice of beef. Another plate was at the same time given, with a moderate proportion of mashed potatoes on it, together with a knife, and a fork on which was stuck a piece of bread. As the waiters passed along, they took occasion to incline their ears to the right and to the left, to receive fresh orders, and also to snatch up empty tumblers, plates, and knives and forks. The multiplicity and rapidity of these orders and movements made me giddy. Had there been one set to receive and forward the orders, and another to put them in execution, we might have seen better through the confusion; but all hands, little and big together, were screaming out with equal loudness and quickness—"Half plate beef, 4!"—"One potato, 5!"—"Two apple pie, one plum pudding, 8!" and so on.

There could not be, I should think, fewer than a dozen boxes, with four people in each; and as everyone seemed to be eating as fast as he could, the extraordinary bustle may be conceived. We were not in the house above twenty minutes, but we sat out t *wo* sets of company, at least.

"Devoid of decency and comfort . . ."

EARLY CINCINNATI

February 10, 1828

FRANCES MILTON TROLLOPE

"*I* venture to say," wrote an early society columnist, "that a young lady could scarcely be found in the United States who would not give you on demand a complete list of our national faults and foibles, as recorded by . . . Trollope. Why, they form the common staple of conversation! Mrs. Trollope quite extinguished the trade in spit-boxes and made fortunes for the fingerglass manufacturers."

Frances Trollope was the mother of the more likable Anthony Trollope, the novelist.

We reached Cincinnati on the 10th of February. It is finely situated on the south side of a hill that rises gently from the water's edge; yet it is by no means a city of striking appearance; it wants domes, towers, and steeples; but its landing-place is noble, extending for more than a quarter of a mile. . . .

We had the good fortune . . . to find a dwelling before long, and we returned to our hotel, having determined upon taking possession of it as soon as it could be got ready. Not wishing to take our evening meal either with the three score and ten gentlemen of the dining room, nor yet with the half dozen ladies of the bar-room, I ordered tea in my own chamber. A good-humoured Irish woman came forward with a sort of patronizing manner, took my hand, and said, "Och, my honey, ye'll be from the old country. I'll see you will have your tay all to yourselves, honey." With this assurance we retired to my room, which was a handsome one as to its size and bed-furniture, but it had no carpet, and was darkened by blinds of paper, such as rooms are hung with, which required to be rolled up, and then fastened with strings very awkwardly attached to the window-frames, whenever light or air were wished for. I afterwards met with these same uncomfortable blinds in every part of America.

Our Irish friend soon reappeared, and brought us tea, together with the never-failing accompaniments of American tea-drinking, hung beef, "chipped up" raw, and sundry sweetmeats of brown sugar hue and flavour. We took our tea, and were enjoying our family talk, relative to our future arrangements, when a loud sharp knocking was heard at our door. My "come in," was answered by the appearance of a portly personage, who proclaimed himself our landlord.

"Are any of you ill?" he began.

"No, thank you, sir; we are all quite well," was my reply.

"Then, madam, I must tell you, that I cannot accommodate you on these terms; we have no family tea-drinkings here, and you must live either with me or my wife, or not at all in my house."

This was said with an air of authority that almost precluded reply, but I ventured a sort of apologistic hint, that we were strangers, and unaccustomed to the manners of the country.

"Our manners are very good manners, and we don't wish any changes from England." . . .

We were soon settled in our new dwelling, which looked neat and comfortable enough, but we speedily found that it was devoid of nearly all the accommodation that Europeans conceive necessary to decency and comfort. No pump, no cistern, no drain of any kind, no dustman's cart, or any other visible means of getting rid of the rubbish, which vanishes with such celerity in London, that one has no time to think of its existence; but which accumulated so rapidly at Cincinnati, that I sent for my landlord to know in what manner refuse of all kinds was to be disposed of.

"Your help will just have to fire them all into the middle of the street, but you must mind, old woman, that it is the middle. I expect you don't know as we have got a law what forbids throwing such things at the sides of the streets; they must just all be cast right into the middle, and the pigs soon takes them off."

In truth the pigs are constantly seen doing Herculean service in this way through every quarter of the city; and though it is not very agreeable to live surrounded by herds of these unsavoury animals, it is well they are so numerous, and so active in their capacity of scavengers, for without them the streets would soon be choked up with all sorts of substances, in every stage of decomposition.

"The bear sprang towards us with open mouth ..."

ONE TOUGH BEAR

April 7, 1828

JEDEDIAH SMITH

Smith, born in New York, opened several passages to and from the west to white explorers. He was the first white man to make the westward crossing through Wyoming, and on his return east made the first passage through the Sierra Nevada (1827). The next year, he made the first land crossing into Oregon.

On two expeditions, most of the party was killed by natives, but he survived. He was killed by Comanches in New Mexico in 1831, just thirty-two years old.

7th April . . . In the vicinity was considerable appearance of game and particularly bear. In the evening we shot several bear and they ran into thickets that were convenient. Several of us followed one that was badly wounded into a thicket. We went on foot because the thicket was too close to admit a man on horse back.

As we advanced I saw one and shot him in the head when he immediately stumbled and fell—apparently dead. I went in to bring him out without loading my gun and when I arrived within four yards of the place where the bear lay the man that was following me close behind spoke and said "He is alive." I told him in answer that he was certainly dead and was observing the one I had shot so intently that I did not see one that lay close by his side which was the one the man behind me had reference to.

At that moment the bear sprang towards us with open mouth and making no pleasant noise.

Fortunately the thicket was close on the bank of the creek and the second spring I plunged head foremost into the water. The bear ran over the man next to me and made a furious rush on the third man Joseph Lapoint. But Lapoint had by good fortune a bayonet fixed on his gun and as the bear came in he gave him a severe wound in the neck which induced him to change his course and run into another thicket close at hand. We followed him there and found another in company with him. One of them we killed and the other went off badly wounded.

I then went on horse back with two men to look for another that was wounded. I rode up close to the thicket in which I supposed him to be and rode round it several times halloeing but without making any discovery. I rode up for a last look when the bear sprang for the horse. He was so close that the horse could not be got underway before he caught him by the tail. The horse being strong and much frightened exited himself so powerfully that he gave the bear no opportunity to close upon him and actually drew him 40 or 50 yards before he relinquished his hold.

The bear did not continue the pursuit but went off and [I] was quite glad to get rid of his company on any terms and returned to camp to feast on the spoils and talk of the incidents.

"The spark that will start the conflagration . . ."

EARLY TEXAS

April 27, 1828

JOSÉ MARÍA SÁNCHEZ

At first, Mexico encouraged settlement in Texas by foreigners, especially Americans. But in less than a decade the Mexicans saw the flaws of that policy. This account shows the conditions leading to the 1830 decree that officially closed the Texas border to American immigrants.

Sánchez was a Mexican draftsman on an expedition to survey the border with Louisiana.

We continued along hills without trees, the ground being wet and muddy, until we arrived at a distance of four or five leagues from the settlement of San Felipe de Austin, where we were met by Mr. Samuel Williams, secretary of the empresario, Mr. Stephen Austin; and we were given lodging in a house that had been prepared for the purpose.

This village has been settled by Mr. Stephen Austin, a native of the United States of the North. It consists, at present, of forty or fifty wooden houses on the western bank of the large river known as Rio de los Brazos de Dios, but the houses are not arranged systematically so as to form streets; but on the contrary, lie in an irregular and desultory manner. Its population is nearly two hundred persons, of which only ten are Mexicans, for the balance are all Americans from the North with an occasional European. Two wretched little stores supply the inhabitants of the colony: one sells only whiskey, rum, sugar, and coffee; the other, rice, flour, lard, and cheap cloth. It may seem that these items are too few for the needs of the inhabitants, but they are not because the Americans from the North, at least the great part of those I have seen, eat only salted meat, bread made by themselves out of corn meal, coffee, and home-made cheese. To these the greater part of those who live in the village add strong liquor, for they are in general, in my opinion, lazy people of vicious character. Some of them cultivate their small farms by planting corn; but this task they usually entrust to their negro slaves, whom they treat with considerable harshness. Beyond the village in an immense stretch of land formed by rolling hills are scattered the families brought by Stephen Austin, which today number more than two thousand persons. The diplomatic policy of this empresario, evident in all his actions, has, as one may say, lulled the authorities into a sense of security, while he works diligently for his own ends. In my judgment, the spark that will start the conflagration that will deprive us of Texas, will start from this colony. All because the government does not take vigorous measures to prevent it. Perhaps it does not realize the value of what it is about to lose.

"The people's day, and the people's president . . ."

JACKSON'S ROWDY INAUGURATION

March 11, 1829
Washington, D.C.

MARGARET BAYARD SMITH

*A*ndrew Jackson became famous for his defeat of the British in the Battle of New Orleans during the War of 1812. Amazingly, the battle was fought two weeks after the war had ended, because news of the peace treaty had not reached the generals in the field. The victory was meaningless. Nonetheless, it was dramatic and made Jackson a national hero. He rode that wave of popularity into the White House in 1828.

Distrustful of the ruling class, Jackson was determined to create a populist government. His inauguration, and the reaction of Washington aristocracy to it, foreshadowed the more substantial changes now termed Jacksonian democracy, such as the removal of property requirements for voting rights.

The inaugural was not a thing of detail or a succession of small incidents. No, it was one grand whole, an imposing and majestic spectacle, and to a reflective mind one of moral sublimity. Thousands and thousands of people, without distinction of rank, collected in an immense mass round the Capitol, silent, orderly, and tranquil, with their eyes fixed on the front of that edifice, waiting the appearance of the President in the portico. The door from the rotunda opens; preceded by the marshals, surrounded by the judges of the Supreme Court, the old man with his gray locks, that crown of glory, advances, bows to the people who greet him with a shout that rends the air. The cannons from the heights around, from Alexandria and Fort Warburton, proclaim the oath he has taken, and all the hills reverberate the sound. It was grand—it was sublime!

An almost breathless silence succeeded, and the multitude was still, listening to catch the sound of his voice, though it was so low as to be heard only by those nearest to him. After reading his speech the oath was administered to him by the Chief Justice. Then Marshall presented the Bible. The President took it from his hands, pressed his lips to it, laid it reverently down, then bowed again to the people—yes, to the people in all their majesty. And had the spectacle closed here, even Europeans must have acknowledged that a free people, collected in their might, silent and tranquil, restrained solely by a moral power, without a shadow around of military force, was majesty rising to sublimity and far surpassing the majesty of kings and princes surrounded with armies and glittering in gold. But I will not anticipate, but will give you an account of the inauguration in more detail. The whole of the preceding day immense crowds were coming into the city from all parts, lodgings could not be obtained, and the newcomers had to go to Georgetown, which soon overflowed, and others had to go to Alexandria. I was told the avenue and adjoining streets were so crowded on Tuesday afternoon that it was difficult to pass.

A national salute was fired early in the morning and ushered in the 4th of March. By ten o'clock the avenue was crowded with carriages of every description, from the splendid coach down to wagons and carts, filled with women and children, some in finery and some in rags, for it was the people's President, and all would see him; the men all walked. Julia, Anna Maria, and I (the other girls would not adventure), accompanied by Mr. Wood, set off before eleven and followed the living stream that was pouring along to the Capitol. The terraces, the balconies, the porticoes, seemed, as we approached, already filled. We rode round the whole square, taking a view of the animated scene. Then, leaving the carriage outside the palisades, we entered the inclosed grounds, where we were soon joined by John Cranet and another gentleman, which offered each of us a protector.

We stood so as to have a clear, full view of the whole scene—the Capitol in all its grandeur and beauty. The portico and grand steps leading to it were filled with ladies. Scarlet, purple, blue, yellow, white draperies and waving plumes of every kind and color among the white pillars had a fine effect. In the center of the portico was a table covered with scarlet; behind it, the closed door leading into the rotunda; below the Capitol and all around, a mass of living beings, not a ragged mob but well dressed and well behaved, respectable and worthy citizens. Mr. Frank Key [Francis Scott Key], whose arm I had, and an old and frequent witness of great spectacles, often exclaimed, as well as myself, a mere novice, "It is beautiful, it is sublime!"

Our party went out at the opposite side of the square and went to Colonel Benton's lodgings to visit Mrs. Benton and Mrs. Gilmore. Here was a perfect levee, at least a hundred ladies and gentlemen, all happy and rejoicing—wine and cake was handed in profusion. We sat with this company and stopped on the summit of the hill until the avenue was comparatively clear, though at any other time we should have thought it terribly crowded, streams of people on foot and in carriages of all kinds still pouring toward the President's house. We went home; found your papa and sisters at the bank, standing at the upper windows, where they had been seen by the President, who took off his hat to them, which they insisted was better than all we had seen. From the bank to the President's house, for a long while, the crowd rendered a passage for us impossible. Some went into the cashier's parlor, where we found a number of ladies and gentlemen and had cake and wine in abundance. In about an hour the pavement was clear enough for us to walk. Your father, Mr. Wood, Mr. Ward, Mr. Lyon, with us, we set off to the President's house, but on a nearer approach found an entrance impossible; the yard and avenue was compact with living matter. The day was delightful, the scene animating; we walked backward and forward, at every turn meeting some new acquaintance and stopping to talk and shake hands. We continued promenading here until near three, returned home unable to stand, and threw ourselves on the sofa. Some one came and informed us the crowd before the President's house was so far lessened that they thought we might enter. This time we effected our purpose.

But what a scene did we witness! The majesty of the people had disappeared, and a rabble, a mob, of boys, Negroes, women, children, scrambling, fighting, romping. What a pity, what a pity! No arrangements had been made, no police officers placed on duty, and the whole house had been inundated by the rabble mob. We came too late. The President, after having been literally nearly pressed to death and almost suffocated and torn to pieces by the people in their eagerness to shake hands with Old Hickory, had retreated through the back way or south front and had escaped to his lodgings at Gadsby's. Cut glass and china to the amount of several thousand dollars had been broken in the struggle to get the refreshments. Punch and other articles had been carried out in tubs and buckets, but had it been in hogsheads it would have been insufficient; ice creams and cake and lemonade for twenty thousand people, for it is said that number were there, though I think the estimate exaggerated.

Ladies fainted, men were seen with bloody noses, and such a scene of confusion took place as is impossible to describe—those who got in could not get out by the door again but had to scramble out of windows. At one time the President, who had treated and retreated until he was pressed against the wall, could only be secured by a number of gentlemen forming round him and making a kind of barrier of their own bodies; and the pressure was so great that Colonel Bomford, who was one, said that at one time he was afraid they should have been pushed down or on the President. It was then the windows were thrown open and the torrent found an outlet, which otherwise might have proved fatal.

This concourse had not been anticipated and therefore not provided against. Ladies and gentlemen only had been expected at this levee, not the people en masse. But it was the people's day, and the people's President, and the people would rule. God grant that one day or other the people do not put down all rule and rulers. I fear, enlightened freemen as they are, they will be found, as they have been found in all ages and countries where they get the power in their hands, that of all tyrants, they are the most ferocious, cruel, and despotic. The noisy and disorderly rabble in the President's house brought to my mind descriptions I had read of the mobs in Tuileries and at Versailles. I expect to hear the carpets and furniture are ruined; the streets were muddy, and these guests all went thither on foot.

"511 fellow-creatures ..."

A SLAVE SHIP IN THE SOUTH ATLANTIC

May 24, 1829

ROBERT WALSH

*W*alsh was active in one of the English abolition societies that had a great influence on the issue in America.

The captain now ordered a gun to be fired to leeward, and the English union flag to be hoisted; we had the wind right aft, and were running right down upon her, distant about four miles. . . . The ball went ricocheting along the waves, and fell short of her stern; in a little time afterwards she hoisted a flag, which we perceived was Brazilian.

We could now discern her whole equipment; her gun streak was distinctly seen along the water, with eight ports of a side; and it was the general opinion that she was a French pirate and slaver, notorious for her depredations. . . .

Our boat was now hoisted out, and I went on board with the officers. When we mounted her decks, we found her full of slaves. She was called the *Veloz,* commanded by Captain Jose Barbosa, bound to Bahia. She was a very broad-decked ship, with a mainmast, schooner-rigged, and behind her foremast was that large formidable gun, which turned on a broad circle of iron, on deck, and which enabled her to act as a pirate, if her slaving speculation had failed. She had taken in, on the coast of Africa, 336 males, and 226 females, making in all 562, and had been out seventeen days, during which she had thrown overboard fifty-five. The slaves were all enclosed under grated hatchways, between decks. The space was so low, that they sat between each other's legs, and stowed so close together, that there was no possibility of their lying down, or at all changing their position, by night or day. As they belonged to, and were shipped on account of different individuals, they were all branded, like sheep, with the owners' marks of different forms. . . . These were impressed under their breasts, or on their arms, and, as the mate informed me, with perfect indifference . . . "burnt with the red-hot iron." Over the hatchway stood a ferocious looking fellow, with a scourge of many twisted thongs in his hand, who was the slavedriver of the ship, and whenever he heard the slightest noise below, he shook it over them, and seemed eager to exercise it. . . .

But the circumstance which struck us most forcibly, was, how it was possible for such a number of human beings to exist, packed up and wedged together as tight as they could cram, in low cells, three feet high, the greater part of which, except that immediately under the grated hatchways, was shut out from light or air, and this when the thermometer, exposed to the open sky, was standing in the shade, on our deck, at 89°. The space between decks was divided into two compartments, 3 feet 3 inches high; the size of one was 16 feet by 18, and of the other 40 by 21; into the first were crammed the women and girls; into the second, the men and boys: 226 fellow-creatures were thus thrust into one space 288 feet square; and 336 into another space 800 feet square, giving to the whole an average of 23 inches, and to each of the women not more than 13 inches. . . . We also found manacles; and fetters of different kinds, but it appears that they had all been taken off before we boarded.

The heat of these horrid places was so great, and the odour so offensive, that it was quite impossible to enter them, even had there been room. They were measured as above when the slaves had left them. The officers insisted that the poor suffering creatures should be admitted on deck to get air and water. This was opposed by the mate of the slaver, who, from a feeling that they deserved it, declared they would murder them all. The officers, however, persisted, and the poor beings were all turned up together. It is impossible to conceive the effect of this eruption—511 fellow-creatures of all ages and sexes, some children, some adults, some old men and women, all in a state of total nudity, scrambling out together to taste the luxury of a little fresh air and water. They came swarming up, like bees from the aperture of a hive, till the whole deck was crowded to suffocation, from stem to stern; so that it was impossible to imagine where they could all have come from, or how they could have been stowed away. On looking into the places where they had been crammed, there were found some children next the sides of the ship, in the places most remote from light and air; they were lying nearly in a torpid state, after the rest had turned out. The little creatures seemed indifferent as to life or death, and when they were carried on deck, many of them could not stand.

After enjoying for a short time the unusual luxury of air, some water was brought; it was then that the extent of their sufferings was exposed in a fearful manner. They all rushed like maniacs towards it. No entreaties, or threats, or blows, could restrain them; they shrieked, and struggled, and fought with one another, for a drop of this precious liquid, as if they grew rabid at the sight of it. There is nothing which slaves, in the midpassage, suffer from so much as want of water. It is sometimes usual to take out casks filled with sea water, as ballast, and when the slaves are received on board, to start the casks, and refill them with fresh. On one occasion, a ship from Bahia neglected to change the contents of the casks, and on the mid-passage found, to their horror that they were filled with nothing but salt water. All the slaves on board perished! We could judge of the extent of their sufferings from the afflicting sight we now saw. When the poor creatures were ordered down again, several of them came, and pressed their heads against our knees, with looks of the greatest anguish, at the prospect of returning to the horrid place of suffering below.

It was not surprising that they should have endured much sickness and loss of life, in their short passage. They had sailed from the coast of Africa on the 7th of May, and had been out but seventeen days, and they had thrown overboard no less than fifty-five, who had died of dysentery and other complaints, in that space of time, though they had left the coast in good health. Indeed, many of the survivors were seen lying about the decks in the last stage of emaciation, and in a state of filth and misery not to be looked at. Even-handed justice had visited the effects of this unholy traffic, on the crew who were engaged in it. Eight or nine had died, and at that moment six were in hammocks on board, in different stages of fever. This mortality did not arise from want of medicine. There was a large stock ostentatiously displayed in the cabin, with a manuscript book, containing directions as to the quantities; but the only medical man on board to prescribe it was a black, who was as ignorant as his patients.

While expressing my horror at what I saw, and exclaiming against the state of this vessel for conveying human beings, I was informed by my friends, who had passed so long a time on the coast of Africa, and visited so many ships, that this was one of the best they had seen. The height, sometimes, between decks, was only eighteen inches; so that the unfortunate beings could not turn round, or even on their sides, the elevation being less than the breadth of their shoulders; and here they are usually chained to the decks, by the neck and legs. . . .

When I returned on board the frigate, I found the captain of the slaver pacing the deck in great agitation. . . . Meantime, his papers were rigidly examined, to ascertain if they bore out his story. He said that he was a Brazilian, from Bahia, and that his traffic was strictly confined to the south of the line, where, by treaty, it was yet lawful. . . . All this, his chart and log corresponded with. As the tale, however, could be easily fabricated, and papers were written to correspond, a strict scrutiny was made into other circumstances. . . .

The instructions sent to king's ships as to the manner of executing the treaty of Brazil, are very ambiguous. They state in one place that "no slave ship is to be stopped to the south of the line, on any pretext whatever." Yet in another, a certain latitude is allowed, if there is reason to suspect that the slaves on board "were taken in, to the north." By the first, the ship could not be detained at all, and it was doubtful if there was just reason for the second. Even if there were the strongest grounds for capturing and sending her to Sierra Leone for adjudication, where the nearest mixed commission sat, a circumstance of very serious difficulty occurred. It would take three weeks, perhaps a month or more, to beat up to windward to this place, and the slaves had not water for more than half that time, and we could not supply her. A number had already died, and we saw the state of frenzy to which the survivors were almost driven, from the want of this element. . . . Under these doubtful circumstances, then, it appeared more legal and even more humane to suffer them to proceed on their course to Bahia, where it is probable, after all, the remnant left alive would be finally sent, after an investigation by the commissioners, as having been taken in, within the limits of legal traffic. It was with infinite regret, therefore, we were obliged to restore his papers to the captain, and permit him to proceed, after nine hours' detention and close investigation. It was dark when we separated, and the last parting sounds we heard from the unhallowed ship, were the cries and shrieks of the slaves, suffering under some bodily infliction.

"*The race was neck and neck, nose and nose . . .*"

AMERICA'S FIRST STEAM ENGINE
RACES A HORSE

September 18, 1830
Baltimore and Ellicott's Mills, Maryland

JOHN HAZELHURST BONVAL LATROBE

*L*atrobe, a lawyer, worked with the Baltimore and Ohio Railroad from its founding. He was the son of Benjamin Henry Latrobe, a distinguished architect and
engineer known for starting the Greek Revival influence in the United States.
(Ironically, the father had been bankrupted by his own interest in steam power,
when a business with Robert Fulton failed. Fortunately for him, the British burning
of Washington, D.C., in 1814 created a lot of new work for architects.)

Mr. [Peter] Cooper was satisfied that steam might be adapted to the
curved roads which he saw would be built in the United States; and he
came to Baltimore, which then possessed the only one on which he could
experiment, to vindicate his belief. He had another idea, which was, that
the crank could be dispensed with in the change from a reciprocating to a
rotary motion: and he built an engine to demonstrate both articles of his
faith. The machine was not larger than the hand cars used by workmen
to transfer themselves from place to place; and as the speaker now recalls
its appearance, the only wonder is, that so apparently insignificant a con-
trivance should ever have been regarded as competent to the smallest
results. But Mr. Cooper was wiser than many of the wisest around him.
His engine could not have weighed a ton; but he saw in it a principle
which the forty-ton engines of to-day have but served to develop and
demonstrate.

The boiler of Mr. Cooper's engine was not as large as the kitchen
boiler attached to many a range in modern mansions. It was of about the
same diameter, but not much more than half as high. It stood upright in
the car, and was filled, above the furnace, which occupied the lower section, with vertical tubes. The cylinder was but three-and-a-half inches in
diameter, and speed was gotten up by gearing. No natural draught could
have been sufficient to keep up steam in so small a boiler; and Mr. Cooper
used therefore a blowing apparatus, driven by a drum attached to one of

the car wheels, over which passed a cord that in its turn worked a pulley on the shaft of the blower. . . .

Mr. Cooper's success was such as to induce him to try a trip to Ellicott's Mills; and an open car, the first used upon the road, already mentioned, having been attached to his engine, and filled with directors and some friends, the speaker among the rest, the first journey by steam in America was commenced. The trip was most interesting. The curves were passed without difficulty at a speed of fifteen miles an hour; the grades were ascended with comparative ease; the day was fine, the company in the highest spirits, and some excited gentleman of the party pulled out memorandum books, and when at the highest speed, which was eighteen miles an hour, wrote their names and some connected sentences, to prove that even at that great velocity it was possible to do so. The return trip from the Mills—a distance of thirteen miles—was made in fifty-seven minutes. This was in summer of 1830.

But the triumph of this Tom Thumb engine was not altogether without a drawback. The great stage proprietors of the day were Stockton & Stokes; and on this occasion a gallant gray of great beauty and power was driven by them from town, attached to another car on the second track— for the Company had begun by making two tracks to the Mills—and met the engine at the Relay House on its way back. From this point it was determined to have a race home; and, the start being even, away went horse and engine, the snort of the one and the puff of the other keeping time and tune. At first the gray had the best of it, for his steam would be applied to the greatest advantage on the instant, while the engine had to wait until the rotation of the wheels set the blower to work. The horse was perhaps a quarter of a mile ahead when the safety valve of the engine lifted and the thin blue vapor issuing from it showed an excess of steam. The blower whistled, the steam blew off in vapory clouds, the pace increased, the passengers shouted, the engine gained on the horse, soon it lapped him—the silk was plied—the race was neck and neck, nose and nose—then the engine passed the horse, and a great hurrah hailed the victory. But it was not repeated; for just at this time, when the gray's master was about giving up, the band which drove the pulley, which drove the blower, slipped from the drum, the safety valve ceased to scream, and the engine for want of breath began to wheeze and pant. In vain Mr. Cooper, who was his own engineman and fireman, lacerated his hands in attempting to replace the band upon the wheel: in vain he tried to urge the fire with light wood; the horse gained on the machine and passed it; and although the band was presently replaced, and steam again did its best, the horse was too far ahead to be overtaken and came in the winner of the race. But the real victory was with Mr. Cooper, notwithstanding. He had held fast to the faith that was in him, and had demonstrated its truth beyond peradventure.

"We now saw beautiful lakes of the purest water . . ."

EXPLORING FLORIDA

January 1832

JOHN JAMES AUDUBON

*A*udubon, *who was born in what is now Haiti, came to the United States in 1803 at age eighteen. He began exploring and drawing a few years later.*

He would probably be denied membership in the society that now bears his name because, like other naturalists of his day, he killed innumerable specimens.

Having heard many wonderful accounts of a certain spring near the sources of the St. John's River, in East Florida, I resolved to visit it, in order to judge for myself. On the 6th of January, 1832, I left the plantation of my friend John Bulow, accompanied by an amiable and accomplished Scotch gentleman, an engineer employed by the planters of those districts in erecting their sugar-house establishments. We were mounted on horses of the Indian breed, remarkable for their activity and strength, and were provided with guns and some provisions. The weather was pleasant, but not so our way, for no sooner had we left the "King's Road," which had been cut by the Spanish government for a goodly distance, than we entered a thicket of scrubby oaks, succeeded by a still denser mass of low palmettoes, which extended about three miles, and among the roots of which our nags had great difficulty in making good their footing. After this we entered the Pine Barrens, very extensively distributed in this portion of the Floridas. The sand seemed to be all sand and nothing but sand, and the palmettoes at times so covered the narrow Indian trail which we followed, that it required all the instinct or sagacity of ourselves and our horses to keep it. It seemed to us as if we were approaching the end of the world. The country was perfectly flat, and, so far as we could survey it, presented the same wild and scraggy aspect. My companion, who had travelled there before, assured me that, at particular seasons of the year, he had crossed the barrens when they were covered with water fully knee-deep, when, according to his expression, they "looked most awful;" and I really believed him, as we now and then passed through muddy pools, which reached the saddle-girths of our horses. Here and there large tracts covered with tall grasses, and resembling the prairies of the western wilds, opened to our view. Wherever the country happened to be sunk a little beneath the general level, it was covered with cyprus trees, whose spreading arms were hung with a profusion of Spanish moss. The soil in such cases consisted of black mud, and was densely covered with bushes, chiefly of the Magnolia family.

We crossed in succession the heads of three branches of Haw Creek, of which the waters spread from a quarter to half a mile in breadth, and through which we made our way with extreme difficulty. While in the middle of one, my companion told me, that once when in the very spot where we then stood, his horse chanced to place his fore-feet on the back of a large alligator, which, not well pleased at being disturbed in his repose, suddenly raised his head, opened his monstrous jaws, and snapped off a part of the lips of his affrighted pony. You may imagine the terror of the poor beast, which, however, after a few plunges, resumed its course, and succeeded in carrying its rider through in safety. As a reward for this achievement, it was ever after honoured with the appellation of "Alligator."

We had now travelled about twenty miles, and the sun having reached the zenith, we dismounted to partake of some refreshment. From a muddy pool we contrived to obtain enough of tolerably clear water to mix with the contents of a bottle, the like of which I would strongly recommend to every traveller in these swampy regions; our horses, too, found something to grind among the herbage that surrounded the little pool; but as little time was to be lost, we quickly remounted, and resumed our disagreeable journey, during which we had at no time proceeded at a rate exceeding two miles and a half in the hour.

All at once, however, a wonderful change took place:—the country became more elevated and undulary; the timber was of a different nature, and consisted of red and live oaks, magnolias, and several kinds of pine. Thousands of "molehills," or the habitations of an animal here called "the salamander," and "goffer's burrows," presented themselves to the eye, and greatly annoyed our horses, which every now and then sank to the depth of a foot, and stumbled at the risk of breaking their legs, and what we considered fully as valuable, our necks. We now saw beautiful lakes of the purest water, and passed along a green space, having a series of them on each side of us. These sheets of water became larger and more numerous the farther we advanced, some of them extending to a length of several miles, and having a depth of from two to twenty feet of clear water; but their shores being destitute of vegetation, we observed no birds near them. Many tortoises, however, were seen basking in the sun, and all, as we approached, plunged into the water. Not a trace of man did we observe during our journey, scarcely a bird, and not a single quadruped, not even a rat; nor can one imagine a poorer and more desolate country than that which lies between the Halifax River, which we had left in the morning, and the undulary grounds at which we had now arrived.

"How I escaped death, I do not know."

LIFE WITH A SLAVE BREAKER

1833
Maryland

FREDERICK DOUGLASS

*D*ouglass *began working for an abolitionist society a few years after escaping slavery in 1838. Eloquent and forceful, he wrote the first of his three autobiographies in part because his outstanding skills as a speaker and writer sparked rumors that he could not have been a slave.*

Master Thomas at length said he would stand it no longer. I had lived with him nine months, during which time he had given me a number of severe whippings, all to no good purpose. He resolved to put me out, as he said, to be broken; and, for this purpose, he let me for one year to a man named Edward Covey. Mr. Covey was a poor man, a farm-renter. He rented the place upon which he lived, as also the hands with which he tilled it. Mr. Covey had acquired a very high reputation for breaking young slaves, and this reputation was of immense value to him. It enabled him to get his farm tilled, with much less expense to himself than he could have had it done without such a reputation. Some slaveholders thought it not much loss to allow Mr. Covey to have their slaves one year, for the sake of the training to which they were subjected, without any other compensation. He could hire young help with great ease, in consequence of this reputation. Added to the natural good qualities of Mr.

Covey, he was a professor of religion—a pious soul—a member and a class-leader in the Methodist church. All of this added weight to his reputation as a "nigger-breaker." I was aware of all the facts, having been made acquainted with them by a young man who had lived there. I nevertheless made the change gladly; for I was sure of getting enough to eat, which is not the smallest consideration to a hungry man.

I left Master Thomas's house, and went to live with Mr. Covey, on the 1st of January, 1833. I was now, for the first time in my life, a field hand. In my new employment, I found myself even more awkward than a country boy appeared to be in a large city. I had been at my new home but one week before Mr. Covey gave me a very severe whipping, cutting my back, causing the blood to run, and raising ridges on my flesh as large as my little finger. The details of this affair are as follows: Mr. Covey sent me, very early in the morning of one of our coldest days in the month of January, to the woods, to get a load of wood. He gave me a team of unbroken oxen. He told me which was the in-hand ox, and which the off-hand one. He then tied the end of a large rope around the horns of the in-hand ox, and gave me the other end of it, and told me, if the oxen started to run, that I must hold on upon the rope.

I had never driven oxen before, and of course I was very awkward. I, however, succeeded in getting to the edge of the woods with little difficulty; but I had got a very few rods into the woods, when the oxen took fright, and started full tilt, carrying the cart against trees, and over stumps, in the most frightful manner. I expected every moment that my brains would be dashed out against trees. After running thus for a considerable distance, they finally upset the cart, dashing it with great force against a tree, and threw themselves into a dense thicket. How I escaped death, I do not know. There I was, entirely alone, in a thick wood, in a place new to me. My cart was upset and shattered, my oxen were entangled among the young trees, and there was none to help me.

After a long spell of effort, I succeeded in getting my cart righted, my oxen disentangled, and again yoked to the cart. I now proceeded with my team to the place where I had, the day before, been chopping wood, and loaded my cart pretty heavily, thinking in this way to tame my oxen. I then proceeded on my way home. I had now consumed one half of the day. I got out of the woods safely, and now felt out of danger. I stopped my oxen to open the woods gate; and just as I did so, before I could get hold of my ox-rope, the oxen again started, rushed through the gate, catching it between the wheel and the body of the cart, tearing it to pieces, and coming within a few inches of crushing me against the gate-post. Thus twice, in one short day, I escaped death by the merest chance. On my return, I told Mr. Covey what had happened, and how it happened. He ordered me to return to the woods again immediately. I did so, and he followed on after me. Just as I got into the woods, he came up and told me to stop my cart, and that he would teach me how to trifle away my time, and break gates. He then went to a large gum-tree, and with his axe cut three large switches, and, after trimming them up neatly with his pocket-knife, he ordered me to take off my clothes. I made him no answer, but stood with my clothes on. He repeated his order and I still made him no answer, nor did I move to strip myself. Upon this he rushed at me with the fierceness of a tiger, tore off my clothes, and lashed me till he had worn out his switches, cutting me so savagely as to leave the marks visible for a long time after. This whipping was the first of a number just like it, and for similar offenses. . . .

I lived with Mr. Covey one year. During the first six months, of that year, scarce a week passed without his whipping me. I was seldom free from a sore back. My awkwardness was almost always his excuse for whipping me. We were worked fully up to the point of endurance. Long before day we were up, our horses fed, and by the first approach of day we were off to the field with our hoes and ploughing teams. Mr. Covey gave us enough to eat, but scarce time to eat it. We were often less than five minutes taking our meals. We were often in the field from the first approach of day till its last lingering ray had left us; and at saving-fodder time, midnight often caught us in the field binding blades.

Covey would be out with us. The way he used to stand it, was this. He would spend the most of his afternoons in bed. He would then come out fresh in the evening, ready to urge us on with his words, example, and frequently with the whip. Mr. Covey was one of the few slaveholders who could and did work with his hands. He was a hardworking man. He knew by himself just what a man or a boy could do. There was no deceiving him. His work went on in his absence almost as well as in his presence; and he had the faculty of making us feel that he was ever present with us. This he did by surprising us. He seldom approached the spot where we were at work openly, if he could do it secretly. He always aimed at taking us by surprise. Such was his cunning, that we used to call him, among ourselves, "the snake." When we were at work in the cornfield, he would sometimes crawl on his hands and knees to avoid detection, and all at once he would rise nearly in our midst, and scream out, "Ha, ha! Come, come! Dash on, dash on!" This being his mode of attack, it was never safe to stop a single minute. His comings were like a thief in the night. He appeared to us as being ever at hand. He was under every tree, behind every stump, in every bush, and at every window, on the plantation. He would sometimes mount his horse, as if bound to St. Michael's, a distance of seven miles, and in half an hour afterwards you would see him coiled up in the corner of the wood-fence, watching every motion of the slaves. He would, for this purpose, leave his horse tied up in the woods. Again, he would sometimes walk up to us, and give us orders as though he was upon the point of starting on a long journey, turn his back upon us, and make as though he was going to the house to get ready; and, before he would get half way thither, he would turn short and crawl into a fence-corner, or behind some tree, and there watch us till the going down of the sun.

Mr. Covey's forte consisted in his power to deceive. His life was devoted to planning and perpetrating the grossest deceptions. Every thing he possessed in the shape of learning or religion, he made conform to his disposition to deceive. He seemed to think himself equal to deceiving the Almighty. He would make a short prayer in the morning, and a long prayer at night; and, strange as it may seem, few men would at times appear more devotional than he. The exercises of his family devotions were always commenced with singing; and, as he was a very poor singer himself, the duty of raising the hymn generally came upon me. He would read his hymn, and nod at me to commence. I would at times do so; at others, I would not. My non-compliance would almost always produce much confusion. To show himself independent of me, he would start and stagger through with his hymn in the most discordant manner. In this state of mind, he prayed with more than ordinary spirit. Poor man! such was his disposition, and success at deceiving, I do verily believe that he sometimes deceived himself into the solemn belief, that he was a sincere worshipper of the most high God. . . .

If at any one time of my life more than another, I was made to drink the bitterest dregs of slavery, that time was during the first six months of my stay with Mr. Covey. We were worked in all weathers. It was never too hot or too cold; it could never rain, blow, hail, or snow, too hard for us to work in the field. Work, work, work, was scarcely more the order of the day than of the night. The longest days were too short for him, and the shortest nights too long for him. I was somewhat unmanageable when I first went there, but a few months of this discipline tamed me. Mr. Covey succeeded in breaking me. I was broken in body, soul, and spirit. My natural elasticity was crushed, my intellect languished, the disposition to read departed, the cheerful spark that lingered about my eye died; the dark night of slavery closed in upon me; and behold a man transformed into a brute!

"A man must leave his conscience at Cape Horn."

SPANISH CALIFORNIA

1835
Monterey, California

RICHARD HENRY DANA

*D*ana descended from a prominent Boston family. (His grandfather, Justice Richard Dana, played a role in the Boston Massacre—see page 56.) He dropped out of Harvard because of failing eyesight and signed on with a sailing ship in hopes that the experience would cure his vision. His famous account of the voyage, *Two Years Before the Mast, offered many Americans their first sense of California under Spanish rule.*

When Dana returned to San Francisco twenty years after his first visit, the Gold Rush town gave him a hero's welcome. His name is still found on landmarks in the city.

The bay of Monterey is very wide at the entrance . . . and the town lay directly before us, making a very pretty appearance; its houses being plastered, which gives a much better effect than those of Santa Barbara, which are of a mud-color. The red tiles, too, on the roofs, contrasted well with the white plastered sides, and with the extreme greenness of the lawn upon which the houses—about an hundred in number—were dotted about, here and there, irregularly.

The *gente de razón,* or aristocracy, wear cloaks of black or dark blue broadcloth, with as much velvet and trimmings as may be; and from this they go down to the blanket of the Indian; the middle classes wearing something like a large tablecloth, with a hole in the middle for the head to go through. This is often as coarse as a blanket, but being beautifully woven with various colors, is quite showy at a distance. Among the Spaniards there is no working class; (the Indians being slaves and doing all the hard work;) and every rich man looks like a grandee, and every poor scamp like a broken-down gentleman. I have often seen a man with a fine figure, and courteous manners, dressed in broadcloth and velvet, with a noble horse completely covered with trappings; without a real in his pockets, and absolutely suffering for something to eat.

The Californians are an idle, thriftless people, and can make nothing for themselves. The country abounds in grapes, yet they buy bad wine made in Boston and brought round by us, at an immense price, and retail it among themselves at a *real* (12½ cents) by the small wineglass. Their hides too, which they value at two dollars in money, they give for something which costs seventy-five cents in Boston; and buy shoes (as like as not, made of their own hides, which have been carried twice round Cape Horn) at three and four dollars.

Generally speaking, each person's caste is decided by the quality of the blood, which shows itself, too plainly to be concealed, at first sight. Yet the least drop of Spanish blood, if it be only of quatroon or octoon, is sufficient to raise them from the rank of slaves, and entitle them to a suit of clothes—boots, hat, cloak, spurs, long knife, and all complete, though coarse and dirty as may be,—and to call themselves Españolos, and to hold property, if they can get any.

Courts and jurisprudence they have no knowledge of. No Protestant has any civil rights, nor can he hold any property, or, indeed, remain more than a few weeks on shore, unless he belong to some vessel. Consequently, the Americans and English who intend to reside here become Catholics, to a man; the current phrase among them being, "A man must leave his conscience at Cape Horn."

Revolutions are matters of constant occurrence in California. They are got up by men who are at the foot of the ladder and in desperate circumstances, just as a new political party is started by such men in our own country. The only object, of course, is the loaves and fishes; and instead of caucusing, paragraphing, libelling, feasting, promising, and lying, as with us, they take muskets and bayonets, and seizing upon the presidio and custom-house, divide the spoils, and declare a new dynasty.

"They must surrender without any guarantee, even of life."

FALL OF THE ALAMO

March 6, 1836
Bexar, Texas

VICENTE FILISOLA

*B*y the mid-1830s, little more than a decade after Stephen Austin founded the first American settlement, about twenty-five thousand Americans had moved to Texas. Santa Anna, who had become dictator of Mexico in 1834, opposed the independent spirit of the new arrivals. War started in 1835. In 1836, the Mexicans attacked San Antonio. The one hundred eighty-seven Texan defenders gathered in the Alamo mission, where they were besieged by three thousand Mexican troops. All the Texans at the Alamo died in the final battle except for six men who were executed by Santa Anna after surrendering.

Filisola was one of Santa Anna's soldiers.

On this same evening, a little before nightfall, it is said that Barret Travis, commander of the enemy, had offered to the general-in-chief, by a woman messenger, to surrender his arms and the fort with all the materials upon the sole condition that his own life and the lives of his men be spared. But the answer was that they must surrender at discretion, without any guarantee, even of life, which traitors did not deserve. It is evident, that after such an answer, they all prepared to sell their lives as dearly as possible. Consequently, they exercised the greatest vigilance day and night to avoid surprise.

On the morning of March 6, the Mexican troops were stationed at 4 o'clock, A.M., in accord with Santa Anna's instructions. The artillery, as appears from these same instructions, was to remain inactive, as it received no order; and furthermore, darkness and the disposition made of the troops which were to attack the four fronts at the same time, prevented its firing without mowing down our own ranks. Thus the enemy was not to suffer from our artillery during the attack. Their own artillery was in readiness. At the sound of the bugle they could no longer doubt that the time had come for them to conquer or to die. Had they still doubted, the imprudent shouts for Santa Anna given by our columns of attack must have opened their eyes. As soon as our troops were in sight, a shower of grape and musket balls was poured upon them from the fort, the garrison of which at the sound of the bugle, had rushed to arms and to their posts. The three columns that attacked the west, the north, and the east fronts, fell back, or rather, wavered at the first discharge from the enemy, but the example and the efforts of the officers soon caused them to return to the attack. The columns of the western and eastern attacks, meeting with some difficulties in reaching the tops of the small houses which formed the walls of the fort, did, by a simultaneous movement to the right and to left, swing northward till the three columns formed one dense mass, which under the guidance of their officers, endeavored to climb the parapet on that side.

This obstacle was at length overcome, the gallant General Juan V. Amador being among the foremost. Meantime the column attacking the southern front under Colonels Jose Vicente Minon and Jose Morales, availing themselves of a shelter, formed by some stone houses near the western salient of that front, boldly took the guns defending it, and penetrated through the embrasures into the square formed by the barracks. There they assisted General Amador, who having captured the enemy's pieces turned them against the doors of the interior houses where the rebels had sought shelter, and from which they fired upon our men in the act of jumping down onto the square or court of the fort. At last they were all destroyed by grape, musket shot and the bayonet.

Our loss was very heavy. Colonel Francisco Duque was mortally wounded at the very beginning, as he lay dying on the ground where he was being trampled by his own men, he still ordered them on to the slaughter. This attack was extremely injudicious and in opposition to military rules, for our own men were exposed not only to the fire of the enemy but also to that of our own columns attacking the other fronts; and our soldiers being formed in close columns, all shots that were aimed too low, struck the backs of our foremost men. The greatest number of our casualties took place in that manner; it may even be affirmed that not one-fourth of our wounded were struck by the enemy's fire, because their cannon, owing to their elevated position, could not be sufficiently lowered to injure our troops after they had reached the foot of the walls. Nor could the defenders use their muskets with accuracy, because the wall having no inner banquette, they had, in order to deliver their fire, to stand on top where they could not live one second.

The official list of casualties, made by General Juan de Andrade, shows: officers 8 killed, 18 wounded; enlisted men 52 killed, 233 wounded. Total 311 killed and wounded. A great many of the wounded died for want of medical attention, beds, shelter, and surgical instruments.

The whole garrison were killed except an old woman and a negro slave for whom the soldiers felt compassion, knowing that they had remained from compulsion alone. There were 150 volunteers, 32 citizens of Gonzales who had introduced themselves into the fort the night previous to the storming, and about 20 citizens or merchants of Bexar.

Finally, the place remained in the power of the Mexicans, and all the defenders were killed. It is a source of deep regret, that after the excitement of the combat, many acts of atrocity were allowed which are unworthy of the gallantry and resolution with which this operation had been executed, and stamp it with an indelible stain in the annals of history. These acts were reproved at the time by those who had the sorrow to witness them, and subsequently by the whole army, who certainly were not habitually animated by such feelings, and who heard with disgust and horror, as becomes brave and generous Mexicans who feel none but noble and lofty sentiments, of certain facts which I forebear to mention, and wish for the honor of the Mexican Republic had never taken place.

In our opinion the blood of our soldiers as well as that of the enemy was shed in vain, for the mere gratification of the inconsiderate, puerile, and guilty vanity of reconquering Bexar by force of arms, and through a bloody contest. As we have said, the defenders of the Alamo, were disposed to surrender, upon the sole condition that their lives should be spared. Let us even grant that they were not so disposed—what could the wretches do, being surrounded by 5,000 men, without proper means of resistance, no possibility of retreating, nor any hope of receiving proper and sufficient reinforcements to compel the Mexicans to raise the siege? Had they been supplied with all the resources needed, that weak enclosure could not have withstood for one hour the fire of our twenty pieces of artillery which if properly directed would have crushed it to atoms and leveled down the inner buildings. . . . The massacres of the Alamo, of Goliad, of Refugio, convinced the rebels that no peaceable settlement could be expected, and that they must conquer, or die, or abandon the fruits of ten years of sweat and labor, together with their fondest hopes for the future.

"There are certain words which are never used in America."

MONEY IN NEW YORK CITY
AND MANNERS IN NIAGARA FALLS

1837

FREDERICK MARRYAT

*M*arryat had followed a distinguished career in the British navy with several successful sea novels before his visit to America.

In New York City he saw the effects of President Andrew Jackson's battle with Nicholas Biddle's Bank of the United States, a semipublic institution that had aroused the anger of several groups because of its conservative policies and great power. Jackson, who wanted to decentralize the lending power of the bank, shut it down. But great speculation followed, and since the country did not have enough gold and hard cash to back the paper currency, hundreds of small banks failed. The crisis lasted six years. As it turned out, the Bank's position was merely replaced with financial institutions that were more private and more powerful.

What Marryat found in Niagara Falls speaks for itself.

NEW YORK

My appearance at New York was very much like bursting into a friend's house with a merry face when there is a death in it. . . .

Two hundred and sixty houses have already failed, and no one knows where it is to end. Suspicion, fear, and misfortune have taken possession of the city. . . .

The militia are under arms, as riots are expected. . . .

Nobody refuses to take the paper of the New York banks, although they virtually have stopped payment;—they never refuse anything in New York;—but nobody will give specie in change, and great distress is occasioned by this want of a circulating medium. Some of the shopkeepers told me that they had been obliged to turn away a hundred dollars a-day, and many a southerner, who has come up with a large supply of southern notes, has found himself a pauper, and has been indebted to a friend for a few dollars in specie to get home again. . . .

The distress for change has produced a curious remedy. Every man is now his own banker. Go to the theatres and places of public amusement, and, instead of change, you receive an I.O.U. from the treasury. At the hotels and oyster-cellars it is the same thing. Call for a glass of brandy and water and the change is fifteen tickets, each "good for one glass of brandy and water." At an oyster shop, eat a plate of oysters, and you have in return seven tickets, good for one plate of oysters each. It is the same every-where.——The barbers give you tickets, good for so many shaves; and were there beggars in the streets, I presume they would give you tickets in change, good for so much philanthropy. Dealers, in general, give out their own banknotes, or as they are called here, shin-plasters, which are good for one dollar, and from that down to two and a-half cents, all of which are redeemable, and redeemable only upon a general return to cash payments.

Hence arises another variety of exchange in Wall street.

"Tom, do you want any oysters for lunch to-day?"

"Yes!"

"Then here's a ticket, and give me two shaves in return. . . ."

NIAGARA FALLS

There are certain words which are never used in America, but an absurd substitute is employed. I cannot particularize them after this preface, lest I should be accused of indelicacy myself. I may, however, state one little circumstance which will fully prove the correctness of what I say.

When at Niagara Falls I was escorting a young lady with whom I was on friendly terms. She had been standing on a piece of rock, the better to view the scene, when she slipped down, and was evidently hurt by the fall: she had, in fact, grazed her shin. As she limped a little in walking home, I said, "Did you hurt your leg much?" She turned from me, evidently much shocked, or much offended,——and not being aware that I had committed any very heinous offense, I begged to know what was the reason of her displeasure. After some hesitation, she said that as she knew me well, she would tell me that the word leg was never mentioned before ladies. I apologized for my want of refinement, which was attributable to having been accustomed only to English society; and added, that as such articles must occasionally be referred to, even in the most polite circles in America, perhaps she would inform me by what name I might mention them without shocking the company. Her reply was, that the word limb was used; "nay," continued she, "I am not so particular as some people are, for I know those who always say limb of a table, or limb of a piano-forte."

There the conversation dropped; but a few months afterwards I was obliged to acknowledge that the young lady was correct when she asserted that some people were more particular than even she was.

I was requested by a lady to escort her to a seminary for young ladies, and on being ushered into the reception-room, conceive my astonishment at beholding a square piano-forte with four limbs. However, that the ladies who visited their daughters might feel in its full force the extreme delicacy of the mistress of the establishment, and her care to preserve in their utmost purity the ideas of the young ladies under her charge, she had dressed all these four limbs in modest little trousers, with frills at the bottom of them!

"A dark spiral cloud was rising above the horizon."

THE TRAIL OF TEARS BEGINS

August 28, 1838

WILLIAM SHOREY COODEY

In 1824 about seventy-seven thousand Indians were living east of the Mississippi River, according to estimates given to the secretary of war. By 1840, almost all the tribes had been "removed," pushed westward to make room for new settlers.

In the series of forced marches that has become known as the Trail of Tears, fourteen thousand Cherokees were driven out of Georgia and Tennessee into Oklahoma. About four thousand died on the way.

Coodey, who witnessed the first of the thirteen drives, described the scene in this letter to a friend.

The entire Cherokee population were captured by the U.S. troops under General [Winfield] Scott in 1838 and marched to, principally, the border of Tennessee where they were encamped in large bodies until the time of their final removal west. At one of these encampments, twelve miles south of the Agency and Head quarters of Genl. Scott, was organized the first detachment for marching under the arrangement committing the whole management of the emigration into the hands of the Cherokees themselves.

The first of September was fixed as the time for a part to be in motion on the route. Much anxiety was felt, and great exertions made by the Cherokees to comply with everything reasonably to be expected of them, and it was determined that the first detachment would move in the last days of August.

I left the Agency on the 27th, after night, and watched the encampment above alluded to, early the following morning for the purpose of aiding in the arrangements necessary to get a portion in motion on that day—the remainder to follow the next day and come up while the first were crossing the Tennessee River, about twelve miles distant.

At noon all was in readiness for moving; the teams were stretched out in a line along the road through a heavy forest, groups of persons formed about each wagon, others shaking the hand of some sick friend or relative who would be left behind. The temporary camp covered with boards and some of bark that for three summer months had been their only shelter and home, were crackling and falling under a blazing flame; the day was bright and beautiful, but a gloomy thoughtfulness was depicted in the lineaments of every face. In all the bustle of preparation there was a silence and stillness of the voice that betrayed the sadness of the heart.

At length the word was given to "move on." I glanced along the line and the form of Going Snake, an aged and respected chief whose head eighty winters had whitened, mounted on his favorite pony passed before me and led the way in advance, followed by a number of young men on horse back.

At this very moment a low sound of distant thunder fell on my ear. In almost an exact western direction a dark spiral cloud was rising above the horizon and sent forth a murmur I almost fancied a voice of divine indignation for the wrongs of my poor and unhappy countrymen, driven by brutal power from all they loved and cherished in the land of their fathers, to gratify the cravings of avarice. The sun was unclouded—no rain fell—the thunder rolled away and sounds hushed in the distance. The scene around and before me, and in the elements above, were peculiarly impressive & singular. It was at once spoken of by several persons near me, and looked upon as omens of some future event in the west.

"The people had only themselves to blame."

BARNUM DISCOVERS TOM THUMB

November 1842
Bridgeport, Connecticut

PHINEAS TAYLOR BARNUM

*A*lthough he may not have actually said "There's a sucker born every minute," *P. T. Barnum proved the truth of that proposition throughout his life. No lie was too big for Barnum, no spectacle too grotesque. He turned sideshow performers such as Tom Thumb into international celebrities. He faked oddities such as the Fiji Mermaid, which he created by attaching the upper half of a monkey to the tail of a fish. He imported wild animals, including the famous elephant Jumbo. He built a huge Roman hippodrome in the middle of New York City. Barnum remained unashamed because the public proved him right every time. As many as twenty million people may have seen Tom Thumb.*

This account comes from his picaresque autobiography—a best-seller, of course.

I had heard of a remarkably small child in Bridgeport; and by my request my brother brought him to the hotel. He was the smallest child I ever saw that could walk alone. He was not two feet in height, and weighed less than sixteen pounds. He was a bright-eyed little fellow, with light hair and ruddy cheeks, was perfectly healthy, and as symmetrical as an Apollo. He was exceedingly bashful, but after some coaxing he was induced to converse with me, and he told me that he was the son of Sherwood E. Stratton, and that his own name was Charles S. Stratton. After seeing him and talking with him, I at once determined to secure his services from his parents and to exhibit him in public.

He was only five years old, and to exhibit a dwarf of that age might provoke the question, How do you know that he is a dwarf? Some license might indeed be taken with the facts, but even with this advantage I really felt that the adventure was nothing more than an experiment, and I engaged him for the short term of four weeks at three dollars per week— all charges, including traveling and boarding of himself and mother, being at my expense.

They arrived in New York on Thanksgiving Day, December 8, 1842, and Mrs. Stratton was greatly astonished to find her son heralded in my Museum bills as GENERAL TOM THUMB, a dwarf of eleven years of age, just arrived from England!

This announcement contained two deceptions. I shall not attempt to justify them, but may be allowed to plead the circumstances in extenuation. The boy was undoubtedly a dwarf, and I had the most reliable evidence that he had grown little, if any, since he was six months old; but had I announced him as only five years of age, it would have been impossible to excite the interest or awaken the curiosity of the public. The thing I aimed at was, to assure them that he was really a dwarf—and in this, at least, they were not deceived.

It was of no consequence, in reality, where he was born or where he came from, and if the announcement that he was a foreigner answered my purpose, the people had only themselves to blame if they did not get their money's worth when they visited the exhibition. I had observed . . . the American fancy for European exotics; and if the deception . . . has done anything toward checking our disgraceful preference for foreigners, I may readily be pardoned for the offense I here acknowledge.

"What hath God wrought!"

THE FIRST TELEGRAPH MESSAGE

March 4, 1843, and May 24, 1844
Washington, D.C., and Baltimore, Maryland

SAMUEL F. B. MORSE

Samuel Finley Breese Morse was better known as a painter when he began working on the telegraph in 1832, collaborating with other inventors to improve on existing ideas. He built a working model, devised his famous code, and solved the problem of long-distance transmission by creating a relay device. But because the invention was not wholly original, he had to spend years defending his patent claim, which the Supreme Court finally upheld in 1854.

I had spent at Washington two entire sessions of Congress, one in 1837–'38, the other in 1842–'43, in the endeavor so far to interest the

Government in the novel Telegraph as to furnish me with the means to construct a line of sufficient length to test its practicability and utility.

The last days of the last session of that Congress were about to close. A bill appropriating thirty thousand dollars for my purpose had passed the House, and was before the Senate for concurrence, waiting its turn on the calendar. On the last day of the session (3d of March, 1843) I had spent the whole day and part of the evening in the Senate-chamber anxiously watching the progress of the passing of the various bills, of which there were, in the morning of that day, over one hundred and forty to be acted upon, before the one in which I was interested would be reached; and a resolution had a few days before been passed, to proceed with the bills on the calendar in their regular order, forbidding any bill to be taken up out of its regular place. As evening approached there seemed to be but little chance that the Telegraph Bill would be reached before the adjournment, and consequently I had the prospect of the delay of another year, with the loss of time, and all my means already expended. In my anxiety, I consulted with two of my senatorial friends—Senator Huntington, of Connecticut, and Senator Wright, of New York—asking their opinion of the probability of reaching the bill before the close of the session. Their answers were discouraging, and their advice was to prepare myself for disappointment. In this state of mind I retired to my chamber, and made all my arrangements for leaving Washington the next day. Painful as was this prospect of renewed disappointment, you, my dear sir, will understand me when I say that knowing from experience whence my help must come in any difficulty I soon disposed of my cares, and slept as quietly as a child.

In the morning, as I had just gone into the breakfast-room, the servant called me out, announcing that a young lady was in the parlor wishing to speak with me. I was at once greeted with the smiling face of my young friend, the daughter of my old and valued friend and classmate, the Hon. H. L. Ellsworth, the Commissioner of Patents. On expressing my surprise at so early a call, she said, "I have come to congratulate you." "Indeed, for what?" "On the passage of your bill." "Oh, no, my young friend, you are mistaken; I was in the chamber till after the lamps were lighted, and my senators assured me there was no chance for me." "But," she replied, "it is you that are mistaken. Father was there at the adjournment last night, and saw the President put his name to your bill; and I asked father if I might come and tell you, and he gave me leave. Am I the first to tell you?" The news was so unexpected that for some moments I could not speak. At length I replied: "Yes, Annie, you are the first to inform me; and now I am going to make you a promise: the first dispatch on the completed line from Washington to Baltimore shall be yours." "Well," said she, "I shall hold you to your promise."

In about a year from that time, the line from Washington to Baltimore was completed. I was in Baltimore when the wires were brought into the office, and attached to the instrument. I proceeded to Washington, leaving word that no dispatch should be sent through the line until I had sent one from Washington. On my arrival there, I sent a note to Miss Ellsworth, announcing to her that every thing was ready, and I was prepared to fulfill my promise of sending the first dispatch over the wires, which she was to indite. The answer was immediately returned. The dispatch was, "What hath God wrought!" It was sent to Baltimore, and repeated to Washington, and the strip of paper upon which the telegraphic characters are printed, was claimed by Governor Seymour, of Hartford, Connecticut, then a member of the House, on the ground that Miss Ellsworth was a native of Hartford. It was delivered to him by Miss Ellsworth, and is now preserved in the archives of the Hartford Museum.

I need only add that no words could have been selected more expressive of the disposition of my own mind at that time, to ascribe all the honor to Him to whom it truly belongs.

"The Day of Judgment was at hand."

WAITING FOR THE END OF THE WORLD

October 22, 1844
Philadelphia

ANONYMOUS

In 1831, William Miller, a New York farmer and lay preacher, predicted the impending arrival of Judgment Day. As the world spun sinfully toward his deadline of October 1844, his faithful followers grew to almost a million.

The excitement in Philadelphia had been growing for two or more years, and by the summer of 1844 it was indescribable. The Millerite Church was on Julianna Street, between Wood and Callowhill, and there Miller's followers met night and day, and watched the stars and sun, and prayed and warned the unrepentant that the "Day of Judgment was at hand."

Many of them began to sell their houses at prices which were merely nominal. Others gave away their personal effects, shut up their business, or vacated their houses. On a store on Fifth Street, above Chestnut, was a placard which read thus:

"This shop is closed in honor of the King of Kings who will appear about the 20th of October. Get ready friends to crown Him Lord of all." . . . People laboring under the excitement went mad.

On one occasion all the windows of a meeting-house were surrounded at night by a crowd of young fellows, and at a given signal the darkness and gloom were made lurid by flaming torches, and the air resounded with the roar of firecrackers. The Saints inside went wild with terror, for they thought the fiery whirlwind was come.

The Sunday before the final day was an eventful one. The Julianna Street Chapel was crowded. A mob of unbelievers on the pavements stoned the windows and hooted at the worshippers. The police of Northern Liberties, and Spring Garden, and a sheriff's posse, headed by Morton McMichael, were on hand to quell the threatened disturbance. The members of the congregation repaired to their homes, and after, in many cases, leaving their doors and windows open, and giving away their furniture, set out for the suburban districts. A large number went over into New Jersey, but their chief party assembled in Isaac Yocomb's field on the Darby Road, three miles and a half from the Market Street bridge. While here a furious hurricane strengthened the faith of the Millerites and struck awful terror to the souls of the timid. It swept over the city, destroying shipping and demolishing houses. . . .

The crowd at Darby was gathered in two tents, but so great was it that the children for two days were obliged to run about the fields, exposed to the pelting of a pitiless storm, and crying for their parents. The parents, clad in their white ascension robes, were almost exhausted for want of food, slept on the cold wet ground, and prayed and hymned and groaned incessantly.

At midnight on the 22d, the Bridegroom was to come, and a rain of fire was to descend from the heavens, and the Saints were to be gathered up in a whirlwind. There they stood on that black, tempestuous October night, shivering with cold and fear—their faces upturned, and every eye strained to catch a beam of the awful light piercing the clouds. The morning broke, and with it came the end of the delusion. The assemblage dispersed in despair, and slunk away silently and downcast to their houses.

"Even woodchucks had some rights."

THOREAU AT WALDEN POND

September 1845
Concord, Massachusetts

JOSEPH HOSMER

"*He is so thoughtful," wrote Ralph Waldo Emerson, Henry David Thoreau's neighbor and literary predecessor, "and does so much more than he bargained to do."*

On the other hand, as Emerson complained, "What is so cheap as politeness? Never had I the least social pleasure with him, though often the best conversation . . . when he is not pugnacious."

Eyewitness Hosmer presents the idealized Thoreau, true to the image that continues to influence so many Americans—independent, stoic, and with an affinity for nature.

Early in September, 1845 (can it be so long) on his invitation I spent a Sunday at his lake side retreat, as pure and delightful as with my mother.

The building was not then finished, the chimney had no beginning, the sides were not battened, or the walls plastered. It stood in the open field, some thirty rods from the lake, and the "Devil's Bar" and in full view of it.

Upon its construction he had evidently bestowed much care, and the proportions of it, together with the work, were very much better than would have been expected of a novice, and he seemed well pleased with his effort.

The entrance to the cellar was thro' a trap door in the center of the room. The king-post was an entire tree, extending from the bottom of the cellar to the ridge-pole, upon which we descended, as the sailors do into the hold of a vessel.

His hospitality and manner of entertainment were unique, and peculiar to the time and place.

The cooking apparatus was primitive and consisted of a hole made in the earth and inlaid with stones, upon which the fire was made, after the manner at the sea-shore, when they have a clam-bake.

When sufficiently hot remove the smoking embers and place on the fish, frog, etc. Our bill of fare included roasted horn pout, corn, beans, bread, salt, etc. Our viands were nature's own, "sparkling and bright."

I gave the bill of fare in English and Henry rendered it in French, Latin and Greek.

The beans had been previously cooked. The meal for our bread was mixed with lake water only, and when prepared it was spread upon the surface of a thin stone used for that purpose and baked. It was according to the old Jewish law and custom of unleavened bread, and of course it was very, very primitive.

When the bread had been sufficiently baked the stone was removed, then the fish placed over the hot stones and roasted—some in wet paper and some without—and when seasoned with salt, were delicious.

He was very much disappointed in not being able to present to me one of his little companions—a mouse.

He described it to me by saying that it had come upon his back as he leaned against the wall of the building, ran down his arm to his hand, and ate the cheese while holding it in his fingers; also, when he played upon the flute, it would come and listen from its hiding place, and remain there while he continued to play the same tune, but when he changed the tune, the little visitor would immediately disappear.

Owing perhaps to some extra noise, and a stranger present, it did not put in an appearance, and I lost that interesting part of the show—but I had enough else to remember all my life.

The land where he raised his beans and other vegetables had been so continuously cropped with rye in the years preceding that the weeds had a stunted and sickly look: this however was favorable, as the crops needed but little cultivation.

Perhaps it was in this "field of glory," strewn with the bones and fur of the wood-chucks and rabbits, that he took his first lessons in combativeness: as he had to contend with the woodchucks by day, and the owls (his faithful allies,) stood sentry by night to keep away the rabbits, (literal fact,) otherwise he would not have harvested a bean.

One of the axioms of his philosophy had been to take the life of nothing that breathed, if he could avoid it: but, it had now become a serious question with him, whether to allow the wood-chucks and rabbits to destroy his beans, or fight.

Having determined on the latter, he procured a steel trap and soon caught a venerable old fellow to the "manor born," and one who had held undisputed possession there for all time.

After retaining the enemy of all beans in "durance vile" for a few hours, he pressed his foot on the spring of the trap and let him go—expecting and hoping never to see him more. Vain delusion!

In a few days after, on returning from the village post-office, on looking in the direction of the bean field, to his disgust and apprehension he saw the same old grey-back disappear behind some brush just outside the field.

On a reconnaissance he discovered that the enemy had taken up a strategic position covered by some brush near his beans, and had entrenched himself by digging a "ride pit," and otherwise made preparations for a determined siege. Accordingly he again set the trap and again caught the thief.

Now it so happened that those old knights of the shot gun, hook and line, Wesson, Pratt and Co., were on a piscatorial visit to the "devil's bar," equipped with all the necessary appliances to allure the finny tribe to destruction. A council of war was held at the "Bar," to determine what should be done with the wood-chuck.

A decision was rendered immediately by that old and popular landlord of the Middlesex, in his terse and laconic manner: "knock his brains out."

This however was altogether too severe on the woodchuck, thought Henry; even woodchucks had some rights that "Squatter Sovereigns" should respect. Was he not the original occupant there? and had he not "jumped" the "wood-chucks claim," destroyed his home, and built his "hut" upon the ruins? After considering the question carefully he took the woodchuck in his arms and carried him some two miles away; and then with a severe admonition at the end of a good stick, he opened the trap, and again let him "depart in peace"; and he never saw him more.

"Heavy white wagons creeping on . . ."

THE OREGON TRAIL

1846

FRANCIS PARKMAN

*F*rancis Parkman was a Harvard professor with a taste for adventure, a man with crippling illnesses who loved to challenge himself in the outdoors. He is considered one of the country's greatest historians, and his several books are still in print more than one hundred years after publication. This account of a trip he *made just after he graduated from Harvard Law School comes from* The Oregon Trail.

We were now arrived at the close of our solitary journeyings along the St. Joseph's Trail. On the evening of the twenty-third of May we encamped near its junction with the old legitimate trail of the Oregon emigrants. . . . As we lay around the fire after supper, a low and distant sound, strange enough amid the loneliness of the prairie, reached our ears—peals of laughter, and the faint voices of men and women. For eight days we had not encountered a human being, and this singular warning of their vicinity had an effect extremely wild and impressive.

About dark a sallow-faced fellow descended the hill on horseback, and splashing through the pool, rode up to the tents. He was enveloped in a huge cloak, and his broad felt-hat was weeping about his ears with the drizzling moisture of the evening. Another followed, a stout, square-built, intelligent-looking man, who announced himself as leader of an emigrant party, encamped a mile in advance of us. About twenty wagons, he said, were with him; the rest of his party were on the other side of the Big Blue [a tributary of the Kansas River]. . . . These were the first emigrants that we had overtaken, although we had found abundant and melancholy traces of their progress throughout the whole course of the journey. Sometimes we passed the grave of one who had sickened and died on the way. The earth was usually torn up, and covered thickly with wolf-tracks. Some had escaped this violation. One morning, a piece of plank, standing upright on the summit of a grassy hill, attracted our notice, and riding up to it, we found the following words very roughly traced upon it, apparently by a red-hot piece of iron:

MARY ELLIS
DIED MAY 7TH, 1845.
AGED TWO MONTHS

Such tokens were of common occurrence. . . .

We were late in breaking up our camp on the following morning, and scarcely had we ridden a mile when we saw, far in advance of us, drawn against the horizon, a line of objects stretching at regular intervals along the level edge of the prairie. An intervening swell soon hid them from sight, until, ascending it a quarter of an hour after, we saw close before us the emigrant caravan, with its heavy white wagons creeping on in their slow procession, and a large drove of cattle following behind. Half a dozen yellow-visaged Missourians, mounted on horseback, were cursing and shouting among them; their lank angular proportions, enveloped in brown homespun, evidently cut and adjusted by the hands of a domestic female tailor. As we approached, they greeted us with the polished salutation: "How are ye, boys? Are ye for Oregon or California?"

As we pushed rapidly past the wagons, children's faces were thrust out from the white coverings to look at us; while the care-worn, thin-featured matron, or the buxom girl, seated in front, suspended the knitting on which most of them were engaged to stare at us with wondering curiosity. By the side of each wagon stalked the proprietor, urging on his patient oxen, who shouldered heavily along, inch by inch, on their interminable journey. It was easy to see that fear and dissension prevailed among them; some of the men—but these, with one exception, were bachelors—looked wistfully upon us as we rode lightly and swiftly past, and then impatiently at their own lumbering wagons and heavy-gaited oxen. Others were unwilling to advance at all, until the party they had left behind should have rejoined them. Many were murmuring against the leader they had chosen, and wished to depose him; and this discontent was fomented by some ambitious spirits, who had hopes of succeeding in his place. The women were divided between regrets for the homes they had left and apprehension of the deserts and the savages before them.

"The city has been converted into a wagon maker's shop."

THE MORMON EXODUS

May 8–10, 1846
Nauvoo, Illinois

ANONYMOUS *DAILY*
MISSOURI REPUBLICAN REPORTER

*J*oseph *Smith founded the Mormons in upstate New York in 1830, but the sect soon became a wandering tribe. After leaving New York, they tried to settle in Missouri. They were expelled by order of the governor, so they settled in Illinois. They stayed there long enough to make the town they built, Nauvoo, the largest and most powerful in the state. But once again the sect's unorthodox beliefs, along with its insularity and prosperity, attracted resentment and fear. Smith's grandiose ambitions did not help. He alarmed many people when he declared himself a candidate*

for president of the United States in 1844. Soon after his stunning announcement,
Smith was arrested for using his private militia to destroy the printing press of dis-
sident Mormons. A mob of non-Mormons charged the prison in Carthage, Illinois,
and shot Smith.

Anti-Mormon violence continued in Illinois until Brigham Young led the Mor-
mons west to Deseret, now Utah. The exodus began in February 1846. By the time
this eyewitness account was written, almost all of the fifteen thousand Mormon res-
idents of Nauvoo had left.

A few days ago, to satisfy ourselves of the actual state of affairs at
Nauvoo, and to ascertain whether the Mormons were really leaving the
country, we spent last Friday, Saturday and portion of Sunday in the city
and surrounding country.

The city and country present a very altered appearance since last fall.
Then, the fields were covered with, or the barns contained, the crops of
the season. Now, there are no crops, either growing or being planted. In
many instances, the fences have been destroyed, houses have been deserted, and the whole aspect of the country is one of extreme desolation
and desertion.

Nearly every workshop in the city has been converted into a wagon
maker's shop. Generally, they are providing themselves with light wagons,
with strong, wide bodies, covered with cotton cloth—in some instances
painted, but mostly white. These are to be met with in every direction,
and contribute greatly to the singular and mournful appearance of the
country.

They appear to be going in companies of four to six and ten wagons,
and some of them are fairly well provided with teams and provisions, but
a very large portion seem poorly provided for long a trip.

In the midst of this scene, the spectator cannot fail to be struck with
the lightness of heart, apparent cheerfulness, and sanguine hopes with
which families bid adieu to their friends, and set out on their journey.
The great mass go forth, sustained and cheered by the promises of their
leaders and a most devout conviction of the truth of their religion, and
the rewards which they are to receive from heaven for their present sacrifice.

Their enthusiasm is stimulated by songs and hymns, in which their
men, women and children join, and containing allusions to their persecu-
tions, and the names of Oregon and California, and the hopes that await
them, are mingled with their religious beliefs and expectations.

As a stranger passes through he will find himself frequently beset,
mostly by women and children, with inquiries, "Do you wish to purchase

a house and a lot?" "Do you wish to buy a farm?" In the city, houses and lots are selling from two to five and ten hundred dollars, which must have cost the owners double that sum. They are willing to sell for cash, or oxen or cattle, or to exchange for such articles of merchandise as they can barter or carry with them. Farmers in other sections, it appears to us, would make profitable investments by exchanging their surplus stock for houses and lots in Nauvoo, or for farms.

In and about Nauvoo there is every indication that the Anti-Mormons are satisfied that the Mormons are going, and are disposed to let them get off without further difficulty. There are, however, some turbulent spirits in the country and particularly some young men, who are willing, at any sacrifice, to keep up the excitement. On Saturday evening a number of persons assembled and resolved to visit Nauvoo and burn down the houses and drive out all those who had not already left. These proceedings were universally condemned by the more intelligent and respectable portion of the anti-Mormon party.

"They commenced to eat the dead people 4 days ago."

THE DONNER PARTY

November 20, 1846–March 1, 1847
Donner Lake, Sierra Nevada

PATRICK BREEN

The Donner party, eighty-seven in all, from several families, had left Spring-field, Illinois, in the summer of 1846. When their untested route to California proved impassable, tensions grew. Petty arguments added to the delay. The party did not start to cross the Sierra Nevada until late October, when the snows had already turned those high mountains into a death trap. The crossing was impossible. They got stuck at Truckee Lake.

In December, seventeen of the party made a desperate attempt to complete the passage to California and send back help. Seven succeeded, but by the time rescue parties could make it back up to the Truckee camp, many of those waiting for help had already died. Others had become cannibals.

Forty-seven of the Donner party survived, but they never escaped their grue-some notoriety.

Friday Nov. 20th 1846   Came to this place on the 31st of last month that it snowed   we went on to the pass   the snow so deep we were unable to find the road, when within 3 miles of the summit   then turned back to this shanty on the Lake, Stanton came one day after we arrived here   we again took our teams & waggons & made another unsuccessful attempt to cross in company with Stanton   we returned to the shanty it continuing to snow all the time we were here   we now have killed most part of our cattle having to stay here untill next spring & live on poor beef without bread or salt   it snowed during the space of eight days with little intermission, after our arrival here, the remainder of time up to this day was clear & pleasant frezeing at night the snow nearly gone from the valleys.

Sat. 21st   Fine morning wind NW   22 of our company are about starting across the mountain this morning including Stanton & his indians, some clouds flying thawed to day wnd E.

Sunday 22nd   Froze hard last night   this a fine clear morning, wind E.S.E.   no account from those on the mountains.

Monday 23rd   Same weather   wind W   the Expedition across the mountains returned after an unsuccessful attempt. . . .

Sunday 29th   Still snowing now about 3 feet deep, wind W   killed my last oxen to day   will skin them tomorrow   gave another yoke to Fosters   hard to get wood.

Monday 30th   Snowing fast   wind W   about 4 or 5 feet deep, no drifts   looks as likely to continue as when it commenced   no living thing without wings can get about.

December 1st   Tuesday   Still snowing   wind W   snow about 5½ feet or 6 deep   difficult to get wood   no going from the house   completely housed up looks as likely for snow as when it commenced, our cattle all killed But three or four them, the horses & Stantons mules gone & cattle suppose lost in the snow   no hopes of finding them alive.

Wedns. 9th   Commenced snowing about 11 o'clock   wind NW snows fast   took in Spitzer yesterday so weak that he cannot rise without help caused by starvation.

Mond. 21   Milt. got back last night from Donos camp sad news. Jake Donno Sam Shoemaker Rinehart, & Smith are dead the rest of them in a low situation   Snowed all night with a strong SW wind   to day cloudy wind continues but not snowing, thawing   sun shining dimly   in hope it will clear off. . . .

Friday 25th   Offered our prayers to God this Christmas morning the prospect is apalling but hope in God   Amen

Jany. 1st 1847   We pray the God of mercy to deliver us from our present calamity if it be his Holy will Amen.

Sund. 3rd   Continues fair in day time   freezeing at night   wind about E   Mrs. Reid talks of crossing the mountains with her children provisions scarce.

Mond 4th   Fine morning   looks like spring   thawing now about 12 o'clock   wind SE   Mrs. Reid Milt. Virginia & Eliza started about ½ hour ago with prospect of crossing the mountain   may God of Mercy help them   left ther children here   Tom with us Pat with Keysburg & Jas with Gravese's folks, it was difficult for Mrs. Reid to get away from the children. . . .

Friday 8th   Fine morning   wind E   froze hard last night   very cold this morning   Mrs. Reid & company came back this morning   could not find their way on the other side of the Mountain   they have nothing but hides to live on   Martha is to stay here   Milt. & Eliza going to Donos Mrs. Reid & the 2 boys going to their own shanty & Virginia   prospects dull may God relieve us all from this difficulty if it is his Holy will Amen. . . .

Thursd. 21   Fine morning   wind W   did not freze quite so hard last night as it has done,   John Battice & Denton came this morning with Eliza she wont eat hides   Mrs. Reid sent her back to live or die on them.

Sund. 7th   Ceasd. to snow last after one of the most severe storms we experienced this winter the snow fell about 4 feet deep.

Frid. 12th   A warm thawey morning   wind SE   we hope with the assistance of Almighty God to be able to live to see the bare surface of the earth once more.   O God of Mercy grant it if it be thy holy will Amen. . . .

Sund 14th   Fine morning but cold before the sun got up, now thawing in the sun   wind SE   Ellen Graves here this morning   John Denton not well   froze hard last night   John & Edwd. E burried Milt. this morning in the snow.

Mond. 15   Moring cloudy untill 9 o'clock   then cleared off warm & sunshine   wind W   Mrs Graves refusd. to give Mrs Reid any hides put Suitors pack hides on her shanty would not let her have them   says if I say it will thaw it then will not, she is a case. . . .

Frid. 19th   Froze hard last night   7 men arrived from California yesterday evening with som provisions but left the greater part on the way to day clear & warm for this region some of the men are gone to day to Donnos Camp   will start back on Monday. . . .

Tuesd. 23   Froze hard last night   to day fine & thawey has the appearance of spring all but the deep snow   wind SSE   shot Towser do day & dressed his flesh   Mrs Graves came here this morning to borrow meat dog or ox   they think I have meat to spare but I know to the contrary   they have plenty hides   I live principally on the same. . . .

Thursd. 25th   Froze hard last night   fine & sunshiney to day   wind W.   Mrs Murphy says the wolves are about to dig up the dead bodies at her shanty, the nights are too cold to watch them, we hear them howl.

Frid. 26th   Froze hard last night   today clear & warm   Wind SE blowing briskly   Marthas jaw swelled with the toothache;   hungry times in camp, plenty hides but the folks will not eat them   we eat them with a tolerable good apetite. Thanks be to Almighty God.   Amen   Mrs Murphy said here yesterday that thought she would commence on Milt. & eat him. I dont that she has done so yet, it is distressing   The Donnos told the California folks that they commence to eat the dead people 4 days ago if they did not succeed that day or next in finding their cattle then under ten or twelve feet of snow & did not know the spot or near it, I suppose they have done so ere this time.

Satd. 27th   Beautiful morning sun shining brilliantly, wind about S.W. the snow has fell in depth about 5 feet but no thaw but in day time it freezing hard every night,   heard some geese fly over last night   saw none.

Sund. 28th   Froze hard last night   to day fair & sunshine   wind SE 1 solitary Indian passed by yesterday   come from the lake   had a heavy pack on his back   gave me 5 or 6 roots resembleing onions in shape taste some like a sweet potatoe, all full of little tough fibres.

Mond. March the 1st   So fine & pleasant   froze hard last night there has 10 men arrived this morning from Bear Valley with provisions we are to start in two or three days & cash our goods here   they say the snow will be here untill June.

"Oh! No. That can't be."

GOLD STRIKE AT SUTTER'S MILL

January 24, 1848
California

JAMES W. MARSHALL

*T*he Gold Rush that created thousands of fortunes bankrupted John Augustus Sutter. His very profitable 50,000-acre estate was overrun with miners, his thousands of heads of livestock were stolen, and his workers ran off to look for gold.

Marshall was the crew boss at the mill construction site, located on the Ameri-

can River at the site of present-day Coloma, California. Although he sets the date of
discovery as January 19, other sources say it was January 24.

While we were in the habit at night of turning the water through the
tail race we had dug for the purpose of widening and deepening the race, I
used to go down in the morning to see what had been done by the water
through the night; and about half past seven o'clock on or about the 19th
of January—I am not quite certain to a day, but it was between the 18th
and 20th of that month—1848, I went down as usual, and after shutting
off the water from the race, I stepped into it, near the lower end, and
there, upon the rock, about six inches beneath the surface of the water, I
discovered the gold. I was entirely alone at the time. I picked up one or
two pieces and examined them attentively; and having some general
knowledge of minerals, I could not call to mind more than two which in
any way resembled this—sulphuret of iron, very bright and brittle; and
gold, bright, yet malleable; I then tried it between two rocks, and found
that it could be beaten into a different shape, but not broken. I then collected four or five pieces and went up to Mr. Scott (who was working at
the carpenter's bench making the mill wheel) with the pieces and said, "I
have found it."

"What is it?" inquired Scott.

"Gold," I answered.

"Oh! no," returned Scott, "that can't be."

I replied positively—"I know it to be nothing else."

Mr. Scott was the second person who saw the gold. W. J. Johnston,
A. Stephens, H. Bigler, and J. Brown, who were also working in the mill
yard, were then called up to see it. Peter L. Wimmer, Mrs. Jane Wimmer,
C. Bennet, and I. Smith, were at the house; the latter two of whom were
sick; E. Persons and John Wimmer, (a son of P. L. Wimmer), were out
hunting oxen at the same time. About 10 o'clock the same morning, P. L.
Wimmer came down from the house, and was very much surprised at the
discovery, when the metal was shown him; and which he took home to
show his wife, who, the next day, made some experiments upon it by
boiling it in strong lye, and saleratus; and Mr. Bennet by my directions
beat it very thin.

Four days afterwards, I went to the Fort for provisions, and carried
with me about three ounces of the gold, which Capt. Sutter and I tested
with nitric acid. I then tried it in Sutter's presence by taking three silver
dollars and balancing them by the dust in the air, then immersed both in
water, and the superior weight of the gold satisfied us both of its nature
and value.

*"They had souls large enough
to feel the wrongs of others."*

THE SENECA FALLS CONVENTION

July 19–20, 1848
Seneca Falls, New York

LUCRETIA MOTT, ELIZABETH CADY STANTON, AND SUSAN B. ANTHONY

T his account comes from the History of the Women's Suffrage Movement, *edited by these pioneers for women's rights.*

"WOMAN'S RIGHTS CONVENTION.—A Convention to discuss the social, civil, and religious condition and rights of woman, will be held in the Wesleyan Chapel, at Seneca Falls, N.Y. on Wednesday and Thursday, the 19th and 20th of July, current; commencing at 10 o'clock A.M. During the first day the meeting will be exclusively for women, who are earnestly invited to attend. The public generally are invited to be present on the second day, when Lucretia Mott, of Philadelphia, and other ladies and gentlemen, will address the convention."

This call, without signature, was issued by Lucretia Mott, Martha C. Wright, Elizabeth Cady Stanton, and Mary Ann McClintock. At this time Mrs. Mott was visiting her sister Mrs. Wright, at Auburn, and attending the Yearly Meeting of Friends in Western New York. Mrs. Stanton, having recently removed from Boston to Seneca Falls, finding the most congenial associations in Quaker families, met Mrs. Mott incidentally for the first time since her residence there. They at once returned to the topic they had so often discussed, walking arm in arm in the streets of London, and Boston, "the propriety of holding a woman's convention." These four ladies, sitting round the tea-table of Richard Hunt, a prominent Friend near Waterloo, decided to put their long-talked-of resolution into action, and before the twilight deepened into night, the call was written, and sent to the Seneca County Courier. On Sunday morning they met in Mrs. McClintock's parlor to write their declaration, resolutions, and to consider subjects for speeches. As the convention was to assemble in three days, the time was short for such productions; but having no experience in the modus operandi of getting up conventions, nor in that kind of literature, they were quite innocent of the herculean labors they proposed. On the first attempt to frame a resolution; to crowd a complete thought, clearly and concisely, into three lines; they felt as helpless and hopeless as if they had been suddenly asked to construct a steam engine. And the humiliating fact may as well now be recorded that before taking the initiative step, those ladies resigned themselves to a faithful perusal of various masculine productions.

The reports of Peace, Temperance, and Anti-Slavery conventions were echoed, but all alike seemed too tame and pacific for the inauguration of a rebellion such as the world had never before seen. They knew women had wrongs, but how to state them was the difficulty, and this was increased from the fact that they themselves were fortunately organized and conditioned; they were neither "sour old maids," "childless women," nor "divorced wives," as the newspapers declared them to be. While they had felt the insults incident to sex, in many ways, as every proud, thinking woman must, in the laws, religion, and literature of the world, and in the invidious and degrading sentiments and customs of all nations, yet they had not in their own experience endured the coarser forms of tyranny resulting from unjust laws, or avocation with immoral and unscrupulous men, but they had souls large enough to feel the wrongs of others, without being scarified in their own flesh.

After much delay, one of the circle took up the Declaration of 1776, and read it aloud with much spirit and emphasis, and it was at once decided to adopt the historic document, with some slight changes such as substituting "all men" for "King George." Knowing that women must have more to complain of than men under any circumstances possibly could, and seeing the Fathers had eighteen grievances, a protracted search was made through statute books, church usages, and the customs of society to find that exact number. Several well-disposed men assisted in collecting the grievances, until, with the announcement of the eighteenth, the women felt they had enough to go before the world with a good case. One youthful lord remarked, "Your grievances must be grievous indeed, when you are obliged to go to books in order to find them out."

The eventful day dawned at last, and crowds in carriages and on foot, wended their way to the Wesleyan church. When those having charge of the Declaration, the resolutions, and several volumes of the Statutes of New York arrived on the scene, lo! the door was locked. However, an embryo Professor of Yale College was lifted through an open window to unbar the door; that done, the church was quickly filled. It had been decided to have no men present, but as they were already on the spot, and as the women who must take the responsibility of organizing the meeting, and leading the discussions, shrank from doing either, it was decided, in a hasty council round the altar, that this was an occasion when men might make themselves preeminently useful. It was agreed they should remain, and take the laboring oar through the Convention.

James Mott, tall and dignified, in Quaker costume, was called to the chair; Mary McClintock appointed Secretary, Frederick Douglass, Samuel Tillman, Ansel Bascom, E. W. Capron, and Thomas McClintock took part throughout in the discussions. Lucretia Mott, accustomed to public speaking in the Society of Friends, stated the objects of the Convention, and in taking a survey of the degraded condition of woman the world over, showed the importance of inaugurating some movement for her education and elevation. Elizabeth and Mary McClintock, and Mrs. Stanton, each read a well-written speech; Martha Wright read some satirical articles she had published in the daily papers answering the diatribes on woman's sphere. Ansel Bascom, who had been a member of the Constitutional Convention recently held in Albany, spoke at length on the property bill for married women, just passed the Legislature [the first of its kind in the United States], and the discussion on woman's rights in that Convention. Samuel Tillman, a young student of law, read a series of the most exasperating statutes for women, from English and American jurists, all reflecting the tender mercies of men toward their wives, in taking care of their property and protecting them in their civil rights.

The Declaration having been freely discussed by many present, was re-read by Mrs. Stanton, and with some slight amendments adopted:

". . . We hold these truths to be self evident: that all men and women are created equal . . . therefore:

"Resolved, That such laws as conflict, in any way, with the true and substantial happiness of woman, are contrary to the great precept of nature and of no validity, for this is 'superior in obligation to any other.'

"Resolved, That all laws which prevent woman from occupying such a station in society as her conscience shall dictate, or which place her in a position inferior to that of man, are contrary to the great precept of nature, and therefore of no force or authority.

"Resolved, That woman is man's equal—intended to be so by the Creator, and the highest good of the race demands that she should be recognized as such. . . .

The only resolution that was not unanimously adopted was the ninth, urging the women of the country to secure to themselves the elective franchise. Those who took part in the debate feared a demand for the right to vote would defeat others they deemed more rational, and make the whole movement ridiculous.

But Mrs. Stanton and Frederick Douglass seeing that the power to choose rulers and make laws, was the right by which all others could be secured, persistently advocated the resolution, and at last carried it by a small majority.

Thus it will be seen that the Declaration and resolutions in the very first Convention, demanded all the most radical friends of the movement have since claimed—such as equal rights in the universities, in the trades and professions; the right to vote; to share in all political offices, honors, and emoluments; to complete equality in marriage, to personal freedom, property, wages, children; to make contracts; to sue, and be sued; and to testify in courts of justice. At this time the condition of married women under the Common Law, was nearly as degraded as that of the slave on the Southern plantation. The Convention continued through two entire days, and late into the evening. The deepest interest was manifested to its close.

The proceedings were extensively published, unsparingly ridiculed by the press, and denounced by the pulpit, much to the surprise and chagrin of the leaders. Being deeply in earnest, and believing their demands pre-eminently wise and just, they were wholly unprepared to find themselves the target for the jibes and jeers of the nation. The Declaration was signed by one hundred men, and women, many of whom withdrew their names as soon as the storm of ridicule began to break. The comments of the press were carefully preserved, and it is curious to see that the same old arguments, and objections rife at the start, are reproduced by the press of today. But the brave protests sent out from this Convention touched a responsive chord in the hearts of women all over the country.

"He's gone!"

MAN OVERBOARD!

October 13, 1849
Atlantic Ocean

HERMAN MELVILLE

*M*elville witnessed this event on a voyage from New York to London a few months before he began to write Moby-Dick.

Rose early this morning, opened my bull's-eye window, and looked out to the East. The sun was just rising, the horizon was red, a familiar sight to me, reminding me of old times. Before breakfast went up to the masthead by way of gymnastics. About 10 o'clock A.M. the wind rose, the rain fell, and the deck looked dismally enough. By dinner time, it blew half a gale, and the passengers mostly retired to their rooms, seasick. After dinner, the rain ceased, but it still blew stiffly, and we were slowly forging along under close-reefed topsails—mainsail furled. I was walking the deck, when I perceived one of the steerage passengers looking over the side; I looked too, and saw a man in the water, his head completely lifted above the waves,—about twelve feet from the ship, right abreast the gangway. For an instant, I thought I was dreaming, for no one else seemed to see what I did. Next moment, I shouted "Man overboard!" and turned to go aft. The Captain ran forward, greatly confused.

I dropped overboard the tackle fall of the quarter-boat, and swung it towards the man, who was now drifting close to the ship. He did not get hold of it, and I got over the side, within a foot or two of the sea, and again swung the rope towards him. He now got hold of it. By this time, a crowd of people—sailors and others—were clustering about the bulwarks; but none seemed very anxious to save him. They warned me, however, not to fall overboard. After holding on to the rope about a quarter of a minute, the man let go of it, and drifted astern under the mizzen chains. Four or five of the seamen jumped over into the chains and swung him more ropes. But his conduct was unaccountable; he could have saved himself, had he been so minded. I was struck by the expression of his face in the water. It was merry. At last he drifted off under the ship's counter, and all hands cried "He's gone!" Running to the taffrail, we saw him again, floating off—saw a few bubbles and never saw him again. No boat was lowered, no sail was shortened, hardly any noise was made.

"I found him alone in a chamber. . ."

HAWTHORNE AND *THE SCARLET LETTER*

1849
Salem, Massachusetts

JAMES T. FIELDS

*F*ields *was editor of* The Atlantic Monthly *and a partner in the energetic Boston publishing house Ticknor, Reed & Fields.*

I first saw Hawthorne when he was about thirty-five years old. He had then published a collection of his sketches, the now famous *Twice-Told Tales.* Longfellow, ever alert for what is excellent and eager to do a brother author a substantial service, at once came before the public with a generous estimate of the work in the *North American Review;* but the choice little volume, the most promising addition to American literature that had appeared for many years, made little impression on the public mind. Discerning readers, however, recognized the supreme beauty in this new writer, and they never afterwards lost sight of him.

In the winter of 1849, I went down to Salem to see him and inquire after his health, for we had heard that he had been suffering from illness. He was then living in a modest wooden house in Mall Street, if I remember rightly the location. I found him alone in a chamber over the sitting-room of the dwelling; and as the day was cold, he was hovering near a stove. We fell into talk about his future prospects, and he was, as I feared I should find him, in a very desponding mood. "Now," said I, "is the time for you to publish, for I know during these years in Salem you must have got something ready for the press." "Nonsense," said he; "what heart had I to write anything, when my publishers have been so many years trying to sell a small edition of the *Twice-Told Tales?*" I still pressed upon him the good chances he would have now with something new. "Who would risk publishing a book for me, the most unpopular writer in America?" "I would," said I, "and would start with an edition of two thousand copies of anything you write." "What madness!" he exclaimed. "Your friendship for me gets the better of your judgment. No, no," he continued; "I have no money to indemnify a publisher's losses on my account." I looked at my watch and found that the train would soon be starting for Boston, and I knew there was not much time to lose in trying to discover what had been his literary work during these last few years in Salem. I remember that I pressed him to reveal to me what he had been writing. He shook his head and gave me to understand he had produced nothing. At that moment I caught sight of a bureau or set of drawers near where we were sitting; and immediately it occurred to me that hidden away somewhere in that article of furniture was a story or stories by the author of the *Twice-Told Tales,* and I became so positive of it that I charged him vehemently with the fact. He seemed surprised, I thought, but shook his head again; and I rose to take my leave, begging him not to come into the cold entry, saying I would come back and see him again in a few days.

I was hurrying down the stairs when he called after me from the chamber, asking me to stop a moment. Then quickly stepping into the entry with a roll of manuscript in his hands, he said: "How in Heaven's name did you know this thing was there? As you have found me out, take what I have written, and tell me, after you get home and have time to read it, if it is good for anything. It is either very good or very bad,—I don't know which." On my way up to Boston I read the germ of *The Scarlet Letter.* Before I slept that night I wrote him a note all aglow with admiration of the marvellous story he had put into my hands, and told him that I would come again to Salem the next day and arrange for its publication. I went on in such an amazing state of excitement when we met again in the little house, that he would not believe I was really in earnest. He seemed to think I was beside myself, and laughed sadly at my enthusiasm.

*"He had overheard some men plotting
how they should kill him."*

POE'S MACABRE DREAM

1849
Philadelphia

JOHN SARTAIN

artain was an illustrator who met Poe when they both contributed to Graham's
Magazine. *The episode he describes occurred only about a month before Poe's
death. Sartain's own magazine, the* Union Magazine of Literature and Art,
published "The Bells," one of Poe's most famous poems, just a few weeks later.

The last time I saw Mr. Poe was late in that same year, 1849, and then
under such peculiar and almost fearful conditions that the experience can
never fade from my memory. Early one Monday afternoon he suddenly
entered my engraving room, looking pale and haggard, with a wild and
frightened expression in his eyes. I did not let him see that I noticed it,
and shaking him cordially by the hand invited him to be seated, when he
began, "Mr. Sartain, I have come to you for a refuge and protection; will
you let me stay with you? It is necessary to my safety that I lie concealed
for a time." I assured him that he was welcome, that in my house he would
be perfectly safe, and he could stay as long as he liked, but I asked him
what was the matter. He said it would be difficult for me to believe what
he had to tell, or that such things were possible in this nineteenth century.

I made him as comfortable as I could, and then proceeded with my
work, which was pressing. After he had had time to calm down a little, he
told me that he had been on his way to New York, but he had overheard
some men who sat a few seats back of him plotting how they should kill
him and then throw him off from the platform of the car. He said they
spoke so low that it would have been impossible for him to hear and understand the meaning of their words, had it not been that his sense of hearing was so wonderfully acute. They could not guess that he heard them,
as he sat so quiet and apparently indifferent to what was going on, but
when the train arrived at the Bordentown station he gave them the slip
and remained concealed until the cars moved on again. He had returned
to Philadelphia by the first train back, and hurried to me for refuge.

I told him that it was my belief the whole scare was the creation of his own fancy, for what interest could those people have in taking his life, and at such risk to themselves? He said, "It was for revenge." "Revenge for what?" said I. He answered, "Well, a woman trouble."

Now and then some fragmentary conversation passed between us as I engraved, and shortly I began to perceive a singular change in the current of his thoughts. From such fear of assassination his mind gradually veered round to an idea of self-destruction, and his words clearly indicated this tendency. After a long silence he said suddenly, "If this mustache of mine were removed I should not be so readily recognized; will you lend me a razor, that I may shave it off?" I told him that as I never shaved I had no razor, but if he wanted it removed I could readily do it for him with scissors. Accordingly I took him to the bathroom and performed the operation successfully.

After tea, it being now dark I saw him preparing to go out; and on my asking him where he was going, he said, "To the Schuylkill" [the Schuylkill Water Works]. I told him I would go too, it would be pleasant in the moonlight later, and he offered no objection. . . . When we had reached the corner of Ninth and Chestnut Streets we waited for an omnibus some minutes, which were passed in conversation, and among the many things he said was that he wished I would see to it after his death that the portrait Osgood had painted of him should go to his mother [Mrs. Clemm, his mother-in-law]. I promised that as far as I could control it that should be done. After getting the omnibus we rode to its stopping-place, a little short of Fairmount, opposite a tavern on the north side of Callowhill Street, at the bend it makes to the north-west to reach the bridge over the river. At that spot a bright light shone out through the open door of the tavern, but beyond all was pitchy dark. However, forward into the darkness we walked. I kept on his left side, and on approaching the foot of the bridge guided him off to the right by a gentle pressure, until we reached the lofty flight of steep wooden steps which ascended almost to the top of the reservoir. There was a landing with seats, and we sat down to rest. All this time I had contrived to hold him in conversation, except while we were labouring breathless up that long, breakneck flight of stairs.

There he told me his late experiences, or what he believed to be such, and the succession of images that his imagination created he expressed in a calm, deliberate, measured utterance as facts. . . . "I was confined in a cell in Moyamensing Prison," said he, "and through my grated window was visible the battlemented granite tower. On the topmost stone of the parapet, between the embrasures, stood perched against the dark sky a young female brightly radiant, like silver dipped in light, either in herself or in her environment, so that the cross-bar shadows thrown from my window were distinct on the opposite wall. From this position, remote as it was she addressed to me a series of questions in words not loud but distinct, and I dared not fail to hear and make apt response. Had I failed once either to hear or to make pertinent answer, the consequences to me would have been something fearful; but my sense of hearing is wonderfully acute, so that I passed safely through this ordeal, which was a snare to catch me. But another was in store.

"An attendant asked me if I would like to take a stroll about the place, I might see something interesting, and I agreed. In the course of our rounds on the ramparts we came to a cauldron of boiling spirits. He asked me if I would not like to take a drink. I declined, but had I said yes, what do you suppose would have happened?" I said I could not guess. "Why, I should have been lifted over the brim and dipped into the hot liquid up to the lip, like Tantalus." "Yes," said I, "but that would have killed you." "Of course it would," said he, "that's what they wanted; but, you see, again I escaped the snare. So at last, as a means to torture me and wring my heart, they brought out my mother, Mrs. Clemm, to blast my sight by seeing them first saw off her feet at the ankles, then her legs to the knees, her thighs at the hips, and so on." The horror of the imagined scene threw him into a sort of convulsion. This is but a very brief sample of the talk I listened to up there in the darkness. I had been all along expecting the moon to rise, forgetting how much it retarded every evening, and the clouds hid the light of the stars. It came into my mind that Poe might possibly in a sudden fit of frenzy leap freely forth with me in his arms into the black depth below, so I was watchful and kept on my guard. I asked him how he came to be in Moyamensing Prison.

He answered that he had been suspected of trying to pass a fifty-dollar counterfeit note. The truth is, he was there for what takes so many there for a few hours only—the drop too much. I learned later that when his turn came in the motley group before Mayor Gilpin, some one said, "Why, this is Poe, the poet," and he was dismissed without the customary fine.

I suggested at last that as it appeared we were not to have the moon we might as well go down again. He agreed, and we descended the steep stairway slowly and cautiously, holding well to the handrails. Being down I kept this time, on our return walk, on his right side, and did not suffer the conversation to flag. On arriving at the omnibus waiting for passengers at the tavern door I pressed gently against him and he raised his foot to the step, but instantly recollecting himself drew back. I urged him in, and being seated beside him said "You were saying?" The conversation was resumed, I got him safe home, and gave him a bed on a sofa in the dining room, while I slept alongside him on three chairs, without undressing.

On the second morning he appeared to have become so much like his old self that I trusted him to go out alone. Rest and regular meals had had a good effect, although his mind was not yet entirely free from the nightmare. After an hour or two he returned, and then told me he had come to the conclusion that what I said was true, that the whole thing had been a delusion and a scare created by his own excited imagination. He said his mind began to clear as he lay on the grass, his face buried in it and his nostrils inhaling the sweet fragrance mingled with the odour of the earth. While he lay thus, the words he had heard kept running in his thoughts, but he tried in vain to connect them with the speaker, and so the light gradually broke in upon his dazed mind and he saw that he had come out of a dream. Being now all right again he was ready to depart for New York. He borrowed what was needful, and I never saw him again.

"Their appearance would at once proclaim them to be fugitives."

ON THE UNDERGROUND RAILROAD

About 1850
Cincinnati, Ohio

LEVI COFFIN

The Underground Railroad may have helped as many as fifty thousand escaping slaves reach haven in free states and Canada. The secret organization seems to have been in place as early as 1786. More than three thousand persons were part of the effort.

Coffin, an Ohio Quaker, was considered by some to be "president" of the railroad for a time.

The fugitives generally arrived in the night, and were secreted among the friendly colored people or hidden in the upper room of our house. They came alone or in companies, and in a few instances had a white guide to direct them.

One company of twenty-eight that crossed the Ohio River at Lawrenceburg, Indiana—twenty miles below Cincinnati—had for conductor a white man whom they had employed to assist them. The character of this man was full of contradictions. He was a Virginian by birth and spent much of his time in the South, yet he hated slavery. He was devoid of moral principle, but was a true friend to the poor slave.

The company of twenty-eight slaves referred to, all lived in the same neighborhood in Kentucky, and had been planning for some time how they could make their escape from slavery. This white man—John Fairfield—had been in the neighborhood for some weeks buying poultry, etc., for market, and though among the whites he assumed to be very pro-slavery, the negroes soon found that he was their friend.

He was engaged by the slaves to help them across the Ohio River and conduct them to Cincinnati. They paid him some money which they had managed to accumulate. The amount was small, considering the risk the conductor assumed, but it was all they had. Several of the men had their wives with them, and one woman a little child with her, a few months old. John Fairfield conducted the party to the Ohio River opposite the mouth of the Big Miami, where he knew there were several skiffs tied to the bank, near a wood-yard. When I asked him afterward if he did not feel compunctions of conscience for breaking these skiffs loose and using them, he replied: "No; slaves are stolen property, and it is no harm to steal boats or anything else that will help them gain their liberty." The entire party crowded into three large skiffs or yawls, and made their way slowly across the river. The boats were overloaded and sank so deep that the passage was made in much peril. The boat John Fairfield was in was leaky, and began to sink when a few rods from the Ohio bank, and he sprang out on the sand-bar, where the water was two or three feet deep, and tried to drag the boat to the shore. He sank to his waist in mud and quicksands, and had to be pulled out by some of the negroes. The entire party waded out through mud and water and reached the shore safely, though all were wet and several lost their shoes. They hastened along the bank toward Cincinnati, but it was now late in the night and daylight appeared before they reached the city. Their plight was a most pitiable one. They were cold, hungry and exhausted; those who had lost their shoes in the mud suffered from bruised and lacerated feet, while to add to their discomfort a drizzling rain fell during the latter part of the night. They could not enter the city for their appearance would at once proclaim them to be fugitives. When they reached the outskirts of the city, below Mill Creek, John Fairfield hid them as well as he could, in ravines that had been washed in the sides of the steep hills, and told them not to move until he returned. He then went directly to John Hatfield, a worthy colored man, a deacon in the Zion Baptist Church, and told his story. He had applied to Hatfield before and knew him to be a great friend to the fugitives—one who had often sheltered them under his roof and aided them in every way he could.

When he arrived, wet and muddy, at John Hatfield's house, he was scarcely recognized. He soon made himself and his errand known, and Hatfield at once sent a messenger to me, requesting me to come to his house without delay, as there were fugitives in danger. I went at once and met several prominent colored men who had also been summoned. While dry clothes and a warm breakfast were furnished to John Fairfield, we anxiously discussed the situation of the twenty-eight fugitives who were lying, hungry and shivering, in the hills in sight of the city.

Several plans were suggested, but none seemed practicable. At last I suggested that some one should go immediately to a certain German livery stable in the city and hire two coaches, and that several colored men should go out in buggies and take the women and children from their hiding-places, then that the coaches and buggies should form a procession as if going to a funeral, and march solemnly along the road leading to Cumminsville, on the west side of Mill Creek. In the western part of Cumminsville was the Methodist Episcopal burying ground, where a certain lot of ground had been set apart for the use of the colored people. They should pass this and continue on the Colerain pike till they reached a right-hand road leading to College Hill. At the latter place they would find a few colored families, living in the outskirts of the village, and could take refuge among them. Jonathan Cable, a Presbyterian minister, who lived near Farmer's College, on the west side of the village, was a prominent abolitionist, and I knew that he would give prompt assistance to the fugitives.

I advised that one of the buggies should leave the procession at Cumminsville, after passing the burying-ground, and hasten to College Hill to apprise friend Cable of the coming of the fugitives, that he might make arrangements for their reception in suitable places.

While the carriages and buggies were being procured, John Hatfield's wife and daughter, and other colored women of the neighborhood, busied themselves in preparing provisions to be sent to the fugitives. A large stone jug was filled with hot coffee, and this, together with a supply of bread and other provisions, was placed in a buggy and sent on ahead of the carriages, that the hungry fugitives might receive some nourishment before starting.

All the arrangements were carried out, and the party reached College Hill in safety, and were kindly received and cared for.

When it was known by some of the prominent ladies of the village that a large company of fugitives were in the neighborhood, they met together to prepare some clothing for them. Jonathan Cable ascertained the number and size of the shoes needed, and the clothes required to fit the fugitives for traveling, and came down in his carriage to my house, knowing that the Anti-Slavery Sewing Society had their depository there. I went with him to purchase the shoes that were needed, and my wife selected all the clothing we had that was suitable for the occasion; the rest was furnished by the noble women of College Hill.

I requested friend Cable to keep the fugitives as secluded as possible until a way could be provided for safely forwarding them on their way to Canada. With little delay they were forwarded on from station to station. I had letters from different stations, as they progressed, and I also heard of their safe arrival on the Canada shore.

". . .Can any man do more than that?"

SOJOURNER TRUTH AT A WOMAN'S RIGHTS CONVENTION

1851
Akron, Ohio

MARIUS ROBINSON

Sojourner Truth was one of the country's most commanding speakers. She had been born a slave in New York State in the 1790s and was freed by the New York Emancipation Act of 1827. She was an evangelist who preached not only for religion but also for abolition and women's suffrage. After the Civil War she worked for the Freedmen's Bureau, a government agency that aided former slaves.

According to historian Nell Irvin Painter, Truth probably never said the famous line—"Ar'n't I a woman?"—attributed to her in an exaggerated account of this 1851 speech. Truth did not speak in a southern slave dialect. She had been raised by a Dutch farming family, so she spoke with something of a Dutch accent as a young woman. She spoke very correct English as an older woman.

Eyewitness Robinson was secretary of the convention.

One of the most unique and interesting speeches of the Convention was made by Sojourner Truth, an emancipated slave. Those only can appreciate it who saw her powerful form, her whole-souled, earnest gestures, and listened to her strong and truthful tones. She came forward to the platform and addressing the president said with great simplicity, "May I say a few words?" Receiving an affirmative answer, she proceeded:

"I want to say a few words about this matter.

"I am a woman's rights.

"I have as much muscle as any man, and can do as much work as any man. I have plowed and reaped and husked and chopped and plowed, and can any man do more than that?

"I have heard much about the sexes being equal; I can carry as much as any man, and can eat as much too, if I can get it. I am as strong as any man that is now.

"As for intellect, all I can say is, if a woman have a pint and man a quart why can't she have her little pint full? You need not be afraid to give us our rights for fear we will take too much—for we can't take more than our pint'll hold.

"The poor men seem to be all in confusion, and don't know what to do. Why children, if you have woman's rights give it to her and you will feel better. You will have your own rights, and they won't be so much trouble.

"I can't read, but I can hear. I have heard the Bible and have learned that Eve caused man to sin. Well if woman upset the world, do give her a chance to set it right side up again.

"But man is in a tight place, the poor slave is on him, woman is coming on him, and he is surely between a hawk and a buzzard."

"He will consider his country insulted. . ."

COMMODORE PERRY OPENS JAPAN

July 12, 1853
Uraga, Japan

OFFICIAL REPORT OF THE EXPEDITION

*J*apan's feudal Tokugawa regime had kept Japan closed from most foreign contact for more than two hundred years when Commodore Matthew Perry arrived on the pretext of negotiating a treaty for aid to shipwrecked sailors.

Perry's strategy was to elicit cordial treatment by acting haughtily. Although his obstinacy led to a diplomatic Abbott-and-Costello routine, it worked.

The day appointed for the reception of a reply from Yedo (now Tokyo) Tuesday, July 12, 1853, had now arrived. Accordingly, at about half past nine o'clock in the morning, three boats were seen to approach the steamer *Susquehanna* from the shores of Uraga. . . . The crews were numerous, there being thirty in the largest boat, and thirteen in each of the others, and their great swarthy frames were clothed in the usual uniform of loose blue dresses slashed with white stripes.

The boat in advance was distinguished, in addition to the government mark of a horizontal black stripe across her broad sail, by the black and white flag, which indicated the presence of some officers of distinction, and such in fact were now on board of her. As she approached nearer to the ship, the governor, Kayama Yezaiman, in his rich silken robes, was recognized, seated on mats spread in the centre of the deck of the vessel, and surrounded by his interpreters and suite.

The advance boat now came alongside, leaving the other two floating at some distance from the *Susquehanna*. His highness Kayama Yezaiman, with his two interpreters . . . were admitted at once on board, and, having been received with due formality, were ushered into the presence of Captains Buchanan and Adams, who were prepared to communicate with them.

The Commodore had previously to the arrival of the governor, written the following letter to the Emperor:—

To his Imperial Majesty the Emperor of Japan.

The Commander-in-chief of the United States naval forces in these seas, being invested with full powers to negotiate treaties, is desirous of conferring with one of the highest officers of the Empire of Japan, in view of making arrangements for the presentation of the original of his letter of credence, as also the original of a letter with which he is charged, addressed to his Imperial Majesty by the President of the United States.

It is hoped that an early day will be appointed for the proposed interview.

The governor's first statement was to the effect that there had been a misapprehension as to the delivery of the translations of the papers before the originals had been received. Although the Commodore was certain that there had been no such misunderstanding, nevertheless he, on the second interview in the course of the afternoon, consented, after much discussion, to deliver the translations and originals, and also a letter from himself to the Emperor, at the same time, provided the latter should appoint a suitable officer to receive them directly from the hands of the Commodore, who repeated that he would consent to present them to no other than a Japanese dignitary of the highest rank. The governor then said that a building would be erected on shore for the reception of the Commodore and his suite, and that a high official personage, specially appointed by the Emperor, would be in attendance to receive the letters. He, however, added that no answer would be given in the bay of Yedo, but that it would be transmitted to Nagasaki, through the Dutch or Chinese superintendents. This being reported to the Commodore, he wrote the following memorandum and directed it to be translated into Dutch, and fully explained to the governor:—

"The Commander in chief will not go to Nagasaki, and will receive no communication through the Dutch or Chinese.

"He has a letter from the President of the United States to deliver to the Emperor of Japan, or to his secretary of foreign affairs, and he will deliver the original to none other: if this friendly letter of the President to the Emperor is not received and duly replied to, he will consider his country insulted, and will not hold himself accountable for the consequences.

"He expects a reply of some sort in a few days, and he will receive such reply nowhere but in this neighborhood."

The governor, in accordance with his promise on leaving in the morning, returned in the afternoon accompanied, as usual by his interpreters and suite. Captains Buchanan and Adams were in readiness to receive the party; the Commodore still preserving his seclusion and communicating with the Japanese only through others. The conversation is here given verbatim as reported:

Present Captains Buchanan and Adams, Lieutenant Contee, Flag Lieutenant, and Yezaiman, governor of Uraga, and interpreters.

YEZAIMAN: As it will take a great deal of time to send up the copies of the letters first, and the originals afterward, I propose that the originals and the copies be delivered together, when the high officer comes. The governor and the high officer will do their best to entertain the Admiral and give him a suitable reception.

CAPT. BUCHANAN: That is not the object of the Commodore: he wishes these communications to go because there is among them a letter to the Emperor from himself, which he desires to send to Yedo with the copies. The reply to the President's letter is not of so much consequence just now. We want a reply to the Commodore's letter which is in the package.

YEZAIMAN: If you send the original letter, we will reply to it as soon as possible. We are here for the purpose of receiving the letter from the President to the Emperor, but now you speak of a letter from the Admiral to the Emperor.

CAPT. B.: The letter from the Admiral is in the package containing the copies of the President's letter. It states that he has in his possession the original letter of the President, and is empowered by the President to deliver it in person to the Emperor, or to a high officer of equal rank with himself, appointed by the Emperor.

YEZAIMAN: We are very sorry that you separate the two; it would be better to send the originals at once with the copies.

CAPT. B.: That is impossible. The letter of the Admiral states that he has the original letter of the President, and is empowered to deliver it, either in person or to an officer of his own rank; when the emperor is aware of the fact that the Admiral has the letter, then he will appoint an officer of the same rank to receive the original, and the Admiral will return at some future day to receive the answer.

YEZAIMAN: Can you not contrive to manage it in such a way that the original letter may be sent with the copies?

CAPT. B.: It cannot be done.

[Captains Buchanan and Adams left to speak with Perry, then returned.]

CAPTAIN B.: Captain Adams and I have just had a conversation with the Commodore. He says that, since you appear to have wholly misunderstood the matter about the letter, if you can show proof that an officer of the proper rank is appointed to receive them, he will waive the matter in dispute, and deliver the original at the same time with the copies. But he requires strict evidence that the officer who shall meet him shall be of the necessary rank, and that he has been specially appointed for the purpose by the Emperor. . . .

Though always preserving a certain gentlemanly aplomb and that self-cultivated manner which bespeaks high breeding, these Japanese dignitaries were disposed to be quite social, and shared freely and gayly in conversation. Nor did their knowledge and general information fall short of their elegance of manners and amiability of disposition. They were not only well bred, but not ill-educated, as they were proficient in the Dutch, Chinese, and Japanese languages, and not unacquainted with the general principles of science and of the facts of the geography of the world. When a terrestrial globe was placed before them, and their attention was called to the delineation on it of the United States, they immediately placed their fingers on Washington and New York, as if perfectly familiar with the fact that one was the capital, and the other the commercial metropolis of our country.

"He might have been an emperor . . ."

CHIEF SEATTLE SPEAKS

1854
Seattle

HENRY A. SMITH

*T*he occasion for the famous speech by Chief Seattle, head of the Suquamish and Duwamish tribes, was a reception for Isaac Stevens, governor of Washington Territory. Stevens wanted to buy lands around Puget Sound from the local tribes.

The speech has been discredited as a result of having been altered by many subsequent editors—one popular version was even concocted for a television script. Yet Cecile Maxwell, a recent chairwoman of the Duwamish tribe, has voiced her disapproval of both the editors and the doubters to the Seattle Times: *"Respect this man," she said. "The Duwamish tribe believes in the truth of that speech. Our chief sat and waited in rags for some compensation for the land taken from his people." There were about five thousand Duwamish living in the Seattle area when white settlers began to arrive. The tribe is now about one-tenth that number.*

This extract, flowery as it is, comes from the most reliable version, set down by Seattle pioneer Dr. Henry A. Smith a few decades after he heard it in Seattle's native language.

Old Chief Seattle was the largest Indian I ever saw and by far the noblest-looking. He stood 6 feet full in his moccasins, was broad-shouldered, deep-chested, and finely proportioned. His eyes were large, intelligent, expressive, and friendly when in repose, and faithfully mirrored the varying moods of the great soul that looked through them. He was usually solemn, silent, and dignified, but on great occasions moved among assembled multitudes like a Titan among Lilliputians, and his lightest word was law.

When rising to speak in council or to tender advice all eyes were turned upon him, and deep-toned sonorous, and eloquent sentences rolled from his lips like the ceaseless thunders of cataracts flowing from exhaustless fountains and his magnificent bearing was as noble as that of the most cultivated military chieftain in command of the forces of a continent. Neither his eloquence his dignity or his grace were acquired. They were as native to his manhood as leaves and blossoms are to a flowering almond.

His influence was marvelous. He might have been an emperor but all his instincts were democratic, and he ruled his loyal subjects with kindness and paternal benignity.

He was always flattered by marked attention from white men, and never so much as when seated at their tables, and on such occasions he manifested more than anywhere else the genuine instincts of a gentleman.

When Governor Stevens first arrived in Seattle and told the natives he had been appointed commissioner of Indian affairs for Washington Territory, they gave him a demonstrative reception in front of Dr. Maynard's office, near the waterfront on Main Street. The bay swarmed with canoes and the shore was lined with a living mass of swaying, writhing, dusky humanity, until old Chief Seattle's trumpet-toned voice rolled over the immense multitude, like the startling reveille of a bass drum, when silence became as instantaneous and perfect as that which follows a clap of thunder from a clear sky.

The governor was then introduced to the native multitude by Dr. Maynard, and at once commenced, in a conversational, plain and straightforward style, an explanation of his mission among them, which is too well understood to require capitulation.

When he sat down, Chief Seattle arose with all the dignity of a senator, who carries the responsibilities of a great nation on his shoulders. Placing one hand on the governor's head, and slowly pointing heavenward with the index finger of the other, he commenced his memorable address in solemn and impressive tones.

"Yonder sky that has wept tears of compassion on our fathers for centuries untold and which, to us, loom eternal, may change. Today it is fair, tomorrow it may be overcast with clouds. My words are like stars that never set. . . .

"The son of the white chief says his father sends us greetings of friendship and goodwill. This is kind, for we know he has little need of our friendship in return because his people are many. They are like the grass that covers the vast prairies, while my people are few, and resemble the scattering trees of a storm-swept plain.

"The great and I presume also good, white chief sends us word that he wants to buy our lands but is willing to allow us to reserve enough to live on comfortably. This indeed appears generous, for the red man no longer has rights that he need respect, and the offer may be wise, also, for we are no longer in need of a great country.

"There was a time when our people covered the whole land as the waves of the wind-ruffled sea cover its shell-paved floor. But that time has long since passed away with the greatness of tribes now almost forgotten.

". . . It matters but little where we pass the remainder of our days. They are not many.

"The Indian's night promises to be dark. No bright star hovers about the horizon. Sad-voiced winds moan in the distance. Some grim Nemesis of our race is on the red man's trail, and wherever he goes he will still hear the sure approaching footsteps of the fell destroyer and prepare to meet his doom, as does the wounded doe that hears the approaching footsteps of the hunter. A few more moons, a few more winters, and not one of all the mighty hosts that once filled this broad land or that now roam in fragmentary bands through these vast solitudes will remain to weep over the tombs of a people once as powerful and as hopeful as your own.

". . . We will ponder your proposition, and when we have decided we will tell you. But should we accept it, I here and now make this the first condition: That we will not be denied the privilege, without molestation, of visiting at will the graves of our ancestors and friends. Every part of this country is sacred to my people. Every hillside, every valley, every plain and grove has been hallowed by some fond memory or some sad experience of my tribe.

". . . And when the last red man shall have perished from the earth and his memory among white men shall have become a myth, these shores shall swarm with the invisible dead of my tribe, and when your children's children shall think themselves alone in the field, the store, the shop, upon the highway or in the silence of the woods, they will not be alone. In all the earth there is no place dedicated to solitude. At night, when the streets of your cities and villages shall be silent, and you think them deserted, they will throng with the returning hosts that once filled and still love this beautiful land. The white man will never be alone. Let him be just and deal kindly with my people, for the dead are not altogether powerless."

Other speakers followed, but I took no notes. Governor Stevens' reply was brief. He merely promised to meet them in general council on some future occasion to discuss the proposed treaty. Chief Seattle's promise to adhere to the treaty, should one be ratified, was observed to the letter, for he was ever the unswerving and faithful friend of the white man. The above is but a fragment of his speech, and lacks all the charm lent by the grace and earnestness of the sable old orator, and the occasion.

"Douglas spoke for himself,
and Lincoln for his cause."

LINCOLN AND DOUGLAS DEBATE

June–July 1858
Illinois

GUSTAVE KOERNER

The famous debates were staged during the 1858 Senate race. Douglas won, but Lincoln attracted the national attention that led him to the presidency two years later.

Koerner was a local politician. (Despite Koerner's estimates, Lincoln's actual height was six feet four inches; Douglas's was five feet four inches.)

On June 15th, the Republican Convention met in Springfield. Twelve hundred delegates attended. Richard Yates was made temporary, and I permanent, chairman. It adopted in the main the Republican State platform of 1856. It disapproved of the Dred Scott decision, maintained the right of Congress to prohibit slavery in the Territories and its duty to exercise it, approved the recent decision of the Supreme Court of Illinois, which declared that property in persons was repugnant to the constitution of Illinois, and that slavery was the creature of local and municipal law. A resolution that Abraham Lincoln was the first and only choice of the Republicans of Illinois was adopted with the most deafening applause. James Miller, the old Republican incumbent, was nominated for State Treasurer and Newton Bateman for Superintendent of Public Instruction.

The Convention met again in the evening. Mr. Lincoln, having been requested to address the Convention, took his stand on the right hand of the President, and delivered the ever memorable speech containing the passage: "A house divided against itself cannot stand. I believe this government cannot endure permanently half slave and half free. I do not expect the Union to be dissolved. I do not expect the house to fall, but I do expect it to cease to be divided. It will become all one thing or all the other. Either the opponents of slavery will arrest the further spread of it, and place it where the public mind shall rest in the belief that it is in the course of ultimate extinction,—or its advocates will push it forward until it shall become alike lawful in all the States, old as well as new, North as well as South. Have we no tendency to the latter condition?"

Other speakers followed him and the Convention adjourned amid the wildest enthusiasm. . . .

The first speech Judge Douglas made was at Chicago. His friends had made the most ample preparations for an ovation. Notice had been given for weeks, half-price excursion trains carried large numbers from the country into town. Bands of music and torch-light processions brought large masses to the front of the Tremont House, from the balcony of which he addressed the crowd. Bengal fires illuminated the scene, and when he appeared he was greeted with tumultuous cheers. He was fighting for his political life. His massive form supported his ample head, covered with a thick growth of black hair. His deep-set, dark blue eyes shed their lustre under his heavy brows. The features of his firm, round face were wonderfully expressive of the working of his feelings. Calm in stating facts, passionate when he attacked, disdainful when he was forced to defend, his gestures were sometimes violent and often exceptionally so. His voice was strong, but not modulated. Bold in his assertions, maledictory in his attacks, impressive in language, not caring to persuade, but intent to force the assent of his hearers, he was the Danton, not the Mirabeau, of oratory. . . .

Lincoln, who happened to be in the city, sat quietly on the same balcony. After Douglas got through, he was loudly called for. He rose and stated that this ovation was gotten up for his friend Judge Douglas, but that if the good people of Chicago would listen to him, he would speak to them to-morrow evening at the same time and place. Without time for parade or showy demonstration the throng that listened to Lincoln next evening, as might have been expected from the political complexion of the city, was larger and really more enthusiastic than the one of the night before.

No greater contrast could be imagined than the one between Lincoln and Douglas. The latter was really a very little giant physically, measuring five feet and nothing, while Lincoln, when standing erect, towered to six feet three inches. Lincoln, awkward in his posture and leaning a little forward, stood calm and collected, addressing his hearers in a somewhat familiar, yet very earnest, way, with a clear, distinct, and far-reaching voice, generally well modulated, but sometimes rather shrill. When unmoved, his features seemed overshadowed by an expression of sadness, though at times he could assume a most humorous, and even comical, look; but, when aroused, he appeared like a prophet of old. Neither he nor Douglas indulged in rhetoric; both were mainly argumentative. But while Douglas, powerful as was his speech, never showed anything like genius, there came from Lincoln occasionally flashes of genius and burning words, revelations as it were from the unknown, that will live as long as the English language lives. Lincoln was deeply read in the Bible and Shakespeare. He did not quote from them, but his style showed plainly his close intimacy with the Scriptures and the great bard. Douglas was eminently talented, Lincoln was original. But what made Lincoln vastly more effective in this contest was that even the most obtuse hearer could see at once that Douglas spoke for himself, and Lincoln for his cause.

"We whirled up one street and down another . . ."

FIRST OVERLAND MAIL REACHES THE WEST COAST

October 9–10, 1858
San Francisco

WATERMAN L. ORMSBY

*O*rmsby *was a reporter for the* New York Herald.

Most drivers would have been content to drive slowly over this spot— a distance of twelve miles and every foot of it requiring the most skillful management of the team to prevent the certain destruction of all in the coach. But our Jehu was in a hurry with the "first States' mail" and he was bound to put us through in good time. I suggested to him that a bad man riding on this road was on the very brink of the bad place and likely to depart thence at almost any moment if anything should break. He said, "Yes, but they didn't expect anything to break," and whipped up his horses just as we started down a steep hill. I expected to see him put down the brakes with all his might but he merely rested his foot on them, saying, "It's best to keep the wheels rolling, or they'll slide"; so he did keep the wheels rolling, and the whole coach slid down the steepest hills at the rate of fifteen—yes, twenty—miles an hour, now turning an abrupt curve with a whip and crack and "round the corner, Sally," scattering the loose stones, just grazing the rocks, sending its rattling echoes far away among the hills and ravines, frightening the slow teamsters on the road and making them haul off out of the way, and nearly taking away the breath of all.

The driver seemed to enjoy the fun, and invited me up to ride with him on the box. I got up, taking off my hat and throwing a blanket over my head; I held on tight as we dashed along—up and down, around the curves, and in straight lines, all at the same railroad speed. The loosening of a nut, the breaking of a strap, the shying of one of the four spirited horses, might—indeed would—have sent us all to "kingdom come" without a chance for saying prayers. . . .

We ran the twelve miles in an hour and five minutes, and, considering the ups and downs, I thought it pretty good travelling. The mountain is covered with stunted oak trees, making it much resemble an orchard. On the east side I noticed very few rocks, and none large. On the west this was made up by huge rusty looking crags, towering high in air, or with heavy boulders on their sides or at their feet, as if just fallen. The road over the mountains is excellent for the place and is much improved by Mr. Firebaugh, who appears to be the enterprising man of the region. He has a toll gate at the base of the mountains charging two dollars for the passage of a single four horse team, which is cheerfully paid in consideration of what he does to the road. . . .

It was just after sunrise that the city of San Francisco hove in sight over the hills, and never did the night traveller approach a distant light, or the lonely mariner descry a sail, with more joy than did I the city of San Francisco on the morning of Sunday, October 10. As we neared the city we met milkmen and pleasure seekers taking their morning rides, looking on with wonderment as we rattled along at a tearing pace.

Soon we struck the pavements, and, with a whip, crack, and bound, shot through the streets to our destination, to the great consternation of everything in the way and the no little surprise of everybody. Swiftly we whirled up one street and down another, and round the corners, until finally we drew up at the stage office in front of the Plaza, our driver giving a shrill blast of his horn and a flourish of triumph for the arrival of the first overland mail in San Francisco from St. Louis. But our work was not yet done. The mails must be delivered, and in a jiffy we were at the post office door, blowing the horn, howling and shouting for somebody to come and take the overland mail.

I thought nobody was ever going to come—the minutes seemed days—but the delay made it even time, and as the man took the mail bags from the coach, at half-past 7 A.M. on Sunday, October 10, it was just twenty-three days, twenty-three hours and a half from the time that John Butterfield, the president of the company, took the bags as the cars moved from St. Louis at 8 A.M. on Thursday, 16th of September, 1858. And I had the satisfaction of knowing that the correspondent of the New York Herald had kept his promise and gone through with the first mail—the sole passenger and the only one who had ever made the trip across the plains in less than fifty days.

"They at once cocked their guns,
and told me I was a prisoner . . ."

JOHN BROWN'S RAID

October 16, 1859
Harpers Ferry, Virginia

JOHN E. DAINGERFIELD

*J*ohn Brown was often described as insane or nearly so. If so, he was, to quote historian Samuel Eliot Morison, "a madman with a method." Yet his goal wasn't crazy. He intended to found a republic with a citizenry of escaped slaves. But his raid at Harpers Ferry ended with his surrender to U.S. Army troops led by Robert E. Lee. He was later tried and hanged.

Daingerfield was one of the hostages captured during the raid. Harpers Ferry is now in West Virginia.

On Sunday night, Oct. 16, 1859, about twelve or one o'clock, the gatekeeper of the bridge over the Potomac leading into Maryland was startled by the steady tramp of many men approaching the gate, having with them wagons, who, upon reaching the gate, ordered it to be opened to them. This the gate-keeper refused to do. They seized him and, presenting a pistol at his head, compelled him to be silent. They then wrenched off the locks and came over, he thinks about sixty strong.

Upon getting over, the first building taken possession of was the depot of the Baltimore and Ohio Railroad, then in charge of a very trusty negro, who slept in the building. Upon Brown's men demanding admittance, he refused to let them come in, saying he was in charge, and his instructions were to let no one in at night. He was then shot down, a negro faithful to his trust being the first victim of those whose mission it was to free the African race from bondage.

Brown's party next proceeded to the hotel, rapped up the landlord, put him under arrest, and placed guards at the doors, so that no one could go out or come in. All this was in perfect quiet at dead of night. They went next to place guards at the arsenal and armories, and fix their pickets at all the streets, so that no one could come or go who was not at once picked up and placed with an armed guard over him and compelled to be silent.

Next they divided their force, sending Cook with some men to seize Colonel Washington and other slaveholders. These gentlemen Brown's party waked from sleep and compelled to go with them as prisoners, at the same time taking all the slaves they could find, carriages, horses, etc. . . .

About daylight one of my servants came to my room door and told me "there was war in the street." I, of course, got up at once, dressed, and went out, my dwelling being immediately on the street. Upon looking round I saw nothing exciting. The only person in view was a man from the country, who was riding rapidly, and I supposed he had lost some of his negroes, who had been stopped at the gate of the bridge and made fight.

I walked towards my office, then just within the armory inclosure, and not more than a hundred yards from my dwelling. As I proceeded I saw a man come out of an alley near me, then another, and another, all coming towards me. When they came up to me I inquired what all this meant; they said, nothing, only they had taken possession of the Government works.

I told them they talked like crazy men. They answered, "Not so crazy as you think, as you will soon see." Up to this time I had not seen any arms; presently, however, the men threw back the short cloaks they wore, and displayed Sharpes's rifles, pistols, and knives. Seeing these, and fearing something serious was going on, I told the men I believed I would return to my quarters. They at once cocked their guns, and told me I was a prisoner. . . .

They said I was in no personal danger; they only wanted to carry me to their captain, John Smith. . . .

Upon reaching the gate I saw what, indeed, looked like war—negroes armed with pikes, and sentinels with muskets all around. When I reached the gate I was turned over to "Captain Smith."

He called me by name, and asked if I knew Colonel Washington and others, mentioning familiar names. I said I did, and he then said, "Sir, you will find them there," motioning me towards the engine room.

We were not kept closely confined, but were allowed to converse with him. I asked him what his object was; he replied, "To free the negroes of Virginia." He added that he was prepared to do it, and by twelve o'clock would have fifteen hundred men with him, ready armed.

Up to this time the citizens had hardly begun to move about, and knew nothing of the raid.

When they learned what was going on, some came out armed with old shot-guns, and were themselves shot by concealed men. All the stores, as well as the arsenal, were in the hands of Brown's men, and it was impossible to get either arms or ammunition, there being hardly any private arms owned by citizens. At last, however, a few weapons were obtained, and a body of citizens crossed the river and advanced from the Maryland side. They made a vigorous attack, and in a few minutes caused all the invaders who were not killed to retreat to Brown inside of the armory gate. Then he entered the engine-house, carrying his prisoners along, or rather part of them, as he made selections among them.

After getting into the engine-house with his men, he made this speech: "Gentlemen, perhaps you wonder why I have selected you from the others. It is because I believe you to be the most influential, and I have only to say now that you will have to share precisely the same fate that your friends extend to my men." He began at once to bar the doors and windows, and to cut port-holes through the brick wall.

Then commenced a terrible firing from without, from every point from which the windows could be seen, and in a few minutes every window was shattered, and hundreds of balls came through the doors. These shots were answered from within whenever the attacking party could be seen. This was kept up most of the day, and, strange to say, no prisoner was hurt, though thousands of balls were imbedded in the walls, and holes shot in the doors almost large enough for a man to creep through.

At night the firing ceased, for we were in total darkness, and nothing could be seen in the engine-house.

During the day and night I talked much with John Brown, and found him as brave as a man could be, and sensible upon all subjects except slavery. Upon that question he was a religious fanatic, and believed it was his duty to free the slaves, even if in doing so he lost his own life.

During a sharp fight one of Brown's sons was killed. He fell; then trying to raise himself, he said, "It is all over with me," and died instantly.

Brown did not leave his post at the port-hole, but when the fighting ceased he walked to his son's body, straightened out his limbs, took off his trappings, then turning to me, said, "This is the third son I have lost in this cause." Another son had been shot in the morning and was then dying, having been brought in from the street. While Brown was a murderer, yet I was constrained to think that he was not a vicious man, but was crazed upon the subject of slavery. Often during the affair in the engine-house, when his men would want to fire upon some one who might be seen passing, Brown would stop them, saying, "Don't shoot; that man is unarmed."

"Here he comes!"

THE PONY EXPRESS

1861

MARK TWAIN

*T*he Pony Express ran from St. Joseph, Missouri, to Sacramento, California. It oper- *ated for just over a year. The completion of the overland telegraph put it out of business in a flash—but not before Mark Twain, heading west in a coach, witnessed it.*

Twain noted the distance covered by each rider and horse as fifty miles. While the riders covered that much ground or more, the horses were changed about every fifteen miles.

In a little while all interest was taken up in stretching our necks and watching for the "pony rider"—the fleet messenger who sped across the continent from St. Joe to Sacramento, carrying letters nineteen hundred miles in eight days! Think of that for perishable horse and human flesh and blood to do! The pony rider was usually a little bit of a man, brimful of spirit and endurance. No matter what time of the day or night his watch came on and no matter whether it was winter or summer, raining, snowing, hailing, or sleeting, or whether his beat was a level straight road or a crazy trail over mountain crags and precipices, or whether it led through peaceful regions or regions that swarmed with hostile Indians, he must be always ready to leap into the saddle and be off like the wind! There was no idling time for a pony rider on duty. He rode fifty miles without stopping, by daylight, moonlight, starlight, or through the blackness of darkness—just as it happened. He rode a splendid horse that was born for a racer and fed and lodged like a gentleman; kept him at his utmost speed for ten miles, and then, as he came crashing up to the station where stood two men holding fast a fresh, impatient steed, the transfer of rider and mailbag was made in the twinkling of an eye, and away flew the eager pair and were out of sight before the spectator could get hardly the ghost of a look. Both rider and horse went "flying light." The rider's dress was thin and fitted close; he wore a roundabout and a skullcap and tucked his pantaloons into his boot tops like a race rider. He carried no arms—he carried nothing that was not absolutely necessary, for even the postage on his literary freight was worth five dollars a letter. He got but little frivolous correspondence to carry—his bag had business letters in it mostly. His horse was stripped of all unnecessary weight too. He wore light shoes or none at all. The little flat mail pockets strapped under the rider's thighs would each hold about the bulk of a child's primer. They held many and many an important business chapter and newspaper letter, but these were written on paper as airy and thin as gold leaf, nearly, and thus bulk and weight were economized. The stagecoach traveled about a hundred to a hundred and twenty-five miles a day (twenty-four hours), the pony rider about two hundred and fifty. There were about eighty pony riders in the saddle all the time, night and day, stretching in a long, scattering procession from Missouri to California, forty flying eastward and forty toward the west, and among them making four hundred gallant horses earn a stirring livelihood and see a deal of scenery every single day in the year.

We had had a consuming desire, from the beginning, to see a pony rider, but somehow or other all that passed us and all that met us managed to streak by in the night, and so we heard only a whiz and a hail, and the swift phantom of the desert was gone before we could get our heads out of the windows. But now we were expecting one along every moment and would see him in broad daylight. Presently the driver exclaims:

"Here he comes!"

Every neck is stretched farther and every eye strained wider. Away across the endless dead level of the prairie a black speck appears against the sky, and it is plain that it moves. Well, I should think so! In a second or two it becomes a horse and rider, rising and falling, rising and falling— sweeping toward us nearer and nearer—growing more and more distinct, more and more sharply defined—nearer and still nearer, and the flutter of the hoofs comes faintly to the ear—another instant a whoop and a hurrah from our upper deck, a wave of the rider's hand, but no reply, and man and horse burst past our excited faces and go swinging away like a belated fragment of a storm!

So sudden is it all and so like a flash of unreal fancy that, but for the flake of white foam left quivering and perishing on a mail sack after the vision had flashed by and disappeared, we might have doubted whether we had seen any actual horse and man at all, maybe.

"Soon afterwards there entered . . . a tall, lank, lean man."

LINCOLN AT THE WHITE HOUSE

March 27–28 and October 9, 1861
Washington, D.C.

WILLIAM HOWARD RUSSELL

*O*n December 20, 1860, shortly after Abraham Lincoln was elected president, South Carolina seceded from the Union. On February 4, 1861—a month before Lincoln was actually inaugurated—the Confederate States of America was formed. The lame duck president, James Buchanan, did not resist.

By Lincoln's inauguration day, the Confederacy had seven members. (In order of secession: South Carolina, Mississippi, Florida, Alabama, Georgia, Louisiana, and Texas.) At first, Lincoln limited his efforts to appeasement. In his inaugural address he upheld the legality of slavery and the fugitive slave laws that called for escaped slaves to be returned to the South. He opposed only secession. Speaking to the citizens of the Confederacy, he said, "In your hands, my dissatisfied fellow-countrymen, and not in mine, is the momentous issue of civil war. The government will not assail you. You can have no conflict without your being the aggressors. You have no oath registered in heaven to destroy the government, while I shall have the most solemn one to 'preserve, protect and defend' it."

British journalist William Howard Russell recorded in his diary these observations of the new president.

MARCH 27

Soon afterwards there entered, with a shambling, loose, irregular, almost unsteady gait, a tall, lank, lean man, considerably over six feet in height, with stooping shoulders, long pendulous arms, terminating in hands of extraordinary dimensions, which, however, were far exceeded in proportion by his feet. He was dressed in an ill-fitting, wrinkled suit of black, which put one in mind of an undertaker's uniform at a funeral; round his neck a rope of black silk was knotted in a large bulb, with flying ends projecting beyond the collar of his coat; his turned-down shirt-collar disclosed a sinewy muscular yellow neck, and above that, nestling in a great black mass of hair, bristling and compact like a ruff of mourning pins, rose the strange quaint face and head, covered with its thatch of wild republican hair, of President Lincoln. The impression produced by the size of his extremities, and by his flapping and wide projecting ears, may be removed by the appearance of kindliness, sagacity, and the awkward bonhomie of his face; the mouth is absolutely prodigious; the lips, straggling and extending almost from one line of black beard to the other, are only kept in order by two deep furrows from the nostril to the chin; the nose itself—a prominent organ—stands out from the face, with an inquiring, anxious air, as though it were sniffing for some good thing in the wind; the eyes dark, full, and deeply set, are penetrating, but full of an expression which almost amounts to tenderness; and above them projects the shaggy brow, running into the small hard frontal space, the development of which can scarcely be estimated accurately, owing to the irregular flocks of thick hair carelessly brushed across it. One would say that, although the mouth was made to enjoy a joke, it could also utter the severest sentence which the head could dictate, but that Mr. Lincoln would be ever more willing to temper justice with mercy, and to enjoy what he considers the amenities of life, than to take a harsh view of men's nature and of the world, and to estimate things in an ascetic or puritan spirit: A person who met Mr. Lincoln in the street would not take him to be what—according to the usages of European society—is called a "gentleman;" and, indeed, since I came to the United States, I have heard more disparaging allusions made by Americans to him on that account than I could have expected among simple republicans, where all should be equals; but, at the same time, it would not be possible for the most indifferent observer to pass him in the street without notice. . . .

MARCH 28

In the conversation which occurred before dinner, I was amused to observe the manner in which Mr. Lincoln used the anecdotes for which he is famous. Where men bred in courts, accustomed to the world, or versed in diplomacy, would use some subterfuge, or would make a polite speech, or give a shrug of the shoulders as the means of getting out of an embarrassing position, Mr. Lincoln raises a laugh by some bold west country anecdote, and moves off in the cloud of merriment produced by his joke. . . .

OCTOBER 9

This poor President! He is to be pitied; surrounded by such scenes, and trying with all his might to understand strategy, naval warfare, big guns, the movements of troops, military maps, reconnaissances, occupations, interior and exterior lines, and all the technical details of the art of slaying. He runs from one house to another, armed with plans, papers, reports, recommendations, sometimes good humoured, never angry, occasionally dejected, and always a little fussy. The other night, as I was sitting in the parlour at head-quarters, with an English friend who had come to see his old acquaintance the General, walked in a tall man with a navvy's cap, and an ill-made shooting suit, from the pockets of which protruded paper and bundles.

"Well," said he to Brigadier Van Vliet, who rose to receive him, "is George in?"

"Yes, sir. He's come back, but is lying down, very much fatigued. I'll send up, sir, and inform him you wish to see him."

"Oh, no; I can wait. I think I'll take supper with him. Well, and what are you now,—I forget your name—are you a major, or a colonel, or a general?"

"Whatever you like to make me, sir."

Seeing that General McClellan would be occupied, I walked out with my friend, who asked me when I got into the street why I stood up when that tall fellow came into the room.

"Because it was the President," [I said.]

"The President of what?"

"Of the United States."

"Oh, come, now you're humbugging me. Let me have another look at him."

He came back more incredulous than ever, but when I assured him I was quite serious, he exclaimed, "I give up the United States after this."

But for all that, there have been many more courtly presidents who, in a similar crisis, would have displayed less capacity, honesty, and plain dealing than Abraham Lincoln.

"I prayed as I never prayed before."

FORT SUMTER IS ATTACKED

April 8–15, 1861
Charleston, South Carolina

MARY BOYKIN CHESNUT

*A*s soon as South Carolina seceded, it tried to negotiate with the Union for the turnover of federal lands in the state, and by the time of Lincoln's inauguration had already seized some federal forts. But the South Carolina government had not yet captured Fort Sumter, the key to controlling Charleston's harbor. When Lincoln refused to give up the fort, the Confederacy attacked and the Civil War began.

Eyewitness Mary Chesnut, one of of the great diarists of the war, was a leading member of southern society.

APRIL 8, 1861

Tried to read Margaret Fuller Ossoli, but could not. The air too full of war news, and we are all so restless.

Went to see Miss Pinckney, one of the last of the old-world Pinckneys. Governor Manning walked in, bowed gravely, and seated himself by me. Again he bowed low in mock-heroic style and with a grand wave of his hand said, "Madam, your country is invaded." When I had breath to speak I asked, "What does he mean?" He meant this: There are six men-of-war outside the bar. Talbot and Chew have come to say that hostilities are to begin. Governor Pickens and Beauregard are holding a council of war. Mr. Chesnut then came in and confirmed the story. Wigfall next entered in boisterous spirits and said, "There was a sound of revelry by night." The men went off almost immediately. And I crept silently to my room, where I sat down to a good cry.

Mrs. Wigfall came in, and we had it out on the subject of civil war. We solaced ourselves with dwelling on all its known horrors, and then we added what we had a right to expect with Yankees in front and Negroes in the rear. "The slaveowners must expect a servile insurrection, of course," said Mrs. Wigfall, to make sure that we were unhappy enough. Suddenly loud shouting was heard. We ran out. Cannon after cannon roared. We met Mrs. Allen Green in the passageway, with blanched cheeks and streaming eyes. Governor Means rushed out of his room in his dressing gown and begged us to be calm. "Governor Pickens," said he, "has ordered, in the plenitude of his wisdom, seven cannon to be fired as a signal to the Seventh Regiment. Anderson [Major Robert Anderson, commander of the fort] will hear as well as the Seventh Regiment. Now you go back and be quiet; fighting in the streets has not begun yet."

So we retired. No sleep for anybody last night. The streets were alive with soldiers, men shouting, marching, singing. Wigfall, the stormy petrel, is in his glory, the only thoroughly happy person I see. Today things seem to have settled down a little. One can but hope still. Lincoln or Seward has made such silly advances and then far sillier drawings back. There may be a chance for peace after all. Things are happening so fast. My husband has been made an aide-de-camp to General Beauregard. . . . Governor Means has rummaged a sword and red sash from somewhere and brought it for Colonel Chesnut, who had gone to demand the surrender of Fort Sumter. And now, patience—we must wait.

Why did that green goose Anderson go into Fort Sumter? Then everything began to go wrong. Now they have intercepted a letter from him, urging them to let him surrender. He paints the horrors likely to ensue if they will not. He ought to have thought of all that before he put his head in the hole.

Anderson will not capitulate. Yesterday's was the merriest, maddest dinner we have had yet. Men were audaciously wise and witty. We had an unspoken foreboding that it was to be our last pleasant meeting. Mr. Miles dined with us today. Mrs. Henry King rushed in saying: "The news, I come for the latest news! All the men of the King family are on the island," of which fact she seemed proud.

While she was here our peace negotiator or envoy came in—that is, Mr. Chesnut returned. His interview with Anderson had been deeply interesting, but Mr. Chesnut was not inclined to be communicative. He wanted his dinner. He felt for Anderson and had telegraphed to President Davis for instructions—what answer to give Anderson, etc. He has now gone back to Fort Sumter with additional instructions. When they were about to leave the wharf, A. H. Boykin sprang into the boat in great excitement. He thought himself ill-used, with a likelihood of fighting and he to be left behind!

I do not pretend to go to sleep. How can I? If Anderson does not accept terms at four, the orders are he shall be fired upon. I count four, St. Michael's bells chime out, and I begin to hope. At half past four the heavy booming of a cannon. I sprang out of bed, and on my knees prostrate I prayed as I never prayed before.

There was a sound of stir all over the house, pattering of feet in the corridors. All seemed hurrying one way. I put on my double gown and a shawl and went too. It was to the housetop. The shells were bursting. In the dark I heard a man say, "Waste of ammunition." I knew my husband was rowing a boat somewhere in that dark bay. If Anderson was obstinate, Colonel Chesnut was to order the fort on one side to open fire. Certainly fire had begun. The regular roar of the cannon, there it was. And who could tell what each volley accomplished of death and destruction?

The women were wild there on the housetop. Prayers came from the women and imprecations from the men. And then a shell would light up the scene. Tonight they say the forces are to attempt to land. We watched up there, and everybody wondered that Fort Sumter did not fire a shot. . . .

We hear nothing, can listen to nothing; boom, boom, goes the cannon all the time. The nervous strain is awful, alone in this darkened room.

APRIL 13   Nobody has been hurt after all. How gay we were last night! Reaction after the dread of all the slaughter we thought those dreadful cannon were making. Not even a battery the worse for wear. Fort Sumter has been on fire. Anderson has not yet silenced any of our guns. So the aides, still with swords and red sashes by way of uniform, tell us. But the sound of those guns makes regular meals impossible. None of us goes to table. Tea trays pervade the corridors, going everywhere. Some of the anxious hearts lie on their beds and moan in solitary misery. Mrs. Wigfall and I solace ourselves with tea in my room. These women have all a satisfying faith. "God is on our side," they say. When we are shut in Mrs. Wigfall and I ask, "Why?" "Of course, He hates the Yankees," we are told, "You'll think that well of Him."

Not by one word or look can we detect any change in the demeanor of these Negro servants. Lawrence sits at our door, sleepy and respectful, and profoundly indifferent. So are they all, but they carry it too far. You could not tell that they even heard the awful roar going on in the bay, though it has been dinning in their ears night and day. People talk before them as if they were chairs and tables. They make no sign. Are they stolidly stupid? or wiser than we are; silent and strong, biding their time?

APRIL 15   I did not know that one could live such days of excitement. Some one called: "Come out! There is a crowd coming." A mob it was, indeed, but it was headed by Colonels Chesnut and Manning. The crowd was shouting and showing these two as messengers of good news. They were escorted to Beauregard's headquarters. Fort Sumter had surrendered! Those upon the housetops shouted to us, "The fort is on fire." That had been the story once or twice before. But it is all confusion. Our flag is flying there. Fire engines have been sent for to put out the fire.

Everybody tells you half of something and then rushes off to tell something else or to hear the last news.

In the afternoon Mrs. Preston, Mrs. Joe Heyward, and I drove out around the battery. We were in an open carriage. What a changed scene—the very liveliest crowd I think I ever saw, everybody talking at once. All glasses were still turned on the grim old fort.

"The whole North arose as one man."

WAR NEWS REACHES THE NORTH

April 14–16, 1861
Boston

MARY ASHTON LIVERMORE

*L*ivermore was a social reformer, remembered mostly as editor of a suffragist journal and as an energetic crusader for temperance.

The day after my arrival, came the news that Fort Sumter was attacked, which increased the feverish anxiety. The threats of its bombardment had been discredited, for the North believed the South to be as deeply rooted in attachment to the Union as it knew itself to be. All its high-sounding talk of war was obstinately regarded as empty gasconade, and its military preparations, as the idle bluster of angry disappointment. When, therefore, the telegraph, which had registered for the astounded nation the hourly progress of the bombardment, announced the lowering of the stars and stripes, and the surrender of the beleaguered garrison, the news fell on the land like a thunderbolt. . . .

The next day, April 14, was Sunday. The pulpits thundered with denunciations of the rebellion. Congregations applauded sermons such as were never before heard in Boston, not even from radical preachers. Many of the clergy saw with clear vision, at the very outset, that the real contest was between slavery and freedom; and, with the prophetic instinct of the seer, they predicted the death of slavery as the outcome of the war. . . .

Monday dawned, April 15. Who that saw that day will ever forget it! For now, drowning the exaltations of the triumphant South, louder than their boom of cannon, heard above their clang of bells and blare of trumpets, there rang out the voice of Abraham Lincoln calling for seventy-five thousand volunteers for three months. They were for the protection of Washington and the property of the government. All who were in arms against the country were commanded to return home in twenty days, and Congress was summoned to meet on the 4th of July. This proclamation was like the first peal of a surcharged thundercloud, clearing the murky air. The South received it as a declaration of war, the North as a confession that civil war had begun; and the whole North arose as one man.

Everywhere the drum and fife thrilled the air with their stirring call. Recruiting offices were opened in every city, town, and village. When, on the morning of Tuesday, volunteers began to arrive in Boston, they were escorted by crowds cheering vociferously. Merchants and clerks rushed out from stores, bareheaded, saluting them as they passed. Windows were flung up; and women leaned out into the rain, waving flags and handkerchiefs. Horse-cars and omnibuses halted for the passage of the soldiers, and cheer upon cheer leaped forth from the thronged doors and windows. The multitudes that followed after, and surged along on either side, and ran before in dense and palpitating masses, rent the air with prolonged acclamations.

As the men filed into Faneuil Hall, in solid columns, the enthusiasm knew no bounds. Men, women, and children seethed in a fervid excitement. "God bless it!" uttered my father in tender and devout tone, as he sat beside me in the carriage, leaning heavily forward on his staff with clasped hands. And following the direction of his streaming eyes, and those of the thousands surrounding us, I saw the dear banner of my country, rising higher and higher to the top of the flagstaff, fling out fold after fold to the damp air, and float proudly over the hallowed edifice. Oh, the roar that rang out from ten thousand throats! Old men, with white hair and tearful faces, lifted their hats to the national ensign, and reverently saluted it. Young men greeted it with fierce and wild hurrahs, talking the while in terse Saxon of the traitors of the Confederate States, who had dragged in the dirt this flag of their country, never before dishonored. . . .

That day cartridges were made for the regiments by the hundred thousand. Army rifles were ordered from the Springfield Armory. Fifteen hundred workmen were engaged for the Charlestown Navy Yard. Enlistments of hardy-looking men went on vigorously, and hundreds of wealthy citizens pledged pecuniary aid to the families of the soldiers. Military and professional men tendered their services to the government in its present emergency. The Boston banks offered to loan the state three million six hundred thousand dollars without security, while banks outside the city, throughout the state, were equally generous in their offers. By six o'clock on the afternoon of Tuesday, April 16, three regiments were ready to start for Washington, and new companies were being raised in all parts of the state. On the afternoon of the next day, the Sixth Massachusetts, a full regiment one thousand strong, started from Boston by rail, leaving the Fourth Massachusetts to follow.

An immense concourse of people gathered in the neighborhood of the Boston and Albany railroad station to witness their departure. The great crowd was evidently under the influence of deep feeling, but it was repressed, and the demonstrations were not noisy. In all hands were evening editions of the daily papers; and as the record of the disloyal behavior of Maryland and Virginia was read aloud, the comments were emphatic in disapproval. With the arrival of the uniformed troops, the excitement burst out into a frenzy of shouts, cheers, and ringing acclamation. Tears ran down not only the cheeks of women, but those of men; but there was no faltering. A clergyman mounted an extemporized platform, to offer prayer, where he could be seen and heard by all, and a solemn hush fell on the excited multitude, as if we were inside a church. His voice rang out to the remotest auditor. The long train backed down where the soldiers were scattered among mothers, wives, sweethearts, and friends uttering last words of farewell.

"Fall into line!" was the unfamiliar order that rang out, clear and distinct, with a tone of authority. The blue-coated soldiers released themselves tenderly from the clinging arms of affection, kissed again, and again, and again, the faces upturned to theirs, white with the agony of parting, formed in long lines, company by company, and were marched into the cars. The two locomotives, drawing the long train slowly out of the station, whistled a shrill "good-bye." Every engine in the neighborhood shrieked back an answering farewell. From the crowded streets, the densely packed station, the roofs of houses, the thronged windows, and the solid mass of human beings lining both sides of the track, further than the eye could see, there rang out a roar of good wishes, and parting words, accompanied with tears and sobs, and the waving of hats and handkerchiefs—and the Sixth Massachusetts was on its way to Washington.

"A gasp of surprise and horror . . ."

LINCOLN TEARS THE FLAG

June 29, 1861
Washington, D.C.

JULIA TAFT BAYNE

Julia Taft, Lincoln's niece, was sixteen years old when she witnessed his inauguration as president.

I went with my mother to see [the] new flag raised by President Lincoln [over the White House], the date, according to my diary, being June 29, 1861. Arriving at our destination, we went to the south portico to pay our respects to the "first lady," and were invited to join the group by Mrs. Lincoln.

There comes before my vision the brilliant group of generals and their aides, some members of the Cabinet, the cluster of ladies in hoopskirts and blossoming bonnets, and in the center the tall spare form of the President, so little known and valued then.

When the moment came for the flag to be raised, the Marine Band began the national anthem and all arose, officers at salute, civilians uncovered. When the President pulled the cord, it stuck. He pulled harder, and suddenly the upper corner of the Union tore off and hung down. A gasp of surprise and horror at the sinister omen went around, but a young staff officer, with great presence of mind, stepped quickly to the group of ladies and extending his hand, hissed imploringly, "Pins! Pins!"

They were supplied at once. Women had more pins in their clothes in those days. Mother took two out of her lace collar and some out of her dress. Mrs. Lincoln and the other ladies did the same, and the officer swiftly and efficiently pinned the corner and the flag was raised.

The band had continued to play and the people on the grounds below, standing at attention, did not notice anything untoward except a slight delay in raising the flag. When we reached home and my father heard of the incident, he warned us not to mention the tearing of the stars out of the flag to any one.

"It will be suppressed," he said. "Some people are so superstitious. It might affect enlistments and we must have troops."

In my father's diary is this comment: "Flag raised on the White House. General B. much disturbed by an unfortunate accident. I trust he will keep his discomposure to himself."

But what do you suppose Lincoln thought when he saw nine stars torn from the flag by his hand, who was its chief defender? I think he felt a sharper pang than any of us, but with his mystic nature there was a strange combination of hard common sense. I suppose he just forgot it.

"Turn back! Retreat!"

FIRST BATTLE OF BULL RUN

July 21, 1861
Manassas, Virginia

WILLIAM HOWARD RUSSELL

R ussell *was the celebrated correspondent of the* Times *of London. For this account of one of the war's early battles, he earned a nickname—Bull Run Russell—and the antagonism of many northerners, including Lincoln.*

Centreville appeared in sight—a few houses on our front, beyond which rose a bald hill, the slopes covered with bivouac huts, commissariat carts, and horses, and the top crested with spectators of the fight.

The scene was so peaceful a man might well doubt the evidence of one sense that a great contest was being played out below in bloodshed. . . . But the cannon spoke out loudly from the green bushes, and the plains below were mottled, so to speak, by puffs of smoke and by white rings from bursting shells and capricious howitzers. . . . With the glass I could detect now and then the flash of arms through the dust clouds in the open, but no one could tell to which side the troops who were moving belonged, and I could only judge from the smoke whether the guns were fired towards or away from the hill. In the midst of our little reconnaissance Mr. Vizetelly, who has been living and, indeed, marching with one of the regiments as artist of the *Illustrated London News,* came up and told us the action had been commenced in splendid style by the

Federalists, who had advanced steadily, driving the Confederates before them—a part of the plan, as I firmly believe, to bring them under the range of their guns. He believed the advantages on the Federalist side were decided, though won with hard fighting.

As I turned down into the narrow road, or lane, there was a forward movement among the large four-wheeled tilt waggons, when suddenly there arose a tumult in front of me at a small bridge across the road, and then I perceived the drivers of a set of waggons with the horses turned towards me, who were endeavouring to force their way against the stream of vehicles setting in the other direction. By the side of the new set of waggons there were a number of commissariat men and soldiers, whom at first sight I took to be the baggage guard. They looked excited and alarmed and were running by the side of the horses—in front the dust quite obscured the view. At the bridge the currents met in wild disorder. "Turn back! Retreat!" shouted the men from the front, "We're whipped, we're whipped!" They cursed and tugged at the horses' heads, and struggled with frenzy to get past.

I got my horse up into the field out of the road, and went on rapidly towards the front. Soon I met soldiers who were coming through the corn, mostly without arms; and presently I saw firelocks, cooking tins, knapsacks, and greatcoats on the ground, and observed that the confusion and speed of the baggage-carts became greater, and that many of them were crowded with men, or were followed by others, who clung to them. The ambulances were crowded with soldiers, but it did not look as if there were many wounded. Negro servants on led horses dashed frantically past; men in uniform, whom it were a disgrace to the profession of arms to call "soldiers," swarmed by on mules, chargers, and even draught horses, which had been cut out of carts or waggons, and went on with harness clinging to their heels, as frightened as their riders. Men literally screamed with rage and fright when their way was blocked up. On I rode, asking all "What is all this about?" and now and then, but rarely, receiving the answer, "We're whipped;" or, "We're repulsed." Faces black and dusty, tongues out in the heat, eyes staring—it was a most wonderful sight.

All the road from Centreville for miles presented such a sight as can only be witnessed in the track of the runaways of an utterly demoralized army. Drivers flogged, lashed, spurred, and beat their horses, or leaped down and abandoned their teams, and ran by the side of the road; mounted men, servants, and men in uniform, vehicles of all sorts, commissariat waggons thronged the narrow ways. At every shot a convulsion as it were seized upon the morbid mass of bones, sinew, wood, and iron, and thrilled through it, giving new energy and action to its desperate efforts to get free from itself. . . . The Federalists, utterly routed, had fallen back upon Arlington to defend the capital, leaving nearly five batteries of artillery, 8,000 muskets, immense quantity of stores and baggage, and their wounded and prisoners in the hands of the enemy!

"Fifty members sprang to their feet . . ."

THE CONFEDERATE CONGRESS

1862–1863
Richmond, Virginia

REUBEN DAVIS

D *avis was a Mississippi lawyer who had served in the U.S. Congress from 1857 to 1861, then became a member of the Confederate Congress.*
The Confederate capital moved from Montgomery, Alabama, to Richmond, Virginia, in July 1861.

Thus dawned upon Richmond and the South the morning of the 22d of February [1862], appointed for the ceremonial of inauguration and the meeting of the two houses of Congress. . . .

I have been often spoken of as a man of an over-sanguine temperament, prone to see things through the medium of my hopes rather than of my fears, but I will confess that at this time I could not be accused of any undue cheerfulness of spirit. Every step taken up to that time had been, as I thought, defeated by tardiness of movement and inadequate preparation, and I could discover no indications of an improved system for the future.

In a conversation which I had about this time with Mr. [Judah] Benjamin, the secretary of war, he said to me, "There is no doubt that the Southern Confederacy will be recognized by England in ninety days, and that ends the war." I asked him if he would not, in the meantime, make vigorous preparations, and endeavor to drive the enemy out of Tennessee.

He replied that it was wholly unnecessary. I then said that even if recognition by England was certain, and that it would certainly end the war, there might be grave questions to be considered, and grave consequences to be provided for. As for example, if the peace should be declared, each party would, of course, claim all the territory held when the war closed. Was Mr. Benjamin prepared to give up Tennessee and Kentucky?

This answer was, "We shall hold from the Memphis and Charleston Road south, and the Northern States can keep what is north of that line." I was astonished by this reply, and told him plainly that if we could hope for no better result than he promised, I, for one, would rather go back in the Union without further bloodshed.

Speaker Bocock was prompt in reporting committees, and I was put upon the military committee. . . . After a few days, I discovered, with sincere regret, that I could not honestly declare myself in harmony with the other members of the committee or with the administration. There was a radical and irreconcilable difference in our views upon all the questions and measures of the war. This sprang from the fact that I was for a bold, aggressive policy, while they advocated caution and delay.

I believed that our only hope was to concentrate all the forces we could raise into two great invading columns, and then boldly carry the war into the enemy's country. I argued that it depended largely upon which side took the initiative steps, which section should be invaded, wasted, and destroyed.

Other members of the committee were confident that the war would be ended in ninety days, and they were opposed to what they considered useless expense. The cry of the demagogue rang long and loud, "The poor people must not be taxed." This is a favorite watchword for those who court popularity, and I have heard it used with some success both before and since that time.

Realizing this condition of affairs, I made application to the House to be relieved from further connection with the committee, upon the ground that I was an obstacle to its progress. I was excused, and had not afterwards any connection with any committee. . . .

In the fall of 1863 [actually 1862] a bill was introduced into the House, exempting from military service any man who owned twenty negroes. It was referred to a committee, and reported back favorably, and a speech of half an hour in length made in support of the bill.

I replied in a speech of the same length in opposition.

I then called for the ayes and noes. The call was granted as a favor to me, and, perhaps, in some derision of the foreseen result. I was very earnest in my opposition to the bill, and warned the House that to pass such a measure would be to disband the army. My vote was the only one cast against it, the House voting for it with some clamor and vociferation. There was some laughter over my isolated stand-point, but I said, "Laugh on, my merry gentlemen, in a short time you will laugh on the wrong side of your faces!"

A few members afterwards changed their votes to "No." The effect of the bill was just what might have been anticipated. No sooner was the news carried to the army than the soldiers became infuriated. The officers had great difficulty in keeping the army together until Congress could meet and repeal the obnoxious law.

I remember well what a scene we had when Congress met, and the Speaker announced the House ready for business. Fifty members sprang to their feet, and offered resolutions to repeal this law, each eager to be before all others in his recantation. The Speaker recognized Mr. Dowdle, of Alabama, sent from some point on the Coosa River. The rules were suspended, and the resolution hastily passed.

It was my turn to laugh then.

"Such a craft as the eyes of a seaman never looked upon before."

BATTLE OF THE IRONCLADS: THE *MERRIMACK* VERSUS THE *MONITOR*

March 9, 1862
Hampton Roads, Virginia

CAPTAIN G. J. VAN BRUNT, U.S.N., AND LIEUTENANT JAMES H. ROCHELLE, C.S.N.

The Merrimack *fought for the South, the* Monitor *for the North. The* Merrimack, *originally a Union ship, had been captured by the South and fitted with iron plates to make it "invincible." (It had also been renamed the* Virginia, *a name that lacks the alliteration we remember today.) The innovative ironclad seemed to give the South a deadly advantage. It quickly won its first battles, with the* Cumberland *and* Congress, *and ran the* Minnesota *aground.*

But in the North inventor John Ericsson had also been building an ironclad ship, from scratch. The odd-looking Monitor *chugged to the rescue of the* Minnesota. *It was little more than a floating gun turret, but it was a match for the* Merrimack. *They fought to a draw. The* Monitor *had to retreat when its captain was partially blinded, but it had saved the* Minnesota.

Captain Van Brunt was commander of the Minnesota. *Lieutenant Rochelle served on the* Patrick Henry, *a Confederate ship that also fought in the battle. (He refers to the* Merrimack *as the* Virginia.*)*

VAN BRUNT

On Saturday, the 8th instant, at 19:45 P.M., three small steamers, in appearance, were discovered rounding Sewell's Point, and as soon as they came into full broadside view I was convinced that one was the iron-plated steam battery *Merrimack,* from the large size of her smoke pipe. They were heading for Newport News, and I immediately called all hands, slipped my cables, and got underway for that point to engage her. While rapidly passing Sewell's Point the rebels there opened fire upon us from a rifle battery, one shot from which going through and crippling my mainmast. I returned the fire with my broadside guns and forecastle pivot. We ran without further difficulty within about 10 miles of Newport News, and there, unfortunately, grounded. The tide was running ebb, and although in the channel, there was not sufficient water for this ship, which draws 23 feet. I knew that the bottom was soft and lumpy, and endeavored to force the ship over, but found it impossible so to do.

At this time it was reported to me that the *Merrimack* had passed the frigate *Congress* and run into the sloop of war *Cumberland,* and in fifteen minutes after I saw the latter going down by the head. The *Merrimack* then hauled off, taking a position, and about 2:30 P.M. engaged the *Congress,* throwing shot and shell into her with terrific effect, while the shot from the *Congress* glanced from her iron-plated sloping sides without doing any apparent damage. At 3:30 P.M. the *Congress* was compelled to haul down her colors.

At 4 P.M. the *Merrimack, Jamestown,* and *Patrick Henry* bore down upon my vessel. Very fortunately the iron battery drew too much water to come within a mile of us. She took a position on my starboard bow, but did not fire with accuracy, and only one shot passed through the ship's bow.

The other two steamers took their position on my port bow and stern, and their fire did most damage in killing and wounding men, inasmuch as they fired with rifled guns; but with the heavy gun that I could bring to bear upon them I drove them off, one of them apparently in a crippled condition. I fired upon the *Merrimack* with my pivot 10-inch gun without apparent effect, and at 7 P.M. she too hauled off, and all three vessels steamed toward Norfolk. The tremendous firing of my broadside guns had crowded me farther upon the mud bank, into which the ship seemed to have made for herself a cradle. From 10 P.M., when the tide commenced to run flood until 4 A.M., I had all hands at work with steam tugs and hawsers, endeavoring to haul the ship off of the bank but without avail, and, as the tide had then fallen considerably, I suspended further operations at that time. At 2 A.M. the iron battery *Monitor,* Commander [Lieutenant] John L. Worden, which had arrived the previous evening at Hampton Roads, came alongside and reported for duty, and then all on board felt that we had a friend that would stand by us in our hour of trial.

ROCHELLE

The night after the battle the Confederate squadron anchored under Sewell's Point, at the mouth of Norfolk Harbor. There was little time for slumber that night, as the conflict was to be renewed the next morning, and it was necessary to make many repairs and preparations. About midnight a column of fire ascended in the darkness, followed by a terrific explosion. The Federal frigate *Congress,* which had been on fire all the evening had blown up, the fire having reached her magazine.

At the first peep of dawn on the 9th of March the Confederate squadron was underway, it having been determined to destroy the *Minnesota,* that vessel being still aground near Newport News. As the daylight increased the *Minnesota* was discovered in her old position, but the *Minnesota* was not the only thing to attract attention. Close alongside of her there lay such a craft as the eyes of a seaman never looked upon before— an immense shingle floating on the water, with a gigantic cheese box rising from its center; no sails, no wheels, no smokestack, no guns. What could it be? On board the *Patrick Henry* many were the surmises as to the strange craft. Some thought it a water tank sent to supply the *Minnesota* with water; others were of opinion that it was a floating magazine replenishing her exhausted stock of ammunition; a few visionary characters feebly intimated that it might be the *Monitor* which the Northern papers had been boasting about for a long time.

All doubts about the stranger were soon dispelled. As the *Virginia* steamed down upon the *Minnesota* the cheese box and shingle steamed out to meet her. It was indeed the *Monitor,* and then and there commenced the first combat that had ever taken place between ironclads. The *Patrick Henry* and the other wooden vessels took little part in the events of the day, except to exchange shots with the *Monitor* at long range as she passed and repassed during her maneuvering with the *Virginia.*

VAN BRUNT

At 6 a.m. the enemy again appeared, coming down from Craney Island, and I beat to quarters, but they ran past my ship and were heading for Fortress Monroe, and the retreat was beaten to allow my men to get something to eat. The *Merrimack* ran down near to the Rip Raps, and then turned into the channel through which I had come. Again all hands were called to quarters, and when she approached within a mile of us I opened upon her with my stern guns and made signal to the *Monitor* to attack the enemy. She immediately ran down in my wake, right within the range of the *Merrimack,* completely covering my ship as far as was possible with her dimensions, and, much to my astonishment, laid herself right alongside of the *Merrimack,* and the contrast was that of a pigmy to a giant. Gun after gun was fired by the *Monitor,* which was returned with whole broadsides from the rebels with no more effect, apparently, than so many pebble-stones thrown by a child. After awhile they commenced maneuvering, and we could see the little battery point her bow for the rebels, with the intention, as I thought, of sending a shot through her bow porthole; then she would shoot by her and rake her through her stern.

In the meantime the rebel was pouring broadside after broadside, but almost all her shot flew over the little submerged propeller, and when they struck the bombproof tower the shot glanced off without producing any effect, clearly establishing the fact that wooden vessels can not contend successfully with ironclad ones; for never before was anything like it dreamed of by the greatest enthusiast in maritime warfare. The *Merrimack,* finding that she could make nothing of the *Monitor,* turned her attention once more to me. . . . By the time she had fired her third shell the little *Monitor* had come down upon her, placing herself between us, and compelled her to change her position, in doing which she grounded, and again I poured into her all the guns which could be brought to bear upon her. As soon as she got off she stood down the bay, the little battery chasing her with all speed, when suddenly the *Merrimack* turned around and ran full speed into her antagonist. For a moment I was anxious, but instantly I saw a shot plunge into the iron roof of the *Merrimack,* which surely must have damaged her. For some time after the rebels concentrated their whole battery upon the tower and pilot house of the *Monitor,* and soon after the latter stood down for Fortress Monroe, and we thought it probable she had exhausted her supply of ammunition or sustained some injury.

"I think the time has come now."

LINCOLN PROCLAIMS EMANCIPATION

September 22, 1862
Washington, D.C.

SALMON P. CHASE

*W*hen Lincoln first became president, he made a point of deferring to the experienced politicians he had gathered for his cabinet. But he soon learned that some decisions had to be made alone and that he had more resolve than the prominent leaders who had earlier left him in awe.

Chase was Lincoln's secretary of the Treasury.

To department about nine. State Department messenger came with notice to heads of departments to meet at twelve. Received sundry callers. Went to the White House. All the members of the Cabinet were in attendance. There was some general talk, and the President mentioned that Artemus Ward had sent him his book. Proposed to read a chapter which he thought very funny. Read it, and seemed to enjoy it very much. . . .

The President then took a graver tone, and said: "Gentlemen, I have, as you are aware, thought a great deal about the relation of this war to slavery, and you all remember that, several weeks ago, I read to you an order I had prepared upon the subject, which, on account of objections made by some of you, was not issued. Ever since then my mind has been much occupied with this subject, and I have thought all along that the time for acting on it might probably come. I think the time has come now. I wish it was a better time. I wish that we were in a better condition. The action of the army against the rebels has not been quite what I should have best liked. But they have been driven out of Maryland, and Pennsylvania is no longer in danger of invasion. When the rebel army was at Frederick I determined, as soon as it should be driven out of Maryland, to issue a proclamation of emancipation, such as I thought most likely to be useful. I said nothing to any one, but I made a promise to myself and (hesitating a little) to my Maker. The rebel army is now driven out, and I am going to fulfill that promise. I have got you together to hear what I have written down. I do not wish your advice about the main matter, for that I have determined for myself. This I say without intending any thing but respect for any one of you. But I already know the views of each on this question. They have been heretofore expressed, and I have considered them as thoroughly and carefully as I can. What I have written is that which my reflections have determined me to say. If there is any thing in the expressions I use or in any minor matter which any one of you thinks had best be changed, I shall be glad to receive your suggestions. One other observation I will make. I know very well that many others might, in this matter as in others, do better than I can; and if I was satisfied that the public confidence was more fully possessed by any one of them than by me, and knew of any constitutional way in which he could be put in my place, he should have it. I would gladly yield it to him. But though I believe that I have not so much of the confidence of the people as I had some time since, I do not know that, all things considered, any other person has more; and, however this may be, there is no way in which I can have any other man put where I am. I am here. I must do the best I can, and bear the responsibility of taking the course which I feel I ought to take."

The President then proceeded to read his Emancipation Proclamation.

**"The staid old town of Wilmington
was turned topsy-turvy."**

ADVENTURES OF A BLOCKADE RUNNER

1862
Wilmington, North Carolina

CAPTAIN JOHN WILKINSON, C.S.N.

*B*lockade running was essential to the Rebel war effort because the undersupplied South needed to sneak goods from Europe through the ports controlled by the Union. It did so with great ingenuity.

Wilkinson had been a U.S. navy officer when the war began. He joined the Confederate navy and served it in many roles.

Although the shifting sands of the North Carolina coast have rendered obsolete many of Wilkinson's nautical reference points, downtown Wilmington still shows signs of the city's Civil War prominence.

The natural advantages of Wilmington for blockade-running were very great, chiefly owing to the fact that there are two separate and distinct approaches to Cape Fear River, i.e., either by "New Inlet" to the north of Smith's Island, or by the "western bar" to the south of it.

From Smithville, a little village nearly equidistant from either bar, both blockading fleets could be distinctly seen, and the outward bound blockade-runners could take their choice through which of them to run the gauntlet. The inward bound blockade-runners, too, were guided by circumstances of wind and weather; selecting that bar over which they would cross, after they had passed the Gulf Stream.

Upon one occasion, while in command of the *R. E. Lee,* we had experienced very heavy and thick weather; and had crossed the Stream and struck soundings about midday. The weather then clearing so that we could obtain an altitude near meridian we found ourselves at least forty miles north of our supposed position and near the shoals which extend in a southerly direction off Cape Lookout. It would be more perilous to run out to sea than to continue on our course, for we had passed through the off shore line of blockaders, and the sky had become perfectly clear. I decided to impersonate a [U.S. Navy] transport bound to Beaufort, which was in the possession of the United States forces, and the coaling station of the fleet blockading Wilmington. The risk of detection was not very great, for many of the captured blockade-runners were used as transports and dispatch vessels. Shaping our course for Beaufort, and slowing down, as we were in no haste to get there, we passed several vessels, showing United States colors to them all. Just as we were crossing through the ripple of shallow water off the "tail" of the shoals, we dipped our colors to a sloop of war which passed three or four miles to the south of us. The courtesy was promptly responded to; but I have no doubt her captain thought me a lubberly and careless seaman to shave the shoals so closely. We stopped the engines when no vessel was in sight; and I was relieved from a heavy burden of anxiety as the sun sank below the horizon; and the course was shaped at full speed for Masonboro' Inlet. . . .

. . . A blockade-runner did not often pass through the fleet without receiving one or more shots, but these were always preceded by the flash of a calcium light, or by a blue light; and immediately followed by two rockets thrown in the direction of the blockade-runner. I ordered a lot of rockets from New York. Whenever all hands were called to run through the fleet, an officer was stationed alongside of me on the bridge with the rockets. One or two minutes after our immediate pursuer had sent up his rockets, I would direct ours to be discharged at a right angle to our course. The whole fleet would be misled, for even if the vessel which had discovered us were not deceived, the rest of the fleet would be baffled.

The staid old town of Wilmington was turned "topsy turvy" during the war. Here resorted the speculators from all parts of the South, to attend the weekly auctions of imported cargoes; and the town was infested with rogues and desperadoes, who made a livelihood by robbery and murder. . . . The agents and employees of the different blockade-running companies, lived in magnificent style, paying a king's ransom (in Confederate money) for their household expenses, and nearly monopolizing the supplies in the country market.

"I will give you half an hour
to show yourself a great general . . ."

GETTYSBURG

July 1–3, 1863

GENERAL ALFRED PLEASONTON AND ANONYMOUS *NEW YORK WORLD* REPORTER

*I*t was the turning point of the war, but it could have been the end. Had Robert E. Lee won, he was close enough to Washington, D.C., to attack the city and perhaps capture it.

Had the Union's General George Meade advanced on Lee's retreating army, he might have finished the Confederacy. Not only did he fail to advance quickly at the end of the battle, he ignored the opportunity when Lee's army was trapped on the banks of the flooding Potomac. Perhaps he was unsure of himself, having gained command of the Union troops just three days before the battle, when he replaced Joseph Hooker.

At Gettysburg, the Union lost about thirty-two hundred men and had about twenty thousand wounded or missing. The Confederacy lost about thirty-nine hundred and had about twenty-four thousand wounded or missing. The worst of the carnage came at the end, when Lee ordered a charge on the Union's center at Cemetery Ridge. Led by Major General George Pickett, about fifteen thousand men stormed forward through a valley, only to be mowed down by the entrenched Union forces on the hills around them. Less than half survived.

Pleasonton was commander of the Cavalry Corps of the Army of the Potomac.

PLEASONTON

The general line of march of the army was too much to the east for a rapid concentration on Gettysburg, and believing that General Lee understood the advantages of that position as well as I did, I was determined to occupy it first. I, therefore, ordered [General John] Buford, with the first division of cavalry, to move from Middletown to Gettysburg, and to hold that position at all hazards until the army could support him. In obedience to these orders, Buford arrived at Gettysburg on the afternoon of June 30th, and obtaining information that Lee was in force on the Cashtown road, he moved out on that road some four miles beyond Gettysburg, and encamped for the night. Early next morning General A. P. Hill attacked him in force, but the nature of the ground was such that Buford, with his splendid fighting, restrained the superior force against him and saved the position to the Army of the Potomac. . . . Buford's judgment in believing he would be attacked in heavy force on the morning of the 1st of July, and going out four miles to meet it the night before, was what saved to us the position. Had he waited an attack at Gettysburg, he would have been driven from the place before any support could have arrived.

NEW YORK WORLD

The battles of Wednesday and yesterday were sufficiently terrible, but in that which has raged today the fighting done, not only by our troops, but by those of Lee's army, will rank in heroism, in perseverance, and in savage energy with that of Waterloo.

The position of Lee at the close of last evening was such that he was forced today to reduce all his energies into one grand, desperate, and centralized attempt to break through our army.

. . . The engagement began by an assault by our troops upon some rifle-pits on the extreme right, which were left in the possession of the enemy last evening. Their fire was returned by the rebels, and the fight immediately became general. Until nearly noon the battle raged without intermission, but with no loss to us, when we finally obtained possession of the rifle-pits—the rebel force which had previously held them retreating. The firing then slackened, but at one-o'clock was renewed at different points along the line with a fierceness premonitory of the terrific engagement that ensued.

Several charges were made by the rebels as feints, their troops falling back after the first rush in every part of the field, except that held by their forces under Gen. Ewell, who was seen to concentrate the infantry and artillery together, and who soon opened a murderous fire of cannon on our left centre. Then the engagement began in earnest. The firing became a continuous roar; battery after battery was discharged with a swiftness amazing; yell on yell from the rebels succeeded each gust of shot and shell, until the valley, overhung with smoke from whence these horrible sounds issued, seemed alive with demons. It appeared at times as though not a foot of air was free from the hail of missiles that tore over and through our ranks, thinned but not shaken. Our men stood the shock with a courage sublime—an endurance so wonderful as to dim even the heroic record of the band that fell upon the acre of Tourney. The corps upon which this deadly fire was mainly directed was the Second, the position being commanded by Gen. Hayes.

The artillery fire continued without intermission for three hours, when suddenly, having been formed under cover of the smoke of their own guns, the rebel troops were hurled against our lines by their officers in masses the very tread of whose feet shook the declivity up which they came, with cries that might have caused less dauntless troops than those who waited the onset to break with terror. Not a man in the Federal ranks flinched from his position. Not an eye turned to the right or left in search of security, not a hand trembled as the long array of our heroes grasped their muskets at a charge, and waited the order to fire.

On and up came the enemy, hooting, crowding, showing their very teeth in the venom of their rage until within thirty yards of our cannon. As the turbulent mass of gray uniforms, of flashing bayonets and gleaming eyes, lifted itself in a last leap forward almost to the very mouths of our guns, a volley of shot, shell, shrapnel, and bullets went crashing through it, levelling it as a scythe. Its overwhelming onward rush was in the next instant turned to the hesitating leap forward of a few soldiers more daredevil than the rest, the wild bounding upwards of more than a few mortally wounded heroes, and the succeeding backward surge of the disjointed remainder, which culminated in a scamper down the slope that was in some instances retarded by the pursuing bullets of our men.

The carnage of this assault among the rebels was so fearful that even the Federal soldiers who rested on their arms triumphant, after the foe had retreated beyond their fire, as they cast their eyes downward upon the panorama of death and wounds illuminated by the sun that shown upon the slope before them, were seen to shudder and turn sickening away.

PLEASONTON

The battle of Gettysburg was over, and in speaking of the subsequent events of the campaign, I do so with reluctance. I was in the position to form a correct opinion of the failure of the army to follow General Lee, having been the constant companion of General Meade from the time he assumed the command at Frederick City. In justice to the General, I can state he did not desire the command, and considered it hazardous to change commanders at that time, and his position was far more difficult than it would have been had he been assigned the command at the commencement of the campaign. Personally very brave, an excellent corps commander, General Meade had not that grasp of mind, when thrown into a new and responsible position, to quickly comprehend and decide upon important events as they occurred. He required time to come to a decision, and this indulgence an active campaign never allows to a commanding general. From the time he assumed command of the army until after the battle of Gettysburg, the most important events were occurring with such rapidity, and with such resistless force, that his decisions were the consequences of these events rather than the operations of his individual intelligence.

From the suddenness of the repulse of the last charge on July 3rd, it became necessary for General Meade to decide at once what to do. I rode up to him, and, after congratulating him on the splendid conduct of the army, I said: "General, I will give you half an hour to show yourself a great general. Order the army to advance, while I will take the cavalry, get in Lee's rear, and we will finish the campaign in a week." He replied: "How do you know Lee will not attack me again; we have done well enough." I replied that Lee had exhausted all his available men; that the cannonade of the two last days had exhausted his ammunition; he was far from his base of supplies; and, by compelling him to keep his army together, they must soon surrender, for he was living on the country. To this the General did not reply, but asked me to ride up to the Round Top with him; and as we rode along the ridge for nearly a mile, the troops cheered him in a manner that plainly showed they expected the advance. When we reached the Round Top everything was still in Lee's position with the exception of a single battery which was firing upon some of our skirmishers to prevent their advancing. I was so impressed with the idea that Lee was retreating that I again earnestly urged General Meade to advance the army; but instead of doing so, he ordered me to send some cavalry to ascertain the fact. Gregg's Division of cavalry started soon after, and at eight o'clock the next morning I received his report, stating that he was twenty-two miles on the Cashtown road, and that the enemy was not only retreating, but it was a rout, the road being encumbered with wounded and wagons in the greatest confusion.

On this report the two other divisions of cavalry were sent to intercept and harass Lee in crossing the Potomac; but the Army of the Potomac did not leave Gettysburg for four or five days after, and then passed by the way of South Mountain to the Antietam creek. In consequence of heavy rains the Potomac river was so much swollen that Lee could not cross, and the two armies were again brought face to face for two days. General Meade declined to attack, and Lee's army escaped.

"Is that all?"

LINCOLN DELIVERS THE GETTYSBURG ADDRESS

November 19, 1863
Gettysburg, Pennsylvania

JOHN RUSSELL YOUNG

The Gettysburg Address was rated by its first audience as a dud. Edward Everett, the popular orator who held the stage before Lincoln spoke, was one of the few who immediately saw its brilliance. He later sent the president a short note: "I should be glad if I could flatter myself that I came as near to the central idea of the occasion in two hours as you did in two minutes."

John Russell Young attended the Gettysburg ceremony, held eighteen weeks after the battle, as a correspondent for the Philadelphia Press. *Just twenty-four at the time (which may account for his impertinent question), he went on to a distinguished career in journalism, then became U.S. minister to China and later the Librarian of Congress. He wrote this account in his memoirs in 1901.*

When we arrived the rainy afternoon settled into a soggy November night. Gettysburg was in chaos over the new invasion, and a corner in a tavern was a crowning mercy. The Presidential party came in about sunset, and we were all on hand to do them honor. They were a straggled, hungry set. Lincoln, with that weary smile, which a poet might have read as a forecast of destiny; Seward, with an essentially bad hat; John Hay, in

attendance upon the President, and much to be troubled by the correspondents, handsome as a peach, the countenance of extreme youth. . . .

Lincoln became invisible to us, and could not be enticed even by serenading parties, who were bewildering the night with music. Seward was
more amenable, and as he came to the door I recall my trouble in reporting him. Nothing better than the note book and a stone step.

I think I was indebted to John Hay, assuredly to some kind friend for a
special audience with Edward Everett. We of this generation do not realize the space which Edward Everett filled, at least in the imagination of
the younger men. He was the embodiment of a noble and stainless fame.
Webster, Clay, Calhoun gone, he was the last of the orators. No more
great men left to us, only Everett. He had welcomed Lafayette; his schol-
arship was our envy and admiration; he had been the friend of Byron, the
guest of Walter Scott, Minister to England, Secretary of State, and we,
even we were permitted to see him.

The procession from the town was a ragged affair, we all seeming to
get there as best we could. A regiment of cavalry, a regiment of infantry, a
couple of batteries clattering about, added to the confusion, and not
much to the dignity of the day. . . .

It was about 11, as I recall it, when we got under way—cavalry, soldiers, statesmen, governors from other States, wounded soldiers, country
folks who knew all about the battle, and teeming with narratives of its
horror and glory. . . .

A rude platform looked out over the battlefield. On one side sat the
journalists. The eminent people had the other side, the President coming
late. There was some little trouble over a Democratic reporter who did
not admire Lincoln, and insisted upon standing near the front with his hat
on and smoking a cigar, and jeering now and then at the ceremonies. No
judicious remonstrance had effect, the reporter claiming his rights in a
free country; even the right to stand around with his hat on and smoke
whenever and wherever he pleased. A summary proposition to treat
him after the manner of Daniel, and throw him over the rails among the
lions, adjusted that incident, and there was nothing unseemly to disturb
the President's reception. As he slowly came up the steps with his famous
company we arose, and as he took his seat there were loud voices of
welcome.

Everett spoke for two hours and was heard with the deepest attention. There was little applause—no invitation to applause. I felt as I
looked at the orator as if he was some antique Greek statue, so finished,
so beautiful, so chaste, so cold, the lines so perfect, the exquisite tracery
of the divine manhood—all there—all evolved and rescued from stone—

the masterful art, something that you ever dwell upon with freshening wonder at the capacity of human genius. But so cold! If it were only alive!

When Everett ceased, exhausted, excited, the two hours talk telling on him, there was a moment of rustle, hands extended in congratulation, the President and Secretary of State among the first, then loving hands carefully enfolding and wrapping him up in shelter from the insidious purposes of the cold November air. The music ran on a bit and the President arose. Deliberate, hesitating, awkward, "like a telescope drawing out," as I heard some one say, the large, bundled up figure untwisting and adjusting itself into reasonable conditions. I do not recall Lincoln as in appearance an imposing man—but impressive. You would turn and look at him a second time on the street. And there was that in his face when you looked closely that might well give one pause—a deep, unfathomable sense of power. He stood an instant waiting for the cheers to cease and the music to exhaust its echoes, slowly adjusted his glasses, and took from his pocket what seemed to be a page of ordinary foolscap paper, quietly unfolded it, looked for the place, and began to read.

My own personal anxieties at the moment were as to whether he would or would not make a speech. I had an easy time with Stockton [the chaplain] and Everett; prayer and oration in type. But what would the President do? My outing was in the hands of Lincoln. Would he speak an hour? Would he speak from notes and memory or read his address? An extempore effort meant a long evening transcribing notes and no Gettysburg battlefield, no useful afternoon of the solemn study of a mighty drama—aught else, for that matter, but close work in a dingy tavern. I am afraid I pestered Hay on the subject for an advance sight of the manuscript, were there one; but Hay, ever generous and helpful, as I remember, either knew no more than I did or would not tell me. So when the President arose there was my uncertainty. I took up the pencil and began to take him in shorthand. The sight of the single sheet of paper was not reassuring. It could only hold the heads or threads of a discourse—a text as it were—and the outing over the battlefield dissolved into the gray wintry skies. Therefore the emotions with which I took down this immortal address were entirely selfish. To my surprise, almost it seemed before Mr. Lincoln had begun to speak, he turned and sat down. Surely these five or six lines of shorthand were not all. Hurriedly bending over the aisle I asked if that was all. "Yes, for the present," he answered. He did not think he could say any more.

Lincoln, as I was saying, when he arose, adjusted his glasses, and, taking out the single sheet of paper, held it close to his face. He began at once in a high key, voice archaic, strident, almost in a shriek. He spoke slowly, with deliberation, reading straight on. I did not write the report which appeared in the *Press,* as the manuscript had been given to the Associated Press, and the transcription of my notes was unnecessary. This report was studded with "applause," but I do not remember the applause, and am afraid the appreciative reporter was more than generous—may have put in the applause himself as a personal expression of opinion. Nor in fact was there any distinct emotion among those around me on the platform after the prayer, and when Lincoln was speaking, but one of sympathy for the forlorn photographer who failed to take his picture. This enterprising artist, by dint of persuasion and making interest with the crowd, had managed to place his camera in front of the President. And as he began to speak the workman began his work, peeping through his lenses, adjusting them, dodging his head to catch a favorable position, fooling with the cloth that covered the lens, staring wistfully at the President, in the hope to make him "look pleasant" in true photographic fashion. But the President was not a good subject. Whether conscious or not of the honor thus impending, he drove on with his speech, ever holding the paper before the face, the dismayed photographer vainly hoping for one glimpse of the face. And as the President summarily turned to sit down, he desperately uncovered the camera, but too late! The flash of sunshine brought him nothing. There was a general ripple of laughter at his dismay.

I have read many narratives of the scenes, of the emotions produced by the President's address, the transcendent awe that fell upon every one who heard those most mighty and ever living words to be remembered with pride through the ages. I have read of the tears that fell and the solemn hush, as though in a cathedral solemnity in the most holy moment of the sacrifice. There was nothing of this, to the writer at least, in the Gettysburg address. Nor were the conditions such as to invite it. The long oration of Everett had made people restless. Bits of the crowd had broken away and were wandering off toward the battle scenes. We were tired and chilly, and even the November sun did not take the place of the heavy wraps. Lincoln, as I said, began at once in a high, strident key, as one who had little to say, and would say it so as to be heard and seen.

"No escape except by death . . ."

ANDERSONVILLE PRISON

July 3–September 7, 1864
Andersonville, Georgia

JOHN L. RANSOM

*T*he infamous Confederate prison at Andersonville held more than 30,000 prisoners at its peak. Almost 13,000 of them died because of the deliberate short-
ages of food, clean water, and medical care. The commander, Captain Henry Wirz,
was tried and executed as a war criminal soon after the war ended.

Andersonville was an extreme case, but prisons in both the North and the
South were horrible. In all, the rebels held about 194,000 Union prisoners, of
which more than 36,000 died. The Union held about 220,000 rebels, of which
more than 30,000 died. The North refused prisoner exchanges for a time, believing
exchanges would benefit the undermanned Confederate army more than the Union
army.

John L. Ransom was brigade quartermaster of the Ninth Michigan Cavalry
when he was captured in Tennessee, in the autumn of 1863, shortly before Andersonville was built. He almost died of illness in the prison, but eventually received a
furlough to a southern hospital, where he was nursed back to health.

July 3. Three hundred and fifty new men from West Virginia were
turned into this summer resort this morning. They brought good news as
to successful termination of the war, and they also caused war after coming among us. As usual, the raiders [some fellow Union prisoners] proceeded to rob them of their valuables, and a fight occurred in which
hundreds were engaged. The cutthroats came out ahead. Complaints
were made to Captain Wirz that this thing would be tolerated no longer;
that these raiders must be put down, or the men would rise in their
might and break away if assistance was not given with which to preserve
order.

Wirz flew around as if he had never thought of it before, issued an
order to the effect that no more food would be given us until the leaders
were arrested and taken outside for trial. The greatest possible excitement—hundreds that have before been neutral and noncommittal are now
joining a police force; captains are appointed to take charge of the squads,

which have been furnished with clubs by Wirz. As I write, this, the middle of the afternoon, the battle rages.

The police go right to raider headquarters, knock right and left, and make their arrests. Sometimes the police are whipped and have to retreat, but they rally their forces and again make a charge in which they are successful.

Can lay in our shade and see the trouble go on. Must be killing some by the shouting. The raiders fight for their very life and are only taken after being thoroughly whipped. The stockade is loaded with guards who are fearful of a break. I wish I could describe the scene today. A number killed. After each arrest a great cheering takes place.

Night. Thirty or forty have been taken outside of the worst characters in camp, and still the good work goes on. No food today and don't want any. A big strapping fellow called "Limber Jim" heads the police. Grand old Michael Hoare is at the front and goes for a raider as quick as he would a Rebel. Patrol the camp all the time and gradually quieting down. The orderly prisoners are feeling jolly.

July 4. The men taken outside yesterday are under Rebel guard and will be punished. The men are thoroughly aroused, and now that the matter has been taken in hand, it will be followed up to the letter. . . .

July 5. Court is in session outside and raiders being tried by our own men. Wirz has done one good thing, but it's a question whether he is entitled to any credit, as he had to be threatened with a break before he would assist us. Rations again today. I am quite bad off with my diseases, but still there are so many thousands so much worse off that I do not complain much, or try not to however.

July 6. Boiling hot, camp reeking with filth, and no sanitary privileges; men dying off over 140 per day. Stockade enlarged, taking in eight or ten more acres, giving us more room, and stumps to dig up for wood to cook with. Mike Hoare is in good health; not so Jimmy Devers. Jimmy has now been a prisoner over a year and, poor boy, will probably die soon. Have more mementos than I can carry, from those who have died, to be given to their friends at home. At least a dozen have given me letters, pictures, etc., to take North. Hope I shan't have to turn them over to someone else.

July 7. The court was gotten up by our own men and from our own men; judge, jury, counsel, etc. Had a fair trial and were even defended, but to no purpose. It is reported that six have been sentenced to be hung, while a good many others are condemned to lighter punishment, such as setting in the stocks, strung up by the thumbs, thumbscrews, head hanging, etc. The court has been severe, but just. Mike goes out tomorrow to take some part in the court proceedings.

The prison seems a different place altogether; still, dread disease is here and mowing down good and true men. Would seem to me that 100 or 400 died each day, though officially but 140 odd is told. About 27,000, I believe, are here now in all. No new ones for a few days. Rebel visitors, who look at us from a distance. It is said the stench keeps all away who have no business here and can keep away. . . .

July 8. Oh, how hot, and oh, how miserable. The news that six have been sentenced to be hanged is true. . . . The camp is thoroughly under control of the police now, and it is a heavenly boon. Of course, there is some stealing and robbery, but not as before. . . . Guards shoot now very open. Boys, as guards, are the most cruel. It is said that if they kill a Yankee they are given a thirty day furlough. Guess they need them as soldiers too much to allow of this. The swamp now is fearful, water perfectly reeking with prison offal and poison. Still men drink it and die. Rumors that the six will be hung inside. Bread today and it is so coarse as to do more hurt than good to a majority of the prisoners. The place still gets worse.

Tunneling is over with; no one engages in it now that I know of. The prison is a success as regards safety; no escape except by death, and very many take advantage of that way. . . .

Guards every half hour call out the time and post, and there is often a shot to make one shiver as if with the ague. Must arrange my sleeping hours to miss getting owly in the morning. Have taken to building air castles of late, on being exchanged. Getting loony, I guess, same as all the rest.

July 11. This morning, lumber was brought into the prison by the Rebels, and near the gate a gallows erected for the purpose of executing the six condemned Yankees. At about 10 o'clock they were brought inside by Captain Wirz and some guards, and delivered over to the police force. Captain Wirz then said a few words about their having been tried by our own men and for us to do as we choose with them, that he washed his hands of the whole matter, or words to that effect. . . .

All during the hanging scene the stockade was covered with Rebels, who were fearful a break would be made if the raiders should try and rescue them. Many citizens, too, were congregated on the outside in favorable positions for seeing. Artillery was pointed at us from all directions ready to blow us all into eternity in short order; Wirz stood on a high platform in plain sight of the execution and says we are a hard crowd to kill our own men.

"The air is filled with flying, burning cinders . . ."

SHERMAN BURNS ATLANTA

November 14–16, 1864

F. Y. HEDLEY, DAVID CONYNGHAM, AND MAJOR GEORGE WARD NICHOLS

*T*wo months after capturing Atlanta, Sherman ordered its citizens to evacuate the city. He wanted to reduce the number of troops he would need to keep the city secure, and to increase the number he could send to fight. Then he decided to march almost his entire army to the coast city of Savannah, 300 miles to the east. He destroyed Atlanta to prevent it from returning to rebel hands.

Hedley, Conyngham, and Nichols were Union soldiers. In 1865, Nichols, who had been a journalist before the war, wrote a popular book, titled Story of the Great March.

HEDLEY

A regiment would scatter along one side of the road, each man picking up the end of a [railroad] tie; then, at the word of command, all would throw the ties end over end, the fall breaking the rails loose. Then ties and telegraph poles were piled up and fired, and the rails thrown across them. The latter were soon red-hot in the middle, and the men would pick them up and wrap them around trees [forming what came to be known as "Sherman's neckties"], or twist them with cant hooks into a corkscrew pattern which it was impossible to straighten. . . .

The men worked with a will, seeming to take a savage delight in destroying everything that could by any possibility be made use of by their enemies. They attained great proficiency in these methods, and, after this fashion, they absolutely destroyed three-fourths of the railroad between Chattanooga and Atlanta. . . . Each detachment, immediately upon accomplishing the work in its own vicinity, marched rapidly toward Atlanta.

On the night of the 14th, the [last detachment] . . . followed the remainder of the army. There was now not a Federal soldier between Atlanta and Chattanooga, and the hills and plains, which had lately echoed the fearful din of artillery and musketry, and had been alive with masses of fiercely contending human beings, were as still and desolate as if a demon of destruction had passed over.

But there were monuments testifying to the fearful struggle—trees riven by cannon shot, and broken-down caissons. Here, there, and everywhere were graves of those who wore the blue and those who wore the gray, each surmounted by a board upon which were rudely cut by knives of comrades the name, company, and regiment of him who lay beneath.

CONYNGHAM

Winship's iron foundry and machine shops were early set on fire. This valuable property was calculated to be worth about half a million of dollars. An oil refinery nearby next got on fire and was soon in a fierce blaze. Next followed a freight warehouse. . . . The depot, turning-tables, freight sheds, and stores around were soon a fiery mass. . . .

Some ruffians ran with brands to fire the churches. . . . The Roman Catholic minister, Father O'Reiley, who was the only minister that remained in town, met them and upbraided them for their impious sacrilege. Even these hardened men of war shrank before virtue and truth, and the good priest not only saved his own church but also . . . his fellow Christians.

The Atlanta Hotel, Washington Hall, and all the square around the railroad depot were soon in one sheet of flame. Drugstores, dry goods stores, hotels, Negro marts, theaters, and grog shops were all now feeding the fiery element. Worn-out wagons and camp equipage were piled up in the depot and added to the fury of the flames.

A stone warehouse was blown up by a mine. . . . The men plunged into the houses, broke windows and doors with their muskets, dragging out armfuls of clothes, tobacco, and whiskey. . . . The men dressed themselves in new clothes, and then flung the rest into the fire.

NICHOLS

A grand and awful spectacle is presented to the beholder in this beautiful city, now in flames. . . . The heaven is one expanse of lurid fire; the air is filled with flying, burning cinders; buildings covering two hundred acres are in ruins or in flames; every instant there is the sharp detonation or the smothered booming sound of exploding shells and powder concealed in the buildings, and then the sparks and flames shoot away up . . . scattering cinders far and wide.

These are the machine shops where have been forged and cast the Rebel cannon, shot and shell that have carried death to many a brave defender of our nation's honor. These warehouses have been the receptacle of munitions of war, stored to be used for our destruction. The city which, next to Richmond, has furnished more material for prosecuting the war than any other in the South, exists no more as a means for injury to be used by the enemies of the Union.

A brigade of Massachusetts soldiers are the only troops now left in town. They will be the last to leave it.

"Many things reminded us of him . . ."

A MISSING BROTHER AT CHRISTMAS

December 26, 1864
Brooklyn, New York

WALT WHITMAN

Three years earlier, Walt Whitman had gone to Virginia to nurse his brother George, who had been wounded in battle. Afterward he volunteered in army hospitals in Washington, an experience he captured in several powerful poems.

I am writing this in the front basement in Portland Avenue, Brooklyn, at home. It is after 9 o'clock at night. We have had a wet day with fog, mud, slush, and the yet unmelted hard-polished ice liberally left in the streets. All sluggish and damp, with a prevailing leaden vapor. Yesterday, Christmas, about the same.

George's trunk came up express early in forenoon today from City Point, Virginia. Lieutenant Babcock, of the 51st, was kind enough to search it out and send it home. It stood some hours before we felt inclined to open it. Towards evening, Mother and Eddy looked over the things. One could not help feeling depressed. There were his uniform coat, pants, sash, etc. There were many things reminded us of him. Papers, memoranda, books, knick-knacks, a revolver, a small diary, roll of his company, a case of photographs of his comrades (several of them I knew as killed in battle), with other stuff such as a soldier accumulates.

Mother looked everything over, laid out the shirts to be washed, the coats and pants to hang up, and all the rest were carefully put back. It made me feel pretty solemn. We have not heard from him since October 3rd, either living or dead, we know not.

I am aware of the condition of the Union prisoners South through seeing them when brought up, and from lately talking with a friend just returned from taking part in the exchange at Savannah and Charleston—of which we received twelve thousand of our sick. Their situation, as of all our men in prison, is indescribably horrible. Hard, ghastly starvation is the rule. Rags, filth, despair, in large, open stockades; no shelter, no cooking, no clothes—such the condition of masses of men—in some places two or three thousand, and in the largest prison as high as thirty thousand confined. The guards are insufficient in numbers, and they make up by treble severity, shooting the prisoners literally just to keep them under terrorism. . . .

I cannot get any reliable trace of the 51st officers at all. I supposed they were at Columbia, South Carolina, but my friend has brought a list purporting to be a complete record of all in confinement there, and I cannot find any of the 51st among them.*

"All appreciated the sadness that overwhelmed him . . ."

LEE SURRENDERS TO GRANT

April 9, 1865
Appomattox Court House, Virginia

HORACE PORTER

" *T*hese oddly different generals," wrote historian Bruce Catton, "represented the strengths of two conflicting currents that, through them, had come into final collision. Lee was tidewater Virginia, and in his background were family, culture, and tradition . . . the age of chivalry transplanted to a New World . . . Lee stood for the feeling that it was somehow of advantage to human society to have a pronounced inequality in the social structure. There should be a leisure class, backed by

---

* George Whitman was alive and returned home safely. After Walt suffered a paralytic stroke in 1873, George cared for Walt just as Walt had cared for him in the army hospital a dozen years earlier. (Ed.)

ownership of land . . . It would bring forth a class of men with a strong sense of obligation to the community; men who lived not to gain advantage for themselves, but to meet the solemn obligations which had been laid on them by the very fact that they were privileged. . . . Grant, the son of a tanner on the western frontier, was everything Lee was not. He had come up the hard way, and embodied nothing in particular except the eternal toughness and sinewy fiber of the men who grew up beyond the mountains. He was one of a body of men who owed reverence and obeisance to no one, who were self-reliant to a fault, who cared hardly anything for the past but who had a sharp eye for the future. . . ."

Yet at Appomattox, nothing was so obvious as one striking similarity. As Catton wrote, "there was the ability, at the end, to turn quickly from war to peace once the fighting was over. . . . No part of either man's life became him more than the part he played in their brief meeting."

Eyewitness Horace Porter was Grant's aide-de-camp. He later was one of Grant's assistants when Grant was president.

General Grant began the conversation by saying: "I met you once before, General Lee, while we were serving in Mexico, when you came over from General [Winfield] Scott's headquarters to visit Garland's brigade, to which I then belonged. I have always remembered your appearance, and I think I should have recognized you anywhere." "Yes," replied General Lee, "I know I met you on that occasion, and I have often thought of it and tried to recollect how you looked, but I have never been able to recall a single feature." After some further mention of Mexico, General Lee said: "I suppose, General Grant, that the object of our present meeting is fully understood. I asked to see you to ascertain upon what terms you would receive the surrender of my army." General Grant replied: "The terms I propose are those statement substantially in my letter of yesterday—that is, the officers and men surrendered to be paroled and disqualified from taking up arms again until properly exchanged, and all arms, ammunition, and supplies to be delivered up as captured property." Lee nodded an assent, and said: "Those are about the conditions which I expected would be proposed." General Grant then continued: "Yes, I think our correspondence indicated pretty clearly the action that would be taken at our meeting; and I hope it may lead to a general suspension of hostilities and be the means of preventing any further loss of life."

Lee inclined his head as indicating his accord with this wish, and General Grant then went on to talk at some length in a very pleasant vein about the prospects of peace. Lee was evidently anxious to proceed to the formal work of the surrender, and he brought the subject up again by saying:

"I presume, General Grant, we have both carefully considered the proper steps to be taken, and I would suggest that you commit to writing the terms you have proposed, so that they may be formally acted upon."

"Very well," replied General Grant, "I will write them out." And calling for his manifold order-book, he opened it on the table before him and proceeded to write the terms. The leaves had been so prepared that three impressions of the writing were made. He wrote very rapidly, and did not pause until he had finished the sentence ending with "officers appointed by me to receive them." Then he looked toward Lee, and his eyes seemed to be resting on the handsome sword that hung at that officer's side. He said afterward that this set him to thinking that it would be an unnecessary humiliation to require the officers to surrender their swords, and a great hardship to deprive them of their personal baggage and horses, and after a short pause he wrote the sentence: "This will not embrace the side-arms of the officers, nor their private horses or baggage." . . . When this had been done, he handed the book to General Lee and asked him to read over the letter. . . .

. . . When Lee came to the sentence about the officers' side-arms, private horses, and baggage, he showed for the first time during the reading of the letter a slight change of countenance, and was evidently touched by this act of generosity. It was doubtless the condition mentioned to which he particularly alluded when he looked toward General Grant as he finished reading and said with some degree of warmth in his manner: "This will have a very happy effect upon my army."

General Grant then said: "Unless you have some suggestions to make in regard to the form in which I have stated the terms, I will have a copy of the letter made in ink and sign it."

"There is one thing I would like to mention," Lee replied after a short pause. "The cavalrymen and artillerists own their own horses in our army. Its organization in this respect differs from that of the United States." This expression attracted the notice of our officers present, as showing how firmly the conviction was grounded in his mind that we were two distinct countries. He continued: "I would like to understand whether these men will be permitted to retain their horses?"

"You will find that the terms as written do not allow this," General Grant replied; "only the officers are permitted to take their private property."

Lee read over the second page of the letter again, and then said:

"No, I see the terms do not allow it; that is clear." His face showed plainly that he was quite anxious to have this concession made, and Grant said very promptly and without giving Lee time to make a direct request:

"Well, the subject is quite new to me. Of course I did not know that any private soldiers owned their animals, but I think this will be the last battle of the war—I sincerely hope so—and that the surrender of this army will be followed soon by that of all the others, and I take it that most of the men in the ranks are small farmers, and as the country has been so raided by the two armies, it is doubtful whether they will be able to put in a crop to carry themselves and their families through the next winter without the aid of the horses they are now riding, and I will arrange it in this way: I will not change the terms as now written, but I will instruct the officers I shall appoint to receive the paroles to let all the men who claim to own a horse or mule take the animals home with them to work their little farms." (This expression has been quoted in various forms and has been the subject of some dispute. I give the exact words used.) . . .

. . . General Lee now took the initiative again in leading the conversation back into business channels. He said:

"I have a thousand or more of your men as prisoners, General Grant, a number of them officers whom we have required to march along with us for several days. I shall be glad to send them into your lines as soon as it can be arranged, for I have no provisions for them. I have, indeed, nothing for my own men. They have been living for the last few days principally upon parched corn, and we are badly in need of both rations and forage. . . ."

. . . General Grant replied: "I should like to have our men sent within our lines as soon as possible. I will take steps at once to have your army supplied with rations, but I am sorry we have no forage for the animals." . . .

. . . At a little before 4 o'clock General Lee shook hands with General Grant, bowed to the other officers, and with Colonel Marshall left the room. One after another we followed, and passed out to the porch. Lee signaled to his orderly to bring up his horse, and while the animal was being bridled the general stood on the lowest step and gazed sadly in the direction of the valley beyond where his army lay—now an army of prisoners. He smote his hands together a number of times in an absent sort of a way; seemed not to see the group of Union officers in the yard who rose respectfully at his approach, and appeared unconscious of everything about him. All appreciated the sadness that overwhelmed him, and he had the personal sympathy of every one who beheld him at this supreme moment of trial. The approach of his horse seemed to recall him from his reverie, and he at once mounted. General Grant now stepped down from the porch, and, moving toward him, saluted him by raising his hat. He was followed in this act of courtesy by all our officers present; Lee raised his hat respectfully, and rode off to break the sad news to the brave fellows whom he had so long commanded.

"I heard the discharge of a pistol . . ."

LINCOLN IS SHOT

April 14, 1865
Washington, D.C.

MAJOR HENRY R. RATHBONE

Rathbone was in the box at Ford's Theatre with the president. He also was wounded by John Wilkes Booth. This account is from his testimony before a tribunal.

On the evening of the 14th of April last, at about twenty minutes past 8 o'clock, I, in company with Miss Harris, left my residence at the corner of Fifteenth and H Streets, and joined the President and Mrs. Lincoln, and went with them, in their carriage, to Ford's Theater, on Tenth Street. On reaching the theater, when the presence of the President became known, the actors stopped playing, the band struck up "Hail to the Chief," and the audience rose and received him with vociferous cheering. The party proceeded along in the rear of the dress-circle and entered the box that had been set apart for their reception. On entering the box, there was a large arm-chair that was placed nearest the audience, farthest from the stage, which the President took and occupied during the whole of the evening, with one exception, when he got up to put on his coat, and returned and sat down again.

When the second scene of the third act was being performed, and while I was intently observing the proceedings upon the stage, with my back toward the door, I heard the discharge of a pistol behind me, and, looking round, saw through the smoke a man between the door and the President. The distance from the door to where the President sat was about four feet. At the same time I heard the man shout some word, which I thought was "Freedom!" I instantly sprang toward him and seized him. He wrested himself from my grasp, and made a violent thrust at my breast with a large knife. I parried the blow by striking it up, and received a wound several inches deep in my left arm. . . . The man rushed to the front of the box, and I endeavored to seize him again, but only caught his clothes as he was leaping over the railing of the box. The clothes, as I believe, were torn in the attempt to hold him. As he went over upon the stage, I cried out, "Stop that man." I then turned to the President; his position was not changed; his head was slightly bent forward and his eyes were closed. I saw that he was unconscious, and, supposing him mortally wounded, rushed to the door for the purpose of calling medical aid.

On reaching the outer door of the passage way, I found it barred by a heavy piece of plank, one end of which was secured in the wall, and the other resting against the door. It had been so securely fastened that it required considerable force to remove it. This wedge or bar was about four feet from the floor. Persons upon the outside were beating against the door for the purpose of entering. I removed the bar, and the door was opened. Several persons, who represented themselves as surgeons, were allowed to enter. I saw there Colonel Crawford, and requested him to prevent other persons from entering the box.

I then returned to the box, and found the surgeons examining the President's person. They had not yet discovered the wound. As soon as it was discovered, it was determined to remove him from the theater. He was carried out, and I then proceeded to assist Mrs. Lincoln, who was intensely excited, to leave the theater. On reaching the head of the stairs, I requested Major Potter to aid me in assisting Mrs. Lincoln across the street to the house where the President was being conveyed. . . .

In a review of the transactions, it is my confident belief that the time which elapsed between the discharge of the pistol and the time when the assassin leaped from the box did not exceed thirty seconds. Neither Mrs. Lincoln nor Miss Harris had left their seats.

*"The President lay, extended on a bed,
    breathing heavily . . ."*

DEATH OF LINCOLN

April 14–15, 1865
Washington, D.C.

GIDEON WELLES

*W*elles *was secretary of the navy.*

APRIL 14

General Grant was present at the meeting of the Cabinet to-day and remained during the session.

Inquiry had been made as to army news and especially if any information had been received from Sherman. None of the members had heard anything, and Stanton, who makes it a point to be late, and who has the telegraph in his department, had not arrived.

General Grant said he was hourly expecting word. The President remarked, it would, he had no doubt, come soon, and come favorable, for he had last night the usual dream which he had preceding nearly every great and important event of the War. Generally the news had been favorable which succeeded this dream, and the dream itself was always the same.

I inquired what this remarkable dream could be. He said it related to your (my) element, the water; that he seemed to be in some singular, indescribable vessel, and that he was moving with great rapidity towards an indefinite shore; that he had this dream preceding Sumter, Bull Run, Antietam, Gettysburg, Stone River, Vicksburg, Wilmington, etc.

"I had," the President remarked, "this strange dream again last night, and we shall, judging from the past, have great news very soon."

I write this conversation three days after it occurred, in consequence of what took place Friday night, and but for which the mention of this dream would probably have never been noted. Great events did, indeed, follow, for within a few hours the good and gentle, as well as truly great, man who narrated his dream closed forever his earthly career.

I had retired to bed about half past ten on the evening of the 14th of April, and was just getting asleep when Mrs. Welles, my wife, said some one was at our door. Sitting up in bed, I heard a voice twice call to John, my son, whose sleeping-room was on the second floor directly over the front entrance.

I arose at once and raised a window, when my messenger, James Smith, called to me that Mr. Lincoln, the President, had been shot, and said Secretary Seward and his son, Assistant Secretary Frederick Seward, were assassinated.

James was much alarmed and excited. I told him his story was very incoherent and improbable, that he was associating men who were not together and liable to attack at the same time. "Where," I inquired, "was the President when shot?" James said he was at Ford's Theatre on 10th Street. "Well," said I, "Secretary Seward is an invalid in bed in his house yonder on 15th Street."

James said he had been there, stopped in at the house to make inquiry before alarming me.

I immediately dressed myself, and, against the earnest remonstrance and appeals of my wife, went directly to Mr. Seward's, whose residence was on the east side of the square, mine being on the north. James accompanied me.

As we were crossing 15th Street I saw four or five men in earnest consultation, standing under the lamp on the corner by St. John's Church. Before I had got half across the street, the lamp was suddenly extinguished and the knot of persons rapidly dispersed. For a moment, and but a moment, I was disconcerted to find myself in darkness, but, recollecting that it was late and about time for the moon to rise, I proceeded. Hurrying forward into 15th Street, I found it pretty full of people, especially near the residence of Secretary Seward.

Entering the house, I found the lower hall and office full of persons, and among them most of the foreign legations, all anxiously inquiring what truth there was in the horrible rumors afloat.

Proceeding through the hall to the stairs, I found one and I think two of the servants there holding the crowd in check. The servants were frightened and appeared relieved to see me.

I asked for the Secretary's room and proceeded to the foot of the bed. Dr. Verdi and, I think, two others were there. The bed was saturated with blood. The Secretary was lying on his back, the upper part of his head covered by a cloth, which extends down over his eyes. His mouth was open, the lower jaw dropping down.

I exchanged a few whispered words with Dr. V. Secretary Stanton, who came after but almost simultaneously with me, made inquiries in a louder tone till admonished by a word from one of the physicians. We almost immediately withdrew and went into the adjoining front room, where lay Frederick Seward. His eyes were open but he did not move them, nor a limb, nor did he speak. Doctor White, who was in attendance, told me he was unconscious and more dangerously injured than his father.

As we descended the stairs, I asked Stanton what he had heard in regard to the President that was reliable. He said the President was shot at Ford's Theatre, that he had seen a man who was present and witnessed the occurrence.

The streets were full of people. Not only the sidewalk but the carriageway was to some extent occupied, all or nearly all hurrying towards 10th Street. When we entered that street we found it pretty closely packed.

The President had been carried across the street from the theatre to the house of a Mr. Peterson. We entered by ascending a flight of steps above the basement and passing through a long hall to the rear, where the President lay, extended on a bed, breathing heavily.

Several surgeons were present, at least six, I should think more. Among them I was glad to observe Dr. Hall, who, however, soon left. I inquired of Dr. H. as I entered the true condition of the President. He replied the President was dead to all intents, although he might live three hours or perhaps longer.

The giant sufferer lay extended diagonally across the bed, which was not long enough for him. He had been stripped of his clothes. His large arms, which were occasionally exposed, were of a size which one would scarce have expected from his spare appearance. His slow, full respiration lifted the clothes with each breath that he took. His features were calm and striking. I had never seen them appear to better advantage than for the first hour, perhaps, that I was there. After that, his right eye began to swell and that part of his face became discolored.

Senator Sumner was there, I think, when I entered. If not he came in soon after, as did Speaker Colfax, Mr. Secretary McCulloch, and the other members of the Cabinet, with the exception of Mr. Seward.

A double guard was stationed at the door and on the sidewalk, to repress the crowd, which was of course highly excited and anxious.

The room was small and overcrowded. The surgeons and members of the Cabinet were as many as should have been in the room, but there were many more, and the hall and other rooms in the front or main house were full. One of these rooms was occupied by Mrs. Lincoln and her attendants, with Miss Harris. About once an hour Mrs. Lincoln would repair to the bedside of her dying husband and with lamentation and tears remain until overcome by emotion.

APRIL 15

A door which opened upon a porch or gallery, and also the windows, were kept open for fresh air The night was dark, cloudy and damp, and about six it began to rain. I remained in the room until then without sitting or leaving it, when, there being a vacant chair which some one left at the foot of the bed, I occupied it for nearly two hours, listening to the heavy groans, and witnessing the wasting life of the good and great man who was expiring before me.

About 6 A.M. I experienced a feeling of faintness and for the first time after entering the room, a little past eleven, I left it and the house and took a short walk in the open air. It was a dark and gloomy morning, and rain set in before I returned to the house, some fifteen minutes later.

Large groups of people were gathered every few rods, all anxious and solicitous. Some one or more from each group stepped forward as I passed, to inquire into the condition of the President, and to ask if there was no hope. Intense grief was on every countenance when I replied that the President could survive but a short time. The colored people especially—and there were at this time more of them, perhaps, than of whites—were overwhelmed with grief.

Returning to the house, I seated myself in the back parlor, where the Attorney General and others had been engaged in taking evidence concerning the assassination.

A little before seven, I went into the room where the dying President was rapidly drawing near the closing moments. His wife soon after made her last visit to him. The death-struggle had begun. Robert, his son, stood with several others at the head of the bed. He bore himself well, but on two occasions gave way to overpowering grief and sobbed aloud, turning his head and leaning on the shoulder of Senator Sumner.

The respiration of the President became suspended at intervals, and at last entirely ceased at twenty-two minutes past seven.

A prayer followed from Dr. Gurley, and the Cabinet, with the exception of Mr. Seward and Mr. McCulloch, immediately thereafter assembled in the back parlor, from which all other persons were excluded, and there signed a letter which was prepared by Attorney General Speed to the Vice-President, informing him of the event, and that the government devolved upon him.

I went after breakfast to the Executive Mansion. There was a cheerless cold rain and everything seemed gloomy. On the Avenue in front of the White House were several hundred colored people, mostly women and children, weeping and wailing their loss. This crowd did not appear to diminish through the whole of that cold wet day. They seemed not to know what was to be their fate since their great benefactor was dead, and their hopeless grief affected me more than almost anything else, though strong and brave men wept when I met them.

At the White House all was silent and sad. As we were descending the stairs, "Tad," who was looking from the window at the foot, turned and, seeing us, cried aloud in his tears, "Oh, Mr. Welles, who killed my father?"

Neither Speed nor myself could restrain our tears nor give the poor boy any satisfactory answer.

"Something unusual was going to take place at the 'big house' . . ."

FREEDOM

April 26, 1865
Franklin County, Virginia

BOOKER T. WASHINGTON

The founder and first president of Tuskegee Institute was nine years old when the Civil War ended. He described that day in his autobiography, Up from Slavery.

Finally the war closed, and the day of freedom came. It was a momentous and eventful day to all upon our plantation. We had been expecting it. Freedom was in the air, and had been for months. Deserting soldiers returning to their homes were to be seen every day. Others who had been discharged, or whose regiments had been paroled, were constantly passing near our place. The "grape-vine telegraph" was kept busy night and day. The news and mutterings of great events were swiftly carried from one plantation to another. In the fear of "Yankee" invasions, the silverware and other valuables were taken from the "big house," buried in the woods, and guarded by trusted slaves. Woe be to anyone who would have attempted to disturb the buried treasure. The slaves would give the Yankee soldiers food, drink, clothing—anything but that which had been specifically entrusted to their care and honor. As the great day drew nearer, there was more singing in the slave quarters than usual. It was bolder, had more ring, and lasted later into the night. Most of the verses of the plantation songs had some reference to freedom. True, they had sung those same verses before, but they had been careful to explain that the "freedom" in these songs referred to the next world, and had no connection with life in this world. Now they gradually threw off the mask; and were not afraid to let it be known that the "freedom" in their songs meant freedom of the body in this world. The night before the eventful day, word was sent to the slave quarters to the effect that something unusual was going to take place at the "big house" the next morning. There was little, if any, sleep that night. All was excitement and expectancy.

Early the next morning word was sent to all the slaves, old and young, to gather at the house. In company with my mother, brother, and sister, and a large number of other slaves, I went to the master's house. All of our master's family were either standing or seated on the veranda of the house, where they could see what was to take place and hear what was said. There was a feeling of deep interest, or perhaps sadness, on their faces, but not bitterness. As I now recall the impression they made upon me, they did not at the moment seem to be sad because of the loss of property, but rather because of parting with those whom they had reared and who were in many ways very close to them. The most distinct thing that I now recall in connection with the scene was that some man who seemed to be a stranger (a United States officer, I presume) made a little speech and then read a rather long paper—the Emancipation Proclamation, I think. After the reading we were told that we were all free, and could go when and where we pleased. My mother, who was standing by my side, leaned over and kissed her children, while tears of joy ran down her cheeks. She explained to us what it all meant, that this was the day for which she had been so long praying, but fearing that she would never live to see.

For some minutes there was great rejoicing, and thanksgiving, and wild scenes of ecstasy. But there was no feeling of bitterness. In fact, there was pity among the slaves for our former owners. The wild rejoicing on the part of the emancipated colored people lasted but for a brief period, for I noticed that by the time they returned to their cabins there was a change in their feelings. The great responsibility of being free, of having charge of themselves, of having to think and plan for themselves and their children, seemed to take possession of them. It was very much like suddenly turning a youth of ten or twelve years out into the world to provide for himself. In a few hours the great question with which the Anglo-Saxon race had been grappling for centuries had been thrown upon these people to be solved. These were the questions of a home, a living, the rearing of children, education, citizenship, and the establishment and support of churches. Was it any wonder that within a few hours the wild rejoicing ceased and a feeling of deep gloom seemed to pervade the slave quarters?

To some it seemed that, now that they were in actual possession of it, freedom was a more serious thing than they had expected to find it. Some of the slaves were seventy or eighty years old; their best days were gone. They had no strength with which to earn a living in a strange place and among strange people, even if they had been sure where to find a new place of abode. To this class the problem seemed especially hard. Besides, deep down in their hearts there was a strange and peculiar attachment to "old Marster" and "old Missus," and to their children, which they found it hard to think of breaking off. With these they had spent in some cases nearly a half-century, and it was no light thing to think of parting. Gradually, one by one, stealthily at first, the older slaves began to wander from the slave quarters back to the "big house" to have whispered conversation with their former owners as to the future.

"You Northern people are making a great mistake . . ."

THE RECONSTRUCTION

1865
Charleston, South Carolina

SIDNEY ANDREWS

*A*ndrews was a journalist from New England.

A city of ruins, of desolation, of vacant houses, of widowed women, of rotting wharves, of deserted warehouses, of weed-wild gardens, of miles of grass-grown streets, of acres of pitiful and voiceful barrenness,— that is Charleston, wherein Rebellion loftily reared its head five years ago, on whose beautiful promenade the fairest of cultured women gathered with passionate hearts to applaud the assault of ten thousand upon the little garrison of Fort Sumter!

We never again can have the Charleston of the decade previous to the war. The beauty and pride of the city are as dead as the glories of Athens. Five millions of dollars could not restore the ruin of these four past years; and that sum is so far beyond the command of the city as to seem the boundless measure of immeasurable wealth. Yet, after all, Charleston was Charleston because of the hearts of its people. St. Michael's Church, they held, was the centre of the universe; and the aristocracy of the city were the very elect of God's children on earth. One marks now how few young men there are, how generally the young women are dressed in black. The flower of their proud aristocracy is buried on scores of battle-fields. If it were possible to restore the broad acres of crumbling ruins to their foretime style and uses, there would even then be but the dead body of Charleston.

Of Massachusetts men, some are already in business here, and others came on to "see the lay of the land," as one of them said. "That's all right," observed an ex-Rebel captain in one of our after-dinner chats,—"that's all right; let's have Massachusetts and South Carolina brought together, for they are the only two States that amount to anything."

There are many Northern men here already, though one cannot say that there is much Northern society, for the men are either without families or have left them at home. Walking out yesterday with a former Charlestonian,—a man who left here in the first year of the war and returned soon after our occupation of the city,—he pointed out to me the various "Northern houses"; and I shall not exaggerate if I say that this classification appeared to include at least half the stores on each of the principal streets. "The presence of these men," said he, "was at first very distasteful to our people, and they are not liked any too well now; but we know they are doing a good work for the city."

I fell into some talk with him concerning the political situation, and found him of bitter spirit toward what he was pleased to denominate "the infernal radicals." When I asked him what should be done, he answered: "You Northern people are making a great mistake, in your treatment of the South. We are thoroughly whipped; we give up slavery forever; and now we want you to quit reproaching us. Let us back into the Union, and then come down here and help us build up the country."

The city is under thorough military rule; but the iron hand rests very lightly. Soldiers do police duty, and there is some nine-o'clock regulation; but, so far as I can learn, anybody goes anywhere at all hours of the night without molestation. "There never was such good order here before," said an old colored man to me.

*"The first glove I ever saw
on the hand of a ball player . . ."*

BASEBALL INNOVATIONS

1866–1876

ALBERT GOODWILL SPALDING

*S*palding was a professional player and one of the men who modernized and standardized the game. He and his brother James also founded the Spalding sporting goods company.

The first glove I ever saw on the hand of a ball player in a game was worn by Charles C. Waite, in Boston, in 1875. He had come from New Haven and was playing at first base. The glove worn by him was of flesh color, with a large, round opening in the back. Now, I had for a good while felt the need of some sort of hand protection for myself. In those days clubs did not carry an extra carload of pitchers, as now. For several years I had pitched in every game played by the Boston team, and had developed severe bruises on the inside of my left hand. When it is recalled that every ball pitched had to be returned, and that every swift one coming my way, from infielders, outfielders or hot from the bat, must be caught or stopped, some idea may be gained of the punishment received.

Therefore, I asked Waite about his glove. He confessed that he was a bit ashamed to wear it, but had it on to save his hand. He also admitted that he had chosen a color as inconspicuous as possible, because he didn't care to attract attention. He added that the opening on the back was for purpose of ventilation.

Meanwhile my own hand continued to take its medicine with utmost regularity, occasionally being bored with a warm twister that hurt excruciatingly. Still, it was not until 1877 that I overcame my scruples against joining the "kid-glove aristocracy" by donning a glove. When I did at last decide to do so, I did not select a fleshcolored glove, but got a black one, and cut out as much of the back as possible to let the air in.

Happily, in my case, the presence of a glove did not call out the ridicule that had greeted Waite. I had been playing so long and had become so well known that the innovation seemed rather to evoke sympathy than hilarity. I found that the glove, thin as it was, helped considerably, and inserted one pad after another until a good deal of relief was afforded. If anyone wore a padded glove before this date I do not know it. The "pillow mitt" was a later innovation.

About this time, 1875–76, James Tyng, catcher for the Harvard Base Ball Club, appeared on the Boston grounds one day, and, stepping to his position, donned the first wire mask I had ever seen. This mask had been invented and patented by Mr. Fred W. Thayer, a Harvard player. . . . Like other protective innovations at that stage of the game, it was not at first well received by professionals. Our catcher, James White, was urged to try it, and after some coaxing consented. I pitched him a few balls, some of which he missed, and finally, becoming disgusted at being unable to see the ball readily, he tore off the mask and, hurling it toward the bench, went on without it.

This wire mask, with certain modifications, is the same that has been used by catchers ever since.

When sliding, as an aid to the base runner, began, I am not prepared to state with authority. I do know, however, that its introduction was not by "King" Kelly, as has sometimes been claimed. As early as 1866 (Kelly began to play as a lad in 1873), at a game at Rochelle, Illinois, Robert Addy startled the players of the Forest Citys by a diving slide for second base. None of us had ever witnessed the play before.

As a matter of fact, from the time of the adoption of regular playing rules by the old Knickerbockers, changes in the technique of Base Ball have been remarkably few in number as compared with the great advances in skill and science of play. The ball has been recently improved, but is still of practically the same size and weight. Bats are substantially of the same form and material as at the beginning of professional Base Ball.

In one department of the game, however, the change has been very marked. Pitching has undergone a complete revolution. Indeed, the word "pitching," which was properly applied to the act of ball delivery at first, is to-day a misnomer. The ball as now presented to the batsman is not pitched, but thrown. Whereas, in the early days, it left the pitcher's hand with a peculiar snap of the wrist from an unbent elbow, and below the hip, now it may be hurled in any manner at the pitcher's option.

Perhaps at this point it may be of interest to consider briefly the causes that resulted in the change from the old-time straight arm pitch to the present unrestricted delivery of the ball. First, then, it must be conceded that the method employed at the beginning was never acquired by many men. It seemed to be a natural gift to a few players in the early seventies and before, but, in spite of the earnest efforts of hundreds to acquire the science of delivery as required by the published rules, less than a dozen pitchers were using it up to 1876, and only half a dozen gained eminence as pitchers at this time.

The fact that so few ball players were ever able to acquire the "knack" of straight arm pitching led to many embarrassments at the beginning of professional Base Ball. The game was rapidly growing in favor, new clubs and new leagues were coming into existence all over the country, but the supply of pitchers did not correspondingly keep pace. Something had to be done. As the rules were unchanged, and as only a dozen legal pitchers were in the country, clubs were forced to put men in the box who attempted the straight arm delivery, but who only succeeded in presenting a very poor imitation. The effect of this course was to put the question up to the umpire, and if he ruled against the pitcher there was a disappointed crowd, no game, or an utterly uninteresting exhibition.

It was not until the change of 1884, removing all bans and permitting the pitcher to use his own option as to his method of delivering the ball, that the need for further change was removed.

The withdrawal of the old-time straight-elbow restraint of course enabled pitchers to devote their talents to the development of new methods of delivery calculated to deceive the batsman, but long before this some efforts in that direction had been made.

Arthur Cummins, of Brooklyn, was the first pitcher of the old school that I ever saw pitch a curved ball. Bobby Matthews soon followed. This was in the early seventies. Both men were very light, spare fellows, with long, sinewy wrists, and having a peculiar wrist-joint motion with a certain way of holding the ball near the fingers' ends that enabled them to impart a rotary motion to the ball, followed by a noticeable outward curve.

In 1874 Tom Bond inaugurated the present style of pitching or, rather, underhand throwing, with its in-curves and out-shoots. This style of delivery was then in violation of the straight-arm pitching rules, but umpires were disposed to let it go, and thus gradually, in spite of legislation, the old style gave way to the new.

In the first year of the existence of the National League several of its pitchers began the delivery of the curved ball, that is, a ball which, after leaving the pitcher's hand, would curve to the right or left, and could be made to deceive the batsman by appearing to come wide of the plate and then suddenly turn in and pass over it; or, appearing to come directly over the plate, to shoot out, missing it entirely.

The result of this work on the part of the pitcher was to make hitting much less frequent and small scores characterized all well-played games. In 1877, as a result of the curved ball, a hot controversy arose into which many scientists were drawn. Distinguished collegians openly declared that the "curved ball" was a myth; that any other deflection of a thrown ball than that caused by the wind or opposing air-currents was impossible. Men high up in the game clung strenuously to the same opinion. Col. J. B. Joyce, who had been a ruling spirit in the old Cincinnati Red Stockings, held to this view. It was absurd, he claimed, to say that any man could throw a ball other than in a straight line. A practical test was made at Cincinnati in the presence of a great crowd to convert the Colonel. A surveyor was employed to set three posts in a row, with the left-hand surface of the two at the ends on a line with the right hand surface of that in the middle. Then a tight board fence about six feet high was continued from each end post, also bearing on the straight line drawn. Will White, one of the most expert twirlers of the day, was selected to convert Col. Joyce. The test took place in the presence of a big crowd and was a success in everything but the conversion. White stood upon the left of the fence at one end, so that his hand could not possibly pass beyond the straight line, and pitched the ball so that it passed to the right of the middle post. This it did by three or four inches, but curved so much that it passed the third post a half foot to the left. Col. Joyce saw the test successfully performed, but he would not be convinced.

"This glorious Alpine view . . ."

EARLY DENVER

June 19, 1866
Colorado Territory

BAYARD TAYLOR

*T*aylor has been described as "perhaps the most widely known American traveler of his day," by virtue of his celebrated reportage. This account was originally published in the New York Tribune.

My fellow-passengers had been loud in their praises of the place, and I therefore said nothing. Suddenly I perceived, through the dust, a stately square Gothic tower, and rubbed my eyes with a sense of incredulity. It was really true; there was the tower, built of brick, well-proportioned and picturesque. Dwellings and cottages rose over the dip of the ridge, on either side; brick blocks began to appear, and presently we were rolling through gay, animated streets, down the vistas of which the snowy ranges in the west were shining fairly in the setting sun.

The coach drew up at the Pacific Hotel, where I found a hearty welcome and good quarters, and in just four days and six hours from Fort Riley I sat down, not to a "square meal," but to an excellent supper. The two days which have since elapsed have given me a good superficial acquaintance with the place. First, let me say that the views which have appeared in the illustrated papers are simply caricatures. Instead of being a cluster of houses on a flat plain, with a range of clumsy mountains in the distance, and Pike's Peak standing alone in the centre thereof, it is built upon a gradual slope, rising eastward from the junction of Cherry Creek with the Platte. It is as well built as any town of equal size in the Mississippi Valley. The Methodist Church and Seminary, the banks and principal business houses, solidly constructed of brick (the former edifice with considerable architectural beauty), give the place an air of permanence, very surprising to one who has just arrived from the East.

Beyond the Platte the land rises with a gentle, gradual slope, to the base of the Rocky Mountains, twelve miles distant, and there is no part of the town which does not afford a view of the great range. Long's Peak, more than 15,000 feet in height, just fills the vista of the principal business street. Pike's Peak is far to the left, overlooking the head of the Cherry Creek Valley; consequently, a view of Denver, in which it is made the prominent feature, does not correctly represent the place.

Although business of all kinds is extraordinarily dull at present, and the people are therefore as much dispirited as Colorado nature will admit, Denver seems to me to have a very brisk and lively air. A number of substantial buildings are going up, there is constant movement in the streets, the hotels are crowded, and the people one meets are brimful of cheerful energy. The stores and warehouses are thoroughly stocked, and prices are lower than one would expect, considering the tedious and expensive land transportation. At the Pacific Hotel you pay four dollars per day,—no more than in New York, and have an equally good table. There may not be such an excessive bill of fare, but I could distinguish no difference in the cooking. Vegetables in the market are plenty and cheap, and appear to be of remarkably fine quality.

The dryness of the climate and occasional extremes of cold in winter, appear to me to be the principal drawbacks. Near the mouth of Cherry Creek there is a grove of venerable cotton-woods, and perhaps a dozen other specimens are dispersed singly through the lower part of the town.

Attempts are now being made to colonize this tree—which makes a green spot, ugly though it be—around the houses in the higher streets, and with a fair prospect of success. The milk, cream, and butter from the adjoining farms are better than they are in most of the Western States. Venison and antelope are abundant, and canned fruits supply the want of fresh.

The situation of Denver is well selected. Were it nearer to the mountains, it would furnish a more convenient depot of supplies for the Clear Creek mining region, but it would not concentrate, as now, so many radiating lines of travel. It lies, apparently, in the centre of the chord of a shallow arc of the mountains governing the entrances of some half-a-dozen different cañons, and overlooking a belt of farming land, fifty miles by ten in dimensions.

Its prosperity, of course, depends on the activity of mining operations in the mountains. There is at present a stagnation, occasioned principally by the enormous price of labor. Although the new methods of reduction promise a much greater production of the precious metals, and fresh discoveries of gold, silver, copper, and lead are being made every day, wages are so high that many companies have been forced to suspend business until the agricultural supplies at home, and the gradual approach of the Pacific Railroad, shall have brought prices down.

I should estimate the population of Denver at about six thousand. Probably no town in the country ever grew up under such discouraging circumstances, or has made more, solid progress in the same length of time. It was once swept away by the inundation of Cherry Creek; once or twice burned; threatened with Secession; cut off from intercourse with the East by Indian outbreaks; deprived of a great portion of its anticipated trade by our war; made to pay outrageously for its materials and supplies—and all this within seven years!

I was interested in noticing how attached the inhabitants are to the place. Nearly every one who had recently been East seemed rejoiced to return. Even ladies forget the greater luxuries and refinements of the Atlantic coast, when they see the Rocky Mountains once more. The people look upon this glorious Alpine view as one of the properties of the town. Every street opens (in one direction, at least) upon it; and the evening drives along the Platte or over the flowering ridges, become as beautiful as any in the world, when the long line of snowy peaks flash down a brighter gold than ever was unpacked from their veins.

I find myself constantly returning to the point which my eyes seek, with unwearied interest, whenever I lift them from the paper. Ever since my arrival I have been studying the mountains. Their beauty and grandeur grow upon me with every hour of my stay. None of the illustrations accompanying the reports of exploration, and other Government documents, give any distinct idea of their variety and harmony of forms. Lovely in color and atmospheric effect, I may recall some mountain chains which equal, but none which surpass them. They hint of concealed grandeurs in all the glens and parks among them, and yet hold you back with a doubt whether they can be more beautiful near at hand than when beheld at this distance.

To-morrow I shall move nearer their bases.

"The Atlantic and Pacific were joined together . . ."

THE LAST SPIKE

March 10, 1869
Promontory Point, Utah

GENERAL GRENVILLE M. DODGE

A counterpoint to the pomp of this ceremony is found in George Templeton Strong's famous diary of New York City: "May 10. The Pacific Railroad was (or was to have been) formally completed today by the laying of its last rail. So there was a Te Deum *at Trinity Church at twelve, by request of Chamber of Commerce. This seems to have been the only public notice in New York of a most important event—national and international."*

On the morning of May 10, 1869, Hon. Leland Stanford, Governor of California and President of the Central Pacific, accompanied by Messrs. Huntington, Hopkins, Crocker and trainloads of California's distinguished citizens, arrived from the west. During the forenoon Vice President T. C. Durant and Directors John R. Duff and Sidney Dillon and Consulting Engineer Silas A. Seymour of the Union Pacific, with other prominent men, including a delegation of Mormons from Salt Lake City, came in on a train from the east. The National Government was represented by a detachment of "regulars" from Fort Douglass, Utah, accompanied by a band, and 600 others, including Chinese, Mexicans, Indians, half-breeds, negroes and laborers, suggesting an air of cosmopolitanism, all gathered around the open space where the tracks were to be joined. The Chinese laid the rails from the west end, and the Irish laborers laid them from the east end, until they met and joined.

Telegraphic wires were so connected that each blow of the descending sledge could be reported instantly to all parts of the United States. Corresponding blows were struck on the bell of the City Hall in San Francisco, and with the last blow of the sledge a cannon was fired at Fort Point. General Stafford presented a spike of gold, silver and iron as the offering of the Territory of Arizona. Governor Tuttle of Nevada presented a spike of silver from his state. The connecting tie was of California laurel, and California presented the last spike of gold in behalf of that state. A silver sledge had also been presented for the occasion. A prayer was offered. Governor Stanford of California made a few appropriate remarks on behalf of the Central Pacific and the chief engineer responded for the Union Pacific.

Then the telegraphic inquiry from the Omaha office, from which the circuit was to be started, was answered: "To everybody: Keep quiet. When the last spike is driven at Promontory Point we will say 'Done.' Don't break the circuit, but watch for the signals of the blows of the hammer. The spike will soon be driven. The signal will be three dots for the commencement of the blows."

The magnet tapped one—two—three—then paused—"Done." The spike was given its first blow by President Stanford and Vice President Durant followed. Neither hit the spike the first time, but hit the rail, and were greeted by the lusty cheers of the onlookers, accompanied by the screams of the locomotives and the music of the military band. Many other spikes were driven on the last rail by some of the distinguished persons present, but it was seldom that they first hit the spike. The original spike, after being tapped by the officials of the companies, was driven home by the chief engineers of the two roads. Then the two trains were run together, the two locomotives touching at the point of junction, and the engineers of the two locomotives each broke a bottle of champagne on the other's engine. Then it was declared that the connection was made and the Atlantic and Pacific were joined together never to be parted.

"The rushing waters break into
great waves on the rocks . . ."

POWELL ENTERS THE GRAND CANYON

August 13–14, 1869

JOHN WESLEY POWELL

*P*owell led the first survey expedition through the Canyon. This account comes *from his book,* The Exploration of the Colorado River.

AUGUST 13

We are now ready to start on our way down the Great Unknown. Our boats, tied to a common stake, are chafing each other, as they are tossed by the fretful river. They ride high and buoyant, for their loads are lighter than we could desire. We have but a month's rations remaining. The flour has been resifted through the mosquito-net sieve; the spoiled bacon has been dried, and the worst of it boiled; the few pounds of dried apples have been spread in the sun, and reshrunken to their normal bulk; the sugar has all melted, and gone on its way down the river; but we have a large sack of coffee. The lighting of the boats has this advantage; they will ride the waves better, and we shall have but little to carry when we make a portage.

We are three quarters of a mile in the depths of the earth, and the great river shrinks into insignificance, as it dashes its angry waves against the walls and cliffs, that rise to the world above; they are but puny ripples, and we but pigmies, running up and down the sands, or lost among the boulders.

We have an unknown distance yet to run; an unknown river yet to explore. What falls there are, we know not; what rocks beset the channel, we know not; what walls rise over the river, we know not. Ah, well! we may conjecture many things. The men talk as cheerfully as ever; jests are bandied about freely this morning; but to me the cheer is somber and the jests are ghastly.

With some eagerness, and some anxiety, and some misgiving, we enter the canyon below, and are carried along by the swift water through walls which rise from its very edge. They have the same structure as we noticed yesterday—tiers of irregular shelves below, and, above these, steep slopes to the foot of marble cliffs. We run six miles in a little more than half an hour, and emerge into a more open portion of the canyon, where high hills and ledges of rock intervene between the river and the distant walls. Just at the head of this open place the river runs across a dike; that is, a fissure in the rocks, open to depths below, has been filled with eruptive matter, and this, on cooling, was harder than the rocks through which the crevice was made, and, when these were washed away, the harder volcanic matter remained as a wall, and the river has cut a gateway through it several hundred feet high, and as many wide. As it crosses the wall, there is a fall below, and a bad rapid, filled with boulders of trap; so we stop to make a portage. Then we go, gliding by hills and ledges, with distant walls in view; sweeping past sharp angles of rock; stopping at a few points to examine rapids, which we find can be run, until we have made another five miles, when we land for dinner.

Then we let down with lines, over a long rapid, and start again. Once more the walls close in, and we find ourselves in a narrow gorge, the water again filling the channel, and very swift. With great care, and constant watchfulness, we proceed, making about four miles this afternoon, and camp in a cave.

AUGUST 14

At daybreak we walk down the bank of the river, on a little sandy beach, to take a view of a new feature in the canyon. Heretofore, hard rocks have given us bad river; soft rocks, smooth water; and a series of rocks harder than any we have experienced sets in. The river enters the granite!

We can see but a little way into the granite gorge, but it looks threatening.

After breakfast we enter on the waves. At the very introduction, it inspires awe. The canyon is narrower than we have ever before seen it; the water is swifter; there are but few broken rocks in the channel; but the walls are set, on either side, with pinnacles and crags; and sharp, angular buttresses, bristling with wind and wave-polished spires, extend far out into the river.

Ledges of rocks jut into the stream, their tops sometimes just below the surface, sometimes rising few or many feet above; and island ledges, and island pinnacles, and island towers break the swift course of the stream into chutes, and eddies, and whirlpools. We soon reach a place where a creek comes in from the left, and just below, the channel is choked with boulders, which have washed down this lateral canyon and formed a dam, over which there is a fall of thirty or forty feet; but on the boulders we can get foothold, and we make a portage.

Three more such dams are found. Over one we make a portage; at the other two we find chutes, through which we can run.

As we proceed, the granite rises higher, until nearly a thousand feet of the lower part of the walls are composed of this rock.

About eleven o'clock we hear a great roar ahead, and approach it very cautiously. The sound grows louder and louder as we run, and at last we find ourselves above a long, broken fall, with ledges and pinnacles of rock obstructing the river. There is a descent of, perhaps, seventy-five or eighty feet in a third of a mile, and the rushing waters break into great waves on the rocks, and lash themselves into a mad, white foam. We can land just above, but there is no foothold on either side by which we can make a portage. It is nearly a thousand feet to the top of the granite, so it will be impossible to carry our boats around, though we can climb to the summit up a side gulch, and, passing along a mile or two, can descend to the river. This we find on examination; but such a portage would be impracticable for us, and we must run the rapid, or abandon the river. There is no hesitation. We step into our boats, push off and away we go, first on smooth but swift water, then we strike a glassy wave, and ride to its top, down again into the trough, up again on a higher wave, and down and up on waves higher and still higher, until we strike one just as it curls back, and a breaker rolls over our little boat. Still, on we speed, shooting past projecting rocks, till the little boat is caught in a whirlpool, and spun around several times. At last we pull out again into the stream, and now the other boats have passed us. The open compartment of the "Emma Dean" is filled with water, and every breaker rolls over us. Hurled back from a rock, now on this side, now on that, we are carried into an eddy, in which we struggle for a few minutes, and are then out again, the breakers still rolling over us. Our boat is unmanageable, but she cannot sink, and we drift down another hundred yards, through breakers; how, we scarcely know. We find the other boats have turned into an eddy at the foot of the fall, and are waiting to catch us as we come, for the men have seen that our boat is swamped. They push out as we come near, and pull us in against the wall. We bail our boat, and on we go again.

The walls, now, are more than a mile in height—a vertical distance difficult to appreciate. Stand on the south steps of the Treasury building, in Washington, and look down Pennsylvania Avenue to the Capitol Park, and measure this distance overhead, and imagine cliffs to extend to that altitude, and you will understand what I mean; or, stand at Canal Street, in New York, and look up Broadway to Grace Church, and you have about the distance; or, stand at Lake Street bridge in Chicago, and look down to the Central Depot, and you have it again.

A thousand feet of this is up through granite crags, then steep slopes and perpendicular cliffs rise, one above another, to the summit.

"What a curious and scientifically interesting scamp!"

NEW MONEY AND ROBBER BARONS

1869–1873
New York City

GEORGE TEMPLETON STRONG

George Templeton Strong, a prominent lawyer, was an invaluable diarist of national and New York affairs. He began his diary in 1835 as a Columbia sophomore and kept it for forty years. (On its thirtieth anniversary he wrote, "Would that every duty of mine had been as faithfully fulfilled.")

James Fisk, the object of so much of his scorn, was an unscrupulous business-man whose stock manipulations earned him the nickname "Barnum of Wall Street." Fisk made the most of the freewheeling financial world that existed prior to the 1929 crash. One of his great coups was snatching control of the Erie Railroad from Cornelius Vanderbilt. Later he tried to corner the gold market with fellow robber baron Jay Gould, but instead triggered the Black Friday stock market crash of September 24, 1869. Even the government investigation of the crash failed to faze him. But a few years later he was shot dead by a former business partner in a quarrel over a shared mistress.

SEPTEMBER 30, 1869

James Fisk, Jr., keeps in some shady place, and is commonly said to have become a *non-est* man at last. He cannot show his ugly face in Wall Street without bodily peril. Old Vanderbilt is no less dearly hated. These great operators and Railroad Kings (or other Vikings of the stock market) will discover some day that ruining their weaker neighbors by a piratical com-bination of capital, though good for the assets, is bad for the bones, per-haps even for the vertebrae of the neck.

NOVEMBER 11

The grand *Vanderbilt* Bronze on the Hudson River Railroad Depot "unveiled" yesterday with much solemnity. There was a prayer and there were speeches. Vanderbilt began life penniless. He acquired a compe-tence—honestly, I assume—by energy, economy, and business tact, and then increased his store to a colossal fortune of sixty millions (as they say) by questionable operations in railroad stocks. Anyhow, he is a millionaire of millionaires. And, therefore, we bow down before him, and worship him, with a hideous group of molten images, with himself for a central figure, at a cost of $800,000.

JANUARY 10, 1871

Jim Fisk's last recorded antic was on New Year's Day. He made calls in a gorgeous chariot drawn by four high-stepping horses, with four smart footmen in flamboyant liveries. When he stopped before any favored house, his mamelukes descended, unrolled a carpet, laid it from the car-riage steps to the door, and stood on either side in attitude of military salute, while their august master passed by.

SEPTEMBER 4

We the people are a low set, without moral virility. Our rulers, Tweed and Company, are about good enough for us. The Alcibiades of New York is Mr. James Fisk. Mr. J. G. Bennett, Jr., who makes money by printing the adver-tisements of abortionists is elected "commodore"—or some such thing— by the aristocratic Yacht Club of New York, and is a leader of fashion in the Belmont clique. John Astor, Willy Duncan, William T. Blodgett, and others sit in the same railroad direction with vermin like Bill Tweed.

JANUARY 7, 1872

The great Fisk died this morning. No loss to the community—quite the reverse—but it's a pity he should have escaped the state prison in this way.

JANUARY 8

Much talk about Fisk. The remains were conveyed to the railroad depot in great state for interment at poor little Brattleboro. What a scamp he was, but what a curious and scientifically interesting scamp! When he "took to the road" a very few years ago and opened his campaign against society he was penniless.

By talent and audacity he raised himself to the first rank among business scoundrels, and (I suppose) to great wealth—certainly to opportunities of great wealth—but then he was reckless in spending. He was opera impresario, "commodore," financier, roue, mountebank, corrupt to the core, with great faculty of corrupting others, judges included, colonel of a regiment of militia, which he uniformed at his own cost and the splendid band of which he supported. He paid its first cornet-player $10,000 a year, it is said.

Illiterate, vulgar, unprincipled, profligate, always making himself conspicuously ridiculous by some piece of flagrant ostentation, he was, nevertheless, freehanded with his stolen money, and possessed, moreover, a certain magnetism of geniality that attracted to him people who were not particular about the decency of their associates. He was liberal to distressed ballet dancers and munificent to unfortunate females under difficulties.

"Half a dozen rescued pianos were watched by delicate ladies . . ."

THE GREAT FIRE AND ITS AFTERMATH

October 8–11, 1871
Chicago

JOSEPH EDGAR CHAMBERLAIN,
ALEXANDER FREAR, LAMBERT TREE,
AND WILLIAM A. CROFFUT

Horace White, editor in chief of the Chicago Tribune at the time of the fire, later wrote: "Nobody could see it all—no more than one man could see the whole of the Battle of Gettysburg. It was too vast, too swift, too full of smoke, too full of danger, for anybody to see it all. . . . It takes all sorts of people to make a great fire."

The sum of the individual stories is an astounding set of statistics: 250 people killed; just under 100,000 left homeless; 17,500 buildings destroyed over more than 2,000 acres. But one prominent story seems to have been concocted by a news-

paper reporter. Although the fire began near the house of Patrick and Catherine O'Leary, authorities found no clear evidence to prove that the O'Leary's cow started the fire by knocking over a lantern. (An ironic footnote to history: the O'Leary's house was one of the few in the neighborhood to survive the blaze.)

Joseph Edgar Chamberlain was a reporter for the Chicago Evening Post. *Alexander Frear was member of the Assembly of the State of New York. Lambert Tree was a judge of the Circuit Court of Cook County. William A. Croffut was managing editor of the* Chicago Evening Post.

JOSEPH EDGAR CHAMBERLAIN

I was at the scene in a few minutes. The fire had already advanced a distance of about a single square through the frame buildings that covered the ground thickly north of DeKoven Street and east of Jefferson Street—if those miserable alleys shall be dignified by being denominated streets. That neighborhood had always been a terra incognita to respectable Chicagoans, and during a residence of three years in the city I had never visited it. The land was thickly studded with one-story frame dwellings, cow stables, pigsties, corncribs, sheds innumerable; every wretched building within four feet of its neighbor, and everything of wood—not a brick or a stone in the whole area.

The fire was under full headway in this combustible mass before the engines arrived, and what could be done? Streams were thrown into the flame, and evaporated almost as soon as they struck it. . . . But still the firemen kept at work fighting the flames—stupidly and listlessly, for they had worked hard all of Saturday night and most of Sunday, and had been enervated by the whisky which is always copiously poured on such occasions.

Ewing Street was crowded with people pouring out of the thickly-settled locality between Jefferson Street and the river, and here the first panic began. The wretched female inhabitants were rushing out almost naked, imploring spectators to help them on with their burdens of bed quilts, cane-bottomed chairs, iron kettles, etc.

The fire had reached a better section, and many people of the better class were among those who had gathered a few of their household goods on that open space. Half a dozen rescued pianos were watched by delicate ladies, while the crowd still surged in every direction. Two boys, themselves intoxicated, reeled about, each bearing a small cask of whisky out of which he insisted upon treating everybody he met. Soon more casks of whisky appeared, and scores of excited men drank deeply of their contents. The result was, of course, that an equal number of drunken men were soon impeding the flight of the fugitives.

And now the scene of confusion had reached its height. Wagons were rushing through the streets laden with stocks of goods, books, valuable papers, boxes of money, and everything conceivable; scores of men were dragging trunks frantically along the sidewalks, knocking down women and children; fabulous sums of money were offered truckmen for conveyances.

But, as large as was the number of people who were flying from the fire, the number of passive spectators was still larger. Their eyes were all diverted from the scurrying mass of people around them to the spectacle of appalling grandeur before them. They stood transfixed, with a mingled feeling of horror and admiration.

ALEXANDER FREAR

I encountered my nephew saying he had one of George Garrison's horses and wanted only a rubber blanket to throw over him to protect him from the sparks. When we went out a man in his shirt-sleeves was unhitching the horse; and when we came up he sprang into the wagon, and would have driven off in spite of us if I had not caught the horse by the head. He then sprang out and struck my nephew in the face, and ran toward State Street.

To add to the terrors, the animals, burnt and infuriated by the cinders, darted through the streets regardless of human obstacles.

The flames from the houses on the west side reached in a diagonal arch quite across the street, and occasionally the wind would lift the great body of flame, detach it entirely from the burning buildings, and hurl it with terrific force far ahead.

We tried to force our way [in the wagon] along the avenue, which was already littered with costly furniture, some of it burning in the streets under the falling sparks, but it was next to impossible. Twice we were accosted by gentlemen with pocketbooks in their hands, and asked to carry away to a place of safety some valuable property. Much as we may have desired to assist them, it was out of our power. Women came and threw packages into the vehicle, and one man with a boy hanging to him caught the horse and tried to throw us out. I finally got out and endeavored to lead the animal out of the terrible scenes.

I was struck on the arm by a bird cage flung from an upper window, and the moment I released the horse he shied and ran into a burning dray-load of furniture, smashing the wheel of the wagon and throwing my companion out on his shoulder. Fortunately he was only bruised. But the horse, already terrified, started immediately, and I saw him disappear with a leap like that of a panther.

We then hurried on toward the St. James Hotel, passing through some of the strangest and saddest scenes it has ever been my misfortune to witness. I saw a woman kneeling in the street with a crucifix held up before her and the skirt of her dress burning while she prayed. We had barely passed before a runaway truck dashed her to the ground. Loads of goods passed us repeatedly that were burning on the trucks, and my nephew says that he distinctly saw one man go up to a pile of costly furniture lying in front of an elegant residence and deliberately hold a piece of burning packing board under it until the pile was lit.

[At the Tremont House] I forced my way upstairs, seeing no fire, and looked into all the open rooms, calling aloud the names of Mrs. Frear's daughters. When I was going down I found one of the men dragging an insensible woman downstairs by her shoulders. She was an unusually large woman, and had on a striped satin dress and a great quantity of jewelry, which I supposed she had put upon her person for safety. I assisted him to carry her down, and when she reached the lower story, to my surprise she suddenly recovered her consciousness and ran away followed by the man.

Around on Lake Street the tumult was worse. Here for the first time I beheld scenes of violence that made my blood boil. In front of Shay's magnificent dry-goods store a man loaded a storetruck with silks in defiance of the employees of the place. When he had piled all he could upon the truck, someone with a revolver shouted to him not to drive away or he would fire at him, to which he replied, "Fire, and be damned!" and the man put the pistol in his pocket again.

In this chaos were hundreds of children, wailing and crying for their parents. One little girl, in particular, I saw, whose golden hair was loose down her back and caught afire. She ran screaming past me, and somebody threw a glass of liquor upon her, which flared up and covered her with a blue flame.

LAMBERT TREE

When we arrived on the lake shore we found thousands of men, women, and children, and hundreds of horses and dogs, who had already fled there for refuge. The grounds were dotted all over at short intervals with piles of trunks, chairs, tables, beds, and household furniture of every description. It seemed as if this great open space, with nothing but the broad lake on the east of us, ought to be safe; and yet there, a few hours later, and for the second time that morning, we nearly perished from suffocation.

One young girl sat near me, with a cage containing a canary bird in her lap, whose life she was seeking to protect. She had covered the cage with her shawl, and from time to time raised it to see if the bird was all right. An hour or two later, while she was moving to a place of greater safety, I saw her little pet tumble from its perch to the bottom of the cage. It was dead; and the poor child, who doubtless had met her first sorrow, burst into tears.

Some persons drove their horses into the lake as far as the poor beasts could safely go, and men, women, and children waded out and clambered upon the wagons to which the horses were attached, while the lake was lined with people who were standing in the water at various depths, from their knees to their waists, all with their backs to the storm of fire which raged behind them.

WILLIAM A. CROFFUT

When the fire was baffled, citizens who had cowered and fled before it in awe arose bravely and said, "We can conquer everything else."

Pieces of iron, writhing in a thousand fantastic forms, and scarcely revealing under their strange disguises the original gas and water pipes, safes, scales, chandeliers, stoves, mantels, and columns they had been were pulled out while still warm, and carried away for foundry purposes. Ashes and broken bricks were carted to the lake and dumped to make more land for an already opulent railroad corporation. Walls were pulled down, and an army of men were employed to completely clear away the debris, and clean and square with a trowel such bricks as could be made available for rebuilding.

The first merchants who returned to the burnt district were, of course, the newsboys, peripatetic of habit and insinuating of demeanor. After the newspaper nomads came an apple-woman on Tuesday morning, who, with an air of mingled audacity and timidity, stationed her handcart at the corner of State and Randolph streets, half a mile within the ashen circle. She was the pioneer of all the trade of the future.

The vast business of the city, suddenly driven into the street, instantly accommodated itself to new locations and conditions. When the crimson canopy of Monday night merged into the dawn of Tuesday morning, it was found that, besides personal property, some thousands of loads of merchandise had been saved, stowed away in tunnels, buried in back alleys, piled up all along the lake shore, strewn in front yards through the avenues, run out of the city in boxcars, and even, in some instances, freighted upon the decks of schooners off the harbor. Two hundred thousand people in the city, and ten times that number out of the city, were in immediate need of goods and compelled to buy.

Many a man who has done a business of half a million a year has invaded his own front parlor on the avenue. Showcases have been arrayed through drawing and dining rooms, and clerks now serve customers with hats, furs, shoes, or jewelry, where they formerly spooned water ices at an evening party.

The burnt district looks as if Cheyenne had waltzed across the alkaline prairies and bestridden our poor disreputable river; but the city for a mile west and south of the fine district looks like Vanity Fair. The carelessness, even recklessness, with which Commerce has dropped down into dwelling-houses, haphazard, is grotesque and whimsical to the last degree. Three or four kinds of business, moreover, are crowded under every roof. A shoe store is in the basement. Upstairs is a button factory. The bedrooms higher up are lawyers', doctors', and insurers' offices; and into the dormer windows of the roof shoot a large quiver full of telegraphic wires.

Ever since the fire, Chicago has been the Mecca of sign painters; and every man commanding a brush and paint pot was sure of constant employment at high wages, whether he could spell or not.

"They was all disguised . . ."

A KU KLUX KLAN TRIAL

November 1871
Columbia, South Carolina

TESTIMONY OF GADSDEN STEEL

*T*he Klan was formed by angry whites in response to the Reconstruction, which turned their society upside down. The members were not just rowdy farm boys. General Nathaniel Forrest of the Confederate army was the KKK's Grand Wizard. General John B. Gordon was Grand Dragon of the Georgia branch. Zebulon Vance, who had been a U.S. congressman before the war, governor of North Carolina during its membership in the Confederacy, then a U.S. senator from 1879 to 1894, was Grand Dragon of the North Carolina branch.

This examination of Gadsden Steel, a witness for the prosecution, took place during a trial of alleged Klan members.

Q. [Did you] vote at the last election?

A. Yes, sir. . . .

Q. What ticket did you vote?

A. Voted the Radical ticket. . . . [The Radicals supported the rights of freed slaves.]

Q. Now, tell the jury about the Ku Klux coming to your house last March, on the night that Jim Williams was killed; what they said and did and what you said, and all about it.

A. They came to my house on a Monday night.

Q. Very well, tell what occurred.

A. They came to my house about ten o'clock, and I was in bed at that time; and I was asleep; and my wife she heard them before I did, and she shook me and woke me up, and told me she heard a mighty riding and walking, and said I had better get up, she thought it was Ku Klux. I jumped up, and put on my pantaloons, and stepped to the door, and looked out, and very close to the door I seen the men, and I stepped right back into the house; so when they knocked the door open they couldn't see me; and they came in and called for me to give up my gun, and I says I has no gun; and when I spoke they all grabbed me, and taken me out into the yard.

Q. What sort of looking people were they?

A. They was all disguised, as far as I could see—they was all disguised, and struck me three licks over the head, with a pistol; and four of them walked around to Mr. Moore and asked Mr. Moore if I had a gun; and he said no, not that he knew of; and they asked if I had a pistol, and he said no; they asked if I belonged to that company; he said no.

Q. What company?

A. Jim Williams' company; asked him was I a bad boy, and run about into any devilment; he said no; I was a very fine boy, as far as he knew; they asked how I voted; he said I voted the Radical ticket; they says, "There, G——d d——n you, I'll kill you for that"; they took me on out in the lane, and says, "come out and talk to Number 6"; they locked arms with me, and one took me by the collar, and put a gun agin me, and marched me out to Number 6; when I went out there, he was sitting on his horse; I walked up to him; he bowed his head down to me, (illustrating with a very low bow), and says, "How do you do," and horned me in the breast with his horns; had horns on the head about so long, (indicating about two feet;) I jumped back from him, and they punched me, and said "Stand up to him, G——d d——n you, and talk to him." I told them I would do so; he told me that he wanted me to tell him who had guns.

Q. Who said that?

A. Number 6; I told him I knew a heap that had guns, but hadn't them now; they had done give them up; well, says he, ain't Jim Williams got the guns? I says I heard folks say that he has them, but I do not know whether he has them or not. Then he says to me: "We want you to go and show us the way to Jim Williams' house." Says I, "I have never been there since he built on that road." Says they, "We want you to go and show us to where his house is; if you don't show us to where his house is we will kill you;" and then one looked up to the moon and says: "Don't tarry here too long with this d——n n——; we have to get back to hell before daybreak. It won't do to tarry here too long." Says he, "get on." There was a man standing to the right of me with his beast; his head was turned from me; I stepped around and got on behind him, and rode on around until they turned towards the school house, about sixty yards down the road, and he asked me did I want to go, and I told him no. Says I, the fix that I am in, if you don't do anything to me, may kill me. I hadn't nothing on but a shirt, pantaloons and drawers. They started in a lope then, and he hollowed to No. 6 that he could not keep up, that I was too heavy. Says he, "this God damned n—— is too heavy." No. 6 hollows back to him, "let him down," and he rode close enough to the fence so that I could get down, and I stepped off; says he, "you go home and go to bed, and if you are not there when we come along, we will kill you the next time we call on you; we are going on to kill Williams, and are going to kill all these damned n——s that votes the Radical ticket; run, God damn you, run." I ran into the yard, and I heard somebody talking near the store, and I slipped up beside the palings, and it was Dr. Love and Andy Lindsey tallying, and Love seen me, and says, "Gadsden, did they hurt you?" "No," says I, "not much; they punched the blood out in two places, and knocked me two or three times about the head, but they did not hurt me very much." Says he, "you go to bed and I don't think they will trouble you very much." I went home and put on my clothes . . . and I waked the others up, and we all went out into the old field and laid there until the chickens crowed for day, and went back to Mr. Moore's, near the house, and lay there till clear daylight, and I goes into the yard there, and Mr. Moore came to me and looked over my face and seen where they had punched the blood out of me, and says then for me to go on to my work and make myself easy, that they should not come and bother me any more; I never seen any more of them after that. . . .

Q. Jim Williams was killed that night, was he?

A. Yes, sir. He was killed that night.

"The Court cannot allow the prisoner to go on . . ."

UNITED STATES V. SUSAN B. ANTHONY—AND VICE VERSA

June 17–18, 1873
Canandaigua, New York

COURT RECORDS

On November 5, 1872, Susan B. Anthony, along with sixteen other women, went to the local polling booth in Rochester to vote in the general election. The note she wrote to her friend Elizabeth Cady Stanton that evening tells the first act of the story: "Well, I have gone and done it!!—positively voted the Republican ticket—Strait—this A.M. at 7 o'clock—& swore my vote in at that . . . All my sisters voted—Rhoda de Garmo too—Amy Post was rejected & she will immediately bring action against the registrars . . . Not a jeer not a word—not a look—disrespectful has met a single woman . . . I hope the morning's telegrams will tell of many women all over the country trying to vote . . . I hope you voted too."

But Anthony's victory was short-lived. She was arrested for violating election laws.

Although she lost her case, and eventually lost her appeal to the U.S. Supreme Court, her followers increased. In 1920, fourteen years after her death, the Nineteenth Amendment to the Constitution was ratified, guaranteeing women the right to vote.

The judge in this case was Ward Hunt. Richard Crowley was the U.S. district attorney. Henry R. Selden and John Van Voorhis defended Anthony.

Mr. Crowley opened the case as follows: May it Please the Court and Gentlemen of the Jury:

On the 5th of November, 1872, there was held in this State, as well as in other States of the Union, a general election for different officers, and among those, for candidates to represent several districts of this State in the Congress of the United States. The defendant, Miss Susan B. Anthony, at that time resided in the city of Rochester, in the county of Monroe, Northern District of New York, and upon the 5th day of November, 1872, she voted for a representative in the Congress of the United States, to represent the 29th Congressional District of this State, and also for a representative at large for the State of New York, to represent the State in the

Congress of the United States. At that time she was a woman. I suppose there will be no question about that. The question in this case, if there be a question of fact about it at all, will, in my judgment, be rather a question of law than one of fact. I suppose that there will be no question of fact, substantially, in the case when all of the evidence is out, and it will be for you to decide under the charge for his honor, the Judge, whether or not the defendant committed the offense of voting for a representative in Congress upon that occasion.

We think, on the part of the Government, that there is no question about it either one way or the other, neither a question of fact, nor a question of law, and that whatever Miss Anthony's intentions may have been—whether they were good or otherwise—she did not have a right to vote upon that question, and if she did vote without having a lawful right to vote, then there is no question but what she is guilty of violating a law of the United States in that behalf enacted by the Congress of the United States.

We don't claim in this case, gentlemen, that Miss Anthony is of that class of people who go about "repeating." We don't claim that she went from place to place for the purpose of offering her vote. But we do claim that upon the 5th of November, 1872, she voted, and whether she believed that she had a right to vote or not, it being a question of law, that she is within the statute.

It is not necessary for me, gentlemen, at this stage of the case, to state all the facts which will be proven on the part of the Government. I shall leave that to be shown by the evidence and by the witnesses, and if any question of law shall arise his Honor will undoubtedly give you instructions as he shall deem proper. Conceded, that on the 5th day of November, 1872, Miss Susan B. Anthony was a woman.

The court, after listening to an argument from the District Attorney, denied the motion for a new trial.

THE COURT: The prisoner will stand up. Has the prisoner anything to say why sentence shall not be pronounced?

MISS ANTHONY: Yes, your honor, I have many things to say; for in your ordered verdict of guilty, you have trampled underfoot every vital principle of our government. My natural rights, my civil rights, my political rights, are all alike ignored. Robbed of the fundamental privilege of citizenship, I am degraded from the status of a citizen to that of a subject; and not only myself individually, but all of my sex, are, by your honor's verdict, doomed to political subjection under this so-called Republican government.

JUDGE HUNT: The Court cannot listen to a rehearsal of arguments the prisoner's counsel has already consumed three hours in presenting.

MISS ANTHONY: May it please your honor, I am not arguing the question, but simply stating the reasons why sentence can not, in justice, be pronounced against me. Your denial of my citizen's right to vote is the denial of my right of consent as one of the governed, the denial of my right of representation as one of the taxed, the denial of my right to a trial by a jury of my peers as an offender against law, therefore, the denial of my sacred rights to life, liberty, property, and—

JUDGE HUNT: The Court can not allow the prisoner to go on.

MISS ANTHONY: But your honor will not deny me this one and only poor privilege of protest against this high-handed outrage upon my citizen's rights. May it please the Court to remember that since the day of my arrest last November, this is the first time that either myself or any person of my disfranchised class has been allowed a word of defense before judge or jury—

JUDGE HUNT: The prisoner must sit down; the Court can not allow it.

MISS ANTHONY: All my prosecutors, from the 8th Ward corner grocery politician, who entered the complaint, to the United States Marshal, Commissioner, District Attorney, District Judge, your honor on the bench, not one is my peer, but each and all are my political sovereigns; and had your honor submitted my case to the jury, as was clearly your duty, even then I should have had just cause of protest, for not one of those men was my peer; but, native or foreign, white or black, rich or poor, educated or ignorant, awake or asleep, sober or drunk, each and every man of them was my political superior; hence, in no sense, my peer. Even, under such circumstances, a commoner of England, tried before a jury of lords, would have far less cause to complain than should I, a woman, tried before a jury of men. Even my counsel, the Hon. Henry R. Selden, who has argued my cause so ably, so earnestly, so unanswerably before your honor, is my political sovereign. Precisely as no disfranchised person is entitled to sit upon a jury, and no woman is entitled to the franchise, so, none but a regularly admitted lawyer is allowed to practice in the courts, and no woman can gain admission to the bar—hence, jury, judge, counsel, must all be of the superior class.

JUDGE HUNT: The Court must insist—the prisoner has been tried according to the established forms of law.

MISS ANTHONY: Yes, your honor, but by forms of law all made by men, interpreted by men, administered by men, in favor of men, and against women; and hence, your honor's ordered verdict of guilty, against a United States citizen for the exercise of "that citizen's right to vote," simply because that citizen was a woman and not a man. But, yesterday, the same man-made forms of law declared it a crime punishable with $1,000 fine and six months' imprisonment, for you, or me, or any of us, to give a cup of cold water, a crust of bread, or a night's shelter to a panting fugitive as he was tracking his way to Canada. And every man or woman in whose veins coursed a drop of human sympathy violated that wicked law, reckless of consequences, and was justified in so doing. As then the slaves who got their freedom must take it over, or under, or through the unjust forms of law, precisely so now must women, to get their right to a voice in this Government, take it; and I have taken mine, and mean to take it at every possible opportunity.

JUDGE HUNT: The Court orders the prisoner to sit down. It will not allow another word.

MISS ANTHONY: When I was brought before your honor for trial, I hoped for a broad and liberal interpretation of the Constitution and its recent amendments, that should declare all United States citizens under its protecting aegis—that should declare equality of rights the national guarantee to all persons born or naturalized in the United States. But failing to get this justice—failing, even, to get a trial by a jury not of my peers—I ask not leniency at your hands—but rather the full rigors of the law.

JUDGE HUNT: The Court must insist— (Here the prisoner sat down.)

JUDGE HUNT: The prisoner will stand up. (Here Miss Anthony arose again.) The sentence of the Court is that you pay a fine of one hundred dollars and the costs of the prosecution.

MISS ANTHONY: May it please your honor, I shall never pay a dollar of your unjust penalty. All the stock in trade I possess is a $10,000 debt, incurred by publishing my paper—*The Revolution*—four years ago, the sole object of which was to educate all women to do precisely as I have done, rebel against your man-made, unjust, unconstitutional forms of law, that tax, fine, imprison, and hang women, while they deny them the right of representation in the Government; and I shall work on with might and main to pay every dollar of that honest debt, but not a penny shall go to this unjust claim. And I shall earnestly and persistently continue to urge all women to the practical recognition of the old revolutionary maxim, that "Resistance to tyranny is obedience to God."

JUDGE HUNT: Madam, the Court will not order you committed until the fine is paid.

"The effect was loud . . ."

THE FIRST TELEPHONE CALL

March 10, 1876
Boston

ALEXANDER GRAHAM BELL

This is the account Bell recorded in his laboratory journal. The notations for the telephone's parts refer to his diagram.

I then shouted into M [the mouthpiece] the following sentence: "Mr. Watson—Come here—I want to see you." To my delight he came and declared that he had heard and understood what I said. I asked him to repeat the words. He answered "You said—'Mr. Watson—Come here—I want to see you.' " We then changed places and I listened at S [the receiver] while Mr. Watson read a few passages from a book into the mouth piece M. It was certainly the case that articulate sounds proceeded from S. The effect was loud but indistinct and muffled. If I had read beforehand the passage given by Mr. Watson I should have recognized every word. As it was I could not make out the sense—but an occasional word here and there was quite distinct. I made out "to" and "out" and "further"; and finally the sentence "Mr. Bell do you understand what I say? Do—you—un—der—stand—what—I—say" came quite clearly and intelligibly.

"A tall well-built soldier
   with yellow hair and mustache . . ."

CUSTER IS KILLED AT LITTLE BIGHORN

June 25, 1876
Little Bighorn, Montana

CHIEF WHITE BULL

*I*n 1875, gold was discovered in the Black Hills, an area the U.S. government
had agreed to protect as a holy land of the Cheyenne and Sioux. But the army
could not or would not stop the rush of prospectors. The Sioux, who had already
seen their hunting grounds diminish as white settlers arrived over the previous
decade, decided to make a stand.

A U.S. Army force of more than a thousand men under the command of General Alfred Terry rode to meet the natives. Terry divided his troops, sending Custer
with the Seventh Cavalry to ride around the natives and prepare for a pincers
movement. But Custer did not wait for Terry to order the advance. He unwisely
divided his forces into three columns and attacked on his own. The whole central
column—more than two hundred men including Custer—was killed in the battle.
The other two columns were able to retreat.

To a point, Custer seemed to understand the Sioux's feelings. He had once written, "If I were an Indian, I would certainly prefer to cast my lot . . . to the free open
plains rather than submit to the confined limits of a reservation, there to be the
recipient of the blessed benefits of civilization with its vices thrown in."

White Bull was a Sioux chief.

I charged in. A tall, well-built soldier with yellow hair and mustache
saw me coming and tried to bluff me, aiming his rifle at me. But when I
rushed him, he threw his rifle at me without shooting. I dodged it. We
grabbed each other and wrestled there in the dust and smoke. It was like
fighting in a fog. This soldier was very strong and brave. He tried to
wrench my rifle from me, and nearly did it. I lashed him across the face
with my quirt, striking the coup. He let go, then grabbed my gun with
both hands until I struck him again.

But the tall soldier fought hard. He was desperate. He hit me with his
fists on jaw and shoulders, then grabbed my long braids with both hands,

pulled my face close and tried to bite my nose off. I yelled for help: "Hey, hey, come over and help me!" I thought that soldier would kill me.

Bear Lice and Crow Boy heard me call and came running. These friends tried to hit the soldier. But we were whirling around, back and forth, so that most of their blows hit me. They knocked me dizzy. I yelled as loud as I could to scare my enemy, but he would not let go. Finally I broke free.

He drew his pistol. I wrenched it out of his hand and struck him with it three or four times on the head, knocked him over, shot him in the head and fired at his heart. I took his pistol and cartridge belt. Hawk-Stays-Up struck second on his body.

Ho hechetu! That was a fight, a hard fight. But it was a glorious battle, I enjoyed it. . . .

On the hill top, I met my relative, Bad Juice [Bad Soup]. He had been around Fort Abraham Lincoln and knew Long Hair by sight. When he came to the tall soldier lying on his back naked, Bad Soup pointed him out and said, "Long Hair thought he was the greatest man in the world. Now he lies there."

"Well," I said, "if that is Long Hair, I am the man who killed him."

"That startling cry in the night . . ."

ALEUTS

June 30–July 2, 1879
Pribilof Islands, Alaska

LIBBY BEAMAN

*S*ecretary of State William Seward bought "Seward's Folly," as Alaska was called afterward, from Russia in 1867. He paid $7,200,000—about two cents an acre.

Beaman, from a prominent Washington, D.C., family, was the first non-native woman to settle in the Pribilof Islands. Her husband was a Treasury Department junior agent who helped oversee the fur trade.

JUNE 30

The Aleuts believe that they are descended from the seals! Never having seen a monkey in their lives, this belief is much more logical for them and is a part of their legend and folklore—that is, what little they have retained of a folklore from the time before the Russians. Dr. Kelly says it is a logical belief and in many ways more valid than ours, because the seal has a far larger brain box in proportion to the body than has a monkey. The seal's eyes express human emotion where a monkey's do not, and since the Aleuts always have worn seal fur, eaten seal meat, and used the skin for boats and the blubber for fuel, they are entirely identified with the seals. If they have any theology left from the old time, their god or gods were no doubt giant seals, and they themselves have been seals in other incarnations.

While they do not have too many legends for their race, they do have a few strange customs that are not Russian. The men wander about at night in a sort of a trance, not *kvas*-induced. Of course the nights are light, so one can see them. They are not frightening, just eerie, moving about unseeing. No one has been able to account for this, and as they never do any harm, no one has ever tried to stop the habit. It is a bit disconcerting to run into one and have him look right through you without acknowledging a greeting. The womenfolk never wander like this and don't seem to mind when the men do. Usually the next day, the man will recount ghostly encounters he has had or visions of almost mythological beasts. I've heard them pad past our windows on occasion and wondered what they could be up to. Sometimes they are actually clairvoyant when they are traipsing about in a dense fog and suddenly scream out, "Ship's light! Ship's light!" which they cannot possibly see with their physical eyes. And always, sure enough, when the fog lifts, a ship is lying offshore!

One screamed "Ship's light!" about two this morning, sending chills up and down our spines. There's a dense, dense fog, but we think the *St. Paul* may be in. She's due within a few days.

JULY 2

The *St. Paul* was riding at anchor when the mists finally dissipated! What a welcome sight! What a truly beautiful sight! A first link with home! . . . I won't ever mind that startling cry in the night, "Ship's light!" again.

"The longer it burned the more fascinated we were . . ."

ELECTRIC LIGHT

October 21, 1879
Menlo Park, New Jersey

THOMAS ALVA EDISON

*O*f Thomas Alva Edison's thousands of inventions and more than one thousand patents, including the phonograph and the movie camera, the greatest is obvious: the incandescent electric light.

In those days, you know, we had arc lamps. I had been down to see Professor Barker, at Philadelphia, and he had shown me one. A little later I had seen another one, and the whole outfit, engine, dynamo and one or two lamps, was traveling around the country with a circus. At that time Wallace and Moses G. Farmer had succeeded in getting 10 or 15 lamps to burn together in series. It happened that I was comparatively at leisure then, because I had just finished working on the carbon button telephone, and this electric light idea took possession of me.

It was easy to see what the thing needed; it wanted to be subdivided. The light was too bright and too big. What we wished for was little lights and a distribution of them to people's houses in just the same way that gas is sent around and burned at your fixture when you want it. . . . It was easy enough to see that the subdivision never could be accomplished unless each light was independent of every other. Now it was plain enough that they could not burn in series; hence they must burn in multiple arc. It was with this conviction that I started. I was fired with the idea of the incandescent lamp as opposed to the arc lamp, so I went to work and got some very fine platinum wire drawn. . . . We tried to make the platinum work but it didn't stand. Then we tried mixing in about 10 per cent of iridium with the platinum, but we couldn't force that high enough without melting it. . . . We went fishing around and trying all sorts and shapes of things to make a filament that would stand. We tried silicon and boron and a lot of things that I have forgotten now. The funny part of it was that I never thought in those days that carbon would answer because a fine hair of carbon was so sensitive to oxidation. Finally I thought I would try it because we had got very high vacuum and good conditions for it. We sent out and bought some cotton thread and carbonized it and made the first filament. . . . We built the lamp and lighted it; it lit up, and in the first few breathless minutes we measured its resistance quickly and found it was 275 ohms—all we wanted. Then we sat down and looked at that lamp; we wanted to see how long it would burn. There was the problem solved—if the filament would last. The day was—let me see—October 21, 1879. We sat and looked and the lamp continued to burn and the longer it burned the more fascinated we were. None of us could go to bed and there was no sleep for over 40 hours; we sat and just watched it with anxiety growing into elation. It lasted about 45 hours and then I said, "If it will burn 40 hours now I know I can make it burn a hundred."

"The imprint of self-reliance,
firmness and dauntless courage . . ."

JESSE JAMES'S BODY

April 3, 1882
St. Joseph, Missouri

ANONYMOUS *WESTERN*
ASSOCIATED PRESS REPORTER

A fter the Civil War, former Rebel guerilla Jesse James formed a gang with his brother Frank and some other outlaws. For fifteen years they robbed banks and trains in the Midwest, becoming folk heroes. Because of the many reported sightings of James after his death a body was exhumed from his grave in 1995 for DNA testing. It was James's.

A great sensation was created in this city this morning by the announcement that Jesse James, the notorious bandit and train-robber, had been shot and killed here in St. Joseph. The news spread with great rapidity, but most people received it with doubts until an investigation established the fact beyond question. Then the excitement became more and more intense, and crowds of people rushed to that quarter of the city where the shooting took place, anxious to view the body of the dead outlaw and to learn the particulars.

The body is that of a man of magnificent physique, who in the pride of health and strength must have been a commanding figure, six feet tall, and weighing 175 pounds, with every muscle developed and hardened by active life. It is a body that would fill with delight the surgeon seeking material for demonstrating anatomy. The features, but little disturbed in death are not unpleasing, and bear the imprint of self-reliance, firmness and dauntless courage. To look upon that face is to believe that the wonderful deeds of daring ascribed to Jesse James have not been exaggerated. The hair is dark brown, the eyes half-opened, glazed, a cold steel gray, upon the upper lip a close-cropped mustache, stained by nasal hemorrhage, and the lower part of the face covered by a close brown beard about four inches long. Over the left eye is the blackened wound caused by the bullet of Robert Ford, the beardless boy whose cunning and treachery, animated by greed of gold, brought to an ignoble end the desperado who has so long snapped his fingers contemptuously at the law and its myriad of agents.

A superficial examination of the body would alone afford strong proof that the dead body is that of Jesse James. He has been literally shot to pieces in his daring exploits, and his old wounds would have killed any one cast in a less rugged mold. Two bullets have pierced the abdomen, and are still in the body. There is a bullet-hole in the right wrist, and another in the right ankle. Two more disfigure the left thigh and knee. The hands are soft and white and unstained by manual labor, and the middle finger of the left hand has been shot away at the first joint. Hundreds of people have passed before the body, and while there was a unanimous expression of relief that the country was rid of so formidable a desperado, there were not a few who did not hesitate to condemn the manner of his taking off. Nevertheless, the young Ford brothers are undeniably the heroes of the hour. As they sat in the County Clerk's office this afternoon awaiting their call before the Coroner's inquest, then progressing in an adjoining room, they were the coolest and most unconcerned persons present, and the very last that a stranger would pick out as the slayers of Jesse James.

"I saw a lighted fuse . . ."

HAYMARKET RIOT

May 1, 1886
Chicago

BARTON SIMONSON

*L*abor battles became increasingly violent at the end of the 1800s. The three
most notorious incidents may be the Homestead strike, against Andrew Carnegie's Pennsylvania steel mills (1894), the Pullman strike, against the Chicago
railroad car builder (1894), and the Haymarket riot, which occurred during a
strike at the McCormick Reaper Company in Chicago.

The day before the riot, a striker had been killed in a fight with police. Union
organizers called for a rally to protest the killing. At the rally a bomb was thrown,
killing seven police officers and wounding sixty. The melee began.

Eight rally leaders were tried as accessories to murder. Although none was
linked to the bomb, all eight were convicted. Four of them were hanged and one
committed suicide. Governor John P. Altgeld pardoned the remaining three in 1893,
at the cost of his political career.

Eyewitness Simonson's mention of "Spies" refers to August Spies, a rally leader.

I reached the Haymarket about 7:30. I found no meeting there. I
walked around among the crowd, which was scattered over the Haymarket, then I went to the Des Plaines Street station and shook hands with
Captain Ward, whom I knew. He introduced me to Inspector Bonfield and
I had a conversation with him. Later on I went back and remained
throughout the whole meeting until the bomb had exploded. The speakers were northeast of me in front of Crane Brothers' building, a few feet
north of the alley. I remember the alley particularly. As far as I remember
Spies' speech, he said: "Please come to order. This meeting is not called to
incite any riot." . . .

I thought Mr. Parsons did say: "To arms, To arms," but in what connection could not remember. Somebody in the crowd said "shoot" or
"hang Gould," and he [Spies] says, "No, a great many will jump up and
take his place. What socialism aims at is not the death of individuals but
of the system."

Fielden spoke very loud, and as I had never attended a Socialist meeting before in my life, I thought they were a little wild. Fielden spoke about a Congressman from Ohio who had been elected by the workingmen and confessed that no legislation could be enacted in favor of the workingmen, consequently he said there was no use trying to do anything by legislation. After he had talked a while a dark cloud with cold wind came up from the north. Many people had left before, but when that cloud came a great many people left. Somebody said, "Let's adjourn"—to someplace—I can't remember the name of the place. Fielden said he was about through, there was no need of adjourning. He said two or three times, "Now in conclusion," or something like that and became impatient. Then I heard a commotion and a good deal of noise in the audience, and somebody said "police." I looked south and saw a line of police. The police moved along until the front of the column got about up to the speaker's wagon. I heard somebody near the wagon say something about dispersing. I saw some persons upon the wagon. I could not tell who they were. About the time somebody was giving that command to disperse, I distinctly heard two words coming from the vicinity of the wagon or from the wagon. I don't know who uttered them. The words were, "peaceable meeting." That was a few seconds before the explosion of the bomb. I did not hear any such exclamation as, "Here come the bloodhounds of the police; you do your duty and I'll do mine," from the locality of the wagon or from Mr. Fielden. I heard nothing of the sort that night. At the time the bomb exploded I was still in my position upon the stairs. There was no pistol firing by any person upon the wagon before the bomb exploded. No pistol shots anywhere before the explosion of the bomb.

Just after the command to disperse had been given, I saw a lighted fuse, or something—I didn't know what it was at the time—come up from a point twenty feet south of the south line of Crane's alley, from about the center of the sidewalk on the east side of the street, from behind some boxes. I am positive it was not thrown from the alley. I first noticed it about six or seven feet in the air, a little above a man's head. It went in a northwest course and up about fifteen feet from the ground, and fell about the middle of the street. The explosion followed almost immediately. Something of a cloud of smoke followed the explosion. After the bomb exploded there was pistol shooting. From my position I could distinctly see the flashes of the pistols. My head was about fifteen feet above the ground. There might have been fifty to one hundred and fifty pistol shots. They proceeded from about the center of where the police were. I did not observe either the flashes of the pistol shot or hear the report of any shots from the crowd upon the police prior to the firing by the police.

The police were not only shooting at the crowd but I noticed several of them shoot just as they happened to throw their arms. I concluded that my position was possibly more dangerous than down in the crowd, and then I ran down to the foot of the stairs, ran west on the sidewalk on Randolph Street a short distance, and then in the road. A crowd was running in the same direction. I had to jump over a man lying down, and I saw another man fall in front of me about 150 to 200 feet west of Des Plaines Street. I took hold of his arm and wanted to help him, but the firing was so lively behind me that I just let go and ran. I was in the rear of the crowd running west, the police still behind us. There were no shots from the direction to which I was running.

I am not and never have been a member of any Socialistic party or association. Walking through the crowd before the meeting, I noticed that the meeting was composed principally of ordinary workingmen, mechanics, etc. . . . In the course of the conversation with Capt. Bonfield at the station before the meeting that night, I asked him about the trouble in the southwestern part of the city. He says: "The trouble there is that these"—whether he used the word Socialist or strikers, I don't know—"get their women and children mixed up with them and around them and in front of them, and we can't get at them. I would like to get three thousand of them in a crowd without their women and children"—and to the best of my recollection he added—"and I will make short work of them."

"Stood there studying
the river-sights in the drizzling rain . . ."

FRANK LLOYD WRIGHT
SEES HIS FIRST CITY

1887
Chicago

FRANK LLOYD WRIGHT

*A*rchitect Frank Lloyd Wright *is celebrated as much for his single-family "prairie" homes as for landmarks like New York City's Guggenheim Museum. His original theories have now become common axioms. He developed the idea of "organic architecture," in which design must be derived from a building's environment and*

from its function and materials. He opened the interior spaces of buildings, allow-
ing rooms to flow into each other.

In his autobiography the Wisconsin native set down his first impressions of
Chicago. Soon after the overwhelming experience he took a job with the man who
would influence him most, Louis Sullivan, the great architect whose elegant early
skyscrapers were already reshaping American cities.

Wells Street Station: Six o'clock in late Spring, 1887. Drizzling. Sputtering white arc-light in the station and in the streets, dazzling and ugly. I
had never seen electric lights before.

Crowds. Impersonal, intent on seeing nothing.

Somehow I didn't like to ask anyone anything. Followed the crowd.

Drifted south to the Wells Street Bridge over the Chicago River. The
mysterious dark of the river with dim masts, hulks, and funnels hung
with lights half-smothered in gloom—reflected in the black beneath. I
stopped to see, holding myself close to the iron rail to avoid the blind
hurrying by.

I wondered where Chicago was—if it was near. Suddenly the clanging
of a bell. The crowd began to run. I wondered why: found myself alone
and realized why in time to get off but stayed on as the bridge swung out
with me into the channel and a tug, puffing clouds of steam, came pushing
along below, pulling at an enormous iron grain boat, towing it slowly
along through the gap.

Stood there studying the river-sights in the drizzling rain until the
bridge followed after and closed to open the street again. Later, I never
crossed the river without being charmed by somber beauty.

Wondered where to go for the night. But again if I thought to ask anyone, there was only the brutal, hurrying crowd, trying hard not to see.

Drifted south.

This must be Chicago now. So cold, black, blue-white and wet.

The horrid blue-white glare of arc-lights was over everything.

Shivering. Hungry. Went into an eating place near Randolph Street
and parted with seventy cents, ten per cent of my entire capital.

Got into the street again to find it colder raining harder.

. . . Wabash Avenue. Cottage-Grove Avenue cable cars were running
there. My first sight of the cable car. So, curious, I got on the grip-car
beside the gripman and tried to figure it all out, going south in the
process until the car stopped and "all out!" That car was going to the barn.

Got on the one coming out headed north now. Not sleepy nor tired.
Half resentful because compelled to read the signs pressing on the eyes

everywhere. They claimed your eyes for this, that, and everything beside. They lined the car above the windows. They lined the way, pushing, crowding and playing all manner of tricks on the desired eye.

Tried to stop looking at them. Compelled to look again. Kept on reading until reading got to be torture.

There were glaring signs on the glass shop-fronts against the lights inside, sharp signs in the glare of the sputtering arc-lamps outside.

HURRAH signs. STOP signs. COME ON IN signs. HELLO signs set out before the blazing windows on the sidewalks. Flat fences lettered both sides, man-high, were hanging out across above the sidewalks and lit by electric lamps. . . .

Supersensitive eyes were fixed by harsh dissonance and recovered themselves: reasoned and fought for freedom. Compelled again—until the procession of saloons, food shops, barber shops, eating houses, saloons, restaurants, groceries, laundries—and saloons, saloons, tailors, dry goods, candy shops, bakeries and saloons, became chaos in a wilderness of Italian, German, Irish, Polak, Greek, English, Swedish, French, Chinese and Spanish names in letters that began to come off, and get about, interlace and stick and climb and swing again.

Demoralization of the eye began: names obliterating everything. Names and what they would do for you or with you or to you for your money. Shutting your eyes didn't end it, for then you heard them louder than you saw them. They would begin to mix with absurd effect and you need take nothing to get the effect of another extravaganza. Letters this time. Another ballet, of A. B. C. D. E. F. G., L. M. N. O. P., X. Y. and Z the premier danseuse, intervening in fantastic dances.

It would have been a mercy not to have known the alphabet. One pays a heavy toll for the joys of being "eye-minded."

Got to bed at the Brigg's House north on Randolph Street, wrapped a sheet around myself—it seemed awfully like a winding sheet as I caught sight of it in the mirror—and slept. . . .

Asleep in Chicago.

A Chicago murderously actual.

Next day I began on Chicago.

My hand in my pocket after breakfast, I could feel sure of three silver dollars and a dime.

Took the city directory and made a list of architects, choosing names I had heard in Conover's office or that sounded interesting. All names, and missed the names of all names important to me. . . . Tramped through street after street now seeing Chicago above the sign-belt.

And where was the architecture of the great city—The "Eternal City of the West"?

Where was it? Behind these shameless signs?

A vacant block would come by. Then the enormous billboards planted there stood up grandly, had it all their own way, obliterating everything in nothing. That was better.

Chicago! Immense gridiron of noisy streets. Dirty . . . Heavy traffic crossing both ways at once, managing somehow: Torrential noise.

A stupid thing, that gridiron: cross-currents of horses, trucks, street cars, grinding on hard rails, mingling with streams of human beings in seeming confusion and clamor. But habit was in the movement making it expert, and so safe enough. Dreary—dim—smoked. Smoked dim and smoking.

A wide, desolate, vacant strip ran along the water front over which the Illinois Central trains incessantly puffed and ground, cutting the city off from the lake.

Terrible, this grinding and piling up of blind forces. If there was logic here who could grasp it?

To stop and think in the midst of this would be to give way to terror. The gray, soiled river with its mists of steam and smoke, was the only beauty. That smelled to heaven.

Young engineer looking for work? Sam Treat looked me over. "University man, eh!" The kindly intellectual face under a mass of gray hair smiled. "Sorry."

Caught a glimpse of a busy drafting room full of men as I came out.

Well!—there was Beers, Clay and Dutton. More tramping through brutal crowds that never seemed to see anything. Mr. Clay came out and looked me over—a twinkle of kindly humor in his black eyes. I have remembered that he seemed to see me and was amused. Why? Was it the longish hair again, or what? Took pity on me, maybe, for he asked me to call again in a few weeks if I found nothing. In a few weeks! And I had just three dollars and ten cents! . . .

The famous Pullman Building had come into view. It looked funny— as if made to excite curiosity. Had passed the Palmer House, on the way down, that famous Chicago Pallazzo. It seemed curious to me: seemed like an ugly old, old man whose wrinkles were all in the wrong place owing to a misspent life. As I went on my way to W. W. Boyington's office I passed the Chicago Board of Trade at the foot of La Salle Street. Boyington had done it. This?—thin-chested, hardfaced, chamfered monstrosity? I turned aside from Boyington's office then and there.

Chicago architecture! Where was it? Not the Exposition Building, a rank, much-domed yellow shed on the lake front. No, nor the rank and file along the streets. The rank and file all pretty much alike, industriously varied but with no variety. All the same thought or lack of it. Were all American cities like this one, so casual, so monotonous in their savage, outrageous attempts at variety? All competing for the same thing in the same way? Another senseless competition never to be won?

"Suddenly the air was pierced with the blast of a bugle . . ."

THE GREAT OKLAHOMA LAND RUSH

April 22, 1889
Guthrie, Oklahoma

HAMILTON S. WICKS

*T*he Homestead Act opened some 2 million acres of Oklahoma territory not already assigned to the "Five Civilized Tribes"—Cherokee, Cocktaw, Chickasaw, Creek, and Seminole. Fifty thousand prospective settlers waited on the border of the Cherokee Strip until noon on April 22, when the rush began to lay claim to the individual allotments of 160 acres.

The plan was a mess. Because people who had jumped the gun—"Sooners"— were already in the territory, it took years to sort out conflicting claims. But it was the essence of freewheeling Americanism.

Wicks participated in the land rush and reported on the event for Cosmo-politan *magazine. The city he saw built in a day was Guthrie. Enid and Oklahoma City were also built that day.*

As our train slowly moved through the Cherokee Strip, a vast procession of "Boomers" was seen moving across the plains to the Oklahoma lines, forming picturesque groups on the otherwise unbroken landscape. The wagon road through the "Strip," extemporized by the Boomers, ran for long distances parallel with the railway, and the procession that extended the whole distance illustrated the characteristics of Western American life. Here, for instance, would be a party consisting of a "prairie schooner" drawn by four scrawny, rawboned horses, and filled with a tat-terdemalion group, consisting of a shaggy bearded man, a slatternly look-ing woman, and several girls and boys, faithful images of their parents, in shabby attire, usually with a dog and a coop of chickens. In striking contrast to this frontier picture, perhaps a couple of flashy real estate men from Wichita would come jogging on a short distance behind, driving a spanking span of bays, with an equipage looking for all the world as though it had just come from a fashionable livery stable.

Our train, whirling rapidly over the prairie, overtook many such contrasted pictures. There were single rigs and double rigs innumerable; there were six-mule teams and four-in-hands, with here and there parties on horseback, and not a few on foot trudging along the wayside. The whole procession marched, rode, or drove, as on some gala occasion, with smiling faces and waving hands. Everyone imagined that Eldorado was just ahead, and I dare say the possibility of failure or disappointment did not enter into the consideration of a single individual on that cool and delightful April day. . . .

As our train neared the Oklahoma border, the "procession" became more dense and in some instances clogged the approaches to the fords of the small streams that crossed its pathway. When we finally slowed up at the dividing line, the camps of the "Boomers" could be seen extending in every direction.

And now the hour of twelve was at hand, and everyone on the *qui vive* for the bugle blast that would dissolve the chain of enchantment hitherto girding about this coveted land. Many of the "Boomers" were mounted on high-spirited and fleet-footed horses, and had ranged themselves along the territorial line, scarcely restrained even by the presence of the troop of cavalry from taking summary possession. The better class of wagons and carriages ranged themselves in line with the horsemen, and even here and there mule teams attached to canvas-covered vehicles stood in the front ranks, with the reins and whip grasped by the "Boomers" wives. All was excitement and expectation. Every nerve was on tension and every muscle strained.

Suddenly the air was pierced with the blast of a bugle. Hundreds of throats echoed the sound with shouts of exultation. The quivering limbs of saddled steeds, no longer restrained by the hands that held their bridles, bounded forward simultaneously into the "beautiful land" of Oklahoma; and wagons and carriages and buggies and prairie schooners and a whole congregation of curious equipages joined in this unparalleled race, where every starter was bound to win a prize—the "Realization Stakes" of home and prosperity.

Here was a unique contest in which thousands participated and which was to occur but once for all time. Away dashed the thoroughbreds, the broncos, the pintos, and the mustangs at a breakneck pace across the uneven surface of the prairie. It was amazing to witness the recklessness of those cowboy riders. They jumped obstacles; they leaped ditches; they cantered with no diminution of speed through waterpools; and when they came to a ravine too wide to leap, down they would go with a rush, and up the other side with a spurt of energy, to scurry once more like mad over the level plain. This reckless riding was all very well at the fore part of the race, but it could not prevail against the more discreet maneuverings of several elderly "Boomers" who rode more powerful and speedy horses.

One old white-bearded fellow especially commanded attention. He was mounted on a coal black thoroughbred, and avoided any disaster by checking the pace of his animal when ravines had to be crossed. But his splendid bursts of speed when no obstructions barred the way soon placed him far in advance of all his competitors. It took but a short time to solve this question of speed among the riders, and after a neck-and-neck race for half a mile or more, they spread like a fan over the prairie, and were eventually lost to our vision among the rolling billows of Oklahoma's far-expanding prairie.

The race was not over when you reached the particular lot you were content to select for your possession. The contest still was who should drive their stakes first, who would erect their little tents soonest, and then, who would quickest build a little wooden shanty.

The situation was so peculiar that it is difficult to convey correct impressions of the situation. It reminded me of playing blindman's buff. One did not know how far to go before stopping; it was hard to tell when it was best to stop; and it was a puzzle whether to turn to the right hand or the left. Everyone appeared dazed, and all for the most part acted like a flock of stray sheep. Where the boldest led, many others followed. I found myself, without exactly knowing how, about midway between the government building and depot. It occurred to me that a street would probably run past the depot.

I accosted a man who looked like a deputy, with a piece of white cord in his hands, and asked him if this was to be a street along here.

"Yes," he replied. "We are laying off four corner lots right here for a lumber yard."

"Is this the corner where I stand?" I inquired.

"Yes," he responded, approaching me.

"Then I claim this corner lot!" I said with decision, as I jammed my location stick in the ground and hammered it securely home with my heel. "I propose to have one lot at all hazards on this town site, and you will have to limit yourself to three, in this location at least."

An angry altercation ensued, but I stoutly maintained my position and my rights. I proceeded at once to unstrap a small folding cot I brought with me, and, by standing it on its end, it made a tolerable center pole for a tent. I then threw a couple of my blankets over the cot and staked them securely into the ground on either side. Thus I had a claim that was un-jumpable because of substantial improvements, and I felt safe and breathed more freely until my brother arrived on the third train, with our tent and equipments.

On the morning of April 23, a city of 10,000 people, 500 houses, and innumerable tents existed where twelve hours before was nothing but a broad expanse of prairie. The new city changed its appearance every twenty-four hours, as day by day the work of construction went on. The tents were rapidly superseded by small frame structures, until at the end of a month there were scarcely any tents to be seen. The small frame structures in turn gave place to larger ones, and a number of fine two-story frame buildings were erected on the principal thoroughfares before the end of the first sixty days.

At the time of writing this article—less than one hundred days from the date of the opening—Guthrie presents the appearance of a model Western city, with broad and regular streets and alleys; with handsome store and office buildings; with a system of parks and boulevards, unsur-passed in point of number, extent, and beauty by any city of twice its size and population in the West; with a number of fine iron bridges spanning the Cottonwood River, which runs through its midst; with a system of waterworks that furnishes hydrants at the corners of all the principal streets and keeps several large sprinkling carts continually busy; with an electric light plant on the Westinghouse system of alternating currents, capable not only of thoroughly lighting the whole city but of furnishing the power for running an electric railway, for which the charter has already been granted by the City Council.

"All were caught in the fearful rush"

THE JOHNSTOWN FLOOD

June 2, 1889
Johnstown, Pennsylvania

ANONYMOUS *PHILADELPHIA PUBLIC
LEDGER* REPORTER

O n May 31, a dam on the Conemaugh River broke. The dam had been built to
create a resort lake for wealthy families, who had been warned that it was too
weak for its load.

The owner of a local hotel later reported, "The water seemed to leap, scarcely
touching the ground. It bounded down the valley, crashing and roaring, carrying
everything before it. For a mile its front seemed like a solid wall twenty feet high."
The flood claimed twenty-two hundred lives. Every surviving citizen of Johnstown
lost a friend or relative.

I have just come from Johnstown proper, over a bridge which was
completed this afternoon. I reached there at 5 o'clock last night, and tell
only what I did see and do know.

The mighty wave that rushed through the Conemaugh Valley on Friday evening cut a swath of death 13 miles long. In its way lay one of the
most thickly populated centers of the Keystone State, and within a few
minutes from the time the dam at Lake Conemaugh broke, houses were
rolling over one another in a mad whirl, as they were carried by the
seething waters down the gorge between the endless hills.

At Johnstown the whole center of the city was cut, as if a mammoth
scythe had passed over the land. At that place was a large stone bridge of
the Pennsylvania Railroad Company, one of the strongest that the company owns. The Conemaugh River is crossed by it at an angle. Into this
angle houses, trees and fences that came down the left side of the river
rushed and were piled on high until rafters and timbers project above the
stone. Then the houses, nearly all crowded with people, crashed, one
after another, until the terrible wreckage extended a half mile up the
stream. No pen can tell the horror of the shrieks of the thousands who
were in the mass of floating ruins.

Shortly after the blockade had formed the dry timbers of the houses caught fire, and the mass nearest the railroad bridge became a glowing furnace. Hundreds of people, who had not been drowned or crushed to death in the mad rush downstream, were burned alive. Their shrieks as the flames reached them made the most stout-hearted wring their hands in agony at their inability to render assistance. The wind blew from upstream. The air became filled with the gruesome odors until at last the horrors to sight, hearing and smell became so great that persons in the vicinity were forced to leave the place. Meanwhile, the greater bulk of the houses had gone down along the right bank. One mad rush carried away a portion of the stone bridge, and then the flood bore down upon the thousands of homes and floated them further westward in the Conemaugh. It was only a little after 5 Friday afternoon when the first warning came, and as it had been raining heavily all day the citizens of Johnstown and the neighboring hamlets thought that the slowly rising waters meant only a light flood.

Thus the inhabitants were either grouped in windows or in the open doors watching what was expected would be an imposing spectacle, but nothing more. No one seemed to think it necessary that they should take to the hills, and so all were caught in the fearful rush. The committee at Johnstown, in their bulletin, place the number of lives lost at 8,000. In doing so they are figuring the inhabitants of their own city and the towns immediately adjoining. But it must be remembered that the flood swept ten miles through a populous district before it even reached the locality over which this committee has supervision. It devastated a tract the size and shape of Manhattan Island. Here are a few facts that will show the geographical lines of the terrible disaster. The Hotel Hurlburt, of Johnstown, a massive three-story building of 100 rooms has vanished. There were in it 75 guests at the time of the flood. Two only are known to be alive. The Merchants' Hotel is levelled. How many were inside it is not known but as yet no one has been seen who came from there or heard of an inmate escaping. At the Conemaugh Round House forty-one locomotives were swept down the stream and before they reached the stone bridge all the iron and steel work had been torn from their boilers.

It is almost impossible in this great catastrophe to go more into details. I stood on the stone bridge at 6 o'clock, and looked into the seething mass of ruin below me. At one place the blackened body of a babe was seen; in another 14 skulls could be counted. Further along the bones became thicker and thicker, until at last at one place it seemed as if a concourse of people, who had been at a ball or entertainment, had been carried in a bunch and incinerated. At this time the smoke was still rising to the height of 50 feet, and it is expected that when it dies down the charred bodies will be seen dotting the entire mass of burned debris. A cable had been run last night from the end of the stone bridge to the nearest point across—a distance of 30 feet. Over this cable was run a trolley and a swing was fastened under it.

A man went over, and he was the first one who visited Johnstown since the awful disaster. I followed him today. I walked along the hillside and saw hundreds of persons lying on the wet grass, wrapped in blankets or quilts. It was growing cold, and a misty rain had set in. Shelter was not to be had, and houses on the hillside that had not been swept away were literally packed from top to bottom. The bare necessities of life were soon at a premium, and loaves of bread sold at fifty cents.

Fortunately, however, the relief train from Pittsburgh arrived at 7 o'clock. Otherwise the horrors of starvation would have been added. All provisions, however, had to be carried over a rough, rocky road a distance of four miles (as I know, who had been compelled to walk it) and in many cases they were seized by the toughs, and the people who were in need of food did not get it.

"The man was alive . . ."

THE FIRST ELECTROCUTION

August 6, 1890
Auburn State Prison, New York

ANONYMOUS *NEW YORK WORLD* REPORTER

*W*illiam Kemmler ran away with a married woman, Tillie Ziegler. But touch turned to shove, and the affair ended when Kemmler murdered Ziegler.

Kemmler's execution became more than just the usual public spectacle. It was the stage for a battle between rival inventors, Thomas Edison and George Westinghouse. Each had patented methods of providing electricity. Each wanted his own method to be deemed safe and the other's to be declared deadly. Neither wanted the distinction of killing Kemmler. Edison's public relations crew even tried to coin a term for the newfangled idea of killing with electricity: "to westinghouse," as in "Kemmler was westinghoused"—or Kemmler "went to the westinghouse." As Edison biographer Neil Baldwin notes, they hoped to make Westinghouse as infamous as Dr. Guillotine. After much political wrangling and backroom dealing, Westing-

house's method—alternating current—was chosen for the first electrocution. We now know that Westinghouse's system was not very deadly, as this gruesome account of the botched job suggests. Westinghouse's verdict: "They could have done better with an axe." His system became the standard.

The first execution by electricity has been a horror. Physicians who might make a jest out of the dissecting room, officials who have seen many a man's neck wrenched by the rope, surgeons who have lived in hospitals and knelt beside the dead and dying on bloody fields, held their breaths with a gasp, and those unaccustomed to such sights turned away in dread.

The doctors say the victim did not suffer. Only his Maker knows if that be true. To the eye, it looked as though he were in a convulsive agony.

The current had been passing through his body for fifteen seconds when the electrode at the head was removed. Suddenly the breast heaved. There was a straining at the straps which bound him, a purplish foam covered the lips and was spattered over the leather head-band.

The man was alive. Warden, physicians, everybody, lost their wits. There was a startled cry for the current to be turned on again. Signals, only half understood, were given to those in the next room at the switchboard. When they knew what had happened, they were prompt to act, and the switch-handle could be heard as it was pulled back and forth, breaking the deadly current into jets.

The rigor of death came on the instant. An odor of burning flesh and singed hair filled the room. For a moment a blue flame played about the base of the victim's spine. One of the witnesses nearly fell to the floor. Another lost control of his stomach. Cold perspiration beaded every face. This time the electricity flowed four minutes.

Kemmler was dead. Part of his brain had been baked hard. Some of the blood in his head had been turned into charcoal. The flesh at the small of his back was black with fire.

"The sounds went right through my body . . ."

MASSACRE AT WOUNDED KNEE

December 29, 1890
Pine Ridge Sioux Reservation, South Dakota

BLACK ELK

W *ounded Knee was the last major battle between Native Americans and U.S. troops. The confrontation began when the federal government banned the Sioux's Ghost Dance, a religious ceremony that the government feared would incite more resistance. The Sioux continued to practice the ceremony, so troops were sent to arrest the native leaders. Tensions rose when Chief Sitting Bull was killed while being arrested on December 15.*

About two hundred Sioux were killed in the massacre, including women and children.

Black Elk, a cousin of Oglala Sioux warrior Crazy Horse, was a Sioux holy man who as a teenager had fought against Custer at Little Bighorn. In 1930 he recounted the oral autobiography from which this account comes, Black Elk Speaks, *to poet and anthropologist John Neihardt.*

That evening before it happened, I went in to Pine Ridge and heard these things, and while I was there, soldiers started for where the Big Foots were. These made about five hundred soldiers that were there next morning. When I saw them starting I felt that something terrible was going to happen. That night I could hardly sleep at all. I walked around most of the night.

In the morning I went out after my horses, and while I was out I heard shooting off toward the east, and I knew from the sound that it must be wagon-guns (cannon) going off. The sounds went right through my body, and I felt that something terrible would happen.

When I reached camp with the horses, a man rode up to me and said: "Hey-hey-hey! The people that are coming are fired on! I know it!"

I saddled up my buckskin and put on my sacred shirt. It was one I had made to be worn by no one but myself. It had a spotted eagle out-stretched on the back of it, and the daybreak star was on the left shoulder, because when facing south that shoulder is toward the east. Across the breast, from the left shoulder to the right hip, was the flaming rainbow, and there was another rainbow around the neck, like a necklace, with a star at the bottom. At each shoulder, elbow, and wrist was an eagle feather; and over the whole shirt were red streaks of lightning. You will see that this was from my great vision, and you will know how it protected me that day.

I painted my face all red, and in my hair I put one eagle feather for the One Above. It did not take me long to get ready, for I could still hear the shooting over there.

I started out alone on the old road that ran across the hills to Wounded Knee. I had no gun. I carried only the sacred bow of the west that I had seen in my great vision. I had gone only a little way when a band of young men came galloping after me. The first two who came up were Loves War and Iron Wasichu. I asked what they were going to do, and they said they were just going to see where the shooting was. Then others were coming up, and some older men.

We rode fast, and there were about twenty of us now. The shooting was getting louder. A horseback [scout] from over there came galloping very fast toward us, and he said: "Hey-hey-hey! They have murdered them!" Then he whipped his horse and rode away faster toward Pine Ridge.

In a little while we had come to the top of the ridge where, looking to the east, you can see for the first time the monument and the burying ground on the little hill where the church is. That is where the terrible thing started. Just south of the burying ground on the little hill a deep dry gulch runs about east and west, very crooked, and it rises westward to nearly the top of the ridge where we were. It had no name, but the Wasichus [white men] sometimes call it Battle Creek now. We stopped on the ridge not far from the head of the dry gulch. Wagon-guns were still going off over there on the little hill, and they were going off again where they hit along the gulch. There was much shooting down yonder, and there were many cries, and we could see cavalrymen scattered over the hills ahead of us. Cavalrymen were riding along the gulch and shooting into it, where the women and children were running away and trying to hide in the gullies and the stunted pines.

A little way ahead of us, just below the head of the dry gulch, there were some women and children who were huddled under a clay bank, and some cavalrymen were there pointing guns at them.

We stopped back behind the ridge, and I said to the others: "Take courage. These are our relatives. We will try to get them back." Then we all sang a song which went like this:

A thunder being nation I am, I have said.
A thunder being nation I am, I have said.
You shall live. You shall live.
You shall live. You shall live.

Then I rode over the ridge and the others after me, and we were crying: "Take courage! It is time to fight!" The soldiers who were guarding
our relatives shot at us and then ran away fast, and some more cavalrymen
on the other side of the gulch did too. We got our relatives and sent them
across the ridge to the northwest where they would be safe.

I had no gun, and when we were charging, I just held the sacred bow
out in front of me with my right hand. The bullets did not hit us at all.

We found a little baby lying all alone near the head of the gulch. I
could not pick her up just then, but I got her later and some of my people
adopted her. I just wrapped her up tighter in a shawl that was around her
and left her there. It was a safe place, and I had other work to do.

The soldiers had run eastward over the hills where there were some
more soldiers, and they were off their horses and lying down. I told the
others to stay back, and I charged upon them holding the sacred bow out
toward them with my right hand. They all shot at me, and I could hear
bullets all around me, but I ran my horse right close to them, and then
swung around. Some soldiers across the gulch began shooting at me too,
but I got back to the others and was not hurt at all.

By now many other Lakotas, who had heard the shooting, were coming up from Pine Ridge, and we all charged on the soldiers. They ran eastward toward where the trouble began. We followed down along the dry
gulch, and what we saw was terrible. Dead and wounded women and
children and little babies were scattered all along there where they had
been trying to run away. The soldiers had followed along the gulch, as
they ran, and murdered them in there. Sometimes they were in heaps
because they had huddled together, and some were scattered all along.
Sometimes bunches of them had been killed and torn to pieces where the
wagon-guns hit them. I saw a little baby trying to suck its mother, but she
was bloody and dead.

There were two little boys at one place in this gulch. They had guns
and they had been killing soldiers all by themselves. We could see the soldiers they had killed. The boys were all alone there, and they were not
hurt. These were very brave little boys.

When we drove the soldiers back, they dug themselves in, and we
were not enough people to drive them out from there. In the evening

they marched off up Wounded Knee Creek, and then we saw all that they had done there.

Men and women and children were heaped and scattered all over the flat at the bottom of the little hill where the soldiers had their wagon-guns, and westward up the dry gulch all the way to the high ridge, the dead women and children and babies were scattered.

When I saw this I wished that I had died too, but I was not sorry for the women and children. It was better for them to be happy in the other world, and I wanted to be there too. But before I went there I wanted to have revenge. I thought there might be a day, and we should have revenge.

After the soldiers marched away, I heard from my friend, Dog Chief, how the trouble started, and he was right there by Yellow Bird when it happened. This is the way it was:

In the morning the soldiers began to take all the guns away from the Big Foots, who were camped in the flat below the little hill where the monument and burying ground are now. The people had stacked most of their guns, and even their knives, by the tepee where Big Foot was lying sick. Soldiers were on the little hill and all around, and there were soldiers across the dry gulch to the south and over east along Wounded Knee Creek too. The people were nearly surrounded, and the wagon guns were pointing at them.

Some had not yet given up their guns, and so the soldiers were searching all the tepees, throwing things around and poking into everything. There was a man called Yellow Bird, and he and another man were standing in front of the tepee where Big Foot was lying sick. They had white sheets around and over them, with eyeholes to look through, and they had guns under these. An officer came to search them. He took the other man's gun, and then started to take Yellow Bird's. But Yellow Bird would not let go. He wrestled with the officer, and while they were wrestling, the gun went off and killed the officer. Wasichus and some others have said he meant to do this, but Dog Chief was standing right there, and he told me it was not so. As soon as the gun went off, Dog Chief told me, an officer shot and killed Big Foot who was lying sick inside the tepee.

Then suddenly nobody knew what was happening, except that the soldiers were all shooting and the wagon-guns began going off right in among the people.

Many were shot down right there. The women and children ran into the gulch and up west, dropping all the time, for the soldiers shot them as they ran. There were only about a hundred warriors and there were nearly five hundred soldiers. The warriors rushed to where they had piled their guns and knives. They fought soldiers with only their hands until they got their guns.

Dog Chief saw Yellow Bird run into a tepee with his gun, and from there he killed soldiers until the tepee caught fire. Then he died full of bullets.

It was a good winter day when all this happened. The sun was shining. But after the soldiers marched away from their dirty work, a heavy snow began to fall. The wind came up in the night. There was a big blizzard, and it grew very cold. The snow drifted deep in the crooked gulch, and it was one long grave of butchered women and children and babies, who had never done any harm and were only trying to run away.

"I have two old peach baskets down in the store room . . ."

THE INVENTION OF BASKETBALL

December 1891
Springfield, Massachusetts

JAMES NAISMITH

C anadian-born Naismith was training Y.M.C.A. instructors when he invented basketball. For most of the rest of his career he was head of physical education at the University of Kansas.

When the fall sports were ended, our attention was again called to the conditions which had previously caused us so much worry. The school at that time was training two classes of leaders, one as physical directors and the other as secretaries.

It soon became evident that the antagonism of the class toward physical work was increasing; at the next meeting of the faculty, Dr. R. A. Clark said that no one could do anything with that group. While we were discussing this condition, I again spoke my mind, saying: "The trouble is not with the men but with the system that we are using."

It was like a bolt of lightning from a clear sky when Dr. Gulick turned to me and said, "Naismith, I want you to take that class and see what you can do with it." Knowing the difficulty of the task that was being assigned to me, I immediately began to make excuses. His mind was made up, however.

As we left the meeting, Dr. Gulick turned to me and said, "Naismith, now would be a good time for you to work on that new game that you said could be invented."

When he had assigned me the class of incorrigibles, I had felt that I was being imposed on; but when he told me to do what all the directors of the country had failed to accomplish, I felt it was the last straw. My fist closed, and I looked up into Gulick's face. I saw there only a quizzical smile. There was little left for me to do but to accept the challenge.

Football was the first game that I modified. In eliminating the roughness, I tried to substitute the tackling of English Rugby for that of the American game. In Rugby, the tackle must be made above the hips, and the endeavor is to stop the runner rather than to throw him. The changing of the tackle did not appeal to the members of the class, who had been taught to throw the runner with as much force as possible, so that if he were able to get up at all, he would at least be in a dazed condition. To ask these men to handle their opponents gently was to make their favorite sport a laughing stock, and they would have none of it.

Soccer, or as it was then called, Association football, was the game that I next attempted to modify. On the gymnasium floor the men were accustomed to wearing soft soled shoes, and I thought, therefore, they would use caution in kicking the ball. Many of the class had played soccer outdoors, and when they saw an opening for a goal, they forgot all about their shoes and drove the ball with all their might. As a result of this, many of them went limping off the floor; instead of an indoor soccer game, we had a practical lesson in first aid.

There was still one more game that I was determined to try, and this was the Canadian game of lacrosse. I have always considered this the best of all games, but it seemed impossible to make an indoor sport of one that required so much space.

In the group there were seven Canadians; and when these men put into practice some of the tricks they had been taught in the outdoor game, football and soccer appeared tame in comparison. No bones were broken in the game, but faces were scarred and hands were hacked.

Two weeks had almost passed since I had taken over the troublesome class. The time was almost gone; in a day or two I would have to report to the faculty the success or failure of my attempts. So far they had all been failures, and it seemed to me that I had exhausted my resources.

With weary footsteps I mounted the flight of narrow stairs that led to my office directly over the locker room. I slumped down in my chair, my head in any hands and my elbows on the desk. I was a thoroughly disheartened and discouraged young instructor.

As I sat there at my desk, I began to study games from the philosophical side. I had been taking one game at a time and had failed to find what I was looking for. This time I would take games as a whole and study them.

My first generalization was that all team games used a ball of some kind; therefore, any new game must have a ball. Two kinds of balls were used at that time, one large and the other small. I noted that all games that used a small ball had some intermediate equipment with which to handle it. Cricket and baseball had bats, lacrosse and hockey had sticks, tennis and squash had rackets. In each of these games, the use of the intermediate equipment made the game more difficult to learn. The Americans were at sea with a lacrosse stick, and the Canadians could not use a baseball bat.

I then considered a large ball that could be easily handled and which almost anyone could catch and throw with very little practice. I decided that the ball should be large and light, one that could be easily handled.

The type of a ball being settled, I turned next to the point of interest of various games. I concluded that the most interesting game at that time was American Rugby. I asked myself why this game could not be used as an indoor sport. The answer to this was easy. It was because tackling was necessary in Rugby. But why was tackling necessary? Again the answer was easy. It was because the men were allowed to run with the ball, and it was necessary to stop them. With these facts in mind, I sat erect at my desk and said aloud:

"If he can't run with the ball, we don't have to tackle; and if we don't have to tackle, the roughness will be eliminated."

I can still recall how I snapped my fingers and shouted,

"I've got it!"

Starting with the idea that the player in possession of the ball could not run with it, the next step was to see just what he could do with it. There was little choice in this respect. It would be necessary for him to throw it or bat it with his hand. In my mind, I began to play a game and to visualize the movements of the players. Suppose that a player was running, and a teammate threw the ball to him.

Realizing that it would be impossible for him to stop immediately, I made this exception: when a man was running and received the ball, he must make an honest effort to stop or else pass the ball immediately. This was the second step of the game.

The game now had progressed only to the point where it was "keep away," and my experience with gymnastic games convinced me that it would not hold the interest of the players. The next step was to devise some objective for the players. In all existing games there was some kind of a goal, and I felt that this was essential. I thought that if the goal were horizontal instead of vertical, the players would be compelled to throw the ball in an arc; and force, which made for roughness, would be of no value.

The following morning I went into my office, thinking of the new game. As I walked down the hall, I met Mr. Stebbins, the superintendent of buildings. I asked him if he had two boxes about eighteen inches square. Stebbins thought a minute, and then said: "No, I haven't any boxes, but I'll tell you what I do have. I have two old peach baskets down in the store room, if they will do you any good."

I told him to bring them up, and a few minutes later he appeared with the two baskets tucked under his arm. They were round and some-what larger at the top than at the bottom. I found a hammer and some nails and tacked the baskets to the lower rail of the balcony, one at either end of the gym.

There were eighteen men in the class; I selected two captains and had them choose sides. When the teams were chosen, I placed the men on the floor. There were three forwards, three centers, and three backs on each team. I chose two of the center men to jump, then threw the ball between them. It was the start of the first basketball game and the finish of the trouble with that class.

The class met at eleven-thirty in the morning, and the game was in full swing by twelve o'clock. Some teachers from the Buckingham Grade School were passing the gym one day, and hearing the noise, decided to investigate. They could enter the gallery through a door that led to the street. Each day after that, they stopped to watch the game, sometimes becoming so interested that they would not have time to get their lunch. These teachers came to me one day and asked me why girls could not play that game. I told them that I saw no reason why they should not, and this group organized the first girls' basketball team.

It is little wonder that the crowd enjoyed the game. If we could see it today as it was played then, we would laugh too. The players were all mature men; most of them had mustaches, and one or two had full beards. Their pants were long, and their shirts had short sleeves. Some-times when a player received the ball, he would poise with it over his head to make sure that he would make the goal. About the time that he was ready to throw, someone would reach up from behind and take the ball out of his hands. This occurred frequently and was a never-ending source of amusement. No matter how often a player lost the ball in this manner, he would always look around with a surprised expression that would plainly say, "Who did that?" His embarrassment only added to the laughter of the crowd.

"Everybody goes to Wanamaker's."

THE FIRST DEPARTMENT STORE

1896
Philadelphia

GEORGE STEEVENS

S teevens was a British writer in America to research his book The Land of the Dollar. *In Philadelphia he saw the huge emporium of John Wanamaker.*

In Philadelphia everybody goes to Wanamaker's. Mr. Wanamaker was once Postmaster-General of the Republic, and I should think he was a rattling good one. His store was already the largest retail drapery and hosiery and haberdashery, and all that sort of business, in the world, when by the recent purchase of a giant establishment in New York he made it more largest still. Now the working of Wanamaker's, as I am informed, is this. It is no use going there to get what you want. You must go to get what Mr. Wanamaker wants to sell. He tells you each morning in the newspapers what he has got today, and if you want it you had better go and get it: the chances are it will be gone tomorrow. The head of each department is entrusted with a certain amount of capital, and buys his goods at his own discretion. But woe unto him if he does not turn over his capital quickly. There is a rule that no stock may be in the house more than, I think, three months; after that off it must go at any sacrifice.

"You can always tell when Mr. Wanamaker's in town," said a shopwalker, "because there's always some change being made." And then he added, in a half-voice of awestricken worship, "I believe Mr. Wanamaker loves change for its own sake." For the sake of custom, I should say; for this formula of change for change's sake is one of the master-keys of American character. Mr. Wanamaker keeps a picture-gallery, with some really fine modern French paintings, to beguile his patrons. To-day he will

have an orchestrion playing, tomorrow a costume exhibition of spinning—girls from all the lands of the earth,—every day something new.
One day, by moving a table six feet, so that people had to walk round it
instead of past it, he increased the sales of an article from three shillings
to hundreds of pounds. If that is not genius, tell me what is.

But the really Napoleonic—I was going to say daemonic—feature of
the Wanamaker system is the unerring skill with which it reaps its profits
out of the necessities of others. Fixing his price according to the economic doctrine of final utility—taking no account, that is, of the cost of
production, but only of the price at which most people will find it worth
their while to buy—Mr. Wanamaker realizes 10 per cent for himself, and
an enormous saving for the consumers. A cargo of rose-trees had been
consigned from Holland to a firm of florists, which failed while the plants
were in mid-ocean. They went a-begging till Mr. Wanamaker bought them
up and put them on the market at about half the rate current in Philadelphia. In ten days not one of the twenty thousand was left. A firm which
manufactured hundred-dollar bicycles found itself without cash to meet
its liabilities. Mr. Wanamaker bought up the stock and altered the maker's
label as well as one peculiarity of the gear. Then he broke the price to
sixty-six dollars, and subsequently to thirty-three. They all went off in a
week or so. He bought the plates of a huge edition of the hundred-dollar
Century Dictionary, altered the title-page, bound them for himself, and
put the article on the market at fifty-one dollars and a half. In six weeks
he had sold two thousand. A firm in California, which manufactures an
excellent kind of blanket, was in difficulties. Mr. Wanamaker bought up
the stock, and sold it at a third of the normal price in three days.

All this is magnificent for the customer, and apparently not unprof-
itable to Mr. Wanamaker. But plainly somebody has to pay, and who? The
small trader. After the rose-tree deal nobody wanted to buy roses of the
florists of Philadelphia. The city is stocked with bicycles and Century Dic-
tionaries, and nobody within a radius of miles will want to buy a pair of
blankets for a generation. Mr. Wanamaker sends out three hundred and
sixty-five thousand parcels to his customers in the slackest month of the
year, and turns over thirteen million dollars annually. The small people, it
is presumed, are ground to powder against the wall.

*"Colonel Roosevelt, on horseback,
    broke from the woods . . ."*

THE ROUGH RIDERS CHARGE SAN JUAN HILL

July 1, 1898
Santiago, Cuba

RICHARD HARDING DAVIS

The Spanish-American War was a "splendid little war," said John Hay, ambassador to Great Britain at the time. America proudly fought on the side of the angels, freeing Cuba from the vicious Spanish colonial government that had established concentration camps to stop a resistance movement. It also made a handsome profit.

Within two months of the sinking of the U.S.S. Maine in Havana harbor— probably caused by an explosion in its own powder magazine, despite headlines decrying a Spanish plot—America had gained control of the Philippines, Guam, Puerto Rico, and Cuba. The U.S. also replaced the Spanish in Cuba with a de facto government of American businessmen controlling the sugar and tobacco fields. And William Randolph Hearst and Joseph Pulitzer sold a lot of newspapers.

It was a cheap investment, as wars go. Of the 275,000 men who served in the war only about 5,500 died, and of those just 379 died in battle. Most of the others died of tropical diseases.

Davis was a prolific and admired journalist and novelist. Mindful of the entertainment value of the war, he neglected to mention that Teddy Roosevelt had to dismount and climb part of the way up the hill.

But at least Roosevelt, assistant secretary of the navy at the time, had a horse. The other Rough "Riders" had to fight on foot, because the ship that took them to Cuba didn't have room for their horses. In fact, of the 1,000 men he selected for his volunteer cavalry regiment, only 560 could fit on the ship. Nonetheless, Roosevelt managed to find room for photographic equipment, including an early motion picture camera. Within two years of his exploits in Cuba, he was President.

The situation was desperate. Our troops could not retreat, as the trail for two miles behind them was wedged with men. They could not remain where they were for they were being shot to pieces. There was only one thing they could do—go forward and take the San Juan hills by assault. It was as desperate as the situation itself. To charge earthworks held by men with modern rifles, and using modern artillery, until after the earthworks have been shaken by artillery, and to attack them in advance and not in the flanks, are both impossible military propositions. But this campaign had not been conducted according to military rules, and a series of military blunders had brought seven thousand American soldiers into a chute of death, from which there was no escape except by taking the enemy who held it by the throat, and driving him out and beating him down. So the generals of divisions and brigades stepped back and relinquished their command to the regimental officers and the enlisted men.

"We can do nothing more," they virtually said. "There is the enemy."

Colonel Roosevelt, on horseback, broke from the woods behind the line of the Ninth, and finding its men lying in his way, shouted: "If you don't wish to go forward, let my men pass, please." The junior officers of the Ninth, with their Negroes [the Ninth and Tenth were black infantry units], instantly sprang into line with the Rough Riders, and charged at the blue block-house on the right.

I speak of Roosevelt first because, with General Hawkins, who led Kent's division, notably the Sixth and Sixteenth Regulars, he was, without doubt, the most conspicuous figure in the charge. General Hawkins, with hair as white as snow, and yet far in advance of men thirty years his junior, was so noble a sight that you felt inclined to pray for his safety; on the other hand, Roosevelt, mounted high on horseback, and charging the rifle-pits at a gallop and quite alone, made you feel that you would like to cheer. He wore on his sombrero a blue polka-dot handkerchief, à la Havelock, which, as he advanced, floated out straight behind his head, like a guidon. . . .

I think the thing which impressed one the most, when our men started from cover, was that they were so few. It seemed as if someone had made an awful and terrible mistake. One's instinct was to call them to come back. You felt that someone had blundered and that these few men were blindly following out some madman's mad order. It was not heroic then, it seemed merely terribly pathetic. The pity of it, the folly of such a sacrifice was what held you.

They had no glittering bayonets, they were not massed in regular array. There were a few men in advance, bunched together, and creeping up a steep, sunny hill, the top of which roared and flashed with flame. The men held their guns pressed across their breasts and stepped heavily as they climbed. Behind these first few, spreading out like a fan, were single lines of men, slipping and scrambling in the smooth grass, moving forward with difficulty, as though they were wading waist high through water, moving slowly, carefully, with strenuous effort. It was much more wonderful than any swinging charge could have been. They walked to greet death at every step, many of them, as they advanced, sinking suddenly or pitching forward and disappearing in the high grass, but the others waded on, stubbornly, fanning a thin blue line that kept creeping higher and higher up the hill. It was as inevitable as the rising tide. It was a miracle of self-sacrifice, a triumph of bulldog courage, which one watched breathless with wonder. The fire of the Spanish riflemen, who still stuck bravely to their posts, doubled and trebled in fierceness, the crests of the hills crackled and burst in amazed roars, and rippled with waves of tiny flame. But the blue line crept steadily up and on, and then, near the top, the broken fragments gathered together with a sudden burst of speed, the Spaniards appeared for a moment outlined against the sky and poised for instant flight, fired a last volley and fled before the swift-moving wave that leaped and sprang up after them.

The men of the Ninth and the Rough Riders rushed to the blockhouse together, the men of the Sixth, of the Third, of the Tenth Cavalry, of the Sixth and Sixteenth Infantry, fell on their faces along the crest of the hills beyond, and opened upon the vanishing enemy. They drove the yellow silk flags of the cavalry and the Stars and Stripes of their country into the soft earth of the trenches, and then sank down and looked back at the road they had climbed and swung their hats in the air. And from far overhead, from these few figures perched on the Spanish rifle-pits, with their flags planted among the empty cartridges of the enemy, and overlooking the walls of Santiago, came, faintly, the sound of a tired, broken cheer.

"Mrs. Nation sent one of the stones whizzing . . ."

CARRIE NATION

December 27, 1900
Topeka, Kansas

ANONYMOUS *TOPEKA DAILY CAPITAL* REPORTER

Mrs. Carrie Nation, president of Barber County Women's Christian Temperance Union, began today a raid on the saloons in Wichita. As a result of her work she is now under arrest and placed behind the bars at the county jail.

At 9:45 this morning she entered the saloon in the basement of the Carey hotel and without a word of warning pulled from a bundle of papers which she carried in her hands two large stones. Before the clerks and bartenders could realize what was going on, Mrs. Nation sent one of the stones whizzing through a large oil painting of Cleopatra nude at the Roman bath. The painting was valued at $100. As a result of the stone hitting the painting the picture is completely spoiled.

After damaging this picture, the woman suddenly turned herself about and with much force sent another large stone through a valuable $1,500 mirror which is situated directly back of the bar. She then left the saloon.

While in the saloon she also broke about $25 worth of bottled goods and also a window. As soon as she left the saloon she was arrested. . . .

Last night Mrs. Nation visited all the saloons in Wichita and demanded that they close their doors. She called at the Carey barroom last night where she saw this costly picture hanging on the wall. She told the bartender to remove it. The bartender refused to do so. Today, while the stones were being hurled, the bartender, Edward Parker, hid himself behind the bar.

Mrs. Nation, when seen by a reporter for the *Capital*, said:

"I am a law abiding citizen and I have not gone out of the bounds of the law. I have a husband who is a lawyer and he says they cannot prosecute me. . . ."

She dared the officers to place her in a cell. She said if they did, she would sue the city for false imprisonment. . . .

Members of the Women's Christian Temperance Union of Wichita who heard of the actions of Mrs. Nation say they do not approve of them, and believe there are other ways to shut up the saloons in Wichita.

Mrs. Nation was removed to the county jail tonight. . . .

"I came to the Governor's town," she said, "to destroy the finest saloon in it, hoping thus to attract public attention to the flagrant violation of a Kansas law, under the very eye of the chief executive of the state."

The damage done to the saloon is hard to estimate. It was finished with stucco secured from the World's Fair buildings and many blocks of it are shattered. The painting of Cleopatra cost Mr. Noble, its author, nine months' time painting it and was still his property, being rented by the saloon. It has been seen at nearly all the street fairs from Canada to the Gulf.

"I came to Wichita expecting to get into trouble and here I am. I have brought my clothes and some eating along so as to be as comfortable as possible. . . . I studied the law and asked competent lawyers if I can be prosecuted for destroying the property of the jointists and they say I cannot for the reason that the saloon men here have no rights under the state laws. I telegraphed my husband this morning not to come here and interfere with my work, but to leave me alone."

The course of Mrs. Nation's fight for temperance started from the cause of the death of her first husband twenty-five years ago, who died from the result of delirium tremens. His name was Dr. Charles Glayd and she was married to him against the wishes of her parents. . . . Word is received in Wichita that Mrs. Nation is well respected in Medicine Lodge [her hometown]. She is considered eccentric at some times.

"The machine would rise suddenly . . ."

THE WRIGHT BROTHERS FLY

December 17, 1903
Kitty Hawk, North Carolina

ORVILLE WRIGHT

*T*he only witnesses to the event were a handful of friends and the lifeguards at the Kill Devil Hills Life Saving Station (who did double duty hauling the Flyer back to the start of the railroad track runway after each flight). At first the press did not believe the story.

The plane weighed 745 pounds, less than half the weight of a modern car. It was powered by just a twelve-horsepower engine.

This account comes from Orville's diary.

When we got up a wind of between 20 and 25 miles was blowing from the north. We got the machine out early and put out the signal for the men at the station. . . . After running the engine and propellers a few minutes to get them in working order, I got on the machine at 10:35 for the first trial. . . . On slipping the rope the machine started off increasing in speed to probably 7 or 8 miles. The machine lifted from the truck just as it was entering on the fourth rail. Mr. Daniels took a picture just as it left the tracks. I found the control of the front rudder quite difficult on account of its being balanced too near the center and thus had a tendency to turn itself when started so that the rudder was turned too far on one side and then too far on the other. As a result the machine would rise suddenly to about 10 ft. and then as suddenly, on turning the rudder, dart for the ground. A sudden dart when out about 100 feet from the end of the tracks ended the flight. Time about 12 seconds (not known exactly as watch was not promptly stopped). The lever for throwing off the engine was broken, and the skid under the rudder cracked. After repairs, at 20 min. after 11 o'clock Will made the second trial. The course was about like mine, up and down but a little longer over the ground though about the same in time. Dist. not measured but about 175 ft. Wind speed not quite so strong. With the aid of the station men present, we picked the machine up and carried it back to the starting ways. At about 20 minutes till 12 o'clock I made the third trial. When out about the same distance as Will's, I met with a strong gust from the left which raised the left wing and sidled the machine off to the right in a lively manner. I immediately turned the rudder to bring the machine down and then worked the end control. . . . At just 12 o'clock Will started on the fourth and last trip.

The machine started off with its ups and downs as it had before, but by the time he had gone over three or four hundred feet he had it under much better control, and was traveling on a fairly even course. It proceeded in this manner till it reached a small hummock out about 800 feet from the starting ways, when it began its pitching again and suddenly darted into the ground. The front rudder frame was badly broken up, but the main frame suffered none at all. The distance over the ground was 852 feet in 59 seconds. The engine turns was 1071, but this included several seconds while on the starting ways and probably about a half second after landing. The jar of landing had set the watch on machine back so that we have no exact record for the 1071 turns. Will took a picture of my third flight just before the gust struck the machine. The machine left the ways successfully at every trial, and the tail was never caught by the truck as we had feared.

After removing the front rudder, we carried the machine back to camp. We set the machine down a few feet west of the building, and while standing about discussing the last flight, a sudden gust of wind struck the machine and started to turn it over. All rushed to stop it. Will who was near one end ran to the front, but too late to do any good. Mr. Daniels and myself seized spars [uprights] at the rear, but to no purpose. The machine gradually turned over on us. Mr. Daniels, having had no experience in handling a machine of this kind, hung on to it from the inside, and as a result was knocked down and turned over and over with it as it went.

His escape was miraculous, as he was in with the engine and chains. The engine legs were all broken off, the chain guides badly bent, a number of uprights, and nearly all the rear ends of the ribs were broken.

"This was their judgment day . . ."

ELLIS ISLAND

1905
New York Harbor

EDWARD STEINER

After first-class and second-class passengers disembarked from their steamships at Manhattan piers, third-class passengers were taken to nearby Ellis Island to be scrutinized. From 1892 until the beginning of World War II, almost 12 million immigrants passed through Ellis Island. The facility was finally closed in 1954. It has since been reopened as a museum.

Steiner imitated a new arrival to research his 1906 book, On the Trail of the Immigrant.

Mechanically and with quick movements we were examined for general physical defects and for the dreaded trachoma, an eye disease, the prevalence of which is greater in the imagination of some statisticians than it is on board immigrant vessels.

From here we pass into passageways made by iron railings, in which only lately, through the intervention of a humane official, benches have been placed, upon which closely crowded, we await our passing before the inspectors.

Already a sifting process has taken place; and children who clung to their mother's skirts have disappeared, families have been divided, and those remaining intact, cling to each other in a really tragic fear that they may share the fate of those previously examined. . . .

The average immigrant obeys mechanically; his attitude towards the inspector being one of the greatest respect. While the truth is not always told, many of the lies prepared proved both inefficient and unnecessary.

The examination can be superficial at best; but the eye has been trained and discoveries are made here, which seem rather remarkable. . . .

Four ways open to the immigrant after he passes the inspector. If he is destined for New York he goes straightaway down the stairs, and there his friends await him if he has any; and most of them have. If his journey takes him westward, and there the largest percentage goes, he enters a large, commodious hall to the right, where the money-changers sit and the transportation companies have their offices. If he goes to the New England states he turns to the left into a room which can scarcely hold those who go to the land of the Pilgrims and Puritans. The fourth way is the hardest one, taken by those who have received a ticket marked P.C. (Public Charge), which sends the immigrant to the extreme left where an official sits, in front of a barred gate behind which is the dreaded detention room. . . .

. . . A Russian Jew and his son are called next. The father is a pitiable-looking object; his large head rests upon a small, emaciated body; the eyes speak of premature loss of power, and are listless. Beside him stands a stalwart son, neatly attired in the uniform of a Russian college student.

"Ask them why they came," the commissioner says rather abruptly.

The answer is: "We had to."

"What was his business in Russia?"

"A tailor."

"How much does he earn a week?"

"Ten to twelve rubles."

"What did the son do?"

"He went to school."

"Who supported him?"

"The father."

"What do they expect to do in America?"

"Work."

"Have they any relatives?"

"Yes, a son and brother."

"What does he do?"

"He is a tailor."

"How much does he earn?"

"Twelve dollars a week."

"Has he a family?"

"Wife and four children."

"Ask them whether they are willing to be separated; the father to go back and the son to remain here?"

They look at each other; no emotion as yet visible, the question came too suddenly. Then something in the background of their feelings moves, and the father, used to self-denial through his life, says quietly, without pathos and yet tragically, "Of course." And the son says, after casting his eyes to the ground, ashamed to look his father in the face, "Of course."

And, "This one shall be taken and the other left," for this was their judgment day.

"Nothing remains of it but memories . . ."

THE GREAT EARTHQUAKE AND FIRE

April 18, 1906
San Francisco

JACK LONDON

S eismologists estimate the tremblor would have hit 7.9 on the current Richter scale. Yet most of the damage was caused by the fire, which burned for three days and leveled twenty-eight thousand buildings—one-third of the city—across almost five square miles. In all, about 450 people died.

Jack London, already one of the world's most famous writers at the time of the earthquake, was a native of San Francisco.

San Francisco is gone! Nothing remains of it but memories and a fringe of dwelling houses on the outskirts. Its industrial section is wiped out. Its social and residential section is wiped out. The factories and ware-houses, the great stores and newspaper buildings, the hotels and the palaces of the nabobs, are all gone. Remains only the fringe of dwelling houses on the outskirts of what was once San Francisco.

Within an hour after the earthquake shock the smoke of San Francisco's burning was a lurid tower visible a hundred miles away. And for three days and nights this lurid tower swayed in the sky, reddening the sun, darkening the sky, and filling the land with smoke. On Wednesday morning at a quarter past five came the earthquake. A minute later the flames were leaping upward. In a dozen different quarters south of Market Street, in the working-class ghetto, and in the factories, fires started. There was no opposing the flames. There was no organization, no communication. All the cunning adjustments of a twentieth-century city had been smashed by the earthquake. The streets were humped into ridge and depressions and piled with debris of fallen walls. The steel rails were twisted into perpendicular and horizontal angles. The telephone and telegraph systems were disrupted. And the great water mains had burst. All the shrewd contrivances and safeguards of man had been thrown out of gear by thirty seconds' twitching of the earth crust.

By Wednesday afternoon, inside of twelve hours, half the heart of the city was gone. At that time I watched the vast conflagration from out on the bay. It was dead calm. Not a flicker of wind stirred. Yet from every side wind was pouring in upon the city. East, west, north, and south, strong winds were blowing upon the doomed city. The heated air rising made an enormous suck. Thus did the fire of itself build its own colossal chimney through the atmosphere. Day and night this dead calm continued, and yet, near to the flames, the wind was often half a gale, so mighty was the suck.

The edict which prevented chaos was the following proclamation by Mayor E. E. Schmitz:

"The Federal Troops, the members of the Regular Police Force, and all Special Police Officers have been authorized to KILL any and all persons found engaged in looting or in the commission of any other crime.

"I have directed all the Gas and Electric Lighting Companies not to turn on gas or electricity until I order them to do so; you may therefore expect the city to remain in darkness for an indefinite time.

"I request all citizens to remain at home from darkness until daylight of every night until order is restored.

"I warn all citizens of the danger of fire from damaged or destroyed chimneys, broken or leaking gas pipes or fixtures, or any like cause."

Wednesday night saw the destruction of the very heart of the city. Dynamite was lavishly used, and many of San Francisco's proudest structures were crumbled by man himself into ruins, but there was no withstanding the onrush of the flames. Time and again successful stands were made by the fire fighters, and every time the flames flanked around on either side, or came up from the rear, and turned to defeat the hard-won victory.

"Now we have taken hold of the job . . ."

BUILDING THE PANAMA CANAL

November 1906
U.S.S. *Louisiana*, at Sea

THEODORE ROOSEVELT

"*T*he creation of the Panama Canal," wrote historian David McCullough in The
Path Between the Seas, "*was far more than a vast, unprecedented feat of
engineering. It was a profoundly important historic event and a sweeping human
drama not unlike that of war. Apart from wars, it represented the largest, most costly
single effort ever before mounted anywhere on earth. It held the world's attention
over a span of forty years. It affected the lives of tens of thousands of people at every
level of society and of virtually every race and nationality. Great reputations were
made and destroyed. For numbers of men and women it was the adventure of a lifetime. . . . It marked a score of advances in engineering, government planning,
labor relations. . . . And yet . . . marked the resolution of a dream as old as the
voyages of Columbus."*

   *The canal runs forty miles, from Cristobal on the Atlantic coast to Balboa on
the Pacific, and cuts the trip from Atlantic to Pacific by seven thousand miles. Its
widest point is three hundred feet across. A ship can cross through the six sets of
locks in seven or eight hours.*

   *The canal is unquestionably one of the greatest engineering feats ever accom-
plished. In the decades required to build it, as many as forty thousand workers
played a part. It also prompted a great medical advance, the conquest of yellow
fever.*

   *Roosevelt wrote this letter to his son Kermit shortly after his gunboat diplo-
macy shortened the rent negotiations with Colombia, which ruled the territory at
the time. He supported an "independent" government for Panama—one that saw
the deal his way.*

   *A bit of trivia: Roosevelt's review of the canal effort was the first international
trip by a U.S. president while in office.*

   The canal was completed in 1914.

Our visit to Panama was most successful as well as most interesting.
We were there three days and we worked from morning till night. The
second day I was up at a quarter to six and got to bed at a quarter of twelve,

and I do not believe that in the intervening time, save when I was dressing, there were ten consecutive minutes when I was not busily at work in some shape or form. For two days there [were] uninterrupted tropic rains without a glimpse of the sun, and the Chagres River rose in a flood higher than any for fifteen years; so that we saw the climate at its worst. It was just what I desired to do.

It certainly adds to one's pleasure to have read history and to appreciate the picturesque. When on Wednesday we approached the coast and the jungle-covered mountains loomed clearer and clearer until we could see the surf beating on the shores, while there was hardly a sign of human habitation I kept thinking of the four centuries of wild and bloody romance, mixed with abject squalor and suffering, which made up the history of the Isthmus until three years ago.

I could see Balboa crossing at Darien, and the wars between the Spaniards and the Indians, and the settlement and the building up of the quaint walled Spanish towns; and the trade, across the seas by galleon, and over land by pack train and river canoe, in gold and silver, in precious stones; and then the advent of the buccaneers, and of the English seamen, of Drake and Frobisher and Morgan, and many, many others, and the wild destruction they wrought. Then I thought of the rebellion against the Spanish dominion, and the uninterrupted and bloody civil wars that followed, the last occurring when I became President; wars, the victorious heroes of which have their pictures frescoed on the quaint rooms of the palace at Panama city, and in similar palaces in all the other capitals of these strange, turbulent little half-caste civilizations.

Meanwhile the Panama railroad had been built by Americans over a half a century ago, with appalling loss of life, so that it is said, of course with exaggeration, that every sleeper laid represented the death of a man. Then the French canal company started work, and for two or three years did a good deal until it became evident that the task far exceeded its powers; and then to miscalculation and inefficiency was added the hideous greed of adventurers, trying each to save something from the general wreck, and the company closed with infamy and scandal.

Now we have taken hold of the job. We have difficulties with our own people, of course. I haven't a doubt that it will take a little longer and cost a little more than men now appreciate, but I believe that the work is being done with a very high degree both of efficiency and honesty; and I am immensely struck by the character of American employees who are engaged not merely in superintending the work, but in doing all the jobs that need skill and intelligence. The steam shovels, the dirt trains, the machine shops, and the like are all filled with American engineers, conductors, machinists, boilermakers, carpenters. From the top to the bottom these men are so hardy, so efficient, so energetic, that it is a real pleasure to look at them. Stevens, the head engineer is a big fellow, a man of daring and good sense, and burly power. All of these men are quite as formidable, and would if it were necessary do quite as much in battle as the crews of Drake and Morgan; but as it is they are doing a work of infinitely more lasting consequence. Nothing whatever remains to show what Drake and Morgan did. They produced no real effect down here. But Stevens and his men are changing the face of the continent, are doing the greatest engineering feat of the ages, and the effect of their work will be felt while our civilization lasts. I went over everything that I could possibly go over in the time at my disposal. I examined the quarters of married men and single men, white men and negroes. I went over the ground of the Gatun and La Boca dams; went through Panama and Colon, and spent a day in the Culebra cut, where the great work is being done. There the huge steam shovels are hard at it; scooping huge masses of rock and gravel and dirt previously loosened by the drillers and dynamite blasters, loading it on trains which take it away to some dump, either in the jungle or where the dams are to be built. They are eating steadily into the mountain cutting it down and down. Little tracks are laid on the side hills, rocks blasted out, and the great ninety-five ton steam shovels work up like mountain howitzers until they come to where they can with advantage begin their work of eating into and destroying the mountainside. With intense energy men and machines do their task, the white men supervising matters and handling the machines, while the tens of thousands of black men do the rough manual labor where it is not worth while to have machines do it. It is an epic feat, and one of immense significance.

The deluge of rain meant that many of the villages were knee-deep in water, while the flooded rivers tore through the tropic forests. It is a real tropic forest, palms and bananas, breadfruit trees, bamboos, lofty ceibas, and gorgeous butterflies and brilliant colored birds fluttering among the orchids. There are beautiful flowers, too. All my old enthusiasm for natural history seemed to revive, and I would have given a good deal to have stayed and tried to collect specimens. It would be a good hunting country too; deer and now and then jaguars and tapir, and great birds that they call wild turkeys; there are alligators in the rivers. One of the trained nurses from a hospital went to bathe in a pool last August and an alligator grabbed him by the legs and was making off with him, but was fortunately scared away, leaving the man badly injured.

I tramped everywhere through the mud. Mother did not do this roughest work, and had time to see more of the really picturesque and beautiful side of the life, and really enjoyed herself.

Your loving father

P.S. The Gatun dam will make a lake miles long, and the railroad now goes at what will be the bottom of this lake, and it was curious to think that in a few years great ships would be floating in water 100 feet above where we were.

*"That night a composer was born,
an American composer . . ."*

THE BIRTH OF THE BLUES

1911
Cleveland, Mississippi

W. C. HANDY

*I*n 1911, *William Christopher Handy altered a campaign song written two years earlier for a local Memphis politician and named it "Memphis Blues." He had to publish it himself because the established companies did not want it. "St. Louis Blues" followed in 1914, then "Beale Street Blues" and about sixty others that helped turn an informal American tradition into an international passion. This account comes from his autobiography,* Father of the Blues.

Southern Negroes sang about everything. Trains, steamboats, steam whistles, sledge hammers, fast women, mean bosses, stubborn mules—all become subjects for their songs. They accompany themselves on anything from which they can extract a musical sound or rhythmical effect, anything from a harmonica to a washboard.

In this way, and from these materials, they set the mood for what we now call blues. My own fondness for this sort of thing really began in Florence [Alabama], back in the days when we were not above serenading beneath the windows of our sweethearts and singing till we won a kiss in the shadows or perhaps a tumbler of good home-made wine. In the Delta, however, I suddenly saw the songs with the eye of a budding composer. The songs themselves, I observed, consisted of simple declarations expressed usually in three lines and set kind of earthborn music that was familiar throughout the Southland half a century ago. Mississippi with its large plantations and small cities probably had more colored field hands than any other state. Consequently we heard many such songs as "Hurry Sundown, Let Tomorrow Come," or

> Boll Weevil, where you been so long?
> Boll Weevil, where you been so long?
> You stole my cotton, now you want my corn.

At first folk melodies like these were kept in the back rooms of my mind while the parlor was reserved for dressed-up music. Musical books continued to get much of my attention. There was still an old copy of Steiner's First Lessons in Harmony purchased back in Henderson for fifty cents. While traveling with the minstrels I had bought from Lyon and Healy a copy of More's *Encyclopedia of Music.* For a time books became a passion. I'm afraid I came to think that everything worthwhile was to be found in books. But the blues did not come from books. Suffering and hard luck were the midwives that birthed these songs. The blues were conceived in aching hearts.

I hasten to confess that I took up with low folk forms hesitantly. I approached them with a certain fear and trembling. Like many of the other musicians who received them with cold shoulders at first, I began by raising my eyebrows and wondering if they were quite the thing. I had picked up a fair training in the music of the modern world and had assumed that the correct manner to compose was to develop simples into grandissimos and not to repeat them monotonously. As a director of many respectable, conventional bands, it was not easy for me to concede that a simple slowdrag and repeat could be rhythm itself. Neither was I ready to believe that this was just what the public wanted. But we live to learn.

My own enlightenment came in Cleveland, Mississippi. I was leading the orchestra in a dance program when someone sent up an odd request. Would we play some of "our native music," the note asked. This baffled me. The men in this group could not "fake" and "sell it" like minstrel men. They were all musicians who bowed strictly to the authority of printed notes. So we played for our anonymous fan an old-time Southern melody, a melody more sophisticated than native. A few moments later a second request came up. Would we object if a local colored band played a few dances?

Object! That was funny. What hornblower would object to a time-out and a smoke—on pay? We eased out gracefully as the newcomers entered. They were led by a long-legged chocolate boy and their band consisted of just three pieces, a battered guitar, a mandolin, and a worn-out bass.

The music they made was pretty well in keeping with their looks. They struck up one of those over-and-over strains that seem to have no very clear beginning and certainly no ending at all. The strumming attained a disturbing monotony, but on and on it went, a kind of stuff that has long been associated with cane rows and levee camps.

Hump-thump-thump went their feet on the floor. Their eyes rolled. Their shoulders swayed. And through it all that little agonizing strain persisted. It was not really annoying or unpleasant. Perhaps "haunting" is a better word, but I commenced to wonder if anybody besides small town rounders and their running mates would go for it.

The answer was not long in coming. A rain of silver dollars began to fall around the outlandish, stomping feet. The dancers went wild. Dollars, quarters, halves—the shower grew heavier and continued so long I strained my neck to get a better look. There before the boys lay more money than my nine musicians were being paid for the entire engagement. Then I saw the beauty of primitive music. They had the stuff the people wanted. It touched the spot. Their music wanted polishing, but it contained the essence. Folks would pay money for it. The old conventional music was well and good and had its place, no denying that, but there was no virtue in being blind when you had good eyes.

That night a composer was born, an American composer. Those country black boys at Cleveland had taught me something that could not possibly have been gained from books, something that would, however, cause books to be written. Art, in the highbrow sense, was not in my mind. My idea of what constitutes music was changed by the sight of that silver money cascading around the splayed feet of a Mississippi string band. Within a day or two I had orchestrated a number of local tunes, among them "The Last Shot Got Him," "Your Clock Ain't Right," and the distinctly Negroid "Make Me a Pallet on Your Floor."

Just as the syncopations and fill-ins have become more elaborate, the form of the three-line stanza has undergone changes. The third line is no longer a repetition; it has taken on the color of an explanation. In my "St. Louis Blues," the line "hate to see de evenin' sun go down" is repeated once, but the third line tells why, "Cause ma baby, he done lef' dis town." Later, too, the simple, natural twelve-measure strain became elaborated into the conventional chorus. So the blues developed into jazz.

I have been called the "Father of the Blues," and I am proud of the title. My old "Memphis Blues" was the first of the blues songs; and the success of the filled-in breaks was established the first time the orchestra played it, when the chorus had to be repeated time after time so that the saxophone, the drum, the violin, all the instruments, could have a share in improvising novel turns. My purpose, however, was not the creation of "hot" numbers. That they have developed so is due to the inherent characteristics of the music itself. My purpose was to capture in fixed form the highly distinctive music of my race. Everything I have written has its roots deep in the folk life of the South.

Although my "St. Louis Blues" is the more popular, I think "Beale Street" has the more interesting history. As I was walking down Beale Street one night, my attention was caught by the sound of a piano. The insistent Negro rhythms were broken first by a tinkle in the treble, then by a rumble in the bass; then they came together again. I entered the cheap cafe and found a colored man at the piano, dog tired. He told me he had to play from seven at night until seven in the morning, and rested himself by playing with alternate hands. He told me of his life, and it seemed to me that this poor, tired, happy-go-lucky musician represented his race. I set it down in notes, keeping faith with all that made the background of that poor piano thumper. If my songs have value, it is not that of dance numbers alone. I have tried to write history, to crystallize a form for the colored workman's personal music, just as the spirituals give form to his religious emotions.

"We saw those people jumping down . . ."

TRIANGLE SHIRTWAIST COMPANY FIRE

March 25, 1911
New York City

PAULINE CUOIO PEPE

The fire in the sweatshop of the Triangle Waist Company (over the years, a small change in the company's name has become common) killed 146 of the 850 people who were trapped inside. Building codes and labor laws were changed after the tragedy.

Pepe told her story to Jeff Kisselhoff, author of the Manhattan oral history, You Must Remember This.

I was nineteen. . . . [A] woman in the building . . . introduced me to the boss, Mr. Blanck. They hired me as a sewing-machine operator for twelve dollars a week. It was easy work. You just sat there and the machine would run the tucking. I was there almost two years before the fire. We loved it. We used to sing while the machine was going. It was all nice young Jewish girls who were engaged to be married. You should see the diamonds and everything. Those were the ones who threw themselves from the window.

I got in at half past eight, and we got out at four o'clock. When we left, we never went out the front door. We always went one by one out the back. There was a man there searching, because the people were afraid we would take something, so that door was always locked.

We were just leaving that Saturday. I was fixing my hair at my machine. The cutters were right there. They generally lit a cigarette when they go out. The man was right there. His match lit the scraps under the table. Suddenly, another cutter said, "C'mon, let's run!"

I said, "Ooh, my God, a fire." I ran and I left everything—pocket-book. I was running and the people were all at the door. I saw the people throwing themselves out the window. I wouldn't dare. I didn't have the courage. "I'm not going out, I'd rather die here," that's what I said.

The door was locked. We were about a hundred people. We were hollering and crying. "Open the door!" Banging and banging quite a long time. We saw quite a lot of people throwing themselves out.

We waited a long time. We didn't feel any of the flames, but it was getting warm. The fires went to the windows. I thought about my mother and father. What would they do if I died?

Then all of a sudden we all fell over. Somebody opened the door. "Thank God!" We were all crying and yelling. The noise was terrible. When I got down, the three flights were blazing. The firemen came up and helped us, but we were tumbling down terrible. We were shivering and crying and holding on. It was terrible.

When we got down the stairs the firemen told us to wait because those young people were still jumping down. When we got out, we saw the ladder was pointing up to the sixth floor. It couldn't go up to the eighth. We saw those people jumping down. And the people in the hotel were yelling, "Don't jump down. Get in!" But they wouldn't listen to us. They had made up their mind. They went right through the glass in the pavement, some of them. There was a big hole there.

They didn't have to throw themselves. Something would have happened. That's too bad all those women died—young girls. . . .

I had a lot of friends who were killed. . . .

We were all torn to pieces. My hair was a mess. My coat was torn. I had no pocketbook or nothing. When my mother saw me, she thought somebody got ahold of me and was killing me. I told them about the fire, and they started hollering terribly. . . .

We were also angry. "What the hell did they close the door for? What did they think we're going out with? What are we gonna do, steal a shirtwaist? Who the heck wanted a shirtwaist?"

*"The man was slipping
the lifebelt off Phillips' back . . ."*

THE *TITANIC* SINKS

April 14–15, 1912
North Atlantic Ocean

HAROLD BRIDE

*M*any prominent Americans were traveling on the maiden voyage of the Titanic, from Southampton, England, to New York City, including John Jacob Astor IV. About fifteen hundred of the twenty-two hundred passengers drowned.

Bride was the surviving wireless operator of the Titanic. *He gave this account to the* New York Times.

On the night of the accident, I was not sending, but was asleep. I was due to be up and relieve Phillips earlier than usual. And that reminds me if it hadn't been for a lucky thing, we never could have sent any call for help.

The lucky thing was that the wireless broke down early enough for us to fix it before the accident. We noticed something wrong on Sunday and Phillips and I worked seven hours to find it. We found a "secretary" burned out, at last, and repaired it just a few hours before the iceberg was struck.

Phillips said to me as he took the night shift: "You turn in, boy, and get some sleep, and go up as soon as you can and give me a chance. I'm all done for with this work of making repairs."

There were three rooms in the wireless cabin. One was a sleeping room, one a dynamo room and one an operating room. I took off my clothes and went to sleep in bed. Then I was conscious of waking up and hearing Phillips sending to Cape Race. I read what he was sending. It was a traffic matter.

I remembered how tired he was and I got out of bed without my clothes on to relieve him. I didn't even feel the shock. I hardly knew it had happened until after the Captain had come to us. There was no jolt whatever.

I was standing by Phillips, telling him to go to bed, when the Captain put his head in the cabin.

"We've struck an iceberg," the Captain said, "and I'm having an inspection made to tell what it has done for us. You'd better get ready to send out a call for assistance. But don't send it until I tell you."

The Captain went away, and in ten minutes, I should estimate the time, he came back. We could hear a terrible confusion outside; there was not the least thing to indicate that there was any trouble. The wireless was working perfectly.

"Send the call for assistance," ordered the Captain, barely putting his head in the door.

"What call shall I send?" Phillips asked.

"The regulation international call for help. Just that."

Then the Captain was gone. Phillips began to send "C Q D." He flashed away at it and we joked while he did so. All of us made light of the disaster.

We joked that way while he flashed signals for about five minutes. Then the Captain came back.

"What are you sending?" he asked.

"C Q D," Phillips replied.

The humor of the situation appealed to me. I cut in with a little remark that made us all laugh, including the Captain.

"Send S O S," I said. "It's the new call, and it may be your last chance to send it."

Phillips, with a laugh, changed the signal to "S O S." The Captain told us we had been struck amidships, or just back of amidships. It was ten minutes, Phillips told me, after he had noticed the iceberg, that the slight jolt that was the collision's only signal to us occurred. We thought we were a good distance away.

We said lots of funny things to each other in the next few minutes. We picked up, first, the steamship *Frankford*. We gave her our position and said we had struck an iceberg and needed assistance. The *Frankford* operator went away to tell his captain.

He came back and we told him we were sinking by the head. By that time we could observe a distinct list forward.

The *Carpathia* answered our signals. We told her our position and said we were sinking by the head. The operator went to tell the Captain and in five minutes returned and told us that the Captain of the *Carpathia* was putting about and heading for us.

Our Captain had left us at this time, and Phillips told me to run and tell him what the *Carpathia* had answered. I did so, and I went through an awful mass of people to his cabin. The decks were full of scrambling men and women. I saw no fighting, but I heard tell of it.

I came back and heard Phillips giving the *Carpathia* fuller directions. Phillips told me to put on my clothes. Until that moment I forgot that I was not dressed.

I went to my cabin and dressed. I brought an overcoat to Phillips. It was very cold. I slipped the overcoat upon him while he worked.

Every few minutes Phillips would send me to the Captain with little messages. They were merely telling how the *Carpathia* was coming our way and gave her speed.

I noticed as I came back from one trip that they were putting off women and children in lifeboats. I noticed that the list forward was increasing.

Phillips told me the wireless was growing weaker. The Captain came and told us our engine rooms were taking water and that the dynamos might not last much longer. We sent that word to the *Carpathia*.

I went out on deck and looked around. The water was pretty close up to the boat deck. There was a great scramble aft, and how poor Phillips worked through it I don't know.

He was a brave man. I learned to love him that night, and I suddenly felt for him a great reverence to see him standing there sticking to his work while everybody else was raging about. I will never live to forget the work of Phillips for the last awful fifteen minutes.

I thought it was about time to look about and see if there was anything to catch that would float. I remembered that every member of the crew had a special lifebelt and ought to know where it was. I remembered mine was under my bunk. I went and got it. Then I thought how cold the water was.

I remembered that I had some boots and I put those on, and an extra jacket, and I put that on. I saw Phillips standing out there still sending away, giving the *Carpathia* details of just how we were doing.

We picked up the *Olympic* and told her we were sinking by the head, and were about all down. As Phillips was sending the message, I strapped his lifebelt to his back. I had already put on his overcoat.

I wondered if I could get him into his boots. He suggested with a sort of laugh that I look out and see if all the people were off in boats, or if any boats were left, or how things were.

I saw a collapsible boat near a funnel and went over to it. Twelve men were trying to boost it down to the boat deck. They were having an awful time. It was the last boat left. I looked at it longingly a few minutes. Then I gave them a hand, and over she went. They all started to scramble in on the boat deck, and I walked back to Phillips. I said the last raft had gone.

Then, came the Captain's voice, "Men, you have done your full duty. You can do no more. Abandon your cabin. Now it's every man for himself. You look out for yourselves. I release you. That's the way of it at this kind of a time. Every man for himself."

I looked out. The boat deck was awash. Phillips clung on, sending and sending. He clung on for about ten minutes, or maybe fifteen minutes after the Captain had released him. The water was then coming into our cabin.

While he worked something happened I hate to tell about. I was back in my room, getting Phillips' money for him, and as I looked out the door I saw a stoker, or somebody from below decks, leaning over Phillips from behind. He was too busy to notice what the man was doing. The man was slipping the lifebelt off Phillips' back.

He was a big man, too. As you can see, I am very small. I don't know what it was I got hold of. I remembered in a flash the way Phillips had clung on—how I had to fix that lifebelt in place, because he was too busy to do it.

I knew that man from below decks had his own lifebelt and should have known where to get it.

I suddenly felt a passion not to let that man die a decent sailor's death. I wish he might have stretched rope or walked a plank. I did my duty. I hope I finished him. I don't know. We left him on the cabin floor of the wireless room and he was not moving.

From aft came a tune from the band. It was a rag-time. I don't know what. Then there was "Autumn." Phillips ran aft, and that was the last I ever saw of him.

I went to the place I had seen the collapsible boat on the boat deck, and to my surprise I saw the boat, and the men still trying to push it off. I guess there wasn't a sailor in the crowd. They couldn't do it. I went up to them and was just lending a hand when a large wave came awash of the deck. The big wave carried the boat off. I had hold of an oarlock and I went with it. The next I knew I was in the boat. But that was not all. I was in the boat, and the boat was upside-down, and I was under it. And I remember realizing I was wet through and that whatever happened I must not breathe, for I was under water. I knew I had to fight for it, and I did. How I got out from under the boat I do not know but I felt a breath of air at last. There were men all around me—hundreds of them. The sea was dotted with them, all depending on their lifebelts. I felt I simply had to get away from the ship. She was a beautiful sight then. Smoke and sparks were rushing out of her funnel. There must have been an explosion, but we heard none. We only saw the big stream of sparks. The ship was turning gradually on her nose—just like a duck that goes for a dive. I had only one thing on my mind to get away from the suction. The band was still playing. I guess all of them went down. They were playing "Autumn" then. I swam with all my might. I suppose I was 150 feet away when the *Titanic,* on her nose, with her afterquarter sticking straight up in the air, began to settle—slowly.

When at last the waves washed over her rudder there wasn't the least bit of suction I could feel. She must have kept going just so slowly as she had been. . . . I felt after a little while like sinking. I was very cold. I saw a boat of some kind near me, and put all my strength into an effort to swim to it.

It was hard work. I was all done when a hand reached out from the boat and pulled me aboard. It was our same collapsible. The same crowd was on it. There was just room for me to roll on the edge. I lay there not caring what happened. Somebody sat on my legs. They were wedged in between slats and were being wrenched. I had not the heart left to ask the man to move. It was a terrible sight all around—men swimming and sinking.

I lay where I was, letting the man wrench my feet out of shape. Others came near. Nobody gave them a hand. The bottom-up boat already had more men than it would hold, and it was sinking. At first the larger waves splashed over my clothing. Then they began to splash over my head, and I had to breathe when I could. As we floated around on our capsized boat and I kept straining my eyes for a ship's lights, somebody said, "Don't the rest of you think we ought to pray?" The man who made the suggestion asked what the religion of the others was. Each man called out his religion. One was a Catholic, one a Methodist, one a Presbyterian. It was decided the most appropriate prayer for all was the Lord's Prayer. We spoke it over in chorus with the man who first suggested that we pray as the leader. Some splendid people saved us. They had a right-side-up boat and it was full to capacity. Yet they came to us and loaded us all into it. I saw some lights off in the distance and knew a steamship was coming to our aid.

"It was like trying to clutch a shadow . . ."

JIM THORPE

November 9, 1912
West Point, New York

ANONYMOUS *NEW YORK TIMES* REPORTER

S portswriters voted James Francis Thorpe the greatest American athlete of the first half of the twentieth century. In 1912 he scored 25 touchdowns and 198 points playing football for his school team, and won Olympic gold medals in both the pentathlon and decathlon. Later he excelled in both professional baseball and professional football.

Jim Thorpe and his redoubtable band of Carlisle Indian gridiron stars invaded the plains this afternoon to match their prowess against the moleskin gladiators of Uncle Sam's Military Academy, and when the two teams crossed the parade ground in the semi-darkness of late afternoon the Cadets had been shown up as no other West Point team has been in many years. They were buried under the overwhelming score of 27 to 6. . . .

Standing out resplendent in a galaxy of Indian stars was Jim Thorpe, recently crowned the athletic marvel of the age. The big Indian Captain added more lustre to his already brilliant record, and at times the game itself was almost forgotten while the spectators gazed on Thorpe, the individual, to wonder at his prowess. To recount his notable performances in the complete overthrow of the Cadets would leave little space for other notable points of the conflict. He simply ran wild, while the Cadets tried in vain to stop his progress. It was like trying to clutch a shadow. Thorpe went through the West Point line as if it was an open door; his defensive play was on a par with his attack and his every move was that of a past master.

Thorpe tore off runs of 10 yards or more so often that they became common, and an advance of less than that figure seemed a wasted effort. His zigzag running and ability to hurl himself free of tacklers made his running highly spectacular. In the third period he made a run which, while it failed to bring anything in points [a penalty was called on a team-mate], will go down in the Army gridiron annals as one of the greatest ever seen on the plains. The Indians had held for downs on West Point's 3-yard line, and Keyes dropped back behind his own goal line and punted out. The ball went directly to Thorpe, who stood on the Army's 45-yard line, about half way between the two side lines. It was a high kick, and the Cadets were already gathering around the big Indian when he clutched the falling pigskin in his arms. His catch and his start were but one motion. In and out, zig-zagging first to one side and then to the other, while a flying Cadet went hurling through space, Thorpe wormed his way through the entire Army team. Every Cadet in the game had his chance, and every one of them failed.

"A man shall never have to take more than one step . . ."

THE FIRST ASSEMBLY LINE

April 1, 1913
Detroit

HENRY FORD

*F*ord had already been building the ingeniously simple Model T for five years
when his engineers developed the assembly line. By 1927, when he halted production of the "Tin Lizzie," more than fifteen million had been sold. His efficient
methods allowed him to pay workers the stunningly generous wage of five dollars
for an eight-hour day, and to start a profit-sharing plan.

A Ford car contains about five thousand parts—that is counting
screws, nuts, and all. Some of the parts are fairly bulky and others are
almost the size of watch parts. In our first assembling we simply started to
put a car together at a spot on the floor and workmen brought to it the
parts as they were needed in exactly the same way that one builds a
house. When we started to make parts it was natural to create a single
department of the factory to make that part, but usually one workman
performed all of the operations necessary on a small part. The rapid press
of production made it necessary to devise plans of production that would
avoid having the workers falling over one another. . . .

The first step forward in assembly came when we began taking the
work to the men instead of the men to the work. We now have two general principles in all operations—that a man shall never have to take more
than one step, if possibly it can be avoided, and that no man need ever
stoop over.

The principles of assembly are these:

(1) Place the tools and the men in the sequence of the operation so that each component part shall travel the least possible
distance while in the process of finishing.

(2) Use work slides or some other form of carrier so that
when a workman completes his operation, he drops the part
always in the same place—which place must always be the most

convenient place to his hand—and if possible have gravity carry the part to the next workman for his operation.

(3) Use sliding assembling lines by which the parts to be assembled are delivered at convenient distances.

The net result of the application of these principles is the reduction of the necessity for thought on the part of the worker and the reduction of his movements to a minimum. He does as nearly as possible only one thing with only one movement. . . .

Along about April 1, 1913, we first tried the experiment of an assembly line. We tried it on assembling the fly-wheel magneto. We try everything in a little way first—we will rip out anything once we discover a better way, but we have to know absolutely that the new way is going to be better than the old before we do anything drastic.

I believe that this was the first moving line ever installed. The idea came in a general way from the overhead trolley that the Chicago packers use in dressing beef. We had previously assembled the fly-wheel magneto in the usual method. With one workman doing a complete job he could turn out from thirty-five to forty pieces in a nine-hour day, or about twenty minutes to an assembly. What he did alone was then spread into twenty-nine operations; that cut down the assembly time to thirteen minutes, ten seconds. Then we raised the height of the line eight inches—this was in 1914—and cut the time to seven minutes. Further experimenting with the speed that the work should move at cut the time down to five minutes. In short, the result is this: by the aid of scientific study one man is now able to do somewhat more than four did only a comparatively few years ago. That line established the efficiency of the method and we now use it everywhere. The assembling of the motor, formerly done by one man, is now divided into eighty-four operations—those men do the work that three times their number formerly did.

"Pure bowshot at 700 meters range . . ."

SINKING THE *LUSITANIA*

May 17, 1915
North Atlantic

KAPITÄN-LEUTNANT WALTER SCHWIEGER

*O*n August 4, 1914, after a week in which many European countries had declared the assortment of wars that became World War I, the United States officially declared its neutrality.

At first, Americans were safe from a war that offered shocking innovations: German submarines, dogfighting airplanes, and chemical weapons such as mustard gas. Then a German U-boat sank the Cunard Line's flagship, Lusitania. Of almost two thousand people on the ship, more than half drowned, including sixty-three infants. More than one hundred Americans were among the dead.

Germany agreed to halt submarine warfare after the Lusitania tragedy. But on January 31, 1917, Germany announced it would resume the practice, to prevent supply shipments to Britain. The German announcement made U.S. involvement in World War I inevitable.

These extracts from the German submarine's log detail the captain's observations through his periscope. The captain did not know what he had sunk until his pilot looked through the periscope and exclaimed, "By God, it's the Lusitania." The ocean liner went down in just eighteen minutes.

3:35 P.M. [GERMAN TIME]

The steamer turns starboard, takes a course to Queenstown and thus makes possible a drawing near for the firing. Up to 3 P.M. ran at high speed in order to get a position up-front.

4:10 P.M.

Pure bowshot at 700 meters range. (G torpedo 3m. depth adjustment), angle of intersection 90°, estimated speed 22 knots. Shot strikes starboard side right behind the bridge.

. . . An unusually heavy detonation takes place with a very strong explosion cloud (far beyond front funnel). The explosion of the torpedo must have been followed by a second one (boiler or coal or powder?). The superstructure above the point of impact and the bridge are torn asunder, fire breaks out, smoke envelops the high bridge. The ship stops immediately and heels over to starboard quickly, immersing simultaneously at the bow. It appears as if the ship were going to capsize very shortly. Great confusion is rife on board; the boats are made ready and some of them lowered into the water. In connection therewith great panic must have reigned, some boats, full to capacity are rushed from above, touch the water with either stem or stern first, and founder immediately.

"The tracer bullets cut a streak of living fire . . ."

WAR IN THE AIR

April 29, 1918
France

CAPTAIN EDDIE RICKENBACKER

*I*n *April 1917, more than two and a half years after the outbreak of World War I, the United States entered the fray. American isolationism had ended as a result of German belligerence that could no longer be ignored: on February 3, Germany had sunk the American ocean liner* Housatonic; *and on February 24, America learned of the Zimmerman telegram, a message from German foreign minister Alfred Zimmerman to the German ambassador to Mexico, proposing that Mexico be asked to join an alliance against the United States.*

When America entered World War I, Eddie Rickenbacker was already famous as a race car driver, with a world speed record of 134 miles an hour. As a pilot, he shot down twenty-six enemy planes and earned the Congressional Medal of Honor.

After the war, he became a successful businessman as a partner in the Indianapolis Speedway and president of Eastern Airlines. His flying partner for this first mission, Captain James Norman Hall, later became famous as the coauthor of Mutiny on the Bounty *and other books.*

Precisely at five o'clock Captain Hall received a telephone call from the French headquarters at Beaumont stating that an enemy two-seater machine had just crossed our lines and was flying south over their heads.

Captain Hall and I had been walking about the field with our flying clothes on and our machines were standing side by side with their noses pointing into the wind. Within the minute we had jumped into our seats and our mechanics were twirling the propellers. Just then the telephone sergeant came running out to us and told Captain Hall to hold his flight until the Major was ready. He was to accompany us and would be on the field in two minutes.

While the sergeant was delivering the message I was scanning the northern heavens and there I suddenly picked up a tiny speck against the clouds above the Forêt de la Reine, which I was convinced must be the enemy plane we were after. The Major was not yet in sight. Our motors were smoothly turning over and everything was ready.

Pointing out the distant speck to Jimmy Hall, I begged him to give the word to go before we lost sight of our easy victim. If we waited for the Major we might be too late.

To my great joy Captain Hall acquiesced and immediately ordered the boys to pull away the blocks from our wheels. His motor roared as he opened up his throttle and in a twinkling both our machines were running rapidly over the surface of the field. Almost side by side we arose and climbing swiftly, soared away in a straight line after our distant Boche.

In five minutes we were above our observation balloon line which stretches along some two miles or so behind the front. I was on Jimmy's right wing and off to my right in the direction of Pont-à-Mousson I could still distinguish our unsuspecting quarry. Try as I might I could not induce the Captain to turn in that direction, though I dipped my wings, darted away from him, and tried in every way to attract his attention to the target which was so conspicuous to me. He stupidly continued on straight North.

I determined to sever relations with him and take on the Boche alone, since he evidently was generous enough to give me a clear field. Accordingly I swerved swiftly away from Captain Hall and within five minutes overhauled the enemy and adroitly maneuvered myself into an ideal position just under his sheltering tail. It was a large three-seater machine and a brace of guns poked their noses out to the rear over my head. With fingers closing on my triggers I prepared for a dash upwards and quickly pulled back my stick. Up I zoomed until my sights began to travel along the length of the fuselage overhead. Suddenly they rested on a curiously familiar looking device. It was the French circular cocard painted brightly under each wing! Up to this time I had not even thought of looking for its nationality, so certain had I been that this must be the Boche machine that had been sighted by the French headquarters.

Completely disgusted with myself, I viraged abruptly away from my latest blunder, finding some little satisfaction in witnessing the startled surprise of the three Frenchmen aboard the craft, who had not become aware of my proximity until they saw me flash past them. At any rate I had stalked them successfully and might have easily downed them if they had been Boches. But as it was, it would be a trifle difficult to face Jimmy Hall again and explain to him why I had left him alone to get myself five miles away under the tail of a perfectly harmless ally three-seater. I looked about to discover Jimmy's whereabout.

There he was cavorting about amidst a thick barrage of black shell-bursts across the German lines. He was half-way to St. Mihiel and a mile or two inside Hun territory. Evidently he was waiting for me to discover my mistake and then overtake him, for he was having a delightful time with the Archy gunner, doing loops, barrels, side-slips and spins immediately over their heads to show them his contempt for them, while he waited for his comrade. Finally he came out of the Archy area with a long graceful dive and swinging up alongside my machine he wiggled his wings as though he were laughing at me and then suddenly he set a course back towards Pont-à-Mousson. Whether or not he knew all along that a German craft was in that region I could not tell. But when he began to change his direction and curve up into the sun I followed close behind him knowing that there was a good reason for this maneuver. I looked earnestly about me in every direction.

Yes! There was a scout coming towards us from north of Pont-à-Mousson. It was about our altitude. I knew it was a Hun the moment I saw it, for it had the familiar lines of their new Pfalz. Moreover, my confidence in James Norman Hall was such that I knew he couldn't make a mistake. And he was still climbing into the sun, carefully keeping his position between its glare and the oncoming fighting plane I clung as closely to Hall as I could. The Hun was steadily approaching us, unconscious of his danger, for we were full in the sun.

With the first downward dive of Jimmy's machine I was by his side. We had at least a thousand feet advantage over the enemy and we were two to one numerically. He might outdive our machines, for the Pfalz is a famous diver, while our faster climbing Nieuports had a droll little habit of shedding their fabric when plunged too furiously through the air. The Boche hadn't a chance to outfly us. His only salvation would be in a dive towards his own lines.

These thoughts passed through my mind in a flash and I instantly determined upon my tactics. While Hall went in for his attack I would keep my altitude and get a position the other side of the Pfalz, to cut off his retreat.

No sooner had I altered my line of flight than the German pilot saw me leave the sun's rays. Hall was already half-way to him when he stuck up his nose and began furiously climbing to the upper ceiling. I let him pass me and found myself on the other side just as Hall began firing. I doubt if the Boche had seen Hall's Nieuport at all.

Surprised by discovering this new antagonist, Hall, ahead of him, the Pfalz immediately abandoned all idea of a battle and banking around to the right started for home, just as I had expected him to do. In a trice I was on his tail. Down, down we sped with throttles both full open. Hall was coming on somewhere in my rear. The Boche had no heart for evolutions or maneuvers. He was running like a scared rabbit. I was gaining upon him every instant and I had my sights trained dead upon his seat before I fired my first shot.

At 150 yards I pressed my triggers. The tracer bullets cut a streak of living fire into the rear of the Pfalz tail. Raising the nose of my aeroplane slightly the fiery streak lifted itself like the stream of water pouring from a garden hose. Gradually it settled into the pilot's seat. The swerving of the Pfalz course indicated that its rudder no longer was held by a directing hand. At 2000 feet above the enemy's lines I pulled up my headlong dive and watched the enemy machine continuing on its course. Curving slightly to the left the Pfalz circled a little to the south and the next minute crashed onto the ground just at the edge of the woods a mile inside their own lines. I had brought down my first enemy aeroplane.

"Our division pressed forward
in irresistible waves to the German trenches."

THE AMERICANS JOIN THE WAR IN EUROPE

September 9–November 8, 1918
France

CORPORAL ELMER SHERWOOD

More than two million American troops, known as the American Expeditionary Force (AEF), went to France in 1917 and 1918, enthusiastically singing that "we won't be back 'til it's over, over there."

At the time, the war in Europe had reached a stalemate, with long trench lines dividing France. The battlegrounds had become muddy graveyards. For instance, during the first Battle of the Somme, which lasted almost five months in 1916, the Allies lost 620,000 French and British troops, and advanced just five miles.

The AEF was commanded by General John J. Pershing. He resisted most efforts of the European commanders to divide the Americans into replacement units for British and French forces. In September 1918 the AEF finally got a chance to take the offensive as an independent unit. Their efforts, combined with new offensives by the French and British, broke the German forces. On the eleventh hour of the eleventh day of the eleventh month—hence the Veteran's Day holiday that is still observed on November 11—the fighting officially ended.

Corporal Sherwood, from Indiana, served in the trenches. He reenlisted during World War II to serve as a brigadier general.

SEPTEMBER 9

This will be the first battle of the war in which the participating troops of our side are to be commanded by Pershing personally, according to the snow [gossip] and it will be the first big all-American drive.

The command may be endeavoring to keep the plans secret. If so, it has not altogether succeeded, because it seems to me everybody in France surmises that we are going to fight to flatten the St. Mihiel salient. Even the French peasants spoke of it as we came up to the front.

This projection of the battlefront is popularly known as the "hernia of St. Mihiel," and it has existed for almost four years. In 1914 the German horde forced its way to this point, which has been held by the enemy ever since.

The salient has an area of some 150 square miles, almost the size of the former Chateau-Thierry salient, and among other things, it contains a very important railway junction. It is a grand and glorious feeling to know that it is the American army which will carry on this operation.

These fellows have so much confidence that they swear they will capture Metz if ordered to, or die in the attempt.

SEPTEMBER 11

We are all set for the party. Unlike the Champagne front, we do not have any reserve positions picked out in case of retreat on this front. Evidently Pershing feels that there is no doubt but that this battle will go our way.

SEPTEMBER 12

The zero hour was 1:05 a.m., the heavy artillery starting it off. The earth seemed to give way when the rest of our guns joined in the stupendous and fierce barrage. The roar was so loud that we could scarcely distinguish the deep intonation of our own howitzers from the reports of the 75s.

For four hours the deafening roar continued as our messengers of death were hurled into enemy territory. Then at 5:00 our infantry preceded by tanks went over the top, making a picture of dash and activity.

Not content with ordinary progress the boys of our division leaped ahead of the clumsy tanks and pressed forward in irresistible waves to the German trenches.

The enemy artillery reply was feeble, though the infantry machine-gun and rifle fire was more menacing.

Our artillery fire in the first place demoralized enemy resistance, and the Boche are surrendering in droves. Surely they must regret giving up these luxurious dugouts and trenches which they have lived in for four years. Many of them even have electric lights and good furniture "requisitioned" from nearby French villages.

We must have slipped up on the enemy because they left a great deal of equipment, ammunition and food. Before we left the battery on detail work, two or three hundred prisoners passed our position. Up here in the advance we pass prisoners in droves of from ten to a hundred with a doughboy in the rear prodding the laggards with a bayonet whenever necessary.

A good many of the Germans are being utilized to carry back wounded. A sedate-looking officer wearing white gloves had to bow his back in the work just as his men did. It seemed to do these enemy enlisted men good to see their officers thus reduced to their own plane. Most of them became quite cheerful after they found that they weren't going to be scalped as they had been led to believe these aboriginal Americans were wont to do.

The condition of the roads is very bad and No Man's Land is a mess of shellholes and mud. A good many enemy dead are lying about and a few of our own men are lying where they were struck down by enemy fire this morning.

The doughboys are still advancing swiftly. In the air we are supreme. We are not in the position of the rat in the cage, as we were at Chateau-Thierry when enemy planes swooped down upon us and threw streams of machine-gun bullets into our ranks. This time the tables are turned. We see our aviators flying over the retreating enemy, dropping bombs and creating havoc.

SEPTEMBER 13

No rest for the weary last night. By inches we progressed to Seicheprey, the town which saw such terrific fighting between the 26th division and the Germans late last winter.

OCTOBER 3

We are now hiking up to the line over newly captured territory. For four years this land had been in German hands.

A doughboy who was under fire for the first time Thursday was on the way back today on some detail. He told me that half of his company was wiped out by gas attack. These fellows, without actual battle experience, didn't detect gas in time, and the officers gave no command to put on masks. By the time they did get their masks on, if indeed they got them on at all, half of them were casualties; many of them died.

I feel sure that we are going to suffer heavy casualties in this drive, due to the nature of the German defense—enemy machine guns scattered through the forests in front of us like snakes in the grass.

OCTOBER 8

This morning Cliff Schwartz awakened us and I rolled out of my blankets hungry and thirsty. Our little signal detail is located in a trench to the left of the battery, just at the bottom of the hill on which the village of Montfaucon stands.

Cliff had obtained a paper from a passing Red Cross worker, and I read the German peace appeal which the enemy had made to President Wilson.

Art Long interrupted me with, "These whiz-bangs Fritz is putting over don't sound like peace to me, any more than the steel we are dousing him with."

"Well, any way you take it, boys, we've got him licked, and I believe that all of us who are lucky enough to live through this battle will get back home," replied Danny Slentz.

I stopped the discussion by announcing that I was going to get some mess.

"You're crazy, Doc," Cliff remarked. "A big H.E. [high explosive shell] will pounce on you and leave nothing but a grease spot. Better wait for a while right here in the trench until things clear up a bit."

Two of our fellows had already been wounded by an explosion near our kitchen this morning, but I was determined to go back for some mess because I was so confounded hungry. Besides, shells seemed to be landing everywhere and one place seemed about as safe as another (or as dangerous), so I climbed out of the trench and made my way carefully back to the clump of bushes where our kitchen was concealed.

I had just got a panful of slum and started eating when I saw part of the temporary trench which I had left screened by an exploding shell. I thought it had come over the trench, but no—just then Smithy and Netterfield jumped out calling for stretchers.

I dropped my mess and ran to the trench and looked in. Poor Art was dead, one arm completely severed from his body. Danny had a hole in his stomach and we placed him on a stretcher and sent him back to the first aid station.

Dan Slentz looked at me with a smile on his face as we loaded him into the ambulance. I gave him a word of cheer and he said, "I don't know, Doc old boy. I've got a pretty bad wound in my stomach. You boys give 'em hell for me." [He died that day.]

I have seen many die, but none have been so close to me as these fellows. I have worked with them and fought beside them every day since I joined the outfit, and they have been my best pals. But we must carry on, whatever happens.

OCTOBER 30

Last night Fritz put on a whale of a bombardment, and I don't see how any of us escaped to tell the story. In the thick of it our communications were knocked out and I was detailed to repair the telephone line. How kind they are to me! Well, I thought of all the mean things I'd done in my life, breathed a little prayer, climbed out of my foxhole, and darted out into the inferno.

Flashes of exploding artillery at intervals lighted up the blackness of the night. Explosions of enemy shells on every hand and the scream of big ones going overhead to back areas added to the thunderous uproar so that I could not have heard my own voice had I dared to speak. Boy! I was glad when I came to that break in the line. I was splicing the wire when— Shriek! Bang! A ton of steel came over me. Just as I finished the job— hell's bells!—another hit knocked the line out in another place.

For once I lost my cocky self-assurance, and I wasn't so certain that I would ever see home and Mother again. But finally, after stumbling over the body of a dead German, I came upon the next break and spliced it in a hurry. Then I raced back to my hole after reporting communications in order.

Jack Skull has just been sent back to the hospital suffering from shell-shock. No wonder nerves give way and normal men go crazy.

NOVEMBER 8 (ADVANCING TOWARD SEDAN)

The battle has changed from a slow, bloody, inch-by-inch fight to a mad chase. The enemy is in full retreat.

"We pitch to better hitters than Ruth ..."

BABE RUTH

October 12, 1923
New York City

HEYWOOD BROUN

As every baseball buff knows, Ruth broke into the majors as a southpaw pitcher for the Boston Red Sox in 1914. He was tough on the mound. He had an 89-46 record with Boston, including seasons of twenty-three wins in 1916 and twenty-four wins in 1917. He had a career 2.28 ERA. Yet when he began with the Yankees in the 1920 season, the team moved him into the field so he could hit every day.

The Yankees won the 1923 World Series, four games to two.

Broun's column for the New York World, *"It Seems to Me," was syndicated across the country. During the Depression he became widely known as a champion of the common American.*

The Ruth is mighty and shall prevail. He did yesterday. Babe made two home runs, and the Yankees won from the Giants at the Polo Grounds by a score of four to two. This evens up the World Series with one game for each contender.

It was the first game the Yankees won from the Giants since October 10, 1921, and it ended a string of eight successive victories for the latter, with one tie thrown in.

Victory came to the American League champions through a change in tactics. Miller Huggins could hardly fail to have observed Wednesday that terrible things were almost certain to happen to his men if they paused anyplace along the line from first to home.

In order to prevent blunders in base running he wisely decided to eliminate it. The batter who hits a ball into the stands cannot possibly be caught napping off any base.

The Yankees prevented Kelly, Frisch, and the rest from performing tricks in black magic by consistently hammering the ball out of the park or into sections of the stand where only amateurs were seated.

Though simplicity itself, the system worked like a charm. Three of the Yankees' four runs were the product of homers and this was enough for a winning total. Erin Ward was Ruth's assistant. Irish Meusel of the Giants also made a home run, but yesterday's show belonged to Ruth.

For the first time since coming to New York, Babe achieved his full brilliance in a World Series game. Before this he has varied between pretty good and simply awful, but yesterday he was magnificent.

Just before the game John McGraw remarked:

"Why shouldn't we pitch to Ruth? I've said before, and I'll say it again, we pitch to better hitters than Ruth in the National League."

Ere the sun had set on McGraw's rash and presumptuous words, the Babe had flashed across the sky fiery portents which should have been sufficient to strike terror and conviction into the hearts of all infidels. But John McGraw clung to his heresy with a courage worthy of a better cause.

In the fourth inning Ruth drove the ball completely out of the premises. McQuillan was pitching at the time, and the count was two balls and one strike. The strike was a fast ball shoulder-high, at which Ruth had lunged with almost comic ferocity and ineptitude.

Snyder peeked at the bench to get a signal from McGraw. Catching for the Giants must be a terrific strain on the neck muscles, for apparently it is etiquette to take the signals from the bench manager furtively. The catcher is supposed to pretend he is merely glancing around to see if the girl in the red hat is anywhere in the grandstand, although all the time his eyes are intent on McGraw.

Of course the nature of the code is secret, but this time McGraw scratched his nose, to indicate: "Try another of those shoulder-high fast ones on the Big Bam and let's see if we can't make him break his back again."

But Babe didn't break his back, for he had something solid to check his terrific swing. The ball started climbing from the moment it left the plate. It was a pop fly with a brand-new gland and, though it flew high, it also flew far.

When last seen the ball was crossing the roof of the stand in deep right field at an altitude of 315 feet. We wonder whether new baseballs conversing together in the original package ever remark: "Join Ruth and see the world."

In the fifth Ruth was up again, and by this time McQuillan had left the park utterly and Jack Bentley was pitching. The count crept up to two strikes and two balls. Snyder sneaked a look at the little logician deep in the dugout. McGraw blinked twice, pulled up his trousers, and thrust the forefinger of his right hand into his left eye. Snyder knew that he meant, "Try the Big Bozo on a slow curve around his knees and don't forget to throw to first if you happen to drop the third strike."

Snyder called for the delivery as directed, and Ruth half topped a line drive over the wall of the lower stand in right field. With that drive the Babe tied a record. Benny Kauff and Duffy Lewis are the only other players who ever made two home runs in a single World Series game.

But was McGraw convinced and did he rush out of the dugout and kneel before Ruth with a cry of "Maestro" as the Babe crossed the plate? He did not. He nibbled at not a single word he has ever uttered in disparagement of the prowess of the Yankee slugger. In the ninth Ruth came to bat with two out and a runner on second base. By every consideration of prudent tactics an intentional pass seemed indicated.

Snyder jerked his head around and observed that McGraw was blowing his nose. The Giant catcher was puzzled, for that was a signal he had never learned. By a process of pure reasoning he attempted to figure out just what it was that his chief was trying to convey to him.

"Maybe he means if we pitch to Ruth we'll blow the game," thought Snyder, but he looked toward the bench again just to make sure.

Now McGraw intended no signal at all when he blew his nose. That was not tactics, but only a head cold. On the second glance, Snyder observed that the little Napoleon gritted his teeth. Then he proceeded to spell out with the first three fingers of his right hand: "The Old Guard dies, but never surrenders." That was a signal Snyder recognized, although it never had passed between him and his manager.

McGraw was saying: "Pitch to the big bum if he hammers every ball in the park into the North River."

And so, at Snyder's request, Bentley did pitch to Ruth, and the Babe drove the ball deep into right center; so deep that Casey Stengel could feel the hot breath of the bleacherites on his back as the ball came down and he caught it. If that drive had been just a shade to the right it would have been a third home run for Ruth. As it was, the Babe had a great day, with two home runs, a terrific long fly, and two bases on balls.

Neither pass was intentional. For that McGraw should receive due credit. His fame deserves to be recorded along with the men who said,

"Lay on, MacDuff," "Sink me the ship, Master Gunner, split her in twain," and "I'll fight it out on this line if it takes all summer." For John McGraw also went down eyes front and his thumb on his nose.

"I heard it as a sort of musical
kaleidoscope of America . . ."

"RHAPSODY IN BLUE"

January 1924
En Route to Boston

GEORGE GERSHWIN

C omposer George Gershwin wrote "Rhapsody in Blue" in three weeks. He didn't have much choice. He had made a throwaway comment about a new idea to Paul Whiteman, an influential bandleader with a background in classical music. Whiteman, eager to establish symphonic jazz, which was played from written scores and more mellow than the improvised jazz of the time, thought the piece was already written, so he advertised the first formal jazz concert ever, to be held in New York City's Aeolian Hall just three weeks later.

The orchestral parts were arranged page by page, as Gershwin delivered them to Whiteman and Ferde Grofé. The title came from Gershwin's lyricist brother, Ira, who changed the prosaic working title, "American Rhapsody." The concert took place on time, with Gershwin himself playing the piano part, and was a huge success.

This account may have been dressed up for publication by an earlier biographer, but it is true to Gershwin's thoughts, according to Charles Schwartz, author of The Life and Music of George Gershwin.

There had been so much chatter about the limitations of jazz, not to speak of the manifest misunderstanding of its function. Jazz, they said, had to be in strict time. It had to cling to dance rhythms. I resolved, if possible, to kill that misconception with one sturdy blow. Inspired by this aim, I set to work composing. No set plan was in my head—no structure to which my music would conform. The rhapsody, as you see, began as a purpose, not a plan.

At this stage of the piece I was summoned to Boston for the premiere of *Sweet Little Devil.* I had already done some work on the rhapsody. It was on the train, with its steely rhythms, its rattle-ty bang that is often so stimulating to a composer. . . . I frequently hear music in the very heart of noise. And there I suddenly heard—and even saw on paper—the complete construction of the rhapsody, from beginning to end. No new themes came to me, but I worked on the thematic material already in mind and tried to conceive the composition as a whole. I heard it as a sort of musical kaleidoscope of America—of our vast melting pot, of our unduplicated national pep, of our blues, our metropolitan madness. By the time I reached Boston I had a definite *plot* of the piece, as distinguished from its actual substance.

"Dayton was simply a great capital like any other ..."

AMONG THE BELIEVERS

July 14, 1925
Dayton, Tennessee

H. L. MENCKEN

*T*he defendant at the Tennessee Monkey Trial was John T. Scopes, a schoolteacher who had been charged with teaching the theory of evolution.

H. L. Mencken, ever the keen observer of American life, called by critic Walter Lippman "the most powerful personal influence" on the intellectuals of his generation, went to Dayton to cover the trial for the Baltimore Sun. *He knew it would offer a chance to send up his favorite target, rural America.*

Scopes was found guilty. The Sun *paid his $100 fine.*

It was hot weather when they tried the infidel Scopes at Dayton, Tenn., but I went down there very willingly, for I was eager to see something of evangelical Christianity as a going concern. In the big cities of the Republic, despite the endless efforts of consecrated men, it is laid up with a wasting disease. The very Sunday-school superintendents, taking jazz from the stealthy radio, shake their fire-proof legs; their pupils, moving into adolescence, no longer respond to the proliferating hormones by enlisting for missionary service in Africa, but resort to necking instead. Even in Dayton, I found, though the mob was up to do execution upon

Scopes, there was a strong smell of antinomianism. The nine churches of the village were all half empty on Sunday, and weeds choked their yards. Only two or three of the resident pastors managed to sustain themselves by their ghostly science; the rest had to take orders for mail-order pantaloons or work in the adjacent strawberry fields; one, I heard, was a barber. On the courthouse green a score of sweating theologians debated the darker passages of Holy Writ day and night, but I soon found that they were all volunteers, and that the local faithful, while interested in their exegesis as an intellectual exercise, did not permit it to impede the indigenous debaucheries. Exactly twelve minutes after I reached the village I was taken in tow by a Christian man and introduced to the favorite tipple of the Cumberland Range: half corn liquor and half Coca-Cola. It seemed a dreadful dose to me, but I found that the Dayton illuminati got it down with gusto, rubbing their tummies and rolling their eyes. I include among them the chief local proponents of the Mosaic cosmogony. They were all hot for Genesis, but their faces were far too florid to belong to teetotalers, and when a pretty girl came tripping down the main street, which was very often, they reached for the places where their neckties should have been with all the amorous enterprise of movie actors. It seemed somehow strange.

An amiable newspaper woman of Chattanooga, familiar with those uplands, presently enlightened me. Dayton, she explained, was simply a great capital like any other. That is to say, it was to Rhea County what Atlanta was to Georgia or Paris to France. That is to say, it was predominantly Epicurean and sinful. A country girl from some remote valley of the county, coming into town for her semi-annual bottle of Lydia Pinkham's Vegetable Compound, shivered on approaching Robinson's drug-store quite as a country girl from upstate New York might shiver on approaching the Metropolitan Opera House. In every village lout she saw a potential white-slaver. The hard sidewalks hurt her feet. Temptations of the flesh bristled to all sides of her, luring her to Hell. This newspaper woman told me of a session with just such a visitor, holden a few days before. The latter waited outside one of the town hot-dog and Coca-Cola shops while her husband negotiated with a hardware merchant across the street. The newspaper woman, idling along and observing that the stranger was badly used by the heat, invited her to step into the shop for a glass of Coca-Cola. The invitation brought forth only a gurgle of terror. Coca-Cola, it quickly appeared, was prohibited by the country lady's pastor, as a levantine and Hell-sent narcotic. He also prohibited coffee and tea—and pies! He had his doubts about white bread and boughten meat. The newspaper woman, interested, inquired about ice-cream. It was, she found, not specifically prohibited, but going into a Coca-Cola shop to get it would be clearly sinful. So she offered to get a saucer of it, and bring it out to the sidewalk. The visitor vacillated—and came near being lost. But God saved her in the nick of time. When the newspaper woman emerged from the place she was in full flight up the street. Later on her husband, mounted on a mule, overtook her four miles out the mountain pike. This newspaper woman, whose kindness covered city infidels as well as Alpine Christians, offered to take me back in the hills to a place where the old-time religion was genuinely on tap. The Scopes jury, she explained, was composed mainly of its customers, with a few Dayton sophisticates added to leaven the mass. It would thus be instructive to climb the heights and observe the former at their ceremonies. . . . But foreigners, it appeared, would have to approach the sacred grove cautiously, for the upland wor-shipers were very shy, and at the first sight of a strange face they would adjourn their orgy and slink into the forest.

. . . Slowly and cautiously we crossed what seemed to be a pasture, and then we stealthily edged further and further. The light now grew larger and we could begin to make out what was going on. We went ahead on all fours, like snakes in the grass.

From the great limb of a mighty oak hung a couple of crude torches of the sort that car inspectors thrust under Pullman cars when a train pulls in at night. In the guttering glare was the preacher, and for a while we could see no one else. He was an immensely tall and thin mountaineer in blue jeans, his collarless shirt open at the neck and his hair a tousled mop. As he preached he paced up and down under the smoking flam-beaux, and at each turn he thrust his arms into the air and yelled "Glory to God!" We crept nearer in the shadow of the cornfield, and began to hear more of his discourse. He was preaching on the Day of Judgment. The high kings of the earth, he roared, would all fall down and die; only the sanctified would stand up to receive the Lord God of Hosts. One of these kings he mentioned by name, the king of what he called Greece-y. The king of Greece-y, he said, was doomed to Hell.

The preacher stopped at last, and there arose out of the darkness a woman with her hair pulled back into a little tight knot. She began so qui-etly that we couldn't hear what she said, but soon her voice rose reso-nantly and we could follow her. She was denouncing the reading of books. Some wandering book agent, it appeared, had come to her cabin and tried to sell her a specimen of his wares. She refused to touch it. Why, indeed, read a book? If what was in it was true, then everything in it was already in the Bible. If it was false, then reading it would imperil the soul. This syllogism from the Caliph Omar complete, she sat down.

Finally, we got tired of the show and returned to Dayton. It was nearly eleven o'clock—an immensely late hour for those latitudes—but the whole town was still gathered in the courthouse yard, listening to the disputes of theologians. The Scopes trial had brought them in from all directions. There was a friar wearing a sandwich sign announcing that he was the Bible champion of the world. There was a Seventh Day Adventist arguing that Clarence Darrow was the beast with seven heads and ten horns described in Revelation XIII, and that the end of the world was at hand. There was an evangelist made up like Andy Gump, with the news that atheists in Cincinnati were preparing to descend upon Dayton, hang the eminent Judge Raulston, and burn the town. There was an ancient who maintained that no Catholic could be a Christian. There was the eloquent Dr. T. T. Martin, of Blue Mountain, Miss., come to town with a truck-load of torches and hymn-books to put Darwin in his place. There was a singing brother bellowing apocalyptic hymns. There was William Jennings Bryan, followed everywhere by a gaping crowd. Dayton was having a roaring time. It was better than the circus. But the note of devotion was simply not there; the Daytonians, after listening a while, would slip away to Robinson's drug-store to regale themselves with Coca-Cola, or to the lobby of the Aqua Hotel, where the learned Raulston sat in state, judicially picking his teeth. The real religion was not present. It began at the bridge over the town creek, where the road makes off for the hills.

"It looked almost magical as it rose ..."

FIRST ROCKET FLIGHT

March 17, 1926
Auburn, Massachusetts

DR. ROBERT H. GODDARD

S *keptics often ridiculed aerospace pioneer Robert Goddard. In 1920, the* New York Times *published an editorial poking fun at Goddard's claim that rockets could fly through the vacuum of space. Even after Goddard began to prove his theories, few American scientists pursued the research.*

In 1969, just before Apollo 11 *landed on the moon, the* New York Times *retracted its earlier comments.*

The first flight with a rocket using liquid-propellants was made yesterday at Aunt Effie's farm in Auburn.

The day was clear and comparatively quiet. The anemometer on the Physics lab. was turning leisurely when Mr. Sachs and I left in the morning, and was turning as leisurely when we returned at 5:30 P.M.

Even though the release was pulled, the rocket did not rise at first, but the flame came out, and there was a steady roar. After a number of seconds it rose, slowly until it cleared the frame, and then at express train speed, curving over to the left, and striking the ice and snow, still going at a rapid rate.

It looked almost magical as it rose, without any appreciably greater noise or flame, as if it said "I've been here long enough; I think I'll be going somewhere else, if you don't mind." . . .

The sky was clear, for the most part, with large shadowy white clouds, but late in the afternoon there was a large pink cloud in the west, over which the sun shone.

One of the surprising things was the absence of smoke, the lack of very loud roar, and the smallness of the flame.

This first flight of a liquid-propellant rocket is of very considerable significance, inasmuch as it demonstrated the possibility of using liquid propellants to secure actual flight, thereby making possible a rocket which could be simple in construction, and of small weight compared with the weight of the propellant.

"She's no clinging vine . . ."

THE FLAPPER

1926

SAMUEL CROWTHER

*C*rowther *was a popular journalist for magazines such as the* Saturday Evening Post.

The real flapper is what used to be known as the "poor working girl,"—who, if the accounts are true, dragged herself off day by day to work until someone came along and married her. Sometimes she was a Cinderella, but more often she graduated a household drudge.

The flapper of to-day is a very different person. In dress she is as standardized as a chain hotel. . . . Barring size, flappers at a hundred feet are as standardized as Ford cars. As far as dress goes, they are a simplified national product. . . . There is no distinction between the town flapper and the farm flapper—the automobile has wiped them out. There is no distinction in the cut of clothing between the rich flapper and the poor flapper—national advertising has attended to that. The rich flapper has better clothing than the poor one, but a block away they are all flappers.

The outstanding characteristic of the flapper is not her uniform but her independence and her will to be prosperous.

She is no clinging vine. I was in the office of the president of a good-sized bank on the Pacific Coast when his daughter and several of her high-school friends burst in—flappers all. We got to talking and I found that these girls, not one of whom had any need to work, all intended to find jobs during the summer, and they thought that most of the girls in school would do the same. They all wanted to know how to make a living—and to have a good time doing it. That seems to be common everywhere.

Girls will no longer marry men who can merely support them—they can support themselves better than can many of the men of their own age. They have awakened to the fact that the "superior sex" stuff is all bunk. They will not meekly bow their heads to the valiant man who roars, "Where is that dress I bought you three years ago?"

The flapper wants to look well, and she is willing to provide for herself—employers everywhere told me that the women were doing better work than the men, and they do seem to be mentally more alert. All of which means that the man who marries the modern flapper has got to provide for her—she will not be merely an unpaid servant. And this in turn means that the men have got to work—than which nothing better could happen for the country. The flapper is to-day our most important national institution.

"You look more handsome over the wire ..."

TELEVISION IS BORN

April 7, 1927
Washington, D.C., and New York City

ANONYMOUS *NEW YORK TIMES* REPORTER

*H*oover was Secretary of the Interior at the time.

Herbert Hoover made a speech in Washington yesterday afternoon. An audience in New York heard him and saw him.

More than 200 miles of space intervening between the speaker and his audience was annihilated by the television apparatus developed by the Bell Laboratories of the American Telephone and Telegraph Company and demonstrated publicly for the first time yesterday.

The apparatus shot images of Mr. Hoover by wire from Washington to New York at the rate of eighteen a second. These were thrown on a screen as motion pictures, while the loud-speaker reproduced the speech. As each syllable was heard, the motion of the speaker's lips and his changes of expression were flashed on the screen in the demonstration room of the Bell Telephone Laboratories at 55 Bethune Street.

When the television pictures were thrown on a screen two by three inches, the likeness was excellent. It was as if a photograph had suddenly come to life and begun to talk, smile, nod its head and look this way and that. When the screen was enlarged to two by three feet, the results were not so good.

At times the face of the Secretary could not be clearly distinguished. He looked down, as he read his speech, and held the telephone receiver up, so that it covered most of the lower part of his countenance. There was too much illumination also in the background of the screen. When he moved his face, his features became clearly distinguishable. Near the close of his talk he turned his head to one side, and in profile his features became clear and full of detail.

On the smaller screen the face and action were reproduced with perfect fidelity.

After Mr. Hoover had spoken, Vice President J. J. Carty of the American Telephone and Telegraph Company and others in the demonstration room at Washington took his place and conversed one at a time with men in New York. The speaker on the New York end looked the Washington man in the eye as he talked to him. On the small screen before him appeared the living face of the man to whom he was talking.

Time as well as space was eliminated. Secretary Hoover's New York hearers and spectators were something like a thousandth part of a second later than the persons at his side in hearing him and in seeing changes of countenance.

The faces and voices were projected from Washington by wire. It was shown a few minutes later, however, that radio does just as well.

In the second part of the program the group in New York saw and heard performances in the Whippany studio of the American Telephone and Telegraph Company by wireless. The first face flashed on the screen from Whippany, N.J., was that of E. L. Nelson, an engineer, who gave a technical description of what was taking place. Mr. Nelson had a good television face. He screened well as he talked.

Next came a vaudeville act by radio from Whippany. A. Dolan, a comedian, first appeared before the audience as a stage Irishman, with side whiskers and a broken pipe, and did a monologue in brogue. Then he made a quick change and came back in blackface with a new line of quips in negro dialect. The loudspeaker part went over very well. It was the first vaudeville act that ever went on the air as a talking picture and in its possibilities it may be compared with the Fred Ott sneeze of more than thirty years ago, the first piece of comedy ever recorded in motion pictures. For the commercial future of television, if it has one, is thought to be largely in public entertainment—super-news reels flashed before audiences at the moment of occurrence, together with dramatic and musical acts shot on the other waves in sound and picture at the instant they are taking place at the studio. . . .

The demonstration of combined telephone and television, in fact, is one that outruns the imagination of all the wizards of prophecy. It is one of the few things that Leonardo da Vinci, Roger Bacon, Jules Verne and other masters of forecasting failed utterly to anticipate. Even interpreters of the Bible are having trouble in finding a passage which forecast television. H. G. Wells did not rise to it in his earlier crystal-gazing. It is only within the last few years that prophets have been busy in this field. Science has moved ahead so rapidly in this particular line that one of the men, who played a major part in developing the television apparatus shown yesterday, was of the opinion four years ago that research on this subject was hopeless. More than twenty years ago, however, Dr. Alexander Graham Bell, the inventor of the telephone, predicted at a gathering in the tower of the Times Building that the day would come when the man at the telephone would be able to see the distant person to whom he was speaking.

The demonstration began yesterday afternoon at 2:15 with General Carty at the television apparatus in Washington. As he held the transmitter in his hand and talked the light of an arc lamp flickered on his face. Small circles of light were moving across his face, one after another, but they were traveling at such high speed that they seemed to bathe his face in a uniform bluish light. By a complicated process these lights were dividing his face into fine squares. Each square traveled as a telegraph signal from Washington to New York. Here, with inconceivable rapidity, these squares were assembled as a mosaic. Each square differs in its amount of illumination. These differences of illumination traced the countenance in light and shadow and registered the least changes of expression. The squares rushed across the wire from Washington at the rate of 45,000 a second. The face was done over every eighteenth part of a second. About 2,500 squares or "units," as they are called—make up each picture.

As General Carty talked his face was thus dissected by light in Washington and reconstructed on the small screen in New York. President Walter S. Gifford of the American Telephone and Telegraph Company was on the New York end of the wire.

"How do you do, General? You are looking well," said Mr. Gifford.

The face of General Carty smiled and his voice inquired after the health of the speaker on the New York end.

"I am instructed to make a little conversation," said President Gifford, "while they are getting the loudspeaker ready. They are having a little power trouble."

"We are all ready and waiting here," said General Carty. "Mr. Hoover is here."

"You screen well, General," said Mr. Gifford. "You look more handsome over the wire."

"Does it flatter me much?" General Carty asked.

"I think it is an improvement," was the reply.

"Suddenly a message spread like lightening . . ."

LINDBERGH CROSSES THE ATLANTIC

May 21, 1927

EDWIN L. JAMES

*C*harles Augustus Lindbergh was an airmail pilot on the St. Louis–Chicago route when a group of St. Louis businessmen agreed to finance his attempt to make the first New York–Paris crossing of the Atlantic. They hoped to be repaid from the $25,000 prize that had been offered for the feat.

Lindbergh bought a Ryan monoplane in San Diego and flew it to Long Island, New York, setting a transcontinental speed record on the way. Then on May 20 he took off from Roosevelt Field and headed east. After 33½ hours and 3,600 miles, he saw Le Bourget airfield, near Paris.

James was a reporter for the New York Times.

Lindbergh did it. Twenty minutes after 10 o'clock tonight suddenly and softly there slipped out of the darkness a gray-white airplane as 25,000 pairs of eyes strained toward it. At 10:24 the *Spirit of St. Louis* landed and lines of soldiers, ranks of policemen and stout steel fences went down before a mad rush as irresistible as the tides of the ocean.

"Well, I made it," smiled Lindbergh, as the white monoplane came to a halt in the middle of the field and the first vanguard reached the plane. Lindbergh made a move to jump out. Twenty hands headed for him and lifted him out as if he were a baby. Several thousands in a minute were around the plane. Thousands more broke the barriers of iron rails round the field, cheering wildly.

As he was lifted to the ground Lindbergh was pale and with his hair unkempt, he looked completely worn out. He had strength enough, however, to smile, and waved his hand to the crowd. Soldiers with fixed bayonets were unable to keep back the crowd.

United States Ambassador Herrick was among the first to welcome and congratulate the hero.

A *New York Times* man was one of the first to reach the machine after its graceful descent to the field. Those first to arrive at the plane had a picture that will live in their minds for the rest of their lives. His cap off, his famous locks falling in disarray around his eyes, "Lucky Lindy" sat peering out over the rim of the little cockpit of his machine.

It was high drama. Picture the scene. Almost if not quite 100,000 people were massed on the east side of Le Bourget air field. Some of them had been there six and seven hours.

Off to the left the giant lighthouse of Mount Valerien flashed its guiding light 300 miles into the air. Closer on the left Le Bourget Lighthouse twinkled, and off to the right another giant revolving glare sent its beams high into the heavens.

Big arc lights on all sides with enormous electric flares were flooding the landing field. From time to time rockets rose and burst in varied lights over the field.

Seven thirty, the hour announced for the arrival, had come and gone. Then 8 o'clock came, and no Lindbergh; at 9 o'clock the sun had set but then came reports that Lindbergh had been seen over Cork. Then he had been seen over Valentia in Ireland and then over Plymouth.

Suddenly a message spread like lightning. The aviator had been seen over Cherbourg. However, remembering the messages telling of Captain Nungesser's flight, the crowd was skeptical.

"One chance in a thousand!" "Oh, he cannot do it without navigating instruments!" "It's a pity because he was a brave boy." Pessimism had spread over the great throng by 10 o'clock.

The stars came out and a chill wind blew.

Suddenly the field lights flooded their glares onto the landing ground and there came the roar of an airplane's motor. The crowd was still, then began to cheer, but two minutes later the landing glares went dark for the searchlight had identified the plane and it was not Captain Lindbergh's.

Stamping their feet in the cold, the crowd waited patiently. It seemed quite apparent that nearly every one was willing to wait all night, hoping against hope.

Suddenly—it was 10:16 exactly—another motor roared over the heads of the crowd. In the sky one caught a glimpse of a white gray plane, and for an instant heard the sound of one. Then it dimmed, and the idea spread that it was yet another disappointment.

Again landing lights glared and almost by the time they had flooded the field the gray white plane had lighted on the far side nearly half a mile from the crowd. It seemed to stop almost as it hit the ground, so gently did it land.

And then occurred a scene which almost passed description. Two companies of soldiers with fixed bayonets and the Le Bourget field police, reinforced by Paris agents, had held the crowd in good order. But as the lights showed the plane landing, much as if a picture had been thrown on a moving picture screen, there was a mad rush.

The movement of humanity swept over soldiers and by policemen and there was the wild sight of thousands of men and women rushing madly across half a mile of the not too even ground. Soldiers and police tried for one small moment to stem the tide, then they joined it, rushing as madly as anyone else toward the aviator and his plane.

The first people to reach the plane were two workmen of the aviation field and half a dozen Frenchmen.

"*Cette fois, ça va!*" they cried. (This time, it's done.)

Captain Lindbergh answered:

"Well, I made it."

An instant later he was on the shoulders of half a dozen persons who tried to bear him from the field.

The crowd crushed about the aviator and his progress was halted until a squad of soldiers with fixed bayonets cleared a way for him.

It was two French aviators—Major Pierre Weiss and Sergeant de Troyer who rescued Captain Lindbergh from the frenzied mob. When it seemed the excited French men and women would overwhelm the frail figure which was being carried on the shoulders of a half dozen men, the two aviators rushed up with a Renault car and hastily snatching Lindy from the crowd, sped across the field to the commandant's office.

Then followed an almost cruel rush to get near the airman. Women were thrown down and a number trampled badly. The doors of the small building were closed, but the windows were forced by enthusiasts, who were promptly ejected by soldiers.

Spurred on by reports spread in Paris of the approach of the aviator, other thousands began to arrive from the capital. The police estimate that within half an hour after Captain Lindbergh landed there were probably 100,000 storming the little building to get a sight of the idol of the evening.

Suddenly he appeared at a window, waving his helmet. It was then that, amid cheers for him, came five minutes of cheering for Captain Nungesser.

Not since the armistice of 1918 had Paris witnessed a downright demonstration of popular enthusiasm and excitement equal to that displayed by the throngs flocking to the boulevards for news of the American flier, whose personality has captured the hearts of the Parisian multitude.

"I have ceased marveling at it . . ."

RADIO AND ITS EVILS ARRIVE

October 24, 1927
New York City

FRANKLIN PIERCE ADAMS

A dams was considered the "father" of the Algonquin Round Table, a salon whose members also included the writers Dorothy Parker, Robert Benchley, and Alexander Woolcott. Its name came from the New York City hotel where the group often met to eat lunch, drink bootleg liquor, and trade insults.

Adams's own column, written under the famous byline "F.P.A.," appeared in newspapers across the country. Each Saturday he recounted the previous week's events in the style of English diarist Samuel Pepys.

So cometh a man to install our radio set, which I did bring with me last night and it worked very well, and I have ceased marveling at it, as I no longer at the telephone nor the electric light, neither of which I understand at all. And I heard some of the radio announcers, and could not believe that I was hearing aright, some of the advertising being pretentious and silly, as when one man spoke many times of the slogan of a company being "You might as well have the best," and I wondered how long it took that concern, and how many conferences were held, before they made that slogan up.

"My rackets are run on strictly American lines ..."

AL CAPONE, PATRIOT

1929
Chicago

CLAUD COCKBURN

*A*t the time of this meeting, Cockburn was a reporter for the Times *of London. He later gained fame as a radical editor and as a writer for the British humor magazine* Punch, *whose editor at the time, Malcolm Muggeridge, once said, "Above everything, Cockburn is a journalist, perhaps the most perfect specimen of the genus ever to exist, certainly the most accomplished I have ever known." This account comes from one of Cockburn's memoirs.*

In Chicago the director of the Illinois Central Bank, to whom I had been putting solemn questions on the subject of car loadings, commodity prices and the like, said moodily, "Hell, boy, the capitalist system's on the skids anyway, let's go and get a drink." I was glad of this attitude on his part because I had not really come to Chicago to discuss commodity prices in the Middle West, but to report the background to a murder. A couple of days before, we in New York had read the news of the killing in broad daylight of Jake Lingle, then crime reporter of the *Chicago Tribune* and—as emerged later—an important liaison officer between the Capone gang and the police department. It was one of the most spectacular and, for many reasons, looked like being one of the most revealing Chicago killings of the period when Al Capone was at approximately the height of his power.

As an assignment to report a murder the reply from *The Times* was probably a classic. "By all means," it said, "Cockburn Chicagowards. Welcome stories ex-Chicago not unduly emphasising crime."

I drove to the Criminal Courts Building and sought the advice of the dean of Chicago crime reporters, the original, I believe, of one of the central characters in Ben Hecht's play *The Front Page*. I showed him my cable. His deep laughter shook the desk. What, he asked, did I want to do? I said I supposed the first thing to do was to interview Mr. Capone. He suggested that I listen in on an extension while he telephoned Mr. Capone at the Lexington Hotel where he then had his offices. Presently I heard Capone's voice on the wire asking what went on. The crime reporter explained that there was a

Limey from the London *Times* who wanted to talk with him. They fixed up an appointment for the following afternoon and just before he rang off the crime reporter said, "Listen, Al, there's just one thing. You know this bird's assignment says he's to cover all this 'not unduly emphasising crime.' " Bewilderment exploded at the other end of the line. "Not what?" Capone said. "You heard me," said the crime reporter. "Not unduly emphasising crime."

The Lexington Hotel had once, I think, been a rather grand family hotel, but now its large and gloomy lobby was deserted except for a couple of bulging Sicilians and a reception clerk who looked at once across the counter with the expression of a speakeasy proprietor looking through the grille at a potential detective. He checked on my appointment with some superior upstairs, and as I stepped into the elevator I felt my hips and sides being gently frisked by the tapping hands of one of the lounging civilians. There were a couple of anterooms to be passed before you got to Capone's office and in the first of them I had to wait for a quarter of an hour or so, drinking whisky poured by a man who used his left hand for the bottle and kept the other in his pocket.

Except that there was a sub-machine gun, operated by a man called MacGurn—whom I later got to know and somewhat esteem—poking through the transom of a door behind the big desk, Capone's own room was nearly indistinguishable from that of, say, a "newly arrived" Texan oil millionaire. Apart from the jowly young murderer on the far side of the desk, what took the eye were a number of large, flattish, solid silver bowls upon the desk, each filled with roses. They were nice to look at, and they had another purpose too, for Capone, when agitated stood up and dipped the tips of his fingers in the water in which floated the roses.

I had been a little embarrassed as to how the interview was to be launched. Naturally the nub of all such interviews is somehow to get around to the question "What makes you tick?" but in the case of this millionaire killer the approach to this central question seemed mined with dangerous impediments. However, on the way down to the Lexington Hotel I had had the good fortune to see, in I think the *Chicago Daily News,* some statistics offered by an insurance company which dealt with the average expectation of life of gangsters in Chicago. I forgot exactly what the average expectation was, and also what was the exact age of Capone at that time—I think he was in his very early thirties. The point was, however, that in any case he was four years older than the upper limit considered by the insurance company to be the proper average expectation of life for a Chicago gangster. This seemed to offer a more or less neutral and academic line of approach, and after the ordinary greetings I asked Capone whether he had read this piece of statistics in the paper. He said that he had. I asked him whether he considered the estimate reasonably accurate. He said that he thought that the insurance companies and the newspaper boys probably knew their stuff. "In that case," I asked him, "how does it feel to be, say, four years over the age?"

He took the question quite seriously and spoke of the matter with neither more nor less excitement or agitation than a man would who, let us say, had been asked whether he, as the rear machine-gunner of a bomber, was aware of the average incidence of casualties in that occupation. He apparently assumed that sooner or later he would be shot despite the elaborate precautions which he regularly took. The idea that—as afterwards turned out to be the case—he would be arrested by the Federal authorities for income-tax evasion had not, I think, at that time so much as crossed his mind. And, after all, he said with a little bit of corn-and-ham somewhere at the back of his throat, supposing he had not gone into this racket? What would he have been doing? He would, he said, "have been selling newspapers barefoot on the street in Brooklyn."

He stood up as he spoke, cooling his finger-tips in the rose bowl in front of him. He sat down again, brooding and sighing. Despite the ham-and-corn, what he said was quite probably true and I said so, sympathetically. A little bit too sympathetically, as immediately emerged, for as I spoke I saw him looking at me suspiciously, not to say censoriously. My remarks about the harsh way the world treats barefoot boys in Brooklyn were interrupted by an urgent angry waggle of his pudgy hand.

"Listen," he said, "don't you get the idea I'm one of these goddam radicals. Don't get the idea I'm knocking the American system. The American system. . . ." As though an invisible chairman had called upon him for a few words, he broke into an oration upon the theme. He praised freedom, enterprise and the pioneers. He spoke of "our heritage." He referred with contemptuous disgust to Socialism and Anarchism. "My rackets," he repeated several times, "are run on strictly American lines and they're going to stay that way." This turned out to be a reference to the fact that he had recently been elected the President of the Unione Siciliano, a slightly mysterious, partially criminal society which certainly had its roots in the Mafia. Its power and importance varied sharply from year to year. Sometimes there did seem to be evidence that it was a secret society of real power, and at other times it seemed more in the nature of a mutual benefit association not essentially much more menacing than, say, the Elks. Capone's complaint just now was that the Unione was what he called "lousy with Black Hand stuff." "Can you imagine," he said, "people going in for what they call these blood feuds—some guy's grandfather was killed by some other guy's grandfather, and this guy thinks that's good enough reason to kill the other." It was, he said, entirely unbusinesslike. His vision of the American system began to excite him profoundly and now he was on his feet again, leaning across the desk like chairman of a board meeting, his fingers plunged in the rose bowls.

"This American system of ours," he shouted, "call it Americanism, call it Capitalism, call it what you like, gives to each and every one of us a great opportunity if we only seize it with both hands and make the most of it." He held out his hands towards me, the fingers dripping a little, and stared at me sternly for a few seconds before reseating himself.

A month later in New York I was telling this story to Mr John Walter, minority owner of *The Times*. He asked me why I had not written the Capone interview for the paper. I explained that when I had come to put my notes together I saw that most of what Capone had said was in essence identical with what was being said in the leading articles of *The Times* itself, and I doubted whether the paper would be best pleased to find itself seeing eye to eye with the most notorious gangster in Chicago. Mr Walter, after a moment's wry reflection, admitted that probably my idea had been correct.

"If only one could drink water there!"

PROHIBITION

1929
New York City

PAUL MORAND

*L*iquor *became illegal in the United States in 1920, following ratification of the 18th Amendment to the Constitution and passage of the Volstead Act in 1919.*

Over half a million people were arrested for smuggling or bootlegging in the next decade, and over three hundred thousand were convicted. But very few, it seemed, went thirsty. After the 1932 elections created a Democratic Party majority in Congress, a special convention was organized to pass the 21st Amendment, making liquor legal again. The whole process took less than a year. It was a marvel of government efficiency that has probably never been matched.

Morand was a French author and diplomat.

Open a book or newspaper of a few years ago and you will seek the term "speakeasy" in vain. It was born of Prohibition. The speakeasy (the name suggests a whispered password) is a clandestine refreshment-bar selling spirits or wine. They must be visited to understand present-day New York. . . . There are a few in the downtown streets, but they are mainly set up between Fortieth Street and Sixtieth Street; they are usually situated downstairs and are identifiable by the large number of empty cars standing at their doors. The door is closed, and is only opened after you have been scrutinized through a door-catch or a barred opening. At night an electric torch suddenly gleams through a pink silk curtain. There is a truly New York atmosphere of humbug in the whole thing. The interior is that of a criminal house; shutters are closed in full daylight, and one is caught in the smell of a cremation furnace, for the ventilation is defective and grills are prepared under the mantelpiece of the fireplace. Italians with a too familiar manner, or plump, blue pseudo-bullfighters, carrying bunches of monastic keys, guide you through the deserted rooms of the abandoned house. Facetious inscriptions grimace from the walls. There are a few very flushed diners. At one table some habitues are asleep, their heads sunk on their arms; behind a screen somebody is trying to restore a young woman who has had an attack of hysteria. . . . The food is almost always poor, the service deplorable; the staff regard you with the eyes of confederates and care not two pins about you. The Sauterne is a sort of glycerine; it has to go with a partridge brought from the refrigerator of a French vessel; the champagne would not be touched at a Vincennes wedding-party.

Yet the speakeasy pervades Manhattan with a fascinating atmosphere of mystery. If only one could drink water there! Some speakeasies are disguised behind florists' shops, or behind undertakers' coffins. I know one, right in Broadway, which is entered through an imitation telephone-box; it has excellent beer; appetizing sausages and Welsh rabbits are sizzling in chafing-dishes and are given to customers without extra charge; drunks are expelled through a sidedoor which seems to open out into the nether world, as in Chicago Nights. In the poorer quarters many former saloons for the ordinary people have secretly reopened. All these secret shrines are readily accessible, for there are, it is said, 20,000 speakeasies in New York, and it is unlikely that the police do not know them; I think myself that they are only forced to close down when they refuse to make themselves pleasant to persons in authority, or when they sell too much poison. . . . The speakeasy is very popular in all classes of society; women go there gladly, even a few young girls. . . .

An intelligent lady remarked to me once that Prohibition was very pleasant. "Before it," she said, "no decent woman could go into a bar, but now nobody is surprised at our being there."

"Will I get in the papers?"

RAID OF AN ABORTION CLINIC

April 15, 1929
New York City

MARGARET SANGER

S anger *helped create the modern birth control movement. Her outrage at the deaths from self-induced abortions in the New York slums, where she worked as a nurse, led her to push for relaxed laws and improved methods. She founded the National Birth Control League in 1914 and opened her first clinic in Brooklyn in 1916. At the time it was illegal for doctors to give advice about birth control, even to married patients. As Sanger expected, she was arrested, and began the public battles for her cause. Her court cases eventually established the right of doctors to discuss contraception and prescribe contraceptive devices. In 1921 she founded the American Birth Control League, one of the organizations that were later merged and named the Planned Parenthood Federation.*

Early in the morning of April 15, 1929, the telephone in my apartment rang, startling me. I was pretty nervous, having been up all night with Stuart, who had mastoiditis. His temperature was running high, and he was suffering with terrible, indescribable pain.

I took off the receiver. "Hello. This is Anna. The police are here at the clinic." Briefly she related how they had descended without warning, stamped into the basement, and were at that moment tearing things to pieces.

With this meager information pounding through my brain I hastened to the street, hailed a taxi, and urged the driver to go as fast as he could to West Fifteenth Street.

The shade to the glass door was pulled down; the door itself was locked. I knocked and a plain-clothes man of the Vice Squad opened it. "Well, who are you?"

"I'm Mrs. Sanger and I want to come in."

My request was passed on to a superior and I heard someone answer, "Let her in."

Inside, in a room more than ordinarily small because partitions had sliced it up to make minute consultation booths, the patients were sitting quietly, some of them weeping. Detectives were hurrying aimlessly here and there like chickens fluttering about a raided roost, calling to each other and, amid the confusion, demanding names and addresses. The three nurses were standing around; Dr. Elizabeth Pissoort was practically in hysterics.

Dr. Stone was aloof, utterly unmoved by the tumult and the noise. I have always admired her attitude. This was the first time in her life she had been arrested, yet she treated it so lightly. "Isn't this fantastic?" she remarked. "Only a few moments ago a visiting physician from the Middle West asked one of the nurses whether we ever had any police interference. 'Oh, no,' the nurse cheerfully replied. 'Those days are over.' "

Stocky Mrs. Mary Sullivan, head of the City Policewomen's Bureau, was superintending the raid in person. Her round, thickset face might have been genial when smiling, but was very terrifying when flushed with anger. She was giving orders to her minions in such rapid succession that it seemed impossible to keep pace with them. I tried to talk to her, asking why she had come and what it was all about.

"You'll see," said Mrs. Sullivan, and went on directing the patrolmen who were removing books from shelves, pictures and diagrams from walls, and sweeping out the contents of medical cabinets. In their zeal I noticed they were seizing articles from the sterilizers, such as gloves and medicine droppers, having no sinister significance whatsoever. They were also gathering up the various strange, weird devices patients had brought us to inquire as to their efficacy, and which we exhibited as curios.

Patrolwoman Anna McNamara, far less assured than her chief, was consulting a list in her hand and turning over the case histories in the files as swiftly as her fingers could move. Many of these contained the personal confessions of women, some of whom had entrusted us with the knowledge that their husbands had venereal disease or insanity. It ran through my mind that dire misfortune could follow in the way of being black-mailed by anyone obtaining the records.

I requested Mrs. Sullivan to show me her search warrant, and saw it had been signed by Chief Magistrate McAdoo. Nevertheless, I cautioned her, "You have no right to touch those files. Not even the nurses ever see them. They are the private property of the doctors, and if you take them you will get into trouble."

"Trouble," she snapped back. "I get into trouble? What about the trouble you're in?"

"I wouldn't change mine for yours."

"Well, this is my party. You keep out."

One of the policemen scooped up all the name cards and stuffed them into a waste basket to be carried off as "evidence." This was a prime violation of medical ethics; nothing was more sacred to a doctor than the confidences of his patients. Immediately Anna telephoned Dr. Robert L. Dickinson at the Academy of Medicine that the police were confiscating the case histories of patients and asked him to recommend a lawyer. He suggested Morris L. Ernst, whom Anna then called.

Doctors, nurses, and evidence were being hustled into the street. The patrol wagon had arrived, but I summoned taxicabs in which we rode to the West Twentieth Street station. On the way I heard part of the story, which accounted for my non-arrest. About three weeks earlier a woman who had registered under the name of Mrs. Tierney had come for contraceptive advice and, on examination, was found by both doctors to have rectocele, cystocele, prolapsus of the uterus, erosions, and retroversion. Although not informed of her exact condition, she was instructed, because another pregnancy would be dangerous, and told to return for a check-up. She had now done so under her rightful name of McNamara, including in her entourage Mrs. Sullivan and a police squad.

Dr. Stone, Dr. Pissoort, and the three nurses were booked for violation of Section 1142, though I attempted to explain the clinic had been active for six years quite legally under the exception, Section 1145. At Jefferson Market Court, to which we next traveled, Magistrate Rosenbluth looked over the warrant and ordered a three-hundred-dollar bond for each.

The succeeding morning I sent Stuart to a hospital for treatment; I had to attend a meeting in Boston, and the day after that go to Chicago for a series of lectures. Again I was obliged to leave him, and this time with even more misgivings. At Buffalo came a telegram saying a mastoid operation had been performed. At Chicago I telephoned the doctor and was reassured. The moment my duties were over I hurried back to be with him, and, incidentally, to attend the hearings.

I still had no idea of the fate of the case histories and had been very worried. Now I learned that the evening after the raid Magistrate McAdoo had been dining with Dr. Karl Reiland, my husband's pastor. Dr. Reiland, much upset, had remarked upon its outrageousness. Justice McAdoo, aghast and horrified to find that, without reading it, he had signed this warrant, just one of many laid on his desk, had called up the police station without delay, saying that all the twenty-four histories must be put in his safe and kept there until he arrived in the morning. He had perceived instantly that those doctors' records were going to be a serious embarrassment.

One hundred and fifty cards, our sole memoranda of names and addresses, were never restored. Catholic patients, whose records had thus been purloined, received mysterious and anonymous telephone calls warning them if they continued to go to the clinic their private lives would be exposed. They came to us asking fearfully, "Will I get in the papers?"

"It came with a speed and ferocity that left men dazed."

CRASH

October 24, 1929
New York City

ELLIOTT V. BELL

Bell was a reporter for the New York Times. *He later became New York State's superintendent of banks.*

October 24, 1929, was not the first day of the big break in stocks, nor was it the last. Nevertheless, it was the most terrifying and unreal day I have ever seen on the Street, and it constitutes an important financial landmark, for that day marked the great decline in the prestige and power of Wall Street over national affairs.

The day was overcast and cool. A light north-west wind blew down the canyons of Wall Street, and the temperature, in the low fifties, made bankers and brokers on their way to work button their topcoats around them. The crowds of market traders in the brokers' board rooms were nervous but hopeful as the ten o'clock hour for the start of trading approached. The general feeling was that the worst was over and a good many speculators who had prudently sold out earlier in the decline were congratulating themselves at having bought back their stocks a good deal cheaper. Seldom had the small trader had better or more uniform advice to go by.

The market opened steady with prices little changed from the previous day, though some rather large blocks, of 20,000 to 25,000 shares, came out at the start. It sagged easily for the first half-hour, and then around eleven o'clock the deluge broke.

It came with a speed and ferocity that left men dazed. The bottom simply fell out of the market. From all over the country a torrent of selling orders poured onto the floor of the Stock Exchange and there were no buying orders to meet it. Quotations of representative active issues, like Steel [U.S. Steel], Telephone [AT&T], and Anaconda, began to fall two, three, five, and even ten points between sales. Less active stocks became unmarketable. Within a few moments the ticker service was hopelessly swamped and from then on no one knew what was really happening. By one-thirty the ticker tape was nearly two hours late; by two-thirty it was 147 minutes late. The last quotation was not printed on the tape until 7:08½ p.m., four hours, eight and one-half minutes after the close. In the meantime, Wall Street had lived through an incredible nightmare.

In the strange way that news of a disaster spreads, the word of the market collapse flashed through the city. By noon great crowds had gathered at the corner of Broad and Wall Streets where the Stock Exchange on one corner faces Morgan's across the way. On the steps of the Sub-Treasury Building, opposite Morgan's, a crowd of press photographers and newsreel men took up their stand. Traffic was pushed from the streets of the financial district by the crush.

It was in this wild setting that the leading bankers scurried into conference at Morgan's in a belated effort to save the day. Shortly after noon Mr. [Charles E.] Mitchell left the National City Bank and pushed his way west on Wall Street to Morgan's. No sooner had he entered than Albert H. Wiggin was seen to hurry down from the Chase National Bank, one block north. Hard on his heels came William C. Potter, head of the Guaranty Trust, followed by Seward Prosser of the Bankers Trust. Later George F. Baker, Jr., of the First National, joined the group.

The news of the bankers' meeting flashed through the streets and over the news tickers—stocks began to rally—but for many it was already too late. Thousands of traders, little and big, had gone "overboard" in that incredible hour between eleven and twelve. Confidence in the financial and political leaders of the country, faith in the "soundness" of economic conditions had received a shattering blow. The panic was on.

At Morgan's the heads of six banks formed a consortium since known as the bankers' pool of October, 1929—pledging a total of $240,000,000, or $40,000,000 each, to provide a "cushion" of buying power beneath the falling market. In addition, other financial institutions, including James Speyer and Company and Guggenheim Brothers, sent over to Morgan's unsolicited offers of funds aggregating $100,000,000. It was not only the first authenticated instance of a bankers' pool in stocks but by far the largest concentration of pool buying power ever brought to bear on the stock market—but in the face of the panic it was pitifully inadequate.

After the bankers had met, Thomas W. Lamont, Morgan's partner, came out to the crowd of newspaper reporters who had gathered in the lobby of his bank. In an understatement that has since become a Wall Street classic, he remarked:

"It seems there has been some disturbed selling in the market."

It was at the same meeting that "T. W." gave to the financial community a new phrase—"air pockets," to describe the condition in stocks for which there were no bids, but only frantic offers. (Mr. Lamont said he had it from his partner, George Whitney, and the latter said he had it from some broker.)

After the meeting, Mr. Lamont walked across Broad Street to the Stock Exchange to meet with the governors of the Exchange. They had been called together quietly during trading hours and they held their meeting in the rooms of the Stock Clearing Corporation so as to avoid attracting attention. Mr. Lamont sat on the corner of a desk and told them about the pool. Then he said:

"Gentlemen, there is no man nor group of men who can buy all the stocks that the American public can sell."

It seems a pretty obvious statement now, but it had a horrid sound to the assembled governors of the Exchange. It meant that the shrewdest member of the most powerful banking house in the country was telling them plainly that the assembled resources of Wall Street, mobilized on a scale never before attempted, could not stop this panic.

The bankers' pool, in fact, turned out a sorry fiasco. Without it, no doubt, the Exchange would have been forced to close, for it did supply bids at some price for the so-called pivotal stocks when, because of the panic and confusion in the market, there were no other bids available. It made a small profit, but it did not have a ghost of a chance of stemming the avalanche of selling that poured in from all over the country. The stock market had become too big. The days that followed are blurred in retrospect. Wall Street became a nightmarish spectacle.

The animal roar that rises from the floor of the Stock Exchange and which on active days is plainly audible in the Street outside, became louder, anguished, terrifying. The streets were crammed with a mixed crowd—agonized little speculators, walking aimlessly outdoors because they feared to face the ticker and the margin clerk; sold-out traders, morbidly impelled to visit the scene of their ruin; inquisitive individuals and tourists, seeking by gazing at the exteriors of the Exchange and the big banks to get a closer view of the national catastrophe; runners, frantically pushing their way through the throng of idle and curious in their effort to make deliveries of the unprecedented volume of securities which was being traded on the floor of the Exchange.

The ticker, hopelessly swamped, fell hours behind the actual trading and became completely meaningless. Far into the night, and often all night long, the lights blazed in the windows of the tall office buildings where margin clerks and bookkeepers struggled with the desperate task of trying to clear one day's business before the next began. They fainted at their desks; the weary runners fell exhausted on the marble floors of banks and slept. But within a few months they were to have ample time to rest up. By then thousands of them had been fired.

Agonizing scenes were enacted in the customers' rooms of the various brokers. There traders who a few short days before had luxuriated in delusions of wealth saw all their hopes smashed in a collapse so devastating, so far beyond their wildest fears, as to seem unreal. Seeking to save a little from the wreckage, they would order their stocks sold "at the market," in many cases to discover that they had not merely lost everything but were, in addition, in debt to the broker. And then, ironic twist, as like as not the next few hours' wild churning of the market would lift prices to levels where they might have sold out and had a substantial cash balance left over. Every move was wrong, in those days. The market seemed like an insensate thing that was wreaking a wild and pitiless revenge upon those who had thought to master it.

The excitement and sense of danger which imbued Wall Street was like that which grips men on a sinking ship. A camaraderie, a kind of gaiety of despair, sprang up. The Wall Street reporter found all doors open and everyone snatched at him for the latest news, for shreds of rumor. Who was in trouble? Who had gone under last? Where was it going to end?

I remember dropping in to see a vice-president of one of the larger banks. He was walking back and forth in his office.

"Well, Elliott," he said, "I thought I was a millionaire a few days ago. Now I find I'm looking through the wrong end of the telescope."

He laughed. Then he said: "We'll get those bastards that did this yet."

"Pedestrians were little more than ants ..."

FIRST VIEW FROM THE EMPIRE STATE BUILDING

May 1, 1931
New York City

ANONYMOUS *NEW YORK TIMES* REPORTER

*C*ritic Edmund Wilson noted with disdain that *"there is a telescope in Madison Square Park for people to look at the tower through, just as they used to look at the moon."*

One thing was hard to find, even with a telescope: occupants. Because the building was built at the beginning of the Depression, there weren't many. For a few years, wags called it the "Empty" State Building. But the observation deck was an immediate hit.

A new view of the metropolitan district—a vast panorama of shimmering water, tall towers, quiet suburban homes and busy Manhattan streets—was unfolded yesterday to visitors who ascended to the observatory above the eighty-fifth floor of the Empire State Building.

From the highest vantage point steamers and tugs, which appeared to be little more than rowboats, could be seen far up the Hudson and the East River. Down by the bay, beyond the Narrows and out to sea a ship occasionally hove into view or faded in the distance.

For miles in every direction the city was spread out before the gaze of the sight-seers. To the north the apartment houses of the Bronx were plainly visible. To the east and southeast lay the green residential sections, the business and factory districts and shorelines of Long Island and Brooklyn; beyond the bay, the hills of Staten Island, and to the west, the smoke of Jersey's industries with wooded slopes hiding a thousand dwellings.

In Manhattan the tall buildings, which from the streets below appeared as monsters of steel and stone, assumed a less awe-inspiring significance when viewed from above. Fifth Avenue and Broadway were little more than slender black ribbons which had cut their way sharply through masses of vari-colored brick. Along them lilliputian vehicles jockeyed for position, halting or moving forward in groups, often like a processional. From a height of more than 1,000 feet pedestrians were little more than ants and their movements hardly could be detected.

Central Park appeared as a flattened rectangle of earth and turf, a welcome relief from the stern irregularity of the skyline and the buildings which hemmed in its lake and trees. The new apartment houses along the East River were pierced by the spire of the Chrysler tower. Some of the modern skyscrapers of white brick and stone stood out in sharp contrast to the darker edifices surrounding them and to the rows of brownstone homes which are rapidly giving way to taller residential buildings.

At night the scene was hardly recognizable as the same which greeted the daytime visitors. Beyond the immediate shadows of midtown Manhattan on the south a million windows glowed with light from the towers of the financial district, although the darkened outline of some of these skyscrapers showed that they had become deserted with the coming of night. Lines of lights and the dim, errant flicker from motor vehicles marked the streets with Broadway as a kaleidoscope of flickering color. Brief rows of brightness, or slight lights, moved slowly up and down the waters around the island.

"The steel doors closed ..."

IN THE DEATH HOUSE WITH THE SCOTTSBORO BOYS

June 1932
State Penitentiary, Kilby, Alabama

LANGSTON HUGHES

The nine Scottsboro "boys" were black men aged thirteen to twenty-one who were arrested for raping two white women on a train traveling through Alabama in 1931, crimes they obviously had not committed. But they were quickly convicted anyway, and each received the death penalty. When the appeals reached the U.S. Supreme Court, the Court ruled they had been denied a fair trial and had to be retried. Again an Alabama jury found them guilty, and again the U.S. Supreme Court found that they had been denied a fair trial. The third time around, charges were dropped against four of the defendants, but the other five received long prison terms.

The exceptional gifts of Hughes, a leader of the Harlem Renaissance movement, extended to poetry, short stories, critical essays, and autobiography. In this account he seems to combine them all. (All elisions are his original punctuation.)

The steel doors closed. Locked. Here, too, was Brown America. Like monkeys in tiered cages, hundreds of Negroes barred away from life. Animals of crime. Human zoo for the cast-offs of society. Hunger, ignorance, poverty: civilization's major defects woven into a noose for the unwary. Men in jail, months and months, years and years after the steel doors have closed. Vast monotony of guards and cages. The State Penitentiary at Kilby, Alabama, in the year of our Lord, 1932.

Our Lord . . . Pilate . . . and the thieves on the cross.

For a moment the fear came: even for me, a Sunday morning visitor, the doors might never open again. WHITE guards held the keys. (The judge's chair protected like Pilate's.) And I'm only a nigger. Nigger. Niggers. Hundreds of niggers in Kilby Prison. Black, brown, yellow, near-white niggers. The guards, White. Me—a visiting nigger.

Sunday morning: In the Negro wing. Tier on tier of steel cells. Cell doors are open. Within the wing, men wander about in white trousers and shirts. Sunday clothes. Day of rest. Cards, checkers, dice, story telling from cell to cell. Chapel if they will. One day of rest, in jail. Within the great closed cell of the wing, visiting, laughing, talking, *on Sunday.*

But in the death house, cells are not open. You enter by a solid steel door through which you cannot see. White guard opens the door. White guard closes the door, shuts out the world, remains inside with you.

THE DEATH HOUSE. Dark faces peering from behind bars, like animals when the keeper comes. All Negro faces, men and young men in this death house at Kilby. Among them the eight Scottsboro boys. Sh-s-s-s! Scottsboro boys? SCOTTSBORO boys. SCOTTSBORO BOYS! (Keep silent, world. The State of Alabama washes its hands.) Eight brown boys condemned to death. No proven crime. Farce of a trial. Lies. Laughter. Mob. Music. Eight poor niggers make a country holiday. (Keep silent, Germany, Russia, France, young China, Gorki, Thomas Mann, Romain Rolland, Theodore Dreiser. Pilate washes his hands. Listen Communists, don't send any more cablegrams to the Governor of Alabama. Don't send any more telegrams to the Supreme Court. What's the matter? What's all this excitement about, over eight young niggers? Let the law wash its hands in peace.)

There are only two doors in the death house. One from the world, in. The other from the world, out—to the electric chair. To DEATH. Against this door the guard leans. White guard, watching Brown America in the death house.

Silence. The dark word is silent. Speak! Dark world:

Listen, guard: Let the boys out.
Guard with the keys, let 'em out.

Guard with the law books, let them out.
Guards in the Supreme Court! Guards in the White House!
Guards of the money bags made from black hands sold in the cotton
*   fields, sold in mines, sold on Wall Street:*
Let them out!

Daily, I watch the guards washing their hands.

The world remembers for a long time a certain washing of hands. The world remembers for a long time a certain humble One born in a manger—straw, manure, and the feet of animals—standing before Power washing its hands. No proven crime. Farce of a trial. Lies. Laughter. Mob. Hundreds of years later Brown America sang: *My Lord! What a morning when the stars began to fall!*

For eight brown boys in Alabama the stars have fallen. In the death house, I heard no song at all. Only a silence more ominous than song. All of Brown America locked up there. And no song.

Even as ye do unto the least of these, ye do it unto Me.

White guard.

The door that leads to DEATH.

Electric chair.

No song.

"The cavalry clattered down Pennsylvania Avenue ..."

GENERAL DOUGLAS MacARTHUR FIRES ON AMERICANS

July 29, 1932
Washington, D.C.

LEE McCARDELL

*T*he Bonus Expeditionary Force took its name from the American Expeditionary Force that had been sent to Europe in World War I. Its "troops" were veterans of World War I and their families, some twenty-five thousand in all, who demanded early payment of the veterans' bonuses the government was scheduled to pay in 1945.

MacArthur, army chief of staff at the time, was a highly capable but immoder-

ate commander. When President Hoover asked him to evict the bonus marchers camped on Capitol Hill, MacArthur saw an opportunity to roust the main camp living across the Anacostia River. Historian William Manchester noted, "A Veterans Administration survey would later show that 94 percent of the bonus marchers had army or navy records, 67 percent had served overseas, and 20 percent had been disabled. MacArthur refused to believe it. He thought 90 percent of them were fakes. And he never changed his mind."

Hoover knew enough about MacArthur's personality and intentions to send two different officers to the general with duplicates of the same order—not to cross the river and engage the marchers there. MacArthur's aide Dwight Eisenhower later recalled his shock when his boss said he was "too busy" to pay attention to anyone "pretending to bring orders."

Two children were among the dead in the attack.

McCardell reported for the Baltimore Sun.

The bonus army was retreating today—in all directions.

Its billets destroyed, its commissary wrecked, its wives and babies misplaced, its leaders lost in the confusion which followed its rout last night by troops of the Regular Army, the former soldiers tramped the streets of Washington and the roads of Maryland and Virginia, foraging for coffee and cigarettes.

. . . The battle really had ended shortly after midnight, when, from the dusty brow of a low hill behind their camp on the Anacostia flats, the rear guard of the Bonus Expeditionary Force fired a final round of Bronx cheers at the tin-hatted infantrymen moving among the flames of Camp Marks.

The powerful floodlights of Fire Department trucks played over the ruins of the camp. In the shadows behind the trucks four troops of cavalry bivouacked on the bare ground, the reins of their horses hooked under their arms.

The air was still sharply tainted with tear gas.

The fight had begun, as far as the Regular Army was concerned, late yesterday afternoon. The troops had been called out after a veteran of the Bonus Army had been shot and killed by a Washington policeman during a skirmish to drive members of the Bonus Army out of a vacant house on Pennsylvania Avenue, two blocks from the Capitol.

The soldiers numbered between seven hundred and eight hundred men. There was a squadron of the Third Cavalry from Fort Myer, a battalion of the Twelfth Infantry from Fort Washington, and a platoon of tanks (five) from Fort Meade. Most of the police in Washington seemed to be trailing after the soldiers, and traffic was tied up in knots.

The cavalry clattered down Pennsylvania Avenue with drawn sabers.

The infantry came marching along with fixed bayonets.

All Washington smelled a fight, and all Washington turned out to see it.

Streets were jammed with automobiles.

Sidewalks, windows, doorsteps were crowded with people trying to see what was happening.

"Yellow! Yellow!"

From around the ramshackle shelters which they had built on a vacant lot fronting on Pennsylvania Avenue, just above the Capitol, the bedraggled veterans jeered.

And other words less polite.

The cavalrymen stretched out in extended order and rode spectators back on the sidewalks. The infantry started across the lot, bayonets fixed.

Veterans in the rear ranks of a mob that faced the infantry pushed forward. Those in front pushed back. The crowd stuck. An order went down the line of infantrymen. The soldiers stepped back, pulled tear-gas bombs from their belts, and hurled them into the midst of the mob.

Some of the veterans grabbed the bombs and threw them back at the infantry. The exploding tins whizzed around the smooth asphalt like devil chasers, pfutt-pfutt-pfutt. And a gentle southerly wind wafted the gas in the faces of the soldiers and the spectators across the street.

Cavalrymen and infantrymen jerked gas masks out of their haversacks. The spectators, blinded and choking with the unexpected gas attack, broke and fled. Movie photographers who had parked their sound trucks so as to catch a panorama of the skirmish ground away doggedly, tears streaming down their faces.

. . . Veterans with automobiles parked in the jungle behind the mob begin to crank up their machines. Others grab rolls of bedding from their shacks. A tin disk sails through the air down at the west end of the square. Another devil chaser pfutt-pfutts across the surface of the street.

But the breeze is still blowing from the south and the gas drifts back against the attacking party. Newspaper reporters and photographers cut and run for fresh air.

. . . A member of the Bonus Army, somewhat the worse for a serious hangover, finds it difficult to steer a straight course down the middle of one street. He wants to turn.

He argues:

"I don't have to—"

A cavalry saber flashes.

Whack!

"Beat it!"

"I don't have to—"

Whack! Whack!

. . . Somebody got a saber over the head. The men on the truck topple over each other, rolling out into the street.

In a filling station across the way a man—a newspaper reporter—is using a telephone.

"Out of there!" yells the trooper.

The man at the phone hangs on.

The trooper tosses a gas bomb into the station. The man comes out.

. . . Meanwhile the infantrymen have applied the torch. The whole camp goes up in smoke.

The blazing camp sends out a great yellow glow that lights up the sky. The wind freshens and the smoke drifts into the faces of the watching Bonus Army. Motorboats with loud radios come chug-chugging in toward shore to watch the fire.

At half-past twelve General MacArthur returns with Secretary of War Hurley. The dapper Secretary of War is attired in white sport shoes and pants and a flapping felt hat and smokes his cigarette in a debonair fashion.

"He was a hog buyer . . . much depressed
by prevailing prices."

DEPRESSION PRICES

1933
Springfield, Illinois

PAUL ANGLE

*A*ngle was a historian from the midwest, director of the Chicago Historical Society.

One day in 1933 I met a friend in a bank in Springfield, Illinois, in the center of the corn belt. He was a hog buyer, much concerned with farm prosperity, much depressed by prevailing prices. During our conversation he took a fifty-cent piece from his pocket and threw it on one of the bank's glass-topped writing tables. "Paul Angle," he exclaimed, "you're a sturdy fellow, but you can't carry out of this bank all the corn that half-dollar will buy!" He was right: there are fifty-six pounds in a bushel of corn, and the price was then ten cents a bushel.

"Something drastic and immediate ought to be done . . ."

ROOSEVELT'S NEW DEAL

March 5, 1933–April 27, 1934
Washington. D.C.

HAROLD L. ICKES

*W*ith one quarter of the workforce unemployed, the economic crisis facing the United States in 1933 was so dire that many people believed democracy might collapse. Thirty years afterward, historian Samuel Eliot Morison wrote that the New Deal "probably saved the capitalist system in the United States: there is no knowing what might have happened under another administration like Hoover's. The German Republic fell before Hitler largely because it kept telling the people, 'The Government can do nothing for you.' "

From the start Roosevelt's confident style reassured the public. "The only thing we have to fear is fear itself," he said in his first inaugural address, just a few days after six states closed banks to stop a financial panic. His leadership had an immediate effect. Thomas Stokes, White House reporter for United Press, quoted a leading Republican congressman, who exclaimed, after an early meeting, "My, that man is refreshing after Hoover! Like a nice, cool highball after drinking stale, flat beer. . . . He was courteous. He deferred here and there. He was good-humored. But all the way through he kept a straight line toward what he wanted. When it was all over, he had got his way. He's smart!"

If you liked Roosevelt, he was smart, or perhaps wily. If you didn't, he was cunning or manipulative. He was all those things, because they were all the same thing: he was a broker, a dealmaker, a professional politician who understood how to make people work together. Biographer Frank Freidel wrote, "Roosevelt felt strongly that he was President of all the American people. Therefore he tried to meet the demands of each of the main blocks of voters. He bridged over strong oppositions between their goals with generalities and compromises . . . [he] proceeded, like *a father dividing favors among clamoring children, hiding contradictions with a smoke screen of swift action and radiant confidence."*

He had the perfect partner in his wife, Eleanor. She was an independent thinker and equal to the president in energy and compassion. To make up for the president's limited ability to travel following his paralysis by polio at age thirty-nine, Eleanor made appearances throughout the country and overseas.

"We must act, and act quickly," he said in his inaugural address, foreshadowing his famous First Hundred Days, in which he created the first programs of the New Deal, including the Public Works Administration, which promoted large construction projects; the Civil Works Administration and Civilian Conservation Corps, which provided jobs for the unemployed; and the Tennessee Valley Authority, which promoted the responsible development of an area three-fourths the size of England.

This account from the diary of Secretary of the Interior Harold L. Ickes reveals the speed with which government was remade by the Roosevelt administration. Notable among the participants were Secretary of Labor Frances Perkins, the first woman member of the cabinet, and Harry Hopkins—admiringly nicknamed "Mr. Root of the Matter" by Winston Churchill—who headed many of the work-relief programs.

MARCH 5, 1933

President Roosevelt called the members of the Cabinet, Vice President [John Nance] Garner, and Speaker-elect [Henry T.] Rainey to meet him at the White House at two-thirty to discuss the acute banking situation and agree on a policy. We considered, and the President decided to issue, the Executive Order which will appear in tomorrow morning's papers, the effect of which will be to close every bank in the United States for a bank holiday of three days, to stop the exportation of gold, and to put into effect other emergency regulations designed to stop the run on the banks and to prevent the hoarding of gold or gold certificates.

MARCH 15, 1933

I attended a meeting in the office of the Secretary of War this morning, together with the Secretary of Labor and the Secretary of Agriculture, to consider further the bill that the President and the Cabinet have had under consideration to take unemployed men out of the crowded areas and put them to work in the national forests, etc. The bill is to be redrafted in one or two important particulars so as to make it clear that it is to apply only to such public works as would not be otherwise undertaken at this time of financial stringency.

APRIL 29, 1933

This afternoon at two o'clock we went into a long session with the President in the White House on the proposed public works bill. Present were the Secretaries of Labor, War, and Agriculture, the Solicitor of the Department of Labor, and the Director of the Budget, in addition to myself. After going over the draft of the bill which called for an appropriation of $5 billion, the President asked what public works there were that would call for the expenditure of such a large sum. Miss Perkins [Frances Perkins, Secretary of Labor] then produced a list prepared by some association of contractors and architects covering the entire country. The President at once turned to the proposals for the State of New York.

I had never before seen the President critical in perhaps a captious way, but he proceeded to rip that list to pieces and Miss Perkins was, in effect, put on trial, although she was not responsible for the list but simply presented it as a suggestion brought in by others. The President was perfectly nice about it all, but I got the impression that he had begun to feel the nervous strain resulting from the extra pressure he has been under as the result of the foreign representatives being here during the last ten days. There was no opportunity to go to Miss Perkins' rescue, much as I wanted to once or twice, not that she needed it, as she was perfectly able to handle it herself, but once or twice I did feel a bit sorry for her. I felt, however, that it would be better all around if the President got out of his system whatever he had in it. In the end we got around to a discussion of the subject matter of the bill and made considerable progress. It is hoped to have the bill perfected and introduced in Congress within ten days.

NOVEMBER 6, 1933

At twelve o'clock Secretaries Wallace [Henry Wallace, Secretary of Agriculture] and Perkins, and Harry Hopkins, Emergency Relief Administrator, came in for a conversation by direction of the President. Professor Rogers was also here at the suggestion of Secretary Wallace. We discussed a plan of Hopkins to put anywhere from two to four million men back to work for standard wages on a thirty-hour-week basis. He would continue to pay on account of these wages what he is now contributing toward relief, and the balance would be made up out of the public works funds. This would amount to a maximum of $400 million for the next sixty days. This would put a serious crimp in the balance of our public works fund, but we all thought it ought to be done.

There was a general feeling that we really are in a very critical condition and that something drastic and immediate ought to be done to bolster the situation. Secretary Wallace believes that the public works fund ought to be increased to $10 billion.

NOVEMBER 7, 1933

Harry L. Hopkins and I lunched with the President to discuss Hopkins' plan of putting four million of the unemployed to work. In order to do this, he is counting upon a certain contribution by municipalities and states. He will put in, out of his emergency relief funds, what it would cost for relief for these men, and Public Works will appropriate about $400 million. Under this plan he will have two million men now on relief work putting in full time by November 15 on various public works throughout the country, the men to receive the normal wages for the type of work they are doing. He will have another two million men at work by December 1, and the money appropriated will run him until February 15.

JANUARY 24, 1934

The Secretary of Labor, Harry L. Hopkins, Dr. [George] Zook, Commissioner of Education, and I had a conference with the President at noon about the educational situation. On account of the depression many thousands of children are being denied educational opportunities in the schools. Many schools are running on part time and thousands of teachers are either unemployed or, if employed, work at salaries, which, if paid, are mere pittances. The President authorized Harry Hopkins to do what he could to relieve the unemployed teachers and also to go as far as possible to help keep in college students who must have help in order to get through. He also indicated that as part of our public works program we might work out a plan for helping to build consolidation schools in those parts of the country where school facilities are very poor, if they exist at all.

APRIL 27, 1934

The President closed the Cabinet meeting today by giving us his views on what he has in mind with respect to social insurance. It is evident that he has thought very deeply on the subject. He is looking forward to a time in the near future when the Government will put into operation a system of old-age, unemployment, maternity, and other forms of social insurance.

"The sideshow motif became evident early ..."

THE LINDBERGH CASE CIRCUS

January 1935
Flemington, New Jersey

STANLEY WALKER

*E*very few years we are treated to a spectacle invariably known as the "Trial of the Century"—the murder of architect Stanford White (1906), the Los Angeles Times bombing (1911), the trial of anarchists Sacco and Vanzetti (1921), the "perfect murder" case of Leopold and Loeb (1924), and so on.

Charles and Anne Lindbergh's baby son was kidnapped in March 1935. Although a ransom of $50,000 was paid, the child was not returned. His body was found in May. In September, carpenter Bruno Richard Hauptmann was found with some of the ransom money and charged with kidnapping and murder. For what it is worth, evidence now shows that Hauptmann, who was executed in 1936, may have been innocent.

Walker reported for the New York Herald Tribune.

The trial of Bruno Richard Hauptmann, for the murder of the Lindbergh baby, which began in Flemington, New Jersey, in the first part of January 1935, was so spectacular, so bizarre, that in retrospect it seems almost incredible that things could have happened as they did. Everything conspired to make the trial dramatic. In its bare, simple outlines the case had all the ingredients of a starkly realistic mystery story. But that was not enough. It remained for the press, the radio, the officials and the spectators to make of it a fantastic extravaganza.

The 300 or more reporters covering the trial filed more than 10,000,000 words. Foreign correspondents sent hundreds of thousands of words by radio, cable and mail. Many radio stations were busy broadcasting transcripts of the testimony. In addition, news commentators and extralegal authorities discussed all aspects of the case. Hearst's *New York Journal,* which was instrumental in employing defense counsel, and which paid the wife of Hauptmann $25 a week, had thirty reporters and a posse of photographers on the scene. The *New York Times* devoted more space to the trial than the other papers, simply because it had more room. It was, surely, the trial of the century.

One of the unforgettable characters of the trial was Edward J. Reilly, a criminal lawyer from Brooklyn, who had been retained as chief of defense counsel. Known as the "Bull of Brooklyn," Reilly had a long, successful record of defending criminals. His strength in his home county usually lay in political pull, oratory or convenient witnesses. As soon as he took over the defense of Hauptmann he began issuing statements. There were, he said, new witnesses. He knew who did the kidnaping. He knew many dark secrets. The forces of the prosecution, headed by David Wilentz, Attorney General of New Jersey, began answering Reilly, and this interchange continued up to the start of the trial.

The sideshow motif became evident early. Sheriff John H. Curtiss, of Hunterdon County, a fat man who came from New England, perceived almost immediately that he could make a good thing out of the trial. His first move was to keep the minions of Mayor Frank Hague of Jersey City out of the scheme. Mr. Hague is a man of considerable dignity, but some of his "boys" have a habit of "muscling in" on important trials, no matter in what part of New Jersey they are held. A committee of reporters, with one of the Hague men at the head, set out for Flemington to discuss seating arrangements. When they arrived, Sheriff Curtiss eyed the Hague fixer with contempt. After some blustering the Hague man departed, leaving the Sheriff in complete power.

The Sheriff informed each reporter, when he came to get tickets for his paper, that there would be a $10 tax on main floor seats and a $5 fee for balcony seats. Most of the reporters paid it, knowing that they could put the item on their expense accounts. But one young fellow from the *New York World-Telegram* telephoned his office before paying; the editor, in crusading mood that morning, ordered a story on the Sheriff's fee-fixing.

Then the fun began. The Board of Freeholders, all Democrats, announced an investigation of the Sheriff, who was a Republican. The Sheriff explained that he was only trying to save the county a little money, and that the "contributions" were merely to meet the cost of installing benches and a temporary press table. He offered free seats to the *World-Telegram*. The reporters, realizing that they would have to keep on good terms with the Sheriff for many weeks, let the matter drop.

Afterward the Sheriff was more cautious. A third person, connected with a telegraph company, could get anyone a ticket for a price. Even Mrs. Ogden L. Mills, wife of the former Secretary of the Treasury, had to pay to get in. Tickets could be obtained for $10, $5, a pint of good bonded rye, or a box of cigars. The Sheriff smoked cigars. Tickets were good for one session only; the reporters were lucky to have received season passes for $10 each. A ticket, of course, did not guarantee a seat.

Many paying customers saw the show from the aisles, radiators and window sills. Panes of several windows were broken by eager spectators, adding a pleasant tinkle of falling glass to the regular trial noises.

On one occasion a woman drove up in front of the courthouse in a Rolls-Royce. Her uniformed chauffeur leaped out and opened the door. The woman, wrapped in mink, stepped out and drew from her pocketbook a $100 bill, which she waved, announcing in a loud, clear voice that she would give all of it for a ticket. She got the ticket.

The first to realize the possibilities in the housing situation was Bert Pedrick, owner of Flemington's only hotel, a ramshackle three-story wooden building. He bought up options on most of the rooms available in the town. He paid the owners $1 a night and charged newspaper men $5 a day for room and board. After the trial Bert paid off the mortgage on the hotel and bought a new sedan.

Everybody in town was out to make money. The Women's Exchange where homemade pastries, breads and rolls were brought by matrons during normal times for sale to their sisters, emerged as a tearoom. The Methodist Episcopal Church became a luncheon spot, with women from the auxiliary serving meals. This enterprise was subsidized by the state, which fed all its witnesses and officers there. After the trial the church bought a new organ. An evangelist from the Middle West saw an opportunity to save some souls while the trial was in progress. The Reverend Fred Bindenberger of Flemington liked the idea and promised the use of his church. Other pastors objected. A compromise was reached under which the visitor agreed not to mention the Hauptmann trial in his exhortations. The revival was a failure.

The souvenir salesmen overran the place. One enterprising fellow made up a batch of miniature ladders. They were simple affairs, about eight inches long and two inches wide, the pine in them being of cigar box thickness. These miniatures were handed out to salesmen, who went about shouting that it was possible to purchase "exact duplicates" of the famous ladder used in the kidnaping for twenty-five cents. The ladders differed greatly from the principal exhibit in the case, but the buyers didn't mind. The ladders sold. One young man, highly excited, bought a ladder and tied it to his lapel with a red ribbon. He said to his companions:

"I'm going to leave it on too, by God! I'll march in on Gertie with it. Then won't she kick herself when she sees what she missed. The double-crossing bitch!"

A man with a metal press did a fair sort of business. He set up for business on the porch of the hotel. He had constructed a die depicting the Hunterdon County courthouse, surrounded by the legend, "Hauptmann

Trial, Flemington, N. J." On the stand beside the press lay several hundred bright new pennies and several fine strips of copper. By running the copper strips through the press, together with the pennies, he turned out Lincoln heads backed by the courthouse and the legend. The pieces sold for five cents each, three for a dime.

The Flemington pottery turned out a set of book ends on which the courthouse appeared. These bits of clay were bought by the more wealthy visitors and today serve as parlor exhibits in many a home. A quick-sketch artist turned out portraits of Hauptmann and other principals of the trial by the dozen; post cards with scenes of Flemington were sold at five cents each; pictures of the jury ranged from a dime to twenty-five cents. The higher-priced jury pictures were "suitable for framing."

Boys from the high school made pocket money running copy for reporters. They had managed to get days off from school. These sharp lads hit upon a scheme of financing their yearbook. The town was overrun with autograph seekers. One day several of the boys appeared in the bar of the hotel with a large drawing board. They went from reporter to reporter and asked for autographs for the yearbook. It seemed that the book was to be dedicated to the reporters who covered the trial. As each man jotted down his name, he was asked for a contribution of twenty-five cents. The reporters didn't feel they could refuse. The boys also got signatures of most of the principals except Colonel Lindbergh and Hauptmann. A week later there was offered for sale at twenty-five cents each, copies of the sheet with the autographs, headed by the inscription, "The Trial of the Century." The youth of Flemington made a lot of money.

The crowds of curious were bad enough on weekdays, but on Sundays they were worse. After the first Sunday, when visitors stole everything in the courthouse they could get their hands on, the Sheriff wanted to close the place on Sundays, but the American Legion and the Kiwanis and Rotary Clubs volunteered to supply guards who would not only stop souvenir hunters but would answer the questions of the sightseers. When the visitors began arriving the second Sunday they found huge placards scattered about the courtroom. Over the chair of the defendant was the sign, "Hauptmann." Likewise there were signs indicating where the judge and jury sat, the witness chair, Colonel Lindbergh's chair, and the spot where Walter Winchell usually kept himself. The crowds were especially eager to see Mrs. Hauptmann and her little son. Every time the two appeared on the street, the crowd would rush for them. Somehow the sightseers seemed to find it astonishing that the child should appear as a pleasant-faced, chubby baby rather than as some sort of monster. Reilly wanted to have the baby brought into the courtroom, but Justice Trenchard, presiding, refused to allow it. Nevertheless, the jury got several glimpses of the child.

A man who got relatively little attention during the trial was Warden Harry O. McCrae, who guarded Hauptmann. Of course he got a few cigars now and then for divulging how Hauptmann had slept, or what he ate but that was about all he got during the trial. Later, however, it developed that McCrae also had entered into the spirit of the thing. Because the officials feared that Hauptmann might attempt suicide if allowed to eat with ordinary knives and forks, he was forced to use paper utensils. The warden supplied this equipment, but when Hauptmann had finished eating the warden hid the utensils in a little basket under his desk. After the trial he handed out paper spoons, forks and plates to any friends who happened to call—each and every one of them guaranteed to have been used by none other than Bruno Richard Hauptmann.

The macabre spectacle finally came to an end. The most dismal scene of all was the courtroom from the time the jury went out until it returned with the verdict of guilty. Justice Trenchard left the bench and went to his chambers to read. Attorney General Wilentz sat in the jury box. Reilly sits in the witness chair. The floor was strewn with papers, cigarette stubs and remnants of sandwiches. Some, with paper bags in their hands, ate sandwiches and cakes and drank coffee, milk or applejack. The more sportive element played games of checkers and tick-tack-toe. Some of the journalists started a dice game in Justice Trenchard's library without his knowledge. Soon reporters, radio men, stenographers, lawyers and Broadway hangers-on were trying their luck. One man won $200 on two passes. A member of the defense counsel collected $75 and said, "That's more than I earned during the whole trial." At this point Justice Trenchard left his chambers and started for the library to get a book. The players, however, were warned. They quickly hid the dice and money and when the old justice entered the library he saw an unusually studious group of young men, all poring over law books. As soon as the justice left, the game was resumed.

Meanwhile, Wilentz, sitting in the jury box, amused his listeners with such jests as, "This is where I should have been in the first place." Reilly, in the witness chair, burlesqued the testimony of state's witnesses. He shot questions at himself, then pretended to be too deaf to hear them. He would cup his hand to his ear and say, "What was that? What? Repeat the question." Reilly is known far and wide as a card, and his barroom stories and repartee were among the most engaging aspects of the Flemington period. Before the jury came in Reilly and a woman reporter stood up in front of the judge's bench and sang "When Irish Eyes Are Smiling."

As soon as the jury had found Hauptmann guilty its members were besought by agents to go on the stage. The foreman was offered $800 a week and the other members $500 a week each. Some of them considered it seriously. So far had the carnival spirit run that many persons could see no impropriety in the jury going on the stage. This attitude was expressed by County Judge Adam O. Robbins, who had relinquished his post in order that Justice Trenchard might sit at the trial. Asked what he thought of the jury accepting the offer, he said:

"Couldn't blame them if they did. You don't make that much farming in a lifetime. Nope, I think it might be a good idea."

The vaudeville scheme collapsed, but the members of the jury did write (or rather, had ghostwritten) articles in which they discussed the trial. They also wrote a book, each contributing a chapter. These twelve men and women had become so impressed with their importance that they found it difficult after the trial to return to their ordinary tasks.

American newspapers were criticized because of the sensational fashion in which the trial was handled. There were many astounding excesses, violations of ethical canons, double-crossings by reporters and officeholders, and an unbelievable amount of trickery. Indeed, sound films of the trial were taken surreptitiously during the first few days, shown at a few theaters and then suppressed. Undoubtedly the press and the radio people overstepped all limits of dignity, but they were not alone. The lawyers in some respects were worse. And there was printed during the trial a long, learned discussion of the evidence in the New York Law Journal, the official law periodical of the First Judicial Department of New York. This article discussed the evidence editorially as it had developed thus far, and pointed out that some of the testimony given was hardly credible. Many old-fashioned lawyers were perturbed at this.

It is difficult to see what could have been done to make the trial a model of decorum. It was too big, and the interest was too great.

"It begins to look like a face . . ."

GUTZON BORGLUM CARVES MOUNT RUSHMORE

September 21, 1936
South Dakota

ERNIE PYLE

B orglum began carving Mount Rushmore in 1927. The job took fourteen years. Shortly after Borglum died, in 1941, his son Lincoln finished the last details.

Pyle is most celebrated for his frontline World War II reports, which appeared in newspapers across the country. The Saturday Evening Post *called him "probably the most prayed-for man with the American troops."*

Do you wonder how an artist can get a sixty-foot stone face to look like George Washington, or Thomas Jefferson, or Abraham Lincoln, or Teddy Roosevelt?

Borglum makes a big plaster cast of all four figures. Then he puts a rod into the top of, say, Washington's head, and drops a plumb line down over the face. Then he measures down the plumb line, and also from the line in toward the face, all over it.

Now, up on the mountain top is another rod, stuck in the rock, and another plumb line dropping down over the stone cliff. So they just multiply the scale figures by twelve, and measure down the face of the rock, write the measurements on with chalk, and the drillers start gouging.

After they've drilled and blasted, purely by measurement, for several months, it begins to look like a face—and, strangely enough, like Washington's face. Then comes the artist's touch. Borglum is up there every day. He looks at the face close up. He goes miles away and looks at it. He starts to mold and shape it. He orders a brow bulged a little more, a hunk taken off the nose. They may blast off a whole carload of rock just for the shading effect on a cheek. . . .

. . . Gutzon Borglum doesn't seem the type of man you'd picture from reading the reports about him. He doesn't spout, nor blow off, nor seem the least bit violent. He doesn't use those artistic phrases that befuddle the layman. He is intensely earnest about Mount Rushmore, and seems to feel a sort of reverence about it.

Borglum is of Danish descent. His father was a Nebraska country doctor. There were no artists in the family before. Gutzon is going on seventy now, but he doesn't look it or act it; he has amazing courage and vitality. He works hard and long. He is medium-short and heavy. His head is bald and he wears a heavy mustache. Around his neck is a scarflike piece of batik, the ends tied down about his waist, like the sling for a broken arm. That's the only artist's effect.

He hates politicians. He swears when he talks about them. He won't let politicians tell him how to do his sculpturing, or how to spend the money. That's what most of his rows have been about. But he isn't just plain bullheaded. I see his point. And I was surprised to learn that he will compromise a small point to get something big. He's a practical genius. . . .

He feels so deeply about the historical greatness of Mount Rushmore that it seemed to me that anything he does after this would be anticlimactic in his career. But he doesn't feel that way about it. He says it took him quite a while to get the artist's feel for dealing with anything as massive as a sixty-foot face on a mountainside. He says even now, after being away during the winter, it takes him a week or two to get adjusted to it. . . .

Borglum, even at seventy, climbs the high mountain several times every day, or rides up in the chicken-coop cable car, high across the valley. . . .

Just now, the whitish sculptured faces stand out brightly against the dark mountain. Borglum says it will take fifty years for the newness to disappear, and twenty thousand years for the elements to harmonize them completely with the gray rock all around. He says the faces will last as long as the mountains last.

Someday, Borglum would like to do a lone face of an Indian on some nearby mountain—a stoic, almost expressionless Indian head, just carved there in stone, looking out forever over the country the white man stole from him.

"I am living very cheaply."

HITTING BOTTOM

Autumn 1936
Hendersonville, North Carolina

F. SCOTT FITZGERALD

Fitzgerald's wife, Zelda, personification of the manic Jazz Age, was in a sanatorium when Fitzgerald hit bottom. He died a few years later, aged forty-four. This is a note to his diary.

In Hendersonville: I am living very cheaply. Today I am in comparative affluence, but Monday and Tuesday I had two tins of potted meat three oranges and a box of Uneedas and two cans of beer. For the food, that totalled eighteen cents a day—and when I think of the thousand meals I've sent back untasted in the last two years. It was fun to be poor—especially if you haven't enough liver power for an appetite. But the air is fine here, and I liked what I had—and there was nothing to do about it anyhow because I was afraid to cash any checks, and I had to save enough for postage for the story. But it was funny coming into the hotel and the very deferential clerk not knowing that I was not only thousands, nay tens of thousands in debt, but had less than forty cents cash in the world and probably a deficit in the bank. I gallantly gave Scotty [his daughter] my last ten when I left her and of course the Flynns, etc., had no idea and wondered why I didn't just "jump into a taxi" (four dollars and tip) and run over for dinner.

Enough of this bankrupt's comedy—I suppose it has been enacted all over the U.S. in the last four years, plenty of times. . . .

The final irony was when a drunk man in the shop where I bought my can of ale said in a voice obviously intended for me, "These city dudes from the East come down here with their millions. Why don't they support us?"

THE WAR OF THE WORLDS

October 30, 1938
New York City

JOHN HOUSEMAN

*T*housands *of listeners who tuned in late to* The War of the Worlds, *a radio adaptation of the H. G. Wells novel about an invasion from Mars, believed the fictional news reports were real. Panics began in several cities at the same time.*

Houseman, a co-founder with Orson Welles and others of the Mercury Theater, tells how the troupe created the accidental spectacle. Wells himself was absent for most of the work because he was preparing a stage play.

Five days before the show, [scriptwriter] Howard Koch telephoned. He was in deep distress. After three days of slaving on H. G. Wells's scientific fantasy he was ready to give up. Under no circumstances, he declared, could it be made interesting or in any way credible to modern American ears. Koch was not given to habitual alarmism. To confirm his fears, Annie, our secretary, came to the phone. She was an acid and emphatic girl from Smith Collage with fine blond hair, who smelled of fading spring flowers. "You can't do it!" she whined. "Those old Martians are just a lot of nonsense. It's all too silly! We're going to make fools of ourselves! Absolute fools!"

For some reason which I do not clearly remember our only possible alternative for that week was a dreary one—*Lorna Doone.* Unable to reach Welles, I called Koch back. I was severe. I taxed him with defeatism. I gave him false comfort. I promised to come up and help.

When I finally got there—around two the next morning—things were better. He was beginning to have fun laying waste the State of New Jersey. Annie had stopped grinding her teeth. We worked all night and through the next day. Wednesday at sunset the script was finished.

Thursday, as usual, Paul Stewart rehearsed the show, then made a record. We listened to it rather gloomily, long after midnight in Orson's room at 8 the St. Regis, sitting on the floor because all the chairs were covered with coils of unrolled and unedited film. We agreed it was a dull show. We all felt its only chance of coming off lay in emphasizing its newscast style—its simultaneous, eyewitness quality.

All night we sat up, spicing the script with circumstantial allusions and authentic detail. Friday afternoon it went over to CBS to be passed by the Network censor. Certain name alterations were requested. Under protest and with a deep sense of grievance we changed the Hotel Biltmore to a nonexistent Park Plaza, Trans-America to Intercontinent, the Columbia Broadcasting Building to Broadcasting Building. Then the script went over to mimeograph and we went to bed. We had done our best and, after all, a show is just a show.

Around six we left the studio. Orson, phoning from the theater a few minutes later to find out how things were going, was told by one of the CBS sound men, who had stayed behind to pack up his equipment, that it was not one of our better shows. Confidentially, the man opined, it just didn't come off.

On Sunday, October 30, at 8:00 P.M., E.S.T., in a studio littered with coffee cartons and sandwich paper, Orson swallowed a second container of pineapple juice, put on his earphones, raised his long white fingers and threw the cue for the Mercury theme—the Tchaikovsky Piano Concerto In B Flat Minor # 1. . . .

Orson stretched both these numbers to what seemed to us, in the control room, an almost unbearable length. We objected. The interview in the Princeton Observatory—the clockwork ticking monotonously overhead, the woolly-minded professor mumbling vague replies to the reporters' uninformed questions—this, too, he dragged out to a point of tedium. Over our protests, lines were restored that had been cut at earlier rehearsals. We cried there would not be a listener left. Welles stretched them out even longer.

He was right. His sense of tempo, that night, was infallible. When the flashed news of the cylinder's landing finally came—almost fifteen minutes after the beginning of a fairly dull show—he was able suddenly to spiral his action to a speed as wild and reckless as its base was solid. The appearance of the Martians; their first treacherous act; the death of Carl Phillips; the arrival of the militia; the battle of the Watchung Hills; the destruction of New Jersey—all these were telescoped into a space of twelve minutes without ever stretching the listener's emotional credulity. The broadcast, by then, had its own reality, the reality of emotionally felt time and space.

The Crossley census taken about a week before the broadcast had given us 3.6 per cent of the listening audience to Edgar Bergen's 34.7 per cent. What the Crossley Institute (that hireling of advertising agencies) deliberately ignored, was the healthy American habit of dial-twisting. Edgar Bergen in the person of Charlie McCarthy temporarily left the air about 8:12 P.M., E.S.T., yielding place to a new and not very popular singer. At that point, and during the following minutes, a large number of listeners started twisting their dials. . . . By this time [in the radio play] the mysterious meteorite had fallen at Grovers Mill in New Jersey, the Martians had begun to show their foul leathery heads above the ground, and the New Jersey State Police were racing to the spot. . . .

In [the real] New York, hundreds of people on Riverside Drive left their homes ready for flight. Bus terminals were crowded. A woman calling up the Dixie Bus Terminal for information said impatiently, "Hurry up please, the world is coming to an end and I have a lot to do." . . .

In Rhode Island officials of the electric light company received a score of calls urging them to turn off all lights so the city would be safe from the enemy. In Minneapolis a woman ran into church screaming, "New York destroyed—this is the end of the world. You might as well go home to die I just heard it on the radio."

The second part of the show was extremely well written and most sensitively played—but nobody heard it. After a stirring musical finale, Welles, in his own person, delivered a charming informal little speech about Halloween, which it happened to be.

I remember, during the playing of the final theme, the phone starting to ring in the control room and a shrill voice through the receiver announcing itself as belonging to the mayor of some Midwestern city, one of the big ones. He is screaming for Welles. Choking with fury, he reports mobs in the streets of his city, women and children huddled in the churches, violence and looting. If, as he now learns, the whole thing is nothing but a crummy joke—then he, personally, is coming up to New York to punch the author of it on the nose! Orson hangs up quickly. For we are off the air now and the studio door bursts open. The following hours are a nightmare. The building is suddenly full of people and dark blue uniforms. We are hurried out of the studio, downstairs, into a back office. Here we sit incommunicado while network employees are busily collecting, destroying, or locking up all scripts and records of the broadcast. Then the press is let loose upon us, ravening for horror. How many deaths have we heard of? (Implying they know of thousands.) What do we know of the fatal stampede in a Jersey hall? (Implying it is one of many.) What traffic deaths? (The ditches must be choked with corpses.) The suicides? (Haven't you heard about the one on Riverside Drive?) It is all quite vague in my memory and quite terrible.

Hours later, instead of arresting us, they let us out a back way. We were on the front page for two days. Having had to bow to radio as a news source during the Munich crisis, the press was now only too eager to expose the perilous irresponsibilities of the new medium. Orson was their whipping boy. They quizzed and badgered him. Condemnatory editorials were delivered by our press-clipping bureau in bushel baskets. There was talk, for a while, of criminal action.

Then gradually, after about two weeks, the excitement subsided. By then it had been discovered that the casualties were not as numerous or as serious as had at first been supposed. One young woman had fallen and broken her arm running downstairs.

Of the suits that were brought against us—amounting to over three quarters of a million dollars for damages, injuries, miscarriages and distresses of various kinds—none was substantiated or legally proved. We did settle one claim, however, against the advice of our lawyers. It was the particularly affecting case of a man in Massachusetts, who wrote:

"I thought the best thing to do was to go away. So I took three dollars twenty-five cents out of my savings and bought a ticket. After I had gone sixty miles I knew it was a play. Now I don't have money left for the shoes I was saving up for. Will you please have someone send me a pair of black shoes size 9B!"

We did.

"Frankly, my dear . . ."

A MOVIE EXECUTIVE PLEADS FOR A FEW FAMOUS LAST WORDS

October 29, 1939
Hollywood, California

DAVID O. SELZNICK

*D*avid O. Selznick was the fiery independent film producer who had staked his *career on the adaptation of Margaret Mitchell's novel,* Gone with the Wind. *Will Hays directed the Hays Office, which maintained the "morality" of motion pictures.*

Dear Mr. Hays—

As you probably know, the punch line of *Gone With the Wind,* the one bit of dialogue which forever establishes the future relationship between Scarlett and Rhett, is, "Frankly, my dear, I don't give a damn."

Naturally I am most desirous of keeping this line and, to judge from the reactions of two preview audiences, this line is remembered, loved, and looked forward to by the millions who have read this new American classic.

Under the code, Joe Breen is unable to give me permission to use this sentence because it contains the word "damn," a word specifically forbidden by the code.

As you know from my previous work with such pictures as *David Copperfield, Little Lord Fauntleroy, A Tale of Two Cities,* etc., I have always attempted to live up to the spirit as well as the exact letter of the producers' code. Therefore, my asking you to review the case, to look at the strip of film in which this forbidden word is contained, is not motivated by a whim. A great deal of the force and drama of *Gone With the Wind,* a project to which we have given three years of hard work and hard thought, is dependent upon that word.

It is my contention that this word as used in the picture is not an oath or a curse. The worst that could be said against it is that it is a vulgarism, and it is so described in the *Oxford English Dictionary.* Nor do I feel that in asking you to make an exception in this case, I am asking for the use of a word which is considered reprehensible by the great majority of American people and institutions. A canvass of the popular magazines shows that even such moral publications as *Woman's Home Companion, Saturday Evening Post, Collier's* and *The Atlantic Monthly,* use this word freely. I understand the difference, as outlined in the code, between the written word and the word spoken from the screen, but at the same time I think the attitude of these magazines toward "damn" gives an indication that the word itself is not considered abhorrent or shocking to audiences.

I do not feel that your giving me permission to use "damn" in this one sentence will open up the floodgates and allow every gangster picture to be peppered with "damns" from end to end. I do believe, however, that if you were to permit our using this dramatic word in its rightfully dramatic place, in a line that is known and remembered by millions of readers, it would establish a helpful precedent, a precedent which would give to Joe Breen discretionary powers to allow the use of certain harmless oaths and ejaculations whenever, in his opinion, they are not prejudicial to public morals.

"He threw in something different, man . . ."

CHARLIE "BIRD" PARKER MAKES THE SCENE

1941
Kansas City

IDREES SULIEMAN

A lto saxophonist Parker pushed jazz toward bebop, and turned the jazz clubs of New York City's 52nd Street into a training ground for the generation of musicians that followed him. With trumpeter Dizzy Gillespie, he also cut the first bop records.

I was with the Carolina Cotton Pickers doing one-nighters for four years. We stopped in Kansas City in 1941, and I met Bird blowing every night at the Kentucky Club. They'd start at four o'clock after the other clubs closed and go, sometimes, to twelve noon.

I didn't recognize [Bird's talent] because there was an alto player we had named Porter Kilbert. So, for us, Porter was the world's best. Because he could do the same thing, too. He had a photographic memory. Play arrangements, and he could play all the solos. We heard about Charlie Parker, and finally when we got to Kansas City, everyone in the band was waiting to see what would happen. So the first night we played, Charlie Parker was there listening to Porter. So we said, "Yeah. He's getting the message."

When we finished they had this jam session, and they both were really blowing. When it was over we said, "We're still with Porter. Porter don't have nothing to worry about."

But Porter said, "Yeah, but he threw in something different, man." So we said, "It's different, yeah, but you played everything he played." And he said, "Yeah, but he thought of it first."

"The Japanese are planning . . . a surprise mass attack."

AN EARLY WARNING

January 7, 1941

AMBASSADOR JOSEPH CLARK GREW

*G*rew, *ambassador to Japan, sent this despatch from Tokyo to the State Department in Washington, D.C.*

There is a lot of talk around town to the effect that the Japanese, in case of a break with the United States, are planning to go all out in a surprise mass attack on Pearl Harbor. I rather guess that the boys in Hawaii are not precisely asleep.

"And then we saw the planes . . ."

PEARL HARBOR

December 7, 1941
Oahu, Hawaii

SENATOR DANIEL K. INOUYE

*I*nouye *was a high school student when Pearl Harbor was attacked. Later, when he learned he had been denied enlistment in the army because he was training to become a doctor, he quit his studies and joined the distinguished 442nd "Go for Broke!" Regiment (see 424). He lost an arm in combat and decided after the war to give up medicine. He was Hawaii's first elected representative in 1959, and in 1962 was elected to the Senate, where he has served more than thirty years.*

The family was up by 6:30 that morning, as we usually were on Sunday, to dress and have a leisurely breakfast before setting out for 9 o'clock services at church. Of course anyone who has some memory of that shattering day can tell you precisely what he was doing at the moment when he suddenly realized that an era was ending, that the long and comfortable days of peace were gone, and that America and all her people had been abruptly confronted with their most deadly challenge since the founding of the Republic.

As soon as I finished brushing my teeth and pulled on my trousers, I automatically clicked on the little radio that stood on the shelf above my bed. I remember that I was buttoning my shirt and looking out the window—it would be a magnificent day; already the sun had burned off the morning haze and glowed bright in a blue sky—when the hum of the warming set gave way to a frenzied voice. "This is no test," the voice cried out. "Pearl Harbor is being bombed by the Japanese! I repeat: this is not a test or a maneuver! Japanese war planes are attacking Oahu!"

"Papa!" I called, then froze into immobility, my fingers clutching that button. I could feel blood hammering against my temple, and behind it the unspoken protest, like a prayer—It's not true! It is a test, or a mistake! It can't be true!—but somewhere in the core of my being I knew that all my world was crumbling as I stood motionless in that little bedroom and listened to the disembodied voice of doom.

Now my father was standing in the doorway listening, caught by that special horror instantly sensed by Americans of Japanese descent as the nightmare began to unfold. There was a kind of agony on his face and my brothers and sister, who had pushed up behind him, stopped where they were and watched him as the announcer shouted on:

". . . not a test. This is the real thing! Pearl Harbor has been hit and now we have a report that Hickam Field and Schofield Barracks have been bombed, too. We can see the Japanese planes. . . ."

"Come outside!" my father said to me, and I plunged through the door after him. As my brothers John and Bob started out, too, he turned and told them: "Stay with your mother!"

We stood in the warm sunshine on the south side of the house and stared out toward Pearl Harbor. Black puffs of anti-aircraft smoke littered the pale sky, trailing away in a soft breeze, and we knew beyond any wild hope that this was no test, for practice rounds of anti-aircraft, which we had seen a hundred times, were fleecy white. And now the dirty gray smoke of a great fire billowed up over Pearl and obscured the mountains and the horizon, and if we listened attentively we could hear the soft crrrump of the bombs amid the hysterical chatter of the ack-ack.

And then we saw the planes. They came zooming up out of that sea of gray smoke, flying north toward where we stood and climbing into the bluest part of the sky, and they came in twos and threes, in neat formations, and if it hadn't been for that red ball on their wings, the rising sun of the Japanese Empire, you could easily believe that they were Americans, flying over in precise military salute.

I fell back against the building as they droned near, but my father stood rigid in the center of the sidewalk and stared up into that malignant sky, and out of the depths of his shock and torment came a tortured cry: "You fools!"

We went back into the house and the telephone was ringing. It was the secretary of the Red Cross aid station where I taught. "How soon can you be here, Dan?" he said tensely.

"I'm on my way," I told him. I felt a momentary surge of elation—he wanted me! I could do something—and I grabbed a sweater and started for the door.

"Where are you going?" my mother cried. She was pointing vaguely out the window, toward the sky, and said, "They'll kill you."

"Let him go," my father said firmly. "He must go."

I went to embrace her. "He hasn't had breakfast," she whispered. "At least have some breakfast."

"I can't, Mama. I have to go." I took a couple of pieces of bread from the table and hugged her.

"When will you be back?" she said.

"Soon. As soon as I can."

But it would be five days, a lifetime, before I came back. . . .

The planes were gone as I pumped furiously toward the aid station, more than a mile away. The acrid smell of the smoke had drifted up from Pearl and people, wide-eyed with terror, fumbling for some explanation, something to do, had spilled into the streets. What would become of them, I agonized, these thousands, suddenly rendered so vulnerable and helpless by this monstrous betrayal at the hands of their ancestral land? In those first chaotic moments, I was absolutely incapable of understanding that I was one of them, that I, too, had been betrayed, and all of my family.

An old Japanese grabbed the handlebars of my bike as I tried to maneuver around a cluster of people in the street. "Who did it?" he yelled at me. "Was it the Germans? It must have been the Germans!"

I shook my head, unable to speak, and tore free of him. My eyes blurred with tears, tears of pity for that old man, because he could not accept the bitter truth, tears for all these frightened people in teeming, poverty-ridden McCully and Moiliili. They had worked so hard. They had wanted so desperately to be accepted, to be good Americans. And now, in a few cataclysmic minutes, it was all undone, for in the marrow of my bones I knew that there was only deep trouble ahead. And then, pedalling along, it came to me at last that I would face that trouble, too, for my eyes were shaped just like those of that poor old man in the street, and my people were only a generation removed from the land that had spawned those bombers, the land that sent them to rain destruction on America, death on Americans. And choking with emotion, I looked up into the sky and called out, "You dirty Japs!"

. . . It was past 8:30—the war was little more than half an hour old—when I reported in at the aid station, two classrooms in the Lunalilo Elementary School. I had gained the first six years of my education in this building and before the day was out it would be half-destroyed by our own anti-aircraft shells which had failed to explode in the air. Even now confusion was in command, shouting people pushing by each other as they rushed for litters and medical supplies.

Somewhere a radio voice droned on, now and then peaking with shrill excitement, and it was in one such outburst that I learned how the *Arizona* had exploded in the harbor. Many other vessels were severely hit.

And then, at 9 A.M., the Japanese came back. The second wave of bombers swooped around from the west and the anti-aircraft guns began thundering again. Mostly the planes hammered at military installations—Pearl, Hickam, Wheeler Field—and it was our own ack-ack that did the deadly damage in the civilian sectors. Shells, apparently fired without timed fuses, and finding no target in the sky, exploded on impact with the ground. Many came crashing into a three-by-five-block area of crowded McCully, the first only moments after the Japanese planes reappeared. It hit just three blocks from the aid station and the explosion rattled the windows. I grabbed a litter and rounded up a couple of fellows I knew.

"Where're we going?" one yelled at me.

"Where the trouble is! Follow me!"

In a small house on the corner of Hauoli and Algaroba Streets we found our first casualties. The shell had sliced through the house. It had blown the front out and the tokens of a lifetime—dishes, clothing, a child's bed—were strewn pathetically into the street.

I was propelled by sheerest instinct. Some small corner of my mind worried about how I'd react to what lay in that carnage—there would be no textbook cuts and bruises, and the blood would be real blood—and then I plunged in, stumbling over the debris, kicking up clouds of dust and calling, frantically calling, to anyone who might be alive in there. There was no answer. The survivors had already fled and the one who remained would never speak again. I found her half-buried in the rubble, one of America's first civilian dead of the Second World War. One woman, all but decapitated by a piece of shrapnel, died within moments. Another, who had fallen dead at the congested corner of King and

McCully, still clutched the stumps where her legs had been. And all at once it was as though I had stepped out of my skin; I moved like an automaton, hardly conscious of what I was doing and totally oblivious of myself. I felt nothing. I did what I had been taught to do and it was only later, when those first awful hours had become part of our history, that I sickened and shuddered as the ghastly images of war flashed again and again in my mind's eye, as they do to this day.

By the time we had removed the dead to a temporary morgue set up in Lunalilo School, more shells had fallen. It was now, by one of those bitter ironies, that our aid station was hit by our own shells, and we lost precious minutes evacuating what was left of our supplies. Nearby, a building caught fire and as the survivors came stumbling out, we patched their wounds as best we could and commandeered whatever transportation that passed to get them to the hospital. For those still trapped inside there was nothing in the world anyone could do. The flames drove us back to the far side of the street, and by the time the firemen brought them under control, there was nothing left alive in that burned-out hulk. Then, carrying corrugated boxes, it became our melancholy duty to pick our way through the smouldering beams and hot ashes and collect the charred, barely recognizable remains of those who had perished. We tried to get one body in each box, but limbs came away as we touched them and it was hard to tell an arm from a leg, and so we couldn't always be sure of who, or what, was in any given box.

There are moments I can never forget. An empty-eyed old lady wandered screaming through the wreckage of a house on King street. A boy of twelve or so, perhaps her grandson, tried to lead her from danger, for she could scarcely keep her footing in the ruins. But the old woman would not be budged. "Where is my home?" she would cry out hysterically in Japanese, or "Where are my things?"

I climbed up to where she tottered on a mountain of wreckage and took hold of her shoulders. "Go with the boy," I said to her.

But it was as though I wasn't there. She looked right through me and wailed, "What have they done to my home?" And without thinking about it, for if I had thought about it I could never have done it, I slapped her twice across the face, sharply. Later, I would be awed by my audacity—my whole life had been a lesson in reverence for my elders—but at that instant I remembered only what I had been taught to do in cases of uncontrollable hysteria. And it worked.

"Go with the boy," I said again, and the light of reason returned to her eyes, and she went.

A man burst into the improvised morgue, snatching at the arms of strangers and begging to know if they had seen his wife and baby. Finally someone recognized him and, gently as such a thing can be said, told him that they were dead. "Where are they?" he cried out, his face torn with anguish. "Let me see them!"

And so he was led to one of the corrugated boxes and he saw them. The woman lay nude, staring back at him sightlessly. One arm ended in a bloody wrist and the hand had been tossed haphazardly into the lower corner of the box. The other arm, rigid in death, clutched the body of a child without legs.

"Yes," the man said softly after a time, "that is my family." And they led him away.

We worked on into the night, and were working still when the new day broke. There was so much to be done—broken bodies to be mended, temporary shelter to be found for bombed-out families, precautions against disease, food for the hungry and comfort for the bereaved—that even our brief respites for a sandwich or a cup of coffee were tinged with feelings of guilt. We worked on into the following night and through the day after that, snatching some broken moments of sleep wherever we happened to be when we could move no further, and soon there was no dividing line between day and night at all.

"A day which will live in infamy . . ."

PEARL HARBOR NEWS REACHES FDR

December 7, 1941
Washington, D.C.

GRACE TULLY

The final tally at Pearl Harbor: nineteen American ships damaged or sunk, 149 planes lost, 1,178 Americans wounded, and 2,403 dead. Simultaneous surprise attacks on the Philippines, Guam, Midway Island, and Hong Kong added to the damage and casualties. The Japanese lost just twenty-nine planes and pilots.

Tully was Roosevelt's secretary.

On Sunday afternoon I was resting, trying to relax from the grind of the past weeks and to free my mind from the concern caused by the very grave tones in which the President dictated that Saturday night message. I was rather abstractedly looking at a Sunday paper when the telephone rang and Louise Hackmeister said sharply:

"The President wants you right away. There's a car on the way to pick you up. The Japs just bombed Pearl Harbor!"

With no more words and without time for me to make a single remark, she cut off the connection. She had a long list of people to notify. In twenty minutes I was drawing into the White House driveway, already swarming with extra police and an added detail of Secret Service men, with news and radio reporters beginning to stream into the Executive Office wing and State, War and Navy officials hurrying into the House. Hopkins, Knox and Stimson already were with the Boss in his second floor study; Hull and General Marshall arrived a few minutes later.

Most of the news on the Jap attack was then coming to the White House by telephone from Admiral Stark, Chief of Naval Operations, at the Navy Department. It was my job to take these fragmentary and shocking reports from him by shorthand, type them up and relay them to the Boss. I started taking the calls on a telephone in the second floor hall but the noise and confusion were such that I moved into the President's bedroom.

General Watson, Admiral McIntire, Captain Beardall, the Naval Aide, and Marvin McIntyre were on top of me as I picked up each phone call and they followed me as I rushed into Malvina Thompson's tiny office to type each message. All of them crowded over my shoulders as I transcribed each note. The news was shattering. I hope I shall never again experience the anguish and near hysteria of that afternoon.

Coding and decoding operations in Hawaii and in Washington slowed up the transmission. But the news continued to come in, each report more terrible than the last, and I could hear the shocked unbelief in Admiral Stark's voice as he talked to me. At first the men around the President were incredulous; that changed to angry acceptance as new messages supported and amplified the previous ones. The Boss maintained greater outward calm than anybody else but there was rage in his very calmness. With each new message he shook his head grimly and tightened the expression of his mouth.

Within the first thirty or forty minutes a telephone circuit was opened from the White House to Governor Joseph B. Poindexter in Honolulu. The Governor confirmed the disastrous news insofar as he had learned it. In the middle of the conversation he almost shrieked into the phone and the President turned to the group around him to bark grimly:

"My God, there's another wave of Jap planes over Hawaii right this minute."

Mr. Hull, his face as white as his hair, reported to the Boss that Nomura and Kurusu were waiting to see him at the exact moment the President called to tell him of the bombing. In a tone as cold as ice he repeated what he had told the enemy envoys and there was nothing cold or diplomatic in the words he used. Knox, whose Navy had suffered the worst damage, and Stimson were cross-examined closely on what had happened, on why they believed it could have happened, on what might happen next and on what they could do to repair to some degree the disaster.

Within the first hour it was evident that the Navy was dangerously crippled, that the Army and Air Force were not fully prepared to guarantee safety from further shattering setbacks in the Pacific. It was easy to speculate that a Jap invasion force might be following their air strike at Hawaii—or that the West Coast itself might be marked for similar assault.

Orders were sent to the full Cabinet to assemble at the White House at 8:30 that evening and for Congressional leaders of both parties to be on hand by 9:00 for a joint conference with the Executive group.

Shortly before 5:00 o'clock the Boss called me to his study. He was alone, seated before his desk on which were two or three neat piles of notes containing the information of the past two hours. The telephone was close by his hand. He was wearing a gray sack jacket and was lighting a cigarette as I entered the room. He took a deep drag and addressed me calmly:

"Sit down, Grace. I'm going before Congress tomorrow. I'd like to dictate my message. It will be short."

I sat down without a word; it was no time for words other than those to become part of the war effort.

Once more he inhaled deeply, then he began in the same calm tone in which he dictated his mail. Only his diction was a little different as he spoke each word incisively and slowly, carefully specifying each punctuation mark and paragraph.

"Yesterday comma December 7 comma 1941 dash a day which will live in infamy dash the United States of America was suddenly and deliberately attacked by naval and air forces of the Empire of Japan period paragraph."

The entire message ran under 500 words, a cold-blooded indictment of Japanese treachery and aggression, delivered to me without hesitation, interruption or second thoughts.

"I ask," he concluded, "that the Congress declare that since the unprovoked and dastardly attack by Japan on Sunday comma December 7 comma a state of war has existed between the United States and the Japanese Empire period end."

As soon as I transcribed it, the President called Hull back to the White House and went over the draft. The Secretary brought with him an alternative message drafted by Sumner Welles, longer and more comprehensive in its review of the circumstances leading to the state of war. It was rejected by the Boss and hardly a word of his own historic declaration was altered. Harry Hopkins added the next to the last sentence: "With confidence in our armed forces—with the unbounded determination of our people—we will gain the inevitable triumph—so help us God."

"You felt like a prisoner."

EVACUATION TO MANZANAR

April 26, 1942
Los Angeles and Manzanar

YURI TATEISHI

A nger over Pearl Harbor led to a fear that Japanese Americans were spies or saboteurs. In March 1942, a presidential order allowed General John De Witt, commander of Western Defense Command, to order more than 110,000 Japanese Americans living on the west coast to be confined to ten inland "relocation centers," actually concentration camps, where many inmates were held until 1945. Most of those removed were American citizens. The others had been barred from seeking citizenship because of earlier alien-exclusion laws.

Some of the men in the camp were later allowed to enlist in the U.S. Army. They became the most decorated unit in its history, the 442nd "Go for Broke" Brigade (see page 424).

In 1988, after years of lobbying by internees and their families, the American government formally apologized and offered reparations.

Tateishi was confined in Manzanar, a camp near Los Angeles.

When the evacuation came, we were renting a home and had four kids. It was terrible because you had to sell everything. We were just limited to what we could take with us, and so everything was just sold for whatever we could get. Our furniture was rather new at that time because we had just bought a living-room and dining-room set. I just finished paying for a refrigerator when I had to sell that. Of course, we got nothing for it, because we had such a limited time. I don't remember how much notice we got, but it seems it was two weeks or something because we had to rush to sell everything. I don't remember how much time we had, but it wasn't very long. Otherwise, we wouldn't be selling at such low prices.

The day of the evacuation was April 26. The day before, we had to sleep on the floor because all the furniture was gone. We all slept on the floor, ate on the floor, and cooked what we could with what few utensils we had. I recall we had to get up very early in the morning, and I think we all walked to the Japanese school because no one had a car then. And everybody was just all over the place, the whole Japanese community was there, the West L.A. community. The Westwood Methodist Church had some hot coffee and doughnuts for us that morning, which helped a lot, and we were loaded in a bus.

Just about the time we were ready to load, my youngest son broke out with measles that morning, and I had him covered up, and then a nurse came up to me and said, "May I see your baby?" He was almost three, but I was carrying him, and she said, "I'm sorry but I'm going to have to take him away." Of course, I thought, he would be sleeping at that time so he wouldn't know, but I thought also that he would wake up in a strange place, he wouldn't know anybody; and he probably would just cry all day or all night. But the neighbors said that they would go and check him, so that kind of relieved me. If he were awake, maybe we would have been able to tell him something, but he was asleep. It was easier for me because he was asleep. I don't know. But when I thought about how he might wake up and be in a strange place, with strange people, I just really broke down and cried. I cried all morning over it, but there was nothing we could do but leave him. He stayed at the general hospital and joined us at Manzanar in three weeks.

When we got to Manzanar, it was getting dark and we were given numbers first. We went to the mess hall, and I remember the first meal we were given in those tin plates and tin cups. It was canned weiners and canned spinach. It was all the food we had, and then after finishing that we were taken to our barracks. It was dark and trenches were here and there. You'd fall in and get up and finally got to the barracks. The floors were boarded, but they were about a quarter to a half inch apart, and the next morning you could see the ground below. What hurt most I think was seeing those hay mattresses. We were used to a regular home atmosphere, and seeing those hay mattresses—so makeshift, with hay sticking out—a barren room with nothing but those hay mattresses. It was depressing, such a primitive feeling. We were given army blankets and army cots. Our family was large enough that we didn't have to share our barrack with another family but all seven of us were in one room.

. . . You felt like a prisoner. You know, you have to stay inside and you have a certain amount of freedom within the camp I suppose, but . . . you're kept inside a barbed-wire fence, and you know you can't go out.

And you don't know what your future is, going into a camp with four children. You just have to trust God that you will be taken care of somehow. It's scary—not in the sense that you would be hurt or anything but not knowing what your future will be. You don't know what the education for the children will be or what type of housing or anything like that. Of course, you don't know how you're going to be able to raise the children.

"A brilliant piece of deception . . ."

A CODEBREAKER'S DARING TRICK

May 20, 1942
Honolulu, Hawaii

REAR ADMIRAL EDWIN T. LAYTON

The battle of Midway was the turning point of the Pacific war. It was almost a mirror image of Pearl Harbor. The Americans surprised the Japanese fleet that had assembled to attack Midway Island, about halfway between the United States and Japan. The Japanese navy lost 17 ships, 275 planes, and almost 5,000 troops. The Americans lost just two ships.

The key players in the surprise attack were the U.S. Navy code breakers based in Hawaii, known by their group name, Hypo. Everyone knew the Japanese were preparing to attack; but no one knew where or when. Determining the date was the Hypo team's job.

As fragments of deciphered code revealed that the attack date was nearing, the code breakers, led by Joseph J. Rochefort, concocted an elaborate deception to test their theory that Midway was the target. The ruse worked.

Rochefort's cryptanalyst team began a marathon review of every intercept. They carefully checked even unimportant routing instructions to transports for hints of the date.

At the beginning of the third week in May, the current decrypts and traffic analysis indicated that the Combined [Japanese] Fleet was still on operational maneuvers south of Japan. But a 20 May decrypt suggested that N-day [the day of attack] could be 2 or 3 June. This was two weeks before the mid-June date that King [Admiral King, head of the U.S. Navy] had predicted, and nearly a week earlier than our original estimates.

Washington refused to buy this new date. There were even those in Washington who suggested that their Hypo rivals had been taken in by an elaborate Japanese deception. They believed that the real Japanese objective was an attack on the west coast. It was to silence the skeptics in Washington that Rochefort embarked on a brilliant piece of deception.

The idea came from one of Joe's assistants, Lieutenant Commander Jasper Holmes. He had studied the Midway Pan Am Airlines facility before the war when he was with the engineering school at the University of Hawaii, and he had been impressed that [Midway] island's entire freshwater supply was obtained from an evaporator plant. On 19 May, after receiving Admiral Bloch's preliminary approval Rochefort brought the scheme over to me.

I took the proposal to Nimitz, who authorized the transmission by submarine cable to Midway of a dispatch that ordered the garrison commander to immediately radio a plain-language emergency request for water. At the same time the report was to be made by one of the strip-cipher code systems we knew the Japanese had captured on Wake. This would make a convincing detailed follow-up to the emergency first-flash report of an explosion in their water distillation system.

The instructions were duly sent out to the Midway commander that same Tuesday. Midway broadcast the messages soon afterward. They were picked up by the Japanese listening post at Kwajalein and flashed to the Owada headquarters of the Special Duty Radio Intelligence Group the same day.

Within hours, the commander of the Japanese air unit destined for Midway was signaling headquarters to supply his force with emergency water supplies.

When the Japanese message was intercepted at Pearl, it surprised even Rochefort's second-in-command, who had not been let in on our secret. "I happened to read the Japanese interception of the water message," Captain Dyer recalled, "and I was so ignorant of the whole affair that I told Rochefort, 'Those stupid bastards on Midway. What do they ever mean by sending out a message like this in plain language.' "

"My first actual piece of war work . . ."

THE HOMEFRONT

1943
West Lynn, Massachusetts

NELL GILES

N ell Giles, a writer for the Boston Globe, *took a job at a General Electric factory to report on the lives of the 5 million women who worked during World War II in jobs traditionally held by men.*

Today our training class was divided into two shifts . . . night and day . . . and put to work on the bench, though what we do is just for practice.

My first job was being taught the value of motions. The foreman sat me down before an arrangement of screws, tiny wires and things called "brackets." With a small "jeweler's screw driver" I was to take fifty of the things apart and then put them together again. Then I was to take them apart for the second time, and on the next assembling I would be timed. Putting them together is supposed to take 36 minutes . . . and can be done by the experts in 23 . . . but it took me 45. Getting them back together again is even worse because the wires get tangled up, and you wouldn't believe a screw driver could slip around so!

Then the foreman assigned me to the ratchet screw driver, which is a wonderful way to let off steam. I was a whiz at that. All you do is exert a little pressure with this "ratchet" which hangs on a spring in front of you, and out pops the screw. It makes a big noise and you feel the house is falling down around your ears and you hope it does! If every home were equipped with a ratchet screw driver, how it would clear the air of verbal steam letting-off!

Every move we make in completing one of these "jobs" has been carefully figured out by the methods department and put on a blue print, which is constantly before us. "With the left hand place new block on table as right hand removes completed block . . ." and so forth, through every move. As far as possible, the duties of each hand are the same, though in opposite directions. You see that there is a rhythm in all this.

Again we are told how to use finger movements, rather than shoulder, because they are twice as fast. . . .

Without thinking, we try to beat the rhythm of the next girl, if we are doing the same kind of work. There are four screws in the block . . . and I tried to keep one p-r-r with the ratchet screw driver ahead of my chum who used to work in an automobile office. That's probably why I made a dozen mistakes. But I could hear her try to catch up with my p-r-r-s . . . and she did!

The foreman walks up and down the room all the time, watching our work and showing us how to do it a little better. He is a long, tall man who's lived in Texas and has kept the drawl. Every now and then he goes to the room next to this one to take a smoke but he's never had more than a puff without hearing the wrong kind of noise from a screw driver and having to come in again.

He knows by the noise whether you are taking a screw in or out, whether you are pressing down too hard or not hard enough and at what angle you're holding the screw driver! Also, he can tell by one or two "p-r-r-s" how long it will take you to do fifty blocks. . . .

Today we were graduated from our training class and assigned to parts of the factory. We are still "in training" but there's quite a difference. This week we were paid a learner's rate per hour for the time we spent in training, but next week we'll be paid according to what we do. I have explained that there is a basic pay per hour. For any pieces you do above a predetermined number you are paid extra, according to the "job." A job is an assignment of work . . . 500 brackets to be assembled, for example. One person does only one operation, though this may entail several parts.

But there is more than a financial difference in our status now. Before today, we have done nothing that will actually be used in aircraft . . . all of it was "practice" and the same material used over again by the next class. But now what we do will go to war. There is no one around to tell us six or seven times how to do something either. . . . I found that out before noon today!

My first actual piece of war work started at 7 minutes past 11. The foreman assigned me to a table and said: "Blow the metal chips off these parts." That may sound like Greek to you. Well, it did to me, too. Blow them off . . . you mean just BLOW them off? In the box were about 500 metal gadgets. The nearest description I can give you is that they looked a little like the thing a typewriter ribbon is wound on, only they were more involved. Just as I was trying to figure out how I'd have enough breath to blow metal chips off all those things, I saw a hose attached to the table . . . and of course it was full of compressed air. It looked very simple to press the button and blow off the chips. But the first blast of air blew the gadget right out of my hand! And then somebody walking by said, "Hey, stop blowing that grease out here!" So I learned to hold the hose down. Then a foreman . . . there are several here . . . said don't be so DAINTY . . . take a fistful and BLOW! . . .

. . . I don't want to give you the impression that people who work in a war production factory are all nice and sweet and patriotic, any more than you must think that all soldiers are brave. Money has much to do with how hard people work in a factory, but I honestly think there is an INCREASE in the spirit determined to win this war.

Not a day passes but you'll hear somebody say to a worker who seems to be slowing down, "There's a war on, you know!"

The foreman of each floor gets a monthly quota for production, which he breaks down into weeks and days or nights. At the present time, our factory is two weeks ahead of schedule, but since war doesn't run on schedule, that is not too comfortable a margin.

In spite of the terrific pressure to get things out in a hurry, the first demand is for quality. Everything must be EXACTLY right.

Tonight I got a much deserved call down for drilling a hole in the wrong place. The set-up man gave me a little metal gadget into which I was to drill seven holes. As usual, there was a fixture to hold the gadget and to indicate where the holes were to go. But unfortunately, the top of the fixture had a pattern for two holes, and I was to drill only one of them. An hour later I began to wonder WHICH one, and of course I'd been drilling the wrong hole.

I said to the man, "Well, maybe these pieces of metal can be used for something else . . ." and he said, "yeah, maybe the Army can use 'em for dust cloths."

"You are with the 'point' of an infantry battalion . . ."

A WALK TO SAN STEFANO

July 31, 1943
Sicily

STAFF SERGEANT JACK FOISIE

*I*n late 1942, American forces invaded North Africa to join the British troops *fighting Germany's Afrika Korps. By May 1943, the Allies controlled the region, and by mid-July were ready to launch an invasion of Italy from it. The first step was to land 250,000 British and American troops on the island of Sicily.*

Foisie, a reporter for the San Francisco Chronicle *before the war, wrote this dispatch for* Stars and Stripes *and his old paper.*

It is not a pleasant walk, these last four miles to San Stefano.

You are with the "point" of Company G of an infantry battalion advancing up the road. You are about two hours behind the retreating Germans. You think another company has come down from the hills and beat you into town, but you're not quite sure.

You march in extended order and you keep looking for snipers in the hills and mines under your feet. Your eyes soon get tired from looking, first at the hills and then at your road.

You come to a blown-out bridge with combat engineers already at work carving out a bypass. There is a sign that reads: "Mines cleared four feet on side." You stay exactly along the middle. After passing the curve you hear a muffled explosion behind you. You run back and find that the rear end of a bulldozer has run off the four-foot safety limit. It was a pressure-type S-mine, designed upon contact to hop up out of the ground and explode at about three feet, throwing out a can full of silverball shrapnel. The bulldozer pretty well pinned down the shrapnel, but one ball did go through an engineer's leg.

A jeep passes you by. It is the first vehicle through the bypass and you think he is going to get into town before you. You curse the mobility of some of the army.

Then comes the second blown-out bridge. Combat engineers are here, too, but they have only been able to clear a footpath. The jeep driver is a daring fellow and he seems determined to beat us into San Stefano; he is retracing his way to where he can reach the railroad tracks that parallel the road. He does and speeds up the tracks. You again curse his mobility.

The jeep enters a tunnel and there is a dull explosion. The medics start to rush down to the tunnel and someone says, "Hey, you'd better let me go first." An engineer with a mine detector begins sweeping a path for them. You are suddenly glad you are a walking infantryman, but only for a minute.

The sun is hot, the straps of the light field pack are cutting through the sweat-soaked wool shirt, and the blue Mediterranean down from the curving highway is tantalizing. You ask for a dry match, since everything in your pockets is wet with sweat. In return, you pass the cigarettes, and they clean out your last pack. On the bend in the road are what look like small shell craters in the asphalt surface. You wonder who did the nice shooting, and then a sergeant says, "Watch out for those soft spots, they're anti-tank mines." An engineer comes along and probes with a bayonet, and it strikes metal.

"Take it easy, Joe," says the guy who is working with him, "those things are touchy." The two get down on their knees around the mine, and from a few yards off it looks like they're shooting craps. If you're a damn fool you come closer, and, looking over their shoulders, you see them digging out the dirt around the mine to see if it's boobied—that is, if it will explode when lifted up. Satisfied, the engineer called Joe lifts out the German Teller mine, and the other guy unscrews the cap and defuses it. "Now it's completely harmless," says Joe, and he lays it down very carefully away off the road. There is soon a pile of these Teller mines; each one looks just like an oversize discus.

You've been walking for over an hour now, and white lines of salt begin to appear in your sweat-soaked shirt. Your canteen is still half full, but the water is warmer than luke-warm. There is a spout of cool mountain water emptying into a cement basin in the Q shade of a grove of big-leaved trees. "How about a 40-minute break?" O.K., but you'd better jump from the asphalt to the bank, those road shoulders are always mined.

So you leap over the soft shoulder and land on the bank, lean back and relax. The weight of the pack leaves your shoulder. The grass is cool and soft. You stretch out flat—and that saves your life. The guy who had been walking in front of you, the fellow carrying the Browning automatic rifle, had been the first to refill his canteen from that spout of cold water, and the first to find that the Germans had put a ring of S-mines around the foot of the basin.

Someone else shoulders the Browning automatic rifle, a medic is left with the wounded man, and a guard is placed near the fountain, and you hike on toward San Stefano. You are still thirsty.

The town has been in sight for some time, but when you get around the last bend there is still a long elbow with the bridge across the river, San Stefano at its joint. The bridge, of course, is blown. One complete section in the middle is just a mass of crumbled bricks in the river bed. It's like a freckled-faced boy with a missing front tooth.

You are tempted to take to the railroad tracks that go straight across into town, but then you remember the jeep in the tunnel. This is good country for snipers and you look for them. The commander of the "point" talks in his walkie-talkie to the company commander, who is perhaps a half mile behind with the main body of men. It is decided to reconnoiter the roadblock at the entrance to the bridge. Two men are selected and you are not one of them. A halt is called while they go ahead. They walk on opposite sides of the road, one 25 yards in front of the other. They disappear around the bend. Two minutes of silence will mean that the roadblock is undefended.

There is a sputtering crackle and then several more in rapid succession. The command "Disperse left and right!" is given. The rifles are no longer on the shoulder; you hear the click of the safety on the rifle of the man next to you. There are several more crackles. Your steel helmet no longer feels heavy; you feel like ducking behind a tree but the others are only dispersed, looking with their eyes and ears. There is another crackle; it seems to come from the direction of the bridge. One of the scouts comes running back.

"Mines. All around the bridge. A patrol from another company coming down from the hills ran into them. Got quite a few. They need a doctor."

"Doctor up front! Pass the word back," orders the point commander. The word is passed back: "Doctor up front!" There is more talk on the walkie-talkie; it is decided to try and get the doc through; the engineers will be up shortly, but there is no time.

It is decided that the doctor and a platoon will attempt to make their way around the roadblock, through the barbed wire entanglements, cut across the river bed 100 yards up from the bridge, scale the opposite bank and then work back around to the bridge.

"Mortar platoon up forward! Pass the word back," orders the point commander. The mortar platoon files past with solemn faces, eyes alert for mines and snipers. The doctor is put in the center and they space out 25 feet between each man. They climb the hill and enter a mushroom growth of pillboxes. They pass a sign which when translated reads: "This is a military zone."

You are the last man in that file and this is one time when you are not anxious to pass anyone. The file is stopped by the first of the barbwire.

Where there is barbwire there are often mines. "A guy only lives once," smiles the leader, and steps forward with the wirecutters. The wires part and the file moves forward. Now you are descending into the river bed and now you are stepping from rock to rock, carefully avoiding soft sand for that is a good place to hide mines.

You reach the other bank and there on the ledge above you is an old Italian civilian, all smiles and a weird mixture of languages. He is wearing sandals made out of rubber tires. Naturally, he announces right off that he lived 23 years in Brooklyn.

Okay, Joe, tell us about that later. What we want to know, can you lead us around the minefield. Yes, he says, he knows all about the minefield. He saw the Germans plant them. Yes, he will show us the way, only he would prefer that someone went in front of him. There is a few minutes of debate on who is going to lead and the old Italian man finally consents for a pack of cigarettes.

He leads you along the bank until you come onto the wounded and the dead about 50 yards in front of you. You were taking the same path that these men had taken.

"For God's sake, get back," screams one of the wounded men. He is lying on the ground in his shorts. They are red with blood. His back is toward you. It has been raked with shrapnel.

There is another man, unwounded, attempting to make the wounded man comfortable. The unwounded man dare not move for fear of setting off another mine. "Get out of here," he shouts, "don't make it any worse than it is." There are other men lying where they fell.

The file backs up. This time the Italian who once lived in Brooklyn is ordered to take us up over the ridge and then swing around to the road. The old man explains that he is very old and cannot make the hill. There is nothing to do but go on without a guide. Shoot the old man, you say? No, remember that he was in the lead and would have been the first to go. Blame it on an old man's mind.

You climb the terraced ridge and then turn toward the road. Your eyes are glued on that soil. You follow in the exact footsteps of the man in front of you. The man in the lead—perhaps he follows in the footsteps of God. Every snap of a twig, each rattle of a pebble makes you twitch and shudder. If you think at all, it is about what you said in your last letter home.

The leader reaches the bank overlooking the road. He jumps and lands on the firm asphalt surface. He is safe. The next one jumps. He is safe. Each one jumps and is safe. You jump and you are safe.

The doctor walks in the middle of the road down to the bridge. There is a cart at the end of the bridge. It was the touching of this cart that set off the first of the mines. The doctor goes to work.

The mortar platoon starts up the last hill into town. You stay in the middle of the road. There is a dead German lying on the side of the road. Perhaps, you say to yourself, he was killed by one of his own mines.

You enter San Stefano. The townspeople, pathetically friendly, come out to greet you. You ask in your best Brooklynese Italian if there are any snipers in town. The people say there are not. You ask if there are any booby traps. The people say there are none.

You pass the back side of your sweaty wrist across your eyes. You no longer look at where you are about to step.

"After my father, he came next . . ."

THE DEATH OF CAPTAIN WASKOW

January 10, 1944
At the Front Lines, near San Pietro, Italy

ERNIE PYLE

*D*avid Nichols, who has edited two collections of Pyle's work, calls this famous elegy Pyle's "best piece ever." The Washington Daily News *devoted its entire front page to the piece.*

Pyle himself was killed by a Japanese sniper on a small island off Okinawa in April 1945.

In this war I have known a lot of officers who were loved and respected by the soldiers under them. But never have I crossed the trail of any man as beloved as Captain Henry T. Waskow, of Belton, Texas.

Captain Waskow was a company commander in the Thirty-sixth Division. He had led his company since long before it left the States. He was very young, only in his middle twenties, but he carried in him a sincerity and a gentleness that made people want to be guided by him.

"After my father, he came next," a sergeant told me.

"He always looked after us," a soldier said. "He'd go to bat for us every time."

"I've never known him to do anything unfair," another said.

I was at the foot of the mule trail the night they brought Captain Waskow down. The moon was nearly full, and you could see far up the trail, and even partway across the valley below.

Dead men had been coming down the mountain all evening, lashed onto the backs of mules. They came lying belly-down across the wooden pack-saddles, their heads hanging down on one side, their stiffened legs sticking out awkwardly from the other, bobbing up and down as the mules walked.

The Italian mule skinners were afraid to walk beside dead men, so Americans had to lead the mules down that night. Even the Americans were reluctant to unlash and lift off the bodies when they got to the bottom, so an officer had to do it himself and ask others to help.

I don't know who that first one was. You feel small in the presence of dead men, and you don't ask silly questions.

They slid him down from the mule, and stood him on his feet for a moment. In the half-light he might have been merely a sick man standing there leaning on the others. Then they laid him on the ground in the shadow of the stone wall alongside the road. We left him there beside the road, that first one, and we all went back into the cowshed and sat on water cans or lay on the straw, waiting for the next batch of mules.

Somebody said the dead soldier had been dead for four days, and then nobody said anything more about it. We talked soldier talk for an hour or more; the dead man lay all alone, outside in the shadow of the wall.

Then a soldier came into the cowshed and said there were some more bodies outside. We went out into the road. Four mules stood there in the moonlight, in the road where the trail came down off the mountain. The soldiers who led them stood there waiting.

"This one is Captain Waskow," one of them said quietly.

Two men unlashed his body from the mule and lifted it off and laid it in the shadow beside the stone wall. Other men took the other bodies off. Finally, there were five lying end to end in a long row. You don't cover up dead men in the combat zones. They just lie there in the shadows until somebody comes after them.

The unburdened mules moved off to their olive grove. The men in the road seemed reluctant to leave. They stood around, and gradually I could sense them moving, one by one, close to Captain Waskow's body. Not so much to look, I think, as to say something in finality to him and to themselves. I stood close by and I could hear.

One soldier came and looked down, and he said out loud, "God damn it!"

That's all he said, and then he walked away.

Another one came, and he said, "God damn it to hell anyway!" He looked down for a few last moments and then turned and left.

Another man came. I think he was an officer. It was hard to tell officers from men in the dim light, for everybody was bearded and grimy. The man looked down into the dead captain's face and then spoke directly to him, as though he were alive, "I'm sorry, old man."

Then a soldier came and stood beside the officer and bent over, and he too spoke to his dead captain, not in a whisper but awfully tenderly, and he said, "I sure am sorry, sir."

Then the first man squatted down, and he reached down and took the captain's hand, and he sat there for a full five minutes holding the dead hand in his own and looking intently into the dead face. And he never uttered a sound all the time he sat there.

Finally he put the hand down. He reached over and gently straightened the points of the captain's shirt collar, and then he sort of rearranged the tattered edges of the uniform around the wound, and then he got up and walked away down the road in the moonlight, all alone.

The rest of us went back into the cowshed, leaving the five dead men lying in a line end to end in the shadow of the low stone wall. We lay down on the straw in the cowshed, and pretty soon we were all asleep.

"It seemed like the whole world exploded."

D-DAY

June 6, 1944
Normandy, France

LIEUTENANT ROBERT EDLIN

*W*hile the Allies advanced northward through Italy, they also prepared to descend southward from Britain and invade German-occupied France. After many debates about where and when to invade, the plan was set: land on the beaches of Normandy on June 6.

Technician fourth grade Andrew A. Rooney, U.S. Army Infantry—better known today as Andy Rooney, the curmudgeonly television commentator—saw D-Day as a reporter for the army newspaper, Stars and Stripes: "There have been only a handful of days since the beginning of time," he later wrote in a memoir, My War, "on which *the direction the world was taking has been changed for the better in one twenty-four-hour period by an act of man. June 6, 1944, was one of them. What the Americans, the British, and the Canadians were trying to do was get back a whole continent that had been taken from its rightful owners and whose citizens had been taken captive by Adolf Hitler's German army. It was one of the most monumentally unselfish things one group of people ever did for another. . . .*

"If you're young, and not really clear what D-Day was, let me tell you, it was a day unlike any other. I landed on Utah Beach several days after the first assault waves went in on the morning of June 6. I am uncertain of the day. When I came in, row on row of dead American soldiers were laid out on the sand just above the high-tide mark where the beach turned into weedy clumps of grass. They were covered with olive-drab blankets, just their feet sticking out at the bottom, their GI boots sticking out. I remember their boots—all the same on such different boys. They had been dead several days and some of them had been killed, not on the beaches, but inland.

"No one can tell the whole story of D-Day because no one knows it. Each of the 60,000 men who waded ashore that day knew a little part of the story too well. To them, the landing looked like a catastrophe. Each knew a friend shot through the throat, shot through the knee. Each knew the names of five hanging dead on the barbed wire in the water twenty yards offshore, three who lay unattended on the stony beach as the blood drained from holes in their bodies. They saw whole tank crews drowned when the tanks rumbled off the ramps of their landing craft and dropped into twenty feet of water. . . .

"Across the Channel in Allied headquarters in England, the war directors, remote from the details of tragedy, were exultant. They saw no blood, no dead, no dying. From the statisticians' point of view, the invasion was a great success. The statisticians were right. They always are—that's the damned thing about it."

One of the sixty thousand men, Lieutenant Robert Edlin, told his story to historian Gerald Astor, author of June 6, 1944: The Voices of D-Day. *Edlin was a platoon leader of the Second Ranger Battalion's Company A, which landed on the Dog Green sector of Omaha Beach, site of the invasion's fiercest fighting. His experience proves Rooney right, as do the statistics: by the end of the first week the Allies had landed more than 325,000 troops, 100,000 tons of supplies, and 50,000 vehicles.*

It seemed like the whole world exploded. There was gunfire from battleships, destroyers, and cruisers. The bombers were still hitting the beaches. As we went in, we could see small craft from the 116th Infantry that had gone in ahead, sunk. There were bodies bobbing in the water, even out three or four miles.

Then there was a deep silence. All the gunfire had lifted; the Navy was giving way to let the troops get on the beaches. The sun was just coming up over the Frenchy coast. I saw a bird—a seagull, I guess—fly across the front of the boat, just like life was going on as normal.

Then there came something like a peppering of hail, heavy hail on the front of the ramp. I realized it was enemy machine-gun fire. All hell broke loose from the other side—German artillery, rockets and mortars. It was just unbelievable that anyone could have lived under that barrage.

Our assault boat hit a sandbar. I looked over the ramp and we were at least seventy-five yards from the shore, and we had hoped for a dry landing. I told the coxswain, "Try to get in further." He screamed he couldn't. That British seaman had all the guts in the world but couldn't get off the sandbar. I told him to drop the ramp or we were going to die right there.

We had been trained for years not to go off the front of the ramp, because the boat might get rocked by a wave and run over you. So we went off the sides. I looked to my right and saw a B Company boat next to us with Lt. Bob Fitzsimmons, a good friend, take a direct hit on the ramp from a mortar or mine. I thought, there goes half of B Company.

It was cold, miserably cold, even though it was June. The water temperature was probably forty-five or fifty degrees. It was up to my shoulders when I went in, and I saw men sinking all about me. I tried to grab a couple, but my job was to get on in and get to the guns. There were bodies from the 116th floating everywhere. They were facedown in the water with packs still on their backs. They had inflated their life jackets. Fortunately, most of the Rangers did not inflate theirs or they also might have turned over and drowned.

I began to run with my rifle in front of me. I went directly across the beach to try to get to the seaway. In front of me was part of the 116th Infantry, pinned down and lying behind beach obstacles. They hadn't made it to the seaway. I kept screaming at them, "You have to get up and go! You gotta get up and go!" But they didn't. They were worn out and defeated completely. There wasn't any time to help them.

I continued across the beach. There were mines and obstacles all up and down the beach. The air corps had missed it entirely. There were no shell holes in which to take cover. The mines had not been detonated. Absolutely nothing that had been planned for that part of the beach had worked. I knew that Vierville-sur-Mer was going to be a hellhole, and it was.

When I was about twenty yards from the seaway I was hit by what I assume was a sniper bullet. It shattered and broke my right leg. I thought, well, I've got a Purple Heart. I fell, and as I did, it was like a searing hot poker rammed into my leg. My rifle fell ten feet or so in front of me. I crawled forward to get to it, picked it up, and as I rose on my left leg, another burst of I think machine gun fire tore the muscles out of that leg, knocking me down again.

I lay there for seconds, looked ahead, and saw several Rangers lying there. One was Butch Bladorn from Wisconsin. I screamed at Butch, "Get up and run!" Butch, a big, powerful man, just looked back and said, "I can't." I got up and hobbled towards him. I was going to kick him in the ass and get him off the beach. He was lying on his stomach, his face in the sand. Then I saw the blood coming out of his back. I realized he had been hit in the stomach and the bullet had come out his spine and he was completely immobilized. Even then I was sorry for screaming at him but I didn't have time to stop and help him. I thought, well, that's the end of Butch. Fortunately, it wasn't. He became a farmer in Wisconsin.

As I moved forward, I hobbled. After you've been hit by gunfire, your legs stiffen up, not all at once but slowly. The pain was indescribable. I fell to my hands and knees and tried to crawl forwards. I managed a few yards, then blacked out for several minutes. When I came to, I saw Sgt. Bill Klaus. He was up to the seaway. When he saw my predicament, he crawled back to me under heavy rifle and mortar fire and dragged me up to the cover of the wall.

Klaus had also been wounded in one leg, and a medic gave him a shot of morphine. The medic did the same for me. My mental state was such that I told him to shoot it directly into my left leg, as that was the one hurting the most. He reminded me that if I took it in the ass or the arm it would get to the leg. I told him to give me a second shot because I was hit in the other leg. He didn't.

There were some Rangers gathered at the seaway—Sgt. William Courtney, Pvt. William Dreher, Garfield Ray, Gabby Hart, Sgt. Charles Berg. I yelled at them, "You have to get off of here! You have to get up and get the guns!" They were gone immediately.

My platoon sergeant, Bill White, an ex-jockey whom we called Whitey, took charge. He was small, very active, and very courageous. He led what few men were left of the first platoon and started up the cliffs. I crawled and staggered forward as far as I could to some cover in the bushes behind a villa. There was a round stone well with a bucket and handle that turned the rope. It was so inviting. I was alone and I wanted that water so bad. But years of training told me it was booby-trapped.

I looked up at the top of the cliffs and thought, I can't make it on this leg. Where was everyone? Had they all quit? Then I heard Dreher yelling, "Come on up. These trenches are empty." Then Kraut burp guns cut loose. I thought, oh God, I can't get there! I heard an American tommy gun, and Courtney shouted, "Damn it, Dreher! They're empty now."

There was more German small-arms fire and German grenades popping. I could hear Whitey yelling, "Cover me!" I heard Garfield Ray's BAR [Browning automatic rifle] talking American. Then there was silence.

Now, I thought, where are the 5th Rangers? I turned and I couldn't walk or even hobble anymore. I crawled back to the beach. I saw 5th Rangers coming through the smoke of a burning LST that had been hit by artillery fire. Col. Schneider had seen the slaughter on the beaches and used his experience with the Rangers in Africa, Sicily, and Anzio. He used the smoke as a screen and moved in behind it, saving the 5th Ranger Battalion many casualties.

My years of training told me there would be a counterattack. I gathered the wounded by the seaway and told them to arm themselves as well as possible. I said if the Germans come we are either going to be captured or die on the beach, but we might as well take the Germans with us. I know it sounds ridiculous, but ten or fifteen Rangers lay there, facing up to the cliffs, praying that Sgt. White, Courtney, Dreher, and the 5th Ranger Battalion would get to the guns. Our fight was over unless the Germans counterattacked.

I looked back to the sea. There was nothing. There were no reinforcements. I thought the invasion had been abandoned. We would be dead or prisoners soon. Everyone had withdrawn and left us. Well, we had tried. Some guy crawled over and told me he was a colonel from the 29th Infantry Division. He said for us to relax, we were going to be okay. D, E, and F Companies were on the Pointe. The guns had been destroyed. A and B Companies and the 5th Rangers were inland. The 29th and 1st Divisions were getting off the beaches.

This colonel looked at me and said, "You've done your job." I answered, "How? By using up two rounds of German ammo on my legs?" Despite the awful pain, I hoped to catch up with the platoon the next day.

"I refuse to accept your order.
You can court-martial me."

GO FOR BROKE!

October 29, 1944
Near Hill 617, Biffontaine, France

STAN NAKAMOTO

*A*s noted above, the 100th/442nd Regimental Combat Team earned more decorations than any military unit in United States history. The unit was nicknamed the Go for Broke Brigade and the Purple Heart Battalion. They were Japanese Americans, many of whom had relatives in American concentration camps such as Manzanar in California and Thule Lake in Washington State.

Their most dramatic effort was the rescue, after five days and nights of fighting, of 275 Texan soldiers who were trapped at the top of a hill, surrounded by Germans. The 100th/442nd suffered more than eight hundred casualties in the effort. It might have been worse, if not for officers such as Lieutenant Allan Ohata. Despite the conversation described here to historian Lyn Crost, author of Honor by Fire, Ohata was not demoted. He was speaking to Major General John E. Dahlquist, commander of the 36th Division.

DAHLQUIST: "How many men do you have here?"

OHATA: "One company, sir."

DAHLQUIST: "That's enough. Here's what you do. We've got to get onto that hill and across it. You get all the men you have and charge straight up that hill with fixed bayonets. That's the only way we can get the Krauts off it."

OHATA: "You want my men to charge up that hill, sir?"

DAHLQUIST: "Straight up. It's the quickest way. There's a battalion going to die if we don't get to it."

OHATA: "You realize what this means for our men, sir? They'll be slaughtered climbing a hill in the face of heavy fire in full daylight."

DAHLQUIST: "It's got to be done."

OHATA: "I refuse to accept your order. You can court-martial me. You can strip me of my rank and decorations but I refuse to accept your order."

DAHLQUIST: "You *refuse?* I'm *ordering* you: take your men and make a bayonet charge up that hill and get those Krauts off it quick."

OHATA: "We'll get them off it *our* way and try to save as many of our men as possible." '

"There is such a thing as dying decently, but not on Iwo."

IWO JIMA

February 1945

EDGAR L. JONES

Thousands of U.S. Marines landed on Iwo Jima on February 19. Four days later they achieved the famous flag-raising on Mt. Suribachi. After three more weeks of fighting they won the entire island.

Jones was reporting for The Atlantic Monthly. *(His reference to D-Day, a standard military designation, is the date of the Iwo Jima landing, not the better known "D-Day" of the Normandy invasion.)*

I went in with a large group of Fourth Division Marines. . . . The Japanese were lobbing shells into supply dumps, ammunition depots, communication centers, and every other place where they saw men or machinery concentrated. No man on the beach felt secure. The Americans held about one square mile of low ground at that point, most of which I toured. Everywhere men were struggling: to keep landing craft from submerging, to dig roads in the deep sand, to push mired trucks onto solid ground, to haul equipment to sheltered locations, and to fight nature for the chance to get on with the battle. And all the time the Japanese shells whined down and tore into sand and flesh with indiscriminate fury.

No one who was at Iwo can analyze the battle objectively. The carnage was so horrifying that the blood and agony of the struggle saturated one's mind, dismally coloring all thought. Iwo was unlike any war I had ever seen. It was a fight to the finish, with no man asking for quarter until he was dead. Of the nearly 20,000 American casualties, approximately two thirds were wounded, but all except a few score of the 20,000 Japanese died where they fell. There is such a thing as dying decently, but not on Iwo. I do not believe anything practical can be achieved by describing men blown apart. Veterans of two and three years of war in the Pacific were sickened. An estimated 26,000 men died in eight square miles of fighting. There were 5000 dead and wounded American and Japanese soldiers for every square mile.

I returned to Iwo on D Day plus six, seven and eight. By that time the Marines had captured territory where Japanese had lain dead in the hot sun for more than a week. I crawled into pillboxes burned out by flame-throwers, and into deep caves where the Japanese had been burning their own dead to conceal the extent of their losses. I was torturing myself to look at the results of war, because I think it is essential for civilians occasionally to hold their noses and see what is going on.

The sight on Iwo which I could not force myself to see again was the section of the beach allotted for an American cemetery. . . . On the afternoon I walked by, there was half an acre of dead Marines stretched out so close together that they blanketed the beach for two hundred yards. The stench was overpowering. . . . The smell of one's countrymen rotting in the sun is a lasting impression.

"I loved him so much."

THE DEATH OF ROOSEVELT

April 12–13, 1945
Warm Springs, Georgia; Paris, France; London, England

MERRIMAN SMITH, JANET FLANNER,
AND MOLLIE PANTER-DOWNES

F ranklin Delano Roosevelt had been president more than twelve years. Many *Americans—especially those of military age—could remember no other.*

His death made people feel they were living a Bible story. Like Moses, who had led his people out of Egypt but died before reaching the Promised Land, Roosevelt had guided the country through World War II until victory in Europe was certain, only to die just before it was officially won.

The sudden news also echoed the tragedy of Lincoln's assassination, eighty years earlier almost to the day, just after the Civil War's end had been assured but before victory could be declared. And although Roosevelt died of natural causes—a stroke, at his vacation home in Warm Springs, Georgia—for most Americans the news was as shocking as Lincoln's death had been to an earlier generation. Roosevelt was just a few months into his fourth term as president, having been reelected by a wide margin the previous November. The general public was not fully aware that he was paralyzed by polio, because the news media reported the fact gingerly, and never photographed him in his wheelchair. When he faked short walks for the newsreel cameras, by holding the arms of men on either side of him, the reporters went along with the ruse. The day after his death, many newspapers reprinted the famous elegy to Lincoln, "O Captain! My Captain!" by Walt Whitman:

> *O Captain! my Captain! our fearful trip is done,*
> *The ship has weather'd every rack, the prize we sought is won,*
> *The port is near, the bells I hear, the people all exulting,*
> *While follow eyes the steady keel, the vessel grim and daring;*
> *But O heart! heart! heart!*
> *O the bleeding drops of red,*
> *Where on the deck my Captain lies,*
> *Fallen cold and dead. . . .*

Merriman Smith was a United Press reporter on the funeral train on April 13, the day after Roosevelt died.

The same day, Janet Flanner, who wrote the "Letter from Paris" for The New Yorker magazine, and Mollie Panter-Downes, who contributed the "Letter from London," saw the effects of the news overseas, where the role of the United States in the war made this American event truly international.

EN ROUTE TO WASHINGTON

Franklin Delano Roosevelt was borne across the hushed Southern countryside today on the long, last journey to the White House and Hyde Park. The eleven-coach funeral train made a slow trip northward from Warm Springs, Ga., where he died Thursday afternoon . . .

The funeral procession from the "Little White House," where the President died, was a pageant of grief. Mr. Roosevelt made his last trip through the grounds he loved so well in a black hearse. An Army honor guard of 2,000 troops marched before it, kicking up red clay dust on the winding country road to the village. Behind the hearse rode Mrs. Roosevelt, sitting stiffly upright. Fala, the President's Scottie, sat quietly at her feet, as if aware that something was wrong. At the end of the thirty-five-minute procession from the cottage to the terminal, Mrs. Roosevelt's eyes were misty. She was fighting hard to retain composure.

. . . The patients [of the Warm Springs Foundation] with whom the President shared such a deep bond were not forgotten. It was Mr. Roosevelt's custom, when he ended each Warm Springs visit, to give a brief call and wave of the hand to those gathered before the foundation's main dormitory. Today, the hearse came to a full stop before the crowded porch. In mute grief, the patients watched. Two hours before the faint beat of drums signaled its approach, some had hobbled out to wait. Some were wheeled out. To them, the President was a magnificent inspiration.

A thirteen-year-old, Jay Fribourg, said: "I loved him so much." He clenched his teeth as he held back the tears. Chief Petty Officer Graham Jackson, a Georgia Negro, a favorite of Mr. Roosevelt, stepped out from the circle with the accordion which he had played often for the President. As the procession approached he began the plaintive strains of "Going Home." Then he played "Nearer My God to Thee." There was scarcely a dry eye.

. . . Farther down the road, troops—overseas veterans—wept openly as [the hearse] passed. When it reached the tiny station, the troops moved into company front and presented arms. The townspeople bared their heads and watched the funeral party board the train. They stood silently as the train gathered speed and rumbled northward. Then it rounded a bend, and all that could be seen was a thin trail of black smoke. Still they stood, with the scorching sun beating down on the row of modest stores that lined the street. Then, finally, they began to leave.

PARIS

Friday morning, when the news was first known here, French men and women approached the groups of Americans in uniform standing on the street corners and in public places and, with a mixture of formality and obvious emotion, expressed their sorrow, sometimes in French, sometimes in broken English. On the Rue Scribe, a sergeant in a jeep held up traffic while he received the condolences of two elderly French spinsters. In the Jardin des Tuileries, an American woman was stopped beneath the white-flowering chestnut trees by a French schoolboy who, with trembling voice, spoke for his father, a dead Army officer, to express his father's love for the dead president.

LONDON

Because the British have been prepared for the last few weeks to receive the good news which obviously nothing could spoil, the bad news knocked them sideways. President Roosevelt's death came as a stupefying shock, even to those Britons whose ideas of the peace do not run much beyond the purely personal ones of getting their children home again, a roof back over their heads, a little car back on the road, and plenty of consumer goods in the shops. To the more internationally minded, the news seemed a crushing disaster. People stood in the streets staring blankly at the first incredible newspaper headlines which appeared to have suddenly remodelled the architecture of the world. . . . On that first shocked day after the President's death, one frequently heard the observation that at this juncture even Mr. Churchill could almost have been better spared than Mr. Roosevelt. It was a strange remark to hear in England, but it was a perfectly sincere one. . . . They glanced at the adjoining headlines, which said that Allied troops were reported only fifteen miles from Berlin, with ironically little apparent emotion and as though Berlin were a village on another planet. . . . No Briton has forgotten those dark times when the only cheerful thing seemed to be Mr. Roosevelt's voice coming over the radio late at night, and no Briton will ever forget. Elderly people with long memories say that they remember no such dazed outburst of general grief over the death of any other foreign statesman, or for that matter, over many English ones. At the end of that sad Friday, innumerable people cancelled whatever plans they had made for the evening and stayed quietly at home because they had no heart for going out. It is all very different from what every one of us had expected the last days of the European War to be like.

*"An excellent chance to save
the peace of the world . . ."*

THE UNITED NATIONS

April 13–June 23, 1945
Washington, D.C., and San Francisco

SENATOR ARTHUR H. VANDENBERG

*A*t first, the death of FDR threatened to derail plans to create the United Nations at a conference in San Francisco. But President Harry S. Truman proved *to be immediately aware of the importance of the U.N. And, as New Yorker writer E. B. White eulogized, "It seems to us that the President's death, instead of weakening the structure at San Francisco, will strengthen it. Death almost always reactivates the household in some curious manner, and the death of Franklin Roosevelt recalls and refurnishes the terrible emotions and the bright meaning of the times he brought us through . . . He now personifies, as no one else could, all the American dead—those whose absence we shall soon attempt to justify. The President was always a lover of strategy; he even died strategically. . . . He will arrive in San Francisco quite on schedule, and in hundredfold capacity, to inspire the nations that he named United."*

Eyewitness Arthur Vandenberg, a leading Republican senator with aspirations to the presidency in 1940, had been an isolationist before Pearl Harbor. Eventually he reversed his views, and after the war helped to establish the U.N. Charter, the Marshall Plan, and NATO, and to move them through the Senate at a time when America was unsure about inheriting from the European powers a role in world affairs that is taken for granted today.

APRIL 13, 1945

. . . With 15 others, I had lunch with Truman this noon. He told me he was not going to Frisco personally (as F.D.R. had intended to do) and that he expects to "leave Frisco to our Delegation." Unquestionably we will have greater freedom—but also greater responsibility.

I am puzzled. Stettinius is now Secretary of State in fact. Up to now he has been only the presidential messenger. He does not have the background and experience for such a job at such a critical time—altho he is a grand person with every good intention and high honesty of purpose. Now we have both an inexperienced President and an inexperienced Secretary (in re foreign affairs). . . .

But I liked the first decision Truman made—namely, that Frisco should go on. Senator Connally immediately prophesied, after F.D.R. died, that Frisco would be postponed. . . . Truman promptly stopped that mistake (which would have confessed to the world that there is an "indispensable man" who was bigger than America).

MAY 23, 1945

Yesterday our Sub-committee unanimously o.k.'ed the final Regional draft. This afternoon, the full Committee did the same. . . .

I am deeply impressed by what has happened. . . . At the outset many of the Nations were far, very far, apart. Our own Delegation was not wholly united. The subject itself was difficult—how to save legitimate regionalism (like Pan-Am) and yet not destroy the essential over-all authority of the International Organization. By hammering it out vis-a-vis, we have found an answer which satisfies practically everybody. In my view, that is the great hope for the new League itself. If we do nothing more than create a constant forum where nations must face each other and debate their differences and strive for common ground, we shall have done infinitely much. . . .

JUNE 23, 1945

We had our final meeting of the American Delegation this morning.

Now that we are at the end of our labors and our tensions are relaxed, I look back upon what I believe to be a remarkable performance not only by our Delegation but by the Conference as a whole. To have attained virtual unanimity under such complex circumstances is a little short of a miracle.

I think Stettinius has done a magnificent job. Without his "drive" we should have been here for two more months.

We have finished our job. I am proud of it. It has been the crowning privilege of my life to have been an author of the San Francisco Charter. It has an excellent chance to save the peace of the world if America and Russia can learn to live together and if Russia learns to keep her word.

"The mountains in the far distance
lit up as if it were daylight."

THE TRINITY TEST

July 16, 1945
Alamogordo, New Mexico

ROBERT KROHN

*V*ictory *in Europe had been won, but the Pacific war continued. The Allies feared they could end the war only by invading Japan. The tens of thousands of casualties suffered in battles on relatively small islands such as Tarawa, Iwo Jima, and*

Guadalcanal convinced civilian and military leaders that an invasion of Japan would lead to a long, bloody endgame.

The atom bomb offered those leaders a chance to limit the casualties to one side, and end the war quickly. But the bomb was only a theory when the war began. Building it required a rapid advance in our knowledge of nuclear fission, and the application of new theories to the assembly of a practical warhead.

The Manhattan Project collected some of the country's best physicists in a high-security compound in Los Alamos, New Mexico, and left them to solve the problems. "Trinity" was the name given to the first practical test of their work, at a site near—but not too near—Los Alamos.

Eyewitness Robert Krohn was one of the physicists working on the project. He told his story to filmmaker Jon Else, creator of The Day After Trinity. *Enrico Fermi, with whom Krohn watched the blast, had directed the efforts in Chicago a few years earlier that produced the first atomic chain reaction.*

To give you an idea of the Trinity site, picture a tower here at ground zero, and now off on the four points of the compass, photographic bunkers, little concrete shelters low in the ground, built to withstand the blast, having cameras in them so that this bomb could be photographed in all directions. A few miles to the south, a control station where the actual equipment to set off the bomb would be placed. A few key people would be there. And then about ten or eleven miles to the south was the base camp where we stayed, where we ate, etcetera. At the time of the shot most people were at base camp. I was there. The preparations for the bar-rage balloons had been made, and I had them flying, had to leave them, and I turned back to base camp just about an hour or so before the shot. At the base camp I sat next to Fermi. We sat down with our back towards the tower. We had been given electric welder's glass, which is very, very, dense, and a pair of dark goggles besides. We were told to put both in front of our eyes. And I was rather dismayed. I thought I was going to miss the whole thing. I turned to Fermi and said, "Look, do you really think we should have all this in front of our eyes, because this is very, very dense," and he said, "I think we better."

. . . And so I did put all that in front of my eyes, and nevertheless the mountains in the far distance lit up as if it were daylight. Just the most spectacular thing you could ever see. Immediately after the first light on the mountains to the south we got up and turned around and watched the rest of the bomb go off, the rest of the explosion I suppose you'd say, and then after a moment we took the welder's glass away and then a little bit later we took the dark glass away. Then pretty soon someone said, "Oh, oh, the blast is coming," because of course the blast would only come at the speed of sound. We didn't know what to expect. It wasn't all that much. It was a sharp blow in the pants leg and that was it. But remember, we were ten or eleven miles away.

There was a great deal of speculation as to what the [explosive] yield of the bomb was going to be. Everybody wanted to guess. And Fermi wanted to make the first estimate. He had torn up a piece of paper into little scraps about an inch square and he had them in his hand and just as the blast wave came along he dropped these pieces of paper. He observed the distance between where he had dropped them, the distance to the ground, how high he had them off the ground, and he made a quick calculation as to the yield. And it was remarkably good. The man was a genius.

. . . When the shot went off, even though we had very, very dark glasses in front of our eyes, the mountains lit up to the south just as if it were daylight. We felt the heat on the back of our necks. When we turned around there was this huge ball of fire going up into the air. It seemed like it was going up and up and up and then the light dropped in intensity but the cloud continued to go way up. There was enough daylight by then that we could watch the cloud go all the way up in the air. A very strange thing happened. There's a thing called a "dust devil" in this country, which is a very small tornado. It's caused by heat. It takes the dust and twirls it around. A dust devil usually goes maybe fifty or a hundred feet into the air. After the cloud disappeared, a dust devil appeared in the Trinity crater. It didn't move across the countryside like they usually do, it just stayed there, and it stayed there about an hour. . . . The heat was so intense there was no reason for it to move away. It was a very tall dust devil, it was probably 200 or so feet high.

"We were not prepared for the awesome sight . . ."

DROPPING THE ATOM BOMB

August 6, 1945
Hiroshima, Japan

COLONEL PAUL W. TIBBETS, JR.

*T*ibbets was the pilot of the Enola Gay, *a B-29 that had been specially fitted to carry the first atom bomb. The plane was named for his mother.*

The bomb leveled four square miles of Hiroshima, an important Japanese industrial city. More than 60,000 people were killed, and 100,000 injured. Permanent shadows were left on stone walls and sidewalks where moments before a person had stood. Illness and death from radiation exposure continued to occur for many years. After a second bomb was detonated over Nagasaki three days later, Japan surrendered.

A peace museum now stands at ground zero of the Hiroshima explosion.

As we approached the city, we strained our eyes to find the designated aiming point. From a distance of 10 miles, [bombardier Tom] Ferebee suddenly said, "Okay, I've got the bridge." He pointed dead ahead, where it was just becoming visible. [Navigator "Dutch"] Van Kirk, looking over his shoulders, agreed. "No question about it," he said, scanning an air-photo and comparing it with what he was seeing. The T-shaped bridge was easy to spot. Even though there were many other bridges in this sprawling city, there was no other bridge that even slightly resembled it.

Van Kirk's job was finished so he went back and sat down. . . . Now it was up to Tom and me. We were only 90 seconds from bomb release when I turned the plane over to him on autopilot.

"It's all yours," I told him, removing my hands from the controls and sliding back a bit in my seat in a not very successful effort to relax. My eyes were fixed on the center of the city, which shimmered in the early morning sunlight.

In the buildings and on the streets there were people, of course, but from six miles up they were invisible. To the men who fly the bombers, targets are inanimate, consisting of buildings, bridges, docks, factories, railroad yards. The tragic consequences to humanity are erased from one's thoughts in wartime because war itself is a human tragedy. Of course, one hopes that civilians will have the good sense to seek protection in bomb shelters. In the case of Hiroshima, I was to learn later that Eatherly's weather plane, over the city three-quarters of an hour before our arrival, had set off air raid sirens but, when nothing happened, [the sirens set off by] ours were ignored.

By this time, Tom Ferebee was pressing his left eye against the viewfinder of the bomb sight . . . "We're on target," he said, confirming that the sighting and release mechanism were synchronized, so that the drop would take place automatically at a precalculated point in our bomb run. At 17 seconds after 9:14 A.M., just 60 seconds before the scheduled bomb release, he flicked a toggle switch that activated a high-pitched radio tone. This tone, ominous under the circumstances, sounded in the headphones of the men aboard our plane and the two airplanes that were with us. . . .

A moment before, [co-pilot] Bob Lewis had made this notation in his informal log of the flight: "There will be a short intermission while we bomb our target."

Exactly one minute after it began, the radio tone ceased and at the same instant there was the sound of the pneumatic bomb-bay doors opening automatically. Out tumbled "Little Boy," a misnamed package of explosive force infinitely more devastating than any bomb or cluster of bombs ever dropped before. . . .

With the release of the bomb, the plane was instantly 9,000 pounds lighter. As a result, its nose leaped up sharply and I had to act quickly to execute the most important task of the flight: to put as much distance as possible between our plane and the point at which the bomb would explode. The 155 degree diving turn to the right, with its 60 degree bank, put a great strain on the airplane and its occupants. Bob Caron, in his tail-gunner's station, had a wild ride that he described as something like being the last man in a game of crack-the-whip.

When we completed the turn, we had lost 1,700 feet and were heading away from our target with engines at full power. . . . I was flying this biggest of all bombers as if it were a fighter plane.

Bob Lewis and I had slipped our dark glasses over our eyes, as I had directed the other crewmen to do, but we promptly discovered that they made it impossible to fly the plane through this difficult getaway maneuver because the instrument panel was blacked out. We pushed the glasses back on our foreheads in a what-the-hell manner, realizing that we would be flying away from the actual flash when it occurred. Ferebee, in the bombardier's position in the nose of the plane, became so fascinated with watching the bomb's free-fall that he forgot all about the glasses. . . .

For me, struggling with the controls, the 43 seconds from bomb release to explosion passed quickly. To some in the plane, it seemed an eternity. [Lieutenant Morris] Jeppson [one of the engineers whose duty was to arm the bomb with uranium] was quoted as saying that he had counted down the seconds in his mind, apparently too fast, and had the sickening feeling that the bomb was a dud.

Whatever our individual thoughts, it was a period of suspense. I was concentrating so intently on flying the airplane that the flash did not have the impact on my consciousness that one might think, even though it did light up the interior of the plane for a long instant. There was a startling sensation other than visual, however, that I remember quite vividly to this day. My teeth told me, more emphatically than my eyes, of the Hiroshima explosion. At the moment of the blast, there was a tingling sensation in my mouth and the very definite taste of lead upon my tongue. This, I was told later by scientists, was the result of electrolysis—an interaction between the fillings in my teeth and the radioactive forces that were loosed by the bomb.

"Little Boy" exploded at the preset altitude of 1,890 feet above the ground, but Bob Caron in the tail was the only one aboard our plane to see the incredible fireball that, in its atom-splitting fury, was a boiling furnace with an inner temperature calculated to be 100 million degrees Fahrenheit.

Caron, looking directly at the flash through glasses so dense that the sun penetrated but faintly, thought for a moment that he must have been blinded. Ferebee, without glasses but facing in the opposite direction from a relatively exposed position, felt as if a giant flashbulb had gone off a few feet from his face.

I continued my course from the target, awaiting the shock wave, which required almost a minute to reach us. . . . We must have been 9 miles from the point of the explosion when the shock wave reached us. This was the moment for which we had been bracing ourselves. Would the plane withstand the blow? The scientists were confident that it would, yet they admitted there were some aspects of the nuclear weapon's behavior about which they were not quite certain.

Caron, the only man aboard the plane with an immediate view of the awesome havoc we had created, tried to describe it to us. Suddenly he saw the shock wave approaching at the speed of sound—almost 1,100 feet a second. Condensing moisture from the heated air at the leading edge of the shock wave made it quite visible, just as one sees shimmering air rising from the ground on a hot, humid day.

Before Caron could warn us to brace ourselves, the wave struck the plane with violent force. Our B-29 trembled under the impact and I gripped the controls tightly to keep us in level flight. . . . At a news conference next day, Bob Lewis told reporters that it felt as if some giant had struck the plane with a telephone pole. . . .

Although Caron had told of a mushroom-shaped cloud, and said that it seemed to be "coming toward us," we were not prepared for the awesome sight that met our eyes as we turned for a heading that would take us alongside the burning, devastated city.

The giant purple mushroom, which the tail-gunner had described, had already risen to a height of 45,000 feet, 3 miles above our own altitude, and was still boiling upward like something terribly alive. It was a frightening sight, and even though we were several miles away, it gave the appearance of something that was about to engulf us.

Even more fearsome was the sight on the ground below. At the base of the cloud, fires were springing up everywhere amid a turbulent mass of smoke that had the appearance of bubbling hot tar. If Dante had been with us in the plane, he would have been terrified! The city we had seen so clearly in the sunlight a few minutes before was now an ugly smudge. It had completely disappeared under this awful blanket of smoke and fire.

A feeling of shock and horror swept over all of us.

"My God!" Lewis wrote as the final entry in his log. . . .

As we viewed the awesome spectacle below, we were sobered by the knowledge that the world would never be the same. War, the scourge of the human race since time began, now held terrors beyond belief. I reflected to myself that the kind of war in which I was engaged over Europe in 1942 was now outdated.

But as I swung southward on the return flight to our base, the feeling of tenseness gave way to one of relief. Our mission, for which we had practiced diligently for so long, had been successful. All doubts about the mystery weapon had been removed.

"I think this is the end of the war," I said to Bob Lewis . . .

"An amazing machine ..."

ENIAC

February 14, 1946
Philadelphia

T. B. KENNEDY, JR.

*T*he acronym ENIAC stood for the Electronic Numerical Integrator and Com- *puter, the first general purpose computer, built by the U.S. Army. (A few earlier machines had been built for specific jobs such as breaking a single code.) It towered ten feet tall, covered the breadth of a large room, and weighed close to 60,000 pounds. ENIAC used eighteen thousand vacuum tubes to register the on-off, binary code now standard in digital computing. The tubes were too unreliable for anything more sophisticated. At the time, one of ENIAC's developers called it a "worst-case" design. But as Robert Calem of the* New York Times *says, "Paradoxically, it also turned out to be the best-case design—and a lasting legacy."*

It would be useless today. Personal computers now have one thousand times the computing power, and many million times as much memory space.

Kennedy wrote for the New York Times.

One of the war's top secrets, an amazing machine which applies electronic speeds for the first time to mathematical tasks hitherto too difficult and cumbersome for solution, was announced here tonight by the War Department. Leaders who saw the device in action for the first time heralded it as a tool with which to begin to rebuild scientific affairs on new foundations.

Such instruments, it was said, could revolutionize modern engineering, bring on a new epoch of industrial design, and eventually eliminate much slower and costly trial-and-error development work now deemed necessary in the fashioning of intricate machines. Heretofore, sheer mathematical difficulties have often forced designers to accept inferior solutions of their problems with higher costs and slower programs.

Dr. Arthur W. Burks of the Moore School explained that the basic arithmetic operations, if made to take place rapidly enough, might in time solve almost any problem.

"Watch closely, you may miss it," he asked, as a button was pressed to multiply 97,367 by itself 5,000 times. Most of the onlookers missed it—the operation took place in less than the wink of an eye.

To demonstrate ENIAC's extreme speed, Dr. Burks next slowed down the action by a factor of 1,000 and did the same problem. Had the visitors been content to wait 16⅔ minutes they could have observed the answer in neon light. The next was multiplication—13,975 by 13,975. In a flash the quotient appeared—195,300,625. A table of squares and cubes of numbers was generated in one-tenth of a second. Next, a similar one of sines and cosines. The job was finished and printed on a large sheet before most of the visitors could go from one room to the next.

The ENIAC was then told to solve a difficult problem that would have required several weeks' work by a trained man. The ENIAC did it in exactly 15 seconds.

"The man is all adventure."

JACKIE ROBINSON IN THE MAJOR LEAGUES

1947–1955
Brooklyn, New York

ROGER KAHN

A few African Americans had played major league baseball before the turn of the century, and in the modern era a few more had passed as Cuban or Native American. But Robinson was the first modern player to meet racism head-on.

Kahn covered the Dodgers for the New York Herald Tribune *and subsequently wrote* The Boys of Summer, *from which this account comes.*

This was the man Branch Rickey hired, proud, as his mother had wanted him to be, fierce in his own nature, scarred because white America wounds its fierce proud blacks. I once asked Rickey if he was surprised by the full measure of Robinson's success and I heard him laugh deep in his chest. "Adventure. Adventure. The man is all adventure. I only wish I could have signed him five years sooner."

As surely as Robinson's genius at the game transcends his autobiography, it also transcends record books. In two seasons, 1962 and

1965, Maury Wills stole more bases than Robinson did in all of a ten-year career. Ted Williams' lifetime batting average, .344, is two points higher than Robinson's best for any season. Robinson never hit twenty home runs in a year, never batted in 125 runs. Stan Musial consistently scored more often. Having said those things, one has not said much because troops of people who were there believe that in his prime Jackie Robinson was a better ball player than any of the others. "Ya want a guy that comes to play," suggests Leo Durocher, whose personal relationship with Robinson was spiky. "This guy didn't just come to play. He come to beat ya. He come to stuff the goddamn bat right up your ass."

He moved onto the field with a pigeon-toed shuffle, Number 42 on his back. Reese wore 1. Billy Cox wore 3. Duke Snider wore 4. Carl Furillo wore 6. Dressen wore 7. Shuba wore 8. Robinson wore 42. The black man had to begin in double figures. So he remained.

After 1948 he had too much belly, and toward the end fat rolled up behind his neck. But how this lion sprang. Like a few, very few athletes, Babe Ruth, Jim Brown, Robinson did not merely play at center stage. He was center stage; and wherever he walked, center stage moved with him.

When the Dodgers needed a run and had men at first and second, it was Robinson who came to bat. Would he slap a line drive to right? Would he slug the ball to left? Or would he roll a bunt? From the stands at Ebbets Field, close to home plate, the questions rose into a din. The pitcher saw Robinson. He heard the stands. He bit his lip.

At times when the team lagged, Robinson found his way to first. Balancing evenly on the balls of both feet, he took an enormous lead. The pitcher glared. Robinson stared back. There was no action, only two men throwing hard looks. But time suspended. The cry in the grandstands rose. And Robinson hopped a half yard farther from first. The pitcher stepped off the mound, calling time-out, and when the game resumed, he walked the hitter.

Breaking, Robinson reached full speed in three strides. The pigeon-toed walk yielded to a run of graceful power. He could steal home, or advance two bases on someone else's bunt, and at the time of decision, when he slid, the big dark body became a bird in flight. Then, safe, he rose slowly, often limping, and made his pigeon-toed way to the dugout.

Once Russ Meyer, a short-tempered righthander, pitched a fine game against the Dodgers. The score going into the eighth inning was 2 to 2, and it was an achievement to check the Brooklyn hitters in Ebbets Field. Then, somehow, Robinson reached third base. He took a long lead, threatening to steal home, and the Phillies, using a set play, caught him fifteen feet off base. A rundown developed. This is the major league version of a game children call getting into a pickle. The runner is surrounded by fielders who throw the ball back and forth, gradually closing the gap. Since a ball travels four times faster than a man's best running speed, it is only a question of time before the gap closes and the runner is tagged. Except for Robinson. The rundown was his greatest play. Robinson could start so fast and stop so short that he could elude anyone in baseball, and he could feint a start and feint a stop as well.

All the Phillies rushed to the third-base line, a shortstop named Granny Hamner and a second baseman called Mike Goliat and the first baseman, Eddie Waitkus. The third baseman, Puddin' Head Jones, and the catcher, Andy Seminick, were already there. Meyer himself joined. Among the gray uniforms Robinson in white lunged and sprinted and leaped and stopped. The Phils threw the ball back and forth, but Robinson anticipated their throws, and after forty seconds, and six throws, the gap had not closed. Then, a throw toward third went wild and Robinson made his final victorious run at home plate. Meyer dropped to his knees and threw both arms around Robinson's stout legs. Robinson bounced a hip against Meyer's head and came home running backward, saying, "What the hell are you trying to do?"

"Under the stands, Robinson," Meyer said.

"Right now," Robinson roared.

Police beat them to the proposed ring. Robinson not only won games; he won and infuriated the losers.

In Ebbets Field one spring day in 1955 Sal Maglie was humiliating the Brooklyn hitters. Not Cox or Robinson, but most of the others were clearly alarmed by Maglie's highest skill. He threw at hitters, as he said, "whenever they didn't expect it. That way I had them looking to duck all the time." The fast pitch at the chin or temple is frightening but not truly dangerous as long as the batter sees the ball. He has only to move his head a few inches to safety.

On this particular afternoon, Maglie threw a fast pitch behind Robinson's shoulders, and that is truly dangerous, a killer pitch. As a batter strides, and one strides automatically, he loses height. A normal defensive reflex is to fall backward. When a pitch is shoulder-high behind a man, he ducks directly into the baseball.

I can see Maglie, saturnine in the brightness of May, winding up and throwing. Robinson started to duck and then, with those extraordinary reflexes, hunched his shoulders and froze. The ball sailed wild behind him. He must have felt the wind. He held the hunched posture and gazed at Maglie, who began fidgeting on the mound.

A few innings later, as Maglie continued to overwhelm the Brooklyn hitters, Pee Wee Reese said, "Jack, you got to do something."

"Yeah," Robinson said.

The bat boy overheard the whispered conversation, and just before Jack stepped in to hit, he said in a voice of anxiety, "Don't you do it. Let one of the others do it. You do enough."

Robinson took his stance, bat high. He felt a certain relief. Let somebody else do it, for a change.

"Come on, Jack." Reese's voice carried from the dugout. "We're counting on you."

Robinson took a deep breath. Somebody else? What somebody else? Hodges? Snider? Damn, there wasn't anybody else.

The bunt carried accurately toward first baseman Whitey Lockman, who scooped the ball and looked to throw. That is the play. Bunt and make the pitcher cover first. Then run him down. But Maglie lingered in the safety of the mound. He would not move, and a second baseman named Davey Williams took his place. Lockman's throw reached Williams at first base. Then Robinson struck. A knee crashed into Williams' lower spine and Williams spun into the air, twisting grotesquely, and when he fell he lay in an awkward sprawl, as people do when they are seriously injured.

He was carried from the field. Two innings after that, Alvin Dark, the Giant captain, lined a two-base hit to left field. Dark did not stop at second. Instead, he continued full speed toward third base and Jackie Robinson. The throw had him beaten. Robinson put the ball into his bare right hand and decided to tag Dark between the eyes.

As Dark began to slide, Robinson faked to his right. Dark followed his fake. Robinson stepped aside and slammed the ball at Dark's brow. To his amazement, it bounced free. He had not gotten a secure grip. Dark, avenging Davey Williams, substituting for Sal Maglie, was safe at third.

Both men dusted their uniforms. Lockman was batting. Staring toward home, Robinson said through rigid lips, "This isn't the end. There'll be another day." But when the game was over, Dark asked a reporter to carry a message into the Brooklyn clubhouse. "Tell him we're even," the Giant captain said. "Tell him I don't want another day."

. . . Watching the deep-set angry eyes, I could not forget that when combat reached close quarters, it was the Southerner not the black who had backed off.

"The ambulances literally lined up outside the place."

JONAS SALK HUNTS FOR A POLIO VACCINE

June 16, 1950–February 23, 1954
Pittsburgh, Pennsylvania

ANONYMOUS NURSES AT MUNICIPAL HOSPITAL

*P*olio was one of the most feared diseases as late as the 1950s. For many victims it seemed to develop, in just a day, from ·a backache to lifetime paralysis or death. It struck mostly children. No one could predict where the next outbreak would occur. Some years it was the nation's leading killer of children.

Salk, building on the work of earlier researchers, started his formal quest to develop a safe vaccine in 1950. By early 1954, he had a vaccine that could be tested on humans.

Two nurses at the hospital where Salk worked told Richard Carter, author of Breakthrough, *what they saw.*

Once in a while Dr. Salk made rounds in the hospital, especially if one of the physicians wanted diagnostic help. He certainly knew what was going on upstairs, and anyone who understands how sensitive he is to suffering can imagine how all his scientific and technical problems must have goaded him under those circumstances. He knew that children were dying within a few yards of him because the problems had not yet been solved. A lot of people thought he was an awfully cold fish. They thought he was remote from the everyday life of the hospital and indifferent to it. This was unfair. His job was to understand polio, not to treat it. He knew what polio did to people and their families. He had been present often enough when decisions were made to remove a child from a respirator because she was going to die anyhow and someone else might benefit from the apparatus. Dr. Salk didn't need to be exposed to that kind of thing repeatedly. He was keyed up enough to begin with. . . .

In all my career there has been no experience like Municipal Hospital before the Salk vaccine. One year the ambulances literally lined up outside the place. There were sixteen or seventeen new admissions every day. One of our resident physicians never went to bed for nights on end, except for stretching out on a cot in his clothes. We nurses could never get home on time, either. To leave the place you had to pass a certain number of rooms, and you'd hear a child crying for someone to read his mail to him or for a drink of water or why can't she move, and you couldn't be cruel enough just to pass by. It was an atmosphere of grief, terror, and helpless rage. It was horrible. I remember a high school boy weeping because he was completely paralyzed and couldn't move a hand to kill himself. I remember paralyzed women giving birth to normal babies in iron lungs. I remember a little girl who lay motionless for days with her eyes closed, yet recovered, and I can remember how we all cried when she went home. And I can remember how the staff used to kid Dr. Salk—kidding in earnest—telling him to hurry up and do something.

"That was one night I didn't get much sleep ..."

NORTH KOREA CHALLENGES THE UNITED NATIONS

June 25, 1950

DEAN ACHESON, PRESIDENT HARRY TRUMAN, AND JOHN HICKERSON

A merican foreign policy turned on a dime when World War II ended. The Soviet Union and China, allies in America's fight against the Axis powers of Germany, Italy, and Japan, suddenly became the enemies in the effort to halt communism. The Korean War—or "police action," as politicians preferred to call it—was an effort to contain communism in Asia, as the Vietnam War would be later.

It was also a test for the new United Nations, which opposed the invasion of South Korea as a breach of international law. It ended in 1953 with a cease-fire agreement and the establishment of a truce line, still defended on both sides, at the thirty-eighth parallel.

Acheson was secretary of state. Hickerson was assistant secretary of state for United Nations affairs.

ACHESON

. . . About ten o'clock [P.M.] I received a telephone call on what we called the white telephone. I had in my office and also in my house a white telephone which was connected directly with the switchboard of the

White House. If one lifted the receiver, one got the switchboard in the White House and could be directly connected with the President or through that switchboard with any other department or Cabinet officer in Washington.

The telephone rang, as I say, about ten o'clock, and I answered it to find on the wire Assistant Secretary of State Jack Hickerson, who had charge of international organization affairs, including the United Nations. He said he was in the State Department with Assistant Secretary Dean Rusk, who is now Secretary of State, and that they had just received an alarming message from Ambassador [John Joseph] Muccio in Seoul. This message was to the effect that there was a serious attack along the whole northern border of South Korea. They were not sure whether this was a determined effort of the North Koreans to penetrate South Korea or whether it was a larger than usual border incident.

But the military mission was alarmed. The Korean forces were alarmed, and the ambassador was standing by to confer with the head of our military mission and let us know more details during the course of the night.

I asked him what recommendations they had, and he said that it was their view that we should call for a meeting of the Security Council of the United Nations for the following afternoon, Sunday, and obtain a resolution requesting or ordering all parties to return within their borders, to cease any aggression, and calling upon all members of the UN to assist in this endeavor.

I said that they were to get in touch with our representatives to the United Nations, have them available in New York the next day, and that in the meantime I would call the President, who was then at his home in Independence. And if the President approved this action, they would already have started on it. If he disapproved it, they could stop it at once. But I thought that time was so pressing that we should not even delay while I spoke to the President.

I told them that I would call them back, but immediately to get in touch with people in the Pentagon to set up a working force which would be there all night . . . so that we could find out more about this situation and be prepared to take further action in the morning.

I then called the President. I gave him this message and told him what I had done, saying that I had done it entirely subject to his approval and that I wished further orders or instructions from him. The President said he approved this action entirely and that I was to proceed with it with the utmost vigor.

PRESIDENT TRUMAN

It was about ten thirty on Saturday night, and I was sitting in the living room reading. The phone rang, and it was Dean Acheson calling from his home in Maryland. He said, "Mr. President, I have serious news. The North Koreans are attacking across the thirty-eighth parallel."

I wanted to get on the plane and fly to Washington right that night, but he said that I shouldn't, that a night flight wasn't necessary. He said that I should stand by for another call from him when he'd have more details. And I agreed.

I also gave my approval to his suggestion to call an emergency session of the United Nations Security Council to consider a declaration that active aggression had been committed against the Republic of Korea.

I went to bed, and that was one night I didn't get much sleep.

HICKERSON

I knew that Ambassador Warren Austin, our permanent representative to the United Nations, was in Rutland, Vermont, for the weekend. So after talking to Secretary Acheson, I called Ambassador Ernest Gross, who was our deputy representative to the United Nations. I called him at his house and was told that he was out to dinner somewhere on Long Island and they did not have the telephone number. I asked that he call me urgently at the State Department as soon as he came in. . . .

At twelve o'clock, not having heard from Ambassador Gross, it seemed to me it would be a good idea to call the Secretary-General of the United Nations, Trygve Lie, and alert him. . . . I got him on the phone at five minutes past twelve. He had been listening to the midnight news, and there was something I had not heard about disturbances on the Korean border. He had some inkling of it but no idea of whether it was simply a minor clash or what. I told him that it was an all-out massive attack from the North Koreans against South Korea.

I shall never forget his words. He listened. And then—Trygve Lie speaks perfect English but with a Norwegian accent—and he said, "My God, Jack, that's war against the United Nations!"

I regret to say that I couldn't think of anything more original to reply than, "Trygve, you're telling me!"

*"You should have fired
the son of a bitch two years ago."*

FIRING MacARTHUR

April 6–9, 1951
Washington, D.C.

PRESIDENT HARRY TRUMAN

*G*eneral Douglas MacArthur, based in Tokyo as supreme commander of allied forces in *the Pacific (among other titles), was looked upon as a demigod by many Americans. His regard for himself was even greater. He clashed several times with Truman, the cabinet, and the Joint Chiefs over his independent announcements of foreign policy. Rather than limit the Korean War to a stalemate, he believed the United Nations forces should advance into China to destroy the communist government. Truman finally decided to fire him, a decision he knew would be widely unpopular.*

Secretary of Defense George Marshall's concerns were voiced in the April 6 cabinet meeting. MacArthur was fired on April 9.

General Marshall was concerned about the reaction of certain Congressmen, and he wanted to think over what he felt the reaction of the troops would be. And so at the end of the meeting I asked him, I said, "General, you go over there and you read all the correspondence that's passed between MacArthur and me for the last two years. Then be in my office at nine in the morning, and if you still feel I shouldn't fire him, I won't."

I knew the general very, very well; we'd been through a lot together, and I knew how his mind worked, and there wasn't a doubt in the world in my mind that when he saw what I'd put up with, that he'd agree with me.

And the next morning at eight fifteen when I got to my office, he was out there waiting for me, which was very unusual. General Marshall was usually a punctual man, but I had never known him to be ahead of time. He worked on a very tight schedule.

But that morning he looked up at me, and he says, "I spent most of the night on that file, Mr. President, and you should have fired the son of a bitch two years ago."

And so we went right ahead, and we did it. There were a good many details to be worked out. I asked General Bradley to be sure we had the full agreement of the Joint Chiefs of Staff, which he got; they were all unanimous in saying he should be fired. And we had to arrange to turn the command over to General Ridgway.

And then, of course, we wanted to be sure that MacArthur got the news through official channels. We didn't want it to get into the newspapers first. I signed all the papers and went over to Blair House to have dinner. Some of the others stayed behind at the White House to decide on exactly how to get the word to Frank Pace [secretary of the army, then in Korea]. Pace was supposed to notify the general.

While I was still at Blair House, Joe Short [press secretary] came in to where the others were, and he said he had heard that the Chicago Tribune had the whole story and was going to print it the next morning.

So General Bradley came over to Blair House and told me what was up, and he says if MacArthur hears he's going to be fired before he officially is fired, before he's notified, he'd probably up and resign on me.

And I told Bradley, "The son of a bitch isn't going to resign on me, I want him fired."

*"What do you want to do,
  put me on the spot?"*

A NEIGHBORHOOD VOTE

February 17, 1952
San Francisco

BERNARD TAPER

*T*his story provoked an outraged response nationally, as well as in the San Francisco Bay area. Over four hundred letters came into the Chronicle, of which only twenty-eight supported the actions of the Southwood homeowners. The story won a Newspaper Guild Award.

Taper, a Chronicle city reporter at the time, subsequently had a long career as a staff member of The New Yorker and journalism professor at the University of California at Berkeley.

Residents of the Southwood District of South San Francisco were triumphant yesterday in their efforts to keep their neighborhood 100 per cent Caucasian.

They achieved this object by the use of one of democracy's most fundamental instruments—the secret ballot.

By a vote of 174 to 26 they told Sing Sheng, a former Chinese Nationalist intelligence officer, that they did not want him, his pretty wife and his small son as neighbors.

They did not want the Shengs as neighbors for a lot of reasons which added up to one big reason: the Shengs are Chinese.

The ballots were counted in a garage in the neighborhood. The long narrow building was crowded with some 100 homeowners and spectators.

Sheng, a young man of 25, dressed in a double-breasted blue suit, sat at the balloting table. His Chinese-American wife sat in the front row. She is pregnant. Her baby is due to be born February 22, Washington's birthday.

The suggestion of putting the matter to a ballot came from Sheng himself after he received numerous objections to his purchase of a house on West Orange Avenue last week. Most of the objections asserted that his presence would depress property values.

"I didn't know about any race prejudice at all until I came to Southwood. I was sure everybody really believed in democracy, so I thought up this vote as a test," he said at that time.

Before the counting of ballots began, Edward Howden, executive director of the San Francisco Council for Civil Unity, told the assembled homeowners he had learned of a scientific study recently made in the Bay Area analyzing the actual effect of non-Caucasian residents on property values. He asked if the group wanted to postpone counting the ballots until they had a chance to consider and discuss this study.

Voices from the back of the garage shouted this down:

"Let's get on with it. Let's not fool around any more."

Each ballot was tallied aloud, read by South San Francisco City Manager Emmons McClung. The ballots were phrased so that the homeowners were asked whether they objected to the purchase of a home in the neighborhood by this Chinese family.

The Shengs heard McClung read the phrase, "I object," 174 times as he tallied the ballots. By the end of the balloting they looked crushed.

A silence followed the final tally. Then Sheng stood up and let it be known that he would abide by the vote.

"We'll have to sell the furniture we bought and go somewhere else to live. I hope you people will be happy in your community and that your property values will increase every day."

The meeting broke up. The homeowners exchanged jubilant remarks as they drifted out of the hall.

Many of them were articulate to this reporter about their reasons for not wanting the Shengs in their district, but not one would permit his name to be quoted in connection with these explanations.

"What do you want to do, put me on the spot?" one of them demanded.

The homeowners were indignant at *The Chronicle* for reporting the story in the first place.

"We have a quiet, respectable neighborhood here and we don't care for publicity," one said.

If Sheng had wished, he could have ignored the vote and insisted on his legal right to move into the house. The U.S. Supreme Court has ruled "restrictive covenant" agreements unconstitutional.

Despite this ruling, the American Homes Development Company of Burlingame—describing itself as "developers of this representative American residential area"—sent a letter to all homeowners in Southwood last week urging them to hold fast to the principle of restrictive covenants in their housing transactions.

"These covenants set forth salutary and beneficial restrictions on the land for those purchasers desiring ownership in a community where they could welcome their neighbor and live in equality."

The Shengs also wrote a letter to the Southwood homeowners before the balloting. It read:

"We wish to express our gratitude for the interest you showed in the welfare of our purchasing the house at 726 W. Orange Avenue.

"Before you reach any decision as to how you will vote in the ballot, allow us to tell you our opinion. The present world conflict is not between individual nations, but between Communism and Democracy. We think so highly of Democracy because it offers freedom and equality. America's forefathers fought for these principles and won the Independence of 1776.

"We have forsaken our beloved China and have come to this country seeking the same basic rights. Do not make us the victims of false Democracy. Please vote in favor of us."

Southwood's homes are in the $10,000 to $12,000 price range. Of the 253 homeowners eligible to vote, 31 did not return ballots and 14 expressed themselves as having no opinion in the matter. Six ballots were void.

The owner of the house, Jack Denson, said after the meeting he would return Sheng's $2,950 down payment. The Densons said they had been subject to "considerable pressure" ever since the sale to the Shengs was announced.

"We were given to understand that if the sale went through people would see to it that we would have a hard time buying another piece of property anywhere on the Peninsula," Mrs. Denson said.

Sheng came to the United States in 1947, intending to study for the diplomatic service. When the Communists took over China, he decided to stay in this country. He is employed as an airline mechanic. He and his family live in an apartment in colorful—but congested—Chinatown, at 47 Eagle Avenue.

This week the Shengs will resume their efforts to find a home. They hope to meet with better success, because this is Brotherhood Week.

"Have you no sense of decency, sir?"

McCARTHY
MEETS HIS MATCH

April 23–June 17, 1954
Washington, D.C.

OFFICIAL RECORDS

Senator Joseph McCarthy of Wisconsin was a demagogue who whipped the country into a frenzy about alleged communists in the United States. America listened to his accusations for more than four years. Few of the people who might have challenged him had the courage to do so, for fear of being labeled a communist. Even President Dwight Eisenhower tiptoed around McCarthy.

McCarthy's downfall came in 1954, when he took on the U.S. Army. He accused many of its leaders, including Secretary of the Army Robert T. Stevens and some highly decorated World War II veterans, of hampering his efforts to drive suspected communists out of the military. The hearings of his investigating committee were televised and exposed the irrationality of McCarthy and his cohort Roy Cohn in a way newspaper reporting had not. The most memorable moment came when McCarthy broke into the questioning of Roy Cohn by Secretary Stevens's defense counsel Joseph Welch, to smear a young man who worked for Welch's law firm. Welch's response prompted the country's rejection of McCarthy—although some offshoots of McCarthyism, such as the Hollywood blacklist, continued for years.

McCarthy was censured by the Senate in December 1954 and died of alcoholism in 1957. Cohn became a notoriously unethical lawyer and power broker in New York City, and was eventually disbarred for several criminal acts.

MR. WELCH: Mr. Cohn, tell me once more: Every time you learn of a Communist or a spy anywhere, is it your policy to get them out as fast as possible?

MR. COHN: Surely, we want them out as fast as possible, sir.

MR. WELCH: And whenever you learn of one from now on, Mr. Cohn, I beg of you, will you tell somebody about them quick?

MR. COHN: Mr. Welch, with great respect, I work for the committee here. They know how we go about handling situations of Communist infiltration. If they are displeased with the speed with which I and the group of men who work with me proceed, if they are displeased with the order in which we move, I am sure they will give me appropriate instructions along those lines, and I will follow any which they give me.

MR. WELCH: May I add my small voice, sir, and say whenever you know about a subversive or a Communist or a spy, please hurry. Will you remember those words? . . .

SENATOR McCARTHY: Mr. Chairman, in view of that question—

SENATOR MUNDT: Have you a point of order?

SENATOR McCARTHY: Not exactly, Mr. Chairman, but in view of Mr. Welch's request that the information be given once we know of anyone who might be performing any work for the Communist Party, I think we should tell him that he has in his law firm a young man named Fisher whom he recommended, incidentally, to do work on this committee, who has been for a number of years a member of an organization which was named, oh, years and years ago as the legal bulwark of the Communist Party, an organization which always swings to the defense of . . . Communists. I certainly assume that Mr. Welch did not know of this young man at the time he recommended him as the assistant counsel for this committee, but he has such terror and such a great desire to know where anyone is located who may be serving the Communist cause, Mr. Welch, that I thought we should just call to your attention the fact that your Mr. Fisher, who is still in your law firm today, whom you asked to have down here looking over the secret and classified material, is a member of an organization, not named by me but named by various committees, named by the Attorney General, as I recall, and I think I quote this verbatim, as "the legal bulwark of the Communist Party." He belonged to that for a sizeable number of years, according to his own admission, and he belonged to it long after it had been exposed as the legal arm of the Communist Party.

Knowing that, Mr. Welch, I just felt that I had a duty to respond to your urgent request that before sundown, when we know of anyone serving the Communist cause, we let the agency know. We are now letting you know that your man did belong to this organization for either three or four years, belong to it long after he was out of law school. . . . I have hesitated bringing that up, but I have been rather bored with your phony requests to Mr. Cohn here that he personally get every Communist out of government before sundown. Therefore, we will give you information about the young man in your own organization.

I am not asking you at this time to explain why you tried to foist him on this committee. Whether you knew he was a member of that Communist organization or not, I don't know. I assume you did not, Mr. Welch, because I get the impression that, while you are quite an actor, you play for a laugh. I don't think you have any conception of the danger of the Communist Party. I don't think you yourself would ever knowingly aid the Communist cause. I think you are unknowingly aiding it when you try to burlesque this hearing in which we are attempting to bring out the facts, however . . .

MR. WELCH: Mr. Chairman, under these circumstances I must have something approaching a personal privilege.

SENATOR MUNDT: You may have it, sir. It will not be taken out of your time.

MR. WELCH: Senator McCarthy, I did not know—Senator, sometimes you say "May I have your attention?"

SENATOR McCARTHY: I am listening to you. I can listen with one ear.

MR. WELCH: This time I want you to listen with both.

SENATOR McCARTHY: Yes.

MR. WELCH: Senator McCarthy, I think until this moment—

SENATOR McCARTHY: Jim, will you get the news story to the effect that this man belonged to this Communist-front organization? Will you get the citations showing that this was the legal arm of the Communist Party, and the length of time that he belonged, and the fact that he was recommended by Mr. Welch? I think that should be in the record.

MR. WELCH: You won't need anything in the record when I have finished telling you this. Until this moment, Senator, I think I never really gauged your cruelty or your recklessness. Fred Fisher is a young man who went to the Harvard Law School and came into my firm and is starting what looks to be a brilliant career with us. When I decided to work for this committee I asked Jim St. Clair, who sits on my right, to be my first assistant. I said to Jim, "Pick somebody in the firm who works under you that you would like." He chose Fred Fisher and they came down on an afternoon plane. That night, when he had taken a little stab at trying to see what the case was about, Fred Fisher and Jim St. Clair and I went to dinner together. I then said to these two young men, "Boys, I don't know anything about you except I have always liked you, but if there is anything funny in the life of either one of you that would hurt anybody in this case you speak up quick."

Fred Fisher said, "Mr. Welch, when I was in law school and for a period of months after, I belonged to the Lawyers Guild," as you have suggested, Senator. He went on to say, "I am secretary of the Young Republicans League in Newton with the son of Massachusetts' Governor, and I have the respect and admiration of my community and I am sure I have the respect and admiration of the twenty-five lawyers or so in Hale and Dorr."

I said, "Fred, I just don't think I am going to ask you to work on the case. If I do, one of these days that will come out and go over national television and it will just hurt like the dickens."

So, Senator, I asked him to go back to Boston. Little did I dream you could be so reckless and so cruel as to do injury to that lad. It is true he is still with Hale and Dorr. It is, I regret to say, equally true that I fear he shall always bear a scar needlessly inflicted by you. If it were in my power to forgive you for your reckless cruelty, I would do so. I like to think I am a gentleman, but your forgiveness will have to come from someone other than me.

SENATOR McCARTHY: Mr. Chairman.

SENATOR MUNDT: Senator McCarthy?

SENATOR McCARTHY: May I say that Mr. Welch talks about this being cruel and reckless. He was just baiting; he has been baiting Mr. Cohn here for hours, requesting that Mr. Cohn, before sundown, get out of any department of Government anyone who is serving the Communist cause. I just give this man's record, and I want to say, Mr. Welch, that it has been labeled long before he became a member, as early as 1944—

MR. WELCH: Senator, may we not drop this? We know he belonged to the Lawyers Guild, and Mr. Cohn nods his head at me. I did you, I think, no personal injury, Mr. Cohn.

MR. COHN: No, sir.

MR. WELCH: I meant to do you no personal injury, and if I did, I beg your pardon.

Let us not assassinate this lad further, Senator. You have done enough. Have you no sense of decency, sir, at long last? Have you left no sense of decency?

*"What really stole the show
was this 20-year-old sensation . . ."*

ELVIS

*May 1955
Orlando, Florida*

JEAN YOTHERS

*Tom Perryman, a local Texas music promoter, described some early Elvis shows to
Last Train to Memphis author Peter Guralnick:"It reminded me of the early
days, of where I was raised in East Texas and going to see these 'Holy Roller' Brush
Arbor meetings, seeing these people get religion. I said, 'Man, that's something.'
You'd see it in the later years with the big sound system and the lights, but Elvis
could do it if there wasn't but ten people. He never realized what he had till later
years. He said, 'Man, this sure is a good crowd in this part of the country. Are they
always this way?' I said, 'No, man. They never seen anything like you.' Nobody had."*

*A few months after Perryman saw Elvis, Jean Yothers, a reporter for the
Orlando Sentinel, caught the fever.*

What hillbilly music does to the hillbilly music fan is absolutely phe-
nomenal. It transports him into a wild, emotional and audible state of
ecstasy. He never sits back sedately patting his palms politely and uttering
bravos of music appreciation like his long-hair counterpart. He thunders
his appreciation for the country-style music and nasal-twanged singing he
loves by whistling shrilly through teeth, pounding the palms together with
the whirling momentum of a souped-up paddle wheel, stomping the floor
and ejecting yip-yip noises like the barks of a hound dog when it finally
runs down a particularly elusive coon.

That's the way it was, friends, at the big Hank Snow show and all-star
Grand Ole Opry jamboree staged last week in Municipal Auditorium to
jam-packed houses both performances. It was as hot as blue blazes within
the tired sanctums of the barnish auditorium, but the hillbilly fans turned
out in droves and seemed oblivious to the heat. . . . The whole shebang
seemed like a cross between the enthusiasm displayed at a wrestling match
and old-fashioned camp meeting. . . . This was my first tangle with a hillbilly jamboree, a poignant contrast to Metropolitan Opera in Atlanta, I
must say. I was awed and with all due respect to opera in Atlanta, I got a

tremendous boot out of this loud, uninhibited music that's sending the country crazy. . . . Ferron [Faron] Young was real sharp singing that ditty about living fast, loving hard, dying young and leaving a beautiful memory, but what really stole the show was this 20-year-old sensation, Elvis Presley, a real sex box as far as the teenage girls are concerned. They squealed themselves silly over this fellow in orange coat and sideburns who "sent" them with his unique arrangement of Shake, Rattle and Roll. And following the program, Elvis was surrounded by girlies asking for autographs. He would give each a long, slow look with drooped eyelids and comply. They ate it up.

"The only tired I was, was tired of giving in."

THE FRONT OF THE BUS

December 1, 1955
Montgomery, Alabama

ROSA PARKS

"*I* *don't think any segregation law angered black people in Montgomery more than bus segregation,*" *Rosa Parks recalled years after this incident, which sparked the Montgomery bus boycott. The two-thirds of the city bus riders who were African Americans were forced to endure humiliating rules, including a requirement that they sit in the back of the bus. Bus drivers, who carried guns, had police power to enforce the regulations. When a local NAACP official requested a change in one of the rules, he was told, "Your folks started it. They do it because they want to."*

Parks was secretary of the local chapter of the NAACP at the time. She has often been described as merely a seamstress who was too tired to move. That poignant version belies the college-educated Parks's long history as a knowledgeable, committed activist. It also ignores the stand she had taken twelve years earlier, in 1943, when a bus driver told her to move to the back. She refused, and the driver forced her off the bus. After avoiding that driver for more than a decade, she found herself on his bus once again. This time she was prepared to see the confrontation through to its end.

The boycott lasted more than a year. The bus company lost two-thirds of its income, and caved in. The action also brought national attention to its leader, Dr. Martin Luther King, Jr.

In December 1956, the U.S. Supreme Court ruled that bus segregation is illegal. The bus driver who forced Parks off the bus in 1943 and 1955 remained in his job until 1972, when he retired.

When I got off from work that evening of December 1, I went to Court Square as usual to catch the Cleveland Avenue bus home. I didn't look to see who was driving when I got on, and by the time I recognized him, I had already paid my fare. It was the same driver who had put me off the bus back in 1943, twelve years earlier. He was still tall and heavy, with red, rough-looking skin. And he was still mean-looking. I didn't know if he had been on that route before—they switched the drivers around sometimes. I do know that most of the time if I saw him on a bus, I wouldn't get on it.

I saw a vacant seat in the middle section of the bus and took it. I didn't even question why there was a vacant seat even though there were quite a few people standing in the back. If I had thought about it at all, I would probably have figured maybe someone saw me get on and did not take the seat but left it vacant for me. There was a man sitting next to the window and two women across the aisle.

The next stop was the Empire Theater, and some whites got on. They filled up the white seats, and one man was left standing. The driver looked back and noticed the man standing. Then he looked back at us. He said, "Let me have those front seats," because they were the front seats of the black section. Didn't anybody move. We just sat right where we were, the four of us. Then he spoke a second time: "Y'all better make it light on yourselves and let me have those seats."

The man in the window seat next to me stood up, and I moved to let him pass by me, and then I looked across the aisle and saw that the two women were also standing. I moved over to the window seat. I could not see how standing up was going to "make it light" for me. The more we gave in and complied, the worse they treated us.

I thought back to the time when I used to sit up all night and didn't sleep, and my grandfather would have his gun right by the fireplace, or if he had his one-horse wagon going anywhere, he always had his gun in the back of the wagon. People always say that I didn't give up my seat because I was tired, but that isn't true. I was not tired physically, or no more tired than I usually was at the end of a working day. I was not old, although some people have an image of me as being old then. I was forty-two. No, the only tired I was, was tired of giving in.

The driver of the bus saw me still sitting there, and he asked was I going to stand up. I said, "No." He said, "Well, I'm going to have you arrested." Then I said, "You may do that." These were the only words we said to each other. I didn't even know his name, which was James Blake, until we were in court together. He got out of the bus and stayed outside for a few minutes, waiting for the police.

As I sat there, I tried not to think about what might happen. I knew that anything was possible. I could be manhandled or beaten. I could be arrested. People have asked me if it occurred to me then that I could be the test case the NAACP had been looking for. I did not think about that at all. In fact if I had let myself think too deeply about what might happen to me, I might have gotten off the bus. But I chose to remain.

Meanwhile there were people getting off the bus and asking for transfers, so that began to loosen up the crowd, especially in the back of the bus. Not everyone got off, but everybody was very quiet. What conversation there was, was in low tones; no one was talking out loud. It would have been quite interesting to have seen the whole bus empty out. Or if the other three had stayed where they were, because if they'd had to arrest four of us instead of one, then that would have given me a little support. But it didn't matter. I never thought hard of them at all and never even bothered to criticize them.

Eventually two policemen came. They got on the bus, and one of them asked me why I didn't stand up. I asked him, "Why do you all push us around?" He said to me, and I quote him exactly, "I don't know, but the law is the law and you're under arrest."

"They are in our school. Oh God . . ."

FIRST DAY OF SCHOOL IN LITTLE ROCK

September 23, 1957
Arkansas

RELMAN MORIN

*T*he U.S. Supreme Court had ordered the Little Rock school system desegregated, but a riot erupted when nine young students arrived to attend the first day of classes.

President Eisenhower sent one thousand army paratroopers to Little Rock the next day to keep the peace and enforce the Supreme Court decision. But similar *incidents occurred elsewhere. A few years later, Governor George Wallace personally tried to block the path of the first black students to attend the University of Alabama. Federal troops had to escort the students inside.*

Morin, an Associated Press reporter, won a Pulitzer Prize for this second-by-second account of the first-day's riot.

It was exactly like an explosion, a human explosion.

At 8:35 A.M., the people standing in front of the high school looked like the ones you see every day in a shopping center.

A pretty, sweet-faced woman with auburn hair and a jewel-green jacket . . . another, holding a white portable radio in her ear. "I'm getting the news of what's going on at the high school," she said. . . . People laughed. . . . A greyhaired man, tall and spare, leaned over the wooden barricade, "If they're coming," he said, quietly, "they'll be here soon." . . .

"They better," said another. "I got to get to work."

Ordinary people—mostly curious, you would have said—watching a high school on a bright, blue-and-gold morning.

Five minutes later, at 8:40, they were a mob.

The terrifying spectacle of 200-odd individuals, suddenly welded together into a single body, took place in the barest fraction of a second. It was an explosion, savagery chain-reacting from person to person, fusing them into a white-hot mass.

There are three glass-windowed telephone booths across the street from the south end of the high school.

At 8:35, I was inside one of them, dictating.

I saw four Negroes coming down the center of the street, in twos. One was tall and big-shouldered. One was tall and thin. The other two were short. The big man had a card in his hat and was carrying a Speed Graflex, a camera for taking news pictures.

A strange, animal growl rose from the crowd.

"Here come the Negroes."

Instantly, people turned their backs on the high school and ran toward the four men. They hesitated. Then they turned to run.

I saw the white men catch them on the sidewalk and the lawn of a home a quarter block away. They were a furious, struggling knot. You could see a man kicking at the big Negro. Then another jumped on his back and rode him to the ground, forearms deep in the Negro's throat.

They kicked him and beat him on the ground and they smashed his camera to splinters. The other three ran down the street with one white man chasing them. When the white man saw he was alone, he turned and fled back toward the crowd.

Meanwhile, five policemen had rescued the big man.

I had just finished saying "Police escorted the big man away—"

At that instant a man shouted, "Look the Negroes are going in."

Directly across from me three Negro boys and five girls were walking toward the side door at the south end of the school.

It was an unforgettable tableau.

They were carrying books. White bobby-sox, part of the high school uniform, glinted on the girls' ankles. They were all nicely dressed. The boys wore open-throat shirts and the girls, ordinary frocks.

They weren't hurrying. They simply strolled across perhaps 15 yards from the sidewalk to the school steps. They glanced at the people and the police as though none of this concerned them.

You can never forget a scene like that.

Nor the one that followed.

Like a wave, the people who had run toward the four Negro men, now swept back toward the police and the barricades.

"Oh, God, they're in the school," a man yelled.

A woman—the one with the auburn hair and green jacket—rushed up to him. Her face was working with fury now.

Her lips drew back in a snarl and she was screaming, "Did they go in?"

"They are in the school," the man said.

"Oh God," she said. She covered her face with her hands. Then she tore her hair, still screaming.

She looked exactly like the women who cluster around a mine head, when there has been an explosion and men are trapped below.

The tall, lean man jumped up on one of the barricades. He was holding on to the shoulders of others nearby.

"Who's going through?" he roared.

"We all are," the people shrieked.

They surged over and around the barricades, breaking for the police.

About a dozen policemen, swinging billy clubs, were in front of them.

Men and women raced toward them and the policemen raised their clubs, moving this way and that as people tried to dodge around them.

A man went down, pole-axed, when a policeman clubbed him.

Meanwhile the women—the auburn-haired one, the woman with the radio, and others—were swirling around the police commanding officers.

Tears were streaming down their faces. They acted completely distraught.

It was pure hysteria.

And they kept crying, "They are in our school. Oh God, are you going to stand here and let them stay in school?"

"The capsule and I went weightless together ..."

SPACE

May 5, 1961

ALAN SHEPARD, JR.

*W*e take astronauts for granted now. They seem to have become anonymous. But in 1961 we knew only the seven Project Mercury astronauts, and they were media stars: Scott Carpenter, Gordon Cooper, John Glenn, Virgil "Gus" Grissom, Walter Schirra, Donald "Deke" Slayton, and the one chosen to be the first American in space, Alan Shepard.

Shepard, a navy admiral and test pilot, flew Freedom 7 to a height of 115 miles in his fifteen-minute flight, traveling in a neat arc that landed him about 300 miles from his Florida launch site.

Ten years later, as part of the Apollo 14 mission, Shepard walked on the moon.

I sort of wanted to kick the tires—the way you do with a new car or an airplane. I realized that I would probably never see that missile again. I really enjoy looking at a bird that is getting ready to go. It's a lovely sight. The Redstone with the Mercury capsule and escape tower on top of it is a particularly good-looking combination, long and slender. And this one had a decided air of expectancy about it. It stood there full of lox [liquid oxygen], venting white clouds and rolling frost down the side. In the glow of the searchlight it was really beautiful.

After admiring the bird, I went up the elevator and walked across the narrow platform to the capsule. . . . I walked around a bit, talking briefly with Gus [Grissom] again and with John Glenn. I especially wanted to thank John for all the hard work he had done as my backup. Some of the crew looked a little tense up there, but none of the Astronauts showed it.

At 5:20 I disconnected the hose which led to my portable air-conditioner, slipped off the protective galoshes that had covered my boots and squeezed through the hatch. I linked the suit up with the capsule oxygen system, checked the straps which held me tight in the couch, and removed the safety pins which kept some of the switches from being pushed or pulled inadvertently. I passed these outside.

John had left a little note on the instrument panel, where no one else could see it but me. It read, "No Handball Playing in This Area." I was going to leave it there, but when John saw me laugh behind the visor he grinned and reached in to retrieve it. I guess he remembered that the capsule cameras might pick up that message, and he lost his nerve. No one could speak to me face to face now. I had closed the visor and was hooked up with the intercom system. Several people stuck their heads in to take a last-minute look around, and hands kept reaching in to make little adjustments. Then, at 6:10, the hatch went on and I was alone. I watched as the latches turned to make sure they were tight.

This was the big moment, and I had thought about it a lot. The butterflies were pretty strong now. "O.K., Buster," I said to myself, "you volunteered for this thing. Now it's up to you to do it.". . . . I passed some of the time looking through the periscope. The view was fascinating. I could see clouds up above and people far beneath me on the ground. When the sun rose, it came right into the scope and I had to crank in some filters to cut down on the glare.

The last few minutes went perfectly. . . . At two minutes before launch, I set the control valves for the suit and cabin temperature, shifted to the voice circuit and had a quick radio check with Deke. I also contacted Chase One and Chase Two—Wally and Scott in the chase planes—and heard them loud and clear. They were in the air, ready to take a high-level look at me as I went past them after the launch. Electronically speaking, my colleagues were all around me at this moment.

Deke gave me the count at T minus 90 seconds and again at T minus 60. I had nothing to do just then but maintain my communications, so I rogered for both messages. At 35 seconds I watched through the periscope as the umbilical which had fed freon and power into the capsule snapped out and fell away. Then the periscope came in and the little door which protected it in flight closed shut. The red light on my instrument panel went out to signal this event, which was the last critical function the capsule had to perform automatically before we were ready to go. I reported this to Deke, and then I reported the power readings. Both were in a "Go" condition. I heard Deke roger for my message, and then I listened as he read the final count. "Ten, nine, eight, seven . . ." At the count of 5 I put my right hand on the stop-watch button, which I had to push at lift-off to time the flight. I put my left hand on the abort handle, which I would move in a hurry only if something went seriously wrong and I had to activate the escape tower.

Just after the count of zero, Deke said, "Lift-off . . . you're on your way . . ."

. . . I was really exhilarated and pleasantly surprised when I answered, "Lift-off and the clock is started."

There was a lot less vibration and noise rumble than I had expected. It was extremely smooth—a subtle, gentle, gradual rise off the ground. There was nothing rough or abrupt about it. But there was no question that I was going, either. I could see it on the instruments, hear it on the headphones, feel it all around me.

It was a strange and exciting sensation. And yet it was so mild and easy—much like the rides we had experienced in our trainers—that it somehow seemed very familiar. I felt as if I had experienced the whole thing before. I knew, of course, that I had not. Nothing could possibly simulate in every detail the real thing that I was going through at that moment. . . .

The engine cutoff occurred right on schedule, at two minutes and 22 seconds after lift-off. Nothing abrupt happened, just a delicate and gradual dropping off of the thrust as the fuel flow decreased. I heard a roaring noise as the escape tower blew off. I was glad I would not be needing it any longer. I had hoped I could see smoke from the explosions blow past the portholes when this happened, but I was too busy keeping track of various events on the instrument panel to take a look. I reported all of these events to Deke, and then I heard a noise as the little rockets fired to separate the capsule from the booster. This was a critical point of the flight, both technically and psychologically. I knew that if the capsule got hung up on the booster, I would have quite a different flight.

Right after leaving the booster, the capsule and I went weightless together and I could feel the capsule begin its slow, lazy turnaround to get into position for the rest of the flight.

The capsule was traveling at about 5,000 miles per hour now, and up to this point it had been on automatic pilot. I switched over to the manual control stick, and tried out the pitch, yaw and roll axes in that order. Each time I moved the stick, the little jets of hydrogen peroxide rushed through the nozzles on the outside of the capsule and pushed it or twisted it the way I wanted it to go.

It was now time to go to the periscope. I had been well briefed on what to expect, and one of the last things I had done at Hangar S before suiting up was to study, with Bill Douglas and John Glenn, some special maps which showed me the view I would get. I had some idea of the huge variety of color and land masses and cloud cover which I would see from 100 miles up. But no one could be briefed well enough to be completely prepared for the astonishing view that I got. My exclamation back to

Deke about the "beautiful sight" was completely spontaneous. It was breath-taking. To the south I could see where the cloud cover stopped at about Fort Lauderdale, and that the weather was clear all the way down past the Florida Keys. To the north I could see up the coast of the Carolinas to where the clouds just obscured Cape Hatteras. Across Florida to the west I could spot Lake Okeechobee, Tampa Bay and even Pensacola. Because there were some scattered clouds far beneath me I was not able to see some of the Bahama Islands that I had been briefed to look for. So I shifted to an open area and identified Andros Island and Bimini. The colors around these ocean islands were brilliantly clear, and I could see sharp variations between the blue of deep water and the light green of the shoal areas near the reefs. It was really stunning.

"You've seen the actual missiles?"

THE CUBAN MISSILE CRISIS

October 16–27, 1962
Washington, D.C.

MINUTES OF THE EXECUTIVE COMMITTEE;
NIKITA KHRUSHCHEV

*I*n the four decades after World War II, American foreign policy focused on the Cold War against communism. The Soviet Union was considered the primary threat, because of its military strength and its control of eastern Europe. As Russia and America built more nuclear missiles, with ever-greater ranges, the tension grew. When Cuban communists led by Fidel Castro overthrew the pro-American government of Fulgencio Batista in 1959, aligning Cuba with the USSR, the Soviet threat suddenly appeared just ninety miles from the Florida Keys.

Shortly after taking office, President John F. Kennedy authorized an invasion of Cuba that had been planned, very poorly, by the previous administration of Dwight D. Eisenhower. The invasion, by a force of about fifteen hundred Cuban exiles, was a fiasco. (In one planning session, the "best and the brightest," as reporter David Halberstam called them in his book of that name, were asked if they knew the size of Cuba. The questioner was a Marine Corps general who had survived the 1943 invasion of Tarawa, a Pacific atoll less than three miles long, which had been won only at the cost of almost one thousand marines and sailors. No one could tell him for certain—an alarming sign—but they guessed it was the size of Long Island, about 120 miles. Cuba is actually 750 miles long. It would stretch from New York City to Chicago.)

In early October 1962, the Cuban Missile Crisis began when U.S. spy planes revealed that the Soviets were building missile and bomber bases in Cuba. On October 22, President Kennedy addressed the nation on television, and Americans waited to see if the crisis would turn into the Armageddon that nuclear doomsayers had predicted. Certainly nuclear war had never been closer. In those days, before satellites linked phones all over the world, President Kennedy and his advisers had to read between the lines of USSR chairman Nikita Khrushchev's public announcements to find a diplomatic solution.

The crisis ended shortly after the turning point of October 27 described in the transcripts below, when Khrushchev agreed to remove the missiles. As Secretary of State Dean Rusk said, "We're eyeball to eyeball, and I think the other fellow just blinked."

Afterward, the White House and the Kremlin installed the "hot line"—a direct teletype communication link—to be used in case of future emergencies.

OCTOBER 16, A.M. MEETING

ARTHUR LUNDAHL [DIRECTOR, NATIONAL PHOTOGRAPHIC INTER-
PRETATION CENTER]: This is a result of the photography taken Sunday, sir.
JFK: Yeah.
LUNDAHL: There's a medium-range ballistic missile launch site and two new military encampments on the southern edge of Sierra del Rosario in west-central Cuba.
JFK: . . . How do you know this is a medium-range ballistic missile?
LUNDAHL: The length, sir.
JFK: The length?
LUNDAHL: The length of it, yes.
JFK: Is it ready to be fired?
SIDNEY GRAYBEAL [CHIEF, GUIDED MISSILE DIVISION, OFFICE OF
SCIENTIFIC INTELLIGENCE, CIA]: No, sir.
JFK: How long before it can be fired?
GRAYBEAL: That depends. . . .
ROBERT McNAMARA [SECRETARY OF DEFENSE]: . . . The question is one of readiness of . . . to fire and—and this is highly critical in forming our plans—that the time between today and the time when the readiness to fire capability develops is a very important thing.

OCTOBER 16, P.M. MEETING

JFK [TO MARSHALL CARTER, DEPUTY DIRECTOR, CENTRAL INTELLI-
GENCE AGENCY]: Uh, General, how long would you say we had, uh,
before these—at least to the best of your ability for the ones we know—
will be ready to fire?

CARTER: Well, our people estimate that these could be fully operational within two weeks. Uh, this would be the total complex. If they're
the oxygen type, uh, we have no—it would be considerably longer since
we don't have any indication of, uh, oxygen refueling there nor any
radars . . . one of 'em, uh, one of them could be operational much
sooner. Our people feel that this has been, being put in since early September. We have had two visits of a Soviet ship that has an eight-foot-hold
capacity sideways. And this is the only delivery vehicle that we would have
any suspicion that they came in on. And that came in late August, and one
in early September. . . .

JFK: There isn't any question in your mind however, uh, that it is an
intermediate-range missile?

CARTER: No, there's no question in our minds at all. . . .

DEAN RUSK [SECRETARY OF STATE]: You've seen actual missiles
themselves and not just the boxes have you?

CARTER: . . . In the picture there is an actual missile. . . . There's no
question in our minds.

PRIVATE NOTE, DATED OCTOBER 26, FROM
CHAIRMAN KHRUSHCHEV TO PRESIDENT KENNEDY

All the the weapons [in Cuba]—and I assure you of this—are of a defensive nature. . . . Mr. President, let us show good sense. I assure you that
the ships bound for Cuba are carrying no armaments at all. The armaments needed for the defense of Cuba are already there. I do not mean to
say that there have been no shipments of arms at all. No, there were such
shipments. But now Cuba has already obtained the necessary weapons for
defense. . . .

Let us therefore display statesmanlike wisdom. I propose: we, for our
part will declare that our ships bound for Cuba are not carrying any
armaments. You will declare that the United States will not invade Cuba
with its troops and will not support any other forces which might intend
to invade Cuba. Then the necessity for the presence of our military spe-
cialists in Cuba will be obviated.

PUBLIC ANNOUNCEMENT MADE OCTOBER 27
BY CHAIRMAN KHRUSHCHEV

. . . How are we, the Soviet Union, our Government, to assess your actions which are expressed in the fact that you have surrounded the Soviet Union with military bases; surrounded our allies with military bases; placed military bases literally around our country; and stationed your missile armaments there? . . . Your missiles are located in Britain, are located in Italy and are aimed against us. Your missiles are located in Turkey.

You are disturbed over Cuba. You say this disturbs you because it [Cuba] is 90 miles by sea from the coast of the United States of America. But Turkey adjoins us.

OCTOBER 27 MEETING

[This meeting was held before Kennedy officially received the second Khruschev statement.]

JFK [READING A NEWS STORY]: "Premier Khrushchev told President Kennedy yesterday he would withdraw offensive missiles from Cuba if the United States withdrew its rockets from Turkey."

[UNKNOWN SPEAKER]: He didn't really say that, did he?

JFK: That may not be—he may be putting out another letter. . . . That wasn't the letter we received, was it?

[UNKNOWN SPEAKER]: No.

JFK: Is he supposed to be putting out a letter he's written me or putting out a statement?

PIERRE SALINGER [PRESIDENTIAL PRESS SECRETARY]: Putting out a letter he wrote you.

RUSK: Well, I think we better get—uh—(words unclear). Will you check and be sure that the letter that's coming in on the ticker is the letter that we were seeing last night. . . .

MCGEORGE BUNDY [SPECIAL ASSISTANT TO THE PRESIDENT]: . . . This would an extremely unsettling business.

JFK: Well this is unsettling now, George, because he's got us in a pretty good spot here, because most people will regard this as not an unreasonable proposal, I'll just tell you that. In fact, in many ways—

BUNDY: But what most people, Mr. President?

JFK: I think you're going to find it very difficult to explain why we are going to take hostile military action in Cuba, against these sites—what we've been thinking about—the thing that he's saying is, if you'll get yours out of Turkey, we'll get ours out of Cuba. I think we've got a very tough one here.

BUNDY: I don't see why we pick that track when he's offered us another track, within the last twenty-four hours. You think the public one's serious? (words unclear)

JFK: Yeah, I think you have to assume that this is their new and latest position and it's a public one.

RUSK: What would you think of releasing the letter of yesterday? (Pause)

BUNDY: I think it has a great deal of virtue.

JFK: Yes, but I think we have to be now thinking about what our position's going to be on this one, because this is the one that's before us, and before the world.

(Short pause)

THEODORE SORENSEN [PRESIDENTIAL COUNSEL]: As between the two I think it clear that practically everyone here would favor the private proposal. . . .

ROBERT F. KENNEDY [ATTORNEY GENERAL]: How are you doing, Bob?

McNAMARA: Well, hard to tell. You have any doubts?

RFK: Well, I think we're doing the only thing we can do and well, you know.

McNAMARA: I think the one thing, Bobby, we ought to seriously (words unclear) we need to have two things ready, a government for Cuba, because we're going to need one (words unclear) and secondly, plans for how to respond to the Soviet Union in Europe, because sure as hell they're going to do something there.

(Mixed voices)

[UNKNOWN SPEAKER]: Suppose we make Bobby mayor of Havana.

(Mixed voices, tape ends)

"I have a dream ..."

DR. MARTIN LUTHER KING, JR.

August 28, 1963
Washington, D.C.

JAMES RESTON

*R*eston was a New York Times *Washington reporter, bureau chief, and columnist for many years.*

. . . It will be a long time before [the nation] forgets the melodious
and melancholy voice of the Rev. Dr. Martin Luther King Jr. crying out
his dreams to the multitude.

It was Dr. King who, near the end of the day, touched the vast audience. Until then the pilgrimage was merely a great spectacle. Only those
marchers from the embattled towns in the Old Confederacy had anything
like the old crusading zeal. For many the day seemed an adventure, a long
outing in the late summer sun—part liberation from home, part Sunday
School picnic, part political convention, and part fish-fry. But Dr. King
brought them alive in the late afternoon with a peroration that was an
anguished echo from all the old American reformers. Roger Williams calling for religious liberty, Sam Adams calling for political liberty, old man
Thoreau denouncing coercion, William Lloyd Garrison demanding emancipation, and Eugene V. Debs crying for economic equality—Dr. King
echoed them all.

"I have a dream," he cried again and again. And each time the dream
was a promise out of our ancient articles of faith: phrases from the Constitution, lines from the great anthem of the nation, guarantees from the
Bill of Rights, all ending with a vision that they might one day all come
true. Dr. King touched all the themes of the day, only better than anybody
else. He was full of the symbolism of Lincoln and Gandhi, and the
cadences of the Bible. He was both militant and sad, and he sent the
crowd away feeling that the long journey had been worthwhile.

"Yes, I was there, I observed that circus ..."

A DISSENTER'S VIEW OF DR. KING'S SPEECH

August 28, 1963
Washington, D.C.

MALCOLM X

M *alcolm X's view may not be a common one, but it reveals the polarization that has always existed in the civil rights movement, whether the debate was between Dr. King and Malcolm X or between Booker T. Washington and W. E. B. DuBois. Integration or separatism? Peaceful protest or violent uprising? Evolution or revolution? The methods of nonviolent resistance that Dr. King adopted from India's Mahatma Gandhi did not satisfy Black Muslim Malcolm X, who called for change "by any means necessary."*

Unfortunately, Malcolm X—born Malcolm Little—met the same end as Dr. King. Malcolm X was assassinated in 1965, shortly after leaving the Nation of Islam and adopting more moderate views; Dr. King was assassinated in 1968.

Not long ago, the black man in America was fed a dose of another form of the weakening, lulling, and deluding effects of so-called "integration."

It was that "Farce on Washington," I call it.

The idea of a mass of blacks marching on Washington was originally the brainchild of the Brotherhood of Sleeping Car Porters' A. Philip Randolph. For twenty or more years the March on Washington idea had floated around among Negroes. And, spontaneously, suddenly now, that idea caught on.

Overalled rural Southern Negroes, small town Negroes, Northern ghetto Negroes, even thousands of previously Uncle Tom Negroes began talking "March." . . .

Any student of how "integration" can weaken the black man's movement was about to observe a master lesson.

The White House, with a fanfare of international publicity, "approved," "endorsed," and "welcomed" a March on Washington. . . .

It was like a movie. The next scene was the "big six" civil rights Negro "leaders" meeting in New York City with the white head of a big philanthropic agency. They were told that their money-wrangling in public was damaging their image. And a reported $800,000 was donated to a United Civil Rights Leadership council that was quickly organized by the "big six."

Now, what had instantly achieved black unity? The white man's money. What string was attached to the money? Advice. Not only was there this donation, but another comparable sum was promised, for sometime later on, after the March. . . . Obviously it all went well.

The original "angry" March on Washington was now about to be entirely changed. . . .

Invited next to join the March were four famous white public figures: one Catholic, one Jew, one Protestant, and one labor boss. . . .

And suddenly, the previously March-nervous whites began announcing they were going.

It was as if an electrical current shot through the ranks of bourgeois Negroes—the very so-called "middle-class" and "upper-class" who had earlier been deploring the March on Washington talk by grass-roots Negroes.

But white people, now, were going to march.

Why, some downtrodden, jobless, hungry Negro might have gotten trampled. Those "integration"-mad Negroes practically ran over each other trying to find out where to sign up. The "angry blacks" March suddenly had been made chic. Suddenly it had a Kentucky Derby image. For the status-seeker, it was a status symbol. "Were you there?" You can hear that right today.

It had become an outing, a picnic.

The morning of the March, any rickety carloads of angry, dusty, sweating small-town Negroes would have gotten lost among the chartered jet planes, railroad cars, and airconditioned buses. What originally was planned to be an angry riptide, one English newspaper aptly described now as "the gentle flood."

Talk about "integrated"! It was like salt and pepper. And, by now, there wasn't a single logistics aspect uncontrolled.

The marchers had been instructed to bring no signs—signs were provided. They had been told to sing one song: "We Shall Overcome." They had been told how to arrive, when, where to arrive, where to assemble, when to start marching and the route to march. First-aid stations were strategically located—even where to faint!

Yes, I was there, I observed that circus. Who ever heard of angry revolutionists all harmonizing "We Shall Overcome . . . Some Day . . ." while tripping and swaying along arm-in-arm with the very people they were supposed to be angrily revolting against? Who ever heard of angry revolutionists swinging their bare feet together with their oppressor in lily-pad park pools, with gospels and guitars and "I Have a Dream" speeches?

"Betty has gone off her rocker ..."

THE FEMININE MYSTIQUE AND THE WOMEN'S RIGHTS MOVEMENT

1963

BETTY FRIEDAN

P erhaps once in a generation, a single book can start a social movement. Betty Friedan's The Feminine Mystique, *published in 1963, was such a book. From its very opening it transformed a widespread but vague discontent into clear, convincing words:"The problem lay buried, unspoken, for many years in the minds of American women. It was a strange stirring, a sense of dissatisfaction, a yearning that women suffered in the middle of the twentieth century in the United States. Each suburban wife struggled with it alone. As she made the beds, shopped for groceries, matched slipcover material, ate peanut butter sandwiches with her children, chauffeured Cub Scouts and Brownies, lay beside her husband at night—she was afraid to ask even of herself the silent question—'Is this all?' "*

Friedan became the leader of the Women's Liberation movement by acclamation, and in 1970 became the founder and first president of the National Organization for Women.

This account comes from the introduction to the tenth-anniversary edition of the book, and from its epilogue.

It seems such a precarious accident that I ever wrote the book at all— but, in another way, my whole life had prepared me to write that book. All the pieces finally came together. In 1957, getting strangely bored with writing articles about breast feeding and the like for *Redbook* and the *Ladies' Home Journal,* I put an unconscionable amount of time into a questionnaire for my fellow Smith graduates of the class of 1942, thinking I was going to disprove the current notion that education had fitted us ill for our role as women. But the questionnaire raised more questions than it answered for me—education had *not* exactly geared US to the role women were trying to play, it seemed. The suspicion arose as to whether it was the education or the role that was wrong. *McCall's* commissioned an article based on my Smith alumnae questionnaire, but the then male publisher of *McCall's,* during that great era of togetherness, turned the piece down in horror, despite underground efforts of female editors. The male *McCall's* editors said it couldn't be true.

I was next commissioned to do the article for *Ladies' Home Journal*. That time I took it back, because they rewrote it to say just the opposite of what, in fact, I was trying to say. I tried it again for *Redbook*. . . . The editor of *Redbook* told my agent, "Betty has gone off her rocker. She has always done a good job for us, but this time only the most neurotic housewife could identify." I opened my agent's letter on the subway as I was taking the kids to the pediatrician. I got off the subway to call my agent and told her, "I'll have to write a book to get this into print."

What I was writing threatened the very foundations of the women's magazine world—the feminine mystique.

. . . When *The Feminine Mystique* was at the printer's, and my last child was in school all day, I decided I would go back to school myself and get my Ph.D. Armed with my publisher's announcement, a copy of my *summa cum laude* undergraduate degree and twenty-years-back graduate record, and the New World Foundation report of the educational project I had dreamed up and run in Rockland County, I went to see the head of the social psychology department at Columbia. He was very tolerant and kind, but surely, at forty-two, after all those undisciplined years as a housewife, I must understand that I wouldn't be able to meet the rigors of full-time graduate study for a Ph.D. and the mastery of statistics that was required. "But I used statistics throughout the book," I pointed out. He looked blank. "Well, my dear," he said, "what do you want to bother your head getting a Ph.D. for, anyhow?"

I began to get letters from other women who now saw through the feminine mystique, who wanted to stop doing their children's homework and start doing their own; they were also being told they really weren't capable of doing anything else now but making homemade strawberry jam or helping their children do fourth-grade arithmetic. It wasn't enough just to take yourself seriously as a person. Society had to change, somehow, for women to make it as people. It wasn't possible to live any longer as "just a housewife." But what other way was there to live? I remember getting stuck at that point, even when I was writing *The Feminine Mystique*. I had to write a last chapter, giving a solution to "the problem that has no name," suggesting new patterns, a way out of the conflicts, whereby women could use their abilities fully in society and find their own existential human identity, sharing its action, decisions, and challenges without at the same time renouncing home, children, love, their own sexuality. My mind went blank. You do have to say "no" to the old way before you can begin to find the new "yes" you need. Giving a name to the problem that had no name was the necessary first step. But it wasn't enough.

Personally, I couldn't operate as a suburban housewife any longer, even if I had wanted to. For one thing, I became a leper in my own suburb. As long as I only wrote occasional articles most people never read, the fact that I wrote during the hours when the children were in school was no more a stigma than, for instance, solitary morning drinking. But now that I was acting like a real writer and even being interviewed on television, the sin was too public, it could not be condoned. Women in other suburbs were writing me letters as if I were Joan of Arc, but I practically had to flee my own crabgrass-overgrown yard to keep from being burned at the stake. Although we had been fairly popular, my husband and I were suddenly no longer invited to our neighbors' dinner parties. My kids were kicked out of the car pool for art and dancing classes. The other mothers had a fit when I now called a cab when it was my turn, instead of driving the children myself. We had to move back to the city, where the kids could do their own thing without my chauffeuring and where I could be with them at home during some of the hours I now spent commuting. I couldn't stand being a freak alone in the suburbs any longer.

At first, that strange hostility my book—and later the movement— seemed to elicit from some women amazed and puzzled me. Even in the beginning, there wasn't the hostility I had expected from men. Many men bought *The Feminine Mystique* for their wives and urged them to go back to school or to work. I realized soon enough that there were probably millions of women who had felt as I had, like a freak, absolutely alone, as a suburban housewife. But if you were afraid to face your real feelings about the husband and children you were presumably living for, then someone like me opening up the can of worms was a menace.

I didn't blame women for being scared. I was pretty scared myself. It isn't really possible to make a new pattern of life all by yourself. I've always dreaded being alone more than anything else. The anger I had not dared to face in myself during all the years I tried to play the helpless little housewife with my husband—and feeling more helpless the longer I played it—was beginning to erupt now, more and more violently. For fear of being alone, I almost lost my own self-respect trying to hold on to a marriage that was based no longer on love but on dependent hate. It was easier for me to start the women's movement which was needed to change society than to change my own personal life.

. . . I went to Washington because a law had been passed, Title VII of the Civil Rights Act of 1964, banning sex discrimination in employment along with race discrimination. The sex discrimination part had been tacked on as a joke and a delaying maneuver by a southern congressman, Howard Smith of Virginia. At the first press conferences after the law went into effect, the administrator in charge of enforcing it joked about the ban on sex discrimination. "It will give men equal opportunity to be *Playboy* bunnies," he said.

In Washington I found a seething underground of women in the government, the press, and the labor unions who felt powerless to stop the sabotage of this law that was supposed to break through the sex discrimination that pervaded every industry and profession, every factory, school, and office. Some of these women felt that I, as a now known writer, could get the public's ear.

One day, a cool young woman lawyer, who worked for the agency that was not enforcing the law against sex discrimination, carefully closed the door of her office and said to me with tears in her eyes, "I never meant to be so concerned about women. I like men. But I'm getting an ulcer, the way women are being betrayed. We may never have another chance like this law again. Betty, you have to start an NAACP for women. You are the only one free enough to do it."

I wasn't an organization woman. I never even belonged to the League of Women Voters. However, there was a meeting of state commissioners on the status of women in Washington in June. I thought that, among the women there from the various states, we would get the nucleus of an organization that could at least call a press conference and raise the alarm among women throughout the country.

Pauli Murray, an eminent black lawyer, came to that meeting, and Dorothy Haener and Caroline Davis from the UAW, and Kay Clarenbach, head of the Governor's Commission in Wisconsin, and Katherine Conroy of the Communications Workers of America, and Aileen Hernandez, then a member of the Equal Employment Opportunities Commission. I asked them to come to my hotel room one night Most didn't think women needed a movement like the blacks, but everyone was mad at the sabotage of Title VII. The consensus was that the conference could surely take respectable action to insist that the law be enforced.

I went to bed relieved that probably a movement wouldn't have to be organized. At six the next morning, I got a call from one of the top token women in the Johnson administration, urging me not to rock the boat. At eight the phone rang again; this time it was one of the reluctant sisters of the night before, angry now, really angry. "We've been told that this conference doesn't have the power to take any action at all, or even the right to offer a resolution. So we've got a table for us all to eat together at lunch, and we'll start the organization." At the luncheon we each chipped in a dollar. I wrote the word "NOW" on a paper napkin; our group should be called the National Organization *for* Women, I said, "because men should be part of it." Then I wrote down the first sentence of the NOW statement of purpose, committing ourselves to "take *action* to bring women into full participation in the mainstream of American society now, exercising all the privileges and responsibilities thereof, in truly equal partnership with men."

. . . I couldn't define "liberation" for women in terms that denied the sexual and human reality of our need to love, and even sometimes to depend upon, a man. . . . It seemed to me that men weren't really the enemy—they were fellow victims, suffering from an outmoded masculine mystique that made them feel unnecessarily inadequate when there were no bears to kill.

. . . On our first picket line at the White House fence ("Rights Not Roses") on Mother's Day in 1967, we threw away chains of aprons, flowers, and mock typewriters. We dumped bundles of newspapers onto the floor of the Equal Employment Opportunities Commission in protest against its refusal to enforce the Civil Rights law against sex-segregated "Help Wanted: Male" ads (for the good jobs) and "Help Wanted: Female" ads (for Gal Friday–type jobs). This was supposed to be just as illegal now as ads reading "Help Wanted: White" and "Help Wanted: Colored." We announced we were going to sue the federal government for not enforcing the law equally on behalf of women (and then called members of our underground in the Justice Department to see if one could do that) and we did.

. . . Our only real office in those years was my apartment. It wasn't possible to keep up with the mail. But when women like Wilma Heide from Pittsburgh, or Karen De Crow in Syracuse, Eliza Paschall in Atlanta, Jacqui Ceballos—so many others—were so determined to have NOW chapters that they called long distance when we didn't answer their letters, the only thing to do was to have them become local NOW organizers.

I remember so many way stations: Going to lunch at the for-men-only Oak Room at the Plaza Hotel with fifty NOW women and demanding to be served . . . Testifying before the Senate against the nomination to the Supreme Court of a sexist judge named Carswell who refused to hear a case of a woman who was fired because she had preschool children . . . Seeing the first sign of a women's underground in the student movement, when I was asked to lead a rap session at the National Student Congress in College Park, Maryland, in 1968 . . . After a resolution for the liberation of women from the mimeograph machines was laughed down at the SDS convention, hearing the young radical women telling me they had to have a separate women's-lib group—because if they really spoke out at SDS meetings, they might not get married . . . Helping Sheila Tobias plan the Cornell intersession on women in 1968, which started the first women's studies programs (how many universities have them now!) . . . Persuading the NOW board that we should hold a Congress to Unite Women with the young radicals despite differences in ideology and style . . . So many way stations.

I admired the flair of the young radicals when they got off the rhetoric of sex/class warfare and conducted actions like picketing the Miss America beauty contest in Atlantic City. But the media began to publicize, in more and more sensational terms, the more exhibitionist, down-with-men, down-with-marriage, down-with-childbearing rhetoric and actions. Those who preached the man-hating sex/class warfare threatened to take over the New York NOW and the national NOW and drive out the women who wanted equality but who also wanted to keep on loving their husbands and children.

. . . The man-haters were given publicity far out of proportion to their numbers in the movement because of the media's hunger for sensationalism. Many women in the movement go through a temporary period of great hostility to men when they first become conscious of their situation; when they start acting to change their situation, they outgrow what I call pseudo-radical infantilism. But that man-hating rhetoric increasingly disturbs most women in the movement, in addition to keeping many women out of the movement.

On the plane to Chicago, preparing to bow out as president of NOW, feeling powerless to fight the man-haters openly and refusing to front for them, I suddenly knew what had to be done. A woman from Florida had written to remind me that August 26, 1970, was the fiftieth anniversary of the constitutional amendment giving women the vote. We needed to call a national action—a strike of women to call attention to the unfinished business of equality: equal opportunity for jobs and education, the right to abortion and child-care centers, the right to our own share of political power. It would unite women again in serious action—women who had never been near a "women's lib" group. (NOW, the largest such group, and the only one with a national structure, had only 3,000 members in thirty cities in 1970.)

The grass-roots strength of NOW went into organizing the August 26 strike. In New York, women filled the temporary headquarters volunteering to do anything and everything; they hardly went home at night. Mayor Lindsay wouldn't close Fifth Avenue for our march, and I remember starting that march with the hoofs of policemen's horses trying to keep us confined to the sidewalk. I remember looking back, jumping up to see over marchers' heads. I never saw so many women; they stretched back for so many blocks you couldn't see the end. I locked one arm with my beloved Judge Dorothy Kenyon (who, at eighty-two, insisted on walking with me instead of riding in the car we had provided for her), and the other arm with a young woman on the other side. I said to the others in the front ranks, "Lock arms, sidewalk to sidewalk!" We overflowed till we filled the whole of Fifth Avenue. There were so many of us they couldn't stop us; they didn't even try. It was, as they say, the first great nationwide action of women (hundreds of men also marched with us) since women won the vote itself fifty years before. Reporters who had joked about the "bra-burners" wrote that they had never seen such beautiful women as the proud, joyous marchers who joined together that day. For all women were beautiful on that day.

"The President was face down on the back seat . . ."

PRESIDENT KENNEDY IS ASSASSINATED

November 22, 1963
Dallas, Texas

MERRIMAN SMITH

*U*nited Press International reporter Smith won a Pulitzer Prize for this account.

It was a balmy, sunny noon as we motored through downtown Dallas behind President Kennedy. The procession cleared the center of the business district and turned into a handsome highway that wound through what appeared to be a park.

I was riding in the so-called White House press "pool" car, a telephone company vehicle equipped with a mobile radio-telephone. I was in the front seat between a driver from the telephone company and Malcolm Kilduff, acting White House press secretary for the President's Texas tour. Three other pool reporters were wedged into the back seat.

Suddenly we heard three loud, almost painfully loud, cracks. The first sounded as if it might have been a large firecracker. But the second and third blasts were unmistakable. Gunfire.

The President's car, possibly as much as 150 or 200 yards ahead, seemed to falter briefly. We saw a flurry of activity in the Secret Service followup car behind the chief executive's limousine.

Next in line was the car bearing Vice President Lyndon B. Johnson. Behind that, another followup car bearing agents assigned to the vice president's protection. We were behind that car.

Our car stood still for probably only a few seconds, but it seemed like a lifetime. One sees history explode before one's eyes and for even the most trained observer there is a limit to what one can comprehend.

I looked ahead at the President's car but could not see him or his companion, Gov. John B. Connally of Texas. Both men had been riding on the right side of the limousine from Washington. I thought I saw a flash of pink, which would have been Mrs. Jacqueline Kennedy.

Everybody in our car began shouting at the driver to pull up closer to the President's car. But at this moment, we saw the big limousine and a motorcycle escort roar away at high speed.

We screamed at our driver, "Get going, get going." We careened around the Johnson car and its escort and set out down the highway, barely able to keep in sight of the President's car and the accompanying Secret Service followup car.

They vanished around a curve. When we cleared the same curve we could see where we were heading—Parkland Hospital, a large brick structure to the left of the arterial highway. We skidded around a sharp left turn and spilled out of the pool car as it entered the hospital driveway.

I ran to the side of the limousine.

The President was face down on the back seat. Mrs. Kennedy made a cradle of her arms around the President's head and bent over him as if she were whispering to him.

Gov. Connally was on his back on the floor of the car, his head and shoulders resting in the arms of his wife, Nellie, who kept shaking her head and shaking with dry sobs. Blood oozed from the front of the governor's suit. I could not see the President's wound. But I could see blood spattered around the interior of the rear seat and a dark stain spreading down the right side of the President's dark gray suit.

From the telephone car, I had radioed the Dallas bureau of UPI that three shots had been fired at the Kennedy motorcade. Seeing the bloody scene in the rear of the car at the hospital entrance, I knew I had to get to a telephone immediately.

Clint Hill, the Secret Service agent in charge of the detail assigned to Mrs. Kennedy, was leaning over into the rear of the car. "How badly was he hit, Clint?" I asked. "He's dead," Hill replied curtly.

I raced down a short stretch of sidewalk, into a hospital corridor. . . . Jiggs Fauver of the White House transportation staff grabbed me and said Kilduff [of the White House press staff] wanted a pool of three men immediately to fly back to Washington on Air Force 1, the presidential aircraft.

Aboard Air Force 1, on which I had made so many trips as press association reporter covering President Kennedy, all of the shades of the larger main cabin were drawn and the interior was hot and dimly lighted.

Kilduff propelled us to the President's suite two-thirds of the way back in the plane. The room is used normally as a combination conference and sitting room and could accommodate eight to ten people seated.

I wedged inside the door and began counting. There were 27 people in this compartment. Johnson stood in the center with his wife, Lady Bird. U.S. District Judge Sarah T. Hughes, 67, a kindly faced woman, stood with a small black Bible in her hands, waiting to give the oath.

The compartment became hotter and hotter. Johnson was worried that some of the Kennedy staff might not be able to get inside. He urged people to press forward, but a Signal Corps photographer, Capt. Cecil Stoughton, standing in the corner on a chair, said if Johnson moved any closer, it would be virtually impossible to make a truly historic photograph.

It developed that Johnson was waiting for Mrs. Kennedy, who was composing herself in a small bedroom in the rear of the plane. She appeared alone, dressed in the same pink wool suit she had worn in the morning when she appeared so happy shaking hands with airport crowds at the side of her husband.

She was white-faced but dry-eyed. Friendly hands stretched toward her as she stumbled slightly. Johnson took both of her hands in his and motioned her to his left side. Lady Bird stood on his right, a fixed half-smile showing the tension. . . .

The brief ceremony ended when Johnson, in a deep, firm voice, repeated after the judge, ". . . So help me God."

Johnson turned first to his wife, hugged her about the shoulders and kissed her on the cheek. Then he turned to Kennedy's widow, put his left arm around her and kissed her cheek.

As others in the group—some Texas Democratic House members, members of the Johnson and Kennedy staffs—moved toward the new President, he seemed to back away from any expression of felicitation.

The two-minute ceremony concluded at 2:38 p.m. CST and seconds later, the President said firmly, "Now, let's get airborne."

When the President's plane reached operating altitude, Mrs. Kennedy left her bedchamber and walked in the rear compartment of the plane. This was the so-called family living room, a private area where she and Kennedy, family and friends had spent many happy airborne hours chatting and dining together.

Kennedy's casket had been placed in this compartment, carried aboard by a group of Secret Service agents.

Mrs. Kennedy went into the rear lounge and took a chair beside the coffin. There she remained throughout the flight.

"How does one go about meeting a Beatle?"

THE BEATLES ARRIVE

February 7–9, 1964
New York City

TOM WOLFE AND WILLIAM WHITWORTH

*T*he New York Herald Tribune *covered the first U.S. tour of the Beatles as something of a parody of a visit by a foreign head of state, with stories throughout the week. Beatlemania was the perfect target of the paper's stylish writers. (The* Tribune *proudly claimed that it beat the heavily staffed* New York Times, *which had a man for every rathole in the city, by hiring a rat for every manhole. Many of its enterprising reporters have become national figures, among them Jimmy Breslin, Liz Smith, Gail Sheehy, Dick Schaap, and the two young reporters quoted in these accounts: Tom Wolfe, now famous for his journalism and fiction, and William Whitworth, longtime editor of* The Atlantic Monthly.)

According to the review of the group's appearance on the Ed Sullivan Show, by television critic John Horn, the Beatles "are more of a sight than a sound. Without their shaggy-dog moptops and their sensational buildup, they would be four nice boys with a total of one weak voice and one weak beat that rolls more than it rocks."

FEBRUARY 7—TOM WOLFE

By six-thirty A.M., half the kids from South Orange, New Jersey, to Seaford, Long Island, were already up with their transistors plugged in their skulls. It was like a civil defense network or something. You could turn anywhere on the dial, WMCA, WCBS, WINS, almost any place, and get the bulletins: "It's B-Day! Six-thirty A.M.! The Beatles left London thirty minutes ago! They're thirty minutes out over the Atlantic Ocean! Heading for New York!"

By one P.M. about 4,000 kids had finished school and come skipping and screaming into the international terminal at Kennedy Airport. It took 110 police to herd them. At one-twenty P.M., the Beatles' jet arrived from London.

The Beatles left the plane and headed for customs inspection and everybody got their first live look at the Beatles' hair style, which is a mop effect that covers the forehead, some of the ears and most of the back of the neck. To get a better look, the kids came plunging down the observation deck, and some of them already had their combs out, taking their hair down over their foreheads as they ran.

Then they were crowding around the plate-glass windows overlooking the customs section, stomping on the floor in unison, some of them beating time by bouncing off the windows.

The Beatles—George Harrison, 20; John Lennon, 23; Ringo Starr, 23; and Paul McCartney, 21—are all short, slight kids from Liverpool who wear four-button coats, stovepipe pants, ankle-high black boots with Cuban heels. And droll looks on their faces. Their name is a play on the word "beat."

They went into a small room for a press conference, while some of the girls tried to throw themselves over a retaining wall.

Somebody motioned to the screaming crowds outside. "Aren't you embarrassed by all this lunacy?"

"No," said John Lennon. "It's crazy."

"What do you think of Beethoven?"

"He's crazy," said Lennon. "Especially the poems. Lovely writer."

In the two years in which they have risen from a Liverpool rock-and-roll dive group to the hottest performers in the record business, they had seen much of this wildness before. What really got them were the American teenage car sorties.

The Beatles left the airport in four Cadillac limousines, one Beatle to a limousine, heading for the Plaza Hotel in Manhattan. The first sortie came almost immediately. Five kids in a powder blue Ford overtook the caravan on the expressway, and as they passed each Beatle, one guy hung out the back window and waved a red blanket.

A white convertible came up second, with the word BEETLES

scratched on both sides in the dust. A police car was close behind that one with the siren going and the alarm light rolling, but the kids, a girl at the wheel and two guys in the back seat, waved at each Beatle before pulling over to the exit with the cops gesturing at them.

In the second limousine, Brian Sommerville, the Beatles' press agent, said to one of the Beatles, George Harrison: "Did you see that, George?"

Harrison looked at the convertible with its emblem in the dust and said, "They misspelled Beatles."

But the third sortie succeeded all the way. A good-looking brunette, who said her name was Caroline Reynolds, of New Canaan, Conn., and Wellesley College, had paid a cab driver $10 to follow the caravan all the way into town. She cruised by each Beatle, smiling faintly, and finally caught up with George Harrison's limousine at a light at Third Avenue and 63rd St.

"How does one go about meeting a Beatle?" she said out of the window.

"One says hello," said Harrison out of the window.

"Hello!" she said. "Eight more will be down from Wellesley." Then the light changed and the caravan was off again.

At the Plaza Hotel, there were police everywhere. The Plaza, on Central Park South just off Fifth Avenue, is one of the most sedate hotels in New York. The Plaza was petrified. The Plaza accepted the Beatles' reservations months ago, before knowing it was a rock-and-roll group that attracts teenage riots.

About 500 teenagers, most of them girls, had shown up at the Plaza. The police herded most of them behind barricades in the square between the hotel and the avenue. Every entrance to the hotel was guarded. The screams started as soon as the first limousine came into view.

The Beatles jumped out fast at the Fifth Avenue entrance. The teenagers had all been kept at bay. Old ladies ran up and touched the Beatles on their arms and backs as they ran up the stairs.

After they got to the Plaza the Beatles rested up for a round of television appearances (the Ed Sullivan Show, Sunday), recordings (Capitol Records), concerts (Carnegie Hall, Wednesday) and a tour (Washington, Miami). The kids were still hanging around the Plaza hours after they went inside. One group of girls asked everybody who came out, "Did you see the Beatles? Did you touch them?"

A policeman came up, and one of them yelled, "He touched a Beatle! I saw him!" The girls jumped on the cop's arms and back, but it wasn't a mob assault. There were goony smiles all over their faces.

FEBRUARY 8 — WHITWORTH

The Plaza Hotel, which seldom knows a louder noise than violin music or the pop of a champagne cork, listened in dismay yesterday to the squeals of the young set. Teen-age girls began trying to crash the hotel about 7:30 yesterday morning, in the hope of getting a look at a Beatle. They were turned away at every door by guards from the Burns Detective Agency. By noon, there was a full-scale demonstration in front of the hotel. About 300 girls, held back by patrolmen and mounted policemen, hollered for the Beatles to come out and face their public. They carried signs saying "We love you," "Come out Beatles," and "Elvis is Dead." They chanted "We want the Beatles, we want the Beatles."

A Beatle, of course, is a British rock 'n' roll singer who looks like an Old English Sheepdog and bays like an American foxhound. There are four of them, and they are a sensation. Luckily for the public peace, the girls did not know that inside the hotel one Beatle lay abed, stricken with a sore throat. They almost certainly would have stormed the police lines and scaled the hotel wall to minister to him.

The Beatles ignored the girls. The three healthy ones slipped out a side door and drove to the Boathouse in Central Park, where they posed for photographers. From there they went to the Columbia Broadcasting System studio at 219 W. 53d St., to rehearse for their appearance tonight on the Ed Sullivan Show. Ed, who has hired everything from trained seals to acrobats, said that he had never seen anything quite like a Beatle.

Neither have the New York police, who must protect the Beatles from all the little girls who'd like to get the singers down and just shampoo them to death, or something.

. . . The Beatles themselves don't know how they do it. Young girls must know, but if you ask them, they just whimper or give you a look that says, if you have to ask questions about it, don't mess with it. Two lucky teen-aged girls with high connections got into the Beatle rehearsal— Kathy Cronkite, thirteen, and Nancy Cronkite, fifteen, daughters of Walter Cronkite, the CBS newsman. They could hardly stand it. They whined and squirmed and covered their mouths with their hands, perhaps to avoid speaking in tongues. They got to meet Ringo Starr, who is the drummer and the shaggiest of the Beatles. Ringo, who looks a lot like one of the original Three Stooges, was described by the girls as "precious and adorable." They said their father didn't especially like their reaction to the Beatles, and that he was no fan of rock 'n' roll.

About 2:15 P.M., four prop men wheeled a set of drums on to the stage of the Columbia Broadcasting System television studio [of the Ed Sullivan Show] at 53d St. and Broadway. It brought the house down.

Fifteen solid seconds of high-pitched, multi-decibel screaming. A sound as though of anguish, death and destruction. Because these weren't just any drums; these drums belonged to Ringo Starr, the hairiest of the Beatles. They were ceremonial objects, like a Beatle boot or Beatle bangs.

The response from the 650 teenagers in the studio set the tone for the afternoon, during which the Beatles gave their first American performance.

Bouncing and yelling like that, the sound inside a girl's head must be a lot like that terrible screech the BMT Astoria train makes as it turns east near 59th St. and Seventh Avenue.

Crew members said there had never been such hysteria on the show, not even for Elvis Presley. Mr. Sullivan had to plead with the girls again and again to be quiet. "Stop it or I'll get a barber," he shouted once.

"I had the best seat in the house ..."

THE VIETNAM WAR BEGINS

August 4–11, 1964
Tonkin Gulf

ADMIRAL JAMES STOCKDALE

*T*he Tonkin Gulf incident led to America's official declaration of war against North Vietnam. However, it is worth noting that thousands of U.S. military "advisers" had already been sent to Vietnam, and the U.S. was already funding most of the effort against the North. As well, the French had been fighting since the 1940s, trying unsuccessfully to maintain the Indochina holdings they had gathered since the 1800s. And the Vietnamese could claim they had been resisting foreign invaders for two thousand years.

Eyewitness Stockdale was commander of Fighter Squadron Fifty-One on the U.S.S. Ticonderoga. *He flew in a real shootout with Vietnamese PT boats that occurred August 2, and was in the air on August 4, the day of a fake "Tonkin incident" concocted by Washington bureaucrats to prompt Congress to start the war.*

He later became the highest-ranking U.S. prisoner of war in North Vietnam, where he was held for six years without proper medical treatment for the considerable wounds he suffered when he was shot down. After returning home he became a fellow at the Hoover Institute in California. In 1992, he was Ross Perot's vice-presidential running mate.

I had the best seat in the house, orbiting a few hundred feet above the two American destroyers, clear of the surface haze and spray that their crews' eyeballs and radars had to penetrate. And when, after a couple of hours, it came to light that no American eyeball, from the air or from the destroyers, had ever detected a PT boat or a wake or a gunflash, a steady stream of messages emanated from that same destroyer commodore who had sent the first [alert of a possible attack]: "Wait, there may have been a mistake, take no action until we have proof. Hold your horses." . . .

The whole scene was loaded for misinterpretation. You had people in Washington who had passed up the opportunity for a show of force two days before. You had a frustrated President who was getting heat on the back channels from Maxwell Taylor and the then current head of state in Saigon—heat for passing up that chance. You had a President who felt inferior and ill at ease in the office, and who had bearing down on him from behind in a hot presidential campaign, Barry Goldwater, whose main plank was that Johnson was soft on Vietnam. And so when the messages started to come in saying that there was a second Tonkin Gulf event, he was elated because here was the reprieve: "My God, two days ago I made an ass of myself and now I can recover and win the election and happy days are here again."

. . . The visibility from the deck of the destroyers was nowhere near as good as it was for me circling around at a thousand feet, surveying the whole area. They later found sailors who claimed to have seen sparkling things in the water, but most of those "sparkling things" sightings were dreamed up a couple of days later, when re-debriefings were conducted after a message from Washington demanded "proof." I know of no responsible person who considers them anything but bunk. Two days before, I'd led the attack against real boats in the daytime and I saw my bullets hit them and even in bright sunlight I could see sparks as they glanced off. I could see their wakes were wider and more pronounced than the destroyers' wakes. Their guns flashed. People say, "Wasn't it a dark night?" Yes, it was dark as hell and that's why I could see so well. The wake would have been luminous. The ricochets would have been sparkling, the gunfire of the PT boats would have been red and bright. I'm sure I'd have seen anything within five miles of those boats during the hour and a half that I was there. No question about it.

No boats were there and when I got back to the ship, the commander of the destroyers had come to the same conclusion. He [cabled Washington,] "Please don't take any rash action until you verify this." In other words, a plea to disregard the [earlier] messages he'd been sending—that weather conditions, the sonar operator's lack of skill and other things had rendered the question wide open and not to take action on it. These cables were part of the same three-hour continuum. And Washington had those in their hands for twelve hours and I'm sure that important people were seeing them. They had twelve hours to change their minds and it still went on.

I went to bed laughing that night. I was very tired and I was laughing in relief. I'd nearly flown into the water and killed myself trying to find these boats. It was the third flight I'd had in one day, it was after midnight, and on the way out there I thought we were going to war and I'd said, "My God, I'm going to be telling my grandchildren about this night." And I finally realized there was nothing to find and came back and they read me the messages that had passed from the destroyers to Washington saying the same thing. And they also sent in my reports. Everybody was saying, "Well, that was the goddamnedest mess we've ever been in. Let's have a cup of coffee and forget about it." If this had happened in the nineteenth century, before radios, that would have been the end of it.

And then I was awakened about two hours later by a young officer and told that they have received word from Washington that we're going to retaliate. And I said, "Retaliate for what?" And he said, "For last night's attack." He didn't know any better. Well, I sat there on the edge of the bed realizing that I was one of the few people in the world that realized we were going to launch a war under false pretenses. And sure enough, the next day we did.

I led this big horde of airplanes over there and we blew the oil tanks clear off the map. . . .

Now it is very important to understand that there was a tinderbox situation in the Western Pacific that was probably going to precipitate war, and a person might say, "What's all the fuss about. It was going to happen anyway, what is so wrong about picking the opportune time to trigger it? No big thing." But there is such a thing as moral leverage, which tilts the argument in the other direction. The Communists have a great nose for moral leverage. Any good bargainer knows the balance of authority has tipped when the other guy has performed some act of which he might be ashamed. And in the case of starting wars it is very, very important that you have that moral leverage behind you.

A leader who starts a war must face the fact that there will later be many times when he wishes he could get out of that war. Because as the caskets move by and grief emerges there is going to be a great temptation, unless he is just an Adolf Hitler, to get out of that. And "to get out of that" that way is a worse mistake usually than getting into it, because it lets everybody down, just like McNamara and Johnson bailed out and left a whole generation of Americans over there to pick up after them.

I'm a warrior and you can see I'm a hawk, but I'm going to tell you that when you get into a war you've got to be very sure that you are on honest, solid rock foundations or it's going to eat you alive. In a real war, you just cannot risk losing moral leverage, which he [Johnson] did. There was no question that Washington knew what they had done and not a lot of question about them knowing it as they did it. . . .

I could have sulked or resigned but I didn't. I would have been ground up like an ant. There would have been no satisfaction in being a martyr. Anyway, I told them what the truth was. A message went out from the ship to Washington right after I had landed, saying that I had seen no boats. But it was a great learning experience. I was forty-one and growing up. I had always thought the government worked just like Poli. Sci. One and Two said it did. And now I realized that this was a goddamned fiasco and I was a part of it. And I thought, "Well, live and learn. This is the way the ballgame is played."

The Tonkin Gulf resolution passed on August 7. That was two days after the flight I'm talking about. And the State Department said that was the functional equivalent of a declaration of war. But it passed on the coat-tails of the second—the false—incident. And McGeorge Bundy later said that Johnson was so much a child of Congress that when he got the resolution he thought the war was over. If Congress was behind him, then it was just a matter of waiting for the curtain to fall.

He signed that thing on August 11. And that day we read at the breakfast table that the Harris poll showed LBJ's popularity jumped fourteen percentage points. And just before noon that same day I was sitting at my desk doing paperwork when suddenly the ship's yodelhorn blared the welcome-aboard honors appropriate for a vice admiral. I remember wondering how that happened out there in the middle of the ocean. And then the phone rang. It was Captain Hutch Cooper. He said, "Jim, a couple of guys just came aboard and say they want to talk to you. I'll send them down with an escort." There were two guys in sports shirts and slacks, one about my age and the other younger. The older one introduced himself as Jack Stempler, special assistant to Secretary McNamara. And he said, "The day before yesterday, I was down with my family at the cottage at Nag's Head. About four in the afternoon I was walking back to the beach and what do I see but a government staff car in the driveway. I was to go right to Washington. So I picked up a bag and away we went. We were sent out here just to find out one thing. Were there any fuckin' boats out there the other night or not?" And this is four hours after they'd signed the "declaration of war."

"I forgot about praying,
and I just turned and ran."

POLICE TRY TO HALT THE SELMA MARCH

March 21, 1965
Alabama

SHEYANN WEBB

*T*he *five-day march from Selma to Montgomery, a voter registration drive orga-*
nized by Martin Luther King, Jr., John Lewis, Hosea Williams, and other mem-
bers of the Southern Christian Leadership Conference, ended with a demonstration
of twenty-five thousand people in front of the State House.

Now the Edmund Pettus Bridge sits above the downtown; you have to walk up it like it's a little hill. We couldn't see the other side: we couldn't see the troopers. So we started up and the first part of the line was over. I couldn't see all that much because I was so little; the people in front blocked my view.

But when we got up there on that high part and looked down, we saw them. I remember [a] woman saying something like, "Oh, my Lord" or something. And I stepped out to the side for a second and I saw them. They were in a line—they looked like a blue picket fence—stretched across the highway. There were others gathered behind that first line and to the sides. . . . And further back were some of Sheriff Jim Clark's posse-men on their horses. Traffic had been blocked.

At that point I began to get a little uneasy about things. I think everyone did. People quit talking: it was so quiet then that all you could hear was the wind blowing and our footsteps on the concrete sidewalk.

Well, we kept moving down the bridge. I remember glancing at the water in the Alabama River, and it was yellow and looked cold. I was told later that Hosea Williams said to John Lewis, "See that water down there? I hope you can swim, 'cause we're fixin' to end up in it."

The troopers could be seen more clearly now. I guess I was fifty to seventy-five yards from them. They were wearing blue helmets, blue jackets, and they carried clubs in their hands: they had those gas-mask pouches slung across their shoulders. The first part of the march line reached them and we all came to a stop. For a few seconds we just kept standing, and then I heard this voice speaking over the bullhorn saying that this was an unlawful assembly and for us to disperse and go back to the church.

I remember I held the woman's hand who was next to me and had it gripped hard. I wasn't really scared at that point. Then I stepped out a ways and looked again and saw the troopers putting on their masks. That scared me. I had never faced the troopers before, and nobody had ever put on gas masks during the downtown marches. But this one was different: we were out of the city limits and on a highway. Williams said something to the troopers asking if we could pray . . . and then I heard the voice again come over the bullhorn and tell us we had two minutes to disperse. . . .

. . . So the next thing I know—it didn't seem like two minutes had gone by—the voice was saying, "Troopers advance and see that they are dispersed." Just all of a sudden it was beginning to happen. I couldn't see for sure how it began, but just before it did I took another look and saw the line of the troopers moving toward us: the wind was whipping at their pants legs. . . .

All I knew is I heard all this screaming and the people were turning and I saw this first part of the line running and stumbling back toward us. At that point, I was just off the bridge and on the side of the highway. And they came running and some of them were crying out and somebody yelled, "Oh, God, they're killing us!" I think I just froze then. . . .

I remember looking toward the troopers and they were backing up, but some of them were standing over some of our people who had been knocked down or had fallen. It seemed like just a few seconds went by and I heard a shout, "Gas! Gas!" And everybody started screaming again. And I looked and I saw the troopers charging us again and some of them were swinging their arms and throwing canisters of tear gas. And beyond them I saw the horsemen starting their charge toward us. . . .

I'll tell you, I forgot about praying, and I just turned and ran. And just as I was turning, the tear gas got me: it burned my nose first, then got my eyes. I was blinded by the tears. So I began running and not seeing where I was going. I remember being scared that I might fall over the railing and into the water. I don't know if I was screaming or not, but everyone else was. People were running and falling and ducking and you could hear people scream and hear the whips swishing and you'd hear them striking the people. . . . It seemed to take forever to get across the bridge. It seemed I was running uphill for an awfully long time. . . . I just knew then that I was going to die, that those horses were going to trample me. . . .

All of a sudden somebody was grabbing me under the arms and lifting me up and running. The horses went by and I kept waiting to get trampled on or hit, but they went on by and I guess they were hitting at somebody else. And I looked up and saw it was Hosea Williams who had me and he was running but we didn't seem to be moving, and I shouted at him, "Put me down! You can't run fast enough with me!" But he held on until we were off the bridge and down on Broad Street and he let me go. I didn't stop running until I got home.

"We have a love story, too ..."

STORY PITCH AT A HOLLYWOOD STUDIO

1967

JOHN GREGORY DUNNE

In 1965, Dunne was granted access to 20th Century Fox for his book, The Studio. *In all, he spent a year at Fox observing studio operations.*

Richard Zanuck was vice president in charge of production at the time. His father, film pioneer Darryl Zanuck, was Fox's president. Darryl Zanuck subsequently fired his son.

Mary Ann McGowan, Richard Zanuck's secretary, came into his office and announced that director Henry Koster, producer Robert Buckner and three William Morris agents were waiting outside.

"What's Buckner's first name?" Zanuck asked.

492 • *Eyewitness to America*

"Robert," Mary Ann McGowan said, as she disappeared out the door. "They call him Bob."

The five visitors filed into Zanuck's office. Zanuck rose and shook the hand of each. "Hello, Bob," he said to Buckner.

Koster, Buckner and two of the agents arranged themselves in chairs in front of Zanuck's desk. The third agent slid onto a couch in the corner of the office. Koster cleared his throat and wiped his forehead with a handkerchief. He is a portly man with thinning hair slicked down on the top of his head and a thick middle-European accent. At one time he had directed a number of pictures for the Studio. "I have a story for you, Dick," he said.

Zanuck nodded. No one spoke for a moment. Koster wiped his forehead again and mashed the handkerchief in his hand.

"I have wanted to bring to the screen a story of great music," he said, "ever since I first came to this country and made 'A Hundred Men and a Girl.' " He looked to Zanuck for encouragement. "With Deanna Durbin," he added.

Zanuck picked up the bronzed baby shoe behind his desk and began to turn it around in his hands. His eyes did not catch Koster's.

"We fade in on Moscow," Koster said. "Behind the credits, we hear one of the world's great symphony orchestras playing—Shostakovich would be good for Moscow. The orchestra has a flamboyant, tempestuous conductor—I think Lenny Bernstein will love this idea. As we finish the credits, we come on on the orchestra and then we close on the cymbals. It is obvious that the cymbal player is sick. The orchestra is supposed to leave Moscow that night for a charity concert in New York." Koster paused for effect. He was sweating profusely. "For crippled children."

One of the Morris agents was examining his fingernails. The head of the agent on the couch began to nod. "When the concert is over, we find that the cymbal player has a contagious disease," Koster said. He wound the handkerchief around his palms. "We can work out the disease later. The orchestra must be quarantined in Moscow. All except the Lenny Bernstein character. I think we can work out that he had the right shots. Anyway we can get Lenny out of Moscow and back to New York. Now here is your problem, Dick. The charity concert must be canceled."

The agent on the couch had now fallen asleep. An abortive snore jolted him awake.

"Unless," Koster continued. He smiled benignly. "There is a youth orchestra in New York and they can take the place of the symphony at the concert. We have, of course, tried to get the Philadelphia and the Cleveland and Ormandy and George Szell would love to do it, but they have commitments. So the Lenny Bernstein character goes to hear the youth symphony and he says, 'No, I cannot conduct them, they are not good enough.' He will not yield, the concert must be canceled, there will be no money for the crippled children." Koster's voice softened. "But then the president of the charity comes to plead with him against cancellation." Koster's head swiveled around, taking in everyone in the room. "In his arms, he is carrying a small boy—with braces on his legs."

Buckner seemed to sense that Zanuck's attention was wavering. "We have a love story, too, Dick," he said.

Koster picked up the cue. "Yes, we have a love story," he said. "There is a beautiful Chinese cellist who does not speak a word of English and a beatnik kook who plays the violin." The words rolled over his tongue. "They communicate through the international language of music."

"Don't forget the jazz," Buckner said.

"We can get jazz into our story, Dick," Koster said. "You see, the concert is only five days away and there are not enough players in the youth orchestra, so the conductor—the Lenny Bernstein character—goes out and hunts them up in a bunch of weird joints."

"Jazz joints," Buckner said.

The top of Koster's head was slick with perspiration. His voice began to quicken. "Working day and night, the conductor molds these untutored players into a symphony orchestra. In just five days." Koster's face grew somber. "Then we get word from Moscow. The quarantine has been lifted. The orchestra can get back to New York in time for the concert."

Zanuck gazed evenly, unblinkingly at Koster.

"Here is the crux of our story, Dick," Koster said. "Will our conductor use the youth symphony, or will he use his own orchestra, thus destroying by his lack of faith this beautiful instrument"—Koster's hands moved up and down slowly—"he has created in just five days?"

Koster sighed and leaned back, gripping both the arms on his chair. There was silence in the office. Zanuck cleared his throat.

"Very nicely worked out," he said carefully. "Very nicely." His jaw muscles began to work as he considered his thoughts. "But I'm afraid it's not for us at the moment." He squared the bronzed baby shoe against the edge of his desk. "We've got a lot of musical things on the schedule right now—The Sound of Music is still doing great business, just great, we've got Dr. Dolittle and we're working on Hello, Dolly—and I don't think we should take on another." He paused, seeking the right words. "And quite frankly, I'm just a little afraid of this kind of music. You'll get the music lovers, no doubt about that, none at all. But how about the Beatle fans?"

Koster made a perfunctory objection, but the meeting was over. As if on cue, the dozing agent awoke, and after an exchange of small talk, agents and clients departed Zanuck's office, hurling pleasantries over their shoulders. For a long time, Zanuck sat chewing on a fingernail, saying nothing.

"Jesus," he said finally.

*"I'm totally surrounded
by you guys. I'm cooperating."*

THE LONG, HOT SUMMER

July 1967
Detroit

JAMES INGRAM

The summer of 1967 was marked by race riots in more than a hundred cities. The worst was the weeklong Detroit riot. Forty-three people were killed, two thousand were injured, and five thousand were left homeless after buildings were burned. President Johnson sent almost five thousand paratroopers to stop the violence.

There had been a huge riot in Watts in 1965, and there would be riots again in 1968, when Dr. Martin Luther King, Jr., was assassinated. But the summer of 1967 was "the long, hot summer."

Ingram, an auto worker at the time, and later a reporter, had been arrested for stopping to buy gasoline on the third day of the riot, after gasoline sales had been halted. His account comes from Voices of Freedom, *an oral history of the civil rights movement compiled by Henry Hampton and Steve Fayers.*

We were taken to the Seventh Precinct—I knew that because the ride was very short—and the doors were flung open and somebody started yelling, "Run, niggers, run." And an officer started slinging us out of the van. I couldn't see that clearly what was going on in front of me, but I was the last one out of the van and I saw my brother in front of me being swung at. There were National Guardsmen on the right and police on the left, and they were swinging rifles and swinging these brightly painted red pickax handles and I was trying to dodge some of the swings. I don't know how I got through there with only being hit hard one time with a rifle barrel. That's what broke my right arm. We sort of ran, I guess as fast as we could. Some of them were really swinging quite wildly, but it was an experience I'll never forget. It was like I was going to myself, What have we done? I mean, we're guilty of Lord knows what in these guys' minds. I mean, they were treating us like we were hardened criminals or something. And all we were doing was attempting to buy some gas in a gas station. We were in the wrong place at the wrong time.

We were placed in a holding cell, which was rather large but still very crowded because there were so many people in there. At one point we were all talking and they brought in this white kid. I guess everybody at that point was black or Hispanic or whatever. And this young white kid came in, and some of the younger black guys, as soon as he got inside that door and the door was slammed shut, just charged him. He apparently was fairly alert, because he knew right away he was going to be dead meat. He literally climbed the steel bars of the door and climbed almost all the way up to the ceiling. I don't even know how he maintained his balance. At that point, Ross Mitchell and myself and several others just kind of prevailed upon the guys. "Leave the kid alone. He's not bothering anybody. He's in here with us. He may have been doing some of the things we were doing, you know, and he may in fact be innocent, so why are you trying to do something to him?" So, at that point, I began to think that this really couldn't be characterized as a race riot, although there was that white-black thing in terms of the schism between the police and those they were locking up. And I guess they were hurling their resentment of the police back at this one kid. And I didn't think that was fair.

Later on they took us to be fingerprinted and I was taken down this corridor with a young guardsman holding a rifle to my head. And I got to the end of the corridor and this really young kid, looked to be no more than sixteen, put a .45 automatic to my right temple. I was led over to this bench where a police officer grabbed my hand and squeezed it real hard and said, "Relax, nigger."

And I said, "I can't relax, this guy's got . . . Why don't you have him take this gun from my temple? What am I, John Dillinger, going to escape? I'm totally surrounded by you guys. I'm cooperating."

And he said, "I'll teach you. I'll show you how to relax," and he put this cigarette out right on my hand. And it was just a pinpoint fire that just seemed to shoot right up my arm. I never knew that kind of pain existed. I mean, it was excruciating. I lost consciousness almost. I remember the one kid with the rifle. He grabbed me and tried to hold me up. And I never was actually fingerprinted.

I left the Seventh Precinct with a burning, raging fury inside of me. These people I'd have thought were guardians of the law and protectors of the people were in fact brutal racist oppressors, and I felt that they had to be wiped out totally. I had a personal mission out of that experience that meant that it was my job in conjunction with others to kill them all and make sure they had no chance of ever reproducing, that they were evil devils, much as the Muslims had said. I along with eleven other people formed something that we called the Order of the Burning Spear, and that was our primary mission—to kill white people, beginning with the police and guardsmen.

"I didn't know I had it in me."

THE MY LAI MASSACRE

March 16, 1968
South Vietnam

VARNADO SIMPSON

When Lieutenant William Calley and his men raided the small village of My Lai they killed an estimated three hundred and forty-seven people, mostly unarmed civilians. The incident was covered up, but one soldier wrote to government officials repeatedly until they investigated. Many of the soldiers were charged, five were court-martialed, and one, Calley, was convicted on charges of premeditated murder of twenty-two civilians. He was sentenced to life imprisonment, but a federal court overturned the decision. The incident helped turn public opinion against the war.

Varnado Simpson was a member of Calley's unit. He told his story to Michael Bilton and Kevin Sim, authors of Four Hours in My Lai.

That day in My Lai, I was personally responsible for killing about 25 people. Personally. Men, women. From shooting them, to cutting their throats, scalping them, to cutting off their hands and cutting out their tongue. I did it. I just went. My mind just went. And I wasn't the only one that did it. A lot of other people did it. I just killed. Once I started, the training, the whole programming part of killing, it just came out. A lot of people were doing it. So I just followed suit. I just lost all sense of direction, of purpose. I just started killing any kinda way I could kill. It just came. I didn't know I had it in me.

But like I say, after I killed the child, my whole mind just went. It just went. And once you start, it's very easy to keep on. Once you start. The hardest—the part that's hard is to kill, but once you kill, that becomes easier, to kill the next person and the next one and the next one. Because I had no feelings or no emotions or no nothing. No direction. I just killed. It can happen to anyone. Because, see, I wasn't the only one that did it. Hung 'em, you know—all type of ways. Any type of way you could kill someone, that's what they did. And it can happen.

"The whole world is watching."

POLICE BREAK UP A STUDENT PROTEST

August 27, 1968
Chicago

STUDS TERKEL

*T*en *thousand protesters had gone to Chicago, site of the Democratic party convention, to create a scene of political theater that would capture the attention of the national television news crews. The Chicago police force more than played its role. Police officers appeared to rampage, beating both protesters and bystanders in front of the cameras. The event became known as a police riot.*

Then came the second act. Eight protest leaders were charged with conspiracy to incite the riots. One of them, Jerry Rubin, later recalled: "It took eight or nine months before the Justice Department made the huge mistake of putting the symbols of a generation on trial in the most publicized trial at that time in history. . . . I remember when I got the indictment. I was thrilled. Thank God! I called it the Academy Award of protest."

The trial was a microcosm of the anarchy in the streets. At one point the National Guard was called in to maintain order outside the courthouse. The defendants, defense lawyer William Kunstler, and Judge Julius Hoffman were so openly antagonistic that Hoffman ordered one defendant, Black Panther Bobby Seale, bound and gagged. Seale was eventually tried separately. Some of the remaining Chicago Seven, as they became known, were convicted on lesser charges, but the convictions were overturned because of judicial bias in 1973.

Chicago reporter Studs Terkel was caught in the second night of rioting.

Last night, a gathering of the young in the park was broken up by Chicago police. Clubs were swung and heads were busted. Several young journalists were among those clobbered. The ministrations in the tent, a moment ago, brought to mind the wild night before. Would there be a repeat performance tonight? The indignant young, and a surprising number of the middle-aged, plan to gather once more in the park. Mayor Daley has ordered the police to disperse all at eleven o'clock. That is the park's official curfew. For years, it has been more honored in the breach than in the observance. For years, smelt fishermen have lingered and hoped all night long for a good catch. They have sat along the banks of the lake, in the area that is officially Lincoln Park, from nightfall to well past dawn. It has been a Chicago ritual ever since the Potawatamies. But tonight, Mayor Daley, with Nestor-like wisdom, has decreed that the curfew shall ring at the appointed hour.

Led by young clergymen of the North Side Ministry, a raggletaggle band is marching toward the park. A huge, rude wooden cross is borne at the head of the parade. James Cameron [a British journalist] and I join the procession. It is a lovely midsummer evening. Thousands are seated upon the grass. Brief speeches are made. Familiar songs are sung. "Amen." "Down by the Riverside." "Come by Here." Even "We Shall Overcome." Cameron is "instantly transported back seven or eight years to Aldermaston." The feeling of dejà vu overcomes a number of others, too, including myself. The occasion is both tender and sad. Cameron notes that this ceremonial of what appears to be genuine dedication, touched by anxiety, anger, and some fear, is almost deliberately masked by outrageous costumes and fancy dress. A few youngbloods, hot out of Radcliffe and Amherst, protest the tranquil spirit. They are gently hooted down by the others. It is something of a religious occasion. Testimony is offered by one or another, caught in the spirit of the occasion. Even I.

A young clergyman recognizes me as one who talks a great deal, to others as well as to himself. At a microphone, one doesn't have to bear too much witness. "I am glad to be here, where life is," I intone preacherlike, "rather than at the Amphitheatre where life ain't." It doesn't really matter; the mike isn't working very well. I am certain, I let James Cameron know, that nothing will happen tonight. After all, last night's bloody encounter was chronicled by the world's press and television. The Whole World Is Watching. It was certainly a black eye for Chicago. Mayor Daley may not be Pericles, but he's not really so dumb as to stage an encore. He'll just let the kids say their say, shout their shouts, sing their songs, and wander off. . . .

James Cameron accepts my word, because I know such things. He and I shall soon wander off ourselves and toast a peaceful night with a martini or two. The era of good feeling is short-lived. About three minutes after my pronouncement, Cameron says, "Look out there." So does the young clergyman at the mike. All eyes peer into the semidarkness across the green field. About two hundred yards away, in what appears to be a ghostly light,from lamps and headlights of cars speeding down Outer Drive, is gathered a Roman legion. So it seems. We see helmets and shields, face shields of plastic. We see no faces. We are, all of us, transfixed. Have I seen this before on some wall tapestry? Or in some well-thumbed pictorial history of ancient times? Here, a band of raggletaggle Christians and all sorts of outcasts. There, a battalion of armed soldiers of the Empire. Or is it a summer festival of young pagans, about to be disrupted by figures out of some primordial myth? One thing is certain: we are dreaming awake.

Several police trucks are faintly visible. From one, a voice on the bullhorn is heard. It is impersonal in tone. "You are ordered to clear out of the park by eleven o'clock." We shall be allowed to go peacefully. Those who remain will be in violation of the law. The young clergyman suggests that those who wish to leave may do so now. We have about an hour to go. Hardly anyone moves. A band of young men uproot the huge cross from its original position, carry it some fifty yards forward, and implant it in the field. It stands between us and them. In the night vapors, it is awesome. Will it, as in medieval times, ward off the devil, wherever he may be? "I have never seen the crucifix more symbolically used," murmurs Cameron. . . . A young man says to Jim and me, "You two elderly people better go. We don't want you hurt. Tear gas is nasty." Cameron and I harrumph indignantly. Elderly, indeed! Yet, our indignation is muted by something deeply felt.

At first, there had been a gratitude expressed by a good number of the young that so many Over Thirty are here, to help them bear some sort of witness. Now, as Cameron observes, they are solicitous. Rather they be hurt than us. Advice is offered by young veterans to middle-aged rookies. When the gas comes, hold your nose. Breathe through your mouth. Moisten your handkerchief. We are waiting. Waiting. . . . It is nearly eleven o'clock. Now, the tension cannot be disguised. The helmeted figures across the field are motionless. So are the trucks. "They always have the advantage," observes Cameron. "The decision is theirs. They can keep us waiting as long as they want." "Eleven o'clock." A last warning from the voice on the bullhorn. Nobody moves. The faceless images come alive. They are coming toward us. So are the trucks. "I don't believe it," somebody says. A sound is heard. Another. And another.

Canisters of tear gas are being shot out from the tanklike trucks. Held noses and wet handkerchiefs do little good. We are coughing, hawking, crying, spitting, phlegming, cursing . . . We are helpless. And humiliated. The humiliating attributes of tear gas are astonishing. We are stumbling, helter-skelter, across the park, toward Clark Street. It is a retreat of stumblebums. James Cameron and I, among others whose presence we hardly sense, are two characters out of Samuel Beckett. We are Estragon and Vladimir. We are Hamm and Clov. We are Krapp. We cling to one another. We cough, we spit, we hawk, we curse. Like blind Pozzo, we stumble on. A canister falls at our feet. A tall young man, of flowing blond beard (I note, tearfully), immediately behind us, kicks the canister away, toward himself. "Are you all right? Are you all right?" he coughs at us, solicitously. "Grrrhhgg," we reply. "Are you sure?" "Grrrhhgg," we insist.

We are huddled, refugees, a good fifty of us, on the safety island in the middle of Clark Street. Sirens are sounding. The whole city, it seems, is possessed by the wailing of banshees. Nobody is in his right mind. Cars are racing past. We see the faces of the occupants. They are crazy with fear. Of us. One car deliberately swerves toward the island, on which we hover. I see the driver's face. It is distorted. Hate and terror. Of us. His hand is on the horn; stuck to it. Noise and confusion. We cry out. The car's fender scrapes against a young islander. It knocks him down. He howls, jumps up, and beats against the window. Others join him. Banging away at the car, they almost overturn it. Sirens. Horns. Rage. Madness.

"A frantic group of marines
worked at keeping me alive ..."

A FORTUNATE SON

October 1968
Viem Dong, Vietnam

LIEUTENANT LEWIS B. PULLER, JR.

*O*n June 23, 1968, shortly before this event took place, the Vietnam War became the longest war in American history. Half a million troops were on duty in Vietnam at the time.

One of those troops, Lewis B. Puller, Jr., was the son of General "Chesty" Puller, the most decorated marine in the history of the corps. He followed his father into the marines but had a very different experience. Pain from the devastating injuries he suffered as a platoon leader in Vietnam led him to a painkiller addiction and then to alcoholism. He fought his way back to sobriety, but his personal life was never the same. He died by his own hand in 1994, a delayed casualty of the war. This account comes from his autobiography, Fortunate Son, *which won a Pulitzer Prize in 1992.*

Captain [Clyde] Woods devised an ambitious operation. . . . As Woods outlined the plan, in effect a cordon and search operation, for his platoon leaders and platoon sergeants a few days after our earlier conversation, I could see several of the men nod their heads and murmur approvingly. We could not be certain of engaging any of our enemies, of course, but our own risk was minimal. If our timing was right, the operation could turn out to be a turkey shoot.

. . . The word came down that the choppers were on their way, and I smoked one last cigarette before assembling the men by squads in their staging area.

As soon as our chopper alighted, the men raced to its yawning tailgate and piled aboard. I made certain we all were accounted for before taking a seat beside the door gunner and giving the crew chief the thumbs-up. As we lifted off, I felt the familiar pull in the pit of my stomach caused by our rapid ascent, and when we leveled off, I relaxed my hold on the side of the craft and watched the blur of foliage passing just beneath us. The sky was streaked with the red of the rising sun, and I realized, as I watched its reflection on the glassy surface of the South China Sea, that at least for today the rain was finished. The pilot nosed down in a clearing between the beach and Viem Dong after only a few minutes aloft, and we scrambled down the gangway and fanned out to take up our positions as he reversed his direction and banked up into the sky.

I concentrated as best I could on making certain that the two squads to my left were on line and in position to hook up with the platoon adjacent to them, but in the confusion and noise from the other helicopter around us, control was almost impossible. . . . After I had gotten my men on line, my next assignment was to connect with his location. Watson followed closely in my tracks with the radio, but the two nearest men to us were at least twenty meters away on either side and for all intents and purposes out of hearing range. As we maneuvered, I scanned the area to my immediate front, which I had been neglecting in my effort to maintain platoon integrity.

Suddenly I saw a squad of green-uniformed North Vietnamese soldiers begin running out of the village and in my direction. They had apparently panicked when the helicopters began landing and were now probing for a way out of the noose we were drawing around them. As they advanced toward me, I was unable to get the attention of the marines near me, and it dawned on me, to my horror, that I was the only obstacle between them and freedom. I raised my rifle to my shoulder and attempted to draw a bead on the lead soldier; but my first bullet was off the mark, and when I pulled the trigger the second time, my rifle jammed. By now the North Vietnamese soldiers had spotted me, and several of them fired wildly in my direction until they abruptly altered their advance and veered off to my left. Standing alone with a malfunctioning weapon and seven enemy soldiers bearing down on me, I was at once seized by a fear that was palpable and all-encompassing. My throat became as dry as parchment, and beads of perspiration popped out on my forehead before coursing down my face. I turned abruptly, with Watson in tow, and ran as fast as I could toward the safety of the bluffs above Viem Dong, where the company headquarters party was to be located.

A narrow trail led up the hill to the headquarters group, and as I approached, it never occurred to me that the thirty meters between my course and the commanders' position had not been secured. I knew only that the firepower advantage of the NVA squad I had just encountered would be neutralized if I could reach the men milling at the crest of the hill. With only a few meters left to cover in my flight, a thunderous boom suddenly rent the air, and I was propelled upward with the acrid smell of cordite in my nostrils.

When I landed a few feet up the trail from the booby-trapped howitzer round that I had detonated, I felt as if I had been airborne forever. Colors and sound became muted, and although there was now a beehive of activity around me, all movement seemed to me to be in slow motion. I thought initially that the loss of my glasses in the explosion accounted for my blurred vision, and I had no idea that the pink mist that engulfed me had been caused by the vaporization of most of my right and left legs. As shock began to numb my body, I could see through a haze of pain that my right thumb and little finger were missing, as was most of my left hand, and I could smell the charred flesh, which extended from my right wrist upward to the elbow. I knew that I had finished serving my time in the hell of Vietnam.

As I drifted in and out of consciousness, I felt elated at the prospect of relinquishing my command and going home to my wife and unborn child. I did not understand why Watson, who was the first man to reach me, kept screaming, "Pray, Lieutenant, for God's sake, pray." I could not see the jagged shards of flesh and bone that had only moments before been my legs, and I did not realize until much later that I had been forever set apart from the rest of humanity.

For the next hour a frantic group of marines awaited the medevac chopper that was my only hope of deliverance and worked at keeping me alive. Doc Ellis knelt beside my broken body and with his thumbs kept my life from pouring out into the sand, until a tourniquet fashioned from a web belt was tied around my left stump and a towel was pressed tightly into the hole where my right thigh had joined my torso. My watch and rifle were destroyed by the blast, and my flak jacket was in tatters; but I did manage to turn my undamaged maps and command of the platoon over to Corporal Turner during one of my lucid intervals. I also gave explicit orders to all the marines and corpsmen hovering around me that my wife was not to be told of my injuries until after the baby was born. There was, of course, no possibility of compliance with my command, but the marines ministering to me assured me that my wishes would be honored.

Because we were on a company-size operation, there were six corpsmen in the immediate area around Viem Dong, and each of them carried a supply of blood expanders, which were designed to stabilize blood pressure until whole blood could be administered. As word spread of my injuries, each of the company's corpsmen passed his expanders to Doc Ellis, who used up the last of them while my men slapped at my face, tried to get me to drink water, and held cigarettes to my lips in an attempt to keep me awake. When the chopper finally arrived, I was placed on a stretcher and gently carried to its entrance, where a helmeted crew chief and medevac surgeon helped me aboard. Someone had located my left boot which still contained its bloody foot and that, too, was placed on the stretcher with me.

As the chopper began its race toward the triage of the naval support hospital in Da Nang, I was only moments from death, but I remember thinking clearly before losing consciousness that I was going to make it. I never again saw the third platoon of Golf Company, a remarkable group of young men with whom I had had the most intense male relationships of my life, and I felt guilty for years that I had abandoned them before our work was finished. I was to feel even worse that I was glad to be leaving them and that, in my mind, I had spent my last healthy moments in Vietnam running from the enemy. I came to feel that I had failed to prove myself worthy of my father's name, and broken in spirit as well as body, I was going to have to run a different gauntlet.

. . . When I regained consciousness, I was in a clean bed with white sheets. An assortment of tubes carried liquids to and from my body, and when I reached up to remove the annoying one affixed to my nose, I found that I could not do so because both my hands were wrapped in bandages the size of boxing gloves. I understood the reason for my bandaged hands because I had seen my right hand with its missing thumb and little finger earlier, and I also knew that my left hand now retained only a thumb and half a forefinger. The word prehensile no longer applied to me. I did not yet know or knew only vaguely that I had lost my right leg at the torso and that only a six-inch stump remained of my left thigh. In addition to the damage to my extremities, I had lost massive portions of both buttocks, my scrotum had been split, I had sustained a dislocated shoulder and a ruptured eardrum, and smaller wounds from shell fragments peppered the remainder of my body. Only my face had been spared. It remarkably contained only one small blue line across my nose from a powder burn.

"I do not feel that I am a piece of property ..."

THE BIRTH OF MODERN SPORTS: CURT FLOOD FIGHTS BASEBALL

October–December 1968
St. Louis

CURT FLOOD

*C*urt Flood had been an all-star second baseman for several of his twelve seasons with the St. Louis Cardinals before the Cardinals traded him to the Philadelphia Phillies in 1970.

But Flood did not want to play in Philadelphia. After much soul-searching, and careful planning, he decided to take the issue to court. His fight against the practice of baseball's team owners to hold perpetual options on a player's service—called the "reserve clause"—probably had a greater impact on modern sports than any single performance by an athlete or team in a game. Baseball owners had evaded previous efforts to strike down the reserve clause, and Flood also lost his court case. But his battle established the path for later cases that won. Free agency reset the balance of power between players and owners in all professional sports.

After the case Flood returned to baseball briefly for the Washington Senators, then retired.

If I had taken inventory before the front office called, I would have compiled a formidable list. Expensive athlete. Painter of oil portraits as negotiable as any currency. Student of the human condition. Impervious to shock. Subdivision: black. Belief in the American dream: lapsed.

Wrong. The dream dies hard. It lay deep within me, dormant but not destroyed . . .

I was an expert on baseball's spurious paternalism. I was a connoisseur of its grossness. I had known that I was out of phase with management. I therefore had known that I might be traded. Yet now, when the industry was merely doing its thing, I took it personally. I felt unjustly cast out. Days passed before I began to see the problem whole.

. . . The more deeply I explored myself, the more determined I became to take baseball to court. I was in luck. Until me, no player had been able to do himself the honor of committing so fundamental an act in behalf of his profession. Danny Gardella, a Giant outfielder blacklisted for playing in the Mexican League, had sued the owners and had won in the Circuit Court of Appeals. But he had been persuaded to settle for cash.

I would not settle out of court for any amount, unless the bargain included employer-employee relations of a kind acceptable to me and the Major League Baseball Players Association. I had little money, but I was fortified by what I am not ashamed to call spiritual resources. I had spent good years with Johnny Jorgensen. I would do us both proud by trying to improve my own corner of society before moving on. Win or lose, the baseball industry would never be the same. I would leave my mark.

. . . On December 24, I fired the opening shot, a letter to Bowie Kuhn, the Commissioner of Baseball. . . . The letter said:

Dear Mr. Kuhn—

After twelve years in the major leagues, I do not feel that I am a piece of property to be bought and sold irrespective of my wishes . . .

"The door crashes open,
  beer cans and bottles hurtle in ..."

STONEWALL

July 3, 1969
New York City

HOWARD SMITH

*T*he gay rights movement began with this riot at a New York bar called the
  Stonewall Inn. The patrons had been harassed by police before, but on this
night they decided to fight back. Many police officers had to barricade themselves
inside the bar to protect themselves as the crowd outside grew.

  Within three years of this incident the number of gay rights groups in the
United States grew from about twenty to about twelve hundred. In 1973, in part as
a result of the efforts of these groups, the American Psychiatric Association stopped
classifying homosexuality as a psychiatric disorder.

  Smith (not to be confused with television reporter Howard K. Smith) was an
unsympathetic Village Voice *reporter.*

During the "gay power" riots at the Stonewall last Friday night, I
found myself on what seemed to be the wrong side of the blue line. Very
scary. Very enlightening. . . .

  The turning point came when the police had difficulty keeping a dyke
in a patrol car. Three times she slid out and tried to walk away. The last
time a cop bodily heaved her in. The crowd shrieked, "Police brutality!"
"Pigs!" A few coins sailed through the air. I covered my face. Pine ordered
the three cars and paddy wagon to leave with the prisoners before the
crowd became more of a mob. "Hurry back," he added, realizing he and
his force of eight detectives, two of them women, would be easily overwhelmed if the temper broke. "Just drop them at the Sixth Precinct and
hurry back."

  The sirened caravan pushed through the gauntlet, pummeled and buf-
feted until it managed to escape. "Pigs!" "Faggot cops!" Pennies and dimes
flew. I stood against the door. The detectives held at most a ten-foot clearing. Escalate to nickels and quarters. A bottle. Pine says, "Let's get inside.
Lock ourselves inside, it's safer."

"You want to come in?" he asks me. "You're probably safer," with a paternal tone. Two flashes: If they go in and I stay out, will the mob know that the blue plastic thing hanging from my shirt is a press card, or by now will they assume I'm a cop too? On the other hand, it might be interesting to be locked in with a few cops, just rapping and reviewing how they work.

In goes me. We bolt the heavy door. The front of the Stonewall is mostly brick except for the windows, which are boarded within by plywood. Inside we hear the shattering of windows, followed by what we imagine to be bricks pounding on the door, voices yelling. The floor shudders at each blow. "Aren't you guys scared?" I say.

"No." But they look at least uneasy.

The door crashes open, beer cans and bottles hurtle in. Pine and his troops rush to shut it. At that point the only uniformed cop among them gets hit with something under his eye. He hollers, and his hand comes away scarlet. It looks a lot more serious than it really is. They are all suddenly furious. Three run out in front to see if they can scare the mob from the door. A hail of coins. A beer can glances off Deputy Inspector Smyth's head.

Pine, a man of about forty and smallish build, gathers himself, leaps out into the melee, and grabs someone around the waist, pulling him downward and back into the doorway. They fall. Pine regains hold and drags the elected protester inside by the hair. The door slams again. Angry cops converge on the guy, releasing their anger on this sample from the mob. Pine is saying, "I saw him throwing something," and the guy unfortunately is giving some sass, snidely admits to throwing "only a few coins." The cop who was cut is incensed, yells something like, "So you're the one who hit me!" And while the other cops help, he slaps the prisoner five or six times very hard and finishes with a punch to the mouth. They handcuff the guy as he almost passes out. "All right," Pine announces, "we book him for assault."

"The moon almost filled our circular window . . ."

ON THE MOON

July 21, 1969

NEIL ARMSTRONG

*L*ess than a decade after President John F. Kennedy promised to put an American
on the moon, the space program had progressed through the Mercury and Gem-
ini projects, and ten Apollo missions.

    *Now three astronauts—Neil Armstrong, Buzz Aldrin, and Michael Collins—
all born within a few years of Charles Lindbergh's first flight across the Atlantic,
planned to fly Apollo 11 into a moon orbit, then deploy a small landing craft
toward the moon's surface.*

    That historic landing craft, Eagle, *was a clumsy vehicle. Its walls were
flimsy—just thin plastic stretched over a frame. Its flight computers, although
advanced for the time, were so rudimentary they would frustrate a child today.*

    *While Collins piloted the command module orbiting the moon, Armstrong and
Aldrin entered* Eagle *and began the landing by following the plan that was supposed to be coordinated with NASA engineers on Earth. But the plan didn't work.
Armstrong saw a large crater and car-sized boulders at the target site, so he had to
look for another place to set the vulnerable* Eagle *down. And the craft was low on
fuel.*

    *While Aldrin called out figures from the flight computer, Armstrong took man-
ual control of the* Eagle. *He was too busy flying to describe the situation to mission
control on Earth. The NASA crew there knew only that Armstrong and Aldrin were
facing something unexpected. "I think we'd better be quiet," one NASA crew member
said.*

    Finally, with just twenty seconds of fuel left, Armstrong settled Eagle *down gen-
tly, then radioed Earth: "Houston, Tranquillity Base here. The* Eagle *has landed."*

It took us somewhat longer to emerge from *Eagle* than we had anticipated but the delay was not, as my wife and perhaps some others have half
jokingly suggested, to give me time to think about what to say when
I actually stepped out onto the moon. I had thought about that a little
before the flight, mainly because so many people had made such a big
point of it. I had also thought about it a little on the way to the moon, but
not much. It wasn't until after landing that I made up my mind what to

say: "That's one small step for a Man, one giant leap for mankind." Beyond those words I don't recall any particular emotion or feeling other than a little caution, a desire to be sure it was safe to put my weight on that surface outside *Eagle*'s footpad.

. . . The most dramatic recollections I have now are the sights themselves, those magnificent visual images. They go far beyond any other visual experiences I've had in my life. Of all the spectacular views we had, the most impressive to me was on the way toward the moon when we flew through its shadow. We were still thousands of miles away but close enough so that the moon almost filled our circular window. It was eclipsing the sun, from our position, and the corona of the sun was visible around the limb of the moon as a gigantic lens-shaped or saucer-shaped light stretching out to several lunar diameters. It was magnificent, but the moon itself was even more so. We were in its shadow so there was no part of it illuminated by the sun. It was illuminated only by the earth, by earthshine. It made the moon appear blue-gray and the entire scene looked decidedly three-dimensional.

I was really aware, visually aware, that the moon was in fact a sphere, not a disk. It seemed almost as if it were showing us its roundness, its similarity in shape to our earth, in a sort of welcome. I was sure then that it would be a hospitable host. It had been awaiting its first visitors for a long time.

"A cosmic accident . . ."

WOODSTOCK

August 15–18, 1969
Near Bethel, New York

RICHIE HAVENS, MIRIAM YASGUR, AND
MYRA FRIEDMAN

E *stimates of the crowd at the Woodstock Music and Art Fair—billed as "Three Days of Peace and Music"—ranged from three to four hundred thousand.*

It wasn't really held at Woodstock. Because citizens of that town were afraid of being overrun by hippies, the promoters moved the event to Bethel, sixty miles away. In keeping with the chaos of the festival, some fans showed up in Woodstock anyway.

As singer Richie Havens recounts, he was the first performer to go on stage. Miriam Yasgur and her husband, Max, owned the farm where the Woodstock Music and Art Fair was held. Myra Friedman worked for Janis Joplin's manager. They told their stories to Joel Makower, author of Woodstock: The Oral History.

RICHIE HAVENS

I call it a cosmic accident myself. I call it a media event, created by the media and not by the promoters, as much as they would like it to have been more in their control. What happened was created by the media. When I did come back, I heard on the radio all around the country about this festival that was going to happen on the East Coast, and the news was, "Well, they found a place to do it." And the next two days the news was, "Well, they don't have a place to do it." So, mind you, all around the country, everybody's hearing this big music news item. When there was a finality of the location, people started to leave their places then. There were people from Alaska, from California—they drove from everywhere.

I actually was afraid to go on first, basically because I knew the concert was late and I knew that people paid for this and maybe it would be a little nuts. Flying over that crowd coming in in that bubble, I knew what being nuts could mean. And I didn't want to be trampled by a billion people. So I said, "Don't put me in front of your problem like this. Don't do this to me, Michael. I'm only one guy. My bass player isn't even here." He was walking on the road for twenty-five miles because the cars were backed up. He made it as I walked off the stage, he came walking up to the stage. They'd left the car on the New York Thruway twenty-five miles back and then walked, along with a lot of other people, and they partied all the way down the line and he got there just as I got off.

. . . I just saw color to the top of the hill and beyond. When my eyes went from the foot of the stage up to the top of the hill and beyond, I went right up to the sky, I went right out to where the whole thing was. The best sound that I have ever played on outdoors to date happened at Woodstock. As a matter of fact, they said they heard it ten miles away in every direction, because they put those towers up there, and it bounced through those mountains. We not only did it for the crowd there, we did it for the whole countryside at that point. So it was a modular saturation level of vibrations into the planet. This was not just in that spot, it went ten miles all around, and that's a big circle of sound wave.

I did about four or five encores, till I had nothing else to sing, and then "Freedom" was created right there on the stage. That's how "Freedom" was created, on the stage. It was the last thing that I could think of to sing. I made it up. It was what I thought of, what I felt—the vibration which was freedom—which I thought at that point we had already accomplished. And I thought, "God, this is a miracle. Thank God I got to see it." . . . My viewpoint of it was I finally crossed over the line where I don't have to worry anymore. About the whole planet, the entire planet.

MIRIAM YASGUR

In my innocence, when they finally got this thing going, a few days before I said to Max, "You know, Joan Baez is going to be there, and I'm going to go up there for the time Joan Baez is there because I have to hear her." Some of the other people weren't as attractive, but she was one, so I had all these nice plans. I was going to go up when Joan Baez was there, maybe one or two of the other people. But, of course, there was no way I was going to get there. That went by the board.

I had to be down at the office and help take care of things. Customers were calling and routes were being diverted, the principals of the festival were getting calls on our lines, and then we had the kooks calling—you know, you would hang up and you would pick up the phone and you would get these people screaming at you and you'd hang up on them and they'd redial and scream at you. It was mostly foul language or "You're ruining the area!" or "You allowed all these hippies in!"—you know, really in more nasty tones than I'm saying. And there were a few people that were so persistent that we called the telephone company, asked them to put a check on our lines and see if they could trace back these calls, because these people were calling up and hysterically screaming on the phone at us so that we couldn't keep our lines open.

So we were involved with that, we were involved with taking food out of the cooler and feeding people, we were involved with trying to keep our business going and I really couldn't push through this. The troopers, when they would go by our office, would stop by, either to get something to drink or whatever—you know, they'd drink orange juice or chocolate milk—and they kept expressing amazement in the fact that they never saw so many youngsters together being so helpful to each other and being so peaceable that their job was really to try and keep things open as much as they could. One car with some troopers got stuck in the road. It went off the road in the crowd, you know, trying to get by, maybe a half a mile west of our office, somewhere in that area. And they said they saw all these kids coming at them and they thought, "Oh, boy." And what these kids did was lift the car and take it and put it back on the road. I had kids come in and say, "You know, there's been a couple of troopers directing traffic on that road for the last few hours. It's so hot; they must be thirsty. Could you give me something for them to drink?" And they would take cartons of chocolate milk and orange juice and go over to the troopers.

MYRA FRIEDMAN

I didn't really know I was going to Woodstock until the last minute, so I thought, "Gee, I really ought to let my mother know because what if she calls and I'm not here and she calls again—" We didn't have answering machines then. My mother lives out in St. Louis and she was a widow and you want to tell your mother where you are—or at least I did. So, I had called and it was a very hurried conversation. I said, "Look, I'm leaving, I'm going out of town for the weekend." She said, "Where are you going?" I said, "I'm going to this big rock festival, Mother, and I'll call you on Monday when I get back."

So, I think Saturday was when they were declaring it a disaster area and I knew that it had to be just terrible in terms of the news—helicopters flying in bringing in food, God knows what, you're dying, you know. So all of a sudden from the blue I think, "Oh my God, my mother!" And I go into a trailer in the back and I called my mother. And she was, indeed, absolutely hysterical. She was frightened out of her wits. She was crying and she said, "Well, they say it's a disaster." I said, "No, no, no. It's really not." And she was just carrying on and I said, "Mother, I got to get off the phone now. I'm knee-deep in mud." And there was a lot of mud out there. She said, "You're knee-deep in mud?" I said, "No, no, no. I'm really O.K." And she kept saying, "Well, where are you?" And I guess that it was Bethel, White Lake, what the hell is this? She wouldn't know where. She couldn't get a focus on it. My mother, by the way, was a highly intelligent person and she wasn't a hysteric either. But the broadcasts were really scary. So I wanted to give her a focus. So I said, "Listen, Mother, I'm just down the road from Grossinger's." And there's this silence and she calms down and says, "Oh. Well, why don't you go *there* for the weekend?"

"Houston, we've got a problem."

APOLLO 13

April 11–17, 1970

JAMES LOVELL AND JEFFREY KLUGER

*A*stronaut Jim Lovell never got to the moon. In 1968, as a crewman on Apollo 8, he had flown in the first moon orbit and mapped possible landing sites. But his next moon mission was unlucky Apollo 13. Two days into that spacecraft's voyage a mysterious explosion, later found to be a ruptured oxygen tank, crippled the ship. Lovell and crewmates Fred Haise and John Swigert, along with the NASA team in Houston, had to improvise a way to get back without their main power before the oxygen supply ran out.

Over four days they solved dozens of complicated problems using whatever equipment and supplies they could adapt to their urgent needs, even though they did not know what had gone wrong on the outside of the ship. They used the small thrusters on the spidery lunar landing module Aquarius, which now would never get to the moon, to direct the ship. They also huddled together in Aquarius, which was not meant to support them for several days, because staying in the command module would have consumed too much of their precious electrical power. Finally the moment came when they would jettison the section of the spacecraft that was wrecked by the explosion, jettison their lifeboat, Aquarius, then lock themselves into the small command module to return to Earth. If they calculated correctly and could steer the ship despite its malfunctioning navigation equipment, they would survive. But an error would either send them into Earth's atmosphere too fast, creating so much heat they would burn to death, or bounce them off the top of the atmosphere, spinning them into space forever.

Lovell's account, written with reporter Jeffrey Kluger for their book Lost Moon, picks up the story just after the crippled section of the ship has been cut loose. In Houston that day, Joe Kerwin, a fellow astronaut, had the capsule communicator (capcom) duty.

At their separate windows, Lovell, Swigert, and Haise leaned anxiously forward, raised their cameras, and flicked their eyes about their patches of sky. Swigert had chosen the big, round hatch window in the center of the spacecraft, but pressing his nose against it now he saw . . . nothing. Jumping to his left, he peered out Lovell's window and there too saw nothing at all. Scrambling across to the other side of the spacecraft, he banged into Haise's porthole, scanned as far as the limited frame would allow him, and there, too, came up empty.

"Nothing, damnit!" he yelled down the tunnel. "Nothing!"

Lovell, at his triangular window, swiveled his head from side to side, also saw nothing, and looked over to Haise, who was searching as frantically as he was and finding just as little. Cursing under his breath, Lovell turned back to his glass and all at once saw it: gliding into the upper left-hand corner of the pane was a mammoth silver mass, moving as silently and smoothly and hugely as a battleship.

He opened his mouth to say something, but nothing came out. The service module moved directly in front of his window, filling it completely; receding ever so slightly it began to roll, displaying one of the riveted panels that made up its curved flank. Drifting away a little more, it rolled a little more, revealing another panel. Then, after another second, Lovell saw something that made his eyes widen. Just as the mammoth silver cylinder caught an especially bright slash of sun, it rolled a few more degrees and revealed the spot where panel four was—or should have been.

In its place was a wound, a raw, gaping wound running from one end of the service module to the other. Panel four, which made up about a sixth of the ship's external skin, was designed to operate like a door, swinging open to provide technicians access to its mechanical entrails, and sealing shut when it came time for launch. Now, it appeared, that entire door was gone, ripped free and blasted away from the ship. Trailing from the gash left behind were sparkling shreds of Mylar insulation, waving tangles of torn wires, tendrils of rubber liner. Inside the wound were the ship's vitals—its fuel cells, its hydrogen tanks, the arterial array of pipes that connected them. And on the second shelf of the compartment, where oxygen tank two was supposed to be, Lovell saw, to his astonishment, a large charred space and absolutely nothing else.

The commander grabbed Haise's arm, shook it, and pointed. Haise followed Lovell's finger, saw what his senior pilot saw, and his eyes, too, went wide. From behind Lovell and Haise, Swigert swam frantically down the tunnel holding his Hasselblad.

"And there's one whole side of that spacecraft missing!" Lovell radioed to Houston.

"Is that right," Kerwin said.

"Right by the—look out there, would you? Right by the high-gain antenna. The whole panel is blown out, almost from the base to the engine."

"Copy that," said Kerwin.

"It looks like it got the engine bell too," Haise said, shaking Lovell's arm and pointing to the big funnel protruding from the back of the module. Lovell saw a long, brown burn mark on the conical exhaust port.

"Think it zinged the bell, huh?" Kerwin asked.

"That's the way it looks. It's really a mess."

. . . The crew followed the module until it had faded to little more than a tumbling star hundreds of yards from the ship. More than twenty minutes after Swigert had thrown the SM JETT switch, the three crew-mates fell away from their windows.

"Man," Haise mumbled to no one in particular, "that's unbelievable."

"Well, James," Kerwin called up, "if you can't take better care of a spacecraft than that, we might not give you another one."

. . . "Thirty seconds to LEM jettison," Swigert said.

"Ten seconds."

"Five."

Swigert reached up to the instrument panel, ripped away his "NO" note, and balled it up in his palm.

"Four, three, two, one, zero."

The command module pilot flipped the toggle switch and all three crewmen heard a dull, almost comical pop. In their windows, the silver roof of the lunar lander began to recede. As it did, its docking tunnel became visible, then its high-gain antenna, then the array of other antennas that bristled from its top like metal weeds. Slowly, the unbound *Aquarius* began a graceful forward somersault.

Lovell stared as the face of the ship—its windows, its attitude-control quads—rolled into view. He could see the forward hatch from which he and Haise would have emerged after settling down in the dust of Fra Mauro. He could see the ledge on which he would have stood while opening his equipment bay before climbing down to the lunar surface. He could see the reflective, almost taunting, nine-rung ladder he would have used to make that final descent. The LEM rolled some more and was now upside down, its four splayed legs pointing up to the stars, the crinkly gold skin of its descent stage shining back at *Odyssey*.

"Houston, LEM jettison complete," Swigert announced.

"O.K., copy that," Kerwin said softly. "Farewell, *Aquarius,* and we thank you."

With the loss of the lander, *Apollo 13* was at last reduced to its irreducible essence. Shorn of the 36-story Saturn 5 booster that had lifted it off the pad, the 59-foot third-stage booster that blasted it toward the moon, the 25-foot service module that was to have provided it with air and power, and finally the 23-foot LEM that was to have carried Lovell and Haise into history, the spacecraft was now nothing more than an 11-foot-tall, wingless pod, heading inexorably toward a free fall through the fast-approaching atmosphere and a collision with the fast-growing ocean.

. . . From the center seat, Jim Lovell turned to look at the men on either side of him and smiled. "Gentlemen," he said, "we're about to reenter. I suggest you get ready for a ride."

Unconsciously, the commander touched his shoulder belts and lap belts, tightening them slightly. Unconsciously, Swigert and Haise copied him.

"Joe, how far out do you show us now?" Swigert asked his capcom.

"You're moving at 25,000 miles per hour, and on our plot map board, the ship is so close to Earth we can't hardly tell you're out there at all."

"I know all of us here want to thank all you guys for the very fine job you did," Swigert said.

"That's affirm, Joe," Lovell agreed.

"I'll tell you," Kerwin said, "we all had a good time doing it."

In the spacecraft, the crew fell silent, and on the ground in Houston, a similar stillness fell over the control room. In four minutes, the leading edge of the command module would bite into the upper layer of the atmosphere, and as the accelerating ship encountered the thickening air, friction would begin to build, generating temperatures of 5,000 degrees or more across the face of the heat shield. If the energy generated by this infernal descent were converted to electricity, it would equal 86,000 kilowatt-hours, enough to light up Los Angeles for a minute and a half. If it were converted to kinetic energy, it could lift every man, woman, and child in the United States ten inches off the ground. Aboard the spacecraft, however, the heat would have just one effect: as temperatures rose, a dense ionization cloud would surround the ship, reducing communications to a hash of static lasting about four minutes. If radio contact was restored at the end of this time, the controllers on the ground would know that the heat shield was intact and the spacecraft had survived; if it wasn't, they would know that the crew had been consumed by the flames.

. . . "*Odyssey*, Houston. We just had one last time around the room, and everyone says you're looking great. We'll have loss of signal in about a minute. Welcome home."

"Thank you," Swigert said.

In the sixty seconds that followed, Jack Swigert fixed his eyes out the left-hand window of the spacecraft, Fred Haise fixed his out the right, and Jim Lovell peered through the center. Outside, a faint, faint shimmer of pink became visible, and as it did, Lovell could feel an equally faint ghost of gravity beginning to appear. The pink outside gave way to an orange, and the suggestion of gravity gave way to a full g. Slowly the orange turned to red—a red filled with tiny, fiery flakes from the heat shield— and the g forces climbed to two, three, five, and peaked briefly at a suffocating six. In Lovell's headset, there was only static.

In Mission Control, the same steady electronic hiss also streamed into the ears of the men at the consoles. When it did, all conversation on the flight controllers' loop, the backroom loops, and in the auditorium itself stopped. At the front of the room, the digital mission clock read 142 hours, 38 minutes. When it reached 142 hours, 42 minutes, Joe Kerwin would hail the ship. As the first two minutes went by, there was almost no motion in either the main room or the viewing gallery. As the third minute elapsed, several of the controllers shifted uneasily in their seats. When the fourth minute ticked away, a number of men in the control room craned their necks, casting glances toward Kranz.

"All right, capcom," the flight director said, grinding out the cigarette he had lit four minutes ago. "Advise the crew we're standing by."

"*Odyssey,* Houston standing by, over," Kerwin called.

Nothing but static came back from the spacecraft. Fifteen seconds elapsed.

"Try again," Kranz instructed.

"*Odyssey,* Houston standing by, over." Fifteen more seconds.

"*Odyssey,* Houston standing by, over." Thirty more seconds.

The men at the consoles stared fixedly at their screens. The guests in the VIP gallery looked at one another. Three more seconds ticked slowly by with nothing but noise on the communications loop, and then, in the controllers' headsets, there was a change in the frequency of the static from the ship. Nothing more than a flutter, really, but a definitely noticeable one. Immediately afterward, an unmistakable voice appeared.

"O.K., Joe," Jack Swigert called.

Joe Kerwin closed his eyes and drew a long breath, Gene Kranz pumped a fist in the air, the people in the VIP gallery embraced and applauded.

"O.K.," Kerwin answered without ceremony, "we read you, Jack."

Up in the no longer incommunicado spacecraft, the astronauts were enjoying a smooth ride. As the ion storm surrounding their ship subsided, the steadily thickening layers of atmosphere had slowed their 25,000-mile-per-hour plunge to a comparatively gentle 300-mile-per-hour free fall. Outside the windows, the angry red had given way to a paler orange, then a pastel pink, and finally a familiar blue. During the long minutes of the blackout, the ship had crossed beyond the nighttime side of the Earth and back into the day.

. . . Thirty seconds later, the astronauts felt a sudden but surprisingly painless deceleration, as their ship—behaving nothing like *Apollo 8*—sliced smoothly into the water. Instantly, the crewmates looked up toward their portholes. There was water running down the outside of all five panes.

"Fellows," Lovell said, "we're home."

"A young man cradled one of the bleeding forms . . ."

KENT STATE

May 4, 1970
Kent, Ohio

JOHN KIFNER

This event eclipsed even the Chicago riot of 1968. At Kent State University, nine protestors were wounded and four were killed.
Kifner reported for the New York Times.

Students here, angered by the expansion of the war into Cambodia, have held demonstrations for the last three nights. On Saturday night [May 2], the Army Reserve Officers Training Corps building was burned to the ground and the National Guard was called in and martial law was declared.

Today's rally, called after a night in which the police and guardsmen drove students into their dormitories and made 69 arrests, began as students rang the iron Victory Bell on the Commons, normally used to herald football victories.

A National Guard jeep drove onto the Commons and an officer ordered the crowd to disperse. Then several canisters of tear gas were fired, and the students straggled up a hill that borders the area and re-treated into buildings.

A platoon of guardsmen, armed—as they have been since they arrived here with loaded M-1 rifles and gas equipment—moved across the green and over the crest of the hill, chasing the main body of protesters.

The youths split into two groups, one heading farther downhill toward a dormitory complex, the other eddying around a parking lot and girls' dormitory just below Taylor Hall, the architecture building.

The guardsmen moved into a grassy area just below the parking lot and fired several canisters of tear gas from their short, stubby launchers.

Three or four youths ran to the smoking canisters and hurled them back. Most fell far short, but one landed near the troops and a cheer went up from the crowd, which was chanting "Pigs off campus" and cursing the war.

A few youths in the front of the crowd ran into the parking lot and hurled stones or small chunks of pavement in the direction of the guards-men. Then the troops began moving back up the hill in the direction of the college.

The students in the parking lot area, numbering about 500, began to move towards the rear of the troops, cheering. Again, a few in front picked up stones from the edge of the parking lot and threw them at the guardsmen. Another group of several hundred students had gathered around the sides of Taylor Hall, watching.

As the guardsmen, moving up the hill in a single file, reached the crest, they suddenly turned, forming a skirmish line and opening fire.

The crackle of the rifle volley cut the suddenly still air. It appeared to go on, as a solid volley, for perhaps a full minute or a little longer.

Some of the students dived to the ground, crawling on the grass in ter-ror. Others stood shocked or half-crouched, apparently believing the troops were firing into the air. Some of the rifle barrels were pointed upward.

Near the top of the hill at the corner of Taylor Hall, a student crum-pled over, spun sideways and fell to the ground, shot in the head.

When the firing stopped, a slim girl, wearing a cowboy shirt and faded jeans, was lying face down on the road at the edge of the parking lot, blood pouring out onto the macadam, about 10 feet from this reporter.

The youths stood stunned, many of them clustered in small groups staring at the bodies. A young man cradled one of the bleeding forms in his arms. Several girls began to cry. But many of the students who rushed to the scene seemed almost too shocked to react. Several gathered around an abstract steel sculpture in front of the building and looked at a .30-caliber bullet hole drilled through one of the plates.

"What would you choose?"

ROE V. WADE

December 13, 1971, and October 13, 1972
Washington, D.C.

COURT RECORDS

*I*n *1970, a pregnant woman in Dallas sought an abortion. It was denied under an 1854 Texas law denying abortions except when the mother's life was at stake. She fought the law, using the pseudonym "Jane Roe." The United States Supreme Court heard her case. (Actually, for technical reasons, it heard the case twice—hence the delay between the two dates of this account.) In 1973, the Court announced its 7–2 vote to strike down the Texas law (and a similar one in Georgia), on the grounds that the Constitution's Fourteenth Amendment protects a woman's right to choice in the matter and the Ninth Amendment reserves to the people all rights not specifically restricted. But as part of the Court's Solomonic ruling, it allowed that the state had an interest in protecting the life of an unborn child after a certain point, which was determined to be the first trimester of pregnancy.*

Sarah Weddington was Roe's counsel. Jay Floyd and Robert Flowers were lawyers on the staff of the attorney general of Texas.

DECEMBER 13, 1971

SARAH WEDDINGTON: Mr. Chief Justice, and may it please the court. . . .

I don't think there's any question but that women in Texas continue to desire abortions and to seek them out, outside our state. . . . The state cannot deny the effects that this law has on the women of Texas. Certainly there are problems regarding even the use of contraception. Abortion now for a woman is safer than childbirth. In the absence of abortion, or legal, medically safe abortions, women often resort to the illegal abortion, which certainly carries risks of death, all the side effects such as severe infection, permanent sterility, all the complications that result. And in fact, if the woman is unable to get either a legal abortion or an illegal abortion in our state, she can do a self-abortion, which is certainly, perhaps, by far the most dangerous. And that is no crime. . . .

If the pregnancy would result in the birth of a deformed or defective child, she has no relief. Regardless of the circumstances of conception, whether it was because of rape, incest, whether she is extremely immature, she has no relief. . . .

I think it's without question that pregnancy to a woman can completely disrupt her life. It disrupts her body, it disrupts her education, it disrupts her employment, and it often disrupts her entire family life. And we feel that because of the impact on the woman, this certainly, inasfar as there are any rights which are fundamental, is a matter which is of such fundamental and basic concern to the woman involved that she should be allowed to make the choice as to whether to continue or to terminate her pregnancy.

FLOYD: Mr. Chief Justice, may it please the Court. It's an old joke, but when a man argues against two beautiful ladies like this, they're going to have the last word. . . . [Nobody laughed.] There are situations in which, of course, as the Court knows, no remedy is provided. Now I think she makes her choice prior to the time she becomes pregnant. That is the time of the choice. It's like, more or less, the first three or four years of our life we don't remember anything. But once a child is born, a woman no longer has a choice, and I think pregnancy may terminate that choice. That's when . . .

COURT: Maybe she makes her choice when she decides to live in Texas.

FLOYD: . . . We say there is life from the moment of impregnation.

JUSTICE THURGOOD MARSHALL: And do you have any scientific data to support that?

FLOYD: Well, we begin, Mr. Justice, in our brief, with the development of the human embryo, carrying it through to the development of the fetus from about seven to nine days after conception.

MARSHALL: Well, what about six days?

FLOYD: We don't know.

MARSHALL: Well, this statute goes all the way back to one hour.

FLOYD: I don't . . . Mr. Justice, there are unanswerable questions in this field.

MARSHALL: I appreciate it.

FLOYD: This is an artless statement on my part.

MARSHALL: I withdraw the question.

FLOYD: Thank you. Or when does the soul come into the unborn, if a person believes in a soul? I don't know. . . . There is nothing in the United States Constitution concerning birth, contraception, or abortion. We think these matters are matters of policy, which should be properly addressed by the state legislature.

OCTOBER 11, 1972

WEDDINGTON: . . . The Court has in the past, for example, held that it is the right of the parents, and of the individual, to determine whether or not they will send their child to private school; whether or not their children will be taught foreign languages; whether or not they will have offspring—the Skinner case; whether, the right to determine for themselves whom they will marry—the Loving case.

Griswold, of course, is the primary case, holding that the state could not interfere in the question of whether or not a married couple would use birth control. And since then this Court, of course, has held that the individual has the right to determine—whether they are married or single—whether they will use birth control. So there is a great body of cases, decided in the past by this Court, in the areas of marriage, sex, contraception, procreation, childbearing, and education of children, which says that there are certain things that are so much a part of the individual concern that they should be left to the determination of the individual. . . .

If a state could show that the fetus was a person under the Fourteenth Amendment, or under some other amendment or part of the Constitution, then you would have the situation of trying . . . you would have a state compelling interest, which in some instances can outweigh a fundamental right.

JUSTICE BYRON WHITE: Well, do I get from this then that your case depends primarily on the proposition that the fetus has no constitutional rights?

WEDDINGTON: It depends on saying that the woman has a fundamental constitutional right and that the state has not proved any compelling interest for regulation in the area. Even if the Court at some point determined the fetus to be entitled to constitutional protection, you would still get back into the weighing of one life against another.

WHITE: And that's what's involved in this case—weighing one life against another?

WEDDINGTON: No, Your Honor. I said that would be what would be involved if the facts were different and the state could prove that there was a person with a constitutional right.

COURT: If it were established that an unborn fetus is a person, within the protection of the Fourteenth Amendment, you would have almost an impossible case here, would you not?

WEDDINGTON: I would have a very difficult case.

COURT: You certainly would.

ROBERT FLOWERS: It is impossible for me to trace, within my allocated time, the development of the fetus from the date of conception to the date of its birth. But it is the position of the state of Texas that upon conception we have a human being, a person within the concept of the Constitution of the United States and that of Texas also.

BLACKMUN: Now how should that question be decided? Is it a legal question, a constitutional question, a medical question, a philosophical question, a religious question, or what is it?

FLOWERS: Your Honor, we feel that it could be best decided by a legislature, in view of the fact that they can bring before it the medical testimony, the actual people who do the research. But we do have . . .

BLACKMUN: You think then it's basically a medical question?

FLOWERS: From a constitutional standpoint, no sir. I think it's fairly and squarely before this Court. We don't envy the Court for having to make this decision.

JUSTICE WHITE: If you're correct that the fetus is a person, then I don't suppose you'd have . . . the state would have great trouble permitting an abortion . . .

FLOWERS: . . . Yes, sir . . .

WHITE: . . . in any circumstance? . . .

FLOWERS: . . . It would, yes, sir . . .

WHITE: . . . to save the life of the mother, or her health, or anything else?

FLOWERS: Well, there would be the balancing of the two lives. And I think that . . .

WHITE: What would you choose? Would you choose to kill the innocent one, or what?

FLOWERS: Well, in our statute the state did choose that way, Your Honor, in protection of the mother. . . . Gentlemen, we feel that the concept of a fetus being within the concept of a person, within the framework of the United States Constitution and the Texas constitution, is an extremely fundamental thing.

COURT: Of course, if you're right about that, you can sit down.

You've won your case, except insofar as maybe the Texas abortion law presently goes too far in allowing abortions.

FLOWERS: Yes, sir. That's exactly right. We feel that this is the only question really that this Court has to answer. We have a . . .

COURT: You think the case is over for you? You've lost your case if the fetus or the embryo is not a person, is that it?

FLOWERS: Yes, sir, I would say so. . . .

JUSTICE MARSHALL: I want you to give me a medical, recognizable medical writing of any kind that says that at the time of conception that the fetus is a person.

FLOWERS: I do not believe that I could give that to you without researching through the briefs that have been filed in this case, Your Honor.

COURT: And the basic constitutional question, initially, is whether or not an unborn fetus is a person, isn't it?

FLOWERS: Yes, and entitled to the constitutional protections.

COURT: That's critical to this case, is it not?

FLOWERS: Yes, sir, it is . . . I think that here is exactly what we're facing in this case: Is the life of this unborn fetus paramount over the woman's right to determine whether or not she shall bear a child? This Court has been diligent in protecting the rights of the minorities, and, gentlemen, we say that this is a minority, a silent minority, the true silent minority. Who is speaking for these children? Where is the counsel for these unborn children, whose life is being taken? Where is the safeguard of the right to trial by jury? Are we to place this power in the hands of a mother, in a doctor? All of the constitutional rights, if this person has the person concept. What would keep a legislature, under this grounds, from deciding who else might or might not be a human being, or might not be a person?

WEDDINGTON: No one is more keenly aware of the gravity of the issues or the moral implications of this case. But it is a case that must be decided on the Constitution. We do not disagree that there is a progression of fetal development. It is the conclusion to be drawn from that upon which we disagree. We are not here to advocate abortion. We do not ask this Court to rule that abortion is good or desirable in any particular situation. We are here to advocate that the decision as to whether or not a particular woman will continue to carry or will terminate a pregnancy is a decision that should be made by that individual. That in fact she has a constitutional right to make that decision for herself, and that the state has shown no interest in interfering with that decision.

*"The real problem here
is whether anything is traceable ..."*

THE WATERGATE COVER-UP BEGINS

June 18, 1972
Key Biscayne, Florida

H. R. HALDEMAN

A little after midnight on June 17, 1972, an alert security guard at Washington's Watergate complex noticed a small piece of tape on a door in the parking garage. It looked as though the tape was holding the lock open. He tore it off. The next time he walked by the door, another piece of tape was there. Although he assumed that there was an innocent explanation—only an incompetent criminal would leave such an obvious sign, not just once, but twice—he checked the building. He found five burglars inside the office of the Democratic National Committee.

The burglars—who were also wiretappers—were arrested. Eventually they were traced to the Committee to Re-elect the President (Richard Nixon) and to the Central Intelligence Agency, setting larger investigations in motion. In addition to the Watergate break-in, those investigations would uncover several paranoid plots with odd leading characters such as martinet G. Gordon Liddy and failed writer E. Howard Hunt.

Within a year, several top members of the administration had resigned, including White House chief of staff H.R. Haldeman, White House counsel John Dean, Attorney General Richard Kleindienst, and White House special assistant on domestic affairs John Ehrlichman.

In May 1973, a Senate committee began televised hearings into the affair. John Dean became the star witness. He linked the burglars to the top members of the administration. In June, a former White House aide revealed that Nixon had taped many conversations with his staff, and the Senate subpoenaed the tapes to confirm Dean's testimony. The president refused to release them. Despite arranging the firing of the special prosecutor appointed to the case, Nixon was unable to stop the Supreme Court from supporting the Senate.

The tapes clearly showed Nixon's direct involvement in the cover-up of the affair. At the end of July 1974, a House committee charged Nixon with defying House subpoenas, violating the constitutional rights of U.S. citizens, and obstructing justice.

On August 9, Nixon became the first U.S. president to resign. He was pardoned a month later by President Gerald Ford, in advance of any possible prosecution.

Liddy, Hunt, Dean, Ehrlichman, and Mitchell were convicted of felonies and served prison sentences for their roles.

Haldeman noted in his diary the first reactions of the administration to the news that the Watergate burglars had been caught.

At Key Biscayne. The P [the President] is still over at Walker's this morning. I talked to him over the phone. I reported to him on Shultz's meeting with [union leader George] Meany yesterday, which came out to be pretty interesting. Meany had called him, wanting to meet with him, and so they had a game of golf during which Meany told him under no circumstances could he possibly support McGovern. That he was working to try and get Humphrey the nomination still, but if that failed he could not support McGovern. The big flap over the weekend has been news reported to me last night, then followed up with further information today, that a group of five people had been caught breaking into the Democratic headquarters (at the Watergate). Actually to plant bugs and photograph material.

It turns out that there was a direct connection (with CRP) [the Committee to Re-elect the President, Nixon's campaign organization], and Ehrlichman was very concerned about the whole thing. I talked to Magruder this morning, at Ehrlichman's suggestion, because he was afraid the statement that Mitchell was about to release was not a good one from our viewpoint. Magruder said that we plan to release the statement as soon as the fact that the Committee is involved is uncovered, which it now has been. It says that we've just learned that someone identified as an employee of the Committee was one of those arrested (James McCord, Jr., CRP's security coordinator). He runs a private security agency and was employed to install the system of security at the headquarters. He has a number of clients. He's not operating on our behalf or with our consent. We have our own security problems, not as dramatic as this but of a serious nature to us. We don't know if they're related but there's no place for this in a campaign. We would not permit or condone such a thing.

The real problem here is whether anything is traceable to Gordon Liddy (formerly with the White House plumbers unit, and then with CRP). He (Liddy) says no, but Magruder is not too confident of that. They were thinking of getting Mardian back to Washington (Mitchell, Mardian, Magruder, and LaRue are out in California) to keep an eye on Liddy. (Mardian was formerly Assistant Attorney General in charge of internal security, now one of Mitchell's assistants at CRP. LaRue was CRP Deputy Director.)

They think that McCord, our security guy, will be okay, but he's concerned about Liddy because of his lack of judgment and reliability. He's also concerned that two or three others are implicated. Apparently there's some cash and Magruder thought it was the DNC's, but it turns out it was ours.

I talked to Ehrlichman after that and he thinks the statement is OK and we should get it out. I talked to Colson to tell him to keep quiet. It turned out that one of the people (implicated) was on our payroll until April 1. A guy named Howard Hunt, who was the guy Colson was using on some of his Pentagon Papers and other research type stuff. Colson agreed to stay out of it and I think maybe he really will. I don't think he is actually involved, so that helps. So far the P is not aware of all this, unless he read something in the paper, but he didn't mention it to me.

"I howled at the top of my lungs . . ."

FEAR AND LOATHING AT THE SUPER BOWL

January 1973
Houston, Texas

HUNTER S. THOMPSON

The iconoclastic Thompson has himself become the icon of "gonzo" journalism. His excuse for joining the Super Bowl festivities was an assignment from Rolling Stone. *In keeping with the party mood surrounding the National Football League championship, a report of the on-field action was almost beside the point.*

". . . and whosoever was not found written into the book of
life was cast into the lake of fire . . ."

—REVELATIONS 20:15

This was the theme of the sermon I delivered off the 20th floor balcony of the Hyatt Regency in Houston on the morning of Super Bowl VIII. It was just before dawn, as I recall, when the urge to speak came on me. Earlier that day I had found—on the tile floor of the Men's Room on the hotel mezzanine—a religious comic book titled "A Demon's Nightmare," and it was from the text of this sleazy tract that I chose the words of my sermon.

The Houston Hyatt Regency—like others designed by architect John Portman in Atlanta and San Francisco—is a stack of 1000 rooms, built around a vast lobby at least 30 stories high, with a revolving "spindletop" bar on the roof. The whole center of the building is a tower of: acoustical space. You can walk out of any room and look over the indoor balcony (20 floors down, in my case) at the palm-shrouded, wood and naugahyde maze of the bar/lounge on the lobby floor.

Closing time in Houston is 2:00 A.M. There are after-hours bars, but the Hyatt Regency is not one of them. So—when I was seized by the urge to deliver my sermon at dawn—there were only about 20 ant-sized people moving around in the lobby far below.

Earlier, before the bar closed, the whole ground floor had been jammed with drunken sportswriters, hard-eyed hookers, wandering geeks and hustlers (of almost every persuasion), and a legion of big and small gamblers from all over the country who roamed through the drunken, randy crowd—as casually as possible—with an eye to picking up a last-minute sucker bet from some poor bastard half-mad on booze and willing to put some money, preferably four or five big ones, on "his boys."

The spread, in Houston, was Miami by six, but by midnight on Saturday almost every one of the two-thousand or so drunks in the lobby of the Regency—official headquarters and media vortex for this eighth annual Super Bowl—was absolutely sure about what was going to happen when the deal went down on Sunday, about two miles east of the hotel on the fog-soaked artificial turf of Rice University stadium.

Ah. . . . but wait! Why are we talking about gamblers here? Or thousands of hookers and drunken sportswriters jammed together in a seething mob in the lobby of a Houston hotel?

And what kind of sick and twisted impulse would cause a professional sportswriter to deliver a sermon from the Book of Revelations off his hotel balcony on the dawn of Super Sunday?

I had not planned a sermon for that morning. I had not even planned to be in Houston, for that matter. . . . But now, looking back on that outburst, I see a certain inevitability about it. Probably it was a crazed and futile effort to somehow explain the extremely twisted nature of my relationship with God, Nixon and the National Football League: The three had long since become inseparable in my mind, a sort of unholy trinity that had caused me more trouble and personal anguish in the past few months than Ron Ziegler, Hubert Humphrey and Peter Sheridan all together had caused me in a year on the campaign trail.

Or perhaps it had something to do with my admittedly deep-seated need to have public revenge on Al Davis, general manager of the Oakland Raiders. . . . Or maybe an overweening desire to confess that I had been wrong, from the start, to have ever agreed with Richard Nixon about any-thing, and especially pro football.

In any case, it was apparently something I'd been cranking myself up to deliver for quite a while . . . and, for reasons I still can't be sure of, the eruption finally occurred on the dawn of Super Sunday.

I howled at the top of my lungs for almost 30 minutes, raving and screeching about all those who would soon be cast into the lake of fire, for a variety of low crimes, misdemeanors and general ugliness that amounted to a sweeping indictment of almost everybody in the hotel at that hour.

Most of them were asleep when I began speaking, but as a Doctor of Divinity and an ordained minister in the Church of The New Truth, I knew in my heart that I was merely a vessel a tool, as it were—of some higher and more powerful voice.

For eight long and degrading days I had skulked around Houston with all the other professionals, doing our jobs—which was actually to do nothing at all except drink all the free booze we could pour into our bodies, courtesy of the National Football League, and listen to an endless barrage of some of the lamest and silliest swill ever uttered by man or beast . . . and finally, on Sunday morning about six hours before the opening kickoff, I was racked to the point of hysteria by a hellish interior conflict.

I was sitting by myself in the room, watching the wind & weather clocks on the TV set, when I felt a sudden and extremely powerful move-ment at the base of my spine. Mother of Sweating Jesus! I thought. What is it—a leech? Are there leeches in this goddamn hotel, along with every-thing else? I jumped off the bed and began clawing at the small of my back with both hands. The thing felt huge, maybe eight or nine pounds, moving slowly up my spine toward the base of my neck.

I'd been wondering, all week, why I was feeling so low and out of sorts . . . but it never occurred to me that a giant leech had been sucking blood out of the base of my spine all that time; and now the goddamn thing was moving up towards the base of my brain, going straight for the medulla . . . and as a professional sportswriter I knew that if the bugger ever reached my medulla I was done for.

It was at this point that serious conflict set in, because I realized—given the nature of what was coming up my spine and the drastic effect I knew it would have, very soon, on my sense of journalistic responsibil-ity—that I would have to do two things immediately: First, deliver the sermon that had been brewing in my brain all week long, and then rush back into the room and write my lead for the Super Bowl story. . . .

Or maybe write my lead first, and then deliver the sermon. In any case, there was no time to lose. The thing was about a third of the way up my spine now, and still moving at good speed. I jerked on a pair of L. L. Bean stalking shorts and ran out on the balcony to a nearby ice machine.

Back in the room I filled a glass full of ice and Wild Turkey, then began flipping through the pages of "A Demon's Nightmare" for some kind of Spiritual springboard to get the sermon moving. I had already decided—about midway in the ice-run—that I had adequate time to address the sleeping crowd and also crack out a lead before that goddamn blood-sucking slug reached the base of my brain—or, even worse, if a sharp dose of Wild Turkey happened to slow the thing down long enough to rob me of my final excuse for missing the game entirely, like last year. . . .

"This is Tania . . ."

THE DOUBLE LIFE OF PATTY HEARST

April 15, 1974
San Francisco

PATRICIA "TANIA" HEARST

*O*n *February 4, 1974, heiress and college student Patricia Hearst was kid-napped from her apartment in Berkeley, California, by a radical group calling itself the Symbionese Liberation Army. In April, Patty reappeared as Tania, a member of the SLA. A few weeks afterward, the nation saw her on the security-camera tapes that recorded the SLA's robbery of a San Francisco bank.*

The hunt for the SLA ended in May 1974 at their Los Angeles hideout. In a police raid and shootout, the building caught fire and eight SLA members died. But Hearst missed the inferno. She and two other members were not in the hideout at the time. Hearst was finally captured in September 1975. She was convicted of var-ious charges and sent to prison, but was subsequently pardoned by President Jimmy Carter. She now lives near New York City, where she is a socialite, novelist, and aspiring actress.

The first account is her announcement following the bank robbery. The second comes from her autobiography, which was written after her release from prison and dedicated to her parents, whom she denounced when she was "Tania."

AS TANIA

Greetings to the people. This is Tania.

On April 15, my comrades and I expropriated $10,660.02 from the Sunset branch of the Hibernia Bank. Casualties could have been avoided had the persons involved kept out of the way, and cooperated with the people's forces until after our departure.

I was positioned so that I could hold down customers and bank personnel who were on the floor. My gun was loaded, and at no time did any of my comrades intentionally point their guns at me. Careful examination of the photographs which were published clearly shows that this was true.

Our action of April 15 forced the corporate fascist state to help finance the revolution. In the case of expropriation, the difference between a criminal act and a revolutionary act is shown by what the money is used for.

As for the money involved in my parents' bad faith gesture to aid the people, these funds are being used to aid the people and to insure the survival of the people's forces in their struggle with, and for, the people.

To the clowns who want a personal interview with me—Vincent Hallinan [a lawyer], Steven Weed [her former fiancé], and the Pig Hearsts:

I prefer giving it to the people in the bank. It is absurd to think that I could surface to say what am I saying now, and still be allowed to freely return to my comrades. The enemy still wants me dead.

I am obviously alive and well. As for being brainwashed, the idea is ridiculous to the point of being beyond belief. It is interesting the way earlier reports characterized me as a beautiful, intelligent liberal, while in more recent reports I am a common girl who has been brainwashed. The contradictions are obvious.

Consciousness is terrifying to the ruling class; and they will do anything to discredit people who have realized that the only alternative to freedom is death; and that the only way we can free ourselves of this fascist dictatorship is by fighting, not with words but with guns.

As for my ex-fiancé, I am amazed that he thinks that the first thing I would want to do, once freed, would be to rush and see him. I don't care if I never see him again.

During the last few months, Steven has shown himself to be a sexist, agist pig. Not that this is a sudden change from the way he always was. It merely became more blatant during the period when I was still a hostage.

Frankly, Steven is the one who sounds brainwashed. I can't believe that those weird words [to the press] were from his heart. They were a mixture of FBI rhetoric and Randy's [her father's] simplicity.

I have no proof that Mr. DeBray's letter [regarding an interview] is authentic. The date and location he gave were confusing in terms of when the letter was published in the papers. How could it have been written in Paris and published in your newspapers on the same day, Adolf?

In any case, I hope that the last action has put his mind at ease. If it did not, further actions will.

To those people who still believe that I am brainwashed or dead, I see no reason to further defend my position. I am a good soldier in the people's army. *Patria o muerte! Venceremos!*

AS PATRICIA HEARST

We all set out together. I left that apartment in a daze, realizing finally what I would scarcely admit to myself before: I was actually going to rob a bank. I felt as one would walking to the gallows. My M-1, with its straight clip, was hidden under my coat, clasped to my side by my left arm. Our two cars were parked about a half block away. This was the first time I had been out of doors since I had been kidnapped two and one half months ago. The fresh air almost overwhelmed me. Like champagne, it made me feel light-headed. The day was so brilliant, sunny, and clear that I had to squint to see my way. I took my assigned seat in a green station wagon, next to the window, behind Zoya, who was in the front passenger seat. Gabi was driving and Cin and Fahizah were in the back with me. The others were following us in a new red Hornet, as our backup and protection. Inside our car, it was all business: the operation had begun. We moved along the streets of San Francisco at a law-abiding pace, observing all the traffic regulations. As we drove through Golden Gate Park, I marveled at the sight of all the greenery, the trees, the bushes, and the grass. We passed a calm pond. Everything looked so beautiful and serene. When we reached Noriega and Twenty-second Avenue, we circled the block around the bank. It looked exactly as I had seen it in the surveillance photographs, a long, white, single-story building facing Noriega Street, with a shorter blank wall on Twenty-second Avenue. Cin spotted what he suspected was an undercover police car and we circled the next block slowly, returning to the bank in time to see the red Hornet in position, parked opposite the bank entrance.

We parked smoothly in the red-lined bus stop and struggled out of the car with our weapons still hidden under our coats. All was calm and quiet on Twenty-second Avenue. I knew exactly what I was supposed to do and I would do it, because I had to survive this. If I did I would survive everything. We rounded the corner, close to the bank building, and with a nod from Cin, I walked into the bank, with Gabi holding the door open and then following right behind me. We strolled together through the length of the bank to that rear writing desk, as if I were going to make out a deposit dip. Within seconds, all hell broke loose in a blur.

I saw Zoya rush into the bank at a gallop, with little Fahizah right behind her. As Fahizah came through the door, her ammunition clip dropped from her submachine gun and clattered to the floor. Some of the bullets scattered. She knelt down to retrieve the banana-shaped clip, and Cinque, charging in, leaped over her, waving his own submachine gun at the startled people in the bank. As they came through the door, I got my own carbine out into the open and pointed it at the assistant bank manager at the rear desk as well as at two women at nearby desks.

At the same time, in a loud, strong voice that just about froze everyone in the bank, Cin shouted: "This is a holdup. The first m—— f—— who don't lay down on the floor gets shot in the head."

Fahizah ran around waving her submachine gun and kicking and hurting customers and screaming: "SLA! . . . SLA! . . . Get down on the floor over there and you won't get hurt." I glanced over my shoulder in time to see Zoya vault beautifully over the partition which separated the tellers and their cash drawers from the customers. She too was screaming and kicking at the tellers who had flopped to the floor too close to the cash drawers.

I don't remember saying or doing anything other than point my carbine at the people on the floor in front of me. The assistant manager said later that he had asked me where he should lie down and that I did not respond. On his own, he joined the others who were bunched together in a group on the floor, belly down, glancing up at me. I happened to notice at this point that the bolt of my carbine was off to one side rather than closed and flat. It struck me that the carbine was not operable. I remembered vividly, however, not to point it toward the front of the bank where the other SLA people were. Cin had positioned us in such a way that we would not accidentally shoot each other. I knew that if my weapon were pointed in his direction, he would shoot me. I glanced up and down the bank, anxious for it all to be over and to get out of there. Everything seemed to be happening so fast with the sounds of bedlam all around me, and yet it also seemed to be taking too much time. I was confused. Then I remembered suddenly that I was supposed to be making a speech. In the loudest voice I could muster, I managed to get out: "This is Tania . . . Patricia Hearst . . ." And I could recall no more of what I was supposed to say.

I heard Cin shouting out numbers and it was time to go. In the same instant, or so it seemed, I heard the rapid shots of a submachine gun and I caught sight of an elderly man stumbling out of the doorway, his back to me. I actually saw his jacket rip open as the bullets struck him. Fahizah was in a crouch, firing away. I don't really know what happened after that. My mind shut down, went blank. But I must have left the bank when my number, Nine, was called. And I must have jumped over the man who had been shot, because he was lying there on the sidewalk, just beyond the front door. But I don't recall seeing him or anything else.

**"They were coming out in boats,
half-sinking boats."**

THE FALL OF SAIGON

April 10–30, 1975

STEPHEN KLINKHAMMER

*T*he fall of Saigon, the capital of South Vietnam, marked the end of the Vietnam War.

President Richard Nixon, upon taking office six years earlier, had begun a program termed "Vietnamization," by which the U.S. would slowly withdraw its combat troops and leave the fighting to the South Vietnamese army. At the same time, the combatants continued the peace negotiations started the year before. But the war dragged on. And in the early 1970s, despite the public appearance of the Nixon administration's policies, the conflict escalated, with a heightened American bombing effort offsetting a reduction in combat troops.

Finally, the diplomats established a cease-fire that took effect in January 1973. But soon after the U.S. withdrew all its combat forces in March of that year, fighting between North and South Vietnam began again.

Although the U.S. had pledged its support to the South Vietnamese government, the Nixon administration, mindful of anti-war sentiment at home, and already coping with the Watergate scandal, did not have the political inclination or will to once again defend what had clearly become a lost cause.

On April 30, the North Vietnamese army captured Saigon, forcing South Vietnam to surrender.

More than 3 million Vietnamese had been wounded, and 2 million had been killed. Perhaps as many as 12 million people became refugees. About 150,000 Amer-

icans had been wounded, and about 58,000 had been killed. As many as 2500 are still listed as missing.

Eyewitness Klinkhammer was a navy hospital corpsman. He told his story to Al Santoli, author of Everything We Had.

The [aircraft carrier] *Midway* was our base of operations. This was about April 10 or 11. We were real close to shore at the time, right off Saigon. We heard that we were taking on a whole bunch of civilians. We would be flying in and out with refugees, with American personnel, with reporters. The Tan Son Nhut airport was being bombed with big rockets. You could see the explosions from the sea. We were flying in and taking on refugees, and they were flying out whatever they could.

They were coming out in boats, half-sinking boats. There were people who had their own airplanes who were flying out. There were all these choppers we had left there; they were using these to fly out, the Vietnamese. The flight deck was so full of choppers that we had to push them overboard because there was no room, we couldn't get our own choppers in.

It was total chaos. The Purple Heart Trail, the road that came into Saigon from the paddies west of the city, was so jammed, from the air I could see columns of people that were at least twenty miles long. A lot of children crying. Some had clothes they picked off dead bodies. Most were barefoot. There were oxcarts and they were hauling what they had. There were wounded men on both sides of the road with battle dressings on. The NVA was lobbing these rockets all over the place, they were wiping out civilians. They were dropping rockets right into the crowds of fleeing people.

A lot of American Marines were activated and had put up a perimeter guard around Tan Son Nhut. The NVA was still lobbing these rockets in. It was really a mess. These rockets are lobbing in and a C-130 took off full of people going out to one of the aircraft carriers and it was blown out of the sky . . . that was all over the runway. There were corpses, there were burnt-out tanks people had used to come in, there were pieces of bodies lying in the fields and on the streets. It was just bananas, total chaos.

They were raiding the American Exchange. The image I have is this one guy holding up one of those ten-packs of Kellogg's cereal and he's waving it. They were throwing American money up in the air.

We were trying to get the wounded first. They were piled in these old ambulances. The refugees were coming up from the Delta as well as from the North. We were trying to get the wounded out first and a lot of them we couldn't. We ended up with three thousand civilians aboard the *Midway*. We had taken all of our squadrons off because they had been there for offensive purposes. The civilians all stayed where the squadrons used to be. There were people sleeping on the floors, all over.

On April 30 Saigon fell. South Vietnam had fallen. The Vice-President, Ky, flew out to the *Midway* in his own Cessna. Ky had with him an immense amount of gold bars. . . .

"He started to worry that
I only liked him for his money . . ."

WARHOL'S WORLD

October 29, 1977–January 17, 1980
New York City

ANDY WARHOL

No one understood the surface of the celebrity-crazy 1960s, '70s, and '80s better than Andy Warhol, the illustrator from Pittsburgh who helped create Pop Art by appropriating graphics from supermarket shelves—exact reproductions of the Brillo box and the Campbell's Soup can, for example—and reselling them in tony galleries.

He worked from the Factory, an industrial-sized office and hangout, instead of a small atelier. The friends and collaborators who gathered there also formed an extended repertory company for Warhol's films.

People who knew him were divided on the issue of Warhol's depth. But when he died suddenly in 1988, and it was revealed that he had kept a secret diary for years, there was little doubt that he was an appropriate chronicler of disco, gender-bending, the fashion world, and the drug culture.

These accounts from the diary record Warhol's impressions of Studio 54, the world's most famous nightclub—for fifteen minutes.

OCTOBER 29, 1977

We dropped off Diana and then Victor and I went over to Studio 54. It was jammed with beautiful people. Now Studio 54 has its liquor license. Stevie took me over to meet Vladimir Horowitz and his wife who's the daughter of Toscanini. He was thrilled to be there. . . .

OCTOBER 30, 1977

At Elaine's Stevie Rubell [an owner of Studio 54] told me he's very rich, but that all his money's in assets or hidden away. People on drugs, you think they don't notice things, but they notice everything. Elaine had a new menu and Stevie noticed the new prices right away. I only noticed because it was clean.

Oh, and after he confessed how rich he was, he started to worry that I only liked him for his money, and I mean, what can I say?

JANUARY 3, 1978

We cabbed up to 86th Street and we finally hit *Saturday Night Fever* at the right time and were able to get in. Well, the movie was just great. That bridge thing was the best scene—and the lines were great. It's I guess the new kind of fantasy movie, you're supposed to stay where you are. The old movies were things like *Dead End* and you had to get out of the dead end and make it to Park Avenue and now they're telling you that it's better off to stay where you are in Brooklyn—to avoid Park Avenue because it would just make you unhappy. It's about people who would never even think about crossing the bridge, that's the fantasy. And they played up Travolta's big solo dance number, but then at the end they made the dance number with the girl so nothing, so underplayed. They were smart. And New York looked so exciting, didn't it? The Brooklyn Bridge and New York. Stevie Rubell wants to do a disco movie, but I don't think you could do another one, this one was so great. But why didn't they do it as a play first? What was this first, a short story? They should have milked it—done it as a play first and it would have run forever.

DECEMBER 14, 1978

The Daily News had just called wanting a quote from me, they said that fifty agents had gone in and raided Studio 54 for income tax and that they'd busted [Studio 54 co-owner] Ian Schrager for two ounces of coke.

DECEMBER 16, 1978

What Halston's been most upset about in the Studio 54 bust is that the IRS agents discovered another little room that nobody knew about, and Halston is hurt because he's such a close friend and Steve hadn't told him about it.

DECEMBER 31, 1979

We went over to Studio 54 and the look was "ice." Ice wall-to-wall and dripping down the walls. Then Steve said, "Let's go down to the basement," so we did. He just about said, "Anybody have any cocaine?" He wanted it to be like the good old days. It was so filthy down there with the garbage and everything.

JANUARY 17, 1980

. . . Halston's limo pulled up and he and Bianca said they were going to Studio 54 for Steve Rubell's farewell party before his sentencing, so my cab followed their limo. When we got there we stood around, and they were taking pictures. Halston was smart, he disappeared. . . .

*"What are you guys going to advise me to do
if they overrun our embassy . . . ?"*

THE IRANIAN HOSTAGE CRISIS: WEEK ONE

November 4–9, 1979
Washington, D.C.

HAMILTON JORDAN

Jordan was President Jimmy Carter's chief of staff. In the first of the 444 days of the hostage crisis he was still focused on Carter's reelection campaign. Soon the hostage crisis became a part of the campaign—and every other aspect of the Carter presidency.

NOVEMBER 4, 1979

About 4:30 A.M. the phone in my room rang. It took me a minute to recall where I was. I grappled in the dark, and on what must have been the tenth ring, managed to answer it.

"Mr. Jordan, this is the duty officer in the Situation Room," the voice on the other end said. "We wanted to advise you that the American Embassy in Tehran has been overrun by demonstrators and the American personnel are believed to be held in captivity."

"My God," I said. "Are there any injuries? Was anyone killed?"

"Not that we know of, Mr. Jordan—but we really don't have complete information. We'll keep you informed."

I asked if the President had been notified and was told that Secretary of State Vance had called him earlier from the Operations Center at the State Department.

I lay in bed thinking about what I had just heard. This could mean war with Iran. And what would it do to the campaign?

NOVEMBER 5, 1979

Everyone at today's meeting was feeling pretty cheerful after the Ted Kennedy fiasco. [Kennedy's poor interview with CBS reporter Roger Mudd.] "It was terrible," someone said. "Fatal," someone else offered. We all snickered.

Then the question of the hostages was raised. "Don't forget," I said, "this same thing happened last February. We're talking to our diplomats at the embassy and Foreign Minister Ibrahim Yazdi and Prime Minister Mehdi Bazargan at the Foreign Ministry. As soon as the government gets its act together, they'll free our people."

NOVEMBER 6, 1979

I walked past [the Oval Office] to the Cabinet Room, where only the President could conduct business.

A long, rectangular room, lined on one side with French doors that look out on the Rose Garden and on the other with two doors that lead back to the main White House offices, the Cabinet Room is separated from the Oval Office by the small room where Presidential guests wait before entering the Oval Office. A large mahogany table runs the length of the room, and each brown leather chair around it contains a small bronze plate with the name of the Cabinet Secretary who sits there. Cabinet officers take their chairs with them when they leave the government.

The President's chair, slightly taller than the others, is at the middle of the table; the rest are arranged in the historical order of the creation of the Cabinet offices. . . .

Vice President Fritz Mondale, Secretary of Defense Harold Brown, National Security Advisor Zbigniew Brzezinski, Press Secretary Jody Powell, Secretary of State Cyrus Vance, Gary Sick, and David Newsom from the State Department had already assembled, waiting for the President. Vance was bringing them up-to-date on developments in Iran, while Navy stewards in blue blazers bearing the Presidential seal moved from chair to chair, quietly serving coffee.

At 8:00 A.M. sharp, the President entered, walking briskly and carrying a notepad and a stack of cables. He didn't speak as he took his seat. Then, turning to Vance on his immediate left, he asked for a report on the hostages.

Harold Brown scribbled on his notepad and slipped it across the table to me: "I am waiting for the President to say 'I told you so.' "

And I was, too. For it was less than three weeks ago, at our regular foreign policy breakfast in the same room with the same group of people, that Carter had made a reluctant decision to allow the former Shah of Iran to come to the United States for medical treatment. . . .

"As long as there is a country where the Shah can live safely and comfortably," the President reasoned [in February 1979], "it makes no sense to bring him here and destroy whatever slim chance we have of rebuilding a relationship with Iran. It boils down to a choice between the Shah's preferences as to where he lives and the interests of our country."

. . . [On October 19] the President argued alone against allowing the Shah in.

. . . I mentioned the political consequences: Mr. President, if the Shah dies in Mexico, can you imagine the field day Kissinger will have with that? He'll say that first you caused the Shah's downfall and now you've killed him.

The President glared at me. "To hell with Henry Kissinger," he said. "I am the President of this country!"

The controversy continued as Zbig and Vance—together this time—stuck to the arguments of "humanitarian principle." It was obvious that the President was becoming frustrated having to argue alone against all of his advisors and against "principle." Finally, he told Vance to "double-check" the Shah's medical condition and needs and determine from the American Embassy in Tehran what the reaction of the Iranian government would be to the entry of the Shah for medical treatment—and to see if they would guarantee the safety of our embassy.

Vance said he would cable immediately.

Carter had the last word: "What are you guys going to advise me to do if they overrun our embassy and take our people hostage?"

NOVEMBER 9, 1979

A somber mood prevailed at our foreign policy breakfast. When the President bowed his head and asked a short blessing, he mentioned the hostages and everyone joined in the amen.

As usual, the meeting opened with Cy Vance's review of all that had been done to date: cables to allies who had close relations with the Iranians, private meetings with ambassadors from the Moslem countries, a meeting with Habib Chatty of the Islamic League (an international organization of Islamic religious leaders), and contact with Moslem religious figures. The efforts that week had been exhaustive and, I thought, impressive: we seemed to have done everything humanly possible to get our people out. But they were still being held, and the rhetoric of both the militants at the compound and Khomeini had become harsher, with demands that the Shah be returned to Iran to stand trial, that his assets be confiscated, and that the U.S. apologize for past "crimes against the Iranian people."

For the first time it dawned on me that the hostage crisis might not end so soon.

Zbig Brzezinski spoke up first following Vance's presentation. "Mr. President, you can't allow this thing to settle into a state of normalcy. If you do," he warned, "it could paralyze your Presidency. Yes, it is important that we get our people back. But," he argued, "your greater responsibility is to protect the honor and dignity of our country and its foreign policy interests. At some point that greater responsibility could become more important than the safety of our diplomats." He continued: "I hope we never have to choose between the hostages and our nation's honor in the world, but Mr. President, you must be prepared for that occurrence. If they're still in captivity at Thanksgiving, what will that say about your Presidency and America's image in the world?"

Glancing first at Brzezinski and then turning to the President, Vance responded quickly. "The hostages have been held only five days," he said. "We're dealing with a volatile, chaotic situation in Iran, and negotiation is the only way to free them. The President and this nation will ultimately be judged by our restraint in the face of provocation, and on the safe return of our hostages," he argued. "We have to keep looking for ways to reach Khomeini and peacefully resolve this." He harked back to the Pueblo incident, which had plagued the Johnson Administration but which had finally been resolved honorably and without loss of life.

"But that went on for a year!" Brzezinski countered.

"And Johnson wasn't in the middle of a reelection campaign," I added.

. . . The President next asked for a military update. Secretary Brown said that our forces in the Indian Ocean were ready to move to the Persian Gulf, if necessary. It was important, he explained, to have a presence that was adequate but not large enough to provoke a Soviet reaction. On the President's order, the Joint Chiefs were preparing both punitive actions against Iran and emergency rescue plans in the event the militants started to execute their prisoners. But, Brown cautioned, Tehran wasn't Entebbe, where the Israelis had been able to fly in and snatch up their citizens from the airfield where they were being held. Our hostages, he explained, were locked up in a compound in the middle of a city of more than four million people, with the nearest airport nine miles away. The opinion of the Joint Chiefs was that a rescue would be extremely difficult but not impossible, and the Secretary recommended that they proceed with their planning.

Carter said that he wasn't inclined either toward the rescue action or punitive measures, but that both needed to be ready and in place for use as a "last resort." "The problem with all of the military options," he said, "is that we could use them and feel good for a few hours—until we found out they had killed our people. And once we start killing people in Iran, where will it end?" he asked quietly.

Later, when I saw the President in the Oval Office after his meeting with the families of the hostages, he looked troubled. I had some encouraging poll results from Pat Caddell, but it didn't seem the right time to talk politics, so I asked if there was anything I could do to help him. He shook his head and settled into his black leather chair behind the large ornate desk.

"You know, it was my duty to see the families," he said, "but I wasn't looking forward to it. I knew that some of them must blame me, but they were very generous and supportive. They don't expect miracles and want their loved ones home, but they want them to come home only on honorable terms." He paused. "You know, I've been worried all week about the hostages as a problem for the country and as a political problem for me. But it wasn't until I saw the grief and hope on the faces of their wives and mothers and fathers that I felt the personal responsibility for their lives. It's an awesome burden," he said quietly.

I slipped out, sensing that he wanted to be alone.

Back in my office, I thought about the President's emotional involvement with the hostages through their family members. Zbig had refused to meet with the families of the hostages on the grounds that, should the time come when the country's honor was pitted against the safety of the hostages, he would be free of emotional pressures. I respected this logic, but I disagreed with it.

"I'm only odd for a president."

RONALD REAGAN IN THE WHITE HOUSE

1980–1988
Washington, D.C.

PEGGY NOONAN

N oonan was a speechwriter for President Reagan and later for President George Bush.

He was to popular politics what Henry James was to American literature: He was the master. No one could do what he did, move people that way, talk to them so that they understood. A demagogue would have begged for that power; he didn't even care. That's part of why he had it. He didn't have to be the man pulling the switch, he wasn't in it for ego; he was actually in it to do good.

He was probably the sweetest, most innocent man ever to serve in the Oval Office. He was a modest man with an intellect slightly superior to the average. His whole career, in fact, was proof of the superior power of goodness to gifts. "No great men are good men," said Lord Acton, who was right, until Reagan.

Toward mankind in general he had the American attitude, direct and unillusioned: He figured everybody is doing as much bad as he has to, as much good as he can. He wasn't artless, or an angel; he didn't seem to expect a great deal.

He was a happy man. He trusted life. But then so much that had happened to him had been lucky and good. His mother loved him. The fellas knew what they had. Once Deaver took Darman aside and said, "Listen, Dick, I don't care what else you do but make sure you do this: Get that face on television. This is a face that when a baby sees it, the baby smiles." Back in '80 in the debate with Carter, it was the little man who winced versus the Emperor of Ice Cream. Carter didn't have a chance.

How to capture him, how to say what you saw and imagined without it being twisted by one side or another. Tell the truth and the left will seize it as a flag, tell the truth and the right will wave it as a banner. No matter what you say about this man it winds up being somebody's propaganda.

Here he is, at his desk in the Oval Office, a bright, rounded room of gravity and weight.

He is answering his mail. He looks up as you enter and blinks his moist eyes. His suit is brown, of a dense, substantial weave, his white shirt as bright and uncreased as a shirt in a department store; a tie striped in earth colors is knotted at his neck. You imagine him patting down the collar and trying out a smile.

"Well," he says, as he stands and rounds the desk. He walks toward you softly (I never remember hearing his footsteps).

"Hello!" you say smiling, as he puts out his hand. As your hands touch and then clasp you think: I am standing here shaking hands with the president of the United States, right now, this second. The thought so takes you that you forget to let go. He lets you keep shaking. He is used to this. He rarely lets go first.

He stands there in his tall brown suit looking down with soft, kind eyes, and you are surprised by the pinkness, the babylike softness of his skin. The soft neck, and something you hadn't expected: the air of frailty.

He gleams; he is a mystery. He is for everyone there, for everyone who works with him. None of them understand him. In private they admit it. You say to them, Who was that masked man?, and they shrug, and hypothesize.

James Baker said, He is the kindest and most impersonal man I ever knew.

An aide said, Beneath the lava flow of warmth there is something impervious as a glacier.

Mother Teresa said, In him, greatness and simplicity are one.

A friend said, Behind those warm eyes is a lack of curiosity that is, somehow, disorienting.

A power source cool at the core. A woman who knew him said, He lived life on the surface where the small waves are, not deep down where the heavy currents tug. And yet he has great powers of empathy. There is a picture of the president and his aides watching TV moments after the shuttle Challenger blew up. It is shot from the angle of the television set.

On the faces of the men around the president we see varying degrees of interest, curiosity, consternation. Only on the face of Reagan do we see horror, and pain.

Through the force of his beliefs and with a deep natural dignity he restored a great and fallen office.

He was so humble and unassuming that his aides were embarrassed a few days after he was shot to find him in a little bathroom off his hospital room, down on his hands and knees on the cold tile mopping up some water he'd spilled from the sink. He hated to make a mess for the nurse, he said. He wanted to clean it up before she came back, and could they get him some more towels?

Imagine a president with no personal enemies. This has never happened before.

Imagine a man nobody hates, or no one who knows him. He was never dark, never mean, never waited for the sound of the door closing to say, "What a fool," didn't seethe, had no malice. People could tell he trusted their motives. It brought out the best in the best of them, who acted better for the compliment, and the worst in the worst of them: They nodded with mild surprise when they saw his trust, looked into his eyes, and saw . . . nothing. They thought he was an empty house, and they were second story men.

I'll tell you something surprising: This sunny man touched so many Americans in part because they perceived his pain. They saw beyond the television image, they saw the flesh and blood, they felt those wounds, they caught that poignance.

The reporters and correspondents and smart guys, they missed it. But the people saw. They thought, Look at the courage it took at his age to be shot in the chest by a kid with a gun and go through healing and therapy and go out there again and continue being president, continue waving at the crowds as he walks to the car. Think of the courage that old man had!

Stop shaking his hand for a moment. Stop loving him. This is what you should say: "So where did you come from, Mr. President, and who are you, really? What are the forces that shaped you, and why are you so odd?"

"I'm not odd," he would say. "I'm only odd for a president."

. . . Reagan withdrew from the White House, staying sealed in the Oval Office and the residence and pretty much ignoring the fact that he worked where Lincoln trod and Jefferson dined. He never took the dimensions of the place, and so he avoided taking possession of it.

He also took refuge in the mail, in writing letters to children who loved him and old ladies who needed him. Ann Higgins, the woman who ran the president's mail operation, used to send him fifty or so letters from the two hundred thousand a week he received in that time, and sometimes—and it wasn't all that rare—he'd call and ask for more.

I think he saw that people pour out their hearts to presidents, and in a democracy, particularly a modern democracy, it's important that they know they have at least a chance to make it through to the top guy. He knew this naturally. He answered letters from citizens with the same kind of care and respect that he gave to a letter from Thatcher or Kohl.

People thought he was their friend. They'd send him pictures of themselves and their families. The original letters would come back to Ann, but she noticed he always removed the pictures. They started showing up in the pockets of his jackets and coats and in the drawers of the lamp tables in the residence.

He got more mail than most presidents, at one point receiving 8 million letters a year, almost twice the presidential average.

He wrote about ten letters a day, not counting those he wrote to personal friends who contacted him at his special post office box. He had a name-card file of people he'd been writing to for half a century, and when he was president he was still writing to them.

When he had surgery, people wrote in and told him of their ailments. "There's something in Americans that makes them describe their sicknesses in loving detail. We know the country's temperature—literally!" Higgins said.

His aides were always getting calls from weekly newspapers out in the hills asking, Did you know the president has promised to look into Mrs. Elma Fogelby's Social Security problem and also invited her to the White House for a cup of coffee, and are you guys always this nice?

The press aide would sigh, and get the Social Security straightened out, and make sure she got in when she came.

Citizens sent him gifts and he used them. When school children in Allingtown, Connecticut, sent him a bunch of yellow notepads with FROM THE DESK OF RONALD REAGAN stamped on top—it was cheap yellow stock, it looked like something they'd done in shop—he used it for years.

A citizen sent him stationery with a nerd with a long nose peeking over a wall and the saying "No More Mr. Nice Guy!" He sent notes to George Shultz on them.

He sent money to strangers and friends. Once he wrote someone a check for a hundred dollars, and the recipient couldn't cash it because it was signed Ronald Reagan and the cashier at the bank said that was worth more than the amount. Ronald Reagan had to call the bank and arrange for it to give the money. This happened a number of times.

And he met with the people he wrote to. Once Ann Higgins asked him to call the Rossow family of Connecticut to congratulate them on their fine family. At the time Mr. and Mrs. Rossow had fourteen children, most adopted and many handicapped. The president not only called but, typically, asked to speak to everyone in the family including five-year-old Benjamin, who was born with only a brain stem. He not only spoke to them, he invited them to visit. A few weeks later two vans drove up and deposited the sixteen Rossows at 1600 Pennsylvania Avenue. They stayed with the Little Sisters of the Poor, who made waffles in their happy kitchen.

This happened all the time in Reagan's White House. You'd walk by the Oval Office and there was a family full of people with no legs nodding hello to a dwarf who was bringing a message from the doorman at the Mayflower, who'd get a reply. No one else ran a White House like this, none of the modern presidents.

"Each of the items left at the
Vietnam memorial tells a story . . ."

OFFERINGS: THE VIETNAM VETERANS MEMORIAL

1982–
Washington, D.C.

CYNTHIA LOOSE

*J*ohn Wheeler, *former chairman of the Vietnam Veterans Memorial, on first impressions: "When we first saw the amateur, pastel sketch of Maya Lin's winning entry in the open competition for the Wall's design, we did not fully grasp its power, how the polished black granite would serve as a true mirror, showing colors, faces, the nearby American flag, and how the reflections at the cleft of the Wall switch back and forth from the Lincoln Memorial to the Washington Monument. It took a child to show me how the mirrored surface links the visitor's image with the names carved in stone. In* *the summer of 1982 as the Wall was being built, we invited families of men named on the first panels to see our progress. While adults chatted, a little girl went alone to the panels and began touching names. Since then, millions have touched the names."*

There are now 58,202 names on the wall. It is the most visited memorial in the nation. More than 30 million people have come to see it since it was dedicated in 1982.

Loose reported for the Washington Post.

The watch that stopped forever at 10:03 came with a note.

"When I held you in my arms you felt so cold," a soldier wrote in the letter left behind at the Vietnam Veterans Memorial. "I would not let them take you from me for as long as I could. And then you were gone."

Someone else left behind a boy-size newspaper delivery bag emblazoned with the emblem of the *Cleveland Plain Dealer*. "Remember a sweeter, gentler time," the anonymous visitor wrote. "We never dreamed serving the people would end this way."

Like many of the 25,000 items left at the memorial and now stored in a cinder-block warehouse, a '60s-vintage television set came with no explanation. "We sometimes play 'I wonder if,' " curator Duery Felton said yesterday as he chose items to show to a dozen visitors during the first of many events scheduled to commemorate the 10th anniversary of the memorial next November.

"I wonder if someone bought this TV in Vietnam, shipped it home safely, but the person did not make it." Felton, himself a Vietnam veteran, said he believes his job is "a sacred trust," and the collection an invaluable and unique account of war through the eyes of those who fought it. It is, he said, "history being written from the bottom up."

America has virtually no tradition of leaving offerings for the dead. No one is quite sure why so many have done so at the Vietnam memorial. Perhaps it is something specific about the memorial, perhaps about the war. "People clearly believe that the spirits of those men and women reside at the memorial," said Jan C. Scruggs, president of the Vietnam Veterans Memorial Fund. Along with the more than 500 dog tags and 1,000 medals left at the memorial are teddy bears, oil portraits, entire family albums, heirlooms, baby pacifers.

Much of the power of the memorial, the most visited in the United States, lies in its ability to individualize the casualties, to remind those who come that the 58,183 men and women named on the wall died one human being at a time. The repository in Lanham individualizes the survivors. It is a reminder that on 58,183 separate occasions, a casualty officer in full dress uniform parked in a neighborhood, followed a path to a home and rang a doorbell.

Officials of the National Park Service, which oversees the repository, said that notes are left at the Wailing Wall in Jerusalem, and origami paper birds are found at the Hiroshima Peace Memorial. But they know of no other site that has spurred such a public outpouring. Each of the items left at the Vietnam memorial tells a story, but sometimes the import is understood only by the giver. There is a purple, high-heeled pump; a lone, highly polished leather boot; a candle in which dog tags are buried; and what appears to be a casualty report.

Sometimes a few questions asked around the office help at least partially to solve the mystery represented by a gift. Felton, for example, was mystified by two pink washcloths fashioned into the forms of two rabbits. A staff member recognized them immediately. "Those are boo-boo bunnies," she told Felton, explaining that her own mother had made such devices for covering the ice she would put on a child's wound. To some mother somewhere, the boo-boo bunny was perhaps a reminder that she had always before helped heal a son's wounds, and would have done so again if it had been in her power.

Apologies are common. "I did all I could," the letters sometimes say. Some assure their buddies they would trade places if they could. One man's written apology seemed to offer to the dead assurances that he had not escaped the war either. He first explained how he spent his childhood along an Indiana lake he loved before piloting a riverboat in Vietnam. "Now every time I get on a boat I only see the red blood running over the deck and into the water. I try to take my two sons fishing but we never stay out long. The fish don't seem to bite when I take them out, like they do with someone else's father. They are too young to understand that their father does not like the reflections he sees in the water." The mementos keep coming in greater volume every year. Those who collect them notice trends. Recently they began seeing more birthday cards, many of them noting that the deceased would have been 40 years old. Grandchildren of the dead are beginning to leave things. For reasons no one understands, there have been a large number of dollar bills torn in half.

Scruggs believes that some of the items represent the final stage of grieving—that point when people reconcile themselves to the death and resolve to return among the living. That may explain the wedding rings, rings that sometimes are boxed along with crystal goblets, silver wedding bells and party favors. Often there are memorabilia and notes in which high school sweethearts describe their children to their first loves. "They often say, 'This is the child that should have been yours,' " Felton said. "There are a lot of unfulfilled dreams represented here."

. . . Felton continues to catalogue and store each item, handling a ragged hat with the same gentle care that he gives an ivory-handled, intricately engraved, silver knife. His personal favorite is a black beret left by the only surviving member of an ambushed platoon. "I can only imagine what he's going through," Felton said.

"Don't give up, be proud of who you are . . ."

LIVING WITH AIDS

1985–1990

RYAN WHITE

*O*n January 17, 1981, novelist and publisher Felice Picano made a short diary entry, one of the very first records of an AIDS death in America. He was noting the passing of a friend, and what was believed at the time to be the strange disease that killed him: "Yesterday a friend, Nick Rock, died. He'd been ill for the past few months with what was finally diagnosed as cat-scratch fever. Hyperallergic for years, his immunological system couldn't cope with it. Before the illness was diagnosed he wasted away, formed lesions on the brain, etc., fell into a coma . . . I valued him as a friend and a good man."

About five months later the Centers for Disease Control published a terse notice of a few isolated, mysterious deaths that had caught the attention of CDC investigators in Los Angeles, and the hunt for the virus, and a cure, began.

Ryan White caught the AIDS virus from the blood-clotting medicine he took to counter his hemophilia. He died in 1990, at age eighteen. The following comes from his testimony before the Presidential Commission on AIDS, given in 1988.

I came face to face with death at thirteen years old. I was diagnosed with AIDS: a killer. Doctors told me I'm not contagious. Given six months to live and being the fighter that I am, I set high goals for myself. It was my decision to live a normal life, go to school, be with my friends, and enjoy day to day activities. It was not going to be easy.

The school I was going to said they had no guidelines for a person with AIDS. . . . We began a series of court battles for nine months, while I was attending classes by telephone. Eventually, I won the right to attend school, but the prejudice was still there. Listening to medical facts was not enough. People wanted one hundred percent guarantees. There are no one hundred percent guarantees in life, but concessions were made by Mom and me to help ease the fear. We decided to meet everyone halfway. . . . Because of the lack of education on AIDS, discrimination, fear, panic, and lies surrounded me. (1) I became the target of Ryan White jokes. (2) Lies about me biting people. (3) Spitting on vegetables and cookies. (4) Urinating on bathroom walls. (5) Some restaurants threw away my dishes. (6) My school locker was vandalized inside and folders were marked FAG and other obscenities.

I was labeled a troublemaker, my mom an unfit mother, and I was not welcome anywhere. People would get up and leave, so they would not have to sit anywhere near me. Even at church, people would not shake my hand.

This brought in the news media, TV crews, interviews, and numerous public appearances. I became known as the AIDS boy. I received thousands of letters of support from all around the world, all because I wanted to go to school. . . . It was difficult, at times, to handle, but I tried to ignore the injustice, because I knew the people were wrong. My family and I held no hatred for those people because we realized they were victims of their own ignorance. We had great faith that, with patience, understanding, and education, my family and I could be helpful in changing their minds and attitudes. . . .

Financial hardships were rough on us, even though Mom had a good job at G.M. The more I was sick, the more work she had to miss. Bills became impossible to pay. My sister, Andrea, was a championship roller skater who had to sacrifice too. There was no money for her lessons and travel. AIDS can destroy a family if you let it, but luckily for my sister and me, Mom taught us to keep going. Don't give up, be proud of who you are, and never feel sorry for yourself.

"The exhaust plume seemed to balloon outward . . ."

SPACE SHUTTLE *CHALLENGER*

January 28, 1986
Cape Canaveral, Florida

WILLIAM HARWOOD

*T*he explosion turned out to be not only predictable, but predicted. Some of the engineers who built the faulty rocket boosters had warned against launching the shuttle in cold weather, but they were ignored.

Challenger *was almost nine miles above the earth when it exploded. The mission lasted just seventy-three seconds. Seven crew members were aboard.*

Harwood, eyewitness to the explosion itself, was United Press International's Cape Canaveral bureau chief.

I witnessed the launch from the Kennedy Space Center press site just 4.2 miles from pad 39B. It was my 19th shuttle launch but my first without the comforting presence of UPI Science Editor Al Rossiter Jr., a space veteran with all of the experience I lacked. He was in Pasadena, Calif., at the Jet Propulsion Laboratory covering *Voyager 2*'s flyby of Uranus.

I arrived at the UPI trailer around 11:30 p.m. Monday night, Jan. 27. I always came to work before the start of fueling on the theory that anytime anyone loaded a half-million gallons of liquid oxygen and liquid hydrogen into anything it was an event worth staffing.

It was bitterly cold that night. I remember cranking up the drafty UPI trailer's baseboard heaters in a futile attempt to warm up while I started banging out copy. I was writing for afternoon, or PM, newspapers that would hit the streets the following afternoon. Because *Challenger*'s launch was scheduled for that morning, the PM cycle was where the action was, the closest thing to "live" reporting that print journalists ever experience. . . . I had written my launch copy the day before and as usual, I spent most of the early morning hours tweaking the story, checking in periodically with NASA public affairs and monitoring the chatter on the bureau's radio scanner. I would occasionally glance toward the launch pad where *Challenger* stood bathed in high power spotlights, clearly visible for dozens of miles around. Off to the side, a brilliant tongue of orange flame periodically flared in the night as excess hydrogen was vented harmlessly into the atmosphere. Back in the UPI trailer, radio reporter Rob Navias rolled in around 4 a.m. A veteran shuttle reporter with an encyclopedic memory for space trivia, Rob and I had covered 14 straight missions together. In keeping with long-standing launch-day tradition, Rob's first comment after stomping into the trailer was "Will it go?" to which I would respond: "Or will it blow?" It was a grim little charade we carried out to mask our constant fear of catastrophe.

As night gave way to day, the launch team was struggling to keep the countdown on track. Problems had delayed fueling and launch—originally scheduled for 9:38 a.m.—for two hours to make sure no dangerous accumulations of ice had built up on *Challenger*'s huge external tank. Finally, all systems were "go" and the countdown resumed at the T-minus nine-minute mark for a liftoff at 11:38 a.m. Battling my usual pre-launch jitters, I called UPI national desk editor Bill Trott in Washington about three minutes before launch. I had already filed the PM launch story to UPI's computer and Trott now called it up on his screen. We shot the breeze. I reminded him not to push the SEND button until I confirmed vertical motion; two previous launches were aborted at the last second and we didn't want to accidentally "launch" a shuttle on the wire when it was still firmly on the ground. But there were no such problems today. *Challenger*'s three main engines thundered to life on schedule, belching blue-white fire and billowing clouds of steam. Less than seven seconds later, the shuttle's twin boosters ignited with a ground-shaking roar and the spacecraft vaulted skyward.

"And liftoff . . . liftoff of the 25th space shuttle mission, and it has cleared the tower!" said NASA commentator Hugh Harris.

"OK, let it go," I told Trott when Harris started talking. He pushed the SEND button and my story winged away on the A-wire.

Four miles away, *Challenger* was climbing majestically into a cloudless blue sky. We could not see the initial puffs of smoke indicating a fatal booster flaw. A few seconds later, the crackling roar of those boosters swept over the press site and the UPI trailer started shaking and rattling as the ground shock arrived. I marveled at the view, describing it to Trott in Washington. We always kept the line open for the full eight-and-a-half minutes it took for a shuttle to reach orbit; should disaster strike, the plan went, I would start dictating and Trott would start filing raw copy to the wire.

But for the first few seconds, it was a moot point. The roar was so loud we couldn't hear each other anyway. But the sound quickly faded to a dull rumble as *Challenger* wheeled about and arced over behind its booster exhaust plume, disappearing from view. NASA television, of course, carried the now-familiar closeups of the orbiter, but I wasn't watching television. I was looking out the window at the exhaust cloud towering into the morning sky.

"Incredible," I murmured.

And then, in the blink of an eye, the exhaust plume seemed to balloon outward, to somehow thicken. I recall a fleeting peripheral impression of fragments, of debris flying about, sparkling in the morning sunlight. And then, in that pregnant instant before the knowledge that something terrible has happened settled in, a single booster emerged from the cloud, corkscrewing madly through the sky.

I sat stunned. I couldn't understand what I was seeing.

"Wait a minute . . . something's happened . . ." I told Trott. A booster? Flying on its own? Oh my God. "They're in trouble," I said, my heart pounding. "Lemme dictate something!"

"OK, OK, hang on," Trott said. He quickly started punching in the header material of a one-paragraph "story" that would interrupt the normal flow of copy over the wire and alert editors to breaking news.

I still didn't realize *Challenger* had actually exploded. I didn't know what had happened. For a few heartbeats, I desperately reviewed the crew's options: Could the shuttle somehow have pulled free? Could the crew somehow still be alive? Had I been watching television, I would have known the truth immediately and my copy would have been more final.

But I wasn't watching television.

"Ready," Trott said.

The lead went something like this: "The space shuttle *Challenger* apparently exploded about two minutes after launch today (pause for Trott to catch up) and veered wildly out of control. (pause) The fate of the crew was not known."

"Got it . . ." Trott said, typing as I talked. Bells went off seconds later as the story starting clattering out on the bureau's A-wire printer behind me.

Out in Pasadena, Rossiter had watched the launch on NASA television. He ran to his computer, checked the wire and urgently called the bureau. He wanted to know why we had "apparently" blown up the shuttle in the precede. On television, there was no "apparently" about it.

Trott and I quickly corrected the time of the accident (my sense of time was distorted all day) and clarified that *Challenger* had, in fact, suffered a catastrophic failure. While we did not yet know what had happened to the crew, we all knew the chances for survival were virtually zero and the story began reflecting that belief.

For the next half hour or so, I simply dictated my impressions and background to Trott, who would file three or four paragraphs of "running copy" to the wire at a time. At one point, I remember yelling "Obits! Tell somebody to refile the obits!" Before every shuttle mission, I wrote detailed profiles of each crew member. No one actually printed these stories; they were written to serve as instant obits in the event of a disaster. Now, I wanted to refile my profiles for clients who had not saved them earlier. At some point—I have no idea when—I put the phone down and started typing again, filing the copy to Washington where Trott assembled all the pieces into a more-or-less coherent narrative. Dozens of UPI reporters swung into action around the world, later funneling reaction and quotes into the evolving story.

For the next two hours or so I don't remember anything but the mad rush of reporting. Subconsciously, I held the enormity of the disaster at bay; I knew if I relaxed my guard for an instant it could paralyze me. I was flying on some kind of mental autopilot. And then, around 2 p.m. or so, I recall a momentary lull. My fingers dropped to the keyboard and I stared blankly out the window toward the launch pad. I saw those seven astronauts. I saw them waving to the photographers as they headed for the launch pad. I remembered Christa McAuliffe's smile and Judy Resnik's flashing eyes. Tears welled up. I shook my head, blinked rapidly and turned back to my computer. I'll think about it all later, I told myself. I was right. I think about it every launch.

"Pounding his fist into his left hand,
he began to cry . . ."

THE RODNEY KING VERDICT AND RIOTS

April 29–May 1, 1992
Los Angeles, California

STAFF OF THE *LOS ANGELES TIMES*

*D*espite an eyewitness's videotape that horrified the nation, defense lawyers *convinced a jury that the beating of Rodney King by four Los Angeles police officers, while other officers watched, was appropriate conduct because King was resisting arrest. The not-guilty verdict from an all-white jury sparked protests across the nation and riots in Los Angeles.*

DEAN E. MURPHY

April 29, 3:45 P.M., the Simi Valley Courthouse It was chaotic. Ten not-guilty verdicts had sent scores of reporters scrambling in every direction, searching for jurors, defendants, prosecutors, attorneys and community activists.

The jury and most of the defendants didn't want to talk. Sgt. Stacey C. Koon was nearly tackled by a throng of reporters and cameramen as he tried to slip away unnoticed. "You're guilty! You're guilty!" protesters shouted at a tight-lipped Koon, as the advancing crowd crushed a photographer against a parked car.

Inside the courthouse, Officer Laurence M. Powell—accused of striking the most blows on Rodney G. King—stood grinning in a klieg-lit second-floor briefing room. "I am very happy, very happy," he declared.

In response to a question, Powell said he had nothing to say to those upset by the verdicts. "I don't think I have to respond to them," he said. "They have to respond to themselves and make their own decision. I don't think there is anything I can do to change their feelings."

KIRK McCOY

April 29, 3:45 P.M., First A.M.E. Church, Mid-City The mood at the First A.M.E. Church was somber. One could still see the shock and disbelief on the faces of the church members and all who gathered to watch as the verdicts were read.

"Not guilty, not guilty, not guilty."

Then I saw the Rev. Cecil (Chip) Murray.

Pounding his fist into his left hand, he began to cry.

"They gave us nothing, nothing. Not even a bone, dear God, not even a bone."

SHAWN HUBLER

April 29, 6:40 P.M., Florence and Normandie Avenues A half-mile from the corner of Florence and Normandie, you could see the helicopters, swarming. Then, closer in, there were clots of people running, and over the scanner, the sound of police and TV crews telling each other, "Get out of there. Now."

There was gridlock. People lined the sidewalk six deep, shouting, gossiping, shaking their fists. Some held cans of beer and soda, some struggled home with children in their arms. They wore shorts and sport shirts. They looked like they had lined up for a Fourth of July parade.

In traffic, drivers were beginning to panic, pulling out into the paths of oncoming cars to make a quick getaway. As each car approached the intersection, young kids—teen-agers—were loping out, taking a look at the people inside and then heaving chunks of concrete and brick at anyone who wasn't black.

They looked so young, too young for the way their faces contorted with rage. Their wrists seemed so thin, their chests so frail. The rocks would slam into car after car, and you could hear the shouts. "Yeah, m—— f——! Oh, yeah!"

KIRK McCOY

April 29, 9 P.M., Manchester and Slauson Avenues   A colleague, Mike Meadows, and I were crisscrossing streets, looking for looters, when we drove by a liquor store at Manchester and Slauson. Four guys were taking what they could and were just beginning to start a fire. I was on the sidewalk across from the store when I heard someone behind me yell "M—— f——, stop taking pictures."

I turned to see a man, standing about 15 feet away, holding a bottle of liquor and aiming a gun at me. He fired. I turned and ran down the street to where Meadows was waiting in the car with the engine running.

The guy fired five or six more shots as I ran.

If he had been sober I don't think I would have made it.

DAVID FERRELL

April 30, 11:45 A.M., Manchester and Vermont Avenues   As we walked, we encountered a shirtless black man and his son, about 7, viewing the rubble. The man, who declined to give his name, talked of having heard all about Watts when he was young. Now, he wanted to show his own son the horrors of lawlessness. "It's stupid," he said bitterly. "It's just stupid."

JOSH MEYER

April 30, 4 P.M., Mid-Town Shopping Center   As a fire nearby raged out of control, several police cars and hook and ladder trucks careened by, not stopping. One woman zoomed up to the front of the building in a late model Seville, a wild look in her eyes and a grin on her face. She jumped out of her car without rolling up the windows, leaving her screaming infant unattended. Then, the well-dressed, professional-looking woman sprinted into the store for her share.

LEE HARRIS

April 30, 11 P.M., Crenshaw Boulevard near Slauson Avenue Something remained orderly even during the riot. Someone had ripped the front end of a Versateller in the Crenshaw Town Center. A crowd of men, women and children gathered and formed a line and began helping themselves to the money. One person would grab a handful of money and move out of the way for the next person.

SHERYL STOLBERG

May 1, 2:30 P.M., Vermont and Manchester Avenues A single tear is rolling down the right cheek of Norman Simplest, a burly black man in jeans and a bulletproof vest. He has just returned to his business, the Commercial SkyPager, to find it looted and burned, despite the spray-painted letters that said "Black Owned."

Simples and his employees—armed with rifles and semiautomatic guns—had guarded it successfully for two nights, but left when the National Guard arrived. His lament was as much about the Guard's failure as it was about black life in Los Angeles. "All it is is building up our hopes for something," he said. "Always building up our hopes for something, to let us down."

MICHAEL MOREAU

May 1, Evening, Simi Valley I headed home to Simi Valley over strangely abandoned freeways. Pulling off the 118 onto 1st Street, I drove the rental car to the garage where my car was being worked on.

While waiting for my bill, a tanned bleached blonde in shorts and a halter top came in and announced: "They say buses of them are supposed to be coming into town tonight." "Buses of who?" the garage owner asked. "Colored people," she said. "They say they're coming up here to start a riot."

I don't know where she got her information, perhaps from the source who told my neighbor the night before that there was looting at the Target store. Coincidentally, the neighbor had just been to Target and hadn't seen a thing.

"Whose teddy is this, Mama . . . ?"

THE QUILT

October 11, 1992
Washington, D.C.

FERN SHEN AND MICHELE NORRIS

Unfortunately, it is the world's largest piece of folk art. The thirty-acre AIDS Quilt would cover almost thirty football fields. It weighs forty tons.

The first name was Marvin Feldman. He was a friend of Cleve Jones, the San Francisco activist who conceived the Quilt. In 1986, Jones noted that the number of San Franciscans killed by AIDS had passed one thousand. Jones, who had been a protégé of San Francisco city supervisor Harvey Milk, arranged for cards proclaiming the names of the victims to be carried by marchers in that year's candlelight vigil marking the 1976 assassinations of Milk and San Francisco mayor George Moscone. At the end of the march, the cards were taped to the Federal Building near City Hall. The image of those names on the building stayed with Jones.

He spray-painted Feldman's name on the first panel. In 1987, when the Quilt was first displayed, there were 1,920 panels. Now there are close to 45,000 with 70,000 names. More than one hundred panels a week arrive at the Names Project office in San Francisco.

In 1996 the complete Quilt was assembled for the final time on the Washington Mall. It will be too large to be displayed in one place in the future.

Shen and Norris reported for the Washington Post.

Whispering, the way people do in churches and museums, Melanie Swieconec and her 10-year-old daughter, K.C., studied the AIDS Memorial Quilt yesterday for silent clues.

"Look, K.C., he must have liked the Hard Rock Cafe," Swieconec said close to her child's ear. "And he liked the Maryland Terps too. See the turtle?"

Suddenly they realized that a man was standing nearby, wiping his eyes. When he turned and spoke to them, it was as if the quilt had come alive. This was my lover," the man said, sobbing. "I made that square for him."

"You should be very proud of yourself, and I'm sure he's proud of you, too," Swieconec, of Annapolis, said. To K.C., who watched with wide eyes, she added: "That man was his best friend. He made the quilt because he loved him."

It was the kind of moment many parents sought this weekend, as they brought their children to see the Quilt, hoping that the immense patchwork would teach many lessons—about life and death, compassion and prejudice, preventing HIV infection and promoting a cure. Officials estimated that about 50,000 came yesterday to view the Quilt, which was spread out late—about 1:00 p.m., because of overnight rain—and then folded early, about 3 p.m., because of a downpour. As many as 90,000 saw it Saturday, the first day of its Washington exhibition. When the drops began to fall, Quilt organizers interrupted the continuous recitation of AIDS victims' names, which had begun Friday night, to mobilize spectators to help with the "emergency rain fold." Within minutes, the Quilt was packed, and the crowd on the Washington Monument grounds erupted into cheers.

It was a joyous moment in a solemn event.

Synethia Jones brought her two children and a nephew to help them understand a disease that has stricken two members of their family.

"I want them to understand that they don't have to be ashamed of their relatives who are sick with this disease," Jones said. "I want them to see that people who die of this disease are remembered fondly . . . They'll know when they leave here that AIDS is not just something that has struck our family." Jones's 3-year-old daughter, Najai Green, stroked a big brown teddy bear that was sewn to a quilt square for an infant victim of AIDS. "Whose teddy is this, Mama?" she asked.

"It belongs to someone who is in heaven now, baby," Jones replied.

As young as they were, many of the children who came to see the Quilt already had known people who had died because of AIDS.

K.C. Swieconec knew someone, a man who had appeared with her in a theatrical production. Her mother said she took K.C. to the man's funeral and was angered by other parents who said, "How could you bring a child to his funeral? How could you let her be around 'those people'?" Swieconec said the funeral and the Quilt were part of raising K.C. "so she doesn't grow up prejudiced."

For other children, for whom this was the first intimate encounter with the epidemic, the most striking discovery was that patches had been made for children like them.

"A baby died of AIDS?" 6-year-old Sasha Hodge asked her mother, after staring for a long time at a doll sewn onto the Quilt.

"Yes, you know that happens to babies if their mothers are sick," replied her mother, Maris Hodge, an AIDS counselor at Kings County Hospital in New York.

"Look, Dad, these must have been twins," said Jahmal James, 16, of Cheverly, as he noticed two matching baby blue quilt squares, one for Octavio Cantrell and the other for Jason Cantrell, "3 years old forever."

Evan Lewis, 10, gazed down at a square made for a child who died at 11, and quietly he began to cry. His father, Lavonce Lewis, bent down and began a conversation he once thought wouldn't be necessary until his boy was old enough to drive.

"Remember when I told you about where babies come from?" Lewis said in a low whisper. "Well, if people aren't careful when they have sexual relations . . . they can get this disease that right now does not have a cure."

Lewis went on to explain explicitly how men can protect themselves and their partners by wearing a condom. His son nodded dutifully when asked if he understood.

"My parents never really talked to me about sex so I found out on my own and wound up having a son when I was 17," Lewis said. "Well, I can't afford to have my son learn those lessons on his own. You have to start early now."

All this talk of death clearly frightened some children.

"I tried to reassure her that it won't hurt her now, but later, when she's older, there'll be some things she can do to keep herself safe," said Patti Conville, of Rockville, who was guiding her 6-year-old daughter, Caitlin, from square to square. "It's very hard; you don't want to hide the seriousness of it, but you don't want to scare them," Conville said.

Others parents concentrated on the political message.

"They still don't have a cure for it, and they haven't been doing enough to find one—a lot of these names might not be on here if they had done more," Geoffrey Grosvenor, of McLean, said to his 9-year-old daughter and her friend.

A few parents acknowledged that their children did not understand the gravity of AIDS, but might find meaning, some day, in memories of seeing the Quilt.

"I felt they needed to see it, and they could always look back on it," said a tearful Deborah Nelson, of Baltimore, whose 6-year-old daughter and 3-year-old son seemed more interested in heading off to a birthday party.

Nancy Bowling said she brought her five children so they could come up with ideas for a square they are making to commemorate an uncle who died because of AIDS. The younger children in the Bowling brood, who ranged in age from 4 to 12, darted from square to square, oohing and aahing over lace inlays, neon lettering and sewn-on tennis shoes. But the older children drifted behind their mother, stopping to read poems and eulogies. "I wasn't prepared for something this large," said 12-year-old Sarah Bowling. "I didn't think it would make me feel sad because we don't know anyone here, but you can't help but feel something when you look out at all this."

Nancy Bowling listened to her daughter and nodded with a slight smile that seemed to say, "Mission accomplished."

" 'You have mail,' the computer said."

GETTING WIRED: E-MAIL FROM BILL

October 1993–January 1994
Seattle and New York City

JOHN SEABROOK

*I*n 1977, Ken Olson, president of computing giant Digital Equipment Corporation, boldly presented his vision of the future: "There is no reason for any individual to have a computer in his home." About the same time, two teenage hobbyists in California were building the first Apple computer. Shortly afterward, another teenager, William Gates IV, wrote a software program to operate another line of personal computers, and dropped out of Harvard University to market his product.

In 1994, Digital was on the rocks. Apple, though beleaguered, was worth billions. And the products of the company Gates founded, software developer Microsoft, were used by tens of millions of people around the world—a few million of whom used computers at home.

The electronic age also made Gates the world's wealthiest businessman. In the past, his wealth and power might have made him difficult to reach. Yet the revolution in which he had a role also provided New Yorker *writer John Seabrook with a route around official corporate channels. The shortcut itself became the point of his piece, and began the experiences that Seabrook chronicled in a recent book,* Deeper: My Two Year Odyssey in Cyberspace.

Sitting at my computer one day, I realized that I could try to communicate with Bill Gates, the chairman and co-founder of the software giant Microsoft, on the information highway. At least, I could send E-mail to his electronic address, which is widely available, not tell anyone at Microsoft I was doing it, and see what happened. I wrote:

Dear Bill,

I am the guy who is writing the article about you for *The New Yorker*. It occurs to me that we ought to be able to do some of the work through e-mail. Which raises this fascinating question— What kind of understanding of another person can e-mail give you? . . . You could begin by telling me what you think is unique about e-mail as a form of communication.

John

I hit "return," and the computer said, "mail sent." I walked out to the kitchen to get a drink of water and played with the cat for a while, then came back and sat at my computer. Thinking that I was probably wasting money, I nevertheless logged on again and entered my password. "You have mail," the computer said.

I typed "get mail," and the computer got the following:

From: Bill Gates <billg@microsoft.com>
Ok, let me know if you get this email.

According to my computer, eighteen minutes had passed between the time I e-mailed Bill and he e-mailed me back. His message said:

E-mail is a unique communication vehicle for a lot of reasons.

However email is not a substitute for direct interaction. . . . There are people who I have corresponded with on email for months before actually meeting them—people at work and otherwise. If someone isn't saying something of interest its easier to not respond to their mail than it is not to answer the phone. In fact I give out my home phone number to almost no one but my e-mail address is known very broadly. I am the only person who reads my e-mail so no one has to worry about embarrassing themselves or going around people when they send a message. Our e-mail is completely secure. . . .

E-mail helps out with other types of communication. It allows you to exchange a lot of information in advance of a meeting and make the meeting far far more valuable. . . .

> E-mail is not a good way to get mad at someone since you can't interact. You can send friendly messages very easily since those are harder to misinterpret.

We began to e-mail each other three or four times a week. I would have a question about something and say to myself, "I'm going to e-mail Bill about that," and I'd write him a message and get a one- or two-page message back within twenty-four hours, sometimes much sooner. At the beginning of our electronic relationship, I would wake up in the middle of the night and lie in bed wondering if I had e-mail from Bill. Generally, he seemed to write messages at night, sleep (maybe), then send them the next morning. We were intimate in a curious way, in the sense of being wired into each other's minds, but our contact was elaborately stylized, like ballroom dancing.

In some ways, my e-mail relationship with Bill was like an ongoing, monthlong conversation, except that there was a pause after each response to think; it was like football players huddling up after each play. There was no beginning or end to Gates' messages—no time wasted on stuff like "Dear" and "Yours"—and I quickly corrected this etiquette breach in my own messages. Nor were there any fifth-grade-composition-book standards like "It may have come to your attention that" and "Looking forward to hearing from you." Social niceties are not what Bill Gates is about, apparently. Good spelling and use of the upper case are not what Bill Gates is about, either. There was no beginning or end to his messages: Thoughts seemed to burst from his head *in medias res* and to end in vapor trails of ellipses. He never signed his mail, but sometimes he put an "&" at the end, which, someone told me, means "Write back" in e-mail language. After a while, he stopped putting the "&," but I wrote back anyway.

. . . After a month of e-mail between Gates and me, my hour in his physical presence arrived. As we shook hands, he said, "Hello, I'm Bill Gates," and emitted a low, vaguely embarrassed chuckle. Is this the sound one e-mailer makes to another when they finally meet in real space? I was aware of a feeling of being discovered. In the front part of Gates' office, we sat down at right angles to each other. Gates had on normal-looking clothes—a green shirt with purple stripes, brown pants, black loafers. He rocked throughout our time together. He did not look at me very often but either looked down as he was talking or lifted his eyes above my head to look out the window in the direction of the campus. The angle of the light caused the purple stripes in his shirt to reflect in his glasses, which, in turn, threw an indigo tinge into the dark circles around his eyes.

The emotional boundaries of our encounter seemed to have been much expanded by the e-mail that preceded it: Gates would be angry one minute, almost goofily happy the next. I wondered if he was consciously using our present form of communication to express feelings that e-mail cannot convey. Maybe this is the way lots of people will communicate in the future: meet on the information highway, exchange messages, get to know the lining of each other's mind, then meet face to face. In each other's physical presence, they will be able to eliminate a lot of the polite formalities that clutter people's encounters now, and say what they really mean. If this happens, it will be a good thing about the information highway: electronic communication won't reduce face-to-face communication; instead, it will focus it.

. . . As we were saying goodbye, Gates said, "Well, you're welcome to keep sending me mail."

I walked out to my car, drove off the Microsoft campus, and headed back over the Evergreen Bridge to Seattle. When I got to my hotel, I logged on and saw I had e-mail from Bill. It had been written about two hours after I left his office. There was no reference to our having just met. He was responding to mail I had sent him several days earlier.

SOURCES AND PERMISSIONS ACKNOWLEDGMENTS

EDITORS WHO HAVE COLLECTED eyewitness accounts for previous generations have been a great help in the preparation of this volume. One man stands out as the grandfather of all of these works: Albert Bushnell Hart, the eminent Harvard professor who in 1899 prepared the five-volume collection *American History as Told by Contemporaries*. A few decades ago historian Samuel Eliot Morison, who had been a student of Hart's before becoming his colleague and friend, said those volumes "had never been surpassed." He could say the same today.

Among the others are Paul Angle, who is also quoted in this volume, John and La Ree Caughey, Bayrd Still, Bulkley S. Griffin, Louis B. Snyder, Richard B. Morris, and Josef and Dorothy Berger. When appropriate, I have noted both the original source and a modern anthology in which the full text of the piece might be found more easily.

Samuel Eliot Morison's *Oxford History of the American People* was invaluable in preparing the introductions to the pieces, as was Webster's *American Biographies,* edited by Charles Van Doren, and *The American Story,* edited by Earl Schenck Miers.

Except where noted the contributor named in the text is the author of the cited source.

SELECT BIBLIOGRAPHY

Angle, Paul, ed. *The American Reader.* New York: Rand McNally, 1958.

Berger, Josef, and Dorothy Berger, eds. *Diary of America.* New York: Simon & Schuster, 1957.

Caughey, John, and La Ree Caughey, eds. *California Heritage.* Los Angeles: The Ward Ritchie Press, 1962.

Cray, Ed, Jonathan Kotler, and Miles Beller, eds. *American Datelines.* New York: Facts on File, 1990.

Davie, Emily, ed., *Profile of America.* New York: Grosset & Dunlap, 1960.

Griffin, Bulkley S., ed. *Offbeat America*. Cleveland and New York: World Publishing Co., 1967.

Handlin, Oscar. *Readings in American History*. New York: Knopf, 1957.

Hart, Albert Bushnell, ed. *American History as Told by Contemporaries*, vols. I–V. New York: Macmillan, 1897–1929.

———. *Source Book of American History*. New York: Macmillan, 1925.

Hofstadter, Richard, and Michael Wallace, eds. *American Violence: A Documentary History*. New York: Knopf, 1970.

Miers, Earle Schenck, ed. *The American Story*. Great Neck, N.Y.: Channel Press, 1956.

Morison, Samuel Eliot. *The Oxford History of the American People*. New York: Oxford University Press, 1965.

Snyder, Louis L., and Richard B. Morris, eds. *A Treasury of Great Reporting*. New York: Simon & Schuster, 1949.

———, and Richard B. Morris, eds. *They Saw It Happen*. Harrisburg, Pa.: Stackpole Co., 1951.

Still, Bayrd. *Mirror for Gotham*. New York: New York University Press, 1956.

NOTES

Introduction: Boorstin from *Hidden History* (1987; New York: Vintage, 1989), pp. 8, 56.

The Old World Discovers the New World, from Richard Hakluyt, *The Principal Navigations, Voyages, Traffiques, and Discoveries of the English Nation* (Edinburgh, 1889).

Columbus Meets the Native Americans, from Hakluyt, *Principal Navigations,* op. cit.

Epidemic at Stadacona, and a Cure, from Hakluyt, *Principal Navigations,* op. cit.

The Founding of St. Augustine, from "Memoir of Francisco Lopez de Mendoza Grajales," Historical Collections of Louisiana and Florida (Philadelphia, 1850), II; in Old South Leaflets No. 89.

Sir Francis Drake Claims a Kingdom, from *The World Encompassed by Sir Frances Drake* (London, 1628), in Caughey.

Virginia, from Hakluyt, *Principal Navigations,* op. cit.

The Lost Colony, from Hakluyt, in Berger.

The Founding of Jamestown, from *A True Relation,* etc., (London, 1608).

Pocahontas Saves John Smith, from *The Generall Historie of Virginia* (London, 1624).

The First Representative Assembly in America, from *Colonial Records of Virginia,* edited by Thomas H. Wynne and W. S. Gilman (Richmond, 1874).

The Pilgrims' Landing and First Winter, from *History of the Plymouth Plantation* (Boston, 1896).

The Maypole of Merry Mount, from *New English Canaan* (Amsterdam, 1637).

Roger Williams Demands Freedom of Religion, from *New-Englands Memoriall* (Cambridge, 1669).

Stuyvesant's Bad Government, from New York Historical Society, Collections, Second Series (New York, 1849), II.

An Angry Slave, from *Two Voyages to New-England* (Boston, 1865), in Handlin.

Jolliet and Marquette Travel the Mississippi, from "Marquette and Joliet's Account of the Voyage to Discover the Mississippi River," *Historical Collections of Louisiana* (Philadelphia, 1850), II.

King Philip's War: Mary Rowlandson Is Captured, from *The Sovereignty and Goodness of God,* etc., in *The Meridian Anthology of Early American Women Writers,* edited by Katharine M. Rogers (New York: Penguin, 1991).

New York and Environs, from *Journal of a Voyage to New York in 1679–80,* Long Island Historical Society, Memoirs (Brooklyn, 1867), I.

Harvard Students, *Ibid.*

Trial of "Witches" Susannah Martin and Mary Lacey, from *Records of Salem Witchcraft,* compiled by William Elliot Woodward (Roxbury, 1864); and Thomas Hutchinson, *The Witchcraft Delusion of 1692* (Boston, 1870).

Freedom of the Press, from *A Brief Narrative of the Case and Tryal of John Peter Zenger, Printer of the New-York Weekly Journall* (New York, 1738).

The March of the Acadians during the French and Indian War, from "Journal of Colonel John Winslow," in *Reports and Collections, 1882–1883,* III, Nova Scotia Historical Society (Halifax, 1883).

James Otis Starts a Fire, from *The Works of John Adams,* edited by Charles Francis Adams (Boston, 1856).

A Mob Confronts a Stamp Distributor, from *Journals of the House of Burgesses, 1762–1765,* lxviii–lxxi; in Angle.

Franklin Argues Against the Stamp Act . . ., from *The Examination of Doctor Benjamin Franklin . . . relating to the Repeal of the Stamp-Act, etc.* (Philadelphia, 1766).

The Boston Massacre, from *Deacon Tudor's Diary,* edited by William Tudor (Boston, 1896).

The Boston Tea Party, from *Letters of John Andrews, Esq., of Boston. 1772–1776,* edited by Winthrop Sargent, in *Massachusetts Historical Society, Proceedings, 1864–1865* (Boston, 1866).

The First Continental Congress, from *The Works of John Adams,* edited by Charles Francis Adams (Boston, 1856).

Patrick Henry's Speech, from *Select Orations Illustrating American Political History,* edited by Samuel Bannister Harding (New York: Macmillan, 1909).

Lanterns in the North Church Steeple, from *Massachusetts Historical Society Proceedings, XVI,* in *The Spirit of 'Seventy-Six,* edited by Henry Steele Commager and Richard B. Morris (New York: Harper & Row, 1958, 1967).

Standoff at Lexington, from *History of Lexington, I,* in *The Spirit of 'Seventy-Six,* edited by Henry Steele Commager and Richard B. Morris (New York: Harper & Row, 1958, 1967).

"The Shot Heard 'Round the World," from appendix to *The Literature of the Nineteenth of April,* edited by James Lyman Whiteney (Concord, 1876).

Washington Is Chosen for Command, from *The Works of John Adams,* edited by Charles Francis Adams (Boston, 1856); in Old South Leaflets, I.

Jefferson Is Selected to Write the Declaration of Independence, from *The Works of John Adams,* edited by Charles Francis Adams (Boston, 1856).

Young Jefferson Gets Some Advice from Ben Franklin, from John Hazelton, *The Declaration of Independence: Its History* (New York, 1906).

The Declaration's Missing Clause, from Hazelton, *ibid.*

Signing the Declaration, from *Letters in American History,* edited by H. Jack Lang (New York: Harmony Books, 1982).

Recruiting Trouble, from Alexander Graydon, *Memoirs* (Harrisburg, 1811).

Winter at Valley Forge, from the *Historical* magazine, May–June, 1861 (New York, 1861).

Yankees Invade Great Britain, from *Journal of John Paul Jones;* in Berger.

John Jones Refuses to Surrender, from Snyder and Morris, *They Saw It Happen.*

Cornwallis Surrenders, from *Correspondence of Charles, First Marquis Cornwallis,* edited by Charles Ross (London, 1859), I, appendix.

The Eve of the Constitutional Convention, from Kate Mason Rowland, *The Life of George Mason* (New York, 1892).

Last-Minute Dissenters . . ., from *Debates on the Adoption of the Federal Constitution,* edited by Jonathan Elliot (Philadelphia, 1861), V.

Jefferson at the White House, from *The First Forty Years of Washington Society* (New York: Scribner, 1906). Bailyn quotation from *Thomas Jefferson,* television broadcast, Arts & Entertainment Network, July 9, 1996.

The Bathtub Dictator Sells Louisiana, from Th[eodore] Iung, *Lucien Bonaparte et ses Mémoires,* translated by George N. Henning (Paris, 1882).

Aaron Burr Kills Alexander Hamilton, from *The New York Post,* July 19, 1804, in Samuel Engle Burr, Jr., *The Burr-Hamilton Duel and Related Matters,* 2d ed. (San Antonio: Naylor Co., 1971).

Lewis and Clark Head to the Pacific, from *History of the Expedition under the Command of Captains Lewis and Clark to the Sources of the Missouri, etc.,* edited by Paul Allen [actually Nicholas Biddle] (Philadelphia, 1814).

First Voyage of the *Clermont,* from *Reminiscences of H. Freeland,* Old South, V.

Tecumseh, from *Tecumseh: Fact and Fiction in Early Records,* edited by Carl F. Klinck (Englewood Cliffs, N.J.: Prentice Hall, 1961).

Dolley Madison Saves Washington's Portrait, from *Letters in American History,* edited by H. Jack Lang (New York: Harmony Books, 1982).

Uninvited Guests Find Dinner at the White House, from *A Narrative of the Campaigns of the British Army at Washington and New Orleans* (London, 1821).

Public Amusements in New Orleans, from *Sketches of America. A Narrative of a Journey of Five Thousand Miles through the Eastern and Western States of America* (London, 1818).

Calhoun and the Missouri Compromise, from *Memoirs of John Quincy Adams,* edited by Charles Francis Adams (Philadelphia, 1875), IV and V; Hart, VI.

Peale's Museum, from *Sketches of History, Life, and Manners, in the United States* (New Haven, 1826).

Lunch in New York City, from *Travels in North America in the Years 1827 and 1828* (Edinburgh, 1829); in Still.

Early Cincinnati, from *Domestic Manners of the Americans* (London, 1832).

One Tough Bear, from *The Travels of Jedediah Smith,* edited by Maurice S. Sullivan (Santa Ana, Calif., 1934); in Caughey.

Early Texas, from "A Trip to Texas in 1828," translated by Carlos E. Castanada, in *Southwestern Historical Quarterly,* April 1926; reprinted in *A Documentary History of the Mexican Americans,* edited by Wayne Moquin with Charles Van Doren (New York: Praeger, 1971).

Jackson's Rowdy Inauguration, from *The First Forty Years of Washington Society* (New York: Scribner, 1906).

A Slave Ship in the South Atlantic, from *Voices of Brazil in 1828 and 1829* (London, 1830).

America's First Steam Engine Races a Horse, from *The Baltimore and Ohio Railroad: Personal Recollections* (Baltimore, 1868); Hart III.

Exploring Florida, from *Delineations of American Scenery and Character* (New York: G. A. Baker & Company, 1926).

Life with a Slave Breaker, from *Narrative of the Life of Frederick Douglass* (Boston, 1845).

Spanish California, from *Two Years Before the Mast* (New York, 1840).

Fall of the Alamo, from Amelia Williams, "A Critical Study of the Siege of the Alamo and of the Personnel of its Defenders," *Southwestern Historical Quarterly,* July 1933; reprinted in *A Documentary History of the Mexican Americans,* edited by Wayne Moquin with Charles Van Doren (New York: Praeger, 1971).

Money in New York City and Manners in Niagara Falls, from *Diary in America* (1839; reprinted, Bloomington: Indiana University Press, 1960).

The Trail of Tears Begins, from John Ehle, *The Trail of Tears: Rise and Fall of the Cherokee Nation* (New York: Doubleday, 1988).

Barnum Discovers Tom Thumb, from *Struggles and Triumphs* (New York: Penguin, 1967).

The First Telegraph Message, from Samuel Prime, *The Life of Samuel F. B. Morse* (New York, 1875).

Waiting for the End of the World, from J. Thomas Scharf and Thompson Westcott, *History of Philadelphia* (Philadelphia, 1884), II; in *The Making of American Democracy.*

Thoreau at Walden Pond, from "Henry D. Thoreau" (Thoreau Annex, 1880), in *Thoreau as Seen by His Contemporaries,* edited by Walter Harding (New York: Holt, Rinehart and Winston, 1960).

The Oregon Trail, from *The California and Oregon Trail* (New York, 1849).

The Mormon Exodus, from *Daily Missouri Republican,* May 13, 1846.

The Donner Party, from *Diary of Patrick Breen,* edited by Frederick J. Teggart (Berkeley: University of California Press, 1910); in Caughey.

Gold Strike at Sutter's Mill, from *Hutchings' California Magazine,* II (1857); in Caughey.

The Seneca Falls Convention, from *The History of Woman Suffrage,* edited by Elizabeth Cady Stanton, Susan B. Anthony, and Matilda Joslyn Gage, vol. I (1881; reprint, New York: Arno, 1969).

"Man Overboard!," from *A Journal of a Visit to London and the Continent, 1849–50,* edited by Eleanor Melville Metcalf (Cambridge: Harvard University Press, 1948); in *A Treasury of the World's Great Diaries,* edited by Philip Dunaway and Mel Evans (New York: Doubleday, 1957).

Hawthorne and *The Scarlet Letter,* from *Yesterdays with Authors* (Boston, 1901); in Angle.

Poe's Macabre Dream, from *The Reminiscences of a Very Old Man, 1808–97;* in Griffin.

On the Underground Railroad, from *Reminiscences* (Cincinnati, 1876).

Sojourner Truth at a Woman's Rights Convention, from Salem *Anti-Slavery Bugle,* June 21, 1851; in *Sojourner Truth: A Life, a Symbol,* by Nell Irvin Painter (New York: Norton, 1996).

Commodore Perry Opens Japan, from "The Narrative of the Expedition of an American Squadron to the China Seas and Japan, Performed in the Years 1852, and 1854, Under The Command Of Commodore M. C. Perry" (Washington: Government Printing Office, 1856); in Old South, VII.

Chief Seattle Speaks, from *Seattle Sunday Star,* October 29, 1887; reprinted in *Seattle Weekly,* September 1, 1993.

Lincoln and Douglas Debate, from *Memoirs of Gustave Koerner,* II; in Angle.

First Overland Mail Reaches the West Coast, from *New York Herald,* October 13, 1858; in Caughey.

John Brown's Raid, from "John Brown at Harpers Ferry, the Fight at the Engine-House, as seen by one of his prisoners," *Century Illustrated Monthly Magazine,* XXX (June 1885); in Hofstadter.

The Pony Express, from *Roughing It* (New York: Harper, 1871).

Lincoln at the White House, from *My Diary North and South* (London, 1863).

Fort Sumter Is Attacked, from *A Diary from Dixie* (New York, 1905).

War News Reaches the North, from *My Story of the War* (Hartford: A. D. Worthington & Co., 1899).

Lincoln Tears the Flag, from *Tad Lincoln's Father* (Boston: Little Brown, 1931); in *A Civil War Treasury of Tales, Legends and Folklore,* edited by B. A. Botkin (New York: Random House, 1960).

First Battle of Bull Run, from the *Times* (London), August 6, 1861.

The Confederate Congress, from *Recollections of Mississippi and Mississippians* (Boston, 1891).

Battle of the Ironclads, from Edward K. Rawson and Robert H. Woods, *Official Records of the Union and Confederate Navies in the War of the Rebellion,* Series I, vol. 7 (Washington: Government Printing Office, 1898).

Lincoln Proclaims Emancipation, from J. W. Schuckers, *Life and Public Services of Salmon Portland Chase* (New York, D. Appleton & Co., 1874).

Adventures of a Blockade Runner, from *The Narrative of a Blockade-Runner* (New York, 1877).

Gettysburg, from *National Intelligencer,* July 7, 1863, in Cray et al. [*New York World* report]; *Battles and Leaders of the Civil War,* edited by Robert Underwood Johnson and Clarence Clough Buel (New York: The Century Co., 1887–1888) [Pleasonton].

Lincoln Delivers the Gettysburg Address, from John Russell Young, *Men and Memories: Personal Reminiscences,* edited by May D. Russell Young; in Griffin.

Andersonville Prison, from *Andersonville Diary* (Auburn, N.Y., 1881).

Sherman Burns Atlanta, from George Ward Nichols, *The Story of the Great March* (New York: Harper & Brothers, 1865); F. Y. Hedley, *Marching Through Georgia* (Chicago: M. A. Donohue & Co., 1884); David Conyngham, *Sherman's March Through the South* (New York: Sheldon & Co., 1865); in Richard Wheeler, *Sherman's March* (New York: T. Y. Crowell, 1978).

A Missing Brother at Christmas, from *Walt Whitman's Civil War,* edited by Walter Lowenfels (New York: Knopf, 1960).

Lee Surrenders to Grant, from *Battles and Leaders of the Civil War,* edited by Robert Underwood Johnson and Clarence Clough Buel (New York: Century Co., 1889), IV.

Lincoln Is Shot, from *The Assassination of President Lincoln and the Trial of the Conspirators,* compiled by Benjamin Pitman (1865); in Hofstadter.

Death of Lincoln, from *Diary of Gideon Welles,* edited by John T. Morse, Jr. (Boston, 1911), II.

Freedom, from *Up from Slavery* (New York, 1901).

The Reconstruction, from *The South Since the War* (Boston, 1866).

Baseball Innovations, from *America's National Game* (1911).

Early Denver, from *Colorado: a Summer Trip* (New York: G. P. Putnam & Sons, 1867).

The Last Spike, from *How We Built the Union Railway;* in Davie.

Powell Enters the Grand Canyon, from *The Exploration of the Colorado River* (1875; reprinted Chicago: University of Chicago Press, 1957).

New Money and Robber Barons, from *Diary of George Templeton Strong,* edited by Allan Nevins and Milton Halsey Thomas (New York: Macmillan, 1952).

The Great Fire and Its Aftermath, from *Reminiscences of Chicago During the Great Fire* (1915); reprinted as *The Great Chicago Fire,* edited by David Lowe (New York: Dover, 1979).

A Ku Klux Klan Trial, from *Proceedings in the Ku Klux Trials at Columbia, S. C., in the United States Circuit Court, November Term, 1871* (Columbia House, 1872); in Angle.

***United States v. Susan B. Anthony*—and Vice Versa,** from *The History of Woman Suffrage,* edited by Elizabeth Cady Stanton, Susan B. Anthony, and Matilda Joslyn Gage, vol. I, (1881; reprint, New York: Arno, 1969).

The First Telephone Call, from Bruce Robert, *Alexander Graham Bell and the Conquest of Solitude* (Boston: Little, Brown, 1973).

Custer Is Killed at Little Bighorn, from *I Have Spoken,* edited by Virginia I. Armstrong (Swallow Press, 1971).

Aleuts, from Betty John, *Libby: the Alaskan Diaries of Libby Beaman, 1879–1880* (Tulsa: Council Oaks Publishing, 1987). Reprinted by permission of Council Oaks Publishing.

Electric Light, from *As I Pass, O Manhattan,* edited by Esther Morgan McCullough (North Bennington, Vt.: Coley Taylor, 1956).

Jesse James's Body, from Western Associated Press, April 3, 1882; in Greene.

Haymarket Riot, from Dyer D. Lum, *Concise History of the Great Trial of the Chicago Anarchists in 1886* (1886); in Hofstadter.

Frank Lloyd Wright Sees His First City, from *An Autobiography—Frank Lloyd Wright* (New York: Duell, Sloan and Pearce, 1932). Copyright © 1996 The Frank Lloyd Wright Foundation. Reprinted by permission of The Frank Lloyd Wright Foundation.

The Great Oklahoma Land Rush, from "The Opening of Oklahoma," *Cosmopolitan,* September 1889.

The Johnstown Flood, from *Philadelphia Public Ledger,* June 4, 1889; in Greene.

The First Electrocution, from the *New York World,* August 7, 1890; in Greene.

Massacre at Wounded Knee, from John G. Neihardt, *Black Elk Speaks* (Lincoln: University of Nebraska Press, 1932). Reprinted by permission of University of Nebraska Press.

The Invention of Basketball, from *Basketball: Its Origin and Development* (New York: Association Press, 1941).

The First Department Store, from *The Land of the Dollar* (New York, 1897).

The Rough Riders Charge San Juan Hill, from *The Cuban and Porto Rican Campaigns* (New York, 1898); in Angle.

Carrie Nation, from *The Topeka Daily Capital,* December 28, 1900; in Greene.

The Wright Brothers Fly, from *The Papers of Wilbur and Orville Wright,* vol. I, edited by Marvin McFarland (New York: McGraw-Hill, 1953).

Ellis Island, from Edward Steiner, *On the Trail of the Immigrant* (New York: Fleming H. Revell, 1906).

The Great Earthquake and Fire, from *Collier's Weekly,* May 5, 1906.

Building the Panama Canal, from *The Letters of Theodore Roosevelt,* selected and edited by Elting E. Morison (Cambridge: Harvard University Press, 1952).

The Birth of the Blues, from *Father of the Blues* (New York: Macmillan, 1941). Reprinted by permission of the Estate of W. C. Handy, courtesy of Minnie Handy Hanson.

Triangle Shirtwaist Company Fire, from Jeff Kisseloff, *You Must Remember This* (New York: Harcourt Brace Jovanovich, 1989). Copyright © 1989 by Jeff Kisseloff. Reprinted by permission of Harcourt Brace Jovanovich, Inc.

The *Titanic* Sinks, from *New York Times,* April 17, 1912; in Greene.

Jim Thorpe, from *New York Times,* November 10, 1912.

The First Assembly Line, from Henry Ford, *My Life and Work* (New York: Doubleday, 1922).

Sinking the *Lusitania*, from Colin Simpson, *The Lusitania* (London: Longman, 1972).

War in the Air, from *Fighting the Flying Circus* (New York: Frederick A. Stokes, 1919); in *The Last Magnificent War,* edited by Harold Elk Straubing (New York: Paragon House, 1989).

The Americans Join the War in Europe, from *Diary of a Rainbow Veteran, Written at the Front* (Terre Haute, Ind.: Moore-Langen Company, 1929). Reprinted by permission of Robert Elmer Sherwood.

Babe Ruth, from the New York *World,* October 13, 1923.

Rhapsody in Blue, from Charles Schwartz, *The Life and Music of George Gershwin* (New York: Bobbs-Merrill, 1973).

Among the Believers, from *The Vintage Mencken,* edited by Alistair Cooke (New York: Vintage Books, 1956). Reprinted by permission of Random House, Inc.

First Rocket Flight, from personal diary of Dr. Robert H. Goddard; in Davie.

The Flapper, from "Aren't We All Rich Now?," *Collier's Weekly,* November 7, 1926.

Television Is Born, from *New York Times,* April 8, 1927; in Cray et al.

Lindbergh Crosses the Atlantic, from *New York Times,* May 22, 1927; in Cray et al.

Radio and Its Evils Arrive, from *Diary of Our Own Samuel Pepys* (New York: Simon & Schuster, 1935).

Al Capone, Patriot, from *A Discord of Trumpets* (New York: Simon & Schuster, 1956). Copyright © 1956 Claud Cockburn. Reprinted by permission of the Cockburn Literary Estate.

Prohibition, from *New York,* translated by Hamish Miles (London: Heinemann); in Still.

Raid of an Abortion Clinic, from *Margaret Sanger: An Autobiography* (New York: Norton, 1938). Reprinted by permission of Sanger Resources & Management Co., Inc.

Crash, from *We Saw It Happen,* edited by Hanson Baldwin and Shepard Stone (New York: Simon & Schuster, 1938). Reprinted by permission of Amelia Bell for the Estate of Elliot V. Bell.

First View from the Empire State Building, from *New York Times,* May 2, 1931. Reprinted by permission of the *New York Times.*

In the Death House with the Scottsboro Boys, from *Opportunity* magazine, June 1932. Reprinted by permission of The National Urban League.

General Douglas MacArthur Fires on Americans, from *The Baltimore Sun,* July 29, 1932. Reprinted by permission of Sun Source/*The Baltimore Sun.*

Depression Prices, from Paul Angle, *The American Reader* (New York: Rand McNally, 1958).

Roosevelt's New Deal, from Harold L. Ickes, *The Secret Diary of Harold L. Ickes,* vol. I (New York: Simon & Schuster, 1954). Reprinted by permission of Harold L. Ickes, Jr.

The Lindbergh Case Circus, from *Mrs. Astor's Horse* (New York: Stokes, 1935). Reprinted by permission of Joan Walker Iams.

Gutzon Borglum Carves Mount Rushmore, from *Ernie's America: The Best of Ernie Pyle's 1930s Travel Dispatches,* edited by David Nichols (New York: Random House, 1989). Reprinted by permission of the Scripps-Howard Foundation.

Hitting Bottom, from F. Scott Fitzgerald, *The Notebooks* (New York: New Directions, 1945); in *A Treasury of the World's Great Diaries,* edited by Philip Dunaway and Mel Evans (New York: Doubleday, 1957).

The War of the Worlds, from *Harper's* magazine, December 1948. Reprinted by permission of Mrs. John Houseman, 1996.

A Movie Executive Pleads for a Few Famous Last Words, from *Memo From: David O. Selznick* (New York: Viking Press, 1972). Copyright © 1992 Selznick Productions Inc.

Charlie "Bird" Parker Makes the Scene, from *Swing to Bop,* edited by Ira Gitler (New York: Oxford University Press, 1985).

An Early Warning, from *Turbulent Era,* vol. II (New York, 1952); in Handlin.

Pearl Harbor, from Daniel Inouye with Lawrence Elliot, *Journey to Washington* (Englewood Cliffs, N.J.: Prentice-Hall, 1967). Copyright © 1968 by Prentice-Hall Inc., renewed 1995 by Senator Daniel K. Inouye. Reprinted by permission of Simon & Schuster, Inc.

Pearl Harbor News Reaches FDR, from *F.D.R. My Boss* (New York: Scribner's, 1949).

Evacuation to Manzanar, from John Tateishi, *And Justice for All* (New York: Random House, 1984). Reprinted by permission of Random House, Inc.

A Codebreaker's Daring Trick, from Edwin T. Layton with Roger Pineau and John Costello, *"And I Was There": Pearl Harbor and Midway* (New York: Morrow, 1985).

The Homefront, from Nell Giles, *Punch In, Susie! A Woman's War Factory Diary* (New York: Harper Brothers, 1943).

A Walk to San Stefano, from *Stars and Stripes,* July 31, 1943.

The Death of Captain Waskow, from Ernie Pyle, *Brave Men* (New York: Henry Holt, 1944). Reprinted by permission of the Scripps-Howard Foundation.

Nichols quotation from *Ernie's War,* edited by David Nichols (New York: Random House, 1986).

D-Day, from Gerald Astor, *June 6, 1944: The Voices of D-Day* (New York: St. Martin's Press, 1994). Copyright © 1994 by Gerald Astor. Reprinted by permission of St. Martin's Press Incorporated. Introduction from Andy Rooney quotation from *My War* (New York: Random House, 1995).

Go for Broke!, from Lyn Crost, *Honor by Fire: Japanese Americans at War in Europe and the Pacific* (Novato, Calif.: Presidio Press, 1994).

Iwo Jima, from "To the Finish; A Letter from Iwo Jima," *The Atlantic Monthly,* 1945; in *The American Spirit,* edited by Thomas A. Bailey (Boston: D. C. Heath, 1963).

The Death of Roosevelt, from *New York Herald Tribune,* April 14, 1945 [Smith], reprinted by permission of the Associated Press; *New Yorker,* April 21, 1945 [Panter-Downes]; April 28, 1945 [Flanner].

The United Nations, from *The Private Papers of Senator Vandenberg,* edited by Arthur H. Vandenberg, Jr. (Boston: Houghton Mifflin, 1952); in Angle.

The Trinity Test, from working transcript of *The Day After Trinity,* a multimedia edition of a film by Jon Else, CD-ROM, (New York: Voyager, 1994). Reprinted by permission of Jon Else.

Dropping the Atom Bomb, from *The Paul Tibbets Story* (Briarcliff Manor, N.Y.: Stein & Day, 1978). Reprinted by permission of Scarborough House Inc.

ENIAC, from *New York Times,* February 15, 1945. Reprinted by permission of the *New York Times.*

Jackie Robinson in the Major Leagues, from *The Boys of Summer* (New York: Harper & Row, 1972). Reprinted by permission of Harper Collins Publisher and the author.

Jonas Salk Hunts for a Polio Vaccine, from Richard Carter, *Breakthrough* (New York: Trident Press, 1966). Reprinted by permission of Richard Carter.

North Korea Challenges the United Nations, from Merle Miller, *Plain Speaking* (New York: Putnam, 1974). Reprinted by permission of the Putnam Publishing Group. Copyright © 1993, 1994 by Merle Miller.

Firing MacArthur, from Merle Miller, *Plain Speaking* (New York: Putnam, 1974). Reprinted by permission of the Putnam Publishing Group. Copyright © 1993, 1994 by Merle Miller.

A Neighborhood Vote, by Bernard Taper, in *The San Francisco Chronicle Reader,* edited by William Hogan and William German (New York: McGraw-Hill, 1962). Reprinted by permission of the author.

McCarthy Meets His Match, from the *Special Senate Committee on Charges and Countercharges involving Secretary of the Army Robert T. Stevens, Eighty-Third Congress, Second Session,* in *Voices of the American Past,* edited by Robert Borden (Lexington, Mass.: Heath, 1972).

Elvis, from the *Orlando Sentinel,* May 16, 1955: in Peter Guralnick, *Last Train to Memphis* (Boston: Little, Brown, 1994). Reprinted by permission of the *Orlando Sentinel.*

The Front of the Bus, from Rosa Parks with Jim Haskins, *Rosa Parks: My Story* (New York: Dial Books, 1992). Reprinted by permission of Penguin Books USA Inc.

First Day of School in Little Rock, Arkansas, from *New York Journal-American* September 23, 1957; in *The Best of Pulitzer Prize News Writing,* edited by W. David Sloan (Columbus, Ohio: Publishing Horizons, 1986). Reprinted by permission of the Associated Press.

Space, from M. Scott Carpenter, L. Gordon Cooper, Jr., John H. Glenn, Jr., Virgil I. Grissom, Walter M. Schirra, Jr., Alan B. Shepard, Jr., Donald K. Slayton, *We Seven* (New York: Simon & Schuster, 1972). Copyright © 1962 by Simon & Schuster, Inc. Reprinted by permission of Simon & Schuster, Inc.

The Cuban Missile Crisis, from *The Cuban Missile Crisis, 1962: A National Security Archive,* edited by Laurence Chang and Peter Kornbluh (New York: The New Press, 1992).

Dr. Martin Luther King, Jr., from the *New York Times,* August 29, 1963. Reprinted by permission of the *New York Times.*

A Dissenter's View of Dr. King's Speech, from Alex Haley and Malcolm X, *The Autobiography of Malcolm X* (New York: Grove Press, 1965). Reprinted by permission of Random House, Inc.

***The Feminine Mystique* and the Women's Rights Movement,** from Betty Friedan, *The Feminine Mystique* (1963; reprinted with additional material, New York: Dell, 1983). Copyright © 1983, 1974, 1973, 1963 by Betty Friedan. Reprinted by permission of W. W. Norton & Company, Inc.

President Kennedy Is Assassinated, from "Veteran Reporter's Eyewitness Account of Assassination. 'One Sees History Explode Before One's Eyes . . . ,' " *The Dallas Times Herald* (Dallas, Tex.), November 23, 1963; in *The Best of Pulitzer Prize News Writing,* edited by W. David Sloan (Columbus, Ohio: Publishing Horizons, 1986). Reprinted by permission of the Associated Press.

The Beatles Arrive, from *New York Herald Tribune,* February 8–10, 1964. Reprinted by permission of Tom Wolfe and William Whitworth.

The Vietnam War Begins, from Kim Willenson with the correspondents of *Newsweek, The Bad War: an Oral History of the Vietnam War* (New York: New American Library, 1987). Copyright © 1987 by Newsweek, Inc. Reprinted by permission of Penguin Books USA Inc.

Police Try to Halt the Selma March, by Sheyann Webb, Rachel West Nelson, and Frank Sikoro, from *Selma, Lord, Selma: Girlhood Memories of the Civil Rights Days* (Tuscaloosa: University of Alabama Press, 1980). Copyright © 1980 The University of Alabama Press. Reprinted by permission of the publisher; in *Ordinary Americans,* edited by Linda R. Monk (Alexandria, Va.: Close Up Pub., 1994).

Story Pitch at a Hollywood Studio, from *The Studio* (1968; reprinted New York: Limelight Editions, 1985). Reprinted by permission of John Gregory Dunne.

"The Long, Hot Summer," from *Voices of Freedom,* edited by Henry Hampton and Steve Fayer with Sarah Lynn (New York: Bantam, 1990). Copyright © 1990 by Blackside, Inc. Reprinted by permission of Bantam Books, a division of Bantam Doubleday Dell Publishing Group, Inc.

The My Lai Massacre, from Michael Bilton and Kevin Sim, *Four Hours in My Lai* (New York: Viking, 1992).

Police Break Up a Student Protest, from *Talking to Myself* (New York: Pantheon Books, 1977). Reprinted by permission of The New Press.

A Fortunate Son, from *Fortunate Son* (New York: Grove Press, 1991). Reprinted by permission of Grove/Atlantic, Inc. Copyright © 1991 by Lewis B. Puller, Jr.

The Birth of Modern Sports: Curt Flood Fights Baseball, from Curt Flood with Richard Carter, *The Way It Is* (New York: Trident Press, 1971).

Stonewall, from *The Village Voice,* July 3, 1969. Reprinted by permission of the author and *The Village Voice.*

On The Moon, from *First On the Moon: A Voyage with Neil Armstrong, Michael Collins, Edwin E. Aldrin, Jr.,* written with Gene Farmer and Dora Jane Hamblin (Boston: Little, Brown, 1970).

Woodstock, from Joel Makower, *Woodstock: The Oral History* (New York: Doubleday, 1989). Copyright © 1989 by Tilden Press Inc. Reprinted by permission of Tilden Press Inc.

Apollo 13, from *Lost Moon* [also titled *Apollo 13*] (Boston: Houghton Mifflin Company, 1994). Reprinted by permission of The Robert Lantz/Joy Harris Literary Agency, Inc., and the William Morris Agency, Inc., on behalf of the authors. Copyright © 1994 by Jim Lovell and Jeffrey Kluger.

Kent State, *New York Times,* May 5, 1970. Reprinted by permission of the *New York Times.*

Roe v. Wade, from *May It Please the Court,* edited by Peter Irons and Stephanie Guitton (New York: New Press, 1993).

The Watergate Cover-up Begins, from H. R. Haldeman, *The Haldeman Diaries* (New York: G. P. Putnam's Sons, 1994).

Fear and Loathing at the Super Bowl, from *Rolling Stone* magazine #128, February 15, 1973; reprinted in Thompson, *The Great Shark Hunt* (New York: Summit, 1979). Reprinted by permission of Hunter S. Thompson.

The Double Life of Patty Hearst, from *The Symbionese Liberation Army, Documents and Communications,* edited by Robert Brainard Pearsall (Amsterdam: Rodopi N.V., 1974), and from Patricia Hearst with Alvin Moscow, *Patty Hearst: Her Own Story* (New York: Avon, 1983). Reprinted by permission of Patty Hearst.

The Fall of Saigon, from Al Santoli, *Everything We Had* (New York: Random House, 1981). Reprinted by permission of Al Santoli.

Warhol's World, from *The Andy Warhol Diaries* (New York: Warner, 1989). Reprinted by permission of Warner Books Inc. Copyright © 1989 The Estate of Andy Warhol. All rights reserved.

The Iranian Hostage Crisis: Week One, from *Crisis* (New York: Putnam's, 1982). Reprinted by permission of The Putnam Publishing Group. Copyright © 1982 by Hamilton Jordan.

Ronald Reagan in the White House, from *What I Saw at the Revolution* (New York: Random House, 1990). Reprinted by permission of Random House, Inc.

Offerings: The Vietnam Veterans Memorial, from "From 'Nam, With Love: Messages, Offerings at the Wall," in *Washington Post,* December 31, 1991 [Loose]; and "Offerings at the Wall: A Decade of Healing in Stone," in *Washington Post,* September 13, 1992 [Wheeler]. Copyright © 1991, 1992 The Washington Post. Reprinted by permission of The Washington Post.

Living with AIDS, from testimony before the Presidential Commission on AIDS, March 1988; in Mary Ellen Hombs, *AIDS Crisis in America* (Santa Barbara, Calif.: ABL-CLIO, 1992).

Space Shuttle *Challenger,* from *AOL News,* on-line service (Vienna, Va.: America Online, 1996). Reprinted by permission of the Associated Press.

The Rodney King Verdict and Riots, from *Understanding the Riots: Los Angeles Before and After the Rodney King Case,* by the staff of the *Los Angeles Times* (Los Angeles, Calif.: Los Angeles Times, 1992). Reprinted by permission of the Los Angeles Times.

The Quilt, from "Youngsters Learn of Life and Death . . .," the *Washington Post,* October 12, 1992. Reprinted by permission of The Washington Post.

Getting Wired: E-Mail from Bill, from *The New Yorker,* January 10, 1994. Reprinted by permission of John Seabrook.

INDEX

ABOUT THE EDITOR

David Colbert is a writer and book editor.
He lives in New York.